CW00557571

≡ PETER JO

TRAVELLER'S (

SOUTH AFRICA

NEW
HOLLAND

The travel, accommodation and other facilities described in this book represent a major portion of those available at the time of going to press in 1995. However, the tourist world is by nature subject to rapid change, and while every effort has been made to ensure accuracy, some of the information will inevitably become outdated during this edition's lifespan. Travellers are therefore advised to consult local publicity associations and other sources before embarking on visits to specific venues. The contact addresses and telephone numbers of these associations and sources appear in the relevant Advisories at the end of each regional chapter.

This edition first published in 1995 by
New Holland (Publishers) Ltd
24 Nutford Place, London W1H 6DQ
First published in the UK in 1992
Reprinted in 1993

ISBN 1 85368 587 9

Managing Editor: Wilsia Metz
Editors: Nune Jende, Allison Murphy,
Laura van Niekerk, Annlerie van Rooyen
Designers: Janice Evans, Tracey Carstens
Design assistant: Lellyn Creamer
Cover design: Abdul Amien
DTP Maps: John Loubser
Picture researcher: Geoff Payne
Indexer: Ethné Clarke
Phototypeset by Struik DTP
Originated by Unifoto (Pty) Ltd
Printed and bound in Singapore by Kyodo Printing Co (Pte) Ltd

CONTENTS

Front cover illustrations (*clockwise from top left*): *Cape Town harbour; Namaqualand wild flowers; Xhosa women of the Transkei; water sport on the Vaal Dam; elephants in the Kruger National Park; historical Kimberley.*
Back cover: *The Houses of Parliament.* Title page: *the famed Blue Train, on its way to Cape Town.* Imprint page: *vervet monkey, Kruger National Park.* Part openers: *bushveld sunset (pages 6 and 7); the Western Cape's Hex River Valley (pages 38 and 39); The Vaal River at Vereeniging (pages 342 and 343).*

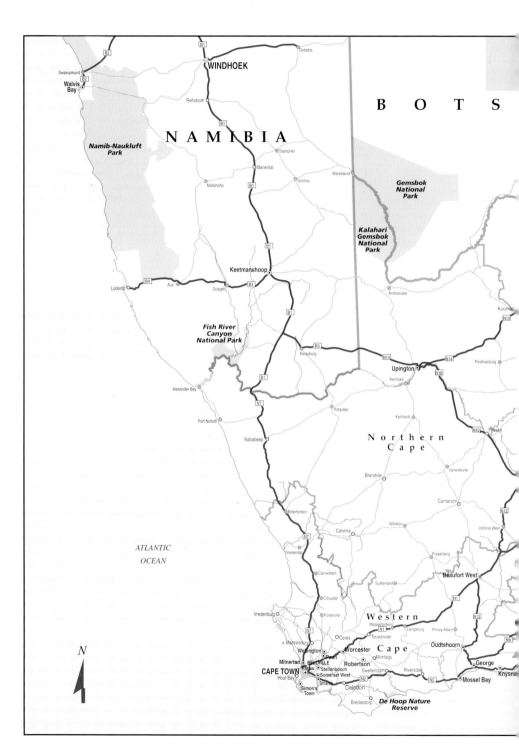

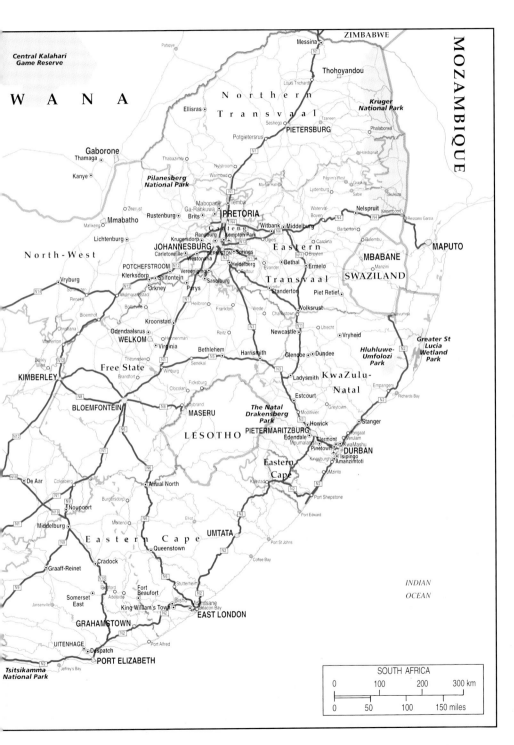

PART ONE

AN INTRODUCTION TO SOUTH AFRICA

AN INTRODUCTION
TO SOUTH AFRICA

THE LAND

South Africa is a big country: five times the size of Britain, about as large as Holland, Belgium, Italy, France and Germany put together. It stretches from the Limpopo River in the north to blustery Cape Agulhas, nearly 2 000 km to the south, from Namaqualand along the barren western seaboard 1 500 km to subtropical KwaZulu-Natal and the humid Indian Ocean coast: a total land area of just under 1,3 million km².

This figure includes the four formerly 'independent' territories, regions that were granted independence in terms of the old regime's 'Grand Apartheid' design, and which are now being painfully reintegrated into the new South Africa. Enclosed within the Republic's borders are the small, separate kingdoms of Lesotho and Swaziland.

To the north-west, beyond the desolate reaches of the Orange River, is Namibia, a vast and beautiful country of diamonds, desert and human division that the League of Nations mandated to South Africa after the First World War and which gained its independence only in 1990. Flanking the Republic's far northern regions are, in clockwise order, the slightly older independent states of Botswana, Zimbabwe and Mozambique. A rich territorial diversity.

Indeed, diversity is probably the single word that best illustrates both South and southern Africa. The canvas is kaleidoscopic; variety, contrast and sometimes conflict are vividly evident in the bewildering mix of race and language, creed, colour and culture. The diversity is there, too, in the nature of the land; in its geological formations and regional climates; its mountains, plains and coasts; its rich farmlands; its bushveld scrub and arid deserts, each of the many different parts supporting its own distinctive plant and animal life. Truly, a world in one country.

A shanty shop in Cape Town's Khayelitsha ('new home'), a vast suburb designed for a community of 250 000 but which will inevitably have to accommodate a lot more.

Plateau and plain

In physical terms a significant portion of the land is very old. The subcontinent comprises 22 physiographic regions – different geological areas. Some of the rock strata in the valley of the Limpopo and in the Northern Transvaal were formed 4 000 million years ago: not all that long, on the geological calendar, after planet earth itself began to cool. Others, those belonging to the Kalahari Group, are a mere two million years old. In between is a score of classifications that, together, tell a large part of the earth's story.

This variety accounts for South Africa's broad-based wealth of mineral resources. The ancient Swazian and Randian formations, for instance, include gold-bearing reefs that, since their discovery just over a hundred years ago, have transformed the once quietly rural Witwatersrand Highveld into a giant conurbation, recognized for the past half century and more as one of the world's mining and financial capitals. More recently extensive reserves of gold were located in the Orange Free State. Also in the north-central region, and farther west, there are rich iron and manganese deposits. Platinum and chrome are found in the North-West Province; coal in the Karoo Sequence; diamonds in the Kimberlite pipes of the Northern Cape; copper, zinc, uranium, cobalt, nickel; the list, 58 commodities in total, extends through almost the entire spectrum of metals and minerals. The only major ingredient that has been missing is oil, and even promising reserves of that, and of natural gas, have been charted off the southern shores and are being exploited.

THE LIE OF THE LAND If you were to look down on South Africa from an orbiting satellite you would see a clear, quite simple topographical pattern. The land falls into two distinctive physical regions: the great interior plateau, semicircular and occupying most of the subcontinent; and the 'marginal zone', which is the relatively narrow coastal and hinterland strip fringing the plateau on three sides. A third, strikingly obvious geographical feature is the division between the two regions: the highly (in the most literal sense) conspicuous and continuous necklace of mountains and hills known as the Great Escarpment.

The plateau is actually the southern tip of the Great African Plateau that rises in the Sahara Desert, some 5 000 km to the north. In southern Africa its altitude varies from the comparatively low 600 m of the Kalahari basin to a impressive 3 400 m in the towering Maluti mountains of Lesotho.

The plateau's rim – the Great Escarpment – begins in the north-east with the craggy Transvaal Drakensberg (highest peak: Mount Anderson 2 316 m), then runs southwards, rising in even more splendid grandeur to the famed Natal Drakensberg's towering faces, some dropping near-vertically 2 000 m to the plains below. Here are Injasuti (3 459 m), Mont-aux-Sources (3 282 m), Champagne Castle (3 377 m), Giant's Castle (3 314 m), charming names for some of the most awesome peaks in the southern hemisphere. So formidable is the range that one 250-km stretch may be traversed by just a single, steep route – the Sani Pass.

Southward still, the escarpment loops inland in a series of smaller ranges: the Stormberg of South African War fame; the Suurberg; the Sneeuberg north of the gracious little eastern Cape town of Graaff-Reinet. It then disappears into flatland for a while – through this opening thrust the major surface communication routes between Cape Town and the north – then rises in the granite formations of the Roggeveld Scarp and the Kamiesberg range (1 707 m) and into the western Namaqualand coastal belt.

Three hundred million years ago, when the single great land mass called Pangaea first began to succumb to continental drift, slowly, over hundreds of millennia, breaking up to create the global land patterns we know today, the stretch and pull of the earth's crust fashioned the most striking portion of South Africa's marginal zone – the Cape Fold Mountains. Legacies of the same mountain-building process are sister ranges in the Argentine and in Antarctica.

This series of Cape mountains, running parallel to each other and rising starkly over wide longitudinal valleys, includes the Olifants River, Drakenstein, Hottentots-Holland and the splendid Cederberg (highest point: the 2 077-m Great Winterhoek north of Tulbagh) ranges in the western parts, and the more in-tensively folded hills of the Langeberg, Outeniqua, Tsitsikamma and Swartberg in the east, an area that also contains the Little Karoo basin, 30 by 60 km in extent.

A much larger basin, the wide, shallow, world-famed Great Karoo, extends from the folded belts of the south and west northwards. Generally flattish but spliced by dramatic gorges, the most spectacular of which is the aptly named Valley of Desolation, it is an arid region ('karoo' is derived from the Hottentot word meaning dry or bare) but not an unproductive one: the Karoo's sparse but sweet grasses and its generous supplies of underground water sustain a scatter of small farming villages and a large percentage of the country's 27 million head of sheep.

WATER IN A DRY LAND Only a part of South Africa is blessed by good and regular rains (see page 13). Just a quarter of the country is nurtured by perennial rivers – they flow across the southern seaboard and eastern section of the plateau. There are no real lakes – the largest expanse of water, called Fundudzi, in the Northern Transvaal, was born of a massive landslide; the tourist-frequented 'lakes' of Zululand and the Knysna district of the Cape are in reality lagoons. Even the flow of the perennial streams and rivers depends on seasonal and, latterly, erratic rains. As for the great spaces of the western interior, their riverbeds fill and flow only after the rare summer storms. In South Africa, water is a precious commodity.

Biggest of the river systems is that of the Orange, running westwards from its headwaters in the Natal Drakensberg for 2 250 km to the Atlantic, plunging magnificently into the granite Augrabies gorge close to the Namibian border (in exceptional seasons the flow is greater than that of the better-known Victoria Falls on the Zambezi River far to the north) before embarking on its last, desolate leg to the sea. Its tributaries include the Caledon and the Vaal, which is actually longer than the Orange but less voluminous. The Orange drains almost the entire plateau – 47% of the country.

The eastern slopes of the plateau, on the other hand, are comparatively well-watered by their small rivers (one of the more substantial is the Letaba, well known to game viewers in the Kruger National Park). They drain just 12% of the country's surface area but contribute 40% of the run-off. Of the plateau's other rivers, Kipling's 'great grey-green, greasy Limpopo' is the most renowned, demarcating South Africa's northern frontiers with Botswana and Zimbabwe, gathering volume and momentum as it makes its way to the Indian Ocean north of the Mozambique capital of Maputo. Despite its legend in literature, however, it is not a major river by African continental standards.

Significant rivers of the marginal zone include the Sundays and Great Fish, both of which were crucial lines in the often violent territorial disputes between white settler and black tribesman in the nineteenth century (see page 22); the beautiful Berg River of the Western Cape; and Natal's Tugela, where some of the most savage and, for the British, unrewarding battles of the South African (or Anglo-Boer) War were fought.

All told, though, South Africa's rivers do not amount to very much in world terms. Put together, their total run-off is equivalent to that of the Rhine at Rotterdam, and to just half that of the mighty Zambezi 1 000 km to the north.

Supplementary to the river systems are hundreds of pans, or 'floors' – shallow stretches of sometimes salty water (the result of evaporation), biggest of which is the 40-by 64-km GrootVloer in the north-western Cape.

But the country's resources remain limited and precious: much of the modest volume is lost through spillage and evaporation in the intense heat, and there is an ever-increasing demand from the farms, the cities and industry. Consequently a number of ambitious hydro-engineering projects have been launched, some completed. Among them is the Orange River scheme, which accumulates an annual 7 500 million m³ of water, irrigates 300 000 ha of farmland and provides 2 200 million m³ for urban use. Its infrastructure includes the huge Vanderkloof (formerly PK le Roux) and Gariep (Hendrik Verwoerd) dams and a system of underground waterways, one of which is 82,5 km long – the world's largest continuous water tunnel.

Even grander in concept and scale is the Lesotho Highlands water scheme, one of the most ambitious civil engineering exercises ever undertaken in the southern hemisphere, one that rivals the famed Australian Snowy Mountains project in its scope and imagination. It is designed to eventually (in the second decade of the 21st century) supply the Pretoria-Witwatersrand-Vaal Triangle (PWV) area and its environs with a massive 63,6 million m³/sec of water, effectively doubling the annual flow into the Vaal basin, and at the same time supply all of Lesotho's electrical power needs. The first of the three phases will, when completed in the late 1990s, produce about 17 million m³/sec of water. The scheme involves the creation of an extensive road network over some of the continent's most rugged terrain, hundreds of kilometres of tunnelling, and a number of the world's largest rock-fill dams.

VEGETATION With the settlement in South Africa of black people from the north and of white colonists who created an enclave at the Cape in the 1650s and then spread steadily eastwards and northwards (see page 22), much of the land was denuded of its natural vegetation, the cover either destroyed or replaced by exotic species. Nevertheless, five major groups, or vegetation communities, are clearly distinguished. They are those of:

THE DESERTS AND SEMIDESERTS Excluding the huge and desolate expanses of the Namib, which are not within the Republic's borders, two areas fall into these categories. South Africa's only true desert region lies along the westward strip – Namaqualand – extending into the lower Orange River Valley, a parched region that averages, depending on the precise locality, a scant 50 to 150 mm of rainfall a year. In some years there is no rainfall at all. Vegetation is appropriately meagre: a thin ground cover of low, hardy, widely spaced shrubs and succulents and, in springtime, a blaze of bright desert annuals.

One notch higher on the vegetation scale is the Great Karoo, an enormous area of semi-desert with an uncertain rainfall averaging between 125 and 375 mm a year. Again, plant life comprises tough shrubs and succulents, though, as mentioned, grasses occur in the more tolerable eastern regions.

THE MEDITERRANEAN (winter-rainfall) areas of the Western Cape. Because of the immense wealth of its plant life, and despite its tiny area, this botanical region is regarded as one of the six floral kingdoms of the world.

Forests are to found only in the wetter *kloofs*, but many evergreen shrubs of various heights occur in this region as well as a vast number of indigenous species known collectivly as *fynbos*. This includes the Western Cape's famed proteas (the king protea is South Africa's national flower), ericas and a marvellous diversity of bulbs. Characteristically, the plants here occur in small, localized areas and are therefore rather rare. They are believed to have ancient origins, and have been able to survive only because the Cape has escaped glaciation for millions of years.

THE BUSHVELD Covering the lower slopes of the plateau and the Lowveld of the Eastern Transvaal – an area that encompasses the great expanse of the Kruger National Park. Flora in the northern parts include marula and umbrella thorn, the elephantine baobab, the fever tree, the ubiquitous dark-green mopani and tall tufted grasses. In the more open Kalahari thornbush country, mainly towards the west, there are hardy acacia and camel-thorn trees and sparse semidesert ground cover.

THE TEMPERATE INTERIOR UPLANDS This is the classical veld, consisting of rolling grassy plains and, probably because of winter droughts and frost, few trees (although some exotic species such as willows and eucalyptus – gum trees – thrive). Tropical-type grasses grow in the lower areas; in the colder upper parts, in the Highveld, the grass is shorter and indigenous trees are a rarity.

THE SCATTERED FORESTS of the year-round rainfall belt, once widespread but victim to the depredations of man over the centuries. The relics of the marginal zone's great woodlands are now protected by law. Most extensive is the strip, 180- by 16-km, along the southern coast where tall ironwood, yellowwood and stinkwood trees occur. Farther to the north, along the Natal coast, there are patches of evergreen subtropical tree species, including palms and, in the swampier areas, mangroves.

Seas and shores

Lapped by two oceans, South Africa's coastline runs 3 000 km from the Atlantic wilderness of the Orange River mouth in the north-west, round the Cape to northern KwaZulu-Natal

The west coast harbour of Lambert's Bay

and the Mozambique border in the east. Large stretches reward the traveller with spectacular scenery; some are a paradise for the angler, surfer, camper and sun-worshipper.

Broadly speaking, the oceans fall into two type-categories: warm, and cooler, the nature of each determined largely by the dominant currents of the subcontinental seas. The warm waters on the east coast emanate from the tropics and flow rapidly south and south-east as the Agulhas Current, which more or less hugs the coast until, near Cape Agulhas, it turns south and east. Along the west coast, the main waterbody comes from the South Atlantic as the north-flowing Benguela Current, and is much cooler.

THE WEST COAST is a strange, barren region of rocky, sand-blown shorelines backed by raised beaches and, stretching inland for anything between 30 and 50 km, terraces of deep, soft, often-shifting sand. Dunes are covered by sparse greenery (technically, dwarf bush vegetation), and the land is classed as 'sandveld'. In the far north, around the mouth of the Orange, the legendary raised beaches are rich in diamonds, swept down by the river over the ages and then distributed by inshore currents.

The country's once-dynamic, now ailing but still enormously productive fishing industry has its home along the length of the west coast. Here, during the upwellings of the Atlantic –

usually in spring and summer – rich plant nutrients are carried to the inshore zone, so favouring the proliferation of plankton, basic to the area's rich stocks of mussels. These shellfish are primary feeders, and in turn support massive populations of rock lobsters, snoek and stockfish (Cape hake). In the south the sea at times abounds with tunny, marlin and yellowtail.

THE SOUTH AND EAST COASTS are much more heavily populated and, in tourist terms, more popular. In the south, one stretch of shoreline with its hinterland is especially beautiful: the 220-km Garden Route that extends roughly from Mossel Bay in the west to the Tsitsikamma Forest and Storms River in the east. This is a green and flowered region of charming bays and beaches, cliffs and pounding surf overlooked by the not-too-distant and quite splendid Outeniqua Mountains.

Equally enticing to holiday-makers are the coasts north and south of Durban in the east: wide, dune-backed sandy strips fringing a remarkably straight shoreline (Durban itself, with its 16-km-long Bluff, is something of an exception).

In fact, there are precious few good natural harbours along the entire length of the Republic's coastline. (Saldanha Bay is the best, but it was passed over by early seafarers in favour of the more exposed but better watered Table Bay.) It is an even coastline, without many pronounced embayments, and most of the otherwise-suitable estuaries are blocked by sandbars, the product of currents and of the heavy sediment brought by rivers with steep gradients and sporadic flow. East London, in the far Eastern Cape, is the country's only river port and its harbour, on the Buffalo, is subject to constant dredging operations. Durban's bar is particularly notorious. The city's port is one of the southern hemisphere's biggest and busiest, but it was only in 1892, after decades of frustrating experiment with breakwaters and sandpumps, that the 2 820-ton *Dunrobin Castle* managed to sail into harbour – the first ocean-going liner to do so.

Climate

Weather patterns, influenced by different ocean currents, by altitude and prevailing winds and by the ever-changing nature of the land, are subject to sharp regional variation. Climatically, South Africa could be half a dozen entirely separate countries.

When it comes to rainfall, however, there are three broad but distinct regions. The south-western tip of the subcontinent, centring on the lovely city of Cape Town, has winter precipitation; the southern and eastern coastal belts enjoy (in good years) perennial showers which are heavy, almost tropical in KwaZulu-Natal. Rains over the rest of the country – on the great central plateau and towards the east – come with sudden summer thunderstorms brought by north-easterly winds.

This is not to say that the land, as a whole, is well-watered. On the contrary, as we've seen, South Africa is one of the world's drier countries: mean annual rainfall is little over 460 mm compared with a global average of 857 mm. The rains, too, tend to be unpredictable; drought has been the norm rather than the exception in recent times. And the farther west one goes the less generous the heavens are: along the shores of the Indian Ocean and in the KwaZulu-Natal hinterland a healthy 1 000 mm of rain can be expected to fall each year; in the western extremities of the country the average tends to be around 200 mm, and some of the thirstlands are lucky if they get 50 mm.

Average annual temperatures are more constant. The northern areas are not, as one might expect, very much hotter than the southern because the land rises to the high central

Kogel Bay, in the south-western Cape

plateau, which is generally cooler than other parts of the world lying within the same lines of latitude. Cape Town can be suffocating and its annual average temperature is 17 °C; Pretoria, a full 1 500 km nearer the tropics, can freeze and its annual average temperature is only half a degree more.

But temperature inversions vary, quite dramatically, from place to place. They are least at the coast and greatest in the interior, where clear-skied winter nights are bitterly cold while the days remain sunny and mild.

South Africa, in fact, is blessed with a great deal of sunshine, the average number of cloud-free hours a day varying (depending on the area) from 7,5 to 9,4 compared with New York's 6,9, Rome's 6,4 and London's 3,8. Some parts of the country, the dust-dry western districts for instance, register a bare ten or so overcast days a year.

The climate of the interior, in the rising lands beyond the Escarpment, is fairly uniform: bone-dry, sunny winters; summer days (from about November to February) of mounting storm clouds and late-afternoon downpours. At least, that is the traditional pattern in the north-central and eastern parts, where, apart from Kimberley in the Northern Cape, the inland cities and most of the towns are situated.

The climates of the different seaboard regions are more variable. The south-western part of the Western Cape – Cape Town, the Peninsula, its coastal extensions and hinterland – is unique within the southern African context in its Mediterranean character. It has dry summers with long, cloudless days which are sometimes – in what are called 'berg wind conditions' (hot air blowing in from the northern interior) – perfect in their somnolent stillness, at other times disturbed by a gusty, unnerving south-easter that often reaches gale-force and can last for up to a week or more. In winter it is wet and cool – downright cold at times. The best Cape months are those of its brief spring (September and October) and autumn (March and April) when colours are changing and the fragile delicacy of the air lifts and sustains the spirit.

Northwards, up the Namaqualand coastal districts, the climate becomes ever drier and hotter until you eventually reach the endless, waterless tracts of the Namib Desert. Springtime in Namaqualand, though, is a lotion for the eyes:

for a few brief weeks the barren-seeming countryside is transformed by multicoloured carpets of small, exquisite flowers.

Along the other coast, stretching east to Port Elizabeth, the climate changes from Mediterranean to temperate. Again the summers are warm (and windy); the winters cool. Here there is rainfall all year round – or there should be: the eastern Cape, like most of the rest of the country, has at times suffered crippling droughts. Following the Indian Ocean coastline as it inclines northwards, one enters the subtropical region of KwaZulu-Natal, where it is hot and stickily humid in summer (though the uplands are cooler and very pleasant); chilly to warm in winter; and rainy throughout, but wetter during the summer months.

THE PEOPLE

South Africa has a total population of about 38 million. One cannot be more exact because although censuses are periodically taken they are soon outdated, and the very nature of society and the mobility – and until recently the downright hostility – of some of its elements have made it difficult, if not impossible, to paint a precise statistical picture.

Of the four major ethnic groups, black people number some 29 million; whites nearly five million; those of Asian origin just under a million; and the mixed-descent (coloured) community between three and four million.

Growth rates vary quite sharply among groups – predictably, since South Africa is anything but homogeneous. Most blacks have their roots in the countryside. They are of peasant farming stock, their traditional communities tribally structured. Cultural taboos and perceived economic necessity inhibit family planning; the extended family is an accepted and effective form of social security. Southern Africa is no different to the rest of the world: the poorer, less educated tend to have large families. With greater urbanization and higher standards of living a decline in the birth rate can be expected. At present, the black population is increasing by 2,7% a year, which projects a total of something close to 40 million by the end of the century. By contrast, the annual white growth rate is 1,5%, indicating (if one discounts the migration factor) a figure of about 5,5 million in the year 2 000.

The face of rural South Africa. The young are flocking to the cities.

CONCENTRATIONS A crucial feature of the past few decades has been urban drift, the migration both of whites and, more importantly, of blacks from the countryside to the cities. Industrial expansion since the Second World War has meant jobs, or at least the prospect of jobs, in and around the major centres, an irresistible lure to hundreds of thousands of blacks who would otherwise have to scratch a meagre living from the soil in areas that are not favoured by many modern amenities, and where, because of drought and overstocking and erosion, much of the land is poor and becoming even poorer.

Biggest of the conurbations is the Pretoria-Witwatersrand-Vereeniging complex, now embraced by the Gauteng region, South Africa's industrial heartland (see page 22). This immense cluster of concrete nuclei, each ringed by its dormitory suburbs, has a population of some eight million: it covers less than 1% of the country's land area but is home to almost a fifth of its people. Soweto – acronym for South Western Townships – started life as a collection of 'locations' housing temporary labour for Johannesburg's giant gold mines. It is now a city in its own right, one of a million souls (that is the official figure – in reality it almost certainly accommodates a great many more), and its commuters include highly qualified people, as well as miners and labourers.

Other centres – Cape Town, Port Elizabeth,

Durban-Pinetown – have grown in a similar fashion if rather less spectacularly.

One source estimates that the ten million urban blacks in South Africa are expected to increase to at least 57 million by the year 2050, posing 'one of the major population problems of the next century'.

Certainly, mass-migration to the cities will not be trouble-free, but urban drift is now regarded not so much a potentially disastrous trend as a natural, unstoppable process that could in fact help short-circuit, or at least alleviate, some of the country's most worrying anticipated ailments: badly needed infrastructure, social and other services, for instance, can be more easily and cheaply created for large concentrations of people than for widely scattered rural populations; it is easier to provide people with jobs, houses and clinics and schools, electric lighting, proper sanitation and all the other ingredients of a decent life if they are close to and part of the established centres.

Moreover, quite apart from their potential as reservoirs of manpower, technical skills and professional expertise, large urban concentrations have a habit of becoming economically self-generative – much to their own and everybody else's benefit.

At some time in the future it will probably be possible to write about the people of South Africa without too much qualification along racial lines, but today's reality is that the ethnic

Making a living in the 'new' South Africa

polygamy); in matters of inheritance and guardianship, and seniority within the clan; in kinship bonds, the social order and the spiritual force of ancestry; and in the assumptions underlying land tenure and in concepts of wealth.

But that is the old Africa. The new co-exists (often uncomfortably) and will in due course supersede. Many of the ten million urban blacks are second and third generation townsmen; hundreds of thousands are migrant workers; all have been dramatically exposed to the blessings and curses of the acquisitive society. The tribal order, in the towns, has been largely eroded, to be replaced by a transitional but distinct subculture that encompasses (engulfs, in many tragic instances) everything from social structure and family life to music, literature and language.

Whether urbanization and its multiple assault on African tradition is a good or a bad thing, it is a complex issue, the conclusion subjective. What is no longer open to question, though, is the inevitability of the process. South Africa is an industrial nation, dependent on the skills of its black people. The blacks for their part are impelled to go – and to live – where there is work. And so the sprawl of the cities continues, shifting the demographic and economic balance.

groups do not share a common heritage and have not, for reasons of law and in some cases of choice, integrated. Any objective summary must therefore take account of the separate identities.

THE BLACK PEOPLE Again, though somewhat less so (there are historical affinities), the blacks of southern Africa are divided by custom, social system and language into a number of groupings. The divisions are not clearly evident in the party-political arena nor in the context of increasingly detribalized urban life, but in other respects the principal black groups can be regarded as distinctive societies. They comprise the Zulu, the Xhosa, the Swazi (all three are related, belonging to the Nguni group of peoples); the Northern Sotho, the Southern Sotho and the Tswana (again, of the same major Sotho group: the Tswana are the western branch); the South Ndebele and the North Ndebele; the Venda and Lemba; and the Shangaan-Tsonga.

These ethnic groupings might suggest that South Africa's black communities have clung tenaciously to traditional African ways and remain outside the mainstream of Western influence, which of course is patently not so. Custom, tradition and ancient loyalties do persist, most obviously in the rural areas. They are enshrined, for instance, in the rules of courtship and marriage (usually those sanctioning

THE ASIAN PEOPLE A need for labour to harvest the crops of KwaZulu-Natal's new and vast sugar plantations in the mid-nineteenth century prompted the importation of tens of thousands of workers from India. They were indentured (contracted) for between three and five years, after which they had the choice of repatriation, of renewing their contracts, or of accepting Crown land and remaining as settlers. Most took up the land option.

The first shipload disembarked in 1860. In due course they were joined by non-indentured 'passenger' immigrants from the Indian subcontinent – British subjects able to travel freely within the Empire, and choosing the sunbathed spaces of KwaZulu-Natal as their future home. Today, South Africa's Asian community numbers some 900 000, most of whom – 85% – live in and around the Verulam-Durban-Pinetown complex. Nearly all the remainder, about 100 000 people of Asian origin, are settled on the Witwatersrand and in Pretoria. Among them are 10 000 or so citizens of Chinese extraction who retain their own cultural identity.

The Indian society, generally a prosperous one, has its own distinct traditions, underpinned by religion and by kutum – the disciplined, patriarchal, extended family which regulates relationships and social interaction. The community as a whole is remarkably unified but also organized according to faith – Hindu and Muslim. The Hindu element is in turn divided into four language groups (Tamil, Telugu, Hindustani and Gujarati) and subscribes to its own strict rules governing modes, manners, ritual, food and drink. The Muslims speak Gujarati – the language of western India – and Urdu, and observe precisely defined codes of belief and behaviour.

Again, though, traditions are being eroded, especially among the younger generation. The izar and qami, the dawni and sari are giving way, if not always to T-shirts and jeans, certainly to the more conservative Western styles of dress; there is movement away from the multiple towards the smaller family; traditional male authority no longer goes unquestioned; young Indian women lead far freer and more diversified lives than their mothers and grandmothers; and English is the main means of communication.

SOUTH AFRICANS OF MIXED DESCENT The country's nearly three million-strong 'coloured' community, the majority of whom live in the Western Cape, has diverse origins. The early Dutch settlers imported slaves from Holland's eastern possessions, from elsewhere in Africa and from some of the islands of the Atlantic and Indian oceans, and admixtures steadily and inevitably followed, Hottentot, Xhosa and white man adding their own progeny over the following decades.

Significant and distinctive subgroups include the Griquas of the eastern Karoo fringes, the product of European-Hottentot miscegenation; the mixed-descent people of KwaZulu-Natal, many of whom trace their ancestry to immigrants from Mauritius and St Helena; and the 200 000 Cape Malays of the Peninsula, a close-knit, homogeneous society that has maintained its strict Islamic ways over the centuries (see page 279).

In general terms, though, the coloured people of South Africa are culturally very much part of the Western world. Some 87% are of the Christian faith; the majority speak Afrikaans; and they are barely separable in lifestyle and social organization from people of exclusively European origin. There seems no good reason why they should have been subjected to any special classification (not that formally imposed ethnic categories of any kind can be justified), and in fact were more or less an integrated part of the Cape community as a whole until fairly recently, enjoying, among other things, the constitutionally entrenched common-roll franchise, until it was removed in the 1950s.

Under the apartheid regime coloured residential areas were delineated; the famed District Six, close to the heart of Cape Town, was demolished and most of its inhabitants moved to the huge, new and somewhat characterless townships such as Mitchell's Plain on the Cape Flats. The callous move created lasting bitterness and the site of District Six remained undeveloped, a scar on Cape Town's landscape and on the minds of its citizens.

THE WHITE PEOPLE White South Africans account for 17,5% of the population, and until the late 1980s they were the politically dominant ethnic group and the controlling influence within the economy. They, in turn, are divided into two major language groups: Afrikaans and English.

THE AFRIKANERS Descendants of the early Cape-Dutch settlers and of the people of the other nationalities they absorbed, number something over 2,5 million.

High Dutch was the stem from which Afrikaans branched, taking on new words and a different shape over three centuries of isolation from the original homeland and, later, from the principal Cape settlement.

The German and French elements are significant (and, linguistically, the black languages as well): the Afrikaners, in fact, have a rich mix of cultures in their blood, one official estimate pegging the ancestral ingredients at only 40% Dutch, a surprising 40% German; 7,5% British (mainly Scottish); 7,5% French and 5% other. The French connection, through the hardy Protestant Huguenots who fled persecution in Europe in the 1680s, can be discerned in names such as Du Plessis, Du Toit and Marais; the Dutch in the 'van' prefixes. Curiously, there seems to be very little that is clearly German in language, custom or nomenclature – assimilation seems to have been total.

Over the decades, the Afrikaner community expanded from very small beginnings, more as a consequence of natural increase than from immigration (hence the proliferation of certain names – the confusing concentration of Bothas in the political arena, for instance). Families have always tended to be large, patriarchal, Calvinistic and close-knit; groups of families clannish – the universal characteristics of colonial pioneers.

Until fairly recently the Afrikaners were a predominantly rural people, but the ravages of the South African War (1899-1902), drought, cattle disease and rapid industrialization led, from the early years of this century, to a large-scale and continuing drift to the cities. This forced migration caused a great deal of hardship: thousands of families with their roots in the countryside found it impossible to adjust to urban life, and few had the skills to compete on the job market. In 1931, at the height of the Great Depression, a Carnegie-funded commission reported that of a total white population of 1,8 million, over 300 000, most of them Afrikaans city-dwellers, could be classed as 'very poor'. Today, however, much of commerce, industry, banking and insurance is in the hands of Afrikaans-speaking businessmen.

THE ENGLISH South Africa is home to just under two million English-speaking whites, and their legacy is entirely different from that of the Afrikaners. The background is colonial rather than pioneer; urban-industrial rather than rural.

The origins of this segment of South African society can be traced, for the most part, to the British occupation of the Cape in the early 1800s, and to the colonial government's 'anglicization' policy, one major consequence of which was the landing, in 1820, of 4 000 British settlers at Algoa Bay, now Port Elizabeth, in the eastern Cape (see page 195). Farther east, the colonization of Natal – a more independently motivated exercise – gathered momentum from the 1840s with a series of privately organized immigration schemes. Thereafter, the discovery first of diamonds in the northern Cape and then of gold on the Witwatersrand attracted an avalanche of 'uitlanders' (foreigners), most of them English-speaking, to the northern areas.

More recently, post-Second World War immigration, and emigrants from Britain's former colonies in East and Central Africa, and especially from rebel Rhodesia (now Zimbabwe), added substantially to the numbers.

The strongholds of the present English-speaking people were thus historically determined. It is no accident that South Africa's 'English' universities are at Cape Town (UCT), Grahamstown (Rhodes University), in Natal (Durban and Pietermaritzburg) and in Johannesburg (Wits). Other than significant English-speaking farming enclaves in the eastern Cape and in the sugar and fruit-growing regions of Natal, it is largely an urban community.

Traces of the colonial psychology persisted until well after the Second World War. In affluent homes along the gracious tree-lined avenues of Constantia in the Cape and in Pietermaritzburg people would speak, in accents indistinguishable from those of upper-middle-class Surrey and Sussex, of England as 'home', toast the Queen on her birthday and eat plum pudding in the heat of a southern Christmas. But these now represent an anachronistic minority. Most English-speaking South Africans have long since detached themselves from their ancestral origins and identify wholly with the country.

WHITE MINORITIES A number of smaller ethnic and linguistic groups make up the remainder of the white community. Most substantial – estimates vary widely but there are probably about 75 000 – are South Africans of Portuguese extraction, most of them former residents of Lisbon's African territories of Mozambique and Angola, both now independent, though a substantial number hail from the Atlantic island of Madeira. In descending numerical order the additional groups are the Germans (40 000); Greek (17 000); Italian (17 000); and French (7 000). Together, other nationalities total some 35 000.

A significant subgroup of English-speaking South Africans are the Jewish people, comprising about 2,5% of the white population. Though relatively small in numbers, Jewish South Africans have contributed disproportionately to the business and industrial development of the country, and to the performing, literary and visual arts.

Where the people live

In 1910 the Crown colonies of the Cape of Good Hope and Natal and the former Boer republics of the Transvaal and Orange Free State were brought together as the four provinces of the Union of South Africa. This territorial structure lasted until 1994, when the country was reorganized into nine provincial divisions in terms of the new federal arrangement. The former 'black homelands' – the quasi-independent republics of Transkei, Ciskei, Bophuthatswana and Ciskei – were reincorporated.

The regions, each with its own premier, parliament and civil service, enjoy a healthy degree of legislative and administrative autonomy. Briefly, they are:

WESTERN CAPE The oldest, most populous and economically advanced segment of the old Cape Province. The region draws its prosperity from Cape Town's great harbour, from the fishing fleets of the seaboard, from the manufacturing and service industries of the metropolitan area, from the wine and fruit of the surrounding Boland region, and from an increasingly flourishing tourism sector.
Area: 129 386 km^2; capital: Cape Town; population: 3.6 million.

EASTERN CAPE A large, heavily populated and unevenly endowed region that takes in the coastal city of Port Elizabeth and surrounding 'settler country', the 'Border' area – so called because it was once at the leading edge of colonial encroachment – and the erstwhile independent (and predominantly Xhosa-speaking) republics of Transkei and Ciskei.

The former homelands are among the poorest parts of the country. Together, they occupy a modest 55 000 km^2 of once-fertile (and still scenically splendid) countryside into which nearly 4 million people have been crammed. Development has been sporadic and inadequate, the land grievously damaged by over-crowding, over-stocking and the pressures imposed by intensive subsistence farming. The coasts, though, are strikingly beautiful and, once things have settled down, could rank among South Africa's prime tourism destinations.
Area: 170 616 km^2; capital: Bisho; population: 6.5 million.

NORTHERN CAPE The largest region in geographical terms but the most sparsely populated and least developed. It extends from the bleak Namaqualand coast in the west to Kimberley in the north-central part of the country. Much of the Northern Cape is covered by the dry, sandy soils of the Great Karoo and, in the far north, beyond the Orange River and the town of Upington, by the Kalahari wilderness.

Valuable crops (cotton, fruit and others) are harvested on the intensively irrigated lands flanking the Orange; sheep-farms occupy much of the east-central drylands; diamonds are extracted in quantity from the deep 'pipes' around Kimberley and from the alluvial fields along the Atlantic seaboard.
Area: 363 389 km^2; capital: Kimberley; population: 740 000.

KWAZULU-NATAL The region corresponds, with some minor adjustments, to the old Natal province and the KwaZulu homeland it incorporated, and it supports the largest of the regional populations: nearly 9 million people are wedged into the narrowish strip that lies between the grandness of the Drakensberg in the west and the warm waters of the Indian ocean.

The majority of its inhabitants are of Zulu (Eastern Nguni) stock; the province's coastal centres are home to most of South Africa's large Indian community.

Aptly known as the Garden Province, KwaZulu-Natal is a well-watered, fertile land of rolling green hills, a magnificent coastline and, towards the north, savanna and wetland conservancies that are immensely rich in plant, animal and bird life.

The warm, southward-flowing Mozambique current ensures high temperatures along the seaboard, which makes possible the cultivation of sugarcane in latitudes more southerly than is usual. Much of the region's income is derived from tourism; major drawcards are the sunlit coastal resorts to either side of Durban; Durban itself; the game reserves of Zululand, and the scenically superb Drakensberg range.
Area: 91 481 km^2; capital: Pietermaritzburg and Ulundi, the traditional Zulu stronghold, were vying for capital status at the time of writing; population: 9 million.

FREE STATE The province, on the high, bare plains of the central plateau between the Orange and Vaal rivers, occupies about a tenth of South Africa's land area, yields a third of its maize and wheat harvests and sustains more than 80% of its sheep and a large percentage of its cattle populations. The land towards the east – that which lies between Bloemfontein and the highlands of Lesotho – is highly productive (fruit orchards feature prominently) as well as scenically lovely. This is a wealthy region: apart from its farms and ranches it has impressive reserves of gold (around the town of Welkom), diamonds, platinum and coal (which supports the massive Sasol synthetic fuel complex). Area: 129 437 km^2; capital: Bloemfontein; population: 2.8 million.

NORTH-WEST This comprises the former western Transvaal, part of the former northern Cape and most of the former 'independent' homeland of Bophuthatswana, and is something of a cinderella region. It has its chrome and platinum mines (the latter concentrated around the pretty little town of Rustenburg), but most of its people are involved in farming: fruit, vegetables and flowers around the beautiful Magaliesberg hills; cattle and great, golden fields of maize elsewhere. It encompasses the magnificent tourist playground of Sun City and the nearby, and superb, Pilanesberg National Park. Area: 118 710 km^2; capital: Mmabatho; population: 3.3 million.

NORTHERN TRANSVAAL A region of bushveld, rich grasslands and enchanting hills (notably the Waterberg and, towards the Limpopo River in the north, the Soutpansberg ranges). There are no major growth points – the Pietersburg area, its largest centre, accounts for just 0.6% of the country's employment – and the province lags far behind in the development stakes. It has excellent tourist potential, though: among other things it encloses half the famed Kruger National Park. Area: 119 606 km^2; capital: Pietersburg; population: 5.2 million.

EASTERN TRANSVAAL The second smallest province with the fastest growing economy. Industry is concentrated around the mining centres of Witbank and Middelburg on the highveld plateau to the west. In the east are the splendid mountains of the Transvaal Escarpment and, beyond, the hot, game-rich lowveld plain and the Kruger National Park. Area: 81 816 km^2; capital: Nelspruit; population: 2.9 million.

GAUTENG was until recently known as the PWV, an acronym for Pretoria-Witwatersrand-Vereeniging. A small, rich, densely populated region that originally drew its wealth from the gold mines of the Witwatersrand – which gave birth to the city of Johannesburg – but now boasts a hugely diverse economy. Urban drift and its attendant socio-economic problems are in greater evidence here than in any other part of the country. Area: 18 810 km^2; capital: Johannesburg; population: 6.9 million.

CITIES The major areas of urban concentration are along the Cape's southern and eastern seaboard, in the KwaZulu-Natal coastal belt, and in the Gauteng region. South Africa's principal cities, in order of age, are:

CAPE TOWN This city had its beginnings in 1652 with the landing of Jan van Riebeeck and his small party of settlers. Greater Cape Town – the magisterial districts of Cape Town, Goodwood, Kuils River, Wynberg and Simon's Town – sprawls over much of the Peninsula and is home to almost three million people. The city's setting, beneath and around the moody grandeur of Table Mountain, is without doubt one of the loveliest in the southern hemisphere. Circumnavigator Francis Drake is said to have described it as 'the fairest Cape in all the circumference of the earth'; later, as one of the busiest harbours on the sea route to India, the town became known as the 'tavern of the seas'.

Cape Town's port is quieter than it was in the heyday of the passenger steamer. Other harbours, much closer to the northern industrial markets, have poached much of its freight traffic. Marine and mercantile enterprises still contribute substantially to the local economy, though. Its wider base includes light engineering and manufacturing, the service industries (many large companies have their headquarters in Cape Town, mainly, it seems, because it is such a pleasant place in which to live) and tourism – the beaches, the attractive wineland-and-mountain hinterland, the history in the stones of the buildings, the calendar of arts, the eating and drinking places, and the undemanding, unhurried lifestyle are powerful attractions. A great many affluent people retire to or near the city. It is 1 463 km from Johannesburg, 1 716 km from Durban, and its residents sometimes tend to feel left out of things.

PORT ELIZABETH It is difficult to say with certainty whether this or Durban is South Africa's second-oldest city. Probably Port Elizabeth, which is where the 1820 Settlers set their optimistic feet ashore – or rather, on the beaches of Algoa Bay, since there was just a dilapidated fort and a tiny cluster of thatched cottages on the site of the city at the time. It is now a great port, but it took decades to grow into anything resembling such. As late as 1838 a visitor could write of 'an ugly, dirty, ill-built, ill-scented hamlet similar to some of the worst fishing villages on the English coast'. But the place did eventually develop (it formally became a city in 1913) into an impressive modern complex of dockyards, motor assembly plants, factories and commercial buildings sustaining, together with its satellites of Uitenhage and Kirkwood, some 300 000 economically active people.

Not far away is Grahamstown, familiarly known as the 'city of saints' because of its many churches. Overlooked by the impressive 1820 British Settlers' Monument, home of Rhodes University and of several famous schools, Grahamstown, keeper of English South Africa's soul, is among the most attractive of the country's smaller centres.

DURBAN On the KwaZulu-Natal coast and third largest of the cities is aptly known as 'South Africa's playground', though it is more reminiscent of Blackpool than of Cannes. Durban is not, however, the capital of KwaZulu-Natal: that honour belongs to the pretty city of Pietermaritzburg some 90 km inland (see page 19).

Durban's origins, and its history, are very English. It started life as the trading and white-hunter outpost of Port Natal when, in 1824, the enterprising Lieutenant Farewell of the good ship *Julia* (he had previously served on the *Beagle* of Darwinian fame) disembarked 40 white settlers, to whom the Zulu king, Shaka, with surprising benevolence, granted 9 000

km² of rich land around the bay. Progress was slow at first (in 1835 there were still only 30 or so residents), but with the launching of immigration schemes in the 1840s the town expanded rapidly. Today, more than one and a half million people inhabit the Durban-Pinetown complex; its 1 668-ha bay area has 15 195 m of quayside that handles bulk cargoes of, among other commodities, grain, coal, manganese, and sugar from the plantations. The local industrial and commercial base is broad, with food-processing and, predictably, marine-orientated businesses such as warehousing and oil storage being prominent.

BLOEMFONTEIN Capital of the Free State and judicial capital of the Republic of South Africa, sprawls over 16 900 ha of dry, treeless central plateau countryside.

The place has a population of some 300 000, and is largely an administrative city (though it has 350 or so light industries, and the largest railway workshops in the country) – 40% of its economically active citizens are employed in social, community or government services. The town is quiet, serious, respectable. It has some fine buildings, notably the Old Raadsaal, or parliament – a dignified mix of Renaissance form and Classical-revival detail – and the splendid new Sand du Plessis theatre complex completed in 1985.

PRETORIA State administrative capital and a place of some one million souls, is known as the 'jacaranda city' because of the 50 000 or so lovely lilac-blossomed trees that grace gardens, parks and about 650 km of well-laid-out streets.

The city has a magnificent general setting, overlooked by the hills on which the renowned architect, Herbert Baker, placed his Union Buildings, model for the grander but no more pleasing seat of the Raj government in New Delhi. There are other impressive structures, especially the turn-of-the-century Palace of Justice, described as 'one of the finest classical public spaces in South Africa'. Church Square has always been Pretoria's hub, but nowadays is not a very attractive one. At the time of Union it could have become one of the architectural glories of the subcontinent, embellished with fountains and flowers and Continental-style paving (this was the citizenry's preference). Instead, the authorities chose to redesign it as a tramway terminus. Says author Vivien Allen: 'Pretoria exchanged its heart for a public transport system'.

JOHANNESBURG Sixty kilometres south of Pretoria is the financial and industrial epicentre of South Africa: the Witwatersrand, with the high-rise city of Johannesburg as *its* centre. In fact there is not much open country between Pretoria and Johannesburg, and there will be even less in the coming decades, during which a brand new city will progressively cover much of the intervening dun-and-green veld. Its focal point is the aptly and charmingly named village of Halfway House but the planners, in their pedestrian fashion, have chosen to call the new metropolis Midrand.

The Witwatersrand has an inner and an outer ring of towns. The former, around metropolitan Johannesburg, comprises the largely dormitory municipalities of Sandton (rich and chic), Randburg, Roodepoort, Edenvale, Germiston, Alberton (the last two somewhat downmarket), Bedfordview and Soweto, the largest 'black' urban complex in the country. The outer zone includes the substantial centres of Krugersdorp, Randfontein, and Westonaria in the west, and Kempton Park (which has a fine racetrack), Benoni, Springs and Boksburg in the east.

These towns are built on gold, discovered just a hundred years ago (see page 23), which still sustains them but not by any means exclusively – nearly 40% of the entire country's gross product is generated by the huge number of mining, manufacturing, commercial and financial enterprises in the area.

Johannesburg itself has a population of between 1,5 and 2 million. Its buildings are tall, new and closely packed (the central flatland area of Hillbrow is the densest residential area in the southern hemisphere).

Nobody can pretend Johannesburg is a beautiful city. It is notably lacking in open space; the mine dumps are an eyesore (though most of them now have thin coats of greenery: an improvement on the dust-blown past). But there is a vibrancy, a bustling, honestly materialistic vitality about the place that does have its appeal. And it has a marvellous climate: it is situated high on the central plateau where the air is rare and heady, the winters clear and not too cold, the summer heat relieved (in good years) by late-afternoon rainstorms that are often cloudbursts of Lear-like proportions. On average Johannesburg gets more rain in little more than four summer months than England's notoriously soggy Manchester does in a full year.

HISTORICAL BACKGROUND

Both the black and the white peoples are relative newcomers to the southern African subcontinent. They were preceded by the San (Bushmen) hunter-gatherers, and by the Khoikhoi (Hottentot) pastoralists.

By the 14th century, however, the first of the Bantu-speaking groups had migrated southwards from the Great Lakes region of Central Africa and were settled in what are now Zimbabwe, Botswana and the western parts of the Transvaal. When the first Europeans set foot on the southern shores in the mid-17th century, Nguni groups (which included the ancestors of the modern Xhosa and Zulu) had long since moved down the Indian Ocean seaboard and were occupying today's Transvaal, Natal and eastern Cape.

Colonization and conflict

Portuguese navigators charted the sea-route round the tip of Africa towards the end of the 15th century, but in the event it was the Dutch who pioneered white settlement. In April 1652, Jan van Riebeeck, commander of the Dutch East India Company's expedition to the Cape, made his landfall at Table Bay to establish a victualling station for Holland's great trading fleets.

The outpost soon grew into a colony, the settlers spreading out into the hinterland – and then eastwards, on a direct collision course with the westward-advancing Xhosa.

Inevitably, competition for grazing and arable land led to open confrontation between black and white farmers and cattle-owners. The first Frontier War broke out in 1779; altogether, there were eight more major conflicts during the next hundred years.

The Dutch remained in control at the Cape until 1795, when they were displaced by the British, who, apart from a further brief period of Dutch rule (1803-6), were to be the dominant force in southern African affairs until the Act of Union established the modern South African state in 1910.

The early British governors of the Cape were anxious to create a colony more English in character, and to resolve the problems between Boer and Xhosa on the eastern frontier. In 1820, in an effort to achieve both ends, shiploads of immigrants were brought from Britain to settle the Albany border district where, it was hoped, they would serve as a 'buffer' against hostile black groups.

The frontier clashes continued, however, and the Boers, their outlying farms vulnerable to attack, felt they were ill-protected by the British military garrisons. Moreover, these independent-minded frontiersmen resented what they perceived as interference in their affairs by a government in far-off Cape Town, especially in the matter of their right to own slaves. In 1834, slavery was abolished.

THE BOER REPUBLICS Deep dissatisfaction among the Boer communities, coupled with a desire for better grazing lands, led many families to sell up, span in their oxen and and seek a new home in the northern interior and on the eastern seaboard – in Natal, where Shaka, the Zulu warrior king, had permitted a British party to establish a trading post (the settlement, inaugurated in 1824, was named Durban, after the Cape governor of the day). This mass-migration of Boers – which started in a small and exploratory way in 1834, gathering momentum over the following decade – became known as the Great Trek.

The eastern trekkers suffered grievously at the hands of Shaka's successor, Dingane, who contrived the massacre of Piet Retief's advance party in February 1838 and then went on to engage the main body of Boers in a series of fiercely fought battles. His impis were finally routed on 16 December 1838, at the Battle of Blood River, and the Trekkers set up their first republic, which they named Natalia. The fledgling state, lasted a bare four years before falling to the British, and the Republic of Natalia became the Crown Colony of Natal.

The northern Voortrekkers enjoyed more success, though their progress was by no means trouble-free. The white man's encroachment was, understandably, bitterly resented by a number of the black peoples, most powerful which were the Matabele, led by Mzilikazi. But superior weaponry prevailed; Mzilikazi's warriors were defeated – at Vegkop and other

places – in 1838 and, after some years of discord and competition for leadership, the Boers finally settled their internal differences and those they had with the British government at the Cape. The Transvaal, the land north of the Vaal River, achieved its independence at the Sand River Convention of 1852 (it later became known as the South African Republic). In 1854, at the Bloemfontein Convention, the Orange Free State, situated between the Orange and Vaal rivers, gained similar status.

DIAMONDS, GOLD AND WAR The Boers were not destined to find lasting peace. Diamonds were discovered in the Griqualand West area in 1869, and a horde of prospectors gravitated to the disputed region just beyond the Cape's northern border. Within two years the mining camp of Kimberley had 50 000 inhabitants – a population larger than that of Cape Town itself. Griqualand West was annexed to the Cape Colony in 1871.

Six years later the British annexed the Transvaal, but in 1880 the Boers rose in revolt and, in February of the following year, soundly defeated the Imperial force at Majuba Hill.

More significant, in 1886 vast deposits of gold were found on the Witwatersrand, close to the South African republic's capital, Pretoria. President Paul Kruger was aware that the arrival of thousands of *uitlanders* (foreigners), most of them English-speaking, posed a threat to the identity of his young republic, and that his country and its newfound wealth could well become a target of British territorial ambition, but his Treasury badly needed the money the mines would generate. He attempted to steer a middle course: Johannesburg, at the centre of the goldfields, was allowed to grow and flourish, but most of its white residents (and all its black inhabitants) were denied full participation in the political process.

In the event, Kruger's fears were to be fully realized. British greed for gold, Imperial expansionism, popular pressure on Britain's leaders to avenge the humiliation of Majuba Hill, the continuing clamour of the *uitlanders* for political rights and Kruger's stubborn reluctance to confer these, all combined to bring matters to a tragically violent head. In October 1899 Britain and the South African Republic, now supported by the Orange Free State, went to war for the second time.

THE COLONIES Meanwhile, the British colonies of the Cape and Natal had been making steady political and economic progress. The Cape achieved Representative Government status in 1854, and Responsible Government status – virtually full control over its internal affairs – in 1872. From about that time, too, the Kimberley diamond fields began to contribute substantially to the colony's prosperity.

Natal's political development followed a similar course: the colony became self-governing in 1893, by which time its white population had grown to 50 000. The whites, though, were then, as now, hugely outnumbered by the indigenous Nguni. The Natal Indian community, too, was to outstrip the whites in terms of numbers. In 1860 the first Indian indentured labourers arrived to work on the newly established sugar plantations, and were followed by a steady stream of ordinary immigrants from the Indian subcontinent (see page 16).

The coming of Union

The Boers lost the war that had erupted in 1899, although they fought with extraordinary skill and determination. They simply lacked the resources of their bigger and more powerful adversary. After more than two and a half years of bitter conflict (a white man's conflict: black people did not feature significantly in the hostilities, though a great many of them suffered profoundly as a consequence), during which large parts of the central and northern regions were reduced to wasteland, the two exhausted sides negotiated the Peace of Vereeniging.

The two republics returned to the Imperial fold as colonies, but goodwill prevailed, and the recommendations of the National Convention – which essentially represented white parties and interests and which, in 1908 and 1909, deliberated on the political future of southern Africa – paved the way for unification. The South Africa Act (Act of Union) came into effect on 31 May 1910. The country's first prime minister was Louis Botha, his lieutenant Jan Smuts. Both had been brilliant guerrilla generals in the war, and were to serve as outstanding statesmen afterwards.

The form of government adopted at Union – the Westminster system, comprising two parliamentary chambers (the Senate acting in a largely advisory capacity), a cabinet of ten, four provincial authorities with considerable local

powers, and a Governor-General representing the Crown – was to remain virtually unchanged until South Africa became a Republic in 1961.

Bechuanaland, Basutoland and Swaziland were not part of the new political arrangement. They would remain within the British fold as High Commission territories until attaining full independence in the 1960s.

Significantly, blacks were excluded from the democratic process; they were to be represented by nominated whites. Only the Cape leadership had pushed for what was call a 'civilization test' (property, income, education), which would enfranchise some blacks and disenfranchise some whites. But the most that liberal-minded men such as WP Schreiner, the enlightened Afrikaner François Malan and Premier JX Merriman could achieve was reluctant agreement to constitutional entrenchment of the 'coloured vote' in the Cape and the right of mixed-descent people to seek election to the Cape Provincial Council. They received only lukewarm support from Natal's traditionally moderate spokesmen and from the British Liberal Ministers, and strong opposition from the powerful northern politicians.

Also significant was the equal status accorded, within the constitution, to the Dutch and English languages. This was a major victory for those Afrikaners who had fought long and hard for all that *de Taal* represented – Afrikaner identity and the emergence of Afrikanerdom as a coherent national political force.

Growth, change and polarization

The years between Union in 1910 and the crucial parliamentary election of 1948 witnessed South Africa's transition from an uneven patchwork of colonial territories to a powerful modern industrial nation. They were also years of war, of profound social change, and of complex political interaction, probably better summarized by broad theme than in chronological sequence:

THE POLITICAL ARENA was dominated, throughout the entire span, by three Afrikaners, each of whom had served as a skilled commander during the Anglo-Boer war.

Louis Botha held the Union premiership until his death in 1919, when the reins passed to Jan

Smuts, his close associate and natural successor. Both were statesmen rather than politicians; both believed in conciliation between the two white cultural groups in South Africa; both were 'Empire men' in the sense that they valued close links with the former colonial power, each leading the country to war against Germany in support of Britain.

The third general, JMB (Barry) Hertzog, was cast in an entirely different mould: a passionate nationalist, determined to entrench Afrikaner power, though towards the end of his political career he was obliged to compromise in the interests of political expediency.

Throughout the tortuous political manoeuvrings of the 1920s and 1930s Smuts and Hertzog occupied centre stage, most of the time in direct opposition to each other but actually coming together in 1933, during the depths of the Great Depression, to form a coalition cabinet with Hertzog as prime minister. At the end of the following year their former parties were fused under the umbrella of the United Party and the two leaders directed the affairs of an increasingly prosperous country until the outbreak of the Second World War in September 1939. At this point Hertzog, anti-British to the last, resigned.

Some Afrikaner nationalists, the hardline conservatives, had refused to follow Hertzog's lead in 1934. Instead, they formed their own 'Purified' National Party under the leadership of Cape clergyman and newspaper editor DF Malan. Smuts, preoccupied with world events during the war and in the years immediately afterwards, badly underestimated the grassroots appeal – among voters of both language groups – of a movement whose doctrinal cornerstone was apartheid, and at the 1948 election his United Party paid the price.

THE YEARS OF WAR Twice during the twentieth century South African troops took to the battlefield in support of the Western allies.

Before marching into German South-West Africa in 1915, Prime Minister Louis Botha was obliged to quell a full-scale insurrection at home. Memories of the concentration camps and the burning farms were still bitter among many Afrikaners: little more than a decade before, their men had been fighting for survival in their own valleys and veld, and now they were being asked to join 'the enemy' in a wider struggle. Altogether, some 11 000 burghers, led by Christiaan de Wet and other former guerrilla heroes, rose against their government in the traditional Boer 'armed protest'.

But the rebels enjoyed too little support in the country as a whole, and the uprising was short-lived: by the beginning of 1915 they had been scattered by disciplined government troops; most of their leaders were arrested and imprisoned; one had drowned in the Vaal River and another was condemned and executed.

Botha could now turn his attention to the real enemy. He personally led a 12 000-man force from Swakopmund, Smuts another from Lüderitzbucht on the western coast; other columns marched in from the Orange River. The terrain was vast, and hostile, but the German occupying garrison was small, and by mid-July it was all over. Observed *The Times* of London: 'To the youngest of the sister nations belongs the glory of the first complete triumph of our arms and the disappearance of Germany from the map of Africa.'

In the long run, though, the new occupation scarcely proved a blessing, certainly not to the international community. Administered by South Africa as a mandate of the League of Nations since 1920, renamed Namibia by the United Nations in 1968, it remained a source of constant diplomatic dispute until 1990.

Other South African theatres of operation in the First World War were East Africa and the European Western Front. In both, the Union forces fought with distinction.

Smuts, appointed commander-in-chief of the Imperial Army in Africa, executed a long and ultimately successful campaign in the east against the German general Paul Emil von Lettow-Vorbeck. Bloodier by far were the battles in Flanders' fields. In one, at Delville Wood in July 1916, 121 officers and 3 032 men of the South African Brigade held their positions against massive bombardment and counterattack, the unwounded survivors numbering just five officers and 750 men.

Once again, in 1939, there was controversy over South Africa's obligations. But Jan Smuts – soldier, statesman, scholar, friend of Winston Churchill and Mohandas Gandhi; member of the Imperial War Cabinet and loyalist (he was one of the prime architects of the Statute of Westminster which, in 1931, proclaimed the Commonwealth of Nations) – carried the parliamentary vote by 80 to 67. Opposition continued throughout the war, its active instrument the underground *Ossewabrandwag*. Generally speaking, though, the opponents of involvement were very much in the minority; whites of both language groups volunteered for active service in large numbers, as did those of mixed descent. South African troops joined the battle against Nazi Germany and its allies, again in East Africa (inflicting a stunning defeat on Mussolini's Italian forces in Abyssinia), in the Western Desert and in Europe, slogging their way up the spine of Italy in one of the hardest and most thankless campaigns of the war.

ECONOMIC GROWTH Exploitation of the Witwatersrand goldfields triggered the move, from the early years of the 20th century, towards industrialization, and by definition urbanization – developments that changed the face of South Africa. Primary industry created the base for an impressive superstructure of heavy secondary industries, most notable of the early ones being Iscor, the massive formerly state-controlled corporation which processes local iron and coal reserves to produce (and export) steel. Iscor came on stream in 1934. The mining industry has expanded steadily throughout the century, providing a solid base for the increasingly sophisticated manufacturing sector. Two global wars and a world greedy for South Africa's raw materials and processed goods reinforced the impetus.

At the same time periodic drought, depression and new, labour-efficient farming techniques were forcing small farmers and tenant *bywoners* off the land and into the cities in droves. The 'poor white' problem (see page 18) was first identified as early as 1890; the Transvaal Indigency Commission reported a few years later that tens of thousands of refugees from the country areas were living 'in wretched shanties on the outskirts of towns', where they competed – largely unsuccessfully – with low-earning black labour being drawn into the industrial system.

This was of course at the depth of the Great Depression, and things would get better. Large-scale government assistance schemes, increasing prosperity, the organized training of skills and the growing manufacturing sector absorbed more and more white labour, and by the end of the 1930s, according to one historian,

'the poor white problem had virtually ceased to exist'. It did, however, leave a painful legacy, especially within official labour policy: the state would borrow from socialism to become the major employer, and job reservation would impose its artificial controls until the 1970s.

South Africa's labour relations story is not an especially happy one. Strikes and unrest were a depressingly regular feature of the industrial scene throughout the decades after Union. Most convulsive was the so-called 'Red Revolt' in 1922. In January of that year 22 000 Rand miners and engineering and power-station workers went on strike and organized themselves into paramilitary commandos, which were soon enough infiltrated by Marxist activists bent on a workers' revolution. Pitched battles broke out; troops were mobilized; 153 people (including 72 of the State forces) were killed, 534 wounded.

This particular upheaval gave graphic point to one of the constants in the social and economic history of modern South Africa: white fear of black encroachment. Times were hard in the 1920s and '30s; black labour extremely cheap (miners earned 2s 2d a day). It was publicly estimated that if 50% of the white labour force could be replaced by blacks the mines would save £1 million a year (a huge amount in those days). Mine managements knew the facts; so did the unions, and the barricades went up as soon as it was announced, in December 1921, that 2 000 semi-skilled white gold-miners would be declared redundant.

Black urbanization, naturally, ran parallel to white. A new proletariat, officially regarded as 'temporary' and composed in part of tens of thousands of migrants from adjacent territories, collected in the enormous townships that began to mushroom around the mining and industrial centres of the Reef, Natal and the eastern Cape from the first years of the century.

The 'social engineers'

The National Party which formed a government – with a slim parliamentary majority of five – under the premiership of Dr DF Malan in 1948 remained in power, virtually unchallenged, for over 40 years, though in the 1980s its composition and some of its ideological tenets underwent radical change.

During the first two decades the formal division, or stratification, of South African society along racial lines provided the thrust of policy. Separate development (later to be called multi-national development) was seen to be the solution to the immense problems of cultural diversity and conflicting group interest. Linchpin of a Draconian and wide-ranging legislative programme was the Group Areas Act of 1950, which segregated, among other things, the country's residential areas. Further statutes included those involving freedom of movement, identity documents, the formal classification of people according to colour, regulation of workplace and a vast arsenal of security laws.

All this was not entirely new: the ingredients of the southern African melting pot had never really melted. They were kept apart, from the early colonial days, by competition, by perhaps irreconcilable cultural distinctions, by fierce informal pressures and by formal edict. In the words of eminent historian TRH Davenport, the Natives (Urban Areas) Act of 1923, for example, 'grew into one of the most complex pieces of control legislation ever developed anywhere' – long before the Nationalists took office in 1948.

Other precedents abound. But from 1949 there were both qualitative and quantitative differences. Now, for the first time, Afrikanerdom was in the driving seat; and for the first time rigid segregation was entrenched within an all-embracing legal code and structured administration.

There were laws, too, affecting the coloured people. In 1951 the Separate Registration of Voters Act, designed to remove coloured voters from the common roll (they were to be represented in Parliament by four white Members) was passed but subsequently declared invalid by the Appellate Division of the Supreme Court. Five controversial years later, however, and after a startling series of constitutional acrobatics, the Act became effective. In 1969 the last vestiges of coloured parliamentary representation ended, to be replaced by the partly-elected, partly-nominated Coloured Persons Representative Council (CRC).

But it was the status and future of the black people that preoccupied the Nationalist government. Under Malan and his successors – JG Strijdom (1954-58) and, especially, Hendrik Verwoerd (1958-66) – the policy of enforced segregation was carried to its logical extremes. In its simplest form, the argument held that the blacks had their own, traditional territories and that it was in these that they should exercise the legitimate rights of citizenship and the vote.

The long, laborious process of creating separate black states began in a modest way with the Black Authorities Act of 1951 (it set up tribal, regional and territorial authorities *within* the Union of South Africa), and reached its legislative zenith in 1959 with the Promotion of Black Self-Government Act. This provided for the establishment of homelands (later known as national states) for the country's main black groups, and for the development in these territories of governmental institutions which would eventually lead, in each case and by predetermined stages, to full independence.

Sharpeville and the Republic

Significantly, DF Malan, just before he assumed office, supported the granting to India of a republican constitution within the Commonwealth. The Nationalists, chafed by the tenuous but irritating Imperial bonds that were the legacy of Union and Dominion status, aspired to the same freedom, and the issue was openly broached by Hendrik Verwoerd in the early months of 1960 (British premier Harold MacMillan's 'wind of change' address to the joint Houses of Parliament in Cape Town reinforced an already strong resolve to cut the ties). A referendum was held later in the year at which the electorate, by a majority of 74 580 votes (1 626 336 were cast), decided in favour of a republican form of government.

In the interim, serious unrest had broken out in parts of the country, the culmination of sporadic riots that had started the year before in protest against the enforced carrying of reference books (passes) and largely orchestrated by the Pan-Africanist Congress (see page 29). On 21 March, 1960 police confronted a large crowd in the township of Sharpeville, near Vereeniging in the Transvaal; shots were fired; 69 blacks were killed and numbers wounded. There were also riots and, soon afterwards, massive protest marches in Cape Town. The PAC and its big brother the African National Congress were banned. A state of emergency was declared.

Sharpeville was a seminal event. Before the shootings the country, for all the criticism levelled at it, was accepted as a member of the international community; after March 1960 it faced increasing isolation.

Exactly a year later Verwoerd flew to London to apply for continued Commonwealth membership for a republican South Africa. Harsh words were exchanged; South Africa withdrew its application, and two months later the Republic was formally established.

Hendrik Verwoerd, Holland-born and Rhodesian-educated, doctrinaire, brilliant, ruthless and uncompromising, died on 6 September 1966 – victim of an assassin's knife (the killer was a parliamentary messenger, subsequently judged unfit to stand trial). Verwoerd had been the chief architect of separate development, designing and constructing a monolithic structure that would become the increasingly sharp focus of critical attention, both inside South Africa and internationally. It would also present his successors with possibly the toughest of political, and moral, challenges.

Dialogue and protest

The man who succeeded Verwoerd, BJ Vorster, was also a hardline conservative, but a pragmatic one who perceived the dangerous consequences of isolation and the need to establish 'normal and friendly relations' with African states (in fact, Verwoerd had also recognized the realities, but too late to translate conviction into action). The Republic was an African country, the most powerful south of the Sahara; some states were economically dependent on it; the whole complex of southern African nations economically interdependent.

This was the era of détente and dialogue, and a significant degree of rapprochement, or at least of contact, was achieved within the southern African context.

Farther afield, however, Vorster enjoyed far less success: South Africa's relations with the international community, with countries beyond her immediate sphere of influence, continued to deteriorate.

Nor was all quiet on the home front. In June 1976 unrest erupted in the sprawling townships of Soweto near Johannesburg and spread to other centres, continuing in varying degrees of intensity for almost eight months. The subsequent commission of inquiry found that the immediate cause was the use of Afrikaans as a teaching medium in black high schools. Discrimination, lack of citizenship, restrictions on

property ownership and a lack of civic facilities were powerful contributory factors.

The riots, however, were not spontaneous incidents but rather part of a sustained, organized campaign, launched by a number of black consciousness organizations, to undermine the social order. In October 1977 the Government reacted sharply, banning 18 of these bodies together with many of their leaders (see page 29).

Opposing forces

The origin of the South African extra-parliamentary opposition movements – if one discounts the lone voices of late nineteenth century black intellectuals such as Tiyo Soga and John Tengo Jabavu – are properly to be found in the years of disenchantment that followed the South African War. British 'non-racial justice', anticipated when the two northern territories returned to colonial rule, simply did not materialize, and a number of black congress-type associations made their appearance in the four British colonies.

Nor, as we have seen, did blacks have a say in the deliberations that created the Union of South Africa in 1910 (see page 24). Despite strenuous representations to the British constitution-makers, the future was shaped without reference to them. In 1912 a Durban lawyer, Dr Pixley Seme, became the moving spirit in the launching of the South African Native National Congress – a body later (in 1925) renamed the African National Congress.

At about the same time, a talented Indian advocate was crusading, successfully, for Asian rights in South Africa. Mohandas K Gandhi had arrived in Durban in 1893 to take up a private legal brief; he founded the Natal Indian Congress a year later and, during two decades of political confrontation (he was imprisoned twice) finally reached an accord with General Jan Smuts. It was during these years that Gandhi evolved his political philosophy and technique, *satyagraha* – commonly termed passive resistance but more literally 'keeping to the truth'. He returned to India in 1914 to work long, hard and ultimately triumphantly for that country's independence.

ORIGINS OF BLACK OPPOSITION The history of the black opposition movement – that is to say, of the African National Congress in particular, although labour and church organizations were active and articulate in the between-war years – is a complicated narrative, most neatly encapsulated perhaps by Professor T Kasis: 'Successively, the ANC retained liberal expectations, became more militant, attempted passive resistance, entered a multi-racial popular front, was overtaken by impatient black nationalism, and moved underground.'

The passive resistance phase came to an abrupt end with the enactment of the Criminal Law Amendment Bill in 1952. The ANC president at the time was Chief Albert Luthuli, a Rhodesian-born Zulu aristocrat and churchman. He was formally 'banned' in 1952 but his moral leadership – he advocated universal suffrage but renounced violence – continued to be acknowledged by the majority of members. Luthuli was awarded the prestigious Nobel Peace Prize in 1961.

After 1952 the ANC, for a time, operated within a loose, nonracial confederation known as the Congress Alliance, whose ideological platform became the Freedom Charter, a code adopted and signed at a rally in Kliptown in 1955. Other signatories were the SA Coloured People's Organization, various Indian congresses and the white Congress of Democrats.

TWO APPROACHES TO BLACK POWER The Freedom Charter is one of the keys to any understanding of the immensely complex political scene in modern South Africa. The signatories and their ideological successors subscribe to a nonracial solution to the country's problems. On the other side of a fundamental divide are those who eschew the Charter, seeking an exclusively black, Marxist-Socialist solution. This lies at the root of many of the divisions within the liberationist movement.

The more militant, mainly younger elements of the ANC, those who walked the black-only path, broke away from the parent body in 1959 to form the Pan-Africanist Congress. A year later Sharpeville brought the rivalry into sharp focus: each organization campaigned vigorously against the pass laws, urging township blacks to leave their reference (pass) books at home, invite unrest, overload the entire security system. On 28 March 1960, both the ANC and the PAC were banned in terms of the Unlawful Organizations Act, and went underground, and

into exile. The ANC formed its military wing, *Umkhonto we Sizwe* ('spear of the nation'): its targets were 'hard' objectives: government installations, communications and so forth. Loss of life was to be avoided. Poqo, the PAC's military counterpart, had more extreme intent.

The sabotage campaign was waged intensively until the mid-1960s. There were arrests; some of the leaders, including Oliver Tambo, went into exile; others, among them Nelson Mandela, remained to continue the struggle on the home front. At the Rivonia Trial in 1964 Mandela and a number of other Congress figures were charged under the General Law Amendment Act (the 'Sabotage Act') and the Suppression of Communist Act and sentenced to life imprisonment.

The arena, during the 1970s, became even more crowded. 'Black consciousness' organizations, led by the younger breed, appeared on the scene.

On 16 June 1976 some 10 000 pupils staged a protest march through the dusty streets of Soweto. Their principal grievance was a Bantu Education Department directive that Afrikaans had to be used as a teaching language at black secondary schools. The regulation added to an already burdensome load of disabilities the African schoolchild had to bear.

For three days many of the black areas around Johannesburg were in a state of virtual siege as police fought it out with stone-throwing students. Lives were lost, buildings and vehicles destroyed. The violence spread to other parts of the country and continued in varying degrees of intensity for a further eight months.

In 1977 a full 18 political bodies were banned, their leaders detained – including black-consciousness activist Steve Biko, who died while in police custody.

The Botha era

The National Party celebrated its thirtieth year in office in 1978 – three controversial decades during which racial separation had been sedulously entrenched. That year, though, was to mark the start of what promised to be a new era. In September BJ Vorster resigned as prime minister to become state president, and was replaced as prime minister by former minister of defence PW Botha. The new premier stated at the outset that he was determined on a reformist course and in August 1979 Botha outlined a 12-point plan to the Natal congress of the National Party: his 'total strategy' for the security and gradual transformation of the social and political order. His constitutional programme made provision for, among other things, an executive president, a Parliament of three Houses (white, Asian and Coloured) and a nonracial Cabinet.

The process of reform got under way, modestly enough, during the first session of the new Parliament. High points were the abolition of the Mixed Marriages Act and Section 16 of the Immorality Act. The perceived significance, though, was that whites and people of colour were for the first time deliberating and legislating together – it was felt by many at the time that the dyke had been breached and the trickle of reform would, eventually, become a flood.

Ironically, or perhaps predictably, this was the time chosen by black opposition organizations and important sections of the international community to intensify pressure on the South African government. The disinvestment debate, sanctions, sporting isolation, township violence and the state of emergency monopolized the headlines.

SIGNS OF CHANGE Over the months, Botha's reform initiative became subordinate to the need to counter the extra-parliamentary opposition. By 1986 security rather than political progress was the central issue.

However, the outlook wasn't entirely gloomy. The 1987 general election indicated that a great many whites did indeed want change. Moreover, there were shortly to be positive moves towards a regional accommodation. In 1988, under joint US-Soviet pressure, the parties involved in the Angolan-Namibian impasse met to negotiate Cuban withdrawal from the subcontinent, Namibian autonomy and a resolution of the Angolan civil war. In March 1990 Namibia became a fully independent state, to take her place in the community of nations. Continued peace moves brought further progress, and for the first time in more than a decade there was real hope of an end to the internal conflicts that had ravaged the former Portuguese territories, and which were bedevilling intra-regional relationships.

These events corresponded with the mood of the times. The wind of change was gusting throughout the world, sweeping away the values, priorities and assumptions of the old order. The Soviet empire was collapsing, bringing down the authoritarian regimes of Eastern Europe, and territorial competition between the major powers had ended. Southern Africa could not of course remain immune from the trends.

Coming together

In January 1989, President PW Botha suffered a mild stroke and, a few weeks later, resigned the leadership of the National Party in favour of FW de Klerk, who had generally been regarded as one of the more conservative influences within the ruling hierarchy.

Later, after fighting a bitter and unseemly rearguard action – against senior politicians who were now agreed that the government's anti-communist 'Total Strategy' had become irrelevant, that the era of the 'securocrats' had passed, that apartheid was an anachronism, and that the time had come for an entirely new dispensation in South Africa – Botha also resigned the presidency.

The changes that followed were rapid, fundamental, dramatic and far-reaching.

On 2 February 1990, at the opening session of the new parliament, President De Klerk announced the unbanning of the African National Congress, the Pan-Africanist Congress and a number of other proscribed organizations. Two weeks later ANC leader Nelson Mandela, by now the world's best-known political prisoner, walked to freedom. He had been incarcerated for 27 years (initially on Robben Island, later in Pollsmoor and finally Victor Verster prison, north of Cape Town).

The decades of white political supremacy were over; the new South Africa, its shape as yet undefined, had been born.

The last mile

The journey towards political settlement and the establishment of a fully democratic order proved long, hard, and fraught with hazard.

Tentative talks between the Nationalist government, the ANC and other organizations began in 1990, and continued more formally during the following year, when the leaders of 19 widely divergent political bodies came together to inaugurate the Convention for a Democratic South Africa (Codesa). Notable absentees from the forum, at least initially, were the Pan-Africanist Congress (which held to its revolutionary principles) and Zulu Chief Mangosuthu Buthelezi's Inkatha Freedom Party.

The issues were complex, some of them seemingly intractable. De Klerk had, from the first, rejected simple majority rule in favour of a power-sharing formula that contained checks against the 'domination of one group by another' – a euphemism for entrenching white minority rights. He also advocated federalism: the devolution of power from the centre to the regions. Conversely, the ANC and its partners wanted, among other things, a unitary state and a winner-takes-all electoral arrangement.

But hopes of a political breakthrough were raised by the positive results of a whites-only referendum held in March 1992, and were maintained despite the setbacks that occurred with depressing regularity in the following months. Among these were:

A rising level of violence, including senseless 'train massacres' and inter-faction slaughter (among the worst was the infamous Boipatong incident of June 1992). Rumours of a 'third force', a sinister covert campaign by white-led reactionaries determined to sabotage the peace process at all costs, gained widespread currency.

The assassination, by maverick right-wingers on 10 April, 1993, of Chris Hani, general secretary of the South African Communist Party and a hero to young black radicals.

The continued intransigence of Chief Buthelezi. The 'Zulu factor' was to be a serious obstacle to settlement until well past the eleventh hour.

The obstructionist tactics of white conservatives determined on their own *Volkstaat*, or people's republic.

Nevertheless, there was steady progress around the negotiating table.

In September 1993 Nelson Mandela called for the lifting of all remaining international sanctions. Two months later he and De Klerk shared the 1993 Nobel Peace Prize.

In December parliament was effectively superceded by a multi-party Transitional Executive Council (TEC), convened in terms of an agreement on an interim constitution, on the reincorporation of the 'homelands' and on a date for a national election.

The last of the obstacles quickly and, it seemed, miraculously evaporated in April 1994 – just days before the polls – when Buthelezi finally agreed to participate.

After a protracted election process, which proved a lively, often chaotic but always (astonishingly in view of past antagonisms) good-humoured affair, the ANC gained a virtual two-thirds majority in the proposed National Assembly.

It also captured healthy majorities in six of the nine regional parliaments, shared the honours in the seventh, lost the Western Cape to the Nationalists (the conservative Coloured vote was decisive) and KwaZulu-Natal to the Inkatha Freedom Party.

Early in May 1994, Nelson Mandela was sworn in as the first president of a liberated, fully democratic South Africa.

SOUTH AFRICA TODAY

South Africa is a region that has seen rapid and fundamental change. Within the space of four years – from 1990 to 1994 – the country negotiated a painful transition from autocratic white minority rule to full democracy. Its political and, to a lesser degree, its economic institutions have been restructured, its society transformed.

Government

South Africa is a republican democracy that has been administered since 1994 by a 'government of national unity'. The constitution introduced in that year operates as an interim arrangement: parliament has until mid-1996 to produce a final formula. However, the constitutional foundations have been laid, embodied in some 30 entrenched principles.

The chief ingredients of the interim constitution are:

☆ A 400-member National Assembly elected on a system of proportional representation.

☆ A 90-member Senate which acts as a watchdog. It may also introduce legislation.

☆ An executive comprising the State President, at least two Deputy Presidents and a cabinet of up to 27 ministers. Parties with 20 or more members in the National Assembly are entitled to a proportionate number of cabinet portfolios. Decision making tends to be by concensus 'in accordance with the spirit of national unity'.

☆ Nine regional administrations, each with its own legislature, premier and cabinet.

☆ A Charter of Fundamental Rights which safeguards the ordinary citizen from unjust action by the State and, in certain instances, by other individuals.

☆ An independent Constitutional Court. The Constitution is the supreme law; statutes enacted by parliament must be in accordance with its clauses, some of which restrict parliamentary discretion.

The Court is the final authority on all constitutional matters.

FOREIGN POLICY South Africa is a minor player on the world stage, but it ranks as a regional superpower and, in Africa, has a crucial rule to fulfill.

The country occupies just three per cent of the continent and is home to a bare five per cent of its population, yet it accounts for:

☆ 40 per cent of Africa's industrial output;

☆ 25 per cent of gross continental product;

☆ 64 per cent of electricity generated;

☆ 45 per cent of mineral production;

☆ 66 per cent of steel production;

☆ 46 per cent of vehicles on Africa's roads, and 36 per cent of its telephones.

The smaller states within the southern subcontinent rely heavily on and co-operate closely with South Africa.

Indeed, the regions of Africa south of the Sahara have a great many shared interests, and they are drawing ever closer together – under southern leadership.

All of which has its wider implications. In Europe and America, South Africa is seen as the best hope for a continent ravaged by poverty, disease, famine and, all too often, civil strife. The industrial world has poured billions of dollars into various forms of disaster relief – unrecoverable funds that could have been used to far better effect on economic development, long-term health care and the badly needed infrastructure.

United States policy towards Africa, unstructured and even opportunistic in the past, now seems to be taking on a definite

shape, best described perhaps by the phrase 'preventive diplomacy'. A great deal more could have been done, so the thinking goes, to pre-empt the horrors of Rwanda, civil war in Angola, disintegration in Somalia, famine in Ethiopia, had more studious forethought been devoted to the ominous trends, and the crises nipped in the bud.

Preventive diplomacy means more than stockpiling food and medicines for the evil day. It calls for a partnership between the United States, together with the other G7 nations, with an enlightened, comparatively powerful regional leadership. South Africa is well placed to assume the part.

NATIONAL SECURITY South Africa maintains a well-equipped, powerful defence force. During the sanctions era, local weapons and equipment manufacture was co-ordinated by the government-sponsored Armscor organization, and the degree of technical sophistication achieved has been impressive by any standards.

Priorities in terms of national security have changed dramatically since the regional peace initiative launched in the late 1980s and South Africa's transition to full democracy in the early 1990s.

The need for a large military establishment, and for well-stocked arsenals of conventional weapons, has diminished. Nevertheless the integration, into the new National Defence Force, of the armed wings of the ANC and PAC and the armies of the former 'homelands' has kept the numbers of service personnel at artificially high levels.

The economy

South Africa is an uncomfortable mix of First World sophistication and Third World underdevelopment.

On the one hand it has immense natural resources, employs advanced technologies and supports complex industrial and commercial structures. On the other hand, educational standards among many of the people are low; there are too few jobs and services for the rapidly expanding population and the 'poverty cycle', if not as horrific as it is in some other African countries, does exist, threatening stability and profoundly affecting the process of economic decision-making.

Relevant to all this are two recent and highly significant changes of direction, shifts in policy designed to strengthen free market forces and generally to expand the productive base. An explanation of their respective backgrounds is appropriate.

In many ways the South African economy is organized along socialistic lines. In the past the emphasis has been on state control; the government has been far and away the largest single employer and the most prolific spender; taxation is high; private initiative has been inhibited and sometimes strangled by red-tape regulations.

Providing intention is translated into decisive action, that will change. A monolithic government presence in the body economic was tolerable enough, perhaps, in good times, when the Rand monetary unit was strong and there was the appearance of financial and social stability. But the economy began to slide, steeply, into recession in 1984; draconian measures to balance the budget, halt inflation and improve the balance of payments, which had looked set for success for a time, were torpedoed by the political unrest that began in 1985, and by international financial sanctions. Meanwhile, the country still needed to create some 300 000

Energy: more than enough for domestic needs

new jobs and build half a million houses a year just to keep pace with minimum black needs – not to mention schools, hospitals, community services and pensions.

Against this background, tentative moves have been made to dismantle the apparatus of state ownership, to transfer sections of present government obligation to the private sector. Specific targets are some of the huge parastatal bodies such as the Iron and Steel Corporation (Iscor), the Electricity Supply Commission (Eskom), state transport undertakings (road, rail and air), health services, housing, education and social services (privatization would act to make pensions portable and more individualized). Some of these, notably Iscor, have already been transferred to the private sector.

Parallel to this has been the abandonment of controls on urban drift. Quite apart from the moral and political implications, influx control was seen to have had damaging socio-economic consequences. Most of the legal barriers have already come down. Also under official attack are the rigid and unrealistically high community standards of the past. The emphasis now is on self-help housing – 'site-and-service' – schemes; closer involvement of the private sector; and encouragement of the 'informal economy', a euphemism for back-yard industry and minimally regulated trading. These developments – if indeed they continue – are fundamental.

With the advent of new political order, too, has come a fundamental change in state spending priorities. Nearly half a century of institutionalized apartheid bequeathed, among other grim legacies, a grossly distorted economy, and there now has to be a significant redistribution of national assets.

The new government's ambitious Reconstruction and Development Programme (RDP) envisages the channelling of billions into education, basic housing, electrification, proper sanitation and clean water supplies, health, social welfare, the creation of jobs. Major prerequisites of the programme's success include the involvement of the private sector, foreign investment and social stability.

ECONOMIC POINTERS The most significant contributions to the Gross Domestic Product are made by the manufacturing industry (about 22%), mining (13%), commerce (11%), trans-

One of South Africa's 25 giant generating plants: most are coal-fired

port and communications (7,5%), electricity and water (4%). Agriculture accounts for a surprisingly modest 5%.

These figures reveal the dramatic transformation from an agrarian-based economy a century ago, before the discovery and exploitation of diamonds and gold, to today's advanced industrialization. For much of the twentieth century mining provided the impetus; after the Second World War there was an impressive growth of manufacturing activity. That sector is now the priority: it is capable of much further expansion (South Africa exports too many raw materials that could be locally fabricated, turned into semi-manufactured or end products) and of absorbing more job-seekers than all the other economic areas put together. This is the vital consideration.

MINING South Africa has the largest known reserves of gold, platinum, high-grade chromium, manganese, vanadium, fluorspar and andalusite in the world, and massive deposits of diamonds, iron ore, coal, uranium, asbestos, nickel and phosphates – a list of natural resources that places the country in the global strategic front line.

Gold production averages some 550 tons a year, roughly 45% of the Western world's output; South Africa's gold mines are the third largest of the world's suppliers of uranium.

Diamonds, discovered in the deep Kimberlite pipes of the northern Cape, launched the country's industrial revolution in the 1870s and generated fabulous wealth over the decades that followed. The country is the world's largest producer of gem diamonds – and of the platinum group of metals (palladium, rhodium, iridium and ruthenium as well as platinum itself). About three-quarters of the earth's known reserves of both platinum and chromium are locked into the immense pre-Cambrian strata of South Africa's bushveld complex.

Probably the most important of the strategic minerals is manganese, vital in the production of steel and found in great quantity (about 80% of the world's reserves, in fact) in the northwestern Cape.

Finally there is coal, of which South Africa has located deposits amounting to 58 billion tons, and which provides the country with much of its electricity and synthetic petroleum (see below). The 100 mines produce about 175 million tons a year, a figure projected to rise to 330 million tons by the year 2000. A healthy proportion of the output is exported, most of it through the east coast port of Richards Bay.

ENERGY Despite the lack of operating oilfields, the republic is a net exporter of energy.

Coal, as mentioned, is the principal source: about 60% of coal-mining output is applied to the generation of electricity; 17% to the production of synthetic fuels; 6% to the conversion of coke and tar. Three great oil-from-coal plants have been built: Sasol 1 in the Orange Free State, and Sasols 2 and 3 at Secunda in the eastern Transvaal. The impetus for the last two came from the international oil crisis of 1973. Together, these establishments consume more than 32 million tons of coal a year and represent the world's first and as yet only commercially viable large-scale synthetic fuel operation. Eventually they will make South Africa self-sufficient in liquid and gas fuels and other coal-based products.

South Africa's largest electricity supply utility, Eskom, which operates 19 coal-fired, two hydro-electric, two pump-storage, one nuclear and three gas-turbine power stations, provides 97% of the electricity consumed (some 140 billion kilowatts annually). Six new coal-fired stations came on stream in the mid-1980s, including the largest dry-cooled plant in the world, at Ellisras in the Transvaal.

Mozambique, Botswana and Zimbabwe are reliant on South African electricity. Eskom generates around 60% of all power produced on the continent of Africa, and could comfortably supply enough electricity for the needs of every country to the south of the Sahara. Eskom's annual turnover is bigger than the gross domestic products of most of the other fifty or so other African states.

Exciting, viable offshore oil and gas fields have been located south of Mossel Bay in the southern Cape, and there are promising indications of further deposits off the west coast.

INDUSTRY A large pool of labour, a wealth of natural resources, technological expertise and, not least, economic and perhaps political necessity have led South Africa towards self-reliance in industrial products.

In the early 1990s, the manufacturing industry employed about 1,6 million people and, as we have noted, contributed about a quarter of the Gross Domestic Product. The larger manufacturing sectors include:

METAL PRODUCTS The Iron and Steel Corporation (Iscor) has three major plants which together produce about six million tons of liquid steel a year, with specialized metal products (for instance carbon and stainless steel, ferro alloys, copper and brass, high-carbon chrome)

turned out by a number of smaller mills. The country's engineering and heavy industrial works manufacture everything from cranes and sugar mills through engines, turbines, machine tools, agricultural equipment, structural steel and cables to specialized industrial machinery and computer products.

NON-METALLIC MINERAL PRODUCTS (largely for the construction industry) have an annual value of about R10 billion.

TRANSPORT AND EQUIPMENT There are a number of vehicle manufacturing and assembly plants in the country, most in and around Port Elizabeth, the 'Detroit of South Africa'. Heavy duty diesel engines for buses are manufactured in Cape Town; gearboxes in Boksburg.

CHEMICALS AND PHARMACEUTICALS The list of basic industrial chemicals produced in the country is long, ranging from fertilizers and pesticides through explosives and petroleum products, plastics and paints.

FOOD PRODUCTS Again, practically the whole range is locally processed. The industry's output is worth about R20 billion, and it employs some 200 000 people. Around 60% of production is exported, principally to EC countries.

CLOTHING AND TEXTILES This industry employs 8% of the national workforce and, because of its labour intensity, is earmarked as one of the key growth points.

AGRICULTURE South Africa is one of the few food-exporting countries in the world – a testament in a sense to the expertise of its farming community and water engineers, because the subcontinent's natural land resources are poor. Rainfall is mainly seasonal and invariably – certainly in recent years – unpredictable. The soil is not especially fertile; erosion over the millennia and the leaching of Africa's earth during the wetter periods of the continent's history have impoverished the nutrient content over large areas (only 12% of the country's surface area is arable).

Despite these built-in drawbacks South Africa has doubled its agricultural output since 1960 and now exports, in an average year, about R10 billion worth of meat, produce, processed foods and forestry and game products and a further R1 billion worth of wool and textiles.

The diversity of climatic conditions (see page 13) enables the country's farmers to grow a wide variety of crops, from the sugar and subtropical fruits of Natal through the huge maize yields of the summer-rainfall areas to the tobacco of the more arid regions; and to rear livestock for beef, pork and dairy products, mutton and wool. A succession of droughts and escalating input costs, however, have placed many of the larger farmers under severe financial strain. The situation within the less developed and generally less well-endowed peasant-farming areas has tended to deteriorate even more rapidly under adverse conditions.

LABOUR The entire structure of labour and labour relations in South Africa underwent a radical transformation following acceptance of the recommendations contained in the seminal reports of the Wiehahn and Riekert commissions of inquiry in the late 1970s. These made provision for full freedom of association of all classes of urban worker, the registration of trade unions, participation in the formal bargaining process, the right to strike, the elimination of discrimination in the workplace, and a comprehensive code regulating conditions of work, minimum wages and social benefits. The Riekert Commission also recommended the encouragement of private enterprise in the 'informal sector'.

The Nico Malan theatre complex, Cape Town

Against the background of over-restrictive labour control that has been a feature of the economy since the early mining days, all this was progress indeed. African workers have been quick to organize and to prove themselves highly skilled in the cut-and-thrust arena of industrial negotiations.

The unions are a powerful force for change. Initially they directed their efforts exclusively to the welfare and material advancement of the workforce but later, in 1985, came together under the umbrella of the Congress of South African Trade Unions. Cosatu has become a prominent player on the political stage.

SOCIAL SERVICES Housing, health and education are in crisis. There are millions of South Africans in desperate need of homes, hospitals and decent schooling: a demand with which the national exchequer is finding it hard to cope. Pre-election promises and the transition to full democracy have both heightened popular expectations and tended to foster a 'culture of entitlement', and the pressures on government to deliver are intense.

The arts, sport and recreation

Culturally, and in the realms of leisure, entertainment and sport, South Africa offers as varied and pleasing a fare as any other middle-sized Western country, and perhaps more so. Its special prides are the game and nature reserves, and the mostly beautiful and often spectacular landscapes. For the visitor, there is a great deal to see and do; the tourist industry is well organized; holiday-makers are able to stay in and travel round the country in comfort and, at rates of exchange prevailing at the time of writing, to do so relatively cheaply.

THE ARTS The scene is lively, and much of it of international standard. Literature, the visual arts, theatre, ballet, opera and classical music thrive in South Africa's major centres.

Much of the activity falls within the ambit of the four state-sponsored performing arts councils. Together they employ over 2 000 artists and theatre technicians and stage around 300 shows of one sort or another each year in a variety of splendid buildings.

Most notable of these are probably the grand Nico Malan theatre complex in Cape Town (opera house, drama theatre, three smaller auditoriums and a full resident orchestra), Pretoria's State Theatre and Bloemfontein's Sand du Plessis theatre complex.

Excellent independent (independent of the arts councils, that is) symphony orchestras are based and give regular performances in Durban, Johannesburg and Cape Town. Also among the more outstanding of the non-government enterprises are the Baxter theatre complex near Cape Town's university and the Market Theatre in Johannesburg.

Music of a different kind – a unique kind – is emerging from the black urban community, a vibrant synthesis of African and western idioms that is beginning to makes its mark beyond the borders of the townships.

South Africa has produced more than its share of gifted instrumentalists, opera singers and ballet dancers. The country, though, finds it difficult to retain its own: universities and other learning centres turn out an unusual wealth of young talent which is often lost to the more sophisticated stages and concert halls of Europe and America.

South Africa can claim few literary giants of the kind that one might expect to have emerged in a country of such beauty, complexity, conflict and tragedy. There has been no Steinbeck to give voice to the wrath of the economically underprivileged; no James Baldwin to bring fiery articulation to ethnic consciousness; no Orwell, no Solzhenitsyn. It could, though, be that very complexity that inhibits the pen. Says Nadine Gordimer, a leading contemporary novelist: 'Living in a society that has been as deeply and calculatedly compartmentalized as South Africa's has been under the colour bar, the writer's potential has unscalable limitations.'

Nevertheless, there have been and are South African writers of real stature: the much underestimated Olive Schreiner; the eccentric Roy Campbell; the mystic Eugene Marais and, of recent vintage, Alan Paton and Laurens van der Post who, each in his own way, has bared the soul of his beloved country; Nadine Gordimer and JM Coetzee; André Brink and Etienne Leroux; the brilliant Athol Fugard and his fellow playwright Gibson Kente.

Among the black people of South Africa there is, too, a powerful tradition of oral literature: the key to their past, and perhaps the door to the country's literary future.

SPORT The country's wonderfully sunny climate favours outdoor activity, and South Africans are enthusiastic and, in competitive terms, increasingly successful sportsmen.

After a decades-long absence, South Africa re-entered the world arena in the early 1990s – with generally modest results. The years of isolation had taken a severe toll; standards had slipped badly. However, the picture is changing dramatically as the country's sportsmen gain experience at international level, and as the immense talent that lies within the hitherto disadvantaged black community is discovered, refined and tested.

Football reigns supreme within black society: it embraces 12 000 soccer clubs and more than a million regular players. Among whites, rugby and cricket have the largest following, though the support base is rapidly widening as energetic development programmes (and television) bring the games into the townships.

RECREATION There are at present 19 national parks and about 500 smaller (some very small) reserves run by regional and local authorities and by private enterprise. The more prominent of these, and of the country's other major recreational attractions – coastal and inland resorts, scenic routes, hiking trails, sporting and leisure facilities and so forth – are covered in some detail in Part 2: 'Exploring South Africa'.

Road running: popular and highly competitive

PART TWO

EXPLORING
SOUTH AFRICA

JOHANNESBURG AND PRETORIA

Just 56 km of somewhat featureless, largely built-up Highveld terrain separates Pretoria, administrative capital of South Africa, and Johannesburg, capital of Gauteng Province and financial heart of the southern African subcontinent. Between the two is Midrand, until recently an unremarkable scatter of villages but now a prime growth point and destined to become a city in its own right.

Pretoria lies in the warm and fertile valley of the Apies ('little ape') River at an altitude of 1 370 m above sea level, the eastern suburbs hugging the foothills of the pleasant Magaliesberg range of hills, the central district overlooked by Meintjes Kop and the imposing neo-classical, semicircular façade of the Union Buildings. It's a substantial city – in terms of both population (546 000) and area (592 km²) – and a handsome one, too, graced by stately buildings and famed for its parks, its jacaranda trees, its roses and its splendid wealth of indigenous flora.

By contrast the vast sprawl of Johannesburg – also known as Jo'burg, Joey's, the Golden City and, by the miners who work the seams deep beneath the surface, as Egoli – has few claims to beauty, though it does have its 'green lung' and some of the suburbs, the northern ones, delight the eye with their embowered avenues and luxuriant gardens. Its appeal lies elsewhere – in its equable climate (see Advisory, page 70), in its vibrancy, its zest for life, its fine hotels, restaurants, shopping malls.

That is the tourist's Johannesburg, a city that, in common with every major metropolis, has its darker side. There is immense wealth here, but also extreme poverty in the surrounding 'black' townships; communities that have suffered generations of deprivation are challenging the old order; the political and social patterns are changing dramatically; the transition process has provoked uncertainty, instability and, at times, confrontation. Johannesburg owes its origins and much of its prosperity to the gold of the Witwatersrand.

Nighttime skyline of the Golden City, financial and industrial heart of South Africa and epicentre of the vast Witwatersrand complex of cities and towns

This 'ridge of white waters' is a modest enough physical feature, barely deserving its rather grand name, but it does form the watershed between the Vaal and the region's northward-flowing rivers (including the Limpopo and the Olifants) and it is the world's richest repository of the precious metal. The Main Reef runs from Nigel in the east to Randfontein in the west in a swathe that encompasses a number of independent, densely-populated municipalities.

Johannesburg and its mining, industrial and dormitory satellites are collectively known as the Witwatersrand or, more simply, as 'the Rand' (and also, confusingly, as 'the Reef'). Nigel, Germiston, Springs, Benoni, Boksburg and Brakpan are among the towns of the East Rand; Randfontein, Krugersdorp, Westonaria, Carletonville and Soweto among those of the West Rand (Soweto is an acronym for South Western Townships).

To the south of Johannesburg, around the Vaal River, is another heavily industrialized area. In fact there isn't all that much open countryside between the two, but the densest of the southern urban concentrations are within the Vaal Triangle, whose 'points' are the flourishing centres of Vereeniging, Vanderbijlpark and, across the river in the Orange Free State (see page 129), Sasolburg.

Together, Pretoria, the Witwatersrand and the Vereeniging conurbation – formerly known as the PWV – is South Africa's economic heartland, occupying just two percent of the country's surface but containing a quarter of its population and generating nearly half its Gross Domestic Product.

JOHANNESBURG

In July 1886 an itinerant Australian prospector named George Harrison, together with his friend George Walker, literally stumbled on the Witwatersrand's reef, the world's richest natural treasure-house; word of the find spread like the proverbial bushfire, and within weeks the first fortune-seekers were camping out on the dry veld. They arrived in their hundreds at first, then in their thousands and finally, when it became clear that this wasn't just another golden bubble, that a new El Dorado was in the making, in their tens of thousands.

These first residents divided themselves into four camps: Ferreira's, Natal (later renamed Jeppestown), Biccardsburg (which became Fordsburg) and Doornfontein. Each was laid out as a self-contained village; collectively they were named (apparently the origin hasn't been firmly established) in honour of three contemporary figures: acting surveyor-general Johannes Rissik, his assistant Johannes Joubert, and Transvaal's president at the time, Stephanus Johannes Paulus Kruger.

During the early years it was commonly believed that the reef, though rich, was limited and would soon enough be mined out, so no real provision was made for future development. The first town plan was simplicity itself; streets ran east-west and north-south, irrespective of the land contours; the first tents and shacks gave way to only slightly more enduring structures of wattle-and-daub.

But as time went by the proven ore reserves, and the mines, grew larger; the magnate JB Robinson found the deeper seams; the new cyanide process revolutionized mining methods, and the residents of Johannesburg began to think seriously about planning for permanence. Conscious of the priorities, they established the first stock exchange (in an open area known as 'Between the Chains') and the first racecourse (at Turffontein) in 1887; the following year saw the inauguration of the first school, the hospital, the Globe Theatre and the famed Wanderers Club. By the early 1890s the

Strolling in the park

'Randlords' – Robinson, Cecil Rhodes, Barney Barnato, Alfred Beit, the Wernher family and others – were adding enormously to their fortunes, creating financial empires that were soon to become household names: the Union Corporation, Johannesburg Consolidated Investments ('Johnnies'), General Mining and Finance. 'Millionaire's Row' developed around Noord Street (the area was later taken up by a grand railway station) and luxurious homes were built 'with skylights and turrets and scrolled verandahs and gilded tips to their fences', most of them equipped with electricity, which had been introduced in 1890.

Not so fortunate were Johannesburg's black residents. By 1904, the year the first 'urban location', Pimville, was formally established, the city's black population numbered 60 000; within the next seven years it would grow to 112 000 (286 000 in the wider Rand area). These were the official figures; the real ones, then as now, were almost certainly much higher. Most of these people were deemed to be temporary workers, migrant labourers who returned each year to the rural areas; wages were low, rentals relatively high, amenities pitifully few, and the seeds of future instability began to germinate at an early stage.

Within three years of its birth, Johannesburg was the country's largest town. In 1928 it became a city, and is now the third biggest on the African continent (after Cairo and Alexandria). It stands 1 740 m above sea level; covers 443 km^2 (excluding the adjacent Witwatersrand centres and the vast municipality of Soweto, separated from its parent in 1983); and enjoys an average of nearly nine hours of sunshine a day throughout the year. In normal times thunderstorms bring almost daily downpours, often torrential ones and sometimes preceded by showers of king-size hailstones, between November and March; winter days are sunny, crisp, the nights frosty.

Johannesburg is home to an impressive number of internationally known mining houses, and to many individual millionaires. It is the industrial, commercial and financial capital of South Africa; its stock exchange, commonly referred to as Diagonal Street, is one of the world's most active. Tertiary education is offered by three universities – Witwatersrand, Rand Afrikaans and the largely black Vista – and by a growing number of technical and teacher-training colleges. The South African Broadcasting Corporation has its headquarters and its main transmission stations at Auckland Park, one of the western inner suburbs. There are a number of museums of note, including the Johannesburg Library's Africana collection and the 'living museum' of Gold Reef City (see next column).

The city is well placed to serve as a base from which one can explore other and perhaps more enticing parts of the country: within comfortable driving distance are the hills of the Magaliesberg, the pleasure-palace of Sun City (see page 117) and the eastern Transvaal's lovely escarpment region and its celebrated game parks (pages 79-109). Johannesburg international airport is at Kempton Park, 20 km from the central area.

The gold mines

Most of the early workings, those established in and immediately around Johannesburg, have long since closed down, leaving only their silent headgear and their dumps, many of them now decently clothed in greenery, to remind one of those heady days – not too long ago – when the place was more of a diggers' camp than a city. The industry has moved to fresh fields, and now exploits the immense underground wealth of the Rand to the east and west.

Visitors interested in the world of gold, both past and present, have a number of sightseeing options. A good place to start is the:

CARLTON CENTRE in Commissioner Street. The building is the city's tallest, and you'll get a very clear idea of just how extensive the mining network is, how pre-eminently it features in the economic life of the region, from the observation platform (the 'Carlton Panorama') on the 50th floor. And of course you'll see a great deal more than the mines: the entire Witwatersrand conurbation lies before you, which, if you're a first-time visitor, will help you establish your bearings. An additional attraction is the Panorama's gold exhibition. Open daily; there's a small admission fee.

AN UNDERGROUND VISIT to a working mine may be arranged through the Chamber of Mines in Hollard Street; Tel. (011) 838-8211. Tours are conducted on Tuesdays, Wednesdays and Thursdays.

'Gumboot' dancers in the streets of Gold Reef City, a living museum of pioneer Johannesburg.

MINE DANCING Traditional African and 'gumboot' dancing displays are held on the first, second and fourth Sunday of each month. Venues vary, so check with the Chamber of Mines (see previous column).

GEORGE HARRISON PARK, at Langlaagte to the south, is the site of the very first claims pegged and registered (see page 72). Harrison was reputed to have sold his share for £10, which probably makes him the biggest loser in mining history. The layers of Main Reef conglomerate that triggered the great rush of 1886 can be clearly seen from the viewing point erected above the shafts; a ten-stamp battery and a cluster of cocopans in the distance provide a bit of atmosphere. Far more evocative of the early years, though, is:

GOLD REEF CITY, a splendidly imaginative reconstruction of pioneer Johannesburg, built on the Crown Mines site 6 km from city centre (it's just off the M1 south highway to the Orange Free State; look for the Xavier Street exit). The Crown is honoured in the annals: it yielded a huge 1,4 million kg of gold during its lifetime – a bounty that would now be worth some R20 billion. The mine also held the world shaft-sinking record for a time.

Visitors can view the gold-pouring process

Visitors can explore the fifth-level underground workings, watch gold being poured, and enjoy traditional (tribal and gumboot) dancing. Some of the many other attractions include train and horse-drawn omnibus trips around the area; a Victorian funfair and tea parlour; a replica of the Theatre Royale; a re-creation of an early brewery, pub, Chinese laundry, tailor's shop, cooperage, apothecary, newspaper office, stock exchange. There are also speciality shops (glassware, pottery, lace, brassware, copperware, leatherware, diamonds, coins, stamps, curios); house museums furnished in period style; restaurants (The Crown is excellent); fast-food outlets; taverns; a beer garden; and a night-club (Rosie O'Grady's). The Gold Reef City Hotel caters for overnight guests (see Advisory, page 72).

Open daily; special group tours are available to foreign-language visitors; for information on these and other facilities, contact Gold Reef City, Private Bag 1890, Gold Reef City 2159; Tel. (011) 496-1400/1600; Fax: (011) 496-1249.

Memorials, museums, landmarks

For a young and reputedly brash city, Johannesburg offers a surprisingly wide selection of cultural venues. Among the more prominent of these are:

ADLER MUSEUM OF THE HISTORY OF MEDICINE (in the grounds of the SA Institute for Medical Research on Hospital Hill). Displays featuring early medicine, surgery, dentistry, pharmacy, African herbal and spiritual medicine. Open weekdays.

MUSEUM AFRICA (located in the Johannesburg Public Library, Market Street). Main features of the complex are exhibits relating to southern African history (Cape colonial settlement; Johannesburg; the Union of 1910); also Cape silver, doll collection, wooden baby-cradles, Victorian peep-show, replicas of early tavern and apothecary. Of special interest to military enthusiasts is the model of the Battle of Rorke's Drift (Anglo-Zulu War, 1879). The Johannesburg Room is worth inspecting at some length, though the place can be a bit stuffy in hot weather.

On the building's first floor is the Geological Museum, housing a formidable collection of minerals. The gold and gold-bearing rock exhibits are especially impressive; children are intrigued by the minerals displayed under ultra-violet lighting. Next door is the Harger Archeological Museum, which focuses on prehistoric southern Africa. Open daily; closed Sunday mornings. Information: Tel. 833-5624.

AFRICANA MUSEUM IN PROGRESS (corner Wolhuter and Bree streets). African (Bantu-speaking and Bushman) cultures superbly displayed in large halls at the Old Market in Bree Street. A must for first-time visitors to southern Africa. Exhibits include beadwork, musical instruments, hunting and military items, religion and custom (the tribal love-letters are fascinating), replicas of decorated huts. Upstairs the ethnic emphasis changes: here there are dolls and dolls' furniture; lead soldiers and needlework are featured. Guided tours can be arranged; museum open daily. Information: Tel. 836-8482/3787.

BENSUSAN MUSEUM OF PHOTOGRAPHY (corner Showground and Raikes roads, Braamfontein). Photography and photographic equipment dating from the earliest days – 1839, to be precise. Notable are the 3D pictures (technically, stereograms) and the material on early Johannesburg and on the Anglo-Boer War (the first major conflict to be covered in earnest by the news photographers, though techniques hadn't advanced far enough for instant action shots, and there were often 'replays' of engagements for the benefit of the cameraman). There's a fine lending and reference library upstairs which is open daily. Information: Tel. 403-1067/3408.

Zoo Lake, a pleasant oasis just north of central Johannesburg

BERNBERG MUSEUM OF COSTUME (corner Jan Smuts Avenue and Duncombe Road, Forest Town). Period costumes and accessories (fans, feathers, parasols, shoes, jewellery) from 1760 to 1929, attractively displayed in the former home of the Bernberg sisters. Open daily. Information: Tel. 646-0716.

CHRIS LESSING BOXING MUSEUM (Old Mutual Centre, corner Church and Harrison streets). Memorabilia (photos, trophies, gloves and so on). Open weekdays; Tel. 834-3088.

FIRST NATIONAL BANK MUSEUM (at 90 Market Street). The world of SA banking since the 1650s; half-hour audio-visual presentation; booking advisable; open Mondays to Fridays. Tel. 836-5887.

JAMES HALL MUSEUM OF TRANSPORT (Pioneers' Park, La Rochelle). All land conveyances are featured except railways (see Railway Museums, page 46): animal-drawn steam-powered vehicles, trams, buses, fire-engines. Open daily; Tel. 435-9718.

JEWISH MUSEUM (Sheffield House, corner Kruis and Main streets). Divided into two sections: ceremonial arts, and the story of Jewry in South Africa from about 1920. Open Mondays to Thursdays; the librarian will show you around. Tel. 331-0331.

JOHANNESBURG ART GALLERY (Joubert Park). Collections include South African, English, French, Dutch works; notable is the print cabinet (just under 3 000 items ranging from Dürer to Rembrandt); also sculpture, ceramics, posters, Japanese woodcuts, textiles, fans, furniture. Regular and special tours; lectures, film shows, concerts, poetry readings, dramatic presentations, seminars, workshops; consult the Press for details, or telephone 725-3180. Open Tuesdays to Sundays.

KLEIN JUKSKEI MOTOR MUSEUM, in Witkoppen Road, Randburg (north of Johannesburg). A superb collection of vehicles, including two rare Lincolns, many Fords and the country's oldest running car, an 1889 Benz. There's a country restaurant on the premises (delicious homemade cakes). Open Wednesdays to Sundays; Tel. 704-1204.

MISSAK CULTURAL CENTRE (for Armenian and Flemish people). Westcliff Drive: an early Johannesburg home, with splendid Belgian furniture; huge library. View by appointment; Tel. 646-2763 (afternoons).

PLACES OF WORSHIP Among several worth visiting are the Anglican Cathedral of St Mary's (corner De Villiers and Wanderers streets; Tel. 23-2537) and the Islamic Mosque (corner Nugget and Market streets; Tel. 833-2270 or 834-8241).

PLANETARIUM (Yale Road, Braamfontein). A journey through space and time, enjoyed in comfort. Programmes change frequently – at the time of writing, the show was entitled 'The Last Question', an adaptation of Isaac Asimov's story about entropy (specifically, what happens when the universe runs out of energy). Informative and entertaining; English alternates with Afrikaans. Book at Planetarium; Tel. 716-3199/3038 or through Computicket; Tel. 331-9991. Night Sky information: Tel. 716-3031.

RAILWAY MUSEUMS The Transnet Museum (formerly the SA Transport Services Museum) is located on the old concourse of the main railway station (De Villiers Street). Displays cover the whole public-transport range: railways (including the Transvaal's first locomotive; and a fascinating collection of model trains); road motor services, harbours, airways, lifeboats, tugboat, a photograph room and an excellent art gallery (35 works by Pierneef). Open Mondays to Fridays; Tel. 773-9114.

Other railway displays – excellent ones – are on view at the Railway Preservation Society's centre near Krugersdorp (see page 111); and at the Transport Museum in Heidelberg's old station (see page 52).

A corner of the Johannesburg Art gallery

SANTARAMA MINILAND (Pioneers' Park, La Rochelle). This miniature city has been modelled on Holland's famed Madurodam. Scale replicas of many prominent South African buildings and landmarks (Cape Town's Castle, Kimberley's Big Hole and so forth), and a full-size reproduction of Van Riebeeck's ship, *Drommedaris*. Open daily; Tel. 435-0543.

SOUTH AFRICAN AIR FORCE MUSEUM (at Lanseria Airport). The story of South African aviation from the pioneer days. Open on weekdays; Tel. 440-9344 or 659-1014 ext 61.

SOUTH AFRICAN MINT (Old Johannesburg Road, Midrand). The museum attached to the Mint houses coins, medals and so forth dating from around 1650. The whole range of SA currency, ancient and modern, is on display. Tours are conducted Mondays to Thursdays; tours of the Mint itself by appointment; Tel. (012) 661-6843/4/5/6. There is an exhibition at Gold Reef City featuring coins of the gold era; Tel. (011) 496-1400/5.

SOUTH AFRICAN NATIONAL MUSEUM OF MILITARY HISTORY (Saxonwold, next to Zoo). A splendid expo of militaria, with special emphasis on the two world wars; weapons, vehicles, aircraft (including the pioneer Messerschmidt BF.262 jet fighter, only one of two in the world to have survived intact). Also South African War memorabilia. Audio-visual presentations on Sundays; Tel. 646-5513; open daily.

SOUTH AFRICAN ROCK ART, MUSEUM OF In the grounds of the Zoo. An open-air display of prehistoric engravings, collected mainly from the southern and western Transvaal and northern Cape. Open daily; Tel. 836-3787.

YAD VASHEM MEMORIAL HALL (Barnato Street, Berea). Dedicated to Holocaust victims; symbolic carvings, taped commentary. Tel. 642-4548 or 331-0331.

THE RAND SHOW An important annual exposition, and something of a showcase for local endeavour, held in March or April at the National Exhibition Centre (part of the National Recreation and Sport Centre, which is still under development) in Baragwanath Road

Joubert Park at night

north of Crown Mines. There's livestock, home industries, jewellery, industrial machinery, house and garden products and much else on display. The show attracts about a million visitors each year.

Visits to working concerns

Among the several commercial, educational and other private organizations that welcome visitors are:

☆ Johannesburg Stock Exchange. By no means the country's first (shares were traded at the Cape as early as 1820; both Kimberley and Barberton had flourishing exchanges in the early 1880s; the JSE was established in 1887, on a patch known as 'Between the Chains'), but now the country's only physical stock and share market, and one of the world's major financial trading centres. It's popularly known as 'Diagonal Street', a vast, sophisticated and fascinating complex open to visitors from Mondays to Fridays (conducted tours at 11h00 and 14h30; Tel. 833-6580). The building also houses the Hall of South African Achievement.

☆ The South African Broadcasting Corporation (SABC), Auckland Park: two-hour tours of the national television and radio headquarters; booking essential; Tel. 714-9111.

☆ Newspapers (*The Star* and *Sunday Star*, Sauer Street): tours of the production line start at 10h45; Tel. Tours Department 633-2341/9111.

☆ ESkom, the giant electricity supply utility, runs an excellent information centre at Eskom

House in Smit Street: the world of energy explained by films, working models and so forth. Tel. 711-9111.

☆ Civic Theatre, city centre: twice daily conducted tours; booking advisable; Tel. 403-3408.

☆ Rand Afrikaans University, Auckland Park: one the country's newest; smallish, very modern; conducted tours on Wednesdays and Fridays; Tel. 726 5000 ext 311 or 489-2171.

☆ University of the Witwatersrand: South Africa's largest English-medium university (16 000 enrollment); the campus is in Braamfontein, near city centre; tours are conducted on the first Wednesday of each month (Tel. 716-3162/1111). Of special note is the Standard Bank collection of African tribal art, housed in the Gertrude Posel Gallery, Senate House: masks, headdresses, fetishes, beadwork, fertility dolls and much else that is disappearing from the cultures. The gallery is also the venue of occasional period exhibitions.

Gardens, parks, reserves

Central Johannesburg isn't known for its greenery: there are few tree-shaded city squares; space is at a premium, and nearly all of it is filled by high-rise development. But first impressions are deceptive: the city council administers over 600 parks and open spaces, most of which grace the suburbs, covering a combined area of some 4 600 ha.

Just outside the central area, for instance, you'll find the Braamfontein Spruit, a stream that slices through the suburbs and northern municipalities, and it is possible to follow its parklike course from Westdene Dam to the Klein Jukskei River – a distance of about 25 km – almost without touching concrete. This is South Africa's oldest and longest urban trail (though there are shorter alternative routes: one can join it at any point), and Johannesburgers count it among their more prized community assets. For specific information on the trail, contact the Johannesburg Hiking Club, Tel. 659-0826.

Some of the area's many other, mainly modest outdoor attractions are:

JOUBERT PARK, in the central area. Laid out in 1887 (just a year after the first diggers' tents went up), it now features a giant open-air chess board, a plant conservatory, floral clock, restaurant; adjacent theatre and art gallery.

JOHANNESBURG ZOO, situated within the Herman Eckstein park, which is located on either side of Jan Smuts Avenue. More than 3 000 animals, birds and reptiles are in residence, 30 of them on the endangered list; the ape house contains gorillas, orang-utans and chimps. Zoo Lake, across the road, is popular among boaters, picnickers, strollers and lazers. Lakeside restaurant; illuminated fountain; open-air art exhibitions; occasional (Sunday afternoon) country-music get-togethers.

BEZUIDENHOUT PARK, in the Dewetshof inner suburb and part of a pre-gold rush farm. The homestead and its attendant graveyard have been preserved; a caravan park, playground, paddling pool and miniature railway added. Pleasant for picnics and walks.

JOHANNESBURG BOTANIC GARDEN, Thomas Bowler Avenue, Emmarentia. Boasts a lovely rose garden (4 000 plants, fountains, pools), rose-trial grounds, herb garden, ground-cover demonstration area, hedge display section, many exotic trees, and the Sima Eliovson Florium, venue for floral exhibitions. Open daily; guided tours at 09h00 on the first Tuesday of each summer month. The grounds are on the western shore of:

EMMARENTIA DAM, where yachtsmen, boardsailors, wind-surfers, scuba-divers and model-boat enthusiasts enjoy themselves.

KINGSTON FROST ALOE RESERVE on Hampton Avenue, Auckland Park, an inner suburb to the west of the city centre. The plants are at their best in June and early July.

MELVILLE KOPPIES, Emmarentia, is a small nature reserve that protects the indigenous flora of the Witwatersrand outcrops, and is open to the public from September to April on the third Sunday afternoon of each month. There's a walking trail; the remains of an Iron-age village and smelting works (the area has in fact been occupied by man for about 100 000 years); guided tours by arrangement; Tel. 646-3612.

MELROSE BIRD SANCTUARY, in the suburb of Melrose, provides sanctuary for some 120 species in its 10 ha of reedbeds. Facilities include benches and a bird-watching hide.

Part of the Sandton City complex, a shopper's mecca to the north of Johannesburg

THE WILDS, Houghton Drive, Houghton. An 18-ha area of rocky ridges, streams and cultivated gardens of indigenous flora (some of it rare) in one of the city's wealthier suburbs. It has four plant houses and a network of sign-posted walking trails.

PIONEERS' PARK, Rosettenville, is a fairly extensive area encompassing the Wemmer Pan (a pleasant stretch of water, used by the local rowing club). A pleasant place for walking, and for viewing Johannesburg's skyline. Also in the park are the transport museum and the Santarama miniature city (see page 46), a steam railway (for members of the Johannesburg Live Steam Club), swimming pool, restaurant, picnic and barbecue area, musical fountain.

KLIPRIVIERSBERG NATURE RESERVE, Fairway Avenue, Mondeor. Covers 550 ha of rocky ridges that are home to about 150 bird and a number of small mammal species. It's strictly a conservation area, though there are guided walking tours on the second Sunday of each month; Tel. 680-4056.

FLORENCE BLOOM BIRD SANCTUARY, between Blairgowrie and Victory Park, is part of the Delta Park conservation centre, headquarters of the Wildlife Society. The sanctuary is haven to about 200 bird species, many of which congregate around the two dams (hides have been established). The bird sanctuary is open at all times.

The Nature Conservation Centre has an auditorium and exhibition halls (superb environmental displays); there is a Natural History Museum, an educational resource complex and a meditation room. Development plans for the future include an astronomical observatory. The area is on the Braamfontein Spruit trail (see page 47). The centre is closed on Sundays; Tel. 782-1531/4723.

HARVEY NATURE RESERVE, in Linksfield, is a small area being developed as a wild flower garden. No facilities, though one can meander freely and most pleasantly along the unmarked paths, enjoying the flora, the birdlife and the views of Johannesburg to the south and the Magaliesberg uplands in the west. One of the many trails leads to:

GILLOOLY'S FARM, a fairly large public park where dog shows are held, where picnickers relax beneath the willows and pines and walkers wander on the koppie. A miniature railway does its rounds in summer; Tel. 407-6111.

OLIFANTSVLEI NATURE RESERVE, to the south-west of Johannesburg, is the largest of Johannesburg's conservation areas: a wildish wetland, south-west of the city, whose reed-beds sustain a prolific birdlife. The reserve is still under development.

AROUND JOHANNESBURG

The city is ringed by a bewildering number of independent municipalities, most of them industrial, and in tourist terms unremarkable. They're all part of what was formerly known as the PWV conurbation (the acronym stands for Pretoria-Witwatersrand-Vereeniging), the haphazard, often rather characterless urban sprawl that stretches west to Krugersdorp, Westonaria and Carletonville (these places are covered, briefly, on pages 111-112), east to Springs and Germiston, north to Sandton and Midrand (beyond which is the city of Pretoria), and south

as far as Vereeniging, Vanderbijlpark and the Vaal River. It's a vast region that defies synopsis, certainly in these few pages. Its more prominent components, however, include:

Sandton and its neighbours

Sandton is a relatively new town (it was granted municipal status in 1969) of fashionable, generally very affluent suburbs that have been developed to retain their open green spaces. Of interest:

SANDTON CITY, the commercial centre, is one of the largest and most sophisticated shopping and business complexes in South Africa and indeed in the southern hemisphere.

MEGAWATT PARK Eskom's large, very modern establishment on Maxwell Drive: horticultural displays; audio-visual presentation on the country's power network; visitors welcome during weekdays; Tel. 800-3487/3120.

POTTERY FACTORY Tours are available to small groups; Tel. 786-1050.

DIE OU KAAPHUIS ('The Old Cape House'), in Main Street, Sandton, north of Johannesburg: a 'living museum' beautifully furnished in Cape Dutch style; adjoining but separate is the exhibition centre, where furniture is for sale. The museum is open on Saturday mornings, other times by appointment; the exhibition centre on Mondays to Saturdays; Tel. 784-2327.

Some way west of Sandton, and accessible from Johannesburg via William Nichol Drive, is the:

LION PARK, where a 10-km driving trail enables you to observe lion, zebra, ostrich, wildebeest, springbok and other game species at close quarters (keep your windows closed, and keep moving). Some visitors enjoy being photographed holding a lion cub; other popular features are the Ndebele village, pets' corner, picnic/barbecue area, swimming pool, curio shop. Light refreshments available.

The small centres to the north and north-east of Sandton – Halfway House, Midrand, parts of the Kyalami area – are strategically positioned between Johannesburg and Pretoria, and have been selected as the growth points of what amounts to a brand-new planned city. Development is large-scale and rapid; new industries, commercial complexes, townships, prestige suburbs are rapidly changing the character of the wider area, which retains the name of Midrand. Recommended ports of call include the:

TRANSVAAL SNAKE PARK, at Halfway House. Here, an intriguing variety of reptiles are on display in an attractive setting; snakes are milked at regular times during the day; there's a curio shop, restaurant and playground; Tel. 805-3116.

At nearby Kyalami is the South African National Equestrian Centre, which among other things trains a bevy of:

LIPPIZANER STALLIONS These lovely white horses perform in the elegantly disciplined style of their colleagues at Vienna's famed Spanish Riding School. The shows are on Sundays at 11h00; bookings through Computicket (see Advisory, page 77). For information, telephone 702-2103.

Roodepoort

Originally an untidy sprawl of miners' tents and shacks clustered around one of the Witwatersrand's first viable gold mines, now a substantial industrial and residential centre of some 200 000 people (it gained city status in 1977) to the west of Johannesburg. It has an excellent small (300-seat) civic theatre, an ice-rink and:

ROODEPOORT MUSEUM, on the ground floor of the handsome Civic Centre. The focus is on early white settlement, gold and the pioneer mining days; features include a Voortrekker outspan and farmstead (complete with reed ceiling and *koffiekonvoor),* a Victorian house and a smithy. There's a restaurant as well. Lunch, a tour of the museum (the staff are knowledgeable and friendly) and a recital in the adjacent theatre makes a pleasant Sunday outing. Closed Mondays and public holidays. Tel. 472-1400/672-2147.

FLORIDA LAKE, born of the local marshes and enlarged by water pumped from the mines, is a large and attractive recreational area that also makes a valuable contribution to conservation: its western shores are protected as a breeding ground for herons; the Hamerkop nature reserve is located at the western inflow. A pleasant walk takes you to the Bennie Reyneke dam 3 km to the north-west and on to the Vivian Rorke park. Facilities include picnic/barbecue

Johannesburg boasts a surprising 600 suburban parks and open spaces

spots, caravan/camping ground, miniature railway, swimming pool. The lake area serves as venue for the Roodepoort International Eisteddfod of South Africa.

Also recommended is the short Helderkruin nature trail: it follows a pretty stream from just north of Roodepoort and through its gorge, passing an impressive 30-m waterfall *en route*. The trail ends just south of the Little Falls gorge, near the:

KLOOFENDAL NATURE RESERVE, a 150-ha area of kloofs, koppies and dam that are home to about 120 bird species. Walks, self-guided trails and picnic/barbecue spots have been established; among the other features are an amphitheatre in which open-air events are staged, and the first mine shaft to produce viable gold (this is now a national monument). Open daily in summer.

WITWATERSRAND NATIONAL BOTANIC GARDEN is a 225-ha area of Roodepoort proclaimed to conserve one of the few surviving patches of the Rand's natural vegetation. A waterfall plunges dramatically into the ravine. Cultivated sections are devoted to comprehensive collections of succulents and ferns; visitors may wander the footpaths freely.

Vereeniging

This large (population: 200 000) town on the Vaal River 58 km south of Johannesburg gained prominence when the peace terms that brought the South African War of 1899-1902 to an end were concluded there (though the treaty itself was signed at Melrose House, Pretoria).

The town's name translates from the Afrikaans as 'company', a reference to its origins as a colliery centre in the early 1880s. The initial impetus for its growth, though, was the establishment of a power station in 1909 and, four years later, the commissioning of the Union Steel Corporation's giant plant. It's now one of South Africa's most flourishing heavy industrial (coal, steel) and manufacturing centres. Its attractions:

VEREENIGING MUSEUM (Leslie Street): weapons, costumes, glassware, and a paleontological section. The peace treaty of Vereeniging is featured in photographs. Open Monday to Saturday; Tel. (016) 22-2251.

The Vaal Dam, popular among Johannesburgers

VAAL DAM AND RIVER These delineate the provincial border between the Transvaal and Orange Free State; the dam is large, deep and bilharzia-free; the river's banks are pleasantly willow-shaded, and both are very popular among holiday-makers and weekenders.

The area is well endowed with resorts, caravan/camping grounds and picnic spots, and with facilities for angling, sailing, power-boating, water-skiing, golf (two courses, one of which belongs to the well-known Maccauvlei club), bowls, tennis and so forth. Some of what's on offer is covered in the chapter on the Free State (page 123-137); for information about amenities on the Transvaal side, contact Vereeniging Public Relations Office or the Johannesburg Publicity Association (see Advisory, page 77).

Vanderbijlpark

On the Vaal River west of Vereeniging and epicentre of what is known as the Vaal Triangle, Vanderbijlpark was built by Iscor (in the late 1940s) to house the employees of its vast foundries and steelworks. It, too, is heavily industrialized, but the place is modern, its development well-planned and, with its wide tree-lined streets and numerous lawned parks, surprisingly attractive. Tours of the foundry (Africa's largest), taking in the entire steel-making process, are conducted on Tuesdays and Thursdays; Tel. (016) 31-1800 ext 2153. There are two resorts within the town itself, and the recreational amenities of the Vaal dam and river are nearby (see page 51).

Heidelberg

Just off the N3 some 50 km south-east of Johannesburg, Heidelberg gained brief prominence when, during the Transvaal War of 1880-81, it served as the seat of the republican government. Among its places of interest are the Klipkerk (the stone church), which houses a small local-history museum in its cellar; and Diepkloof House, a beautifully restored settler home dating from 1850 situated within the Suikerbosrand nature reserve 20 km away (see below), and the:

TRANSPORT MUSEUM, housed in Heidelberg's old station, the first to be built in the Transvaal. The museum's several halls feature exhibits ranging from vintage cars, vehicles and bicycles, quadricycles, gadabouts, push-chairs, and a train and walk-through dining car. Closed on Mondays.

SUIKERBOSRAND NATURE RESERVE The land here – 13 500 ha of grassy plain, hills, gorges, sugarbush and acacia woodland set in one of South Africa's most highly industrialized and densely populated regions – has been painstakingly restored to its original condition, which represents a notable triumph for conservation.

The reserve is a haven for zebra, eland (an especially large herd, and an impressive sight in the lush summer months), kudu, oribi, black wildebeest, blesbok, springbok, mountain reedbuck and the occasional cheetah, aardwolf and brown hyena, and for 220 species of bird, including a pair of black eagles. Of interest in the area are the remains of a number of stone kraals, once home to the ancestral Tswana.

Two pleasant resort camps (caravan/camping grounds; recreational facilities) have been established in the reserve, and a third is being developed. Other facilities include a 60-km game-viewing route, a hiking trail (one to six days; 6 gaslit overnight huts and a 'meditation hut'), charted day-walks (ranging from the two-hour Cheetah to the all-day Bokmakierie), picnic spots, visitors' centre. Information: Officer-in-Charge, Private Bag H616, Heidelberg 2400; Tel. (0151) 2181/2/3.

Nigel

A fast-growing gold-mining and industrial centre on the Far East Rand. Among its modest attractions are the recently built dam just to the north (watersports, picnic spots); the Piet Wagener game park just to the east (ostriches, springbok and other antelope, and a varied birdlife); and, 8 km north-east of town, the:

MARIEVALE BIRD SANCTUARY, one of the Transvaal's most important avian reserves. Among the approximately 300 species recorded in the reedbeds of this 1 400-ha expanse of wetland (partially a product of mining operations) are greater and lesser flamingos, spurwing geese (huge flocks of them in winter), pelicans, most of the duck species and other waterfowl. There are three bird-watching hides in the sanctuary and a pleasant picnic area.

Springs

'Capital' of the East Rand, Springs began life as a coal-mining town, declined after much larger coal reserves were discovered around Witbank farther to the east, and then took on a new lease of life with the extension of the Witwatersrand's gold-mining industry. Among its social assets are the HF Verwoerd theatre (one of the very few venues for live performances outside Johannesburg and Pretoria); the handsome civic centre (which also hosts the performing arts); the 20 000-seat Pam Brink stadium; the Alexander dam and its adjacent man-made lake (sailing, bird-watching in the small sanctuary) and Springs Park, a pleasant place of man-made water-features and picnic spots.

Boksburg

Another major gold- and coal-producing centre (population: 163 000) boasting the southern hemisphere's largest shopping complex (the Hypermarket). Boksburg's first administrative officer, Montagu White, made herculean efforts to beautify the area, creating, among other things, a splendid dam. Its lake (which featured prominently in the anti-apartheid campaign of the late 1980s) is now a most pleasant place of tree-shaded lawns, terraces and an expanse of water much favoured by dinghy-sailors (there are also barbecue spots and restaurants, children's playground, miniature railway, and 'artists in the sun' performances by tribal dancers, pipe bands and so on).

Other outdoor attractions include Rolfe's Pan Bird sanctuary, a 100-ha haven for about 130 species, including sacred ibis and the country's largest inland breeding community of grey-headed gull; Bokkie Park (which introduces urban youngsters to the world of farmyard animals); the La Grange Bird Park (tea-garden, picnic spots, bird-watching) and Wild Waters, where nine water activities are on offer, including a wave pool and the 'raging rapids'. Indoor entertainment at the Fun Factory (ice-rink, ten-pin bowling) and the spacious Warehouse Disco on North Rand Road.

A flea-market is held outside the civic centre on the first Saturday of each month.

Benoni

The Biblical name, which means 'son of my sorrows', was conferred by an early surveyor because of the town's awkward shape. Benoni is one of the largest of the East Rand centres (the last census, in 1985, pegged its population at 215 000) and one of the region's more attractive: a chain of reservoirs, created from water pumped from the mines (all of which have now closed) to areas of natural marsh provide excellent recreational facilities. Picnicking, angling, boating and watersports can be enjoyed at Homestead Lake (only for members of the local yachting club and their guests), Kleinfontein Lake on whose northern shore is the sociable Danie Taljaard Park, where 'lapas' may be hired; Tel. (011) 845-1650; Rynfield Dam, and at the Middle and Civic lakes.

Bunny Park, a children's favourite, is home to a variety of farmyard animals and pets (it also offers thatched rondavels and picnic/barbecue spots). Of interest to visitors is the pottery tour (hand-painted ware; Tel. (011) 54-9615); the flea-market, held at the civic centre on the last Saturday of each month; and Jatniel, a self-contained village and headquarters of the international Pentecostal Christian Organization (its temple seats 3 000). On the Westdene Pan just south of the golf course is the:

KORSMAN BIRD SANCTUARY, whose shallow pan hosts a huge number of flamingos. Other residents include sacred ibis, guinea fowl, ostrich and a number of small buck. The hide is reserved for members of the Witwatersrand Bird Club, but you can see everything on your walk or drive around the perimeter.

Germiston

The city (it gained this status in 1950) began life in 1886 as a group of gold-mining villages on the main reef and grew into the sixth largest of South Africa's urban centres. It boasts the world's biggest gold refinery and is the country's most extensive railway junction; its lake is the Witwatersrand's largest; its Hermann Immelman stadium ranks among the southern hemisphere's most sophisticated sports complexes; its Gosforth Park racecourse serves as headquarters of the Thoroughbred Breeders' Association of South Africa. At the Simmer and Jack museum (named after the partners who owned the original mining company) visitors can view the processes by which gold is mined and refined. Outdoor venues of note include:

GERMISTON LAKE, 10 km outside town on the N2: a pleasant place for angling, boating, watersports, picnicking, strolling.

RONDEBULT BIRD SANCTUARY, one of the country's most important urban wildfowl reserves, comprises a series of man-made pans whose waters (the levels are controlled) and reeded islands attract flamingos, geese, black-winged stilt, avocet, sacred ibis and many other waterbirds. Observation hides (five of them) and short walks have been established; guided visits may be arranged through the Witwatersrand Bird Club.

GETTING AROUND

Johannesburg's layout is fairly symmetrical, the thoroughfares running roughly east-west and north-south.

Getting around the city, though, can be a confusing and, in rush-hour (seven to nine in the morning, four to six in the afternoon) thoroughly irritating business, partly because the traffic is dense and slow-moving, partly because there are so many one-way streets.

Once you escape from city centre, however, things become much easier. The urban freeway system, comprising the M1 North and South and the M2 East and West, is linked to the national bypass freeways and to the main routes north to Pretoria and south to the Orange Free State. Other major routes are well signposted, the numbers appearing against a blue background and, armed with a good map of the Witwatersrand, you should have little difficulty in finding your way around Johannesburg's suburbs and the adjoining towns.

As we've suggested (see page 43), an excellent way to establish your bearings is from the 'Carlton Panorama' observation deck on the Carlton Office Tower's 50th floor. The views are both splendid and informative; strategically placed telescopes enhance the vistas; a 'talking' lift introduces you to the city on your way up; a sight-and-sound show entitled 'A Day in Johannesburg' completes the briefing. Information; Tel. (011) 331-6608.

There are also fine views of the city and of the Magaliesberg to the north from Aasvoëlkop ('peak of vultures') on Northcliff Ridge, highest of Johannesburg's natural features. The viewpoint is off Lucky Street.

PARKING On-street parking is at a premium in central Johannesburg.

One can usually find a berth, though, in one of the city's six municipal and seven or eight major parking garages (information can be obtained from the hotel reception, or call 832-2411), and in a goodly number of open-air parking grounds.

PARK-AND-RIDE is probably the cheapest and least harrowing means of access, enabling you to leave your car at a designated parking ground outside the central area – at one of the more than 20 suburban sites – and use the regular and frequent bus service into town. Information from the Johannesburg Transport Department; Tel. 836-2061 ext 241/327.

BUSES The services are adequate, the fares relatively low, most of the routes pass through Eloff Street. Routes, though, radiate out from city centre, and cross-suburban bus travel can be tricky. Information: Tel. 836-2061.

Daily Multi-journey coupons (in blocks of ten, which represent a considerable saving), timetables and other information available from the ticket office, City Hall, on the corner of Market and Loveday streets. Telephone enquiries: 836-2061 ext 241/327.

Weekend bus services (Saturday 14h00 to Monday morning) leave from Vanderbijl Square, corner of Main and Rissik streets. A half-hourly airport bus connects the SAA's Rotunda city terminal with Johannesburg international airport (see Advisory, page 71).

This city-centre mall features speciality shops

TAXIS Johannesburg is a big and busy enough city to warrant fleets of cruising taxis, but they steadfastly stick to their ranks, which are located outside the Carlton Hotel in Main Street, in Commissioner Street near the Rand Club, outside the Johannesburg Sun Hotel in Jeppe Street and at other sites. It's more usual, though, to book by phone: consult hotel reception or the Yellow Pages; some 24-hour numbers: 337-5858/60; 725-3333; and 23-4555.

The so-called 'black taxi' minibuses do cruise, along certain routes, and can be hailed. They're fast (some much too fast) and tend to be crowded.

TRAINS Generally speaking, suburban train services link the city with the high-density dormitory areas and are not geared to the needs of the average visitor. Regional services connect Johannesburg with Pretoria (a good, fast run) and other major centres in the Pretoria-Witwatersrand-Vaal Triangle (PWV) area.

Entrance to Johannesburg railway station (sometimes called Park Station) is in Wolmarans Street. For enquiries and reservations, see Advisory, page 71.

CAR HIRE The major, internationally-known rental companies are well represented, as are competitive local firms. Consult hotel reception or the Yellow Pages.

Campers and motor homes may also be rented; Tel. 789-2327 or 787-9105.

Walks and hikes

Central Johannesburg is not really a place for walking: the pavements are thronged during business hours, not recommended to casual strollers after hours.

For those who do want to combine sightseeing with some healthy exercise, though, the Publicity Association (see Advisory, page 77), will supply details of three recommended 'historical walkabouts' (the Blue, Green and Orange routes).

Farther afield, there are pleasant rambles in the various parks and reserves (see page 47) and along the Braamfontein Spruit trail (see page 47), which has been conveniently divided into seven sections. For details of these and other suggested walks, consult the Publicity Association or, better still, obtain an excellent little book entitled *Day Walks in and Around Johannesburg & Pretoria* by Brendon Ryan (Struik Publishers, Cape Town), available from leading bookstores.

Tours

Several touring companies operate in and around the Witwatersrand, and the options are virtually limitless. Some sample short excursions on offer:

☆ Around Johannesburg: Johannesburg Municipality runs two tours on a Sunday afternoon; the buses depart at 14h30 from Vanderbijl Square; Tel. 836-2061.

☆ To the sprawling city of Soweto: (see page 56).

☆ Through the northern suburbs to the Lion Park, Heia Safari Ranch (tribal dancing), the organic Village Market and Aloe Ridge Zulu Kraal (Action Tours).

☆ To a gold mine, diamond mine and Gold Reef City (Nawa Safaris).

These are just a few. And, of course, there are a great number and variety of tour packages (coach and air: sightseeing; photographic and hunting safaris and so forth) taking in places much farther afield: Johannesburg is within comfortable driving distance of the Kruger National Park and other major wilderness areas; of the Magaliesberg, the Sterkfontein Caves and Sun City to the west, and of the Vaal River and its dam to the south.

Also on offer are walking, cycling, adventurous river-boating, or 'Wildwater', safaris (Tel. 788-5120); hot-air balloon safaris over the Magaliesberg (Tel. 705-3201), and pleasant steamtrain trips. For information on the latter, contact the Historic Transport Association, PO Box 1864, Johannesburg 2000 (Tel. 640-4739), the Live Steam Train Club (Tel. 646-3481), or the Railway Society of SA's Preservation Group (Tel. 888-1154).

TOUR OPERATORS Offices in the Witwatersrand area include: Welcome Tours and Safaris (Tel. 403-2562) ☆ Nawa Safaris (337-6200; 888-1562/9 and, after hours, 673-0386;

Part of the dormitory city of Soweto. The housing shortage remains critical.

SOWETO

South Africa's largest and best-known 'black' city (though the demise of the Group Areas Act will render the term obsolete), Soweto sprawls across 95 km² of dusty terrain to the south-west of Johannesburg – its name is in fact a contraction of South Western Townships – and it is home to well over a million people, perhaps as many as three million. The place has functioned, uncomfortably, as an independent municipality with its own elected councillors and administration, but the system was imposed by the government and has not proved popular with the residents.

Much of Soweto is now electrified; some roads have been properly surfaced, schools, clinics and hospitals built (the 2 000-bed Baragwanath hospital at Diepkloof is one of the southern hemisphere's largest).

In 1987 the Soweto campus of Vista University was inaugurated. The more affluent Sowetans – the increasing number of entrepreneurs, professional people and highly qualified executives – have substantial and attractive homes. But development has been both haphazard and slow, and most people live in grossly overcrowded conditions.

Soweto has functioned primarily as a dormitory city, neglected (for reasons of law rather than choice) by big business; commercial activity resides in the more than 3 000 shops and stores, and in the multiplicity of small enterprises within the so-called 'informal economy', that have been established. Social life tends to revolve around the football stadiums and grounds, the huge number of shebeens (social drinking and conversation clubs), and the community halls and recreation centres of various kinds, from which is emerging, among other things, a distinctive and vibrant musical culture.

With the disintegration of the apartheid system, and given political stability, it is likely that industries will be attracted to the area by the huge and increasingly skilled labour pool, and commerce by the massive buying power of the community. So one can expect dramatic improvements in the range of amenities available to Sowetans and, hopefully, in the quality of their lives.

Tours of the city are laid on by the Soweto council (they depart from the Carlton Hotel) and others, taking in the housing developments, schools, workshops, the Sangoma Centre, 'cultural kraal', workshop for the handicapped and so forth. Information and bookings: Tel. 331-5072; 331-4911 ext 245; or 932-000 ext 2020.

☆ Action Tours (783-0342) ☆ Tour-Rite (802-7592) ☆ Springbok Atlas (403-6466) ☆ Wildlife Safaris (886-4065) ☆ Born Free Safaris (29-8831) ☆ Rand Coach Tours (339-1658) ☆ Grosvenor Tours (708-1777) ☆ Touring Africa CC (403-4368) ☆ Tourlink (404-2617).

Day drives

Again, plenty of options; among the favoured destinations are Sun City via the Magaliesberg and Rustenburg (see page 113); the Vaal River around Vereeniging (see page 51); and the Suikerbosrand nature reserve (see page 52). If you're in the self-guided touring business, arm yourself with a detailed regional guide and a good map, and spare some time to chat to either Satour or the Automobile Association (see Advisory, page 77) about itineraries. Maxwell Leigh's *Touring in South Africa* (Struik Publishers, Cape Town) and Reader's Digest's *Off the Beaten Track*, both available in major bookshops, are also quite excellent sources of information.

Two local excursions, though, merit special mention: first, about 20 suburban artists and craftspeople – members of the so-called Studio Route – open their studios and workshops (some of which also function as galleries and shops) to the public on the last Sunday of each month, and at other times by appointment. The range of endeavour is wide, taking in painting, sculpture, graphic art, pottery, stoneware, silkscreening, calligraphy, jewellery, stained-glass, African art and crafts, spinning, weaving, clothing design, fibre art, quiltwork, needlecraft. Details of the route and its participants are available from the Johannesburg Publicity Association (see Advisory, page 77).

Second, the 40-km trip west to Heia Safari Ranch is worth making for its 'authentic' Zulu village, and for the Zulu dancing (by the Mzumba Dance Troupe). Open daily; a typical South African barbecue entices visitors on Sundays.

CITY LIFE

Johannesburg has all the amenities of a major modern city: excellent shopping outlets both in the central area and, especially, in the large and glitzy suburban malls; a range of restaurants to suit most tastes; generally good and sometimes innovative theatre; orchestral music, ballet and opera of a fair standard; an explosively adventurous jazz/rock/new wave/indigenous music scene, and an art world searching for an identity.

Johannesburg's vague equivalent of Greenwich Village and Montmartre is Hillbrow, a densely populated, cosmopolitan area of apartment blocks, eateries, nightspots, shops and streets that seldom sleep. The inner suburb, just to the north-east of city centre, may not have the charm of its more renowned counterparts, but what it lacks in that respect it certainly makes up for in sheer exuberance.

Shopping

Major concentrations of general and speciality outlets – 'worlds in one' that encompass restaurants and cinemas, banks, travel agents and other services as well as shops – are the Carlton Centre in Commissioner Street; Rosebank Mall and The Firs on Cradock Avenue, Rosebank; the giant Eastgate Centre on Broadway Extension, Bedfordview; Hyde Park Corner on Jan Smuts Avenue; the Killarney Mall on Riviera Road, Killarney; the Sanlam Centre on Hill Street, Randburg, and, queen of them all, the supremely sophisticated Sandton City in the northern municipality of Sandton.

There are a great many outlets in and around Johannesburg that cater specially for the visitor, offering an array of African craftwork, curios, hides and skins, locally made pottery and so forth. One of the more rewarding is the African Market in the Atrium Centre, Rivonia Road, Sandton.

The city's more prominent art galleries and craft outlets are the Everard Read Gallery in Rosebank (probably Johannesburg's leading dealer; Tel. 788-4805) ☆ The Sanderling Gallery in the Smal Street Mall (Tel. 29-3791) ☆ Gallery 21 in Victory House, Commissioner Street (Tel. 838-6630) ☆ The Market Art and Photographic Gallery in the Market theatre complex (Tel. 832-1641) ☆ Totem Meneghelli Primitive Arts & Antiques in the medical centre, Jeppe street (Tel. 29-4891) ☆ The Soweto Art Gallery in Victory House, Commissioner Street (Tel. 836-0252) ☆ The Fuba Gallery opposite the Market Theatre (experimental township dynamics; Tel. 834-7139) ☆ Primitive Art and Antiques in Rosebank (Tel. 447-1409) ☆ Yursin Art in the Smal Street Mall (paintings

and sculptures by black artists; Tel. 29-1540) ☆ African Magic in Rocky Street, Bellevue ; (Tel. 648-4548), and ☆ Village Curios at the Sandton Holiday Inn (Tel. 783-1540).

Among shopping areas with something different to offer are Rockey Street in Yeoville ☆ The Village Flea Market in Hillbrow's Pretoria Street (jewellery, bric-a-brac, books, leatherwork, clothes) ☆ The Market Theatre mall (within the multi-purpose theatre complex: see page 58; the pretty shopping arcade includes an antique and collectibles corner and a flower market) ☆ Smal Street, the modern pedestrian mall linking the Johannesburg Sun and Towers with the Carlton Hotel (sophisticated shops, restaurants, outdoor cafés) ☆ Diagonal Street, near the Stock Exchange (small shops selling wares ranging from fruit and vegetables to spices, African blankets and traditional medicines) ☆ The African Market in Rivonia (here craftspeople, dressed in traditional fashion, can be seen at work), and two largish and rather unusual complexes:

ORIENTAL PLAZA, the Indian market in Main Road, Fordsburg (there's also access from Bree Street and Lilian road) is a colourful cluster of some 270 stores, stalls, eateries and a flower, fruit and vegetable market that beckon the bargain hunter. The emphasis is generally though not exclusively on eastern merchandise; some of the fabrics are exquisite; a minaret clock-tower and peacock fountain add atmosphere. Highly recommended.

FISHERMAN'S VILLAGE A new development, created on the shore of Bruma Lake in Bedfordview and billed as a 'Mediterranean oasis'. The concept is certainly imaginative, the content appealing, most of it taken up by boutiques and speciality stores, coffee shops and restaurants (about 15 of them in all, including Greek, Italian, Portuguese, Israeli establishments) fronting on cobbled, flower-bedecked streets and alleyways. There's also a boardwalk, and boating and wind-surfing on the lake.

MARKETS South Africa's largest produce market is the complex of six halls and 39 cold storage chambers that does business (from Monday to Saturday; starting at six in the morning) at City Deep. Hall 2 is reserved for the fish traders (this is the country's first and to date only inland fish market) and general dealers; meat, eggs and groceries are also on sale. There are banks (five of them), cafeterias and a filling station; parking is plentiful; most of the business conducted is on wholesale (bulk) basis but the complex welcomes individual buyers, the staff are expert and helpful and the merchandise (such seafood exotics as smoked marlin, live crayfish and queen prawns are popular buys) is top quality.

Next door is the Multiflora Market, the country's largest flower auction. Also on sale are pot plants and garden requisites. Other open-air shopping venues include:

☆ The Johannesburg Flea Market, held each Saturday in Mary Fitzgerald Square, in front of the Market Theatre: more than 400 stalls sell everything from handicrafts to cockatiels; buskers entertain you.

☆ The Organic Village Market in Culross Road, Bryanston: cottage industries; handicrafts; natural-fibre clothing; African carpets; organically grown vegetables; fruits; spices. The market is held from Thursday to Saturday; evening markets on nearest Tuesday to the full moon.

☆ The Artists' Market, Zoo Lake (see page 48): an art and craft expo held on the first weekend of each month.

☆ The National Exhibition Centre, a huge area on Baragwanath Road, Crown Mines, and venue of the People's Show – a 700-stall 'shoppers' carnival' – every Saturday.

Theatre

The performing arts are alive and doing very well in Johannesburg; the daily newspaper *The Star* gives details of what's currently on in its 'Tonight' section; the monthly magazine *Hello Johannesburg* is available from the Publicity Association and from most hotels and many of the shops.

Many of the grander shows – drama, opera, ballet, orchestral – are staged by the Performing Arts Council of the Transvaal (Pact) on a regular basis at the Civic, Arena and Alexander theatres.

There are a number of other, smaller but lively and talented companies, some of them of the highly enterprising, informally experimental workshop type.

Among the latter are productions conceived, written and performed by black artists largely for black audiences, a distinct art form termed 'black theatre' and noted for its sparkling spontaneity, an element rooted in African tradition: performers tend to share in the creation of a work rather than follow a predetermined script. Despite this looseness, though, some of the shows have enjoyed international as well as wide local acclaim.

Until recently much of black theatre reflected, and protested against, the harshness of life under the apartheid system, but it is now tending to move away from racial introspection and towards more universal themes.

Johannesburg's principal venues are the:

☆ Market theatre complex, which houses four auditoriums, restaurant, bar, coffee bar, art and photographic gallery, exclusive bookshop and a precinct (next door, but part of the whole) noted for its shopping arcade, bistro and for its unusual 'Kippies' jazz bar. The 80-year-old building formerly did duty as the Indian Fruit and Citrus Market, and is full of character. The theatres cater for all tastes: there's a lot of local, sometimes experimental drama on offer, but the line-up can also include drawing-room comedy. Bookings through Computicket.

☆ Civic Theatre, Braamfontein: Johannesburg's biggest (1 120-seat; its orchestra pit accommodates 100 musicians) and most prestigious auditorium; venue for opera, ballet, operetta, musical comedy productions, solo recitals and orchestral concerts (and for

Basket-ware stall at a city flea-market

The Market Theatre complex comprises auditoriums, shops, bistros, gallery and jazz bar

marionette shows, which are something of a speciality). Its Chamber Theatre, in an adjoining hall, provides playwrights, directors and actors with a well-equipped workshop. It's also a venue for exhibitions (in the large foyer), conferences and seminars; there's a good restaurant (the Symposium) on the premises. The municipal car park is across the road; book at Computicket.

☆ The Alhambra in Beit Street, Doornfontein, is Johannesburg's oldest theatre. A 370-seat auditorium, it is now part of a group run by Pieter Toerien Productions. Among others in the group are the Leonard Rayne (upstairs at the Alhambra; 160-seat capacity; 34 supper seats; one can also watch the show from the bar), and the André Huguenot in Kapteijn Street, Hillbrow (400-seats; full bar services). Generally, these three present straight drama, though there's the occasional musical show. Bookings through Computicket.

☆ Alexander Theatre, Siemens Street, Braamfontein; 550 seats; leased by Pact; bookings through Computicket.

☆ Arena Theatre, Cradock Avenue, Rosebank: quite small; used by Pact for innovative productions.

☆ Wits Theatre, University of the Witwatersrand: very modern; venue for university drama productions. Bookings through Computicket.

☆ La Parisienne Theatre and Restaurant, Braamfontein: review-type dinner and show entertainment for an audience-clientele of 100. Bookings through Computicket.

Music and entertainment

The National Symphony Orchestra of the SABC presents two Johannesburg and three Pretoria seasons each year, giving something over 60 symphony concerts – at, among other venues, the Johannesburg City Hall – and a number of gala, campus, special-event, choral (with the SABC choir) and symphonic-pop performances. Seasonal programme available from the Johannesburg Publicity Association; bookings through Computicket.

Opera, ballet, oratorio and orchestral performances are staged at a number of venues by the Performing Arts Council of the Transvaal. Details of these, and of the various chamber music, celebrity recital and other musical presentations, are given in the daily press; also consult the Johannesburg Publicity Association (See Advisory, page 77).

JAZZ Standards are high, the scene is lively and innovative, and it's informatively covered in the *Saturday Star*'s jazz column. The privately run and well-supported Johannesburg Jazz Club meets on Sunday evenings at Plumb Crazy; overseas talent is often featured. Enquiries: Tel. 23-5358/29-1809.

Among Johannesburg's jazz venues (they tend to change from month to month, so do check) are AJ's, in the Cresta Centre, Randburg (Monday nights; Tel. 678-9841) ☆ Cheers, in Langerman Drive, Kensington (Sundays; Tel. 616-4415) ☆ Clyde's Jazz Club, in Melville (Saturday afternoons; Tel. 482-2477) ☆ Fat Cats, in

Rosebank (Wednesday to Saturday nights; specialist jazz on Sunday nights; Tel. 788-5536) ☆ Hard Rock Café, in Oxford Road, Illovo (jazz-rock on Thursday nights and Sunday afternoons; Tel. 447-2583) ☆ The Jameson Bar, in Commissioner Street (weekday lunchtime, early evening and night sessions; Saturday afternoons; Tel. 826-6002) ☆ Kippies, in the Market Theatre precinct (Tuesday to Saturday evenings; Tel. 832-1641) ☆ The Pantry, in Windsor (Wednesday and Sunday nights; Tel. 678-6815) ☆ Rakes Wine Bar, in Parktown (Saturday afternoons; 'flashback' 50s and 60s music on Sundays; Tel. 484-1714), and ☆ Roxy Rhythm Bar, in Melville (Thursday and Friday nights; Tel. 716-6019).

NIGHTLIFE Johannesburg, like any big city, offers a wide variety and large number of nightspots. A few examples:

Nightclubs include Bella Napoli, in Hillbrow (Tel. 642-5062); the large and popular Caesar's Palace (booking essential; Tel. 403-2420); Sardis, in the Ster Cine complex, corner Claim and Plein streets (Tel. 23-5411); and the Tavern Bar, Balalaika Village Walk, Sandown (Tel. 884-1400).

Cabaret At the Black Sun, in Louis Botha Avenue (Tel. 728-3280) ☆ The Village Manor Theatre, Balalaika Hotel, Sandown (Tel. 884-1400) ☆ No 58, in Pretoria Street, Hillbrow (Tel. 642-0243) ☆ The Café le Chic, in Melville ☆ Romance Nightclub, which offers topless waitresses, bar ladies, strip shows and easy sociability as well as cabaret (Tel. 23-7815).

Dinner dancing Capri Hotel (big-band session every two Wednesdays; Tel. 786-2250) ☆ The Coconut Grove, in Orange Grove (Tel. 483-1672) ☆ The New Jaggers, in Rosebank (loud and crowded; Tel. 788-1718) ☆ Villa Borghese, in Villiers Street (Tel. 23-1793) ☆ Coimbra, at the corner of Troye and President streets (Tel. 29-4276) ☆ Owen's, in La Rochelle (Tel. 435-3546/436-2905) ☆ Johannesburg Junction, in Parktown (Tel. 643-1870) ☆ Moçambique, in Noord Street (Tel. 23-5022), and ☆ Grayston, in the Sandton Holiday Inn (Tel. 783-5262).

Dining out

Johannesburg is extremely well endowed with restaurants. A select list appears in the Advisory, page 74.

SPORT AND RECREATION

Johannesburg offers the full range of sporting activities, and the amenities are excellent: within the city's bounds are 67 bowling greens, three 18-hole golf courses, 30 public swimming pools, 26 tennis courts, 135 sportsfields; and of course there are many more venues in the surrounding centres. Information on visitor facilities is available from the Johannesburg Publicity Association; Satour (see Advisory, page 77) publishes a 'Sports Fact Sheet'.

First class (international and provincial) rugby matches are played on the 100 000-capacity Ellis Park ground in Doornfontein; cricket at the Wanderers' Club in Corlett Drive, football at a number of venues, including the huge Soccer City arena. The Ellis Park tennis stadium seats 5 000; the new Standard Bank indoor tennis arena 8 000.

HORSE-RACING the leading racecourses are at Turffontein, Gosforth Park and Newmarket.

MOTOR RACING Formula One and other events are held at the international-class Kyalami track.

GOLF most clubs welcome visitors; for guidance, contact the Johannesburg Publicity Association (see Advisory, page 77) or the Transvaal Golf Union (Tel. 640-3714). The city offers a number of driving ranges and putting greens, including those at Huddle Park in Linksfield. The 18-hole mashie golf course next to the Roosevelt Park recreation centre is open to members of the public; the fees are minimal.

BOWLS, SQUASH AND TENNIS There are numerous venues; consult the Johannesburg Publicity Association (see Advisory, page 77).

SAILING on Wemmer Pan and Emmarentia Dam (for club members) and on a number of other pleasant stretches of water beyond the city limits. Some dams, though, are restricted; for advice, contact either the SA Yachting Association, Tel. 337-9250, or the Board-sailing Association of SA, Tel. 726-7076.

FISHING in Wemmer Pan, Emmarentia Dam, Rhodes Park lake, Zoo Lake (see Gardens, parks, reserves: page 47), and at many splendid spots in the general region. Licences are obtainable from sports shops; catches are subject to limits; no live bait may be used; there's no closed season for trout.

For information, contact the Rand Piscatorial Society, Tel. 837-2770; the SA Anglers' Union, PO Box 1456, Johannesburg 2000, Tel. 834-1211; or the SA Freshwater Angling Association, PO Box 700, Vereeniging 1930, Tel. (016) 22-1552 after hours.

WALKING AND HIKING Some fine trails and walks have been established in and around the city (see page 55), the most notable perhaps the Braamfontein Spruit route (see page 47). For information, contact Johannesburg Hiking Club, PO Box 2254, Johannesburg 2000, Tel. 52-8311; the Publicity Association, or Satour (see Advisory, page 77), which publishes a handy little brochure entitled 'Follow the Footprints'.

The really keen hiker will find Jaynee Levy's *The Complete Guide to Walks and Trails in Southern Africa* and Brendan Ryan's *Day Walks in and around Johannesburg & Pretoria*, available from leading bookstores, both informative and useful.

CYCLING Visitors welcome on group outings; contact the Transvaal Pedal Power Association, PO Box 3521, Randburg 2125.

TENPIN BOWLING at the Ponte Bowl, Berea; Northcliff Bowl, on DF Malan Drive; and at the Bracken City Centre, Brackenhurst.

PRETORIA

Pretoria became the official capital of the independent Voortrekker republic of the Transvaal (or, more correctly, the South African Republic) in 1860, though the settlement's origins went back a further two decades. The first homestead belonged to a farmer called Bronkhorst, who settled in the Fountains Valley area in 1840 (a few stones and fragments of his house can still be seen).

Later, more families put roots down in and around the nearby village of Elandspoort which, in 1854, was proclaimed the 'kerkplaas' for the central Transvaal – the focal point for 'nagmaal' (communion), baptisms and weddings. The following year it was renamed Pretoria Philadelphia ('Pretoria Brotherhood') in honour of Andries Pretorius, the victor of Blood River (see page 175).

With capital status came a degree of elegance: some fine buildings were erected in the later decades of the 19th century, most of them fronting onto Church Square, though for a long time the place was noted more for its wealth of greenery and the brightness of its flowers than for its structures. The climate encouraged luxuriant growth, roses were the favoured plantings and, according to one early traveller, 'every garden, hedge, stoep and even waterfurrow' was festooned with ramblers. Later the famed jacarandas made their appearance: the first two, costing £10 apiece, were imported from Rio de Janiero in 1888 by a JD Cilliers and planted on his Myrtle Grove property. Some 70 000 of these feathery, lilac-foliaged trees now grace parks, gardens and about 650 km of its streets. They display their magnificent colours in spring; Pretoria is known as the 'Jacaranda City'.

Modern Pretoria retains many features that have significance in white South African history. They include the old Raadsaal (parliament) of the Zuid-Afrikaansche Republiek; the house where President Paul Kruger lived; the Voortrekker Monument just outside the city and, on the hill above it, the Union Buildings, which houses government establishments.

Pretoria is first and foremost an administrative centre, but it is also the hub of an important rail network, and its advanced industrial complex, originally based on the giant Iscor steelworks just to the south-west, includes engineering, food processing and, principally at nearby Cullinan, diamond mining. The city's population at the last census (1985) was estimated at 450 000.

Memorials, museums, landmarks

Pretoria grew up around Church Square, at the intersection of Church and Paul Kruger streets (the city's two principal arteries). The square is dominated by Anton van Wouw's splendid bronze statue of Oom Paul, patriarch, president of the South African Republic (from 1883 until his flight into exile in 1900) and generally regarded as the 'Father of Afrikanerdom'. Church Street, incidentally, is one of the world's longest urban thoroughfares: it measures a full 26 km from end to end.

The square's northern face is vaguely reminiscent of the Place de la Concorde in Paris or the southern face of London's Trafalgar Square, though of course these two places are a great deal grander. Among the buildings of note are the Old Raadsaal, or parliament, completed in 1889 in French Renaissance style with a sprinkling of classical features; the graceful Palace of Justice; the South African Reserve Bank (designed by Herbert Baker), and, in sharp contrast, the modern Transvaal Provincial Administration building (in which works by leading artists are displayed). Guided tours of the square may be arranged; Tel. 814-911, or 201-3223. Along Church Street three blocks west of the square is:

KRUGER HOUSE, a modest, single-storeyed building with a wide verandah. The house was presented to Paul Kruger by the *volk* in 1884, and here the old man held open court, receiving his people in informal fashion on the stoep for a decade and a half until the guns of the advancing British drove him away. The place has been faithfully restored to something very like its original character; on view are Kruger's furniture, personal belongings, various memorabilia and, behind the house, his carriage and a stinkwood trek wagon. Open daily.

THE VOORTREKKER MONUMENT, on Monument Hill 6 km south of the city centre, commemorates the Great Trek of the 1830s, and is regarded as a shrine by most of the Afrikaner community: a memorial to the founders of their republics and a symbol of Afrikaner national identity. Its status within the heritage of the new South Africa is controversial.

The monument was completed in 1949 (although the foundation stone was laid 11 years earlier, during the Voortrekker centenary celebrations), and it comprises a monolithic 40-m-high block ringed by a 'laager' of 64 granite oxwagons. At the entrance is Anton van Wouw's striking bronze sculpture of a Voortrekker mother and children. Within the main block are two chambers: the domed, 30-m-high Hall of Heroes, its walls lined by a frieze of 27 marble panels (their combined length is 92 m) depicting the Trek's main events; and a lower hall. The latter features a granite cenotaph – so sited that a ray of sunshine falls on the inscription 'Ons Vir Jou, Suid-Afrika', at noon on 16 December each year (the date of the Battle of Blood River) – and a niche holding an ever-burning flame.

Part of the elegant Union Buildings

There are fine views from the dome and roof parapets, reached by a circular stairway of 260 steps. Across the road is the Voortrekker Monument Museum, among whose exhibits are costumes, antiques, tapestries, models of Trek scenes and, at the entrance, a Trek camp. Facilities include a restaurant. Open daily.

UNION BUILDINGS Designed by the celebrated architect Herbert Baker and completed in 1913, the magnificent, crescent-shaped red sandstone edifice looks over the city from the heights of Meintjes Kop, from where there are panoramic views. Features of note, apart from the graceful architecture, are the statues (of generals Botha, Smuts and Hertzog), the impressive Garden of Remembrance, the Delville Wood memorial and the Pretoria war memorial. The grounds have been beautifully landscaped in terraces.

NATIONAL CULTURAL HISTORY MUSEUM (Boom Street) is well worth a visit for its fine collections of Cape Dutch and late-19th century furniture, coins, medals, silverware, glassware, the ethnological display, and an archeology room (which features, among other things, a 2 000-year-old Egyptian mummy). Information: Tel. 323-3128; open daily.

TRANSVAAL MUSEUM OF NATURAL HISTORY (Paul Kruger Street). An extensive series of displays, most prominent of which are the 'Life's Genesis' exhibition and the Austin Roberts Bird Hall. The former tells an integrated story of life on earth, the latter houses a superb array of southern African birds.

The renowned archeologist Robert Broom and his successors did much of their pioneering work on the man-apes (*the Australopithecines*: see page 111)) at the museum; the appropriate displays are fascinating. Special features include informative audio-visual presentations, and an excellent bookshop. Information: Tel. 322-7632; open daily. Next to the Transvaal Museum is the :

MUSEUM OF GEOLOGICAL SURVEY, which features impressive displays of precious and semi-precious stones (some inlaid into a splendid Italian mosaic table); an exposition of rock formations; a fossil collection. Open weekdays.

FORT SCHANSKOP AND FORT KLAPPERKOP These two 19th century bastions were built just before the South African War of 1899-1902 to protect the vulnerable little Boer republic from the British (in the event they proved irrelevant: Imperial troops entered Pretoria in May 1900 without opposition) and now serve as military museums. The former is sited on a hilltop near the Voortrekker Monument, the latter on Jan Rissik Drive; both house interesting displays of weaponry and other militaria. Open daily.

MELROSE HOUSE (in Jacob Maré Street, opposite Burgers Park), an elegant 19th century home set in attractive gardens, was the site chosen for the signing of the historic Peace Treaty of Vereeniging which brought the bloody South African War to an end on 31 May 1902. It's now a museum housing fine period furniture (though some of the contents were badly damaged by rightwing elements in 1989). It also serves as occasional venue for chamber music concerts and art exhibitions. Open daily.

PIONEER OPEN-AIR MUSEUM (Pretoria Street, Silverton). A 3-ha area containing a restored Voortrekker farmstead (house and stables), implements, a Norse mill, threshing floor and so forth. It's on the banks of the Moroleta Stream; picnic/barbecue facilities provided. Open daily.

MUSEUM OF SCIENCE AND INDUSTRY (Didacta Building, Skinner Street). The only museum of its kind in the country; displays include

The University of South Africa. Over 60 000 students are tutored by correspondence.

features on nuclear physics, space, aviation, water research, forestry. Information: Tel. 322-6404; open weekdays.

TRANSVAAL EDUCATION MUSEUM (Gerard Moerdyk Street) covers the South African educational scene from the 1830s to the 1960s. Open weekdays; Tel. 44-3337.

POST OFFICE MUSEUM (in the Post Office's headquarters at the corner of Bosman and Proes streets). The story of written communication, mail, postage stamps, the telegraph and telephone, broadcasting, space communication. Information: Tel. 293-1066/1053; open Mondays to Saturdays.

POLICE MUSEUM (Compol Building, Pretorius Street) features major criminal cases; gambling and smuggling displays; weaponry and so forth. Tel. 21-1678/9, ext 7. The SA Police Dog Training School also put on (at a separate venue) some fascinating demonstrations of canine talent.

PRETORIA ART MUSEUM (Schoeman Street) contains works by leading South African artists (Pierneef, Van Wouw, Frans Oerder), part of the renowned Michaelis collection of Dutch and Flemish paintings and an art library. Guided tours may be arranged; Tel. 344-1087; open Tuesdays to Sundays.

JANSEN AFRICANA COLLECTION (Struben Street) houses a collection of South African period furniture; silver, Chinese porcelain and other displays. Open daily.

ANTON VAN WOUW HOUSE (Clark Street, Brooklyn) was the home of Van Wouw (1862-1945), arguably South Africa's most highly regarded modern sculptor. Some of his smaller works, less formal and melancholy than his monumental sculptures, are on display here. Open Mondays to Saturdays.

PIERNEEF MUSEUM (Vermeulen Street). Jacob Pierneef (1886-1957), is generally acknowledged as the country's finest landscape painter; a collection of his works is on display in this pleasant late-19th century house, which is open Mondays to Fridays. There is a tearoom on the premises.

PLACES OF WORSHIP include the Miriammen (Sixth Street, Asiatic Bazaar), oldest of Pretoria's Hindu temples, and the beautiful Muslim mosque, accessible through an arcade in Queen Street. Both places require visitors to remove footwear before entering.

STAATS MODEL SCHOOL (Van der Walt Street) is a good example of Transvaal republican architecture, and holds modest historical interest as the place where the young Winston Churchill was imprisoned during the South African War, and from which he made a daring escape. It now houses the provincial library.

OTHER PLACES OF INTEREST The Pretoria Publicity Association (see Advisory, page 77) has all the sightseeing details. Worthwhile visits:
☆ The University of Pretoria (Lynwood Road), the country's largest residential university (enrolment is around 18 000). Of note is the Exploratorium, a physics department workroom full of intriguing equipment; 'personal participation' is encouraged. Most attractive building on campus is the 'Ou Letteregebou', designed in late French Renaissance style. Tel. 420-2637 or 420-2251/2735.
☆ University of South Africa (on Muckleneuk Ridge, outside the city). The largest institution of higher learning in South Africa and largest correspondence university in the world: it has over 60 000 students, including 3 000 from neighbouring states and farther afield, and it conducts examinations in 760 centres. The buildings are splendidly futuristic; behind the library is an interesting cycad garden.
☆ Medical University of Southern Africa (Medunsa) some distance north of Pretoria on the Rosslyn-Brits road, was established in 1980, when 'grand apartheid' still dictated educational policy, to train black doctors, veterinarians and paramedics. The buildings are ultra-modern, the 355-ha grounds pleasantly developed, their showpieces the Poison Garden (created to help in the identification and study of poisonous plants) and the Biblical Garden. The latter is functional as well as ornamental: it features many plants that are mentioned in the Scriptures and many that grow in today's Holy Land (papyrus, Nile oleander, Jericho balsam and so forth). Tours by arrangement; contact the public relations officer; Tel. (012) 58-2844 or 529-4111.

☆ State Library (Vermeulen Street). One of South Africa's two national libraries and a vast repository of books, periodicals, documents. Visitors welcome; guided tours by appointment; Tel. 21-8931.
☆ South African Bureau of Standards. Informative tours of laboratories and testing facilities may be arranged (two weeks' notice required). Tel. 428-7911.
☆ South African Mint: interesting tours of the Mint Museum and coin-making production line (two weeks' notice required); Tel. (012) 325-4813/326-2619 (a/h).
☆ Porcelain factory tours are available Mondays to Thursdays; Tel. 58-1533.
☆ South African Motor Corporation (Samcor) in Chrysler Way may be toured by prior arrangement; Tel. 83-1121.

Gardens, parks, reserves

The Pretoria Zoo in Boom Street, formerly the National Zoological Gardens, ranks among the largest and best in existence: it is home to about 3 500 southern African and exotic animals, including the four great apes, a host of mammals, the rare South American maned wolf and the only known giant eland in captivity. The zoo's antelope collection is thought to be the world's most comprehensive.

Within the zoo's aegis is the 4 000-ha game-breeding centre near Lichtenburg in the western Transvaal (see page 116), which has successfully bred the scimitar-horned oryx and the banteng; and the De Wildt cheetah breeding area (see page 112). Indeed, about 20 rare species have been bred under the zoo's supervision, among them the first aardwolf to be raised in captivity.

Much can be seen from the lookout points, which are reached by cable-car. Seals are fed mid-morning and mid-afternoon, carnivores mid-afternoon. Services provided include guided tours (Saturday mornings; booking essential) and courses on ecology and bird recognition. Stalls outside the main entrance offer a wide selection of handicrafts. Information: Tel. 28-3265/6020. Next door to the Zoo is the:

AQUARIUM AND REPTILE HOUSE, in which a great many freshwater and marine species are imaginatively displayed. Also a splendid sea-shell collection and variety of snakes, lizards, iguanas, crocodiles. Tel. 28-3265/6020.

AUSTIN ROBERTS BIRD SANCTUARY (Boshoff Street, New Muckleneuk) is a 11-ha park that protects about 170 species, many of them waterbirds (blue crane, sacred ibis, heron: there are two well-stocked dams), all of which can be observed from the hide. Also in residence are some small mammals. Open daily; public access to the hide confined to weekends and holidays. Tel. (012) 344-3840.

PRETORIA NATIONAL BOTANICAL GARDEN (Cussonia Avenue, 10 km from city centre), administered by the Botanical Research Institute, features more than 5 000 indigenous plant species in its 77 ha. The displays are sensibly grouped (according to major vegetation and climate type); tours last just over two hours and include a slide show and a visit to the normally inaccessible nursery. Tel. 86-1165. Complementing the Botanical Garden is the National Herbarium, a worthwhile port of call for visiting botanists, and indeed for anyone interested in identifying and preserving indigenous flora. Tel. 86-1180/1165.

WONDERBOOM NATURE RESERVE (on the Voortrekker Road, 10 km north of city centre) was established specifically to protect a single 'wonder tree' – a 1 000-year-old, 23-m-high wild fig (*Ficus salicifolia*) which, together with its 13 'daughters' and 'granddaughters' – the fruits of self-propagation – measures 50 m in diameter. A nature trail wanders through the 90-ha area; there are pleasant picnic spots near the tree. Open daily.

FOUNTAINS VALLEY NATURE RESERVE (on the Verwoerdburg Road, 5 km south of city centre). A 60-ha picnic, barbecue and recreational area at the source of the Apies River and popular among Pretorians. A further 500 ha has been set aside as a game and bird sanctuary. Attractions include walking trails, camping and picnic sites, restaurant, swimming pool, small lake (full of swans and other waterfowl), playpark, miniature steam locomotive. Open daily.

MORELETA SPRUIT The stream rises near the Rietvlei Dam to the south-east of Pretoria and joins the Hartbeest Spruit north of the Derdepoort regional park (see page 66). A nature trail follows its course through the city's eastern suburbs, passing through:

☆ Faerie Glen nature reserve, a 100-ha area of natural vegetation and home to a number of bird species. Plants include the cabbage tree ('kiepersol'), wild plum, aloes, proteas.

☆ Meyers Park nature reserve: a small (7-ha) sanctuary distinguished by its birdlife.

☆ Struben Dam, a 10-ha reserve also noted for its birds, among which are some rare species. Fishing is permitted from the small pier.

DERDEPOORT REGIONAL PARK (on the Pietersburg highway) is a 115-ha expanse of bushveld that boasts two dams, picnic/barbecue spots, and a farmyard to which the public has access.

BURGERS PARK (corner of Van der Walt and Jacob Maré streets) was established in 1882 and named after the South African Republic's second president. Its florarium is fairly impressive: a complex of separate glass sections each with its own climate and vegetation.

PROTEA PARK (Queen Wilhelmina Avenue, Groenkloof). On view are aloes and flowering plants as well 130 protea species.

Pretoria in profile

OTHER PRETORIA PARKS include the Springbok (between Pretorius and Schoeman streets; stinkwood trees and attractive shrub species); the Wenning (also in Schoeman Street; its rosarium, which features among many others the new 'City of Pretoria' rose, is well worth a visit); and, a perennial favourite of children, Magnolia Dell (in Queen Wilhelmina Avenue; a place of charmingly landscaped grounds, springflowering magnolias, a dam, and statues of Peter Pan and Wendy).

AROUND PRETORIA

The region to the west of the city is covered in the chapter on the North-West (beginning page 111). For the rest, the bushveld countryside offers pleasant day drives and some points of interest. Worth exploring is:

Verwoerdburg

This large residential town to the south-east of Pretoria was established in 1964 when the township of Lyttelton Manor merged with the villages of Irene and Doringkloof to create a single municipality named after Dr HF Verwoerd, one of the leading architects of the apartheid system, after his assassination in 1966. Verwoerdburg is a rapidly developing centre of modern buildings and fine sporting amenities (including the Centurion Park provincial cricket ground). Its pride is the new Verwoerdburg City shopping complex and its dam, whose fountain is a fantasia of 30-m-high, multi-coloured, 'musical' water-jets. The adjacent Water Park is a popular recreation area.

The small village suburb of Irene, now a centre of the local film industry, was founded as an agricultural research centre and (later) a model farm in the 1890s. Nearby is:

DOORNKLOOF FARM, the family home of Jan Christiaan Smuts, soldier, statesman, politician, philosopher, naturalist, and arguably the century's greatest South African. The remarkably modest house, built of wood and galvanized iron (salvaged from a post- First World War military camp) has been restored to its endearingly informal original condition and now serves as a museum in which Smuts's simple furniture and various memorabilia are displayed. The house and grounds are open daily; among the facilities are picnic/barbecue spots, a tearoom and a camping site.

Pretoria's 70 000 jacaranda trees come into glorious bloom in springtime

VAN RIEBEECK NATURE RESERVE, nearby, is an area of rich vegetation that nurtures zebra, eland, steenbok, red hartebeest, the common duiker and the uncommon oribi. Entry is limited to groups of visitors on foot; the Rietvlei Dam, within the reserve, is popular among anglers and picnickers; walking trails have been established; entry permits are required; Tel. (012) 313-7694.

Cullinan-Bronkhorstspruit

The small village of Cullinan, about 30 km east of Pretoria, was named after Sir Thomas Cullinan who, in 1902, discovered rich volcanic diamond pipes in the vicinity and developed the famed Premier mine which, in 1905, yielded the massive, 3 016-carat Cullinan Diamond (now part of the British Crown Jewels) and, later, the smaller but very beautiful Premier Rose stone. Many of the original miners' cottages still exist, lending a certain charm to the village; the mine management lays on conducted tours from Tuesdays to Fridays; Tel. (01213) 3-0050.

Just off the Cullinan-Bronkhorstspruit road is a cave complex around which a small resort has been established. Attractions include some pleasant walks around caves and river, a swimming pool, caravan-camping ground and self-catering chalets. Tel. (012) 82-1323. Also accessible from this road are the Loopspruit vineyards, wine cellars and wine shop. Conducted tours by arrangement; Tel. (012) 325-3300.

WILLEM PRINSLOO AGRICULTURAL MUSEUM at Rayton, 10 km north of Cullinan, is a well-preserved 1880 farmstead comprising house, stables, outbuildings, domestic animals and display rooms featuring old implements. Early farming methods are demonstrated on Sundays; also of interest is the Ndebele village and the dam; facilities include picnic/barbecue spots and a cafeteria. Tel. (012162) 215.

BRONKHORSTSPRUIT DAM NATURE RESERVE, a popular (perhaps too-popular) 1 285-ha game park and recreational area off the Witbank Highway. In autumn, though, the wild flowers – especially the cosmos – are lovely. Among the wildlife residents are black wildebeest, blesbok and an impressive number of waterfowl and other bird species. The dam is used by anglers and water-sportsmen; two pleasure resorts, caravan/camp sites and picnic spots have been established. Information: Tel. (01212) 2-1621 or 2-0140/0173.

North of Pretoria

The scenically rather featureless countryside between Pretoria and the Waterberg range of hills to the north is not among the more popular tourist destinations: Pretorian holiday-makers and weekenders tend to hurry through it on their way to the resorts at Warmbaths and points beyond (discussed on pages 101-103). Worth calling in at on the way, though, are two pleasant wilderness areas:

ROODEPLAAT DAM NATURE RESERVE, 16 km from the city, reached via the road that branches off to Cullinan (the R513). The bilharzia-free dam, centrepiece of a 1 700-ha expanse of proclaimed bushveld, is popular among fisher-men and owners of small sailing and motor boats; wildlife includes zebra, kudu, waterbuck, the stately sable and other antelope, and an impressive 224 species of bird; some rare plants, including *Aloe pretoriensis*, can be seen growing in the open grasslands. Among the reserve's other attractions are game-viewing roads, walking trails, picnic spots equipped with fireplaces; a restaurant, swimming pool and a cluster of chalets. Information: Tel. (012) 808-1164, 82-1547 or 28-5761/2/3/4.

RUST DE WINTER DAM NATURE RESERVE, farther to the north (40 km along the N1, then eastwards for 30 km) is similar in size to Roode-plaat but rather less developed for tourism. Anglers are drawn to the waters of the dam (beware bilharzia and crocodiles); birdlife is prolific. Accommodation is restricted to a camp-site. Information: Tel. (0121712), and ask for 2422, or contact the Transvaal Division of Nature Conservation on (012) 201-2565.

Just off the Great North Road, 30 km from Pretoria on the Springbok Flats, is the small settlement of:

HAMMANSKRAAL, centre of the local and nor-mally prosperous maize and groundnut indus-tries. The place is undistinguished save for the nearby Pretoria Salt Pan, the crater of an extinct volcano, and, approximately a dozen kilo-metres farther north, by the Papatso (market place). Here you'll find a replica of an Ndebele

village, an attractive selection of African han-dicrafts and, on request, demonstrations of tri-bal dancing.

GETTING AROUND

Pretoria offers all the amenities of a largish modern city, though perhaps it's a quieter, more conservative place than most. The city's hub is Church Square (see page 61), its principal thoroughfares Church Street (east-west) and Paul Kruger Street (north-south).

BUSES City transport arrives at and departs from the Church Square terminal (Tel. 28-3562). There is an hourly commuter ser-vice linking the city with Johannesburg air-port at Kempton Park, 45 km to the south-east (see Advisory, page 71); the ter-minal is at De Bruyn Park, Andries Street.

For details of available coach tours around the city and its environs, consult the Pretoria Infor-mation Bureau (see Advisory, page 77).

Luxury bus services to major cities in South Africa: Greyhound, Tel. (011) 403-6460; Trans-lux, Tel. (012) 294-2007; Transcity, Tel. (012) 294-2121.

TAXI AND CAR-RENTAL services are similar to those of Johannesburg (see page 54).

PARKING Pretoria is a busy city, and on-street parking is often difficult. The main covered parking areas are De Bruyn Park (corner Ver-meulen and Andries streets); Louis Pasteur Building (corner Schoeman and Prinsloo streets); President Arcade (Schoeman Street, be-tween Andries and Van der Walt streets); Saam-bou Centre (Andries Street, between Church and Pretorius streets); Volkskas centre (corner of Pretorius and Van der Walt streets), and Wilson Parking (Proes Street, between Paul Kruger and Andries streets).

TRAINS The main railway station is situated at the corner of Paul Kruger and Scheiding streets; there is a fast and comfortable train service between Pretoria and Johannesburg, and an adequate service to other Witwatersrand centre. For information on the local network, telephone (012) 315-2007/2835. The famed Blue Train departs from and arrives at Pretoria; Reservations: Tel. (012) 315-3038 (see also Advisory, page 71).

CITY LIFE

Shopping

Pretoria offers an inviting variety of general and speciality outlets, shopping malls, arcades, markets.

The principal city-centre complexes are De Bruyn Park (corner of Vermeulen and Andries streets); Sanlam Centre (Pretorius, Andries and Schoeman streets); and the Standard Bank Centre (corner of Church and Van der Walt streets). The major suburban shopping complexes are the Arcadia Centre (corner of Beatrix, Vermeulen and Proes streets); Jacaranda Centre (corner of Michael Brink Street and Frates Road); Menlyn Park (in Atterbury Road); Sunny Park (corner of Esselen and Mears streets); Verwoerdburg City (in Verwoerdburg); and Wonderpark (in Wonderboom).

Most of if not all these centres have speciality outlets of particular interest to visitors: African handicrafts (beadwork, handspun carpets and rugs, pottery, woodwork); hides and skins; ceramics and so forth.

Worth special mention, though, are the crafts on sale outside the Zoo (see page 65). A flea-market is held each Saturday on the square in front of the State Theatre.

Theatre and entertainment

Major dramatic, operatic and ballet productions, choral and symphony concerts are staged, principally at the State Theatre complex, by the Performing Arts Council of the Transvaal (Pact). A number of other theatre companies present live shows, in various auditoriums, ranging from the experimentally serious to the light and bright. For details of what's on offer, consult the local newspapers (the Pretoria News is the leading English-language daily) or the Pretoria Information Bureau.

The splendid State Theatre complex in Church Street encompasses five auditoriums, good if rather ostentatious restaurants and the Applause coffee bar, from which tours set out each Wednesday (morning and afternoon) and Friday (morning). Bookings through Computicket, or Tel. 322-1665.

NIGHTLIFE Consult the local newspapers.

WINING AND DINING A list of select restaurants appears in the Advisory, page 76.

SPORT AND RECREATION

Rugby tends to preoccupy, even obsess, much of white Pretoria; the provincial side (Northern Transvaal, also known as the Blue Bulls) has regularly swept the trophy boards in recent years; the provincial stadium is the 85 000-seat Loftus Versfeld on Kirkness Street. First class cricket matches are played at Berea Park on Van Boeshoten Avenue and at Centurion Park in Verwoerdburg.

GOLF Pretoria and its surrounds boast excellent golf courses; the clubs welcome visitors. For guidance, contact the Northern Transvaal Golf Association, Tel. 320-1410.

TENNIS Contact the Northern Transvaal Tennis Association, Tel. 344-3771.

SQUASH Contact the Northern Transvaal Squash Association, Tel. 28-2231.

TENPIN BOWLING At Kingsley's bowling centre in Beatrix Street, Arcadia, Tel. 44-5314.

FRESHWATER FISHING (see page 105 for general conditions). For specific guidance, telephone the Northern Transvaal branch of the South African Freshwater Angling Association on 70-2009.

SWIMMING City pools include the Central in Park Street (Tel. 341-4418) and the Hillcrest (Olympic standard) in Duncan Street (Tel. 43-4044). Information: Tel. 21-3411.

OTHER WATERSPORTS Pretoria Sailing Club (Rietvlei Dam), PO Box 359, Pretoria 0001, Tel. 46 8839 or 293-1422; Northern Transvaal Power Boat Association, Tel. (012) 64 6962 or (011) 805-3204; Pretoria Canoe Club, Tel. 47-3171; Northern Transvaal Water-Skiing Association, Tel. (012) 86 2189 or (011) 493-2900; South African Windsurfer Class Association, Tel. (012) 46-3245.

WALKING AND HIKING For guidance, consult the Pretoria Information Bureau (see Advisory, page 77); the National Hiking Way Board, Private Bag X447, Pretoria 0001, Tel. 310-3911; the Hiking Federation of South Africa, PO Box 17247, Groenkloof, Pretoria 0027, Tel. 323-7526 ext 6.

ADVISORY: JOHANNESBURG AND PRETORIA

CLIMATE

Summer-rainfall region. On most days from December to February and sometimes into March thunderstorms begin to build up after lunch to produce torrential late-afternoon downpours; the deluge is accompanied by a great deal of noise and fierce flashes of lighting, and occasionally preceded by brief but violent (and destructive) showers of hail.

Summer days tend to be breathlessly hot, the nights less so; winter days are crisp, invigorating; winter nights are chilly and sometimes bitter. Pretoria (1 370 m above sea level) has a somewhat warmer and more humid climate than Johannesburg (1 750 m); its northern parts are frost free. Both cities enjoy, on average, nearly nine hours of sunshine a day.

Johannesburg temperatures (Pretoria in brackets): January average daily maximum 26,3 °C (28,8 °C), daily minimum 14,3 °C (16,4 °C); July average daily maximum 16,5 °C (20,2 °C), daily minimum 4,1 °C (2,6 °C); extremes 35,0 °C (38,2 °C) and -5,6 °C (-4,7 °C). Rainfall: January average monthly rainfall 137 mm (134 mm), July 11 mm (9 mm); highest recorded daily rainfall 100 mm (125 mm).

MAIN ATTRACTIONS

Johannesburg: □The gold mines □Excellent hotels, restaurants, nightlife □All the amenities of a modern city □Easy access to the Magaliesberg and Sun City to the west □The game reserves and scenic delights of the eastern Transvaal.

Pretoria, just 60 km to the north, is also well positioned for expeditions farther afield. A quieter, more relaxed and physically more attractive place: originally and commonly known as the 'City of Roses' and later as the 'Garden City', its current and very apt soubriquet is 'Jacaranda City'. In addition to these lovely trees with their spectacular displays of purple flowers (October brings them to their full glory), Pretoria's streets, parks and gardens are graced by a wealth of indigenous flora: proteas and aloes, acacias, wild figs, fever trees and white stinkwoods.

TRAVEL

Johannesburg is 56 km from Pretoria, 334 km from Pietersburg, 364 km from Nelspruit, 426 km from Bloemfontein, 484 km from Kimberley, 529 km from Pietermaritzburg, 534 km from Messina near the Zimbabwe border, 608 km from Durban, 789 km from Upington, 983 km from Grahamstown, 994 km from East London, 1 075 km from Port Elizabeth, and 1 450 km from Cape Town.

Road. The two cities are connected by the N1 national route (M1 north out of Johannesburg), and by the rather more roundabout R21 through Kempton Park and Verwoerdburg; both are well served by national and regional highways (see page 53): good, fast roads that link them to all of southern Africa's major centres.

Driving into Johannesburg from the airport can be a bit confusing for the first-time visitor; follow the signs to Germiston, then loop right onto the N2 running along the southern fringe of the city. For the rest, well-signposted ring roads provide quick access to suburban destinations. Traffic

The Witwatersrand and Pretoria are served by a fine network of highways

tends to be both heavy and fast but generally Transvaal drivers are courteous.

Buses (see pages 54 and 68); The Johannesburg-Durban bus departs from Leyds Street, near the Rotunda, on weekday mornings (07h00 or 08h00, depending on the season). Information on municipal services: telephone Johannesburg (011) 836-2061 or Pretoria (012) 28-3562; on the Johannesburg-Durban service: (011) 834-3692.

Coach travel is comfortable, even luxurious, and relatively cheap; tour operators with offices in Johannesburg and Pretoria offer a wide range of coach and coach/air packages covering the major southern African tourist destinations; consult the appropriate publicity bureau or a travel agent (see also page 55).

Rail. Adequate train services link Johannesburg and Pretoria with the many, but by no means all, the surrounding centres; a fast and comfortable train connects the two cities. Reservations for all train services are best made personally at the respective station booking offices or through a travel agent. Information: telephone Johannesburg (011) 773-5878 or Pretoria (012) 315-2401-6.

The world-renowned Blue Train plies between Pretoria and Cape Town, taking in Johannesburg and the Great Karoo *en route*. Information: Tel. (012) 315-3038 or the relevant publicity bureau (see page 77); reservations at the respective station booking offices or through a travel agent.

Air. Johannesburg international airport, located at Kempton Park, north-east of Johannesburg and 45 km south-east of Pretoria, serves both cities. South African Airways and an increasing number of other national airlines operate scheduled flights to all five continents; SAA and the private airlines operate frequent scheduled flights to major domestic centres and tourist destinations (including Sun City and the Kruger National Park; see pages 117 and 84).

The glittering well of the Sandton Sun

Facilities at the terminal buildings have proved barely adequate in recent years; customs and immigration procedures have drawn considerable criticism from the travelling public. It was announced in 1990 that the airport is to be given a partial though very costly facelift.

Information: (011) 975-9963 (international arrivals and departures); (011) 978-3171 (international and domestic enquiries).

Reservations: (011) 333-6504; (012) 28-3215 (business hours) or (012) 326-7028 (evenings).

A regular airport bus service connects the airport with Johannesburg's Rotunda in Leyds Street (half-hourly service) and Pretoria's De Bruyn Park (hourly service).

SUBSIDIARY AIRPORTS

Charter airlines operate from Lanseria, located on the Hartbeespoort Dam Road; Tel. (011) 659-2750/1014 ext 61, and Wonderboom, off the N1 north of Pretoria; Tel. (012) 57-1188. Rand Airport, one of the country's busiest, is controlled by the Johannesburg City Council and offers a wide range of general aviation facilities (private airline scheduled services, pilot training, aircraft sales, maintenance, helicopter and charter services and so forth). Tel. (011) 827-8884.

ACCOMMODATION

The following is a representative but by no means exhaustive selection of graded hotels. Full details of all types of accommodation can be obtained from Satour, who publish a comprehensive booklet entitled *Where to Stay – A World in One Country* or from a travel agent.

Select hotels

JOHANNESBURG: CITY AND FRINGES

Braamfontein Protea ★★★★ Fairly central; 308 suites; conference facilities for 300; pool. PO Box 32278, Braamfontein 2017; Tel. (011) 403-5740; Fax: (same).

Carlton Hotel and Carlton Court ★★★★★ One of southern Africa's best; 663 rooms; conference facilities for 1 200; 3 restaurants, 2 cocktail bars; pool, gym, hairdressing salon. PO Box 7709, Johannesburg 2000; Tel. (011) 331-8911; Fax: (011) 331-3555.

Devonshire ★★★★ Fairly central. 64 rooms, 2 suites; conference facilities. PO Box 31197, Braamfontein 2017; Tel. (011) 339-8316.

Diplomat ★★ Central. 72 rooms; several restaurants and bars; live entertainment. PO Box 10250, Johannesburg 2000; Tel. (011) 29-2161/5.

Down Town Holiday Inn ★★★ Fairly central. 224 rooms; conference facilities. PO Box 11026, Johannesburg 2000; Tel. (011) 333-8511.

Gold Reef City Hotel ★★★★★ In re-created early mining town (see page 43); 39 rooms, 6 suites; conference facilities for 230; à la carte and table d'hôte, several cocktail bars. PO Box 61, Gold Reef City 2159; Tel. (011) 496-1626; Fax: (same).

Hillbrow Protea ★★★ In cosmopolitan downtown area. 121 rooms; conference facilities. PO Box 17145, Hillbrow 2038; Tel. (011) 643-4911; Fax: (same).

Johannesburg Sun and Towers ★★★★★ Twin-tower complex; hotels linked by common access. 666 rooms, 126 suites; conference facilities for 900; SAA check-out counter; several restaurants and bars; heated pool, gym, squash courts, jogging track, hairdressing salon. PO Box 535, Johannesburg 2000; Tel. (011) 29-7011; Fax: (011) 29-0515.

Karos Johannesburger ★★★ Central. 385 rooms; conference facilities for 250; à la carte restaurant, carvery, bar (live entertainment); pool. PO Box 23566, Joubert Park 2044; Tel. (011) 725-3753; Fax: (011) 725-6309.

Mariston ★★★ Central. 172 rooms, 3 suites; conference facilities for 200; 3 restaurants; pool. PO Box 23013, Joubert Park 2044; Tel. 725-4130; Fax: (011) 725-2921.

Milpark Holiday Inn ★★★ Auckland Park, 5 km from city centre. 224 rooms, 2 suites; conference facilities for 250; à la carte restaurant, 3 cocktail bars; pool, hairdressing salon. PO Box 31556, Braamfontein 2017; Tel. 726-5100; Fax: (011) 726-8615.

New Library ★★ Central. 25 rooms, 3 suites; conference facilities for 45. 67 Commissioner Street, Johannesburg 2001; Tel. (011) 832-1551.

Park Lane ★★★ In downtown Hillbrow; very modern; 129 rooms; conference facilities for 150; à la carte restaurant, carvery/buffet, several cocktail bars. PO Box 17855, Hillbrow 2038; Tel. (011) 642-7425; Fax: (011) 643-4111.

Protea Gardens ★★★★ Garden setting, in Berea near downtown Hillbrow. 214 rooms, 95 suites; one floor set aside exclusively for female guests (security and privacy ensured); à la carte restaurant, pool, sauna, health studio, hairdressing salon. PO Box 17528, Hillbrow 2038; Tel. (011) 643-6611; Fax: (011) 484-2622.

Rand International ★★★ Central. 143 rooms; conference facilities for 40; à la carte restaurant and 2 cocktail bars. PO Box 4235, Johannesburg 2000; Tel. (011) 29-2724; Fax: (011) 29-6815.

JOHANNESBURG: NORTHERN SUBURBS AND MUNICIPALITIES

Ascot ★★★ Small and excellent; 15 rooms. PO Box 95064, Birnham, Randpark 2051; Tel. (011) 483-1211.

Balalaika Protea ★★★ In Sandton. 60 rooms; excellent à la carte restaurant; pool. PO Box 65327, Benmore 2010; Tel. (011) 884-1400; Fax: (011) 884-1463.

Capri ★★★ Close to northern business areas. 50 rooms; conference facilities for 350; à la carte restaurant, separate Kosher kitchen for functions; pool. 27 Aintree Ave, Savoy Estate, Johannesburg 2192; Tel. (011) 786-2250; Fax: (011) 887-2286.

City Lodges. These two-star, no-trimmings hotels are conveniently sited in major centres and offer excellent value. City Lodges in the Witwatersrand area are located in Edenvale (near Johannesburg airport): PO Box 448, Isando 1600; Tel. (011) 392-1750; in Randburg: PO Box 423, Cramerview 2060; Tel. (011) 706-7800; and in Sandown: PO Box 781643, Sandown 2146; Tel. (011) 884-5300.

Indaba Hotel and Conference Centre ★★★ 25 km from city, near the popular Bryanston shopping centre. 114 rooms; conference facilities for 200; à la carte restaurant; pool. PO Box 67129, Bryanston 2021; Tel. (011) 465-1400; Fax: (011) 705-1709.

Rosebank Hotel ★★★★ Inner suburb (10 km from city centre). Sophisticated, busy; 193 rooms, 19 suites; conference facilities for 400; à la carte restaurants; pool, hairdressing salon. PO Box 52025, Saxonwold 2132; Tel. (011) 788-1820; Fax: (011) 788-4123.

Sandton Holiday Inn ★★★ Conveniently situated near Sandton City complex. 248 rooms; à la carte restaurant; personal domestic staff accommodated; access for handicapped. PO Box 781743, Sandton 2146; Tel. (011) 783-5262; Fax: (011) 783-5289.

Sandton Sun ★★★★★ One of the best; part of Sandton City complex (see page 49). 296 rooms; conference facilities for 1 000; 4 restaurants, 4 cocktail bars; pool and health centre. PO Box 784902, Sandton 2196; Tel. (011) 783-8701; Fax: (same).

Sunnyside Park ★★★ In exclusive Parktown; elegant former residence of High Commissioner Lord Milner. 75 rooms, 12 suites; conference facilities for 650; 4 restaurants; pool, hairdressing salon. 2 York Road, Parktown 2193; Tel. (011) 643-7226; Fax: (011) 642-0019.

KEMPTON PARK (JOHANNESBURG AIRPORT)

Airport Sun ★★★ One km from the airport; 237 rooms; conference facilities for 300; 2 à la carte restaurants; pool and sauna. Private Bag 5, Johannesburg airport 1627; Tel. (011) 974-6911; Fax: (011) 974-8097.

Holiday Inn Johannesburg International ★★★ 358 rooms, 4 suites; conference facilities for 250; à la carte restaurant; pool, hairdressing salon. PO Box 388, Kempton Park 1620; Tel. (011) 975-1121; Fax (011) 975-5846.

EAST RAND AND BEYOND

Hotel Boulevard ★★★ In coal-mining area. 71 rooms; pool. PO Box 1270, Witbank 1035; Tel. (0135) 2424.

Highveld Protea ★★★ Far East Rand. 71 rooms; conference facilities for 150. PO Box 2280, Evander 2280; Tel. (0136) 2-4611.

Hotel van Riebeeck ★★ Central Benoni. 19 en-suite rooms; conference facilities for 70; à la carte and table d'hôte. PO Box 399, Benoni 1500; Tel. (011) 849-8917.

Secunda Inn ★★ 122 en-suite rooms; conference facilities for 150; à la carte restaurant; pool. PO Box 1533, Secunda 2302; Tel. (0136) 1121.

VAAL TRIANGLE

Riverside Holiday Inn ★★★ On banks of Vaal, 5 km from Vanderbijlpark. 173 rooms; conference facilities for 700; à la carte restaurant; pool, tennis courts, health hydro. PO Box 740, Vanderbijlpark 1900; Tel. (016) 32-1111.

Riviera International Hotel and Country Club ★★★★ Vereeniging. 100 rooms; conference facilities for 400 (5 venues); à la carte restaurant and carvery/buffet; cocktail bar and action bar; pool, golf course, tennis courts, bowling greens. PO Box 64, Vereeniging 1930; Tel. (016) 22-2861.

PRETORIA

Farm Inn ★★★ 44 rooms, 2 suites; conference facilities. PO Box 71702, Die Wilgers 0041; Tel. (012) 807-0081; Fax: (same).

Hotel Boulevard ★★★ City centre. 77 rooms, à la carte restaurant. PO Box 425, Pretoria 0001; Tel. (012) 326-4806; Fax: (012) 326-1366.

Hotel Burgerspark ★★★★ Central. 232 rooms, 6 suites; conference facilities for 350; 2 restaurants; pool; hairdressing salon. PO Box 2301, Pretoria 0001; Tel. (012) 322-7500; Fax: (012) 322-9429.

Holiday Inn ★★★ Fairly central. 241 rooms; conference facilities for 600; pool, hairdressing salon; squash, tenpin bowling, golf and mini-golf nearby. PO Box 40694, Arcadia 0007; Tel. (012) 341-1571; Fax: (012) 44-7534.

Karos Manhattan Hotel ★★★ Central. 264 rooms; pool, sauna, squash court. 247 Scheiding Street, Pretoria 0002; Tel. (012) 322-7635; Fax: (012) 320-0721.

Palms ★★★ Suburban. 69 rooms, 4 suites; conference facilities for 400. PO Box 1, Silverton 0127; Tel. (012) 87-1612.

Protea Hof Hotel ★★★ Centrally situated. 116 rooms; conference facilities for 150; excellent traditional Cape restaurant, 2 cocktail bars. PO Box 2323, Pretoria 0001; Tel. (012) 322-7570; Fax: (012) 322-9461.

Ungraded accommodation

Bed and breakfast: Central Booking Office, 5th floor - JCC House, Cnr. Empire Road and Owl Street, Milpark 2092, PO Box 91309, Auckland Park 2006; Tel. (011) 482-2206/7; Fax: (011) 726-6915; Telex: 4 50027 BANDB. East Rand: Tel. (011) 849-3009; Fax: (011) 849-2508. West Rand: Tel. (011) 952-1141; Fax: (011) 952-1085. Pretoria: Tel. (012) 47-3597; Fax: (012) 43-6021.

Johannesburg: Dorchester, 121 Twist Street, PO Box 17223, Johannesburg 2000; Tel. (011) 642-4491/5 (rondavels, rooms). Vistaero, 12 Mitchell Street, Berea, PO Box 9699, Johannesburg 2000; Tel. (011) 643-4954 (flats). Witberg Executive Apartments, Corner Tudhope Ave and Olivia Road, Berea, PO Box 17200, Hillbrow 2038; Tel. (011) 484-2500 (flats).

Pretoria: Majella, 564 Pretorius Street, Arcadia 0083; Tel. (012) 44-6370 (flats, rooms). Malvern House, 575 Schoeman Street, Arcadia 0083; Tel. (012) 341-7212 (rooms).

Caravan/camping and self-catering accommodation

Johannesburg: Safari caravan park, PO Box 27533, Bertsham 2013; Tel. (011) 942-1404 (caravans may also be hired).

Pretoria: Polkadraai caravan park, PO Box 913042, Voortrekkerhoogte 0143; Tel. (012) 666-8710. Pretoria caravan park, PO Box 609, Pyramid 0120; Tel. (012) 545-0808. Roodeplaat Dam nature reserve, PO Box 15163, Lynn East 0039; Tel. (012) 808-0510. Roodeplaat Dam Public Resorts, Baviaanspoort Road, PO Box 15980, East Lynne; Tel. (012) 808-0361/2 (caravan/camping, self-catering chalets and 80-bed youth hostel).

A typical shopping-mall eatery

SELECT RESTAURANTS

JOHANNESBURG

Johannesburg and its immediate environs are blessed with a dazzling array of eating houses catering for practically all culinary tastes, from *haute cuisine* through Cape traditional and other ethnic fare to good, plain steakhouses. Among the latter are members of The Longhorn, Porterhouse, Mike's Kitchen and Squire's Loft chains of eateries, all of which offer value for money.

In most cases it's advisable if not essential to reserve a table in advance. If you're uncertain about where to go or can't get into the place of your choice, try the centralized booking service (it has 300 eating houses on its list) on 788-1516.

CITY AND FRINGES

Anton van Wouw, Sivewright Ave, Doornfontein (Tel. 402-7916/7812). Very South African; good food, tasteful décor.

Butler's, Braamfontein Hotel (Tel. 403-5740). Continental cuisine; restful setting.

The Centre Court, Standard Bank Arena, Ellis Park (Tel. 402-7747). Delicious dishes, surprisingly cheap.

Chez Rachel, Fortesque St, Yeoville (Tel. 648-4114). Delicious Moroccan fare; take your own wine (Kosher only).

Club Room, Carlton Court (Tel. 331-8911). Exclusive; lavish décor; classic and nouvelle cuisine.

Cranks, Hillbrow (Tel. 725-5934). Upwardly mobile; take your own wine.

Deales Wine Bar, Diagonal St (Tel. 838-5441). Lunches only; pub-like and excellent.

Delfini, Hunter St, Yeoville (Tel. 648-3500). The best of Greek food and hospitality.

Denton's, Marlborough House, Fox St (Tel. 331-3827). Lunches only; top of the range Continental cuisine; efficient service.

Dragon Tower, Twist St, Hillbrow (Tel. 725-1710). Mandarin Chinese, and excellent.

Fat Frank's Southern Diner, Biccard St, Braamfontein (Tel. 339-7057). What its name suggests; excellent Cajun fare.

Fisherman's Grotto, Plein St (Tel. 834-6211). Marvellously lavish; superb seafood; fine wine cellar. Heartily recommended.

Garbo's, Claim St, Hillbrow (Tel. 642-0614). Decorative place, decorative people.

Gatrile Son & Co, De Villiers Street (Tel. 29-0485). Superb English food; fine wines; very popular.

Golden Capital, Commissioner Street (Tel. 834-6886). Chinese; wonderful value; take your own wine.

Gramadoelas, Bok St, Joubert Park (Tel. 725-1663). Lovely traditional Cape décor; Cape Malay and other local dishes.

Harridan's, Market Theatre, Bree St (Tel. 838-6729). Imaginative Continental dishes, superbly cooked; pleasing environment.

Kapitan's, Kort St (Tel. 834-8048), Indian restaurant with an international reputation.

La Lanterna, Rockey St, Yeoville (Tel. 648-7201). Italian, sociable, excellent, young clientele.

Leipoldt's, Juta St, Braamfontein (Tel. 339-2765). A cornucopia of traditional SA dishes, served from buffet; very popular.

Linger Longer, Juta St, Braamfontein (Tel. 339-7814). Emphasis on traditional French cuisine; superb service.

Suki Hama, Johannesburg Sun and Towers (Tel. 29-7011). Exquisite Japanese dishes.

The St James, Johannesburg Sun (Tel. 29-7011). Joburg's equivalent of London's Savoy Grill: Continental emphasis; supremely good in all respects.

The Three Ships, Carlton Hotel (Tel. 331-8911). Elegant; faultless cuisine, service and appointments.

OUTSKIRTS

Alexander's, City Lodge, Randburg (Tel. 787-6519). New Orleans setting, all-purpose menu.

Al Theatro, Melville (Tel. 726-3602). Italian; sociable; excellent.

Baccarat, Admiral's Court, Rosebank (Tel. 880-1835). Plush and popular; à la carte and buffet.

Balducci's, Rosebank (Tel. 447-3157). Fashionable; delicate dishes; take your own wine.

The Baytree, Prospecta Centre, Linden (Tel. 782-7219). Very French, very good.

Belem Infante, Belem Bldg, Regents Park (Tel. 435-1004). Authentic Portuguese, simple and very good.

Bougainvillea, Standard Bank Bldg, Rosebank (Tel. 788-4883). Continental cuisine; sophisticated.

Casa Linga Ristorante Italiana, Muldersdrif Rd, Honeydew (Tel. 957-2612). Rural (ask for detailed directions); most attractively appointed; good Italian fare.

Chaplins, 4th Ave, Melville (Tel. 726-2507). Austrian cuisine; intimate; pleasant courtyard.

Chapters, Sandton Sun Hotel (Tel. 783-8701). Very elegant; emphasis on French cuisine; superb service.

Chardonnay's, Joshua Doore Centre, Wynberg (Tel. 887-0269). Creative French cuisine.

Chez Germain, Grant Ave, Norwood (Tel. 483-2200). *Haute cuisine* in bistro atmosphere; take your own wine.

Coachman's Inn, Lyme Park, Sandton (Tel. 706-3059). English pub atmosphere, excellent French food.

Coco de Mer, Main St, Melville (Tel. 726-4104). French Creole and other dishes; fine food. Take your own wine.

Cortina, Hyde Park Corner, Jan Smuts Ave (Tel. 788-1284). Italian excellence; family atmosphere.

The Crown, Gold Reef City (Tel. 835-1181). Evocative setting; gourmet venison dishes, seafood specialities.

Daruma, Park Gallery, Melrose North (Tel. 447-2260). The finest of Japanese foods, beautifully presented; décor not well conceived.

Dickens Inn, Craig Park Centre, Craighall (Tel. 787-7219). Sumptuously English.

Dino's, Bedford centre, Bedfordview (Tel. 622-3007). Imaginative menu, comfortable setting.

The Fiddler, Montagu House, Rivonia (Tel. 803-2611). For the discerning food-lover; excellent wine cellar.

Freddie's of Melville, Main Rd, Melville (Tel. 726-1908). French and other dishes, all very good; genuinely hospitable.

Front Page, Main Rd, Melville (Tel. 726-1917). Newspaper theme; solid value.

Gatrile's, Sandown, Sandton (Tel. 883-7398) as for Gatrile Son and Co page 74, with attractive variations.

Grayston, Sandton Holiday Inn (Tel. 783-5262). Smart.

Hard Rock Café, Illovo Centre, Illovo (Tel. 447-2583). Trendy; popular.

The Herbert Baker, Winchester Rd, Parktown (Tel. 726-6253). Smart; superb wine cellar; astonishing choice of beers.

Hertford, Pelindaba Rd, Lanseria (Tel. 659-0496/67). More English than England; smart. Take your own wine.

Ile de France, Dunkeld West shopping centre (Tel. 442-8216). What its name suggests; excellent.

Koala Blu, 7th St, Melville (Tel. 482-2477). South Pacific and other dishes; full of fun; a bit noisy. Take your own wine.

La Mama's, Videolab Centre, Blairgowrie, Randburg (Tel. 787-2701). Delectable range of Italian specialities; friendly.

La Margaux, Illovo Square, Illovo (Tel. 788-5264). Continental food; smart.

La Rochelle Beer Hall, 6th St, La Rochelle (Tel. 435-3809). Portuguese; earthy; fun.

Le Chablis, Sandown centre, Sandown (Tel. 884-1000). English atmosphere, marvellous French food.

Les Marquis, Fredman Drive, Sandown (Tel. 783-8947). *Haute cuisine*; smart.

Lien Wah, Rosebank Hotel (Tel. 788-1820). Delicate Cantonese fare.

Lord Prawn, 11th St, Parkmore (Tel. 783-9214). Lively; seafood specialities.

Lupo's, Dunkeld West centre (Tel. 880-4850). Italian, smart, popular; extensive menu. Take your own wine.

Ma Cuisine, corner 7th and 3rd avenues, Parktown (Tel. 880-1946). French fare, for the gourmet.

Manana, 4th Ave, Melville (Tel. 726-2012). Young clientele, very informal and sociable. Take your own wine.

Manhattan, Northlands Centre, Illovo (Tel. 880-4435). Very popular, rather noisy, fairly cheap; eclectic menu.

Norman's Grill, Main Rd, Jeppe (Tel. 618-1320). Tacky area; superb seafood.

Palm Court, Admiral's Court, Rosebank (Tel. 447-2979). A fine restaurant; cosmopolitan; sociable.

Paros, Rosebank Boulevard (Tel. 788-6211). Greek; cheerful; good value.

The Partridge Country Restaurant, Old Kempton Park Rd, Olifantsfontein (Tel. 316-3155). Stately home in pleasant surrounds; venison specialities; French undertones; has blazon of the Chaîne des Rôtisseurs.

PD's, Illovo Centre, Illovo (Tel. 788-4865). Informal; Italian emphasis.

Pearl Garden, 9th Ave, Edenburg (Tel. 803-1781). Chinese excellence.

The Prospect, Sunnyside Hotel, Parktown (Tel. 643-7226). Thoughtfully conservative, even aristocratic.

Risky Business, 7th St, Melville (Tel. 726-8142). Indian food, cozy atmosphere. Take your own wine.

The Ritz, 3rd Ave, Parktown North (Tel. 880-2470). Despite its name, unpretentious; imaginative menu.

Sausalito, Linden Rd, Sandown (Tel. 783-3305). Very imaginative food and décor; take your own wine.

Seawave Inn, Sovereign St, Bedfordview (Tel. 615-3708). Seafood with appealing French undertones; rather special.

The Silver Tree, Rosebank Hotel (Tel. 788-1820). Elegant; Continental cuisine.

Tastevin, Sunnyside Hotel, Sunnyside Park (Tel. 643-7226). Dignified, tasteful setting; gourmet fare.

The Tent, Rivonia Square, Rivonia (Tel. 803-7025). Theatrically Middle Eastern; interesting food. Take your own wine.

Thermann's, Louis Botha Ave, Orange Grove (Tel. 728-2771). Cape-style décor; French cuisine; take your own wine.

Trattoria Roma, 4th Ave, Melville (Tel. 726-3402). Delectably Italian; take your own wine.

Virgilius, Rosebank gallery (Tel. 788-3415). Splendid seafood; conservative setting.

The Wine Café, Stanley Ave, Richmond (Tel. 482-1872). American-ish menu; reasonably priced; fine cellar.

Zoo Lake, Zoo Lake Gardens, Parkview (Tel. 646-8807). Superb Continental cuisine and wine cellar, complemented by the view.

PRETORIA

Pretoria can't match Johannesburg in the number and variety of its restaurants, but there's more than enough on offer to suit most tastes. The following are some suggestions:

Allegro, State Theatre, Church St (Tel. 322-1665). Elegant setting; ambitious menu.

Ambassadeur, Burgerspark Hotel (Tel. 322-7500). Gourmet French fare.

Caponero, Beatrix St, Arcadia (Tel. 326-4147). Good Italian food; family hospitality.

Chez Patrice, Riviera (Tel. 70-8916). Imaginative French cuisine.

Ella's at Toulouse, Fountains Valley, Groenkloof (Tel. 341-7511). Sophisticated; *haute cuisine* in parklike surrounds.

Goldfields, State Theatre, Church St (Tel. 322-1665). Lavish food and décor.

Henriette, Lizjohn St, Lynnwood Ridge (Tel. 807-1059). Fine French fare, Cape hospitality and furnishings. Take your own wine.

La Madeleine, Esselen St (Tel. 44-6076). Charming little Belgian bistro.

La Perla, Skinner St (Tel. 322-2759). Continental cuisine at its best; popular for lunch.

Lombardy, Tweefontein Farm, Lynnwood Road Extension, Pretoria East. (Tel. 87-1284). Some distance from city; a conservative establishment in dignified, tree-shaded surrounds; Continental food.

Ming Woo, Lakeside Terrace, Verwoerdburg (Tel. 663-1888). Superb Chinese dishes in pleasantly unpretentious surrounds.

Oude Kaap, Protea Hof Hotel, Pretorius St (Tel. 322-7570). Wide variety of dishes (à la carte and a groaning buffet), including Cape fare.

Stadt Hamburg, Brae St, Willow Brae, De Wilgers (Tel. 83-3273). Thatched German-style farmhouse; Continental cuisine; excellent.

Tutti Pasta, The Willows Centre, Rossouw St, The Willows (Tel. 87-2056). Lively, informal, friendly; delicious Italian fare.

Viktor's, Church St, Arcadia (Tel. 326-8282). Superb Continental cuisine; blazon of Chaîne des Rôtisseurs.

USEFUL ADDRESSES AND TELEPHONE NUMBERS

Automobile Association Johannesburg city office: Mutual and Federal Bldg, 44 Simmonds St; Tel. (011) 836-7391. Pretoria city office: Sanlam Plaza, Schoeman St; Tel. (012) 322-9033. Randburg office: Tel. (011) 789-1529. Sandton office: Tel. (011) 883-1541. Centralized advisory and emergency services (breakdown; locksmith; international motoring advice, reservations, roads and weather information): dial Toll Free 08001 11999.

Computicket Bookings and information services: Johannesburg (011) 331-9991; Pretoria (012) 322-7460.

Embassies and consulates In Pretoria (dial code 012): Australia 325-4315; Austria 322-7790; Belgium 44-3201; Canada 324-3970; France 43-5564; Germany 344-3854; Israel 421-2222; Italy 43-5541; Japan 342-2100; Netherlands 344-3910; Portugal 79-4147; Switzerland 43-7788; United Kingdom 43-3121; United States 28-4266.

Emergency numbers National ambulance number (linked to local Metro emergency service) 1-0177.

Hospitals Johannesburg 488-4911; Johannesburg northern and north-eastern areas 882-2400; Johannesburg southern areas 435-0022; Pretoria HF Verwoerd 21-3211; Pretoria West 79-1801. *Fire brigade* Johannesburg 331-2222; Bedfordview 616-4321; Randburg 789-1111; Sandton 883-2800; Pretoria 323-2781. *Poison information centre* Johannesburg 642-2417 or 488-3108. *Police flying squad* 1-0111; *Life Line* (local equivalent of Samaritans): Northern Transvaal (012) 343-9180; Southern Transvaal (011) 728-1347; Johannesburg 728-1347; Pretoria 343-8888; *Alcoholics Anonymous* Johannesburg 836-8735; Pretoria 322-6047.

In the event of difficulties with an emergency call, dial 1022.

Johannesburg Publicity Association Visitors' Information Bureau, ground floor, Markwell House, corner of Market and Von Wiellgh streets; PO Box 4580, Johannesburg 2000. The Association operates a 24-hour tele-tourist information service; Tel. (011) 29-4961; Fax: 29-4965.

Pretoria Information Bureau Munitoria Building, corner of Vermeulen and Van der Walt streets; PO Box 440, Pretoria 0001; Tel. (012) 313-7980/ 7694/8180.

Satour (South African Tourism Board) offices are located at:

☆ International Arrivals Hall, Johannesburg airport 1627; Tel. (011) 970-1669.
☆ Suite 4611, Carlton Centre; PO Box 1094, Johannesburg 2000; Tel. (011) 331-5241.
☆ Shop 153, Nedbank Plaza, Beatrix Street; PO Box 26500, Arcadia 0007; Tel. (012) 28-7154/5.

Welcome Johannesburg, a supplementary and most helpful visitor information service, has offices in the Markade, 84 President Street; Tel. 29-4961.

ANNUAL EVENTS

Johannesburg

Rand Show: March/April □ Braamfontein Spruit Day: August □ International Eisteddfod (Roodepoort ; biennial), Rothman's Derby, Star Life Expo: October □ SA Grand Prix (Kyalami): November.

Pretoria

Agricultural Show: February □ Pretoria Campus Festival: April □ Music Festival, TED Arts Festival □ French Film Festival: June □ Pretoria Show: August □ Spring Carnival: September □ German Oktoberfest: September/October □ Jacaranda Festival: October □ Arts and Crafts Fair: December.

EASTERN AND NORTHERN TRANSVAAL

Mountain and bushveld are the twin and compelling features of the regions far to the east of the Witwatersrand across the great highveld plateau.

The route eastward, to begin with, has little to commend it. The roads lead from Pretoria and Johannesburg to converge near Witbank, 100 km distant and focal point of Africa's biggest coalfields. About 75 million tons of the black gold lie just beneath the surface and is exploited, easily and profitably, by the 22 collieries of the region. This is industrial, not tourist country.

Beyond Witbank, though, the route (now the N4 highway) becomes a lot more interesting as the gently undulating grasslands and scattered rocky outcrops give way to hills, and then to mountains that sweep up in a splendidly imposing ridge, part of South Africa's Great Escarpment and here known as the Transvaal Drakensberg.

A thousand metres high on average, the mountain range runs in a north-south direction for about 300 km from a point north of Nelspruit to the town of Tzaneen and the high Wolkberg and Magoebaskloof in the northeast. The heights are not so dramatically massive as their counterparts to the south, in Natal, but, by the same token, are less intimidating, more accessible to the ordinary traveller and the vistas are just as lovely.

The Transvaal Drakensberg's eastern faces are especially steep, plunging hundreds of metres to the coastal plain that rolls away through the Kruger National Park and Mozambique to the Indian Ocean.

The plain below is known as the Lowveld: a fierce land, sun-blistered and heat-hazed in the long summer months, dry and dun-coloured for much of the year, but with a beauty and fascination of its own. Here, you really do feel you're in Africa.

Two of the Kruger National Park's 1 500-strong lion community. The Kruger sprawls over nearly 20 000 km² of Lowveld savanna countryside; among its many other residents are leopard and cheetah, elephant, rhino and buffalo.

THE HIGH COUNTRY

For sheer scenic beauty, few parts of the southern African subcontinent compare with the Transvaal Drakensberg.

The geological origins of the region are remote, stretching back a full 2 000 million years to the time when the highland plateau, such as it then was, came under colossal seismic pressures, forcing up layers of granite, shale and quartzite; strata which were then covered by immense outpourings of volcanic rock. This igneous matter consolidated, forming a mantle so massive that it bore down on the lower, older levels, tipping their eastern rim upwards to create the Escarpment.

Over the aeons the forces of erosion, the relentless action of wind and rain and river, have created from this geological diversity a spectacular wonderland of massif and buttress, strangely sculpted peak and deep ravine, and of verdant valleys along which run the Olifants and the Crocodile rivers and a score and more of their tributaries. One of the latter, the Blyde River, flows through a canyon that ranks as one of Africa's great scenic splendours (see page 80).

This diversity carries through to the vegetation: scattered among the often mist-wreathed hills are yellowwood and black ironwood, cabbage tree and white peach, wild lemon and bastard onionwood, poison olive, notseng, silky bark and bachelor's refuge and much else, all combining to create something of a tree-lover's paradise. The rich woodland green is invariably and attractively counterpointed by the scarlet flash of aloe and the colours of myriad wild flower species. Along the streams and beside the waterfalls are ferns and creepers, conifers and ancient cycads.

This is the indigenous flora, and it is far less prolific than it was a hundred years ago. There has been steady and in places massive encroachment, most notably by the pines, wattles and eucalyptuses of some of the world's largest man-made forests. The plantations are a relatively recent feature of the region, a product of modern commercial initiative - but they are beautiful nevertheless.

THE PRESENCE OF MAN Long before the colonial era the Escarpment had served and sustained both the San (Bushmen) and much later, groups of Bantu-speaking black peoples. The San were hunter-gatherers who used the upland caves for shelter, decorating some of them with their vibrant, timeless art. The Bantu-speakers hunted, too, but also kept livestock and, in simple fashion, farmed the land. And they were miners, digging the earth for iron and copper. A few years ago archeologists found, at what is known as the 'Head Site' near Lydenburg, a scatter of pottery shards, which they meticulously pieced together. The artifacts – seven sinister-looking masks that evoke ancient and nameless rituals – are now in the South African Museum in Cape Town, though visitors to the eastern Transvaal can see replicas at the Lydenburg museum.

The first Europeans to penetrate the region were Portuguese explorers and traders. They were followed by the path-finding vanguard of the Voortrekkers, hardy people who reached the Transvaal in the mid-1830s. A few of them, under their leader Louis Trichardt, set an eastward course in search for a route to the sea. Trichardt's odyssey ended, tragically, in Lourenço Marques (now Maputo, capital of Mozambique) in 1840, but other Boer parties followed hard on their heels.

Then came the pick-and-shovel prospector, in the 1870s, when the purse-strings of diamond-rich Kimberley were steadily being tightened by rich and powerful interests (see page 259) and the small man was turning his steps towards the golden lode. The gold was there, found and panned in the streams and creeks of the Escarpment and, a little later, farther south and lower down at Barberton, but the alluvial deposits were soon extracted and most of the diggers moved west, to the newly discovered and much richer Witwatersrand fields. Fairly large-scale mining operations did continue at Pilgrim's Rest for three or four decades but here, too, the returns diminished to the point where the companies were forced to look elsewhere for long-term profits.

They found it in the soil, and in the seed of *Pinus patula*, a species of tree native to South America but ideally suited to the eastern Transvaal's upland regions. The hills now support 170 000 ha of pines and nearly 100 000 of eucalyptus – a later introduction.

TRAVELLING CONDITIONS Touring the Escarpment is anything but arduous: most of the roads are tarred, in generally excellent condition and well signposted. Climate: equable, the air cool even in summer, crisp in winter. The rains fall, often torrentially and accompanied by lightning and thunder of Olympian proportions during the hotter months (November through February) but the storms tend to be brief, and there are few days without long hours of sunshine.

The Blyde River Canyon

In 1840 a group of Voortrekkers camped on the banks of a small stream that wound its way through and down the uncharted Escarpment. In due course the men set off to explore the route ahead, but failed to return by the agreed day, so their womenfolk, resigned to widowhood, named the stream Treur (Afrikaans for 'sorrow'). But the men did return eventually, the reunion taking place beside another watercourse. This, in commemoration, they named Blyde, which means 'Joy'.

The rivers in themselves are insignificant, but below their confluence is one of the great natural features of the southern subcontinent: the Blyde River Canyon, a majestically massive red sandstone gorge whose cliff faces plunge nearly a kilometre and almost sheer to the waters below. Overall, the river falls a full thousand metres in a short 20-km stretch. It has been dammed at the gorge by a 70-m wall, and the lake so created is an especially lovely expanse of water, serene and reflective, home to hippo and crocodile.

There are excellent viewing sites overlooking the gorge: Lowveld Lookout, Wonder View, World's End, easily reached from the main tarmac road (the R532). From these, you can gaze across the immensity of the lowland plain and, higher and closer, at the formidable Mariepskop massif and the hump-like peaks known as the Three Rondavels, and down at the dizzying depths of the canyon itself. The Three Rondavels are so named because they resemble in shape the circular hut traditional to some African rural communities. Mariepskop takes its name from Maripi, a folk hero of the Pulana group who, in one of the bloodiest battles of the pre-colonial era, held the natural fortress against the repeated onslaughts of a raiding Swazi army.

RESERVE AND RESORT Above the gorge is the Blyde River Canyon (or Blyderivierspoort) nature reserve, a 22 700-ha stretch of lovely countryside, often rising steeply in sheer quartzite cliffs, which sustains an unusually varied plant life: vegetation ranges from the subtropical bushveld of the lower slopes through grassland and rainforest to stunted mountain cover.

You won't see big game here, but minor characters abound: among the antelope there are klipspringer, red and grey duiker, bushbuck and kudu and grey rhebok, oribi, steenbok, Sharpe's grysbok; primates include baboon, vervet, the rare samango monkey and the galagos (bush-baby and night-ape), and such members of the cat family as caracal and serval, civet, genet and, occasionally, the shy leopard. Among the large and varied bird population (227 species altogether) is the imposing black eagle, the martial eagle, the purple-crested, Knysna and grey louries, the brown parrot, and the endangered bald ibis. The reserve is also the habitat of two rare proteas: the Blyde sugarbush, identified only in 1970, and the Transvaal mountain sugarbush.

The Blyde River Canyon reserve offers some rewarding rambles and nature and hiking trails (see page 104) and, for the horse-rider, pleasant bridle paths. The Swadini reptile park lies just outside the boundary, near the Sybrand van Niekerk resort (see below). Near the Blyde-Treur confluence, inside the park, are Bourke's Luck Potholes, an intriguing fantasia of rock shapes and colours representing one of the weirder consequences of water erosion and named after early prospector Tom Bourke (despite the implication of good fortune, he didn't find any gold, though he accurately predicted its presence in the area). The holes, hollowed out of the smooth rock and 6 m deep in some cases, are almost unnaturally cylindrical.

Within the reserve are two resorts, the Sybrand van Niekerk camp on the northern side of the river and the Blydepoort to the southwest. Both are run by the semi-official Overvaal organization (see page 106). In fact they are more like small villages than camps: tarred streets, and modern, solidly built and fully equipped bungalows (bedrooms, bathroom, kitchen, toilet, verandah, carport, a patch of lawn and barbecue facilities). At the Blydepoort there's a supermarket, à la carte restaurant, library, petrol station and airstrip.

Pilgrim's Rest

Gold was discovered in the high Escarpment, early in 1873, in a stream to the south of what is today the town of Sabie, and within days the inevitable throng of hopeful diggers congregated, setting up camps at Spitzkop and Mac-Mac (so called for the number of Scotsmen who had arrived on the scene). Later that year news broke of a much bigger strike, made by a dour Caledonian called Wheelbarrow Alec (he carried all his worldly possessions around in a barrow) in a small tributary of the Blyde a little to the north, and within months a gold town had been established and was flourishing. It was named Pilgrim's Rest because here, at last, after so many false trails and faded dreams, the nomadic diggers had found a firm and profitable base – a home.

The place grew: tents and wattle-and-daub shacks were replaced by solid, iron-roofed cottages; women (some of them wives) came to settle; traders and canteen owners set up shop; a school, a church and a newspaper made their appearance; and the Royal Hotel opened its welcoming doors to the polyglot and thirsty community.

A lot of gold was found, including the 6 038-g Reward Nugget, and Pilgrim's Rest, for a time, was a thriving, vibrant little frontier settlement that enjoyed itself to the full, mostly peacefully, sometimes eccentrically, occasionally in outrageous style. But before long the alluvial deposits began to run out, the syndicates and companies moved in to dig deeper, to sink shafts and tunnel adits into the hillsides, and the town retired into a quieter and more respectable routine. The last of the mines, the Beta, closed in the 1970s (though, depending on the gold price, some mines could reopen). Long before then, in the 1920s, the owners had spread their investment, diversifying into large-scale forestry.

Pilgrim's Rest, still a prosperous village of several hundred residents, has a special place in the traveller's itinerary: in 1974 the Transvaal provincial authorities bought the entire place, lock, stock and barrel, and over the years since then it's been turned into a 'living museum', the buildings meticulously restored to the charming condition they were in during the period 1880 to 1915. Among them are the miners' cottages, the Masonic Church, the old Bank House, the fascinating Miner's House – a perfect period-style re-creation – and the premises of *The Pilgrim's and Sabie News*.

And, of course, the Royal Hotel, which still plays amiable host to residents and visitors. Its pub – whose fittings graced a chapel in far-off Lourenço Marques until 1893, when they were hauled up the Escarpment to serve an entirely different kind of congregation – is well patronized; the rooms you sleep in are very much as they were a century ago, complete with brass bedsteads, quilted covers and pressed-steel ceilings. Also available to guests are some of the miners' cottages, a short way up the hill.

There are guided tours around the village, to the old Reduction Works, to the Diggings Museum (gold-panning demonstrations) and around Alanglade, the early mine manager's home. The house is furnished in both the art nouveau and art deco styles and has been described as 'a showpiece illustrating the opulence of the gold industry'.

Towns of the Escarpment

Just to the east of Pilgrim's Rest is the pretty little forestry village of:

GRASKOP ('Grassy Hill'), perched on a spur of the Escarpment and close to a small indigenous forest, called Fairyland, which is much visited by naturalists. Close to town is Kowyn's Pass, a spectacular mountain throughway leading down to the Lowveld and a route well worth taking when you're out on a leisurely drive.

The general area boasts some of the Escarpment's most delightful waterfalls (see panel, page 84).

SABIE, a more substantial centre of the forestry industry, and originally a wayside camp for adventurous prospectors and the transport riders who followed them to the diggings, lies 25 km to the south of Graskop.

Gold was discovered near Sabie in 1895 – accidentally, by a party of picnickers indulging in target shooting (one of the bullets chipped gold-bearing rock) and, during the next 55 years, well over a million ounces of the yellow metal were extracted from the seam. But it was the giant mines of the Witwatersrand, and their voracious appetite for timber pit-props, that sustained the settlement over the decades. The Sabie region now supports the biggest single block of man-made forest – and the biggest

sawmill – in South Africa, supplying about half the country's needs. When in town, try to visit the Cultural History Forestry Museum, which displays 370-plus exhibits, including petrified tree-trunks, antique implements and a 'talking tree', and in which there are six visitors' 'participation areas'.

Lying some way to the west is the fairly large town of:

LYDENBURG The Afrikaans name translates as 'place of suffering', an unhappy epithet derived from the hardships of the eastern Voortrekkers, whose first settlement, Ohrigstad, sited in an unhealthy area 50 km to the north, had been devastated by fever and abandoned by the survivors (it was resettled almost exactly a century later, in the 1940s).

Lydenburg, though, turned out to be anything but a suffering place: it thrived, and is now a substantial and attractive centre. It has, among its other assets, the oldest school building in the Transvaal (built in 1851) and an interesting little museum. Just outside town are the noted trout hatcheries, where freshwater fish species are bred to supply the Escarpment's rivers and dams (the aquarium is open daily from 08h00 to 16h00) and, farther away, on the road east to Long Tom Pass, the Gustav Klingbiel nature reserve. This 2 200-ha sanctuary, on the slopes of Mount Anderson, is home to a variety of antelope ranging from the tiny steenbok up to the stately eland and to over 100 bird species.

Also within the reserve are an interesting collection of Later Stone Age ruins, picnic sites (with fireplaces) and three most pleasant nature walks. A large map at the corner of Lydenburg's Voortrekker and Viljoen streets directs visitors to the waterfalls and other special attractions of the area.

One other small town in the general region deserves a mention, and a visit. If you're a keen angler, try to spend a day or so in:

DULLSTROOM, set on the western slopes of the Escarpment south-west of Lydenburg, in an area renowned for its troutstreams. Its two other claims to modest fame are its railway station, at 2 077 m above sea level the highest in southern Africa; and its proximity to Die Berg, the Transvaal's highest peak. There are two quite charming hotels in the village.

The view from Long Tom Pass. The scenically spectacular route runs between Lydenburg and Sabie.

Kloof and cave

Long Tom Pass, the most spectacular part of the road linking Lydenburg and Sabie, was named after the huge 150-mm Creusot field gun used during the South African War (1899-1902), by the Boer forces with – for the British – annoying effect during General Buller's advance after the relief of Ladysmith in 1900. The pass is notable for its steep and tortuous gradients, its grand views and for the Knuckles, which are four unusually shaped peaks.

Speaking of passes, make a point of including the Abel Erasmus on your sightseeing drive. The R36 highway runs through it north of Lydenburg, the steepest section twisting its way through thickly vegetated orange and yellow sandstone cliffs (and through the JG Strijdom tunnel) from a point high above the Ohrigstad River down 700 m to the Olifants. Again, there are stunning vistas of river and, beyond, the Lowveld. At the bottom of the pass there's a pleasant tree-shaded tearoom.

A short distance off the R36, at the head of the Molopong Valley (this is before you get to the pass on the northward route), are the Echo Caves, an intriguing sequence of formations that includes a cavern fully 100 m long and 50 m high. If you tap some of the dripstone formations (stalagmites and stalactites) they'll echo with disproportionate loudness; hence the name. There are two entrances, though only one is open to the public; the other leads to the gruesomely named and forbidding Cannibal Cave, a large chamber that accommodates millions of bats.

The caves, and others in the vicinity, once sheltered communities of Middle and Later Stone Age people. Relics of their occupation – excavated sites and rock paintings – can be seen at the nearby open-air Museum of Man.

Mount Sheba

One of the loveliest nature reserves in the entire eastern Transvaal is part of a private estate: Mount Sheba, set in a deep green valley and entirely surrounded by the grandness of high hills, a little over 20 km west-southwest of Pilgrim's Rest.

To get there, one travels over what is known as Robber's Pass (R533), bearing left at the signposted turn-off to continue down a tortuous 11-km incline. The last section of the track is a bit rough, but well worth undertaking: at the journey's end there's a warm welcome at the Mount Sheba Hotel, an elegant cluster of thatched buildings set amid trim lawns and, above and beyond, tier upon tier of magnificently wooded mountain slopes.

The rainforests here are in what is termed 'climax condition' – the trees are left to mature and to die of old age without interference. It's an unusually stable floral community which, together with its indigenous fauna (birds, and the small animals) form a complete ecosystem.

LAND OF WATER

The Escarpment is renowned for its many and beautiful streams and cascades, hidden in secret places among the woodland glens. Some of the most charming are concentrated in the Sabie/Graskop area, and include:

☆ The Sabie: situated within the town's boundary; a 73-m chasm spanned by a bridge which serves as a viewing platform.

☆ The Bridal Veil: drive 7 km north of Sabie, then walk through the indigenous forest. The name evokes its delicate perfection.

☆ The Mac-Mac: twin cascades, just off the road from Sabie to Graskop; 56 m into a deep-green ravine dense with trees and ferns. A short distance from the falls, and close to the Escarpment's earliest gold diggings, are the Mac-Mac Pools. The name derives from the unusually large number of Scotsmen who arrived on the scene in the 1870s.

The pools are in an exquisite setting; there are picnic and barbecue sites, and swimming in clear mountain water (there are changing rooms).

☆ The Lone Creek: 10 km west of Sabie; one can drive to the base of the falls, which are 68 m high; the spray nurtures a rainforest.

☆ The Horseshoe: about a km beyond Lone Creek, on the same road. The falls are a proclaimed national monument.

☆ The Lisbon: another splendid double waterfall, situated on the western side of the R532 north of Graskop, reached by gravel road. Semicircular in shape – the water collects in pools before spilling over the rim – and in a setting of great beauty. Pleasantly sited picnic spot.

☆ The Berlin: also reached by gravel road off the R532, about 3 km north of the Lisbon. One takes a path up to a viewing platform above the falls.

Over a thousand plants and trees have already been identified in the Mount Sheba forest reserve, and many more await the exploratory botanist. Some of the yellowwoods are almost a millennium old, and there's a wealth of Cape chestnut, massive cussonias, red pears, and towering, incredibly hard black ironwoods. Signposted paths lead through the forest glades (map and literature available from the hotel), and many of the individual trees are labelled. Rambles range from the gentle 2-km Golagola Walk (crisscrossing mountain streams) to the 5-km stroll to Marco's Mantle, which is a most attractive waterfall, and to the trout and aloe pools. The latter has some steep slopes but provides wonderful views of gorge and river.

THE KRUGER NATIONAL PARK

South Africa's premier reserve covers an immense slice of Lowveld territory – 19 488 km² of it, which is about the size of Wales, larger than the state of Israel. It lies in the savanna-type bushveld between the Crocodile River in the south and the Limpopo, 350 km to the north (the Limpopo is South Africa's common border with Zimbabwe). To the east, along the Lebombo mountains, is Mozambique. The park's dogleg western perimeter borders on a trio of large, privately-owned Transvaal wilderness areas (see page 93).

The Kruger has no pretensions to exclusivity: it takes an unashamedly popular approach to the business of introducing South Africans to their natural heritage. Comfort and easy accessibility to the superb array of wildlife are the keynotes, and there is very little of the classic African safari about one's holiday there.

The park plays host to around 3 000 people daily, and for the inexpensive family vacation it is probably unsurpassed anywhere. The 19 rest-camps, differing in size and character (see page 88), are pleasant, tree-shaded oases in a magnificent setting, linked to each other by a 2 000-km road network; within leisurely driving distance of each camp are waterholes, viewsites, picnic spots and a wealth of scenic and wildlife splendour.

Despite all this, though – despite the massive tourist presence – the Kruger remains unspoilt. Everything introduced by man – the rest-camps, the 'designated areas', the routes and the 'visual bands' that run along either side of them – takes up less than three percent of the total area. The remaining 97% belongs to Nature. The camps and roads, as one writer puts it, are 'merely windows looking out into the wilderness'.

The making of a park

The southern African interior, and in particular the grasslands of the northern and north-eastern regions were, not too long ago, one of the world's great treasure-houses of wildlife. Until about the middle of the 19th century huge herds of buffalo, wildebeest and springbok roamed the sunlit veld, free to follow ancient migratory paths, their numbers kept in check only by seasonal drought, by predators, and by the modest needs of the scattered tribespeople.

Then came the white farmer to settle and fence the land, and the hunter with his guns and his lust for the killing sport. Between them they took a devastating toll of the game. Especially destructive, and wantonly so, was the hunter: it is estimated that by 1880 over two million hides had been exported to Europe – a tragic enough figure by any reckoning, but one that does not reflect the true scale of the slaughter. The Victorian 'sportsman' shot indiscriminately, for the highest possible tally, and only a very small fraction of the spoils served any commercial purpose. The remaining, untold numbers of carcasses, were simply left on the ground for the hyena, the vulture and the burning African sun. Something, clearly, had to be done.

The Transvaal republican government had in fact been conscious of a dwindling natural heritage from the early 1850s, when hunters were officially (and ineffectually) forbidden to kill more than could be consumed, but it wasn't until the 1890s that there was any serious attempt to establish sanctuaries north of the Vaal River. Thereafter, events moved rapidly: on the ageing President Paul Kruger's initiative two reserves were proclaimed – the Pongola (later closed down following an outbreak of stock disease) and the Sabi.

Under Warden James Stevenson-Hamilton's firm guidance the Sabi fulfilled its promise, developing into one of the world's largest and finest game reserves. In 1926, when it became the Union of South Africa's first national park, it was renamed in honour of its principal founder.

The park today

The Kruger is a haven for more varieties of wildlife than any other game sanctuary in Africa: 137 species of mammal, 112 species of reptile (including 50 of snake), 49 of fish (not counting an ocean-living shark that has been found in one of the rivers), 33 of amphibian and 227 of butterfly.

For the bird-watcher, especially, the Kruger has enormous appeal: 493 avian species have been recorded, including ostrich, fish eagle,

vulture, bateleur, secretary bird, lourie and lilac-breasted roller, oxpecker and woodpecker, owl, francolin, hawk, babbler, hornbill, korhaan, Cape glossy starling. It's a fascinating region, too, for the botanist and lover of trees: there are about 400 species of the latter, many with evocative names – mountain syringa, live-long, velvet bushwillow, bride's bush, peeling plane, sumach bean, ironwood and yellowwood, fever tree and mahogany. Not to mention the myriad of shrubs, grasses, worts, bulbous plants and aloes.

All these forms of life, together with the uncountable insects and the micro-organisms, combine to create a coherent habitat, a system of gene pools in infinitely delicate balance, and in which the cycle of life is sustained by collective dependence.

The game complement, naturally, includes the 'big five': lion, leopard, elephant, buffalo, rhino (see page 94). Most numerous of the larger species are the impala, some 120 000 head in total: medium-sized buck that one sees everywhere (but worth more than a passing glance: they are graceful animals, and remarkable ones in flight – the whole herd moves in beautifully synchronized fashion, leaping prodigiously and in concert over the ground).

Other game figures (approximate ones, since censuses are taken at regular intervals and the numbers change) are: zebra 30 500; wildebeest 13 500; kudu 10 500; giraffe 5 000; waterbuck 4 000; warthog 3 000; hippo 3 000; sable antelope 2 000; reedbuck 1 000; tsessebe 900; eland 800; wild dog 300.

Details of these and of the scores of other animal, bird and plant species in the Kruger, may be found in a number of excellent publications, available in South African bookshops and at the larger Kruger camps.

VEGETATION Broadly speaking, the Kruger can be quartered according to plant type. South of the Olifants River, which more or less bisects the park, the western section is distinguished by its acacia, combretum, marula and red bushwillow species, while to the east are the broad grazing lands of buffalo grass and red grass shaded by knobthorn. Fairly tall, butterfly-leafed mopane trees and the rugged bushwillow dominate the lands north-west of the Olifants, stunted mopane the north-east.

Distinct from all these are the strips of dense

WILDLIFE PHOTOGRAPHY: SOME HINTS

✫ Don't arrive in the Kruger with brand-new, unused equipment. It may be the latest and best in the fully automatic range, but it will also be intricate and you'll need to be familiar with its workings. Animals don't pose for the camera and there's often very little time to think about focus, aperture and speed.

✫ Lenses are a matter of personal preference. The standard 35 mm or 50 mm are fine for big game close-ups but need to be augmented by telephoto lenses (say one of 200-250 mm or, preferably, a 135 mm and a 300 mm) for small and distant subjects. Zoom lenses are an excellent option, particularly if combined with a tele-extender – a device that doubles lens magnification.

✫ Film: decide at the outset whether you want prints or transparencies. It is possible to convert one to the other, but to do so is expensive and you'll lose quality. Colour film comes in speeds up to 1 000 ASA, but 100 ASA is suitable for most purposes in the invariably sunlit Kruger. Film may be purchased at the rest-camp shop.

✫ The light is at its best in the early mornings and late afternoons; heat-haze is a problem during the middle part of the day. Bear in mind, too, that the animals tend to retire to shade in the hotter hours.

✫ Remember, telephoto work requires special care, principally to avoid 'camera shake': the lens magnifies not only the subject but also the slight but inevitable unsteadiness of your hand. Two options: use as fast an exposure as conditions allow, and/or support the camera. The latter option need not involve a cumbersome arrangement of tripods and mounts (impractical, anyway, in areas where you have to stay in your vehicle); a cushion placed between camera and car window frame will serve admirably.

✫ Don't attempt to take telephoto pictures from a moving vehicle, nor, indeed, while stationary but with the engine running. The vibrations will seriously affect results. Switch off, and ask the other passengers to sit quite still while you take your shots.

✫ Keep your photographic equipment with you at all times. Theft is uncommon in the Kruger, but not unknown.

✫ You'll find that the smaller creatures, and some not so small (birds, vervet monkeys, rodents, lizards and so forth) are often unusually tame around the rest-camps. They provide excellent subject matter for close-up work – quite literally on your doorstep.

Giraffes enjoy their sundowners. The Kruger's waterholes are a photographer's paradise.

riverine vegetation, often graced by sycamore fig and Natal mahogany.

Far to the north, around Pafuri and Punda Maria, the climate and cover changes. This is a unique and, in geophysical terms, quite remarkable region, the meeting place of fully nine of Africa's major ecosystems. Here there is bushveld and wetland, sandveld, grassy plain and green forest, rolling woodland and broad lava flat, granite hill and spectacular gorge. A land of stunning contrasts, the kaleidoscopic elements complemented by a startling variety of animals and birds, bushes and trees. Many species are found in few other areas. Especially notable are the mahogany and ebony trees, and the groves of ghostly fever trees standing pale in the silent riverine jungle; the Mashikiri's giant and ancient baobabs; the massive Lebombo ironwoods, and the prolific game of the Hlamalala plain.

THE SEASONS The Kruger's climate is generally subtropical. Summer temperatures often reach a high 40 °C and more, though the daytime average is around 30 °C, cooling down to just below 20 °C at night.

Summer is also the wet season: on a typical day during the months from November to February the storm clouds, great billowing masses of cumulonimbus, will begin building up from about lunchtime to release their full fury in late afternoon. These thunderstorms are generally brief, but are accompanied by torrential rain and can be of quite frightening proportions while they last.

Rainfall tends to be heavier in the southern regions, averaging around 740 mm at Pretorius-kop camp, in contrast to the fairly modest 440 mm in the northern Luvuvhu River area, though the charmingly old-fashioned Punda Maria, the northernmost camp, is set on relatively high ground and enjoys better than average precipitation.

Winters are dry, the days pleasantly warm and the nights and early mornings cool, often downright cold, the temperature falling to below zero.

All this has its relevance in deciding when to visit the park, though it is difficult to offer an unqualified recommendation. In winter the streams (there are six perennial rivers and numerous seasonal watercourses in the Kruger area) are reduced to a trickle, the wildlife tends to congregate around what water there is, and

the vegetation is sparser, so it's easier to see the animals, and see them in greater numbers, in the cooler months.

But in many ways the park is at its worst during the winter, the earth parched and dusty, the colours drab.

In startling contrast is the green abundance of spring and summer, when the rivers flow, the pools fill and the bushveld takes on a rich luxuriance, nurturing the game back to health and vitality, drawing the migrating flocks of birds. Climate, of course, largely determines the nature of the vegetation, which in turn has a major influence on the distribution of wildlife.

Travelling to and in the park

The Kruger has eight public entrance gates. They are, clockwise from the south-eastern corner, Crocodile Bridge, Malelane, Numbi, Paul Kruger, Orpen, Phalaborwa, Punda Maria and Pafuri. The Numbi, used by 19% of the park's half a million and more annual visitors, is the busiest.

The Kruger is open throughout the year, though some low-lying routes may be closed during the summer rains. Altogether, there are nearly 2 000 km of main (tarred) and secondary (graded gravel) roads.

In the interests of safety – of both the visitor and the animals – travel within the park is restricted to daylight hours. The gates and camps have set opening and closing hours, which vary slightly with the season.

There are petrol filling stations at all the gates except Malelane and Paul Kruger, and at all the public rest-camps (see next page).

Speed limits vary between 40 and 50 km/h. Vehicle breakdown services are available at Skukuza and Letaba.

FLYING IN Many visitors to the Kruger, and especially those from overseas, prefer to make their way to the park by air, either on a conducted package tour, or travelling privately. Car and minibus hire services are available at Phalaborwa and Skukuza camp.

Scheduled Comair flights operate on a daily basis between Johannesburg international airport and Skukuza and Phalaborwa. Aircraft used include the 44-seater Twin Fokker Friendship and the smaller, 11-seater, Twin Cessna. Comair will also arrange special large-group flights from Durban and, of course, aircraft may be chartered.

DAY VISITS For those who really like their comforts and who plan to include visits to the Kruger as part of a more general Eastern Transvaal holiday, there are some excellent fairly hotels and country hideaways within fairly short driving distances of one or other of the park's gates (see Advisory, page 107).

The rest-camps

The Kruger offers an impressive variety of accommodation, ranging from the simple to the luxurious, in its 24 camps, five of which are small, private clusters of huts and chalets available only on a block-booking basis and one of which is reserved for campers. They are refreshingly restful places, fenced against the animals, neatly laid out, graced by trees and flowering plants and stretches of lawn. Many of the rondavels and bungalows are air-conditioned, surprisingly spacious, attractively thatched. Each camp incorporates a caravan and camping area (with communal facilities).

Camp routine is informal and undemanding, the emphasis on low-cost outdoor living. One usually cooks one's own meals – indoors, if the bungalow has its own kitchen, or on the braai (barbecue) unit just outside. There are also communal field kitchens, and braai facilities at the designated picnic spots. You can either stock up before you arrive or at the camp's shop, which will sell you fresh meat, groceries, beer, wines and spirits, dry goods, photographic film, reading matter, curios and oddments.

A pleasant mealtime alternative is the camp's licensed restaurant, a rather casual place that serves adequate food in a friendly atmosphere. Many of the Kruger's restaurants are strategically sited to overlook river or deep valley, and pre-dinner drinks on the terrace, taken as the sun dips low and the golden light spreads, fill a magical hour of the day.

Most comfortable of the different types of units available are the guest cottages, built by private organizations or affluent individuals for their own occupancy but available for hire when not in use. They vary in size and style; some are large (designed for up to nine people) and, usually, beautifully fitted out. There are guest cottages at Berg-en-Dal, Letaba, Lower Sabie, Olifants, Pretoriuskop, Satara, Shingwedzi and Skukuza. Bookings should be made at least three months in advance.

There is, though, plenty of less exclusive but very adequate accommodation. A typical family cottage is air-conditioned and comprises two two-bed rooms, bathroom, toilet, small kitchen (gas stove, fridge, cutlery and crockery, utensils) and gauzed-in verandah. Lower down the scale are one-room two- and three-bed units with shower and toilet, and the rather basic two- to five-bed huts (handbasin only, cold water) close to an ablution block.

From the general to the specific. In alphabetical order, the Kruger's camps are:

BALULE On the Olifants River in the central region. A small cluster of three-bed rondavels, caravan camp and ablution block. Firewood and a communal freezer on site. Shop, restaurant and filling station at nearby Olifants camp, Letaba or Satara (see page 89). Check in at Olifants (and, at the same time, ask about the terrain and wildlife of the area).

BATELEUR A new camp (named after one of the region's more notable raptors), situated northwest of Shingwedzi in the northern part of the park. Family cottages are available.

BERG-EN-DAL (the Afrikaans name means 'mountain and valley'). A newish, moderate-sized camp offering family cottages (6 beds), 2-and 3-bed chalets (bathroom, kitchen), some specially designed for paraplegics; well-appointed guest cottages and caravan/camp sites. General layout and architectural style are most pleasing: accommodation units are spaced out in natural bush; there is clever and attractive use of natural building materials. The camp overlooks a dam.

Conference facilities, swimming pool, petrol filling station, shop (fresh produce), licensed restaurant, laundry. There is a visitor centre and an interpretive trail suitable for blind people in the camp.

CROCODILE BRIDGE Sited charmingly on the Crocodile riverbank next to one of the park's two southern gates. Smallish: about 20 3-bed chalets (bath, fridge, no kitchen); shop (limited range of stock); petrol filling station. This is acacia country, the sweet grasses sustaining large numbers of buffalo, wildebeest, zebra, impala, kudu. Hippo Pool can be found 8 km on the route to Malelane.

LETABA Beautifully situated above a sweeping bend in the central region's Great Letaba River. Lawns, shade trees (mlala palms, Natal mahogany), aloes, flowering bushes and, for game-viewing, well-sited terraces make this one of the park's most attractive camps. It's also strategically placed – at the junction of three major routes – for drives to the north, west and south. Six-bed family cottages (bathroom, kitchen), 2- and 3-bed huts (bathroom, fridge); one guest cottage (9 guests); caravan sites. Shop (fresh produce), unusually good licensed restaurant, laundromat, petrol filling station; AA garage and workshop.

LOWER SABIE A medium-size camp overlooking the Sabie River; generally a prime game area; nearby are the Mnondosi and Nhlanganzwane dams. Neat lawns and shade trees are features. Five-bed family cottages (bathroom, kitchen); 2- and 3-bed chalets (bathroom, fridge); three well-appointed guest cottages. Shop, licensed restaurant, petrol filling station.

OLIFANTS Splendid position atop cliffs rising 100 m above the river, with spectacular views to distant hills and the game-rich, lushly evergreen valley below – lovely vistas at all times, magical at sunrise and sunset. There's an especially well-sited viewing point built on a promontory a short distance along the heights. A modern, pleasantly laid-out camp, the accommodation built along rising, aloe-decorated terraces (all with views) and offering guest cottage (4 bedrooms), family cottage, chalets (some with kitchen, some with fridge only, all with bathroom); shop, licensed restaurant (self-service), petrol filling station, museum and information centre, amphitheatre (film shows).

ORPEN A small, restful camp near the Orpen gate in the west. Pleasant grounds (rock gardens and aloes, tall acacia and marula trees, red bushwillows). Two and 3-bed chalets; communal ablution and kitchen facilities; shop; petrol. No restaurant. Nearby, on the banks of the Timbavati River, is the Marula caravan camp.

PRETORIUSKOP Situated 9 km from the Numbi gate in the south-west (petrol and first-aid station at the gate), Pretoriuskop is the Kruger's oldest and fourth largest camp. Family cottages, 2- and 3-bedroom chalets (bathroom,

fridge); less sophisticated huts of various sizes (fridge, no bathroom). Shop, licensed restaurant, swimming pool (natural rock), petrol filling station.

PUNDA MARIA Named after the wife of an early ranger and situated in the far north-west, in tropical country not far from the Luvuvhu River (see page 87). A smallish, rather old-fashioned, unassuming camp in a very pretty setting of rocky hill and evergreen grove and with a pronounced wilderness feel about it. Take the short Mahogany loop drive on the evening you arrive: it's an excellent introduction to the area, and the waterhole *en route* is a gem. Four-bed family cottages, 2-bed chalets (bathroom, fridge); caravan/camping. Shop, licensed restaurant, petrol filling station.

SATARA The second largest camp, situated in the central region and, though it doesn't enjoy any specially good views, it's popular for its sociable atmosphere, its terrace, its prolific and attractive birdlife (buffalo weavers, cheeky sparrows and what seems to be a million and more starlings) and its most pleasant self-service restaurant (next to waterhole). This is lion country, but there's also an abundance of zebra, buffalo, elephant, kudu, impala, wildebeest, waterbuck. Six-bed family cottages; 2- and 3-bedroom chalets (bathroom, fridge); 3 larger guest cottages; caravan/camping sites. There is accommodation specially designed for paraplegics. Shop, licensed restaurant, laundry facilities; petrol and garage/workshop, information centre.

SHINGWEDZI The largest of the three northern region rest-camps, Shingwedzi is notable for its spacious grounds, lovely trees (mainly mopane but also palms) and bright pink-and-white impala lilies, its somewhat old-fashioned bungalows (though they are quite modern inside) and its swimming pool. Many possible drives, but especially recommended is that to the south-east (towards Letaba), on the secondary road that leads along the Shingwedzi River. The well-patronized Kanniedood dam is on this route. Accommodation: 2-, 3- and 4-bedroom chalets (bathroom, fridge), self-contained guest cottage; caravan/camping sites. Shop, licensed restaurant and cafeteria, petrol filling station, information centre.

SKUKUZA The 'capital' of the Kruger and more of a thriving little town than a bush camp, Skukuza is named after the park's first warden (see page 85) – the word in translation means 'he who sweeps clean', a reference to Stevenson-Hamilton's ruthless and successful war against poachers.

The camp's focal point is the newly constructed reception and restaurant area, said to be Africa's and perhaps the world's largest thatched building. Accommodation ranges through the spectrum, from self-contained and very well appointed guest cottages through chalets to accommodation specially designed for paraplegics, dormitories for school parties and an extensive caravan/camping area. Amenities and services: supermarket and curio shop, restaurant, 'Train Restaurant' (converted dining and lounge car) and snack bar, post office, bank, airport, Comair and Avis offices, police station, doctor, petrol filling station and workshop, AA service. The information centre houses a good library and an exhibition hall. Well worth visiting is the nursery, which sells baobabs, cycads, palms and other indigenous flora at most reasonable prices.

THE PRIVATE CAMPS These are secluded, small – the largest can take up to 19 people – but with fully equipped accommodation. They are for groups, and must be booked en bloc. Petrol, shop and restaurant are accessible at the nearest of the larger rest-camps. The five are:
☆ Boulders: 12 guests; check in at Letaba. Set against massive boulder formation; beautifully designed, unfenced, the thatched buildings raised on stilts, pleasant verandahs. Solar power provides electricity. Four 2-bed cottages (bath, shower, toilet) and 4-bed family cottage. Kitchen-cum-entertainment area. Domestic help available.
☆ Jock of the Bushveld: 12 guests, check in at Berg-en-Dal. An atmospheric little camp, recalling the early days of gold and the transport riders (see page 91). Neat, rustic, white-painted, tree-shaded buildings set above the sandy Mntomene riverbed. Three self-contained 4-bed cottages. Solar panels provide electricity and refrigeration.
☆ Malelane: 18 guests; check in at Berg-en-Dal. Southern Kruger; once a public camp, now converted. Five well-appointed cottages in neat tree-shaded grounds. Large outside communal kitchen (stove, fridge, freezer).
☆ Nwanetsi: 16 guests, check in at Satara. Set on the banks of the Nwanetsi River, close to the Mozambique border, with the Lebombo Mountains not too far away. An especially tranquil place: the name, in the Shangaan language, means 'reflections of the moon'. Four 3-bed huts, two 2-bed (shower, toilet) bungalows; communal kitchen (with fridge) and a summerhouse for relaxation.
☆ Roodewal: 19 guests, check in at Olifants. Sited on the Timbavati River between the Olifants and Satara camps, in excellent game-viewing area; tree-shaded A-frame buildings; fully equipped 4-bed family cottage; three 5-bed huts (shower, toilet); communal kitchen with stove and fridge.

A splendid new luxury rest-camp, Narina, will shortly be completed (it was still under development at the time of writing) on the Sabie River only 6 km from Skukuza. Narina is designed to offer all the comforts and amenities of a five-star bush hotel, complete with large swimming pool and top-class restaurant. The pleasant air-conditioned chalets – two-bedroom, two-bathroom units, each with its own balcony – are sited at least 15 m from each other to ensure privacy.

THE BUSHVELD CAMPS These are smaller, less sophisticated clusters of accommodation for the more casual visitor. In brief:
☆ Bateleur: 43 km south-west of Shingwedzi, near the Tsange lookout point on the banks of the Shingwedzi River. Offers four 4-bed and three 6-bed family cottages.
☆ Shimuwini: situated west of the tarred road between Phalaborwa and the Mooiplaas picnic spot on the banks of the Shimuwini dam, on the Letaba River. Shimuwini is equipped with one 6-bed and five 4-bed family cottages.
☆ Talamati: on the banks of the Nwaswitsontso River near the Kruger's western boundary. It has ten 6-bed and five 4-bed family cottages. The nearest park entrance is the Orpen gate.
☆ Mbyamiti: set on the banks of the Mbyamiti Spruit, 5 km from its confluence with the Crocodile River. Equipped with ten 5-bed and five 4-bed family cottages.
☆ Sirheni: near the park's western boundary, on the banks of the Nwaswitsontso River. Accommodation comprises ten 6-bed and five 4-bed family cottages.

JOCK'S BUSHVELD

Until the early decades of the 20th century the Lowveld was savagely inhospitable terrain for both man and his cattle. It had few permanent inhabitants; settlers were discouraged by the constant threat of malaria and the dreaded nagana, the 'sleeping sickness' borne by the tsetse fly, and up to quite recent times the acacia-thorn and mopane scrubland, with its fertile soil and sweet grasses, was left relatively undisturbed to serve as refuge for lion and leopard, elephant and rhino and the countless head of antelope.

Not quite undisturbed, though, for the risk of fever receded in the coolness of winter and it was then that the professional hunters embarked on safari in quest of ivory and hides – and the transport riders set out across the wide plains to the coast. There, at Delagoa Bay, they loaded their long, half-tented buckwagons with 3 000 kg or more of provisions – food, equipment and, most important, whisky – for the isolated diggings of Barberton and the Escarpment.

One of the more notable of these intrepid traders was Percy FitzPatrick, who had arrived at Pilgrim's Rest as a storekeeper in 1884 but soon tired of the humdrum life and, together with his Zulu driver Jim and his dog Jock, plied the fever route for two years. Later he recounted his adventures to his young children, telling of the beauty and menace of the Lowveld wastes, their rivers and swamps and hidden places, of its predators and prey, and of the eccentric characters he encountered on his travels. Many of the stories were about Jock, the runt of the litter who became the bravest of hunters and most resourceful of companions.

Much later still, in 1907, and encouraged by his friend Rudyard Kipling, FitzPatrick published the tales. His book, *Jock of the Bushveld*, became an immediate bestseller and has since enthralled generations of youngsters.

Today a number of commemorative plaques and cairns can be seen at various points along the old transport routes. Most notable of these trails is, perhaps, the game-viewing Voortrekker Road that leads from the Kruger park's Pretoriuskop camp south-eastwards and past many of the well-known early landmarks, including Ship Mountain. Under development, too, is the Ox-wagon Trail, which also passes through the Kruger, following the original transport-riders' track from Lydenburg to Delagoa Bay (now Maputo). Hikers walk alongside and occasionally ride in an ox-wagon, outspanning at night in authentic fashion.

The veld at last light

Game-viewing

This is of course how one spends most of one's waking hours in the Kruger. Some suggestions to help make the holiday as enjoyable as possible:

✫ The Kruger is low-lying country, and can be uncomfortably warm and humid in summer. Most of the wildlife tends to rest up during the heat of the day, and so do the majority of visitors. Best times to set off on your drives are the early mornings (first light, up to 10h30) and late afternoons (15h30 to dusk). Conversely, winter mornings can be cold, and you'll need warm clothing.

✫ Before starting out, decide where your particular interests lie and what you would like to see. Elephant, lion, leopard; croc and hippo; giraffe; zebra; birds of prey – each species has its favourite haunts. Arm yourself with a good map, and a guidebook containing a game distribution list. These will be available from the rest-camp's shop, together with a useful array of specialist publications describing the Kruger's wildlife in detail.

✫ Also on sale is a checklist of the park's 300 tree species. Many of the more prominent individual specimens you'll see during your drives have been numbered to correspond with the listed items.

✫ Generally, waterholes are more rewarding than the exploratory drive. One has to be patient, but there's always something to be seen – a hornbill, a mongoose, perhaps a brace of warthog – and sooner or later the larger and rarer animals will be on parade. There are plenty of waterholes to choose from; two of the more pleasant are the Orpen dam (near Tshokwane) and the Mlondozi dam (near Lower Sabie), each of which has a shady viewing point complete with chairs.

✫ The chances of spotting lion – most commonly seen in the central region – are better just after sunrise than at other times.

✫ If you do have a choice of vehicle, bear in mind that a minibus is ideally suited for game-viewing.

✫ Take along more than one pair of binoculars, if possible one for each member of the family or party. Having to share – especially when something really special comes into view – can cause irritation.

✫ As in any public place, visitors are asked to observe a few basic rules and a number of less formal conventions in the interests of safety, health, the convenience and comfort of others and for the protection of the environment:

Do stick to the speed limits. If you exceed them you won't see much game, and will risk collision with a crossing animal. Remember that game has right of way.

Do remember to take anti-malaria pills. The disease, transmitted by two species of anopheles mosquito, has been largely but not entirely eradicated and one can still contract it during the wet summer months. The early symptoms are similar to those of influenza. There's little risk if properly treated, but obviously prevention is better than cure. Tablets are available at the Kruger's gates and camps, though doctors recommend that the course be started before you arrive.

Don't throw cigarettes (or any litter for that matter) from the car, especially in the dry winter months. The fire hazard is very real, and the consequences of carelessness can be truly disastrous.

Don't alight from your vehicle in an undesignated area. Picnic sites, water-holes and viewing points are clearly marked, everywhere else is a no-go area. This is wild country, and although some of the game is thoroughly accustomed to and nonchalant about the human presence, appearances can be deceptive: that lazy lion basking at the roadside can spring to lethal life within a split second.

Don't feed the animals. If a baboon gets used to easy pickings he'll become a nuisance – and possibly a danger to other travellers – and may have to be shot.

Do stick to the roads; don't drive down firebreaks or closed routes. If you do so and the car breaks down, you'll be stranded without any guarantee of early rescue.

There is a full list of do's and don'ts on the entrance permit.

Wilderness trails

Most visitors to the Kruger see the park in comfort, through the windows of the family car or combi. Some, though, want a closer and more intimate experience of one of Africa's most splendid reserves and, for these, six wilderness trails have been established. These foot safaris are led by rangers who know a great deal about the ways of the wild and are able and most willing to share their knowledge.

There's nothing competitive or challenging about these walks: they are designed simply to stimulate the mind and the eye, to provide enjoyment, relaxation and good companionship, and they tend to be undemanding, go-where-you-will affairs. The ranger will be guided in his choice of route by the character and collective energy of his charges, and he will lead them wherever mood and interest dictate, stopping now and again, perhaps to examine a flower, a tree, an insect, a herd of antelope, or to take in an especially lovely vista, and to talk about the lore of the wilderness. He has an intimate knowledge of the countryside, and of the ways of the wild.

Accommodation is fairly rudimentary but it has the basics: bedding, food and utensils are provided; one takes one's own liquid refreshment. Evenings spent in conversation and anecdote, around the camp-fire with the bright stars and the sounds of the veld all around, are times to be savoured and remembered.

The trails are:

☆ The Wolhuter (named after a local hero, ranger Harry Wolhuter, who in 1903 killed a marauding, full-grown lion with his sheath-knife) in the southern region. This trail is notable for its large herds of game, its rarer mammals (roan, sable, reedbuck) and its rhino and lion. Base camp; thatched A-frame huts.

☆ The Bushman, south of the Wolhuter (see above) and an hour's drive from Berg-en-Dal. Pleasant base camp of thatched huts; environment and game similar to the Wolhuter; special attraction is the proliferation of Bushman paintings.

☆ The Olifants, in the central region. Base camp pleasantly sited on the riverbank. Flattish grasslands attract large herds; elephant, crocodile and hippo in riverine areas.

☆ The Metsi-Metsi, in the central region, near Satara and Tshokwane, a densely populated game region. Four days; base camp of A-frame huts.

☆ The Nyalaland, in the far north, near the Luvuvhu River. Base camp sited among striking kuduberry trees; superb game, floral and bird region (see page 87).

☆ The Sweni Wilderness trail. Completed in 1990, offers A-frame huts. Prolific wild life including many lion. East of Satara.

☆ The Balule. This is a five-day, four-night hike in the bush; more arduous than the others and, according to one writer, 'the nearest we have

to a true wilderness trail; it surely has to be the best trail in Africa'. In contrast to the other trails, hikers do not return to their base camp every night.

WEST OF THE KRUGER

The Kruger National Park takes up a large portion of the Eastern Transvaal's Lowveld region but by no means all of it. Sprawled along the park's western boundaries are Timbavati, Klaserie and the Sabi-Sand game reserve, three of the world's largest privately owned game sanctuaries. Beyond them, to the west, are the foothills of the Escarpment, the pleasant towns of Barberton and Nelspruit, and some of South Africa's most fertile farmlands.

The private reserves

Each of these huge areas comprises a number of farms and independent game properties, some of whose owners have combined resources to create and operate commercial camps. Each is different, with its own distinctive personality, but all are professionally run, supremely comfortable, tend to be expensive, and they provide, at a price, the holiday of a lifetime.

Mala-Mala is perhaps the best known: it offers the ultimate in game-viewing luxury, and its reputation extends far beyond South Africa's borders. The ingredients of its success: a spacious Out-of-Africa (but air-conditioned) bush lodge, excellent cuisine and five-star service; neatly thatched and luxuriously appointed chalets (two bathrooms, fitted carpets) nestling among shade trees and trim lawns, the whole complex set in a wilderness area that boasts the largest concentration of big game on the continent. Special mention should be made of the Sable Suite, a self-contained and ultra-luxurious little complex next to the camp proper, designed for groups of up to 16. It has its own lounge, pool and *boma* (outside dining enclosure), though guests can use all the facilities at the main lodge. Ideal for big-business getaways.

Mala-Mala has room for about 50 people, and there are ten rangers to look after them, which, if you work it out, amounts to very personalized service indeed. The rangers are courteous, helpful, knowledgeable, and always with you. The clientele, obviously, falls into the upper income bracket, many of the guests jetting in from Europe and North America for a brief but memorable taste of Africa as it once was.

THE BIG FIVE

Lion, elephant, rhino, buffalo, leopard – these, for most visitors, are at the top of the game-viewing list, and with patience and a little luck you'll be able to spot the first four in the Kruger.

The fifth species, leopard, is very hard to find: it's a shy, solitary, secretive creature, a nocturnal hunter that hides away during the daylight hours among the rocks of an outcrop or in dense bush or in the branches of a tree. Occasionally it will venture into open ground, but is still difficult to discern: its tawny-yellow body is spotted with black rosettes, creating a colour pattern that enables it to blend beautifully into its surroundings. There are just under a thousand leopards in the Kruger.

In somewhat greater evidence are the park's 250 or so cheetah, fastest of all land mammals, able to reach sprint speeds of around 75 km/h in short, explosively dramatic bursts of movement. Their numbers are few because of competition from the larger predators, and the fact that the Kruger doesn't have too many patches of clear grassland, which this plains-loving species needs in order to run down its prey. But it hunts in the open, usually just after dawn or at dusk, so it is more often seen than its cousin. The two are sometimes mistaken for each other, especially in bad light and at a distance, but in fact they're quite dissimilar. Cheetah have longer legs than leopard, smaller heads with rounded ears and, perhaps their most distinguishing feature, 'tear-marks' running down from eyes to mouth.

LION The park is sanctuary to about 1 500 of these big cats, territorial animals that live in prides of up to six, though larger groups of a dozen and more are sometimes found. Occasionally, too, one chances upon the hunt and kill, but this is a rare spectacle indeed. Generally the lion is a nocturnal predator, its prey ranging from massive giraffe and buffalo down to the small mammals.

The hunt is a complex process, one in which the female plays the leading role: the male tends to be somewhat indolent. But his strength, when he chooses to use it, is phenomenal. He is the largest of Africa's carnivores, fully a metre high at the regally maned shoulder, has a mass of 200 kg or more and can break a wildebeest's neck with one swipe of his massive paw. He is, too, able to show a quite remarkable turn of speed, covering 100 m in just four to six seconds.

Lion have no natural enemies, but mortality is high among the prides, the biggest toll taken by starvation among the cubs during lean times, and by a number of parasite-borne diseases that affect cubs in poor condition. Lions are also prone to injury during the hunt, often from the horns of buffalo, from the lethal kick of a giraffe and, oddly enough, from too-familiar contact with the humble porcupine – the needle-sharp quills will pierce the flesh to set up an infection that spreads, debilitates and leads to slow death from starvation.

Kruger's lion are to be found throughout the park but are most common in the central areas, in the general vicinity of Satara camp, and in the south-eastern region, between Lower Sabie and Crocodile Bridge.

ELEPHANTS in the Kruger number about 8 000 and are renowned for the size of their tusks – one recent count revealed more than 20 individuals bearing tusks of 60 kg in weight. They are scattered throughout the park, usually grouped in herds, and 'tame' enough for you to approach to within a few metres. Herds of 100 or more individuals are often found, but they tend to be smaller in the south of the park, comprising about 30 individuals. Solitary bulls or bull groups are also seen. Approach elephants with caution, don't make any unnecessary movement or noise, and be prepared to drive on quickly if warning signs appear – if, that is, one of the adults turns head on to you, raises its trunk and flaps its ears.

Elephant, like lion, have no natural enemies – except man. And in Africa, that's enemy enough. Poaching has been a serious problem throughout the continent in recent years, depleting, and in the case of some countries, seriously endangering the national herds. During the past 15 years Africa's elephant population has fallen from 1,3 million to about 600 000. The recent international ban on the ivory trade – the Convention on Trade in Endangered Species, signed in October 1989 by 103 nations – should slow if not halt the tragic decline. Indeed, within three months of the embargo ivory prices had plunged from US $144 to just $5 a kilo.

The ban itself has been the subject of a lot of heart-searching, and it has its critics among naturalists. Countries like South Africa and its northern neighbour Zimbabwe have a fine record when it comes to conservation in general and the management of elephant populations in particular, and their elephant herds, far from diminishing over the years, have remained healthy and large, to the point where they have to be periodically culled – reduced in size. Until 1989 ivory from the culled carcasses was sold on the open market, the proceeds devoted to schemes that help preserve the subcontinent's priceless wildlife legacy. That source of income has now disappeared, and the game parks of southern Africa are the poorer for it.

Ivory is a sensitive issue. So too is culling, an unpleasant process but an ecologically necessary one.

Elephants can be incredibly destructive: a single adult can consume up to 300 kg of grass, shoots and stripped bark each day and will topple a tree to get at the few tender leaves from the crown. The consequences for the environment can – if the herd is allowed to become too large for the area to which it is confined – be devastating, posing a threat both to the elephant's wellbeing and to the survival of other species. Surplus animals simply have to be killed off in order to protect the habitat.

BUFFALO This large and powerful relative of the antelopes, distinguished by its 800-kg bulk and by the bony boss at the top of the head from which its great horns curve upward, is a common resident of the Kruger. About 25 000 are distributed throughout the park, many of them congregated in herds of well over 200.

Treat the buffalo with respect: he may appear to be docile, but hunters regard him as one of the most dangerous and cunning of Africa's game species. Solitary males, exiled from the herd after losing a mating battle and often seen close to streams and waterholes, can be especially bad-tempered and unpredictable. Ordinary visitors to the park, though, are not at risk, provided they stick to a simple set of rules (see page 92).

RHINO are relative newcomers to the Kruger – or rather, they became locally extinct some decades ago and have only recently been reintroduced to the region.

The first few white rhino were brought in from Zululand in 1961, a translocation that proved so successful that a further 300 were imported ten years later. Incidentally, the prefix 'white' is misleading: the animal is in fact a dark-grey colour, and the term is thought to be a corruption of the Afrikaans word *wyd*, or wide, a reference to its square-lipped mouth – an evolutionary adaptation to its grazing habits. It could also refer to the animal's appearance after a mud- or dustbath.

By contrast, the black rhino (again the term has little meaning, invented simply to distinguish it from its cousin) is a browser, its pointed mouth well suited to feeding on the leaves and branchlets that comprise most of its diet. It is also the smaller of the two species, reaching a mass of about 1 500 kg, but should be viewed with caution, especially but not exclusively in the breeding season: it has poor eyesight, is easily provoked by unfamiliar sounds or smells, and has been known to charge without warning. It is also astonishingly agile for its bulk, capable of speeds up to 45 km/h and of wheeling with lightning speed.

The buffalo: docile in appearance, dangerous when threatened

Almost as famous is Sabi-Sabi, renowned for its game-viewing but also for its good food and its marvellously sociable evenings. A typical menu will offer an impressive selection of fresh salads, four meat dishes (including venison, of course), a 'ranger's platter' of cheeses, home-made bread and sherry trifle to finish. It's the traditional braaivleis (barbecue) dinner, though, that one remembers. This is held in the reed-enclosed *boma*, fire-lit and filled with good cheer and animated chat. The rangers, who join you for the meals, are young and, for all their familiarity with the bush and dedication to their work, full of fun. Shangaan women provide the intermezzo, performing tribal dances and singing with superb gusto. When the dancing is over they resume, somewhat incongruously, their main role and serve food. The atmosphere is informal, cheerful and entertaining; the evenings invariably turn into a roaring party.

Much of one's day at Sabi-Sabi, all but the hottest hours, is spent in a Land-Rover in the company of a ranger-tracker team. These trips provide endless fascination: the team's bush-craft skills are astonishing, the search exacting as one follows, say, the spoor of lion; the climax – first sight of the pride – exhilarating. There are also strategically placed hides overlooking a water-hole and stream and, for the more adventurous, guided walks through the bush.

The other lodges have similar routines, and are equally attractive and hospitable, though each has its own style and special drawcards. Ngala, in the southern Timbavati, operates its own three-aircraft charter service to ferry guests to and from camp (others of course arrive by road). M'bali lodge comprises 'habi-tents' over-looking the Nhlaralumi River – canvas-roofed hides built on stilts and reminiscent of Kenya's famed Tree-Tops. Tanda Tula, also in the Tim-bavati reserve, is one of the smallest, an un-pretentious cluster of buildings catering for just 14 people at a time, and is run by Pat Donald-son, a man with a 'big' personality, a feeling for the real Africa, and an acute perception of what one wants out of a bush holiday. Londolozi is world famous for both its excellence and its highly successful efforts to combine tourism with game conservation and good land management. Londolozi's Dave Varty is internationally known for his study of, and films on, the reserve's leopards.

Gambule is a brand new game lodge, and unusual in that it's a joint venture between the national state of KaNgwane's park's board, the Mpakeni tribe and the Club Africa Lodge and Travel Group. It is tucked away in KaNgwane territory just outside the Kruger's south-western boundary within the 20 000-ha Mthethomu-sha game reserve, and is unique in its setting: high atop a large granite buttress. Lovely views, good game country.

THE PRECIOUS LAND Fairly expensive though they may be, the original impetus behind the establishment of these lodges wasn't financial gain but, rather, a genuine desire to conserve, and in many cases to restore, the indigenous animal and plant life of the region, to protect the land from the encroachment of alien species and from the depredations of man, and indeed from the very presence of man in large numbers.

The desire is a dedication in some instances – the Varty brothers of Londolozi, for example, have undertaken what amounts to a crusade to preserve their natural heritage. The job is a tough one, because the countryside is under simultaneous assault from a number of different, though related, quarters. There are the pressures of population growth and land hunger, a proliferation of roads, tracks and powerlines, and the spread of pollution. The game is confined to specific areas and, despite the enormous size of the reserves, it can no longer move freely with the seasons, which in turn upsets the infinitely delicate balance of predator and prey.

In short, the entire ecosystem is under threat, and to minimize this, to sustain the game, to root out the dense, choking patches of alien bush and return the land to its pristine condition, is a hugely expensive business. Hence the lodges, and the high rates that visitors pay.

AMONG THE FOOTHILLS
The countryside west of the Kruger and the private game reserves, on the plains proper and on the lower slopes of the Escarpment, is given over to woodland plantations and to intensive farming: the soils are rich, the climate warm, often humid, and the land yields marvellously bountiful harvests of bananas and other subtropical fruits, winter vegetables, nuts, tea, coffee and much else.

Barberton

Set in the attractive De Kaap valley well south of the Escarpment and close to the Swaziland border, Barberton is the oldest of the region's towns and one of the earliest of South Africa's gold-mining centres.

A prospector named Auguste Robert, better known as 'French Bob', discovered the first of the reefs in 1883, attracting fortune-seekers in their thousands, among them one Graham Barber and his cousins Fred and Harry, who found and worked Barber's Reef and gave their name to the place.

In its heyday, in the mid-1880s, Barberton was a large and lively settlement, a typical Wild West-type boom town of corrugated iron shanties, music halls and hotels, scores of drinking dens, two stock exchanges and 20 000 people – a citizenry that included almost as many fringe characters as honest diggers. Among them were adventurers, con-artists and various other types of fly-by-night, dealers in liquor and fraudulent stock, and the inevitable ladies of pleasure: Florrie, the Golden Dane and the inimitable Cockney Liz, who would of an evening, in the bar of the Phoenix (still a going concern, but now much quieter), auction herself to the highest bidder. In 1885 the rich Sheba Reef was discovered 16 km away and many of the miners moved to the new camp, which they called Eureka City. This, too, boasted its canteens and vaudeville halls and, in addition, had its own racetrack.

Then the 'Barberton Bubble' burst. The gold was solid enough, but too much money had chased the limited resources, and an exodus to the giant, newly-discovered Witwatersrand goldfields (see page 41) began in 1887.

Eureka City is now billed as a 'ghost town', but in reality it amounts to little more than a rather sad scatter of overgrown ruins. Of the old Barberton more remains, and the town is a pleasant place to visit. A must when you're in the area is the Belhaven House museum, restored and preserved as an especially fine example of turn-of-the-century elegance and good taste. The Barberton Museum (in the public library, Pilgrim Street) has displays of the early days, collectively entitled 'From the Valley of Death to the Valley of Gold'.

Other attractions include the Barberton nature reserve and its contiguous neighbour, the 56 000-ha Songimvelo nature reserve.

The countryside around Barberton is flattish, without too much to recommend it to the casual eye, but the hills are not far away and there are some lovely drives in the area – to the Pioneer Reef, to the waterfall at the Agnes mine, and across the Swaziland border (passports required, but otherwise the formalities are minimal) to the woodland magic of Havelock and Pigg's Peak.

The road to the latter is a bit rugged, but scenically spectacular; at Pigg's Peak itself there's a luxury hotel and casino complex set in lovely surrounds.

Lone Tree Hill near Barberton is one of the finest hang-gliding launch points in the country; Tel. (01314) 3151. To the east, around Komatipoort (a sleepy little town, and in summer one of the hottest in South Africa) there's fine sport for tiger-fishing enthusiasts (contact local police for advice on the best stretches of water). Incidentally, the Mozambique Café in Komatipoort is reputed to serve the most tasty prawn dishes you'll find anywhere.

The Nelspruit area

North of Barberton is Nelspruit, capital of the Eastern Transvaal and a pleasant, prosperous-looking place of clean-lined buildings, wide streets and tree-garlanded suburbs. It's the last major centre on the main west-east highway from Johannesburg and Pretoria (the N4) and the jumping-off point for tourists arriving by both road and air (it has a small but modern airport).

There are good hotels and restaurants in and around town (for a meal out, try the Arkansas Spur or the Costa do Sol), and some sophisticated shops; curios, handwoven rugs, carvings, leather goods are on sale in specialist outlets and the larger stores; fresh produce in season is sold by the many farm stalls along the region's roads.

Among Nelspruit's other attractions are the Lowveld Botanic Gardens, one of eight branches of the National Botanic Gardens (see Kirstenbosch, page 289), sited on the banks of the Crocodile River and haven for a fascinating variety of Lowveld floral species – about 500 of them. Of interest – to the layman as well as botanist – is the adjacent Lowveld Herbarium. A walk through the gardens will bring you to the Cascades viewsite, a platform overlooking rock and river.

Quite delightful, too, is the countryside around Nelspruit, especially along the immensely fertile Crocodile valley. This is the second largest of South Africa's citrus-growing regions. Bright green, scented groves of oranges are everywhere. Scattered among them are fields of subtropical fruits, plantations of pine, wattle and eucalyptus and a splendid abundance of other trees and shrubs, indigenous and exotic, to delight the eye, including the lovely Pride of De Kaap (*Bauhinia galpinii*) and the fragrant yellow-blossomed *Acacia karroo*, which blooms just after Christmas.

TO THE NORTH of Nelspruit is White River, a pretty little farming centre in the in-between region as you pass from Lowveld to Escarpment, in some of the country's richest agricultural land. More than 3 000 smallholders cultivate the soil within a 10-km radius of town, growing, among other things, flowers and tropical fruits. If you're staying in the general area (it has a fine selection of country hotels and guest lodges; see page 107), you'll find White River both convenient and excellent for shopping. Excellent fishing in the Danie Joubert and Longmere dams; 4 km south of town is the Orange Winery (open weekdays, guided tours).

TO THE WEST of Nelspruit, 70 km along the N4, are the charming twin villages of Waterval Boven and Waterval Onder – respectively 'above' and 'below' the waterfall. The falls in question are the magnificent cascades of the Elands River, well worth visiting for their splendour and indeed for the scenic beauty of terrain that marks the abrupt transition from Transvaal Highveld to Lowveld.

The area, too, is steeped in railway history. Paul Kruger, president of the land-locked Transvaal Republic in the 1880s and 1890s, was profoundly suspicious of the British at the Cape and in Natal and determined on his own route to the Indian Ocean. He commissioned a line that was finally completed after a decade of setbacks and, for the construction workers, of tragedy, in 1895. It is said that one man died – of fever, drink or from the ravages of wild animals – for every sleeper laid on the track, and of all the sections on the 700-km route this was probably the most difficult. From Waterval Boven the railroad plunges down a dramatic

1:20 gradient (this necessitated a racked, or cogged, line) to the Elands River valley, along which it passes by way of a 213-m-long tunnel.

If you're heading back to Nelspruit from here, take the secondary road through the enchanting Schoemanskloof valley. This loops north and then west before rejoining the main highway after 60 km, and it's a pleasant drive indeed, especially towards evening when the sun slants gently onto the valley floor, creating an infinite subtlety of colour.

SUDWALA CAVES Not far away from the junction of the two roads – a little to the north off the R539 – is a complex of caverns hollowed out of the Mankelekele ('crag-on-crag') massif. The network is thought to burrow its way through the dolomite rock for 30 km and more, but visitors may explore, or be guided through, just 600 m or so of the complex – which in fact is quite extensive enough to reveal the caves as a magnificent tourist attraction.

The complex comprises a series of linked chambers festooned with cream-coloured (though some are reddish or brownish, from the iron and manganese in the limestone)

The Montrose Falls, west of Nelspruit

stalactites and stalagmites, many with fanciful but highly descriptive names – The Weeping Madonna, Lot's Wife, The Space Rocket, etc. Most impressive of the chambers is the PR Owen Hall, a natural theatre complete with sloping-floor 'stalls' rising to a 'gallery' 37 m in diameter. The ceiling is dome-like, the acoustics so good that the hall has been used for choral recordings and public concerts. For some reason, as yet not fully explained, the air in the caves remains at a constant temperature of 20 °C, day and night throughout the year.

Sudwala's surrounds are just as impressive: the entrance area and flanking cliff-like slopes are cloaked in evergreen forest and a wealth of colourful indigenous flora, including yellow aloe, white pear blossom and the scarlet kaffirboom to name but a few.

Below the entrance is a pleasant resort offering comfortable accommodation, à la carte fare, tennis, swimming, and a healthy selection of nature walks.

Nearby is the Dinosaur Park, an unusual and fascinating open-air display featuring life-size replicas of the giant extinct reptiles that ruled the earth around 250 million years ago. The setting is equally primitive: flora includes the primeval cycad – the 'living fossil' that resembles both a fern and a palm and whose origins can be traced back 180 million years, to the Mesozoic era. Cycads, of which there are nine genera and about 100 species worldwide, are vigilantly protected in South Africa.

THE NORTHERN REGIONS

For ease of description, let's assume you're on a motoring holiday, driving northward along and beyond the Escarpment. The route you'd take is the R36, though the Abel Erasmus pass (see page 83), over the Olifants River – wide here, with pools in which hippo and crocodile are often seen – and on, for a long 150 km or so, to the town of Tzaneen, the main commercial centre of the immensely fertile and very lovely Letaba district.

The town (named after the local baTzaneng people) started as a research station for tropical and subtropical crops, and later became the headquarters of the anti-malaria campaign which, in the 1930s, led to the virtual eradication of the disease, paving the way for the creation of a thriving agricultural economy in the region.

This is largely tea-producing country, the rich, intensively irrigated plantations sprawling to the far distances and the air, in the long harvesting months from September through to May, aromatic with the fresh leaves. Not just tea though: the region has a tropical feel about it, a quality acquired from its position at the foot of the Transvaal plateau, its high rainfall and soils that sustain citrus and avocados, mangoes and bananas, lichis and pawpaws, tomatoes, coffee, macadamia and pecan nuts, cotton and winter vegetables. Flowering trees are everywhere, and huge timber plantations clothe the hills and valleys.

West of Tzaneen

A little to the west of the town are the misty, thickly-wooded heights of the Magoebaskloof, accessible via a good tarred road, which rises some 600 m in a short 6-km stretch. The name is taken from the late-19th century Batlou tribal chieftain Makgoba, who refused to pay taxes to the white settler administration and led 500 of his people into hiding in the dense upland reaches of the kloof. He was eventually – after more than a year – tracked down by a government-recruited Swazi impi and beheaded. Summary injustice, as it were.

Most of the uplands are the domain of the forestry department, much of it under plantation, but some substantial patches of natural woodland remain. Indeed, the Transvaal's largest indigenous forests are in the area. Perhaps the loveliest expanse is the Woodbush, a few kilometres north of Magoebaskloof's summit (1 370 m) – it's a short drive to the forest station, but one that offers superb views of the Lowveld to the east. Woodbush is haven to magnificent redwoods, to giant 40-m-high ironwoods, to cabbage trees, yellowwoods, red stinkwoods. A place for walking, and for communing with restful spirits in the deep green silence. Just to the east of the station are the:

DEBEGENI FALLS, entrancing in their forest setting and in the surge and clarity of their waters. It's a pleasant spot to picnic. And farther east still, close to Tzaneen's town limits, is more water in the attractive shape of the Fanie Botha dam and its attendant nature reserve, a 1 200-ha expanse of lake and grassland surrounded by pine plantations. The setting is splendid, more reminiscent of the great North American wilderness areas than of Africa. The dam is popular among anglers for its black bass, tilapia and yellowfish; and among boating enthusiasts and bird-watchers. Altogether, there are some 150 species of bird in the reserve, including tropical waterfowl and the fish eagle.

Farther to the west, along the road to Pietersburg, is the hamlet of:

HAENERTSBURG, near which is an especially lovely farm on which azaleas and cherries are cultivated in three large nurseries. In springtime the displays are quite breathtaking, but check the exact flowering period – it varies, depending on how good the rains have been – before visiting: Tel. (0152222), and ask for 1823. Also a delight to the eye is the Haenertsburg Spring Fair, which coincides with the Cherry Blossom Festival (arts and crafts as well as flowers). Information: (0152222), ask for 83.

North of Tzaneen

The road leads through the colourful little village of Duiwelskloof ('Devil's Cleft' or pass) and then, beyond, to the turn-off to Modjadji, realm of the mysterious Rain Queen.

The best-selling author Rider Haggard based his novel *She* on the legends that wreathe Modjadji – on her powers over man and the elements, and on her immortality. The original Queen, it is thought, was a 16th century princess of the Karanga people of what is now Zimbabwe, who fled before her enemies, southward across the Limpopo to found the Lobedu clan in a part of the north-eastern Transvaal famed for its giant cycad plants. She and her successors, guardians of the rain-magic, were respected, at one time even feared throughout southern Africa: even the great warrior king Shaka held her in awe, and she and the Lobedu remained unscathed during the bitter wars of the black peoples in the early 1800s.

There is a Rain Queen still – the title is ritualistically and mystically passed down through the generations – though the image is more romantic than the reality. She lives in seclusion, in her royal residence on the slope of the hill, and she may be visited by the favoured few. In times of drought many people, white as well as black, ask for her intercession.

And her domain still encompasses the cycad forest, where literally thousands of these ancient and now-precious plants thrive –

indeed, this is the largest concentration of *Encephalartos transvenosus* (also known as the Modjadji palm) in the world. There are pleasant picnic and barbecue facilities in the forest reserve; cycads may be purchased at a nursery about 5 km to the south.

South of Tzaneen

Principal features of the area are the Ebenezer dam (picnicking, boating, fishing, wind-surfing) in the Letaba river valley; George's Valley (George was an early road-builder who loved the hills, and made gratuitous detours so that travellers could enjoy the finest of views), and the splendid New Agatha state forests, through which the Rooikat nature trail makes its circular and entrancing way.

The forest station serves as jumping-off point for the:

WOLKBERG WILDERNESS AREA, a 22 000-ha expanse of peak and valley, forest and grassland which lies a little farther to the south, beckoning the hiker and lover of untouched Africa. The highest point, Ararat, is 2 050 m above sea level; the countryside wild and lonely. Game is sparse in the Wolkberg – much of it was shot out years ago by the dagga (cannabis) growers who hid in the valleys, away from prying eyes, and lived off the land – though duiker, reedbuck and klipspringer can sometimes be seen. Leopard and the rare brown hyena are also present, as are several types of snake, including the dangerous berg adder, the puff adder and the black mamba.

A lot more rewarding is the birdlife: the reserve is home to a great many species, including Egyptian goose, black eagle, rock kestrel, Goliath heron, white stork and hamerkop.

The last-mentioned is also known as the 'bird of doom', a large, curious-looking creature much feared by the more superstitious of the rural people, though the reason isn't too clear. It may have something to do with its cry, a high-pitched, eerie, tormented whistle. Hamerkops are commonly seen standing still in shallow water, watchful for the frogs and fish they feed on, or searching the muddy water's edge for smaller fry. But for all its apparent awkwardness, the bird is one of nature's most accomplished architects: its nest is a large and ingenious affair, nothing much to look at from the outside but the dimensions are spacious.

The interior, domed and neatly plastered with mud, is divided into three chambers (the lowest level is a concealed-entrance 'reception area', the middle for fledglings, the top for the adults), the whole edifice so strongly built that it can bear the weight of a grown man.

For the rest, the Wolkberg is known for its mists, its clear, cool streams, its rugged mountain slopes and for its many waterfalls. These, and especially the Thabina, on the Mohlapitse River, are certainly worth more than a passing glance. Visitors to the area need a permit (from the State Forester) and the rules are strict: no fires, no fishing, no soap or detergents in the streams.

East of Tzaneen

The region is dominated by the Murchison range of hills, where payable gold was discovered (by 'French Bob' of Barberton fame: see page 97) in 1888. Thousands of claims were pegged, the small town of Leydsdorp established and a 330-km railway began to snake its way north from Komatipoort in the southeastern Lowveld.

But the seams soon gave out, work on the railway stopped (the project, called the Selati line had in any case been plagued by greed and sharp practice; it was belatedly completed in 1922) and Leydsdorp became a ghost town (though there's still a lot of mining in the area – of mica and of the world's largest deposits of the strategic metal antimony). One relic of the old diggers' days, apart from Leydsdorp itself, is the huge, hollow and renowned baobab tree which once served as a pub for the thirsty prospectors. It is recorded that more than a dozen men would huddle *inside* its trunk to take their tipple.

THE HANS MERENSKY RESERVE North of the Murchison range is an island in the Letaba River from which a thermal spring rises at a warm and constant temperature. The river's southern bank is part of the Hans Merensky nature reserve, 5 200 ha of fairly level terrain (except along the eastern boundary, where leopard hunt in the Black Hills) covered by typical Lowveld vegetation: a mix of mopane, grassland and combretum woodland with scatters of weeping boer-bean, jackalberry and red bush-willow.

The game population includes giraffe, the stately sable antelope, zebra, eland, kudu, tsessebe and Sharpe's grysbok.

The river, its hippo pool, the thermal spring and the reserve are a splendid setting for the resort that has been established there and which is called, for obvious reasons, Eiland. The resort offers excellent accommodation: 100-plus self-contained rondavels (bathroom, fully equipped kitchen, some units with lounge/dining room), all thoughtfully laid out among the tree-shaded lawns to give you a welcome degree of privacy. There are also mineral pools, Hidro Spa, a hotel, a licensed restaurant, entertainment hall, tennis, fishing, horse-riding, shops and, of course, the mineral-rich pools in which you can wallow.

Casual visitors are welcome in the reserve: you can't take your car in, but there are bus tours, guided walks, two- and three-day nature trails, and trips to the open-air museum. This last is a re-creation of a typical Tsonga village, enlivened by demonstrations of pottery-making, weaving and woodcraft. The Kruger Park is an hour's drive away.

THE FAR NORTH AND VENDA

A great many South Africans travel up the national highway (the N1) from the Witwatersrand to take their holidays in a part of the country often ignored by the overseas tourist. Some of them go farther, turning eastward through the culturally fascinating and once – during the 'Grand Apartheid' years – independent region of Venda to enter the Kruger National Park through its northernmost gates.

The Great North Road

Along the N1 there are pleasant little towns and resort areas, and a lot to see and do. Places of interest include:

WARMBATHS The town, 93 km from Pretoria, is renowned for its curative springs; for water therapy, the Hidro Spa compares with the best in the world. On offer: underwater massage pool; well appointed Overspa complex and water playground; hot-water outdoor pool; pleasant restaurants; cosmetic, health and slimming salons. A small nature reserve adjoins the resort. Accommodation ranges from a good hotel and luxurious and fully-equipped chalets to more modest apartments. It's very much a 'people-place', busy and at times crowded.

THE TRANS-ORANJE BIRD SANCTUARY, near the small centre of Naboomspruit. The reserve has an impressively diverse range of both indigenous and exotic species. Close by (10 km southwest of town) is the 5 000-ha Mosdene private reserve, home to 450 different kinds of bird.

THE POTGIETERSRUS NATURE RESERVE, a somewhat unusual wildlife enterprise: it's part of the National Zoological Gardens, and serves as a breeding unit for exotic wildlife species – including the blackbuck and hog deer from Asia, banteng wild cattle and mouflon wild sheep, South American llama and pygmy hippo – as well as for indigenous South African fauna (white and black rhino). Visitors are most welcome.

PIETERSBURG, the Northern Transvaal's principal town, and a most pleasant place. Features of tourist interest in the area include:
✩ The art collection at the municipal offices; the open-air exhibition of historical relics (steam locomotive, farming implements and so forth) in Landdros Street; and the open-air display of abstract art at the northern entrance to town. There is also an excellent little photographic museum, housed in the restored and converted Dutch Reformed church.
✩ Nine km south of town, on the Chuniespoort/Burgersfort road, is the Bakong Malapa open-air museum – a kraal in which traditional skills are displayed. Also rock paintings, Iron Age remains; conducted tours, picnic area.
✩ The Pietersburg nature reserve, close to town, is one of the largest municipal sanctuaries in the Transvaal, haven for white rhino, eland, red hartebeest, blesbok, gemsbok, impala and Burchell's zebra. Accommodation at adjacent Union Park (fully equipped chalets; caravan/camping ground).

THE CITRUS ESTATES OF ZEBEDIELA, 45 km east of the town of Potgietersrus. They're the largest in South Africa (more than half a million trees, 500 million oranges). Visit at harvest time: August-October for Valencias; April-June for Navels.

THE SOUTPANSBERG range of hills in the far north, between the grasslands of the Pietersburg Plateau and the warm savanna plains of the northern bushveld. The uplands are densely wooded with exotic plantations and natural forest (yellowwood, stinkwood, wild fig, Cape chestnut, waterberry tree, cycad, tree fern, and well watered (some parts enjoy 2 000 mm of rain a year). The attractive bird life includes the crowned and black eagles. There are some lovely scenic drives here, taking in the forest reserve.

In the region south of the town of Louis Trichardt is the Ben Lavin nature reserve: rest camp; game drives and walks; giraffe, zebra, impala, blue wildebeest and prolific birdlife, including Wahlberg's eagle. Accommodation: 4-bed fully equipped lodges (with bathroom); less sophisticated larger huts; caravan/camping ground; tents and stretchers can be hired.

To the west of Louis Trichardt, high on the southern slopes of the Soutpansberg, is Buzzard Mountain Retreat, a small, privately-run enterprise offering pleasant cottages, scenic beauty, and forest and other trails. To the east is the:

HONNET NATURE RESERVE and the Tshipise resort complex, similar to its sister spa in the Hans Merensky nature reserve (see page 101). Tropical setting: floral features include flamboyant, frangipani, jacaranda, bougainvillea, and a 30- by 20-m baobab tree estimated to be 4 500 years old.

Numbered among the game are giraffe, sable, tsessebe, blue wildebeest. Amenities: spa, hotel, self-catering chalets, swimming pools, bowling greens, riding stables; game trails and drives, bus tours, guided horse trails. The Baobab hiking trail winds its way through the reserve.

A little over a kilometre from the resort is the Greater Kuduland Safaris luxury camp, its two bush camps and its 10 000-ha private reserve. On offer are guided game trails, hiking trails, game drives, hunting safaris, swimming, canoeing – all in somewhat exclusive style.

MESSINA, South Africa's northernmost centre, set close to the great and grey Limpopo River (though greater in Kiplingesque legend than in fact) is a town virtually surrounded by its nature reserve, proclaimed to protect the baobabs of the area.

Other tree species number about 350, some not yet identified. Within the reserve are outcrops of what is known as Sand River Gneiss. The rock strata were formed 3 825 million years ago – when the earth itself was still comparatively young – and are among the world's most ancient geological formations.

Some 75 km from Messina, in the Vhembe nature reserve at the confluence of the Limpopo and Shahsi rivers, is:

MAPUNGUBWE HILL, a massive rock feature accessible only by way of a concealed crevice, and a natural fortress that once served as sanctuary for the people of the archeologically important Mapungubwe culture (AD 950-1200). The area is also a magnet for naturalists; the reserve home to lion, leopard, elephant and many other species. Bungalows and tents available.

The country of the Venda

Until 1994 Venda was the smallest of the four states granted independence by the apartheid government. The region, now fully reintegrated into the country as part of the Northern Transvaal, covers 6 500 km^2 and accommodates a population of about half a million.

Money earned by its migrant workers contributes much to the region's income. The remainder comes from mining (copper, coal, magnetite, phosphates, corundum, graphite), the nascent manufacturing industries (textiles, sisal, tea processing), and from agriculture. Fruit, tea and coffee grow well in the red soil and in the high, humid temperatures of summer and during the temperate, frost-free winters. Timber, from indigenous hardwoods and plantations of pine and eucalyptus, is an increasingly profitable export, tourists a significant import. People visit Venda for the lush, bright beauty of the scenery; for the gambling and fun to be had at the country's largest hotel; for easy access to the Kruger National Park, and for a glimpse of an old culture that remains largely intact.

THE PEOPLE The Venda are something of a mystery – perhaps because they don't all share a common ancestry. Most of them are thought to have originated in the Great Lakes region of East Africa, moving in slow migratory waves through the Congo into, and through, present-day Zimbabwe. Some may have crossed the Limpopo as early as the 12th century; others stayed, and shared the power and prosperity of Great Zimbabwe before they, too, moved farther south. These were the Makhwinde group of the Rozwi, who brought with them elements

Venda women with water pots

of Zimbabwean culture (the stone enclosures, for instance) and imposed their unifying authority on the clans already living in what later became the northern Transvaal regions. Recorded history shows them as a tough and independent people, able to resist Boer incursions (and in one instance to annihilate a large Voortrekker settlement), Swazi, Pedi and Tsonga invasions.

CRAFTS Cottage industries add to the collective income – some 3 500 craftspeople ply their trade in Venda – and to the country's attractiveness. The products are generally of a high standard, especially the pottery and woodcarvings. The former is more or less restricted to large, geometrically patterned traditional pots, ornamental rather than functional. The carvings have greater variety, the range including bowls and dishes, kieries, pots, spoons, walking sticks. For the rest, there's basketry and mat-making (raw materials here are sisal, cane, reed, bark, and ivory-palm leaves), and a developing school of ethnic art (painting and, especially, sculpture). When in Thohoyandou, the capital, try to visit Ditike craft centre.

EXPLORING VENDA Small though it is, the region is remarkable both for the variety of its scenery and the beliefs and legends of its people. Probably the most striking of its natural features is Lake Fundudzi, one of the largest in southern Africa, though technically it is not a true lake but rather the product of a massive landslide that occurred aeons ago. Fundudzi is an intriguing place: swathed in myth, lair of the python god of fertility, sinister in its associations with sacrifice. It is sacred to the people of the region.

Water, indeed, is the essence of Venda's upland attractiveness. Streams and waterfalls (the Mahovhohovho and the Phiphidi are the most prominent, but there are many lesser ones) nurture the richly-treed hills of the Soutpansberg, which in one part is called the Thathe Vondo. Here is the Vondo dam (well stocked with bass; visitors welcome) and the Holy Forest, a dense expanse of indigenous woodland which has served as a sacred burial place and which one may look at but not explore. Thermal springs are everywhere. One, at Sagole, is the focal point of a small resort, though perhaps the most beautiful is that at Munwamadi, which is remote and difficult for the casual visitor to locate but worthwhile if one can get there: the water bubbles up through the roots of ancient fig trees, and the setting is magical.

Venda has one national park: the Nwanedi, some 65 km north of Thohoyandou. It offers self-contained chalets, a caravan park, a restaurant and a block of comfortable family rooms.

Two of its principal attractions are the twin dams, Nwanedi and Luphephe, where you can angle for yellowfish, barbel and bream. Game includes white rhino, giraffe, kudu, eland, klipspringer and other buck; lion and cheetah can be seen in enclosures. The rest-camp is shaded by lovely trees; there's a teach-yourself walking trail, and swimming in the natural pool below the waterfall.

Much of what you do and see in Venda is related to the people's spiritual heritage, some of which is only reluctantly revealed to the outsider. There are trained guides to show you around, and if you want to explore the country, you're advised to make use of them.

GETTING AROUND

Day drives

River and waterfall, peak and valley and splendid viewsite – wherever you travel in the Escarpment region you'll find an embarrassment of scenic riches. There is, though, one standard, or at least widely recommended and most pleasant drive called the:

Panorama (or Summit) route, a circular drive with deviations. It varies in its details according to the traveller's preferences and available time, but generally speaking starts from Sabie and takes in: The Mac-Mac Pools and waterfall; The Lisbon Falls; God's Window; The bathing pools in the Blyde River; The Berlin Falls; The flower- and fern-festooned picnic and bathing site at Watervalspruit in the Blyderivierspoort nature reserve (page 81); On through the pine plantations to the crossroads at Vaalhoek (petrol; tearoom); Northwards to Bourke's Luck Potholes and the Blyde River Canyon; Back down to the crossroads, bearing right along the valley of Pilgrim's Creek to Pilgrim's Rest; And on south to Sabie.

For the rest, there are some pleasant scenic drives in the Barberton area and truly superb ones around Waterval Boven and the Schoemanskloof valley in the south-west and, in the north, in the woodland magic of the Magoebaskloof and New Agatha Forest region.

Walks and hikes

The Eastern and Northern Transvaal are a walker's paradise, and an impressive number of formal trails have been established.

Among those in the Escarpment region, two are especially recommended for those with energy and time to spare::

☆ The five-day, 65-km Blyderivierspoort hiking trail starts at God's Window – an unusually formed cleft, at the very edge of the Escarpment, which affords a magnificent view over the eastern lowlands – and then leads you northwards along the rim of the 'Berg', taking in the reserve and the gorge and ending at Swadini, near the Sybrand van Niekerk resort, in the Lowveld. Fairly hard going, but worth every step.

☆ The Fanie Botha trail is longer (79 km), and also takes five days, though there are permutations and one can opt for much shorter routes. The trail meanders from the Ceylon state forest

FISHING AND HIKING: SOME DO'S & DONT'S

The Escarpment and its foothills, and parts of the northern Transvaal, are prime angling areas (yellowfish, tilapia, bream, bass and, above all, trout). There is no closed season, but summer rains tend to discolour many of the streams and pools. Best angling months: March through September.

Fixed spool reels are prohibited; artificial nonspinning (trout) flies are mandatory. Licences are obtainable at a modest fee from major sports outlets. Information: Sabie Rainbow Trout Angling Club, or the Transvaal Division of Nature Conservation (see Advisory, page 109, for addresses).

Hiking: Again, this is excellent walking country (see page 104 and below). Points to note:

☆ The Transvaal trails are very popular, so book well in advance.

☆ Information and detailed route maps are available from the South African Hiking Way Board, Private Bag X447, Pretoria 0001; Tel. (012) 299-9111. Satour publishes a very useful booklet entitled *Follow the Footprints*, available from regional offices (see Advisory).

☆ Take warm clothing (nights can be chilly, especially on the Escarpment) and, in summer, rainwear; a good rucksack (but one that doesn't weigh more than a third of your body mass); woollen socks; strong and well broken-in walking shoes or boots.

☆ Please don't pick wild flowers (all species are protected), and please don't litter.

☆ Don't digress from designated routes: you could get lost, with tragic results.

---

near the town of Sabie, westward to the slopes of Mount Anderson (2 284 m) and then northward to the Mauchsberg (2 114 m), ending up with the Blyderivierspoort trail. Walkers see the Escarpment at its best: the path leads through the oldest and stateliest of the vast pine plantations, which are interspersed here and there with patches of lovely indigenous forest. Along the way there are breathtaking vistas and, for the naturalist, a fine floral diversity (including tree ferns and entrancing displays of flowering plants), a great many different types of butterfly, and some out-of-the-ordinary bird species (among them white stork and crowned eagle).

☆ The 44-km, two-day Nugget trail, along which there are many reminders of the old mining days. For the less ambitious, there's the 2-km Fontana Mine Walk, which crosses Barberton's Indigenous Tree Park (100 species).

☆ In the Waterval Boven area: the Elandskrans two-day circular hike and the shorter, one-day nature walk: waterfalls, rock pools, lovely scenery, labelled indigenous trees, and – unusual – a train ride. The Elandskrans holiday resort (chalets, camping) is at the trailhead.

Among the attractive walking options in the northern region:

☆ In the Hans Merensky nature reserve: walks range from the 1-km Letaba to the 37-km Giraffe route.

☆ In the Tzaneen area: the 11-km Rooikat nature trail leads you through the rugged Wolkberg wilderness (see page 100). There is also the fairly strenuous but very beautiful Magoebaskloof hiking trail, which is divided into three longish sections.

☆ In the Pietersburg-Potgietersrus area: nature trails in the attractive Percy Fyfe reserve; and a moderately demanding 40-km, two-day walk through and around the Pietersburg game park (page 102).

☆ In the far northern and border areas: rewarding short rambles in the Ben Lavin nature reserve (page 102); and in the Soutpansberg (page 102), where a major, 91-km trail has been established (though there are shorter variations, including an 18-km circular walk). The Honnet reserve (page 102) offers 25 km of nature walks and four-hour horse trails.

Tours

A wide variety of attractive packages are on offer from, among others, Thompsons, Rand Coach Tours, Grosvenor, Springbok Atlas, Afro Ventures, Plusbus and Comair. The options and permutations are too numerous to allow any meaningful summary; all one can usefully say here is that both the Escarpment and the Lowveld are well covered, with the emphasis, predictably, on the Kruger National Park. Several tour operators have working arrangements with the prestigious private reserves situated in the big-game country just west of the Kruger (see page 93). Information can be obtained from your travel agent or from the various tour companies.

ADVISORY: EASTERN AND NORTHERN TRANSVAAL

CLIMATE

Summer-rainfall region; generally hot in summer, very hot in the Lowveld. Thunderstorms usually occur in late afternoon and last an hour or so at most. Winter: cold nights and early mornings on the Escarpment; cool nights and warm days in the Lowveld.

MAIN ATTRACTIONS

Game-viewing □ Bird-watching □ Sightseeing □ Scenic drives □ Fine fishing – especially for trout, but also bream, tilapia, yellowfish, bass, barbel – throughout the Escarpment, its foothills and in the Tzaneen area □ Hiking □ Rambling □ Climbing □ Horse riding □ Boating in the dams □ Rock-collecting, especially in the Murchison range □ Swimming: the Escarpment and most Northern Transvaal waters are bilharzia-free; avoid Lowveld rivers and pools; pool bathing at hotels, lodges and resorts □ Golf, bowls, tennis, squash: excellent facilities throughout the region.

Hunting. The Eastern Transvaal Lowveld is splendid big-game country. Year-round hunting facilities are provided by several private reserves, though the cooler months (March through September) are the best. There are strict rules, especially in regard to licences and quotas. The services of professional hunters, trackers, skinners and taxidermists are available; a number of firms offer organized hunting safaris. For detailed information, contact the Professional Hunters' Association of SA (see Useful Addresses further on).

TRAVEL

Road. Distances in km from Johannesburg and Pretoria respectively: Barberton 368 and 357; Graskop 394 and 370; Louis Trichardt 441 and 387; Lydenburg 323 and 299; Messina 534 and 480; Nelspruit 358 and 334; Numbi Gate (Kruger) 409 and 385; Orpen Gate (Kruger) 519 and 495; Phalaborwa 510 and 483; Pietersburg 331 and 277; Potgietersrus 274 and 220; Punda Maria 581 and 527; Sabie 379 and 360; Skukuza 486 and 442; Tzaneen 422 and 368; Warmbaths 156 and 102.

The region has an excellent network of roads. From Johannesburg to Nelspruit and the Escarpment, take the R22 and then the N4 near Witbank; from Pretoria, take the N4 direct. From Nelspruit north into the Escarpment, take the R40 and then follow the signs. For the northern and north-eastern regions, take the N1 national highway from Pretoria; turn right at Pietersburg on the R71 for the Tzaneen area and the central Kruger (Phalaborwa); for Venda and the northern Kruger, turn right at Louis Trichardt on the R524.

Car and minibus hire: There are Avis offices at Skukuza and Phalaborwa which, together with Comair facilities (see below) allow a great deal of travel and sightseeing flexibility. Reservations: through travel agent, Avis or Comair; Kruger Park contact numbers: Skukuza (0131252) 141; Phalaborwa (01524) Avis 5169, Comair 2801.

Coach travel: A luxury coach service operates between Johannesburg (leaving Tues and Thurs) and Nelspruit (leaving Mon, Wed and Fri). Consult your travel agent for details of these and other coach services.

Air. Scheduled flights between Johannesburg international airport and Nelspruit; Skukuza, Phalaborwa (these are daily, enabling visitors to fly to the Kruger just for the day, or, of course, for longer), Pietersburg and Tzaneen (this links up with Phalaborwa flights).

Weekday scheduled flights between Johannesburg and Durban. Also special Comair large-group flights to the Kruger from Durban.

A new airport at Malelane, on the Kruger's southern boundary and capable of taking such aircraft as the Magnum Metroliner and the twin-engine Chieftain, came into operation early in 1990.

Private reserves: Comair arranges trips to Inyati, Mala-Mala, Motswari, Motswari-M'bali, Ngala, Sabi-Sabi, Tanda Tula and Umbabat.

ACCOMMODATION

ESCARPMENT AREA

Hotel accommodation is available in Sabie and Lydenburg, and there are some exceptionally pleasant, mostly small, country hotels and lodges in and within easy driving distance of the Escarpment area.

The semi-official Overvaal organization runs a number of resorts throughout the Transvaal, including those at the Blyde River Canyon (see page 80) and the whole of Pilgrim's Rest (including the Royal Hotel, see page 81). For booking and information on these, contact Central Reservations, PO Box 3046, Pretoria 0001; Tel. (012) 346-2277; Fax: (012) 346-2276.

Select hotels

Hulala Lakeside Lodge ★★★ Overlooking Degama lake. Elegant country-house atmosphere and hospitality. PO Box 1382, White River 1240; Tel. (01311) 5-1710.

Mount Sheba ★★★ 23 km west of Pilgrim's Rest. Medium-small luxury hotel and time-share complex, exquisitely set in its own forest reserve (see page 83). Cottages, suites; conference facilities; outstanding cuisine. PO Box 100, Pilgrim's Rest 1290; Tel. (0131532), and ask for Pilgrim's

Rest 17. Central reservations, Tel. (011) 883-5674.

Select hideaways

Critchley Hackle Lodge, Dullstroom. Small (10-suite) stone-built luxury getaway in Scottish Highland-type setting; cozy and welcoming; much patronized by trout fishermen; *cordon bleu* cuisine. P.O.Box 141, Dullstroom 1110; Tel. (01325) 4-0145.

Cybele Forest Lodge, in deep forest setting not far from Hulala. Cozy cottage-style rooms, superb cuisine. PO Box 346, White River 1240; Tel. (01311) 5-0564/5-0565.

Jatinga Country Lodge. Graciously converted farmstead; rondavels. Jatinga's cuisine is renowned. PO Box 77, Plaston 1244; Tel. (01311) 3-1932.

Old Joe's Kaia, Schoemanskloof valley. Rustic, cozy, friendly, superb food. PO Box 108, Schagen 1207; Tel. (0131232), and ask for 52 or 53.

KRUGER NATIONAL PARK

A description of the various rest-camps appears on pages 88-90. Reservations for accommodation or for a place on one of the wilderness trails: contact The Chief Director National Parks Board, Reservations, PO Box 787, Pretoria 0001; Tel. (012) 343-1991; or Cape Town: P.O.Box 7400, Roggebaai 8012; Tel. (021) 419-5365; or southern Cape: P.O.Box 774, George 6530; Tel. (0441) 74-6924/5; or call personally at the National Parks Board offices in Leyds St, Muckleneuk, Pretoria.

Book well in advance: the park is an extremely popular tourist venue, especially during the Transvaal school holidays (early December to mid-January; first 3 weeks of April; most of July). Give an indication of your preference for camp or camps, and type of accommodation. There are reduced rates for senior citizens. The Parks Board will send you a voucher, which should be presented when entering the Kruger and the camp. Rest-camp bookings, though, are fairly flexible: one can often relocate, after entering the park, with the help of the reception office.

WEST OF THE KRUGER

Select hotels

Bambi Protea ★★★ Near Schoemanskloof valley (page 98); favoured by trout fishermen. Rooms and chalets; conference facilities. PO Box 98, Machadodorp 1170; Tel. (013242), and ask for 101 or 102.

Casa do Sol ★★★ Hazyview area. Imaginatively unusual: as much a small village as a hotel –

cobbled and cloistered walkways, patios, courtyards, fountains, archways, Cordoba-tiled roofs. Plenty laid on for guests; lovely grounds; conference facilities. Central reservations: PO Box 52890, Saxonwold 2132; Tel. (011) 880-2000 or (0131243), and ask for 22.

Drum Rock ★★ Popular, lively hotel 9 km from Nelspruit overlooking Crocodile River valley. 77 en-suite rooms; pool, squash courts, etc., conference facilities for 250. PO Box 622, Nelspruit 1200; Tel. (01311) 58-1217.

Impala Inn ★★★ Close to Phalaborwa gate; 49 rooms, conference facilities for 80. PO Box 139, Phalaborwa 1390; Tel. (01524) 5681/2.

Malaga ★★★ In Elands river valley; Mediterranean-style design and décor; 52 en-suite rooms, 2 suites; conference facilities; good trout fishing in the area. PO Box 136, Waterval Boven 1195; Tel. (013262) 431/2/3.

Malelane Lodge ★★★★ New luxury hotel on Crocodile River, near the Kruger's Malelane gate. 101 rooms, 2 suites; conference facilities for 150. PO Box 392, Malelane 1320; Tel. (013133) 2294.

Ngwane Valley Inn ★★★ 24 km east of Nelspruit, near the Kruger. Comfortable, friendly, well-appointed. 42 en-suite rooms, 1 suite; conference facilities. PO Box 162, Nelspruit 1200; Tel. (013164) 5213.

Paragon ★★★ In Nelspruit; 45 rooms; conference facilities for 70; pool etc. PO Box 81, Nelspruit 1200; Tel. (01311) 5-3205/6/7/8.

Pine Lake Inn ★★★ Set on lake's edge in White River area; excellent sports facilities, golf. En-suite rooms; conference facilities. PO Box 94, White River 1240; Tel. (01311) 3-1186.

Sabi River Hotel and Country Club ★★★ Close to Kruger gate; subtropical grounds; own 18-hole golf course. En-suite rooms; conference facilities. PO Box 13, Hazyview 1242; Tel. (0131242), and ask for 160 or Central Reservations, Tel. (011) 883-5674.

Hotel Winkler ★★★ In White River area; spacious grounds; own farm and dam; unusual architecture; en-suite rooms; conference facilities. PO Box 12, White River 1240; Tel. (01311) 3-2317/8/9.

Private Reserves

Some of these are featured on pages 93-96; contact direct or through travel agent. Bookings for and information about Inyati, Londolozi, Mohlabetsi, M'Bali, Ngala, Mala-Mala, Sabi-Sabi and Tshukudu lodges are handled by, among others,

Game Lodge Reservations, PO Box 782597, Sandton 2146; Tel. (011) 883-4345/6/7; Fax: (011) 783-7931.

Tanda Tula (page 96): contact Safariplan, PO Box 4245, Randburg 2125; Tel. (011) 886-1810/1/2/3/4; Fax: (011) 783-7931. Gambule Lodge (page 96): Tel. (011) 803 7400; Fax: (011) 803- 7411.

NORTHERN REGIONS

The semi-official Overvaal organization administers the spa complex at Warmbaths (page 101) and the resort and hotel complexes of Eiland (Hans Merensky reserve, page 101) and Tshipise (Honnet reserve, page 102). Central Reservations: PO Box 3046, Pretoria 0001; Tel. (012) 346-2277; Fax: (012) 346-2276.

Select hotels

The Coach House ★★★★ Consistently adjudged SA's best country hotel. Set above the New Agatha state forest outside Tzaneen (page 100); prides itself on its exclusivity; personal attention lavished on guests. 35 rooms, all with splendid views of mountain and forest; five-star cuisine. Conference facilities. PO Box 544, Tzaneen 0850; Tel. (01523) 2-0100 or 2-0170/1.

Lalapanzi Hotel ★ On the N1 to the north of Pietersburg. A cluster of English-village cottages in an exquisite garden setting. Very sociable Bull and Bush pub. PO Box 5, Bandelierkop 0800, Tel. (0020) 9908.

Magoebaskloof ★★★ Between Tzaneen and Haenertsburg, overlooking a wooded kloof of stunning beauty. First-class all-round country hotel. Courtesy and cuisine are of the best. 58 en-suite rooms; conference facilities. PO Magoebaskloof 0731; Tel. (0152222) 82/83.

Pietersburg Holiday Inn ★★★; 179 en-suite rooms, conference facilities. PO Box 784, Pietersburg, 0700; Tel. (01521) 91-2030.

Protea Park Hotel ★★★ 28 km south of Potgietersrus on main highway. The hotel has its own 18-hole golf course. En-suite rooms; conference facilities for 400. PO Box 1551, Potgietersrus, 0600; Tel. (01541) 3101/2.

Ranch ★★★ On the N1 near Pietersburg. Largish and lively hotel; plenty laid on for guests; 2 restaurants, 4 bars. En-suite rooms; conference facilities. PO Box 77, Pietersburg 0700; Tel. (01521) 7-5377.

Venda Sun, Thohoyandou. Conveniently placed half-way between Louis Trichardt and northern Kruger. One of the smaller links in the Sun International chain; busy, lively; tropical setting, splendid pool area; excellent restaurants; small but animated casino. En-suite rooms; conference facilities. PO Box 766, Sibasa, Venda, Tel. (015581) 2-1011/5. Central reservations: Tel. (011) 783-8750.

Private Reserves

Mabula Bush Lodge, 35 km west of Warmbaths. One of the best-stocked, most enterprising and hospitable of the Transvaal's private game parks/ lodges. Game includes the 'big five'. Private Bag 1665, Warmbaths 0480; Tel. (015334) 616 or 717.

Caravan/camping and self-catering accommodation

EASTERN TRANSVAAL

Barberton: Barberton caravan park, PO Box 780, Barberton 1300, Tel. (01314) 2-3323.

Elandshoek: Montrose Falls hotel and caravan park, PO Box 20, Elandshoek 1208, Tel. (0200), ask for Montrose 3. Situated 32 km from Nelspruit on the main road, close to Montrose Falls. 30 caravan/tent stands.

Graskop: Graskop municipal tourist resort, PO Box 18, Graskop 1270, Tel. (0131522) 126. Self-catering bungalows and 70 grassed stands for caravans. The park is beautifully situated beside a dam on the Motsitse River.

Hazyview: Numbi hotel and caravan park, PO Box 6, Hazyview 1242, Tel. (0131242), and ask for 6; Fax: (0131242) 326 (bungalows and caravans for hire – no tents allowed). Sanbonani Lowveld resort, PO Box 112, Hazyview 1242, Tel. (0131242) 94. Self-catering accommodation; 30 caravan and 10 tent stands.

Hoedspruit: Overvaal Blydepoort. Situated on the Blyde River Pass, 50 km from Graskop and 80 km from Sabie. Private Bag 368, Ohrigstad 1122, Tel. (013231) 901 or 881; Fax: (013231) 881.

Kruger National Park: offers outstanding accommodation facilities for visitors, in luxury or standard self-catering units and caravan/camping sites. Bookings: Chief Director, National Parks Board, PO Box 787, Pretoria 0001, Tel. (012) 343-1991 or PO Box 7400, Roggebaai 8012, Tel. (021) 419-5365.

Lydenburg: Uitspan caravan park, PO Box 391, Lydenburg 1120, Tel. (01323) 2914.

Nelspruit: Come Together Guest Farm, Post Office Alkmaar 1206, Tel. (0131232) 2831. Nelspruit Holiday Resort, PO Box 45, Nelspruit 1200, Tel. (01311) 59-9111.

Phalaborwa: Koos Lubbe caravan park, PO Box 67, Phalaborwa 1390, Tel. (01524) 2111; Fax: (01524) 2726.

Sabie: Castle Rock caravan park, PO Box 61, Sabie 1260, Tel. (0131512) 9905. Merry Pebbles Holiday Resort, PO Box 131, Sabie 1260, Tel. (0131512) 323 or 326.

Schagen: Sudwala Park Holiday Resort, PO Box 30, Schagen 1207, Tel. (0131232) 3913 or (01311) 2-8185.

Waterval Boven: Elangeni Holiday Resort, PO Box 254, Waterval Boven 1195, Tel. (013262) 141.

White River: Bundu Park, PO Box 1750, White River 1240, Tel. (01311) 3-3802; Fax: (same).

NORTHERN TRANSVAAL

Haenertsburg: Lakeside Holiday Resort, PO Magoebaskloof 0731, Tel. Haenertsburg (0152222), and ask for 53 or 80. .

Louis Trichardt: Ben Lavin Nature Reserve, PO Box 782, Louis Trichardt 0920, Tel. (01551) 3834.

Messina: Municipal caravan park, Private Bag X611, Messina 0900, Tel. (01553) 2170.

Naboomspruit: Maroela Holiday Resort, PO Box 194, Naboomspruit 0560, Tel. (01534) 3-0327).

Nylstroom: Eurosun caravan park, PO Box 2087, Nylstroom 0510, Tel. (01531) 71-1328.

Tzaneen: Fanie Botha dam nature reserve, PO Box 1397, Tzaneen 0850, Tel. (01523) 5641 (65 caravan/tent stands).

Warmbaths: Klein Kariba Holiday Resort, PO Box 150, Warmbaths 0480, Tel. (015331) 2388. Linga Longa Holiday Farm, PO Box 258, Warmbaths 0480, Tel. (015331) 4300 (caravan/camping, lodging at farmhouse, chapel).

USEFUL ADDRESSES AND TELEPHONE NUMBERS

Barberton Publicity Bureau Tel. (01314) 2-2121.

Lydenburg tourist information Tel. (01323) 2121.

Messina tourist information Tel. 01553) 2209.

Pilgrim's Rest tourist information Tel. (0131532) 28 or 50.

Potgietersrus tourist information Tel. (01541) 2244.

Professional Hunters' Association of SA PO Box 781175, Sandton 2146, Tel. (011) 706-7724.

Satour (SA Tourist Board). Lowveld: Cnr Vorster and Landdros Maré streets, PO Box 2814, Pietersburg 0700; Tel. (01521) 3025. Northern Transvaal: Cor Vorster and Landdros streets, PO Box 2814, Pietersburg 0700; Tel. (01521) 3025.

Transvaal Division of Nature Conservation Private Bag X209, Pretoria 0001; Tel. (012) 201-2361.

Tzaneen area tourist information Tel. (01523) 3246.

Venda Tourism Department VDC Building, Thohoyandou; Tel. (015581) 2-1131.

Warmbaths tourist information Tel. (015331) 2111.

ANNUAL EVENTS

Tzaneen: Bass Masters' Angling Competition: April □Nelspruit: Jock of the Bushveld golf tournament: May □Nelspruit: Lowveld Agricultural Show: August □Tzaneen: Agricultural and Industrial Show: August □Tzaneen: Harvest Festival: September □Tzaneen: Silver Mist golf tournament: September □Haenertsberg: Cherry Blossom and Azalea Festival: springtime.

WESTERN GAUTENG AND THE NORTH-WEST

The region to the west of the Pretoria-Johannesburg axis is one of the great granaries of southern Africa. Here the soils are deep and fertile and, when the rains are generous, hugely productive, yielding a bounty comparable to that from the world's richest food-growing lands. A vast, hot, flattish country of bushveld and thorn, of lonely farmsteads shaded by eucalyptus and bright green willow, of fields of sunflowers and groundnuts, tobacco and citrus, maize, maize and more maize, and villages that sleep soundly in the sun.

Towards the east, though, the horizons change, the land ascending to the heights of the Magaliesberg, a modest but attractive and in places enchanting range of hills which, each weekend, plays amiable host to thousands of city-dwellers.

To the north of the Magaliesberg there are attractions of a quite different kind. Here you will find the splendid Pilanesberg National Park and, nearby, the glittering Sun City hotel, casino and entertainment complex, Africa's most lavish resort.

WEST OF THE WITWATERSRAND

The principal town of the largely (though by no means entirely) industrial West Rand, occupying the Witwatersrand's highest point and situated 30 km from Johannesburg, is

Krugersdorp

A largish centre that enjoys the distinction of having hosted the world's first mining enterprise (West Rand Consolidated) to produce uranium as a by-product of gold – a technological breakthrough that has contributed significantly to the country's economic muscle.

This busy, pleasant, tree-shaded place has – apart from its mines, its modern shopping centres and some good restaurants – a modest number of attractions to offer the visitor, among them the African Fauna and Bird

Bringing in the maize harvest. The region serves as one of the country's great granaries, but often – too often – there is drought.

Park (in Koedoe Street), where there are picnic and barbecue spots and a variety of animals and birds on view. Worthwhile ports of call just outside town are:

THE RAILWAY SOCIETY MUSEUM, a must for anyone with even a passing interest in the story of transport generally and the age of steam in particular. On display: historic locomotives; vintage and veteran vehicles.

KRUGERSDORP GAME RESERVE, a 1 400-ha expanse of open grassland that sustains white rhino, giraffe, buffalo, kudu, sable, the rare roan and several other types of antelope; more than 160 species of bird, and the carefully preserved plant life that covered the region before man came with his mining madness to devastate the land. There's a 200-ha lion camp within the reserve; the rhino and buffalo also have their own enclosures.

Accommodation comprises self-contained chalets and a caravan/camping ground. For the day-visitor: tearoom; swimming pool; a pleasant 16-km prepared game-drive and an undemanding (7-10 km) 'educational trail'.

Just under 10 km north-west of Krugersdorp are the:

STERKFONTEIN CAVES, once described by the great Dr Robert Broom as the 'anthropological treasure-house of the world', a mantle later assumed by Leakey's fossil-rich Olduvai Gorge in Tanzania. Broom began excavating in 1896, though it was to be fully four decades before he unearthed his most important find, the million-year-old fossilized cranium of an ape-man, which he named *Plesianthropus transvaalensis* – informally and universally known as 'Mrs Ples'. Later and closer study revealed that it belonged to the same species of hominid as that discovered by Broom's colleague Raymond Dart, at Taung in the northern Cape, and it was renamed *Australopithecus africanus*. The two discoveries revolutionized scientific theory on the origins of man. There are daily conducted tours of the caves. Next door is the Robert Broom museum, housing fossilized exhibits and displays of prehistoric animal and birdlife.

The site, though, offers more than scientific interest: part of the cave complex consists of six cathedral-like chambers, largest of which is the dripstone-decorated Hall of Elephants, 23 m high and 91 m long, and an underground lake of still-unknown depth with an air of enchantment about it. The lake features prominently in local African lore.

Hartbeespoort Dam

The dam, fed by the Magalies and Crocodile rivers and a favourite playground of the Witwatersrand's city dwellers, lies among the foothills of the Magaliesberg range (see page 113) some 35 km to the west of Pretoria. The waters cover 12 km² of attractive countryside (about 45 km of canals irrigate the surrounding farmlands) and the area is a favourite haunt of water-sportsmen, angling and boating enthusiasts, weekenders, family day-trippers, caravanners and campers, and the more popular recreational spots can be crowded and noisy. However, there are some lovely corners where one can relax in peace; and the views you get from the road that winds around the perimeter, and from the Cableway, the eastern Magaliesberg's highest point, are most pleasant. Specific points of interest include the:

HARTBEESPOORT DAM NATURE RESERVE, comprising the dam itself and a scatter of small conservation areas, though the indigenous vegetation (mixed bushveld, with white stinkwood, wild olive and other notable tree species) is hard put to withstand the substantial human presence. The Oberon segment is noted for its birdlife; the Kommandonek portion has an enclosed game camp (kudu, bushbuck, Burchell's zebra). Both these areas have camping grounds, and there is more formal accommodation nearby. Open daily; Tel. (01205) 921.

AQUARIUM, 3 km from the dam: local and exotic freshwater fish, performing seals, waterbirds, crocodiles. Open daily.

ZOO AND SNAKE PARK, boasting reptiles and a variety of animals; snake, chimpanzee and seal 'shows' are held on Sundays and public holidays; the zoo serves as the starting point for ferry trips around the dam. Open daily.

TAN' MALIE SE WINKEL (Aunt Malie's Shop), near the dam wall, sells all manner of traditional and specialist goodies, including handicrafts, pottery, curios, preserves, farm food.

Carletonville area

Some of the world's deepest and richest gold mines are situated around this Far West Rand town (the main shaft at Western Deep Levels extends down beyond the 3,5-km mark). Underground and surface tours can be arranged; telephone the Town Clerk's office, (01491) 7-2131. Carletonville is also one of the country's leading centres of the maize industry, but is otherwise unremarkable. Just under 10 km from town, though, is the:

ABE BAILEY NATURE RESERVE, a huge 6 000-ha stretch of grassy terrain and wetland that attracts large numbers of waterbirds. Over 250 bird species have been recorded here, including the endangered Cape vulture, which breed in the rocky Magaliesberg region to the northwest. Several kinds of buck have been introduced into the reserve, among them red hartebeest, black wildebeest and springbok. Visits by prior arrangement; Tel. (01491) 2908.

Brits area

A fertile and pleasant part of the western Transvaal to the north of, and irrigated by, the Hartbeespoort Dam. Crops grown on the fertile farmlands include tobacco, wheat, vegetables, flowers and citrus; the warm air is sweet with the scent of orange blossom. The town itself is rather industrial and ordinary, but nearby and worth visiting are:

THE DE WILDT CHEETAH BREEDING STATION, on the R513. This research centre is renowned throughout the zoological world for its successes in breeding (and studying) cheetah, king cheetah, brown hyena and that most fascinating of hunting animals the wild dog. Tours by arrangement; Tel. (01204) 921 or 927.

THE HERBAL CENTRE, on the Pretoria North Road, cultivates an intriguing number and variety of medicinal, culinary and aromatic herbs. On site is a traditional apothecary's shop, nursery, herbarium, pottery workshop. Tours by appointment; potpourri demonstrations; dayworkshops; Tel. (01204) 729.

THE MAGALIESBERG

The ridge of the Magaliesberg runs from a point near Pretoria due westwards for 120 km to and just beyond the attractive town of Rustenburg. It isn't by any definition a major range of hills – it rises little more than 300 m above the surrounding and rather flattish countryside – but it has a woodland beauty of its own and, in the more precipitous parts, even grandeur. Below the ridge, the land lies at a lower level than that of the Witwatersrand to the east, and the climate is kind: the air warm and limpid even in winter, and the rainfall relatively high, feeding the many streams and rivulets that tumble down the slopes and into the park-like valleys. The warmth and the water sustain the region's wonderfully rich crops of peaches and oranges, subtropical fruits, tobacco, vegetables and flowers.

The Magaliesberg is one of the last remaining havens of the shy and stately Cape vulture, a species now on the endangered list: the birds depend for survival on the bones of carcasses crunched to digestible size by the strong jaws of the hyena, and hyenas have all but disappeared from the western Transvaal, pushed out by the encroaching farmlands. But the vultures may still be seen, wheeling elegantly in the thermals above the hills. They are largely sustained by the 'vulture restaurants' established in the area and, in the breeding season (May to October), by their forays into such game-rich terrain as the Pilanesberg park to the north (see page 117).

Predictably, the Magaliesberg area is something of a magnet for people who live in the suffocating urban jungles of the Witwatersrand, just an hour's drive away. Some come for its strategic position – its western end is conveniently placed halfway between the Johannesburg-Pretoria conurbation and Sun City to the north (see page 117), but most are enticed by the tranquillity of the hills and valleys, by the lovely scenic drives and gentle walks, by the charm of the vistas, and by the hospitality of the hotels and lodges of the area. Among the more pleasant of these are Valley Lodge, Hunter's Rest, and Mount Grace Country House, one of southern Africa's most inviting country hideaways (see Advisory, page 120).

COTTAGE CRAFTS The peace and beauty of the Magaliesberg and, closer to Johannesburg, the valley of the Crocodile River have attracted a wealth of artistic talent – sculptors and painters, potters and cabinet-makers, cutlers, workers in leather, stone, wood and textiles have settled in the area in their dozens, their cottage-studios yielding a delightful number and variety of highly individualistic and often exquisite products. Many of the studios are concentrated along the Crocodile, reached via Honeydew (north from Johannesburg along DF Malan Drive) and the Muldersdrift road. Most of them welcome visitors, and keep open house during the first weekend of each month. The studios can provide you with a map of the general area showing the whereabouts of the various artists on the 'route'.

The Rustenburg area

A substantial country town at the western end of, and overlooked by, the red-tinged heights of the Magaliesberg range, Rustenburg is a pleasant 112-km drive from Johannesburg, 105 km from Pretoria. The name means 'town of rest' and was well chosen, for this is indeed a relaxing and attractive place. The countryside around is well-watered, blessed with an average nine hours of sunshine a day throughout the year, and these elements combine to nurture a marvellous profusion of exotic plants in street and garden: jacaranda and frangipani, hibiscus, poinciana and poinsettia and billows of bougainvillea.

Rustenburg is the centre of a thriving agricultural region (maize and wheat, tobacco and cotton, fruit and flowers) and a mining town of note: the two nearby platinum mines are the largest single producers of the metal in the world. Tours by arrangement; Tel. (0142) 9-1011. Visitors are also welcomed at the nearby Tobacco Research Institution; Tel. (0142) 9-3171 and at the Citrus packing house; Tel. (0142) 2-2300.

The area has a significant place in the annals of Afrikanerdom. It was here that the two headstrong Voortrekker rivals, Andries Pretorius and Andries Hendrik Potgieter, finally – in 1852 – made their peace with each other. And here, seven years later, under a syringa tree in town (a granite replica of the stump now marks the spot), the Reformed Church was founded as a body separate from the bigger Dutch Reformed Church. To the former belonged Paul Kruger, patriarch of the Transvaal during the later 19th century. Kruger settled on the farm Boeken-houtfontein in the 1860s, and some 30 ha of the property – on which stand a cottage dating from 1841 (this the oldest surviving house in the province), Oom Paul's original homestead and a house the old man built for his son – have been preserved as a museum. Among other features of interest in and around town are:

THE RUSTENBURG MUSEUM in Van Staden Street: historical, cultural and archeological exhibits; open daily.

PAUL BODENSTEIN PARK, on the eastern outskirts of town: notable for its bronze animal sculptures and a colourful variety of avian life, including waterbirds.

RUSTENBURG KLOOF, on the western perimeter: a pleasant municipal resort, in a setting of indigenous Magaliesberg flora. Restaurant, tearoom, sports facilities, nature rambles, an especially attractive circular swimming pool, and a number of natural pools and mountain streams (bathing permitted). Accommodation: fully equipped chalets; Tel. (0142) 3-1062.

KWAGGAPAN PARK, on the eastern outskirts: giraffe, buck; lovely views from the lookout tower; picnic spots.

RETIEF'S KLOOF, a lovely scenic area some way to the east of town, attracts the keener naturalist and rock-climber. The area is distinguished by its deep ravines, crystal pools and waterfalls.

OLIFANTSNEK DAM, 3 000-ha lake that irrigates the citrus and tobacco plantations. The dam wall, 1 344 m of 24-m-high concrete, captures the rush of the Hex River as it plunges through a narrow mountain pass. Pleasant teas at and vistas from the hotel on the banks of the lake; even more splendid views from the Olifantsnek Pass.

RUSTENBURG NATURE RESERVE is a 4 250-ha expanse of upland terrain straddling part of the Magaliesberg's northern plateau (it was established on the farm Rietvlei, which also belonged to Paul Kruger). The reserve is distinguished by its striking landscapes, its steep rock faces, tumbling streams and attractive patches of syringa, acacia and boekenhout.

Among the 115 different types of tree and bush are a number of rare species – the succulent *Frithia pulchra* for instance, and *Aloe peglerae*. Animals to be seen include the oribi, reedbuck, mountain reedbuck, kudu, sable and – if you're lucky – leopard, brown hyena, black-backed jackal. Birds: over 230 species have been recorded, among them the black and martial eagles; a Cape vulture breeding colony has made its home just to the east of the reserve.

For the energetic visitor, there's the two-day Rustenburg hiking trail (see page 119); for the less so the 3-km, self-guided, circular Peglerae stroll. Other facilities: information centre; picnic spots; caravan/camping ground.

SOUTH OF RUSTENBURG

Potchefstroom

Set on the banks of the Mooi River 120 km from Johannesburg, Potchefstroom is the Transvaal's second oldest town. It was founded in 1838, a short while after the so-called Nine Days Battle between AH Potgieter's Voortrekkers and Mzilikazi's Ndebele warriors – an epic struggle notable for the Ndebele's ingenious use of oxen as cavalry, and for its final confirmation that raw courage was no match for the guns and horses of the whites. Mzilikazi retreated north with his people to the land beyond the Limpopo River, where they settled to become the Matabele nation.

Potchefstroom's Totius House museum. 'Totius' was the pen-name of J.D. du Toit (1877-1953), theologian and leading Afrikaans literary figure.

Klerksdorp miners coming off shift

Klerksdorp

A major mining town some 50 km west of Potchefstroom, and scene of one of the earliest and most frenetic gold rushes. The boom began in 1885, lasted a bare year and, overnight, transformed the little village (the oldest white settlement in the region; founded in 1837) into a flourishing mining camp of iron shanties, over 200 stores, 70 drinking dens and a stock exchange. The easily accessible gold was soon depleted and most of the diggers left town, but recovery techniques improved over the years to the point where the big companies could move in to exploit the deeper and more difficult – and very substantial – reserves of gold and platinum.

Among the notable features in and around town are the:

KLERKSDORP MUSEUM, at the corner of Lombaard and Margaretha Prinsloo streets: historical, cultural, archeological and geological exhibits; open daily.

PREHISTORIC ROCK ENGRAVINGS, on a hill at Bosworth, some 18 km north of Klerksdorp. The origins of these intriguing artifacts are something of a mystery, though it's thought they date from the Later Stone Age.

FAAN MEINTJIES NATURE RESERVE, a 1 300-ha stretch of open plain and sandy ridge about 10 km from town. The sanctuary is very well stocked; game includes white rhino, buffalo, giraffe, eland, sable and a variety of other bovids. The game thrives, and some of the herds are periodically culled, which provides hunters with opportunities for their sport. A rest-camp is being developed. Tel. (018) 2-3635 or 2-5700.

Klerksdorp is at the centre of a busy mining region that includes the towns of Orkney (which has a pleasant recreational resort, popular among anglers and water-sportsmen) and Stilfontein. From the latter, one may embark on interesting tours of the Hartbeestfontein, Stilfontein and Buffelsfontein gold mines; information from the Chamber of Mines, Tel. (011) 838-8211.

Beyond Klerksdorp, on the R29 to the southwest, is Wolmaransstad and, farther on, Bloemhof, its large dam and nature reserve, the Vaal River and Christiana (see Orange Free State, page 128).

Potchefstroom served as the capital of the old South African Republic until 1860, when Pretoria replaced it as the young country's principal centre. The town, though, retained its cultural importance; a theological seminary was established in 1905, later developing into Potchefstroom University for Christian Higher Education. Other assets include a music conservatory and a fine library. Shades of the rather serious past can be discerned in some of the historic buildings, prominent among which are the Old Fort, the Powder Magazine and the Hervormde Kerk (Reformed Church). Among the museums are the President Pretorius House (the restored presidential residence), Totius House (honouring one of Afrikanerdom's leading literary figures) and, most notable, the:

POTCHEFSTROOM MUSEUM, on the corner of Wolmarans and Gouws streets. Well worth a visit for its excellent displays of Voortrekker wagons (including one used in the Battle of Blood River, see page 175), old weapons, household items, and paintings by the representational artist Otto Landsberg.

THE FAR WEST

The big country beyond Rustenburg, to the west, tends to be ignored by the holiday-maker and visiting tourist, and perhaps with good reason: it's a sun-blistered, unadorned, functional region, largely the preserve of hardy farmers who do daily battle with a land that is often harsh and unforgiving. In good summers, when the rains arrive on time, the cattle fatten and the maize fields stretch green and pleasant to far horizons, but too often there is drought, and life is a struggle. So tourism doesn't rate too high among the priorities of the local communities.

Still, for those with time and petrol to spare and a liking for silence, sunlit spaces and sleepy villages, it's certainly worth exploring.

Mampoer country

The Marico district extends from the village of Groot Marico to Mafikeng in the west and from a line through the Bakerville area to Zeerust and beyond in the north.

The region has been enshrined in South Africa's literary annals by the eccentric genius of Herman Charles Bosman, who lived and worked and set some of his finest stories in and around Marico: it was here, among the lucerne and maize fields, the tobacco lands and orange groves, that the simple, earthy characters of *Mafeking Road* and *Jurie Steyn's Post Office* played out their whimsical parts, speaking in English but conveying the essence of rural Afrikaans. And it is an area long famed for the quality of its mampoer, a powerful home-brew distilled by the practised and expert hands of the locals from peaches, apricots and other kinds of fruit (though not from grapes), and from karee-tree berries, a variety that, said Bosman's Oom Schalk Lourens, 'is white and soft to look at, and the smoke that comes from it when you pull the cork out of the bottle is pale and rises up in slow curves ...'.

A 'mampoer route' has recently been established, which helps give visitors some sort of focus on the area. This starts at Groot Marico, ends at Zeerust (where an annual Mampoer Festival is held), is about 60 km in length and, besides introducing outsiders to the secrets of the distilling process, takes in a trout breeding farm, a game farm and pleasant holiday resort. Those interested should contact the Zeerust municipality on (01428) 2- 1081.

Lichtenburg

A modern, good-looking country town, Lichtenburg is notable for its gracious karee-shaded central square, on which stands a striking equestrian statue of General Koos de la Rey, the 'Lion of the North', who fought the British to a standstill in the early part of the South African War and then led his commandos with distinction in the guerrilla campaigns that followed.

The Lichtenburg area, and more specifically the farm Elandsputte to the north, provided the setting for one of the world's last and greatest diamond rushes. News of the first find broke in March 1926 and spread like wildfire, and within months more than 100 000 diggers were working the alluvial ground (and scarring it for ever); at the height of the boom more than 30 000 people took part in an official claim-pegging race – a single, frenzied mass scramble for the wealth of the bushveld. Some splendid stones were unearthed, but the madness lasted a bare decade, and by the mid-1930s Lichtenburg had settled back into its older, quieter routines. Displayed in the town's museum are some fascinating relics and mementos of the diamond years.

Lichtenburg also boasts an unusual nature reserve, a 6 000-ha area that serves as a breeding centre for the National Zoological Gardens. Among its rare and exotic species are Hartmann's mountain zebra, scimitar oryx, pygmy hippo, Indian water-buffalo, Pere David and axis deer – altogether, 35 species of mammal. There's also a cheetah enclosure, and shallow pans near the reserve's entrance attract a large number and variety of waterbird. Accommodation: camping site. Open throughout the year; Tel. (01441) 2-2818.

Some 80 km south-west of Lichtenburg, on the R47, is the:

Barberspan Nature Reserve

The Transvaal's largest waterfowl sanctuary, central feature of which is an 1 800-ha pan nurtured by the Harts River. Here one can see a hugely prolific birdlife – some 350 species in all, including heron, red-knobbed coot, egret, wader, wild duck and, especially, great flocks of flamingos. Bird-watchers are able to use the hide specially constructed for visitors, or stroll along the prepared trail. There are also picnic sites and angling spots, and a camping ground. Tel. (01443) 1202 or 1323.

NORTH OF RUSTENBURG

Drive up the R565 from Rustenburg and you'll enter a region that, until 1994, existed as an independent 'homeland' republic though its autonomy, granted by the apartheid government, wasn't recognized outside southern Africa. It was known as Bophuthatswana, a long word that translates as 'that which binds the Tswana'.

The name was carefully chosen: the Tswana people, nearly three million strong, comprise some 60 different groups who speak the same language and, in general, share a cultural heritage but otherwise tend to be clannish. The local Tswana are kinsmen of the people of Botswana, further to the north, and of the Sotho of Lesotho far to the south-east.

To the casual eye the region looks poor, and a great many of its inhabitants do indeed live in poverty, but in fact the land is wealthy: it contains much of the earth's highly priced platinum-group metals. Of these, rhodium, palladium and platinum itself are the most valuable, finding their way into jewellery, electronics, precision instruments, laboratory ware and, in a world ever more conscious of pollution, into car exhaust systems. The rich soil of the region's northern parts sustains crops of wheat, maize and sunflowers; much of the rest is good cattle country.

The old homeland seat of government and now the North-West provincial capital is Mmabatho, situated due west of Rustenburg and next to the historic town of Mafikeng (formerly known as Mafeking, of Anglo-Boer War siege fame). In fact Mmabatho began life as an appendage of Mafikeng and, today, comprises little more than an administrative and legislative buildings, some pleasant residences, a large stadium, and the by-now standard Sun International hotel and casino, around which revolves the social and business life of the area. The hotel is designed around a huge palm-fringed and quite lovely swimming pool.

A lot more popular among tourists is that part of the region that lies directly to the north of Rustenburg, and which is home to the extraordinary Sun City complex and to the:

Pilanesberg National Park

One of the strangest of southern Africa's geological features rises skywards from the flat plains of the region. This is the Pilanesberg range, an aeons-old relic of volcanic convulsion that comprises a series of four concentric mountain rings. The loftiest peak is the Pilanesberg itself, towering 600 m above Mankwe lake. Mankwe is at the dead centre of the volcano's bowl, a circular area 27 km in diameter and site of the huge, 55 000-ha national park – one of southern Africa's major tourist attractions.

This flourishing reserve is the product of 'Operation Genesis', launched in the 1970s and rated among the most imaginative and successful of the world's game-stocking enterprises. Eland were brought in from Namibia, Burchell's zebra from the Transvaal, white and the endangered black rhino from the eastern Cape's Addo (see page 201) and, today, some 10 000 head of game graze, hunt and scavenge in the dense bush and wooded valleys of the park. They include, in addition to the animals mentioned, giraffe and hippo, waterbuck, tsessebe, impala, red hartebeest, gemsbok and sable; cheetah, leopard and brown hyena, and the area is haven to fully 300 bird species.

Flora includes the extremely rare Transvaal red balloon tree (*Erythrophysa transvaalensis*), of which about a hundred specimens grow in the park and fewer than ten elsewhere. There are about 100 km of well-surfaced game-viewing roads; hides; picnic spots.

Accommodation: luxury chalets at the Tshukudu rest-camp, less sophisticated shelter at the four other sites. Amenities include restaurants, swimming pool, shop. The Kwa Maritane lodge (see Advisory, page 120) is a hotel and time-share development within the park, near the southern boundary – a beautifully appointed place conveniently sited to serve its two major purposes: it provides a supremely comfortable base from which to enjoy a taste of the wide-open bushveld spaces on the one hand, and on the other to sample, just a few minutes drive away, the many delights of:

Sun City

This complex is the flagship of Sun International's fleet of hotel-casino resorts: an enormous, glamorous complex set rather incongruously in one of the bleaker, less developed parts of the subcontinent. But for all the contrast, the splendour among the relative poverty, Sun City has proved a blessing to the region: it provides work for more than 3 000 people, most of them local Tswana, and for

Sun City's luxurious Cascades Hotel. The grounds, 50 000 km² in extent, have been lavishly landscaped.

every person on its staff there are five others who gain indirect employment. Local businesses benefit hugely from its proximity; many of the millions generated in the casino, restaurant and entertainment centre go towards the building and maintaining of the region's roads, schools and clinics.

The Sun City site is 150 km in circumference, and what it sets out to do – divert, amuse, entertain, spoil the holiday-maker – it does on a big scale, and in style. Its major components at present (there are expansion plans: see next column) are:

☆ Three hotels, ranging from the plush Cascades through the middle-of-the-range Sun City Hotel to the Cabanas, designed mainly for families. The Cascades is a 15-storey, twin-pyramid edifice, completed in 1984 at a cost of some R50 million, and it offers the ultimate in luxury. Its grounds are extensive and lovely: over 50 000 m² of the surrounding countryside have been landscaped to produce an imaginatively sculpted fantasia of lawn, pool, grotto, waterfall, tropical plant and exotic birdlife. The flower-beds alone cover nearly 6 000 m². The Cascades backs onto the:

☆ Entertainment Centre, a vibrant concentration of restaurants, bars, discos, conference rooms, cinemas, a 200-seat computerized bingo hall and the 620-seat Extravaganza Theatre. Its core is the multi-purpose Superbowl, used for conventions, banquets for up to 1 300 people at one sitting, lavish promotions,

ice-skating, big-name shows and international-class sporting events, including world title fights. An integral part of the Entertainment Centre is the:

☆ Casino, gaming rooms offering the standard range: roulette, blackjack, craps, a *salon privé* for punto banco and chemmy. And of course there are the ubiquitous speciality slot machines.

Sun City sporting facilities include horse-riding, squash, swimming, bowls and tennis. Much revolves around the various and attractive stretches of water within the grounds. Among the prominent outdoor features are:

☆ The 23-m-high Waterscape, made up of three interlinked swimming pools, 1 050 m of low weirs and 2 000 m of walkways that lead you through gardens and over, and under, rock formations. Among the permanent residents of the Waterscape are swans and herons and the rare South African black duck.

☆ Waterworld, a large, 750-m-long man-made lake, fringed with lush vegetation and designed for both the idler and the sporting enthusiast (skiing, wind-surfing, para-sailing, ordinary sailing, jetskis, wetbikes, pedaloes, etc).

☆ The Gary Player Country Club and its superb golf course, on which most of the world's greats have played and which hosts the annual Million Dollar Golf Challenge.

☆ Kwena Garden, a reptile park and ranch, notable for its unique beehive-style architecture and its lushly tropical surrounds – and for the Nile crocodiles it keeps. Open daily; feeding time is around 16h30. There's an auditorium in which video shows describe the ways of these awesome creatures; a restaurant, and an African art and craft shop.

THE LOST CITY This, the most recent addition to Sun City, is a splendidly imaginative, R650-million development that, when it was inaugurated in 1992, emphatically confirmed the complex's status as Africa's (and one of the world's) biggest and most opulent resorts.

Central ingredient of the Lost City is its Palace Hotel, an ornately elaborate affair of domes and minarets, columns and curlicues reminiscent (vaguely) of the Raj at its most extravagent. The hotel boasts 350 luxurious rooms and suites, an entrance hall rising three storeys, and two fine restaurants, one set on an island surrounded by cascades, the other embowered by jungle foliage.

The Valley of Waves, which links The Palace with the Entertainment Centre, has its own 'instant' forest of 3 500 trees and incorporates 22 different zones of vegetation, ranging from a rocky outcrop of ancient baobabs to lush tropical jungle. There's also a 100 by 60-metre swimming pool with 1,8-metre high artificially created waves, water chutes for the adventurous, and a second, Arizona-style golf course. Other features: coral reefs, waterfalls, and streams that flow among sculptured walls and toppled columns.

GETTING AROUND

Day drives

The region offers a number of attractive motoring options. For the specifics of your itinerary you'll need a good touring map and a detailed regional guide. Meanwhile, some pointers:

DRIVE 1 Travel from Johannesburg to Potchefstroom (see page 114) via the R41 to Randfontein. Go south on the R28 past Westonaria, then turn right on the R29 and right again on the R501 to Carletonville (page 112). Continue to Potchefstroom and then back to Johannesburg via the R29.

DRIVE 2 From Johannesburg to the Magaliesberg. Drive to Hartbeespoort Dam (page 112) on the R511 and R27, via Hennops Pride recre-

ational area, the Animal Kingdom Safari Park and the Lion and Cheetah Safari Park (see Johannesburg and Pretoria, page 49). Explore the dam area, and then continue west on the R27, which takes you past the northern slopes of the Magaliesberg (page 113) to Rustenburg (page 113). Return on the R24 past Olifantsnek Dam (page 114) and the southern slopes of the Magaliesberg to Hartbeespoort Dam.

DRIVE 3 From Rustenberg travel west on the R27 to Groot Marico and the 'mampoer route' (page 113). Go through Zeerust to Mmabatho and Mafikeng (page 111). Return via Lichtenburg (page 111). If there's time, digress to the south on the R47 from Lichtenburg to the Barberspan nature reserve (page 116). Travel back to Rustenburg via the R52.

Walks and hikes

There are some lovely rambles, walks and climbs in the Magaliesberg area (see page 113). The establishment of a formal hiking trail along the entire length of the range has been proposed; meanwhile, fairly strict controls are maintained in some parts.

Contact the relevant local authorities for permits and be careful not to trespass on private land. Specific options include:

☆ The two-day, 20,5-km Rustenburg nature reserve hiking trail (see page 114). Very popular, and deservedly so. Attractions: the game animals, protected plants, birdlife, superb mountain terrain. Information and bookings: The Officer-in-Charge, Rustenburg Nature reserve, PO Box 511, Rustenburg 0300; Tel. (0142) 3-1050. Literature is available at the reserve's information centre. Alternatively, or in addition, you can take the much shorter Peglerae interpretive trail, on which there's an excellent booklet, also available at the information centre.

☆ Sterkfontein Caves, near Krugersdorp (see page 111). An hour's self-guided or (preferably) conducted walk will lead you through part of this extensive and impressive network of chambers and underground lake. It's important to stick to the demarcated trail. Literature available at the shop.

☆ Krugersdorp Game Reserve (page 111). Variable trails, usually taking about four hours, are conducted on Saturday and Sunday mornings by the Wildlife Society. Tel. (011) 660-1076.

ADVISORY: WESTERN, GAUTENG AND NORTH-WEST

CLIMATE

Summer rainfall region. The climate is similar to that of Johannesburg and Pretoria (see page 70) but generally warmer and, in the farther western regions, drier.

MAIN ATTRACTIONS

Scenic and sightseeing drives (Magaliesberg) □Walking, trailing, rock-climbing □Horse-riding □Game-viewing □Bird-watching □Angling □Watersports (Hartbeespoort Dam, Sun City) □Golf (Magaliesberg; Sun City) □Gambling (Sun City) □Poolside relaxation.

TRAVEL

Road. Good tarred roads connect all the centres. Distances in km from Johannesburg and Pretoria respectively: Krugersdorp 29 and 82; Rustenburg 116 and 105; Sun City 167 and 152; Potchefstroom 113 and 185; Klerksdorp 182 and 214; Lichtenburg 215 and 251; Mmabatho 285 and 330.
  Coach travel: daily between Johannesburg and Sun City. Information: bookings through Computicket, Tel. (011) 331-9991, or contact your travel agent for details.

Air. There are frequent Sun Air flights between Johannesburg international airport and Sun City; special day excursions available; Mmabatho Air also links Johannesburg with Mafikeng (Mmabatho) airport. Information: contact Sun International or Sun Air, Tel. (011) 339-2314. (see Useful Addresses and Telephone Numbers on page 121).

ACCOMMODATION

Select hotels

SUN CITY

Cascades ★★★★★ Luxurious. 234 rooms, 11 suites. PO Box 7, Sun City 0316, Bophuthatswana; Tel. (014651) 2-1000; Fax: (014651) 2- 1483; Telex: 0937 74032 BP, or contact Central Reservations (see page 121).

Kwa Maritane Lodge ★★★ Luxury hotel and timeshare, situated in Pilanesberg National Park, close to Sun City. Conference facilities: 4 venues. PO Box 39, Sun City 0316, Bophuthatswana; Tel. (014651) 2-1820; Telex: 0397 4027 BP.

Sun City Cabanas ★★★ Billed as 'a haven of peace and quiet on the lakeside'. 284 standard and de luxe rooms; steakhouse and terrace buffet. PO Box 3, Sun City 0316, Bophuthatswana; Tel.

(014651) 2-1000; Fax: (014651) 2-1590; Telex: 0937 4012 BP, or contact Central Reservations (see page 121).

Sun City Hotel ★★★★★ Five-star accommodation, facilities and service. 300 en-suite rooms, 40 suites; conference facilities: 14 venues. PO Box 2, Sun City 0316, Bophuthatswana; Tel. (014651) 2- 1000; Fax: (014651) 2-1470; Telex: 0937 4000 BP, or contact Central Reservations (see page 121).

Sundown Ranch ★★★ A large, pleasant, good-value hotel near, and offering a complimentary shuttle service to Sun City. 101 rooms; conference facilities for 400; PO Box 139, Boshoek 0301; Tel. (0142) 2-8320; Telex: 0938 4001 BP.

RUSTENBURG AND MAGALIESBERG AREA

Belvedere ★★ Outside Rustenburg. 22 en-suite rooms; conference facilities. PO Box 1298, Rustenburg 0300. Tel. (0142) 9-2121; Telex: 344 185 BELHO SA.

Cashane ★★ In Rustenburg. 48 rooms; facilities for small conferences. PO Box 1487, Rustenburg 0300; Tel. (0142) 2-8541.

Hunter's Rest ★★★ Excellent 100-room country hotel; conference facilities for 250. PO Box 775, Rustenburg 0300; Tel. (0142) 9- 2140; Telex: 344-025.

Karos Safari ★★ In Rustenburg. 60 en-suite rooms, 42 suites; conference facilities for 200. PO Box 687, Rustenburg 0300; Tel. (0142) 3-1053/4; Telex: 344-161.

Mount Grace Country House ★★★★ In the Magaliesberg; very special country hospitality. 44 rooms and suites; conference facilities for 120. PO Box 251, Magaliesburg 2805; Tel. and Fax: (01382), and ask for 119 or 129 or 197; Telex: 346-042.

Valley Lodge ★★★ Inviting country hideaway. 37 rooms, 7 suites; conference facilities for 200. PO Box 13, Magaliesburg 2805; Tel. (01382), and ask for 1 or 230; Telex: 346 244 VAL SA.

KLERKSDORP AREA

Klerksdorp Hotel ★★ 62 rooms; conference facilities for 60. PO Box 109, Klerksdorp 2750; Tel. (018) 2-3521.

Picardi ★★ 20 en-suite rooms; conference facilities for 50. PO Box 1048, Klerksdorp 2570; Tel. (018) 2-4501.

Three Fountains ★★ 27 rooms; conference facilities for 50. PO Box 55, Stilfontein 2550; Tel. (018) 4-1771/2.

Van Riebeeck ★★ 17 en-suite rooms, 4 suites. PO Box 10547, Klerksdorp 2570; Tel. (018) 2-9451.

KRUGERSDORP AREA

Aloe Ridge ★★★ 72 en-suite rooms, 4 suites; conference facilities for 125. Associated with and adjacent to Heia Safari Ranch and Zulu 'living village'. PO Box 3040, Krugersdorp 2040; Tel. (011) 957-2070; Telex: 422-655.

LICHTENBURG

Elgro ★★ 56 rooms, 1 suite. PO Box 365, Lichtenburg 2740; Tel. (01441) 2-3051.

MMABATHO

Mmabatho Sun Luxurious Sun International hotel and casino; 'ethnic' architectural theme. 146 rooms, 4 suites; extensive conference facilities. PO Box 600, Mafikeng 8670, Bophuthatswana; Tel. (01401) 2-1142/4; Fax: (01401) 2-1661; Telex: 0937 3065 BP, or contact Central Reservations.

POTCHEFSTROOM

Elgro ★★ 104 rooms, 3 suites; conference facilities for 500. PO Box 1111, Potchefstroom 2520; Tel. (0148) 2-5411/9.

ZEERUST

Abjaterskop ★★ 17 rooms. PO Box 390, Zeerust 2865; Tel. (01428) 2-2008.

Caravan/camping and self-catering accommodation

Hartbeespoort Dam area: Hennops Pride, 22 km south of dam: Tel. (012) 40-1556; Magalies Kloof, 8 km north of dam: Tel. (012042) 1541; Zanandi, 8 km west of dam: Tel. (01211) 3-1307.

Klerksdorp area: Water Paradise, east of town: Tel. (018) 2-0160; Orkney-Vaal holiday resort on Vaal River: Tel. (018) 3-3228, 3-3270.

Krugersdorp area: Game Reserve (page 111): Tel. (011) 660-1076; Pines Resort, in town: Tel. (011) 664-4613.

Lichtenburg: Municipal caravan park, 2 km from town: Tel. (01441) 2-4349.

Magaliesberg area: Die Olienhoutboom, 12 km north-east of Magaliesburg village: Tel. (01382) 1232; Lover's Rock, 5 km north of village: PO Box 79, Magaliesburg 2805; Tel. (01382) 87 or 134; Ananda caravan park, 9 km west of Rustenburg: PO Box 15, Rustenburg 0300, Tel. (0142) 97-2335; Rustenburg Kloof Holiday Resort (page 114): PO

Box 16, Rustenburg 0300, Tel. (0142) 97-1351; Rustenburg nature reserve (page 114), Tel. (0421) 3-1050. Montana Guest-farm; PO Box 107, Kroondal 0350, Tel. (0142722) ask for 1413.

USEFUL ADDRESSES AND TELEPHONE NUMBERS

Automobile Association, Klerksdorp: Tel. (018) 2-4781; Krugersdorp: Tel. (011) 666-7101; Potchefstroom: Tel. (0148) 5434; Rustenburg: Tel. (0142) 6225.

Bop Air, Tel. (011) 975-3901 or 339-2314.

Bophuthatswana Directorate of Tourism, Garona Government Offices, Private Bag X2008, Mafikeng 8670, Bophuthatswana; Tel. (01401) 29-2000 or 29-2666/7/8/9/70.

Carletonville Tourist Information, The Town Clerk, PO Box 3, Carletonville 2500; Tel. (01491) 7-2131.

Klerksdorp Tourist Information Centre, Plant House, Cor Pretoria and Emily Hobhouse streets, Klerksdorp 2570; Tel. (018) 2-6220.

Krugersdorp Publicity Association, PO Box 1575, Krugersdorp 1740; Tel. (011) 660-1058/7324.

Potchefstroom Tourist Information, The Town Clerk, PO Box 113, Potchefstroom 2521; Tel. (0148) 2-5112 ext 114.

Professional Hunters Association of SA, PO Box 781175, Sandton 2146; Tel. (011) 783-0920.

Rustenburg Publicity and Tourism Bureau, Municipal Offices, Plein Street, Rustenburg 0300; Tel. (0142) 2-8411 ext 238.

Satour, Johannesburg office: Suite 4611, Carlton Centre, PO Box 1094, Johannesburg 2000; Tel. (011) 331-5241; Telex: 4-89281 SA. Also at Johannesburg airport; Tel. (011) 970-1669.

Sun International group, Head Office, PO Box 784487, Sandton 2146; Tel. (011) 783-8750; Central Reservations: PO Box 784 487, Sandton 2146; Tel. (011) 783-8660. Toll Free: 0140 81 0660

Transvaal Division of Nature Conservation, Private Bag X209, Pretoria 0001; Tel. (012) 201-2361 or 28-5761/2/3/4.

ANNUAL EVENTS

Sun City: Annual million dollar golf challenge.
□Zeerust: Mampoer festival (see page 116): contact the Zeerust Town Clerk, Tel. (01428) 2-1080 for dates and venues.

THE FREE STATE

The province comprises a mostly flat, tree-less and rather bleak 130 000-km^2 expanse of grassland plains country straddling the east-central portion of the great interior plateau. Its boundaries are the Vaal River in the north, the kingdom of Lesotho in the east, and the Northern Cape in the south and west.

Part of the Free State's southern boundary is formed by the Orange River, far and away the country's biggest watercourse and the prime element in an enormous water storage and distribution network. Two of South Africa's largest dams have been built along its course.

In the very early days of white colonialism the territory was known as Trans-Orangia, and then as the British-protected Orange River Sovereignty, and finally, when the Voortrekker settlers of the region were granted their own republic – at the Bloemfontein Convention of 1854 – as the Orange Free State.

Long before then, though, the lands between the Orange and Vaal rivers had been occupied by the San (Bushmen), and by the Tswana and elements of the Sotho people. Later, new groups entered the territory, driven westwards by the bloody upheaval known as the Difaqane, and it was partly in response to this that a brilliant Sotho warrior chieftain called Mosh-weshwe (the name is an imitation of the cut-ting sounds of a knife, a reference to his forceful personality) led his people, in the 1820s, into the fastness of the eastern highlands. At Thaba Bosiu ('mountain of the night') he built a strong-hold, an almost impregnable fortress which he successfully defended against everything his adversaries – Boer, Briton, Ngwane, Ndebele – could throw against him.

In the south of the territory at that time were the Griqua, a well-armed and semi-nomadic people of mixed origin who held closely to their part-Dutch heritage – to the Dutch lan-guage and to the military commando system introduced by the white settlers. Between the Griqua and the Sotho, around Thaba Nchu, lived the Barolong, a Tswana tribe which,

The golden countryside of the eastern Orange Free State. This road leads from Ficksburg to Fouriesburg.

under its leader Moroka, received the north-ward-migrating Boer trekkers of the mid-1830s in peace and with hospitality.

Such, in brief, is the ethnic background.

For its first fifteen years the impoverished little Boer republic struggled to maintain its integrity and its boundaries – against British imperialism and, with perhaps less justice, against Moshweshwe's Sotho nation. Then dia-monds were discovered, in the Kimberley area just to the west, and the country began to prosper. In the 1890s, though, it found itself drawn into the Boer-Briton diplomatic con-frontation that led, in October 1899, to the nearly three-year-long South African War. De-feated and occupied by the armies of Roberts and Kitchener, the Free State reverted to colo-nial status and was twice reconstituted as one of the country's provinces – at the Act of Union in 1910, and then with the advent of the new South Africa in 1994.

LAND AND WEALTH The plains of the central plateau slope gently towards the south-west, bare and windswept for the most part, the visual tedium occasionally relieved by dykes and sills of dolerite 'kopjes' (rocky outcrops). Surface water is scarce, but the soils are deep and rich, the grasses sweet, nurturing great numbers of sheep and cattle.

By contrast, the land in the east is scenically spectacular, rising in magnificent fashion in a series of picturesquely weathered sandstone hills. This too is a fertile region, kind to the growers of maize and wheat, golden sun-flowers, vegetables and fruit (cherries and yel-low peaches are prominent harvests).

Indeed, the Free State is one of the wealthier segments of the subcontinent: in addition to its agricultural bounty it has massive mineral re-sources. Gold, diamonds, platinum and coal are mined in the province; the goldfields, around Welkom, are among the world's big-gest; the coalfields supply the world's first viable synthetic fuel plant, established in 1951 at Sasolburg in the far north.

The capital of the Orange Free State, and the country's judicial capital, is Bloemfontein, situ-ated at an altitude of 1 392 m above sea level and astride the national north-south highway (the N1) that connects Cape Town with Johannesburg, Pretoria and points beyond. Of the province's relatively few other major urban centres, the young mining city of Welkom is the largest, followed by Kroonstad and Sasolburg and, in the eastern areas, Bethlehem and Harrismith.

CLIMATE The Free State is within the summer-rainfall region; the rainfall is lower in the east than in the west, where Witsieshoek receives the highest annual average. Summer months can be hot but seldom unbearably so: the heat is moderated by the plateau's altitude and by the coolness brought by cloud cover and thunderstorms. Winter days are clear and sunny, the nights bitterly cold. During the harsher spells temperatures often plunge well below zero, and the countryside is rimed with frost and, sometimes, mantled by snow.

Climatic indices for Bloemfontein include: ☆ Average January (summer) rainfall: 87 mm; ☆ Average June (winter) rainfall: 8 mm; ☆ Highest monthly rainfall recorded: 105 mm; ☆ Average daily maximum temperature, January: 29,8 °C; ☆ Average daily minimum temperature, January: 15,4 °C; ☆ Average daily maximum temperature, June: 16,6 °C; ☆ Average daily minimum temperature, June: 0,7 °C; ☆ Highest temperature recorded: 37,6 °C; ☆ Lowest temperature recorded: -8,8 °C.

BLOEMFONTEIN

The origin of the name is something of a mystery: the obvious explanation is that 'flower fountain' refers to a very attractive spring near the Modder River, but it seems more likely that it commemorates a cow called Bloem, owned by trekker Rudolph Brits, who had settled in the area in 1840. Bloem was given to jumping fences and eventually she paid the penalty: she was eaten by a lion. Brits is said to have named his farm after the late and lamented animal.

The property was later bought (for £37.10s) by the local British agent and, in 1854, its tiny cluster of houses became the capital of the new Orange Free State republic – and a tiny capital it was: the first village management board met to deliberate on civic matters only in 1859; the first national parliament building, or raadsaal, was a small, unadorned, single-storeyed, thatched structure that had served as the village school.

But the place developed, solidly and undramatically, around Naval Hill (so called since the British mounted naval guns on its crest). Proximity to the diamond fields of the Northern Cape and, a little later, in the 1880s and 1890s, to the gold mines of the Witwatersrand, contributed much to Bloemfontein's prosperity; so too did its position on the routes north from the coastal ports, and some fine buildings were completed during this period (notably the new Raadsaal, and the Anglican Cathedral). By the end of the century a visiting Englishman was able to write that 'the town is one of the neatest and, in a modest way, best appointed capitals in the world. Gardens are planted with trees that are now so tall as to make the whole place seem to swim in green'.

The description more or less still fits, though of course Bloemfontein is now a great deal bigger, its growth hugely stimulated by the discovery and exploitation, in the 1950s, of the Free State goldfields 160 km to the north-east and by the massive Orange River Project launched in 1962 (see page 131). Among its more prominent points of interest are:

NATIONAL BOTANICAL GARDENS, a 45-ha floral sanctuary on Rayton Road, 10 km from city centre. The gardens, dominated by impressive dolomite outcrops, include formal displays as well as an area of natural vegetation. Other features: a herbarium, an orange-blossom arbour, nursery, summer house, potsherds dating from the Iron Age, and a petrified tree reckoned to be between 150 and 300 million years old. Guided walks by arrangement; tearoom; bulbs sold by prior arrangement; open daily. Best months: September through November and February through May.

NAVAL HILL There are fine views of the city from the road that winds around the summit. At the top is the Lamont Hussey Observatory, whose staff discovered over 7 000 binary stars (double-star systems) before its American sponsors closed it down in 1972. The buildings have been converted into a theatre and cultural centre.

Some 200 ha of Naval Hill have been set aside as the Franklin nature reserve, home to a number of game species (eland, springbok, red hartebeest, blesbok, Burchell's zebra). Open daily.

At the foot of the hill, in Union Avenue's Hamilton Park, is the impressively modern Orchid House, with its transparent domed roof, (adjustable for temperature control; internal climatic conditions and the watering of plants are controlled by computer). Inside there are pools, bridges, waterfalls, weathered stone, and over 3 000 lovely orchids. Open daily. Best months to visit: May through September.

HISTORIC BUILDINGS The Old Raadsaal is Bloemfontein's most venerable structure, site of the Free State's first school, church, social venue and seat of government. The small, dung-floored building, now a national monument, is in St George's Street.

The Fourth Raadsaal, completed in 1893 and the last seat of government of the old Republic, is an especially fine piece of architecture, a dignified building which reflects the classical revival: Greek in detail and Renaissance in form.

Inside there are vaulted spaces, floors of Devon marble, and an impressive principal chamber, rooflit by coloured glass. Statuary includes busts of the six Free State presidents and, at the entrance, Coert Steynberg's representation of a mounted Christiaan de Wet, most renowned of the Republic's military sons.

The Old Residency, home of three of the republican presidents, is a splendid edifice in President Brand Street. It now serves as a museum (featuring the trappings of presidential office) and centre for art exhibitions, musical evenings, theatrical performances.

ANGLICAN CATHEDRAL, St George's Street. The foundation stone of the cathedral was laid in 1850 but it wasn't until Herbert Baker came onto the Free State scene, in the first years of the new century, that the building assumed its present, elegantly imposing form. Well worth a visit.

MUSEUMS Bloemfontein has a number of excellent permanent exhibitions. Among the more prominent are:
☆ The National Afrikaans Literary Museum and Research centre, President Brand Street. Devoted to the works and lives of leading Afrikaans writers (manuscripts, photographs, memorabilia). The building, which served as the third Raadsaal, also houses the theatre and music museums (costumes, theatre paraphernalia, musical instruments, personalia). In the grounds is a 'sculpture garden'.
☆ The National Museum, Aliwal Street. Extensive exhibition of fossils; local history and art displays.
☆ Military Museum of the Boer Republics, Monument Road. Devoted to the story of the Boer forces during the South African War (1899-1902): weapons; special displays depicting military, prisoner-of-war and concentration-camp lifestyles; personalia. The museum has an excellent research facility (Africana; war photographs). Close by is the:

NATIONAL WOMEN'S MEMORIAL, on a commanding site in Monument Road. Created in memory of the nearly 27 000 Boer women and children who died (mainly of disease) in British camps during the South African War. The monument comprises a 37-m sandstone obelisk and a pedestal supporting statues (by the noted sculptor Anton van Wouw) of two women, one holding a dying child, the other gazing out over the plains of the Free State. The ashes of Emily Hobhouse, the British woman who campaigned so effectively on behalf of the Boer internees, are buried at the base of the obelisk.

KING'S PARK, situated along Kingsway and 346 ha in extent is the city's principal public garden. During the first decade of the century over 125 000 trees were planted, and they're now in their full and glorious maturity. The park incorporates Loch Logan (a largish lake, flanked by a 500-m rose pergola and a most pleasant picnic and recreational area); the zoo (animals include a large number of monkeys, and a 'liger' – a cross between a lion and a tiger), and the well-known Rose Garden. The latter was inaugurated by the Prince of Wales (the future King Edward V111) in 1925 and boasts more than 4 000 rose trees (floribundas, hybrid teas, miniatures, and a special bed of Zola Budd roses, planted in 1985). Best months to see the roses: October and November, during which time the Rose Festival is held. King's Park is the venue for an open-air market, held on the first Saturday of each month.

Next door is State President Swart Park, comprising the 35 000-seat Free State Stadium, public pool (heated), tennis courts, caravan park.

The spectacular Mushroom Rocks, a prominent feature of the Golden Gate park

SAND DU PLESSIS THEATRE, in Markgraaff Street, a splendidly modern complex completed in 1985 at a cost of R60 million. Worth visiting for the works of art that contribute to the décor. Tours are available; contact the city publicity office (see Advisory, page 137). The main theatre (capacity: 964) and the smaller André Huguenet theatre (capacity: 300) are venues for some fine dramatic, operatic, ballet and concert performances.

THABA NCHU

Until re-incorporated in 1994, a small area some 60 km east of Bloemfontein formed one of the scattered segments of the 'independent' homeland of Bophuthatswana, its principal centre the town of Thaba Nchu ('black mountain'). The place has its modest historical significance: it served as the stronghold of the Morolong people, whose chief Moroko befriended the Voortrekkers on their way north in the 1830s. Today it's a rather ordinary little administrative and trading centre, noted mainly for the handknitted Aran jerseys made locally, for its charming church, and for the:

THABA NCHU SUN hotel and casino complex. This gambling and recreational resort is one of the subcontinent's most attractive: it's décor is based vaguely on traditional African designs; it has all the glitter and luxury, and the amenities, of its larger Sun cousins elsewhere in quasi-independent southern Africa, and it lies within the:

MARIA MOROKA NATIONAL PARK, which extends over much of the Thaba Nchu mountain and includes the large Groothoek dam. The region is scenically most attractive; the sweet grasses of the plains, set against a majestic highland backdrop, nurture springbok and eland, red hartebeest and zebra, steenbok and blesbok. Among its 150 species of bird is the rare blue korhaan.

THE EASTERN HIGHLANDS

Scenic splendour, a number of important nature reserves, a proliferation of San (Bushman) rock art, rewarding day drives and invigorating hikes are the principal attractions of a region that is often, and quite undeservedly, bypassed by tourists.

Golden Gate Highlands National Park

A 12 000-ha expanse of dramatically-sculpted sandstone ridges, peaks, cliffs, caves and weirdly shaped formations, situated south of Harrismith, in the valley of the Little Caledon River and at the foot of the Maluti Mountains. The colours are quite remarkable: sandstone and iron oxides have combined to create a wonderful array of reds, oranges, yellows and golden browns. The Golden Gate itself is a massive, strikingly-hued cliff face.

The park is essentially a scenic reserve, but mountain reedbuck, grey rhebok and oribi are long-time residents of the area and other species – eland, blesbok, red hartebeest and zebra – have been reintroduced. Birdlife comprises some 160 species, including black eagle, bearded vulture, blue crane, jackal buzzard, secretary bird. Willows grace the river-banks; the veld is sometimes bright with red-hot poker, fire lily, watsonia and arum lily.

The Golden Gate has two rest-camps (Brandwag and Glen Reenen) offering self-contained accommodation ranging from two-bed chalets with bathroom to huts with communal ablution facilities. There is also a caravan/camping ground, two restaurants, a ladies' bar, curio shop, laundromat, information centre. Recreation: some lovely scenic and game drives; walks (including the two-day Rhebok hiking trail); climbing; scrambling; trout-fishing; horse-riding (mounts may be hired); swimming; tennis; golf.

Information and bookings: National Parks Board, PO Box 787, Pretoria 0001. Tel. (012) 343-1991.

Harrismith

One of the major centres on the national highway (the N3) between the Witwatersrand and the Natal coastal resorts, the town was founded in 1849 and named after the flamboyant Cape governor and Waterloo veteran Sir Harry Smith. A busy little place, unremarkable in itself though the scenically attractive area offers some pleasant distractions. Among them:

HARRISMITH BOTANIC GARDEN (formerly Drakensberg botanic garden), situated 5 km from town, at the foot of the Platberg, a well-defined height much favoured by walkers and picnickers. The 114-ha garden is a sanctuary for more than 1 000 plant species occurring on the Drakensberg range to the south. There are picnic spots, two dams and some interesting walks.

MOUNT EVEREST GAME RESERVE encompasses 1 000 ha of mountain and plains countryside, and 22 species of game. One may drive or ride (Land-Rovers and horses for hire) or walk (but watch out for the rhino) through the area. Accommodation: one luxury log cabin; family huts; rondavels; mountain huts.

PRESIDENT BRAND PARK, a resort area on the Wilge river-banks: camping/caravanning; 'trimpark'; attractive picnic sites; menagerie; bird sanctuary.

STERKFONTEIN DAM, 25 km south-west of town, is a clear and most inviting stretch of water, popular among trout-fishermen and water-sportsmen.

Bethlehem

The eastern Free State's most important farming and commercial centre, set in golden upland countryside, founded by the hardy Voortrekkers of the 1840s and named after both the birthplace of Christ and the region's wheat-growing potential (Bethlehem means 'town of bread'). Its beginnings may have been rather dour but it's now a surprisingly lively and modern little place offering a suitably varied calendar of arts and entertainment and some good restaurants. Of note are its pleasant

Sterkfontein Dam, near Harrismith. The waters are much favoured by trout fishermen.

sandstone buildings, many of them historic; its museum; the champagne quality of its air and, in the general area, a number of attractive outdoor venues, including the:

WOLHUTER NATURE RESERVE, 6 km south of town: an 800-ha haven for a wide variety of buck. Also prolific birdlife; a dam; patches of thick pine forest, and pleasant picnic spots. Recommended are three circular scenic and game-viewing drives (map available at the entrance).

PRETORIUSKLOOF NATURE RESERVE, within the town (entrance from Church Street): a small, cliff-flanked sanctuary. Small mammals, birds, walks along the Jordan River.

LOCH ATHLONE, a storage dam on the Jordan River, and a very popular recreational area: organized sport and entertainment during the December-January holiday season; boating; swimming; tennis; angling; waterskiing; picnicking; braaiing. The ship-shaped Athlone Castle restaurant is an unusual feature.

Qwaqwa

The smallest and poorest of the former 'national states', created by the Nationalist government as a component of its 'grand apartheid' design, is situated below the high mountains south of Harrismith, close to the Lesotho border. The name, an ironic one in the circumstances, means 'whiter than white', a reference to a prominent sandstone hill. Altogether a beautiful corner of South Africa, but an overcrowded and impoverished one. The principal town is Phuthaditjhaba; the only other major centre is Witsieshoek, astride the tumbling Elands River. Of interest to visitors:

☆ Local (Batlokwa and Bakwena, both belong to the baSotho ba Bonwa, or South Sotho group) handicrafts: mohair wall-hangings, karakul carpets, hand-painted pottery and basketware.

☆ The Qwaqwa conservation area is a 30 000-ha expanse of largely mountainous and largely unspoilt terrain, home to some antelope and to a number of fairly rare bird species (the bearded and Cape vulture, bald ibis and wattled crane). Good for walking, but stick to daylight hours unless you're part of a group. Just outside the area is the:

☆ Bergwood resort complex: luxury and family chalets among the Drakensberg foothills; heated pool; excellent restaurant; unsurpassed views and, for the energetic, a hiking trail to the top of Mont-aux-Sources (see page 184). The noted Metsi Matso trail connects Bergwood with the:

☆ Swartwater Dam, about 20 km from Phuthaditjhaba: popular among anglers.

Information: see Advisory, page 137.

LAND OF THE VAAL

The Vaal River rises on the western slopes of the Drakensberg range and flows south-westwards, forming the boundary between the Free State and three of the northern provinces before entering the Northern Cape and, 300 km farther on, joining the Orange.

The total catchment area of the Vaal River is 200 000 km^2; the mean annual run-off 5,6 billion m^3, and it is the Orange's most important tributary, its water intensively exploited for irrigation, for hydro-electric generation, for industry – and for recreation: the Vaal and its willow-shaded banks provide a pleasant playground for thousands of holiday-makers and weekenders, most of them from Johannesburg and the Witwatersrand area.

Along the middle reaches there are resorts, caravan parks and camping grounds, and hotels.

A few of the latter are of international standard, but generally the area's attractions and amenities have few pretensions to sophistication: people come for the long, leisurely days of undemanding relaxation in the sunshine, for the watersports, for family-type diversion and entertainment.

Much of this activity (and inactivity) takes place along the river's northern banks (see Pretoria and Johannesburg, page 51). Pleasant venues on the southern (Free State) side include:

THE VAAL DAM, a 300 km^2 stretch of water, 32 km^2 of which is ideal for a wide range of sports. The waters are deep, bilharzia-free and much favoured by anglers.

On the southern banks of the dam is the Jim Fouché holiday resort, comprising caravan/camping sites, picnic and barbecue spots, restaurant, shop, tennis courts, swimming pool, riding stables.

VILLIERS AND DENEYSVILLE, on the eastern and western sides of the dam respectively, are two attractive little resort villages that offer simple accommodation and the standard range of family leisure amenities (pools, playgrounds, miniature golf and so forth). Watersports – fishing, boating, swimming, skiing – are the main enticements.

SASOLBURG An industrial town, site of the country's first, giant, synthetic fuel project, Sasol ('Sasol' is an acronym for the Afrikaans version of South African Coal, Oil and Gas Corporation) was founded in 1954. But it's by no means the dark and satanic place its name suggests – on the contrary, the planners have done an excellent environmental job: the town is blessed with green belts and pleasant open spaces, a great many trees (over 70 000 to date, including 14 varieties of oak), and some lovely parks, among them the Highveld Garden (on President Brand Street). Next to this, and well worth a visit, is the Bird Park.

Just outside Sasolburg, on the Vaal riverbank, is the Abrahamsrust holiday resort: log cabins, caravan sites, mobile units; picnic, barbecue and fishing spots; pool, water-chute, model steam-train, miniature golf and, nearby, one of the southern hemisphere's largest ice-rinks. Not exactly stylish, but something of a paradise for families with children.

PARYS A largish, attractive town set on a part of the river that has been segmented into numerous streams and rivulets. They flow around green and embowered islands, and beckon the contemplative fisherman. In the vicinity are some enchanting little parks, gardens and picnic spots, and some lively holiday areas, including:
☆ Mimosa Gardens: sophisticated camping ground; luxury chalets; restaurant, beergarden, fun-fair, discos and the rest.
☆ Golf Island, to the north-east of town.
☆ The Feesgrond, to the north-east of Sasolburg: a splendid caravan park in pleasant surrounds; highly rated among water-sportsmen.

BLOEMHOF DAM, near the town of that name and just below the confluence of the Vaal and Vet rivers, has an impressive 5-km-long dam wall. The waters – much favoured by anglers (yellowfish, carp, barbel, mudfish) – nurture two fairly important nature sanctuaries:
☆ The Bloemhof Dam nature reserve (on the Transvaal side of the river) comprises just over 22 000 ha of flattish, open grassland that sustains white rhino, black wildebeest, zebra, springbok, blesbok, eland and ostrich. The reserve is also a game-hunting area; two of its gates are closed during the May-through-August hunting season. Accommodation is limited to a camping ground.
☆ The Sandveld nature reserve, on the southern banks of the dam, covers 14 700 ha of unusual terrain: sandy Kalahari thornveld, which properly belongs to the semi-desert regions far to the north-west. The sweet grasses sustain giraffe and blue wildebeest, eland, gemsbok, red hartebeest, springbok, ostrich and over 170 species of bird have been recorded within its boundaries, including white-backed vulture, pygmy falcon, hornbills and, on the dam, flocks of geese and ducks.
Accommodation: campsite, with basic ablution facilities; recreation: game-viewing, picnicking; angling, boating (there's a boathouse on the dam) and hunting.

CHRISTIANA is a pleasant little Vaal River town, south-west of Bloemhof, whose attractions include the Rob Ferreira spa and resort: luxury rooms, chalets (bathroom, fully equipped kitchen), camping/caravanning area; heated mineral and private pools, shop, restaurant; bowls, tennis, boating, angling; and a game reserve in which white rhino, eland, red hartebeest and gemsbok may be seen.

THE FREE STATE GOLDFIELDS
Though geologists suspected the presence of gold in the northern Free State in the later 1930s, it wasn't until April 1946 that an immensely rich seam – what transpired to be an extension of the fabulous Witwatersrand reef far to the north – was unearthed on the farm Geduld. The region now produces about a third of South Africa's vast output of the yellow metal. Its principal centre is:

Welkom
A new, well-planned, fast-developing mining and industrial city of modern buildings, pleasant parks, wide and easily negotiable thoroughfares (there are 23 traffic circles), shopping malls, an airport, good restaurants and a lively

Flamingos are among the more prolific residents of Welkom's pans

theatre (the 750-seat Oppenheimer, situated in the plush Civic Centre), and, in the early 1990s, an unhappy record of racial tension – a symptom of South Africa in transition.

Highlight of any visit to Welkom must be a surface and underground tour of one of the area's gold mines, some which are household names within the investment world – President Brand, Harmony, Virginia, Lorraine, Freddies, Free State Geduld, Free State Saaiplaas, Welkom, St Helena, President Steyn. Full-day tours are conducted; features of interest incidental to the mining and gold-pouring processes include African dances (sometimes) and, curiously and rather charmingly, an underground wine-cellar. Book well in advance; information from the Welkom Publicity Association (see Advisory, page 137).

Among the other points of note in and around the city are the extraordinarily prolific, and attractive, birdlife of the pans and dams (filled with mine-water, and salty from evaporation) of the area. Notable species include pink flamingo (thousands of them), the sacred ibis, Egyptian goose, maccoa (Muscovy) duck, marsh owl and, most unexpected, a great many seagulls, even though Welkom is around 400 km from the nearest coast.

The two most popular of these stretches of water are the Flamingo Pan (picnic and braai spots, lawns, playgrounds, nature trails, and of course bird-watching and bird photography) on the airport road, and the Theron Pan, within the town's limits and developed as a municipal park.

Theronia is a popular boating and angling venue, complete with yacht club (and licensed restaurant), boathouse and jetty.

Around Welkom

VIRGINIA is a smaller but equally pleasant mining centre (it's billed as a 'garden town') about 20 km south-east of Welkom. Again, a visit to one of the mines (e.g. Harmony, Western Holdings) is a must. Tourist amenities include the 90-ha Virginia Park resort on the Sand River (good hotel; self-catering chalets; caravan/camping sites, and excellent fishing).

The Orange River's giant Gariep Dam (Hendrik Verwoerd). Resorts and reserves fringe its shores.

WINBURG, on the N1 highway, south-east of Welkom, was the first 'capital' of the territory that is now the Orange Free State. Founded in 1842, the name means 'town of victory' – which commemorates, not a feat of arms or some grand political triumph but the conclusion of an argument among the founders about where exactly to build the village. Worth visiting is the Voortrekker Monument and its adjacent museum.

WILLEM PRETORIUS GAME RESERVE, also on the N1, between Winburg and Ventersburg, is a 9 300-ha sanctuary proclaimed around the large Allemanskraal Dam. Numbered among the game are white rhino, giraffe, buffalo, wildebeest, many types of buck and about 220 bird species (waterbirds on the dam, game birds on the grasslands; breeding martial and fish eagles may be seen).

A public resort, established on a rocky hill overlooking the dam, offers pleasant self-contained family accommodation, well-equipped flats, camping/caravanning facilities, licensed restaurant, shop, pool, tennis courts, 9-hole golf course, bowling green, jetty. Hiking enthusiasts can go on one of the nature trails, and there is also good angling on the dam (yellowfish, bass, carp). Information: Tel. (01734) 4229 (resort) and (01734) 4168 (game reserve).

SOUTHERN FREE STATE

Vast, bare plains country that supported millions of head of game until the white farmers and hunters arrived in the 19th century. Sterling efforts are now being made to reintroduce some of the animal species.

The Orange (see panel, page 134), the country's principal watercourse, is the dominant natural feature of the region, flowing from the Lesotho highlands in the east to and through the northern Cape in the west, its waters massively harnessed to meet the growing demands of cities, and of industry and agriculture, within the framework of what is known as the Orange River Project (ORP). The scheme's main components are worth noting: two major dams (the Gariep and the Vanderkloof); the Orange-Fish tunnel (the world's largest continuous water tunnel, 85 km long and driven through an entire mountain range); the Van der Kloof and Fish-Sundays canals (which irrigate the citrus orchards of the Sundays River valley in the Eastern Cape) and the Welgedacht barrage (which supplies water to Bloemfontein and other Free State centres).

Gariep Dam

Formerly known as the Hendrik Verwoerd, the Gariep has a storage capacity of about 6 billion m^3 and covers an area of 374 km^2.

Around the northern shores is the dam's 11 237-ha nature reserve, home to the country's largest population of springbok, and to black wildebeest, mountain reedbuck, blesbok, steenbok, and a breeding herd of Cape mountain zebra.

On the reserve's western boundary is a pleasant holiday resort, a holiday centre of self-contained, well-appointed family rondavels and a shady caravanning/camping area. Fine views of water and veld and hills; powerboating, sailing and fishing on the dam; game-viewing; an 18-hole golf course, bowling green, riding stables; a restaurant and shopping centre, post office and petrol filling station. Information: Tel. (052172), and ask for 45 (resort), 26 (dam).

To the east, covering a 21 000-ha triangular expanse of land at the confluence of the Orange and Caledon rivers, is the:

TUSSEN-DIE-RIVIERE GAME FARM, on which visitors may see a number of game species introduced to the area in an impressive relocation exercise launched in the 1970s. The game, now prolific, includes white rhino, Burchell's zebra, blue and black wildebeest, blesbok, kudu, springbok, eland, red hartebeest, mountain reedbuck, gemsbok. Birdlife is varied and interesting (both game and water species are present, the latter mostly on the floodplain to the west). Accommodation: simply fitted-out chalets (communal ablution facilities) and a camping/caravanning area. There are picnic sites, and a network of game-viewing roads and short (3 to 4 km) nature trails.

The farm is open to the general public from September through April. In the winter months it plays host to hunters – about ten each week, or 300 during a season. Information: Tel. (05862) 2803.

OVISTON NATURE RESERVE, 13 000 ha in extent (of which 3 500 ha is accessible to the public) flanks the dam's southern (Cape) shore. Proclaimed mainly to protect the region's scrub and grassland vegetation (known as the False Upper Karoo ecosystem) and to sustain breeding herds of buck species (for relocation to other areas), it offers a guided overnight trail; shorter trails and walks, and about 50 km of game-viewing track. Information: Tel. (0553) 5-0000.

Vanderkloof Dam

Some 150 km downstream from the Gariep, the Vanderkloof (formerly known as the PK le Roux) is South Africa's second biggest dam. Close by are two sanctuaries:

DOORNKLOOF NATURE RESERVE, a largish expanse of wilderness running along 75 km of the dam's south-eastern shoreline. This is a relatively new reserve, established in 1981 to help the land recover from overgrazing, and as yet there hasn't been any serious attempt to re-stock it with game, though you can spot kudu and mountain reedbuck, steenbok and duiker and (occasionally) the rare brown hyena. Camping and fishing are permitted; guided trails by arrangement; and a strenuous five-day hike to the:

ROLFONTEIN NATURE RESERVE, along the western portion of the dam. The area has a good network of game-viewing roads, leading to viewing points and picnic spots, but can probably be better seen and enjoyed on foot. This is rugged country (part of what is called the Renosterberg), and it contains fully 13 major plant communities, 14 types of grass, and a quite unusual variety of wildlife – 57 mammal species alone, 16 of which are carnivores (including cheetah and brown hyena). Among the birds are herons, cormorants and fish eagles. There are overnight huts for hikers, and slightly more sophisticated accommodation at nearby Vanderkloof and Petrusville.

For information on the reserve and bookings for its two-day guided hiking trails, contact the officer-in-charge, Vanderkloof, Tel. (05782), and ask for 160.

GETTING AROUND

Day drives

Much of the Free State is virtually devoid of scenic or indeed any other kind of interest. However, fairly rewarding drives can be undertaken from Bloemfontein to and along the Vaal River in the north (see page 128); to the Orange River, its dams and nature reserves in the south (page 131), and to the Thaba Nchu mountain, nature reserve and hotel-casino complex (page 126).

A marked exception to the scenic tedium is the eastern highlands region (page 126).

DRIVE 1 If you're in the Bethlehem/Harrismith area (page 127) and have time to spare, a pleasant day-excursion would take in:

Bethlehem south on the R711 to the picturesque hamlet of Clarens ☆ Turn left for and through the Golden Gate Highlands National Park (page 126) to ☆ Witsieshoek in Qwaqwa (and the nearby, flat-topped sandstone Mount Qwaqwa, centrepiece of a ruggedly attractive region), and on to ☆ Harrismith (see page 127) ☆ Return to Bethlehem via the R49, through Kestell and a countryside of rolling grasslands and bountiful maize- and wheat-fields.

DRIVE 2 Still in the east, but this time you will need your passport. Start from Bloemfontein, drive for 68 km on the R64 to and then through Thaba Nchu to Ladybrand, close to the Lesotho border. Visit: Catherine Brand museum (rock paintings; Stone and Iron-age relics) ☆ Turn north on the Clocolan road (R26); turn left after 8,7 km for Modderspruit: sandstone cave-art, and a highly unusual mission-station cave church ☆ Back on the R26 and continue through Clocolan to Ficksburg, headquarters of South Africa's cherry industry. The town is notable for its sandstone buildings and lovely gardens; it's also a key element in the massive Lesotho Highlands Water Scheme.

To digress briefly: the scheme is one of the most ambitious of its kind in the southern hemisphere, designed eventually – in the second decade of the 21st century – to supply Gauteng (formerly known as the PWV) and its environs, with a huge 63,6 m³/sec flow-rate of Lesotho's abundant water, effectively doubling the annual flow into the Vaal basin. It will also meet the whole of Lesotho's power needs. The three-phase project involves: ☆ An extensive road network over some of Africa's most difficult terrain; ☆ Hundreds of km of tunnels linking some of the biggest rock-fill dams in the world to the Vaal River system near Bethlehem; and ☆ An enormous hydro-electric generating plant. The first phase of the scheme, which will produce what has been described as a 'mere trickle' of 17 m³/sec, will be completed in 1995. But back on the road:

On to Fouriesburg, near which is the southern hemisphere's biggest sandstone cave; turn right on the road signposted ☆ Butha Buthe

and drive to the Lesotho border post at Caledon Poort Bridge (Butha Buthe itself is unremarkable); turn right after the border post and follow the spectacular scenic route south-westwards, through Lerike and Teyateyaneng (which has an impressive local weaving industry, begun as a project for the underprivileged and now a large and lucrative factory), to ☆ Maseru, capital of Lesotho (see page 358), and back to Bloemfontein via Ladybrand.

Walks and hikes

The Free State was largely ignored by the hiking and trailing fraternity until fairly recently, but the attractions of the eastern 'Little Switzerland' region and the southern (Orange River) area are beginning to receive the attention they deserve. Among the longer of the established trails are:

☆ The 50-km, two-day Rhebok hike through the Golden Gate Highlands National Park (see page 126). The trail's quite strenuous: the countryside is mountainous (en route, you ascend the 2 757-m Generaalskop, which affords magnificent views of the Free State and Lesotho). Information: National Parks Hiking Way (see page 351).

☆ The 37-km, two-day Houtkop hike. Much less demanding than the Rhebok, this starts from the Loch Athlone holiday resort near Bethlehem and meanders through the grasslands. Main attractions are the birdlife (waterfowl, weavers, Cape vultures) and indigenous flora. Information: the Hoogland Wildlife Society in Bethlehem; Tel. (01431) 3-2800.

☆ The Imperani hiking trail, a scenic two-day, one-night walk (though one can hurry it through in a single day) in the Ficksburg area. Sandstone mountain scenery; lovely views; interesting birdlife. Information: Municipality of Ficksburg; Tel. (0563) 2122/3/4.

☆ The Steve Visser nature walk, a leisurely, two-day, 15-km trail from the Leliehoek pleasure resort near Ladybrand. Magnificent scenery, and attractive trees and shrubs of the Maluti mountains; there are also some Bushman caves to explore.

Rambles: gentler and shorter walks can be enjoyed in the ☆ National Botanic Gardens in Bloemfontein (see page 124); ☆ The Harrismith Botanic Gardens (page 127); ☆ The Tussen-die-Riviere game farm near Bethulie in the southern Free State (page 132).

EXPLORING THE GREAT RIVER

The Orange rises in Lesotho's Maluti Mountains to the east and flows for 2 250 km across the subcontinent's high central plateau, passing through the magnificent Augrabies gorge (see page 265), close to the Namibian border, before negotiating the last, desolate stretch to the Atlantic seaboard. It is by far the country's largest river, draining fully 47% of South Africa's total land area.

The river was once known as the Gariep (from the Khoisan word Garib, meaning Great River) but was renamed, in 1779, in honour of the Prince of Orange. Its islands, of which there are many, have an especially colourful history: in the 1880s some of them served as suitably inaccessible hideaways for bands of rustlers and brigands, notorious 'river pirates' who were finally, and with difficulty, dislodged by colonial forces sent up from the Cape.

The waters are erratic, the flow dictated by seasonal rains. When the summers have been generous the river becomes a swift-moving torrent sweeping across the land in a swathe nearly 10 km wide. At other times it is benign, even sluggish.

For almost its entire length the Orange flows through dry, sometimes arid countryside, generally flattish and dun-coloured but enlivened by fringes of bright greenery along the riverbanks and, increasingly, by irrigated farmlands that yield harvests of cotton, lucerne, dates, raisins and sultanas.

The terrain around the river's lower reaches is rich in semi-precious stones, many of which lie on the surface, literally waiting to be picked up: tiger's eye and amethyst; amazonite, rose quartz, garnet and beryl; tourmaline, agate, jasper and onyx. Diamonds are found, and still mined and panned, in the inland gravels; around the estuary – in the coastal areas of Namaqualand and Namibia – are some of the world's largest alluvial fields (see page 328).

TAKING TO THE WATERS One of the more rewarding and intrepid ways to explore the Orange River (indeed, probably the only way to explore it thoroughly) is by canoe, raft or 'rubber duck', as a member of a water-safari group led by an expert guide. Several outfits conduct expeditions, offering four- and six-day trips (scenic variety, exercise, some element of challenge, and companionable camp life) at surprisingly cheap rates. They include:

Felix Unite River Adventures, Johannesburg (011) 463-3167 and Cape Town (021) 689-8728/9 ☆ Orange River Adventures, Cape Town (021) 685-4475 ☆ River Runners, Cape Town (021) 706-3300/3311 and Johannesburg (011) 403-2512 ☆ Venture Trails (they run an especially spectacular 'Orange River Escape'): Cape Town (021) 25-2886 or 531-2785, or write to: PO Box 231, Howard Place 7450; ☆ River Rats, Cape Town (021) 73-5111.

Sundown and sociability on the banks of the Orange

ADVISORY: FREE STATE

CLIMATE

Summer rainfall region. Summers: hot, but the plateau is high and the heat seldom too intense for comfort; thunderstorms bring the rains, but too infrequently in recent years. Winters: bone-dry; cold nights; cool and sometimes warm days. See also page 124.

TRAVEL

Road. Bloemfontein is 175 km from Kimberley; 108 km from Maseru; 411 km from Johannesburg; 469 km from Pretoria; 614 km from East London; 643 km from Port Elizabeth; 653 km from Durban; 966 km from Beit Bridge on the Zimbabwe border, and 1 007 km from Cape Town.

Bloemfontein is on the main N1 north-south highway that links Cape Town and the Johannesburg-Pretoria area. Good tarred roads connect the city with all major centres, including Welkom (R700 and R710); Kimberley (R64); Maseru in Lesotho (R64); East London (R30). Most of the larger car-hire firms have offices in Bloemfontein (city and airport) and Welkom.
 Coach travel: Contact Rennies travel for Greyhound bus services to the major centres, Tel. Bloemfontein (051) 30-2361 and Translux (051) 408-3242.

Rail. Bloemfontein is a key point on the national rail network; the railway station is in Maitland Street. For principal passenger services contact, Information: Tel. (051) 408-2111, Reservations: Tel. (051) 408-2941. Welkom, Parys and other larger Free State towns also have efficient rail links with the country's main centres.

Air. Bloemfontein airport is situated 14 km from city centre. Daily flights to and from major South African centres. There is no bus service between city and airport. Information: SAA, Prudential Building, St Andrews St, Tel. (051) 47-3811. Link Airways, Tel. (051) 33-3255 or (011) 973-2941/643-4824. Welkom also has a modern airport; daily flights between city and Johannesburg international airport. Welkom airport, Tel. (0171) 7-1250.

ACCOMMODATION

Select hotels

BLOEMFONTEIN

Bloemfontein Sun ★★★★ Standard Southern Sun luxury hotel, located in central business district. 110 rooms, 5 suites; conference facilities for 200.

PO Box 2212, Bloemfontein 9300; Tel. (051) 30-1911; Fax: (051) 47-7102; Telex: 2-67039.

Cecil ★★ Central. 56 en suite rooms; conference facilities for 195. PO Box 516, Bloemfontein 9300; Tel. (051) 48-1155.

Halevy House ★★★ A Protea hotel; central, situated corner Charles and Markgraaff streets. 22 luxury rooms; à la carte restaurant, 3 bars; full conference facilities. PO Box 1368, Bloemfontein 9300; Tel. (051) 48-0271; Telex: 26-7129.

Holiday Inn ★★★ Fairly central (in Union Avenue, 2 km from CBD). Park-like setting. 145 rooms, conference facilities for 600. PO Box 1851, Bloemfontein 9300; Tel. (051) 30-1111; Fax: (051) 30-4141; Telex: 26-7645.

Landdrost Sun ★★★★ Stylish Southern Sun hotel, in suburb of Brandwag, close to university; 147 rooms, 4 suites; each unit faces onto shady courtyard; conference facilities for 200. PO Box 12015, Brandhof 9324; Tel. (051) 47-0310; Fax: (051) 30-5678.

Maitland ★★ 77 en-suite rooms, 5 suites; conference facilities for 50; excellent à la carte restaurant. PO Box 221, Bloemfontein 9300; Tel. (051) 48-3121.

BETHLEHEM

Park Hotel ★★ 44 en-suite rooms; conference facilities. PO Box 8, Bethlehem 9700; Tel. (01431) 3-5191.

CLARENS

Maluti Lodge ★★ 14 en-suite rooms. PO Box 21, Clarens 9707; Tel and Fax: (014326) 661.

HARRISMITH

Holiday Inn ★★ 119 rooms; conference facilities for up to 200. PO Box 363, Harrismith 9880; Tel. (01436) 2-1011; Fax: (01436) 2-2770.

HENDRIK VERWOERD DAM

Hendrik Verwoerd Dam Motel ★★ 23 rooms. PO Box 20, Hendrik Verwoerd Dam 9922; Tel. (052172), and ask for 60; Telex: 26-7857.

KROONSTAD

Toristo Protea Hotel HH 2 km outside town (which is half-way between Bloemfontein and Johannesburg). 48 rooms; conference facilities for 200; restaurant: country-style cuisine. Postal address: Corner of Du Toit and Rautenbach streets, Kroonstad 9501; Tel. (01411) 2-5111; Fax: (01411) 3-3298.

PARYS

Riviera Protea Inn ★★ 38 en-suite rooms; conference facilities for 100; à la carte restaurant. PO Box 90, Parys 9585; Tel. (01601) 2143.

THEUNISSEN

Algro Hotel ★★ 32 en-suite rooms; pool; à la carte restaurant. PO Box 37, Theunissen 9410; Tel. (0175) 3-0381/2/3.

VIRGINIA

Virginia Protea ★★ 30 en-suite family rooms; conference facilities for 100. PO Box 673, Virginia 9430; Tel. (01722) 2-2211.

VREDE

Balmoral ★★ 17 en-suite rooms; conference facilities. PO Box 13, Vrede 2455; Tel. (01334) 3-1008.

WELKOM

Golden Orange ★★ 62 rooms (51 en-suite); conference facilities. PO Box 718, Welkom 9460; Tel. (0171) 2-5281/2/3.

Holiday Inn ★★★ Fairly central (1 km from business and shopping centres). 120 rooms; conference facilities for 200. PO Box 887, Welkom 9460; Tel. (0171) 7-3361; Fax: (0171) 2-1458; Telex: 26-3024.

Hotel 147 ★★ 42 en-suite rooms; conference facilities for 100. PO Box 1834, Welkom 9460; Tel. (0171) 2-5381/3.

Welkom Hotel ★★★ 77 rooms, 5 suites; conference facilities for 200. Pool, sauna, several restaurants & bars. PO Box 973, Welkom 9460; Tel. (0171) 5-1411.

BOPHUTHATSWANA

Thaba Nchu Sun. Luxury hotel and casino complex, built into the mountainside, overlooking an attractive lake, and situated in a private game reserve (see page 126). 116 rooms, 2 suites, conference facilities. Pool, solarium, sauna, gymnasium, whirlpool bath, massage room; floodlit tennis courts; casino; cinema and live entertainment. PO Box 114, Thaba Nchu, Bophuthatswana; Tel. (05265) 2161.

Ungraded accommodation

For less sophisticated accommodation – one-star and ungraded hotels, guesthouses and lodges – contact the relevant publicity office: see Useful Numbers, opposite page.

Bed and Breakfast Central Booking Office: 5th Floor – JCC House, Cnr. Empire and Owl Street, PO Box 91309, Auckland Park 2006, Tel. (011) 482-2206/7; Fax: (011) 726-6915; Telex: 4 50027 BANDB.

BLOEMFONTEIN

Bed and Breakfast: Unitas Herberg, Logeman St 22, Universitas, Tel. (051) 22-6874. City Inn, Eddisonstreet (Pasteur Ave), PO Box 7589, Tel. (051) 22-6284/5.

Chester Hill, cor. Gordon St and St George St, Tel. (051) 47-8476/47-8845/6.

City Lodge, cor. Parfitt Ave. and Voortrekker St, Tel. (051) 47-9888.

Die Herberg, 12 Barnes St, Tel. (051) 30-7500.

J & I Cloud 9 Chalets (N1 coming from Winburg), PO Box 3659, Tel. (05214) 2157/8.

Stanville The Inn, Zastron St, PO Box 3391, Tel. (051) 47-7471/2.

Tuis Huis, 88 Voortrekker St, Tel. (051) 48-3182.

Caravan/camping and self-catering accommodation

Bethlehem: Loch Athlone Holiday Resort, PO Box 551, Bethlehem 9700, Tel. (01431) 3-5732 ext 171.

Bethulie: Bethulie Dam Resort, PO Box 7, Bethulie 9992, Tel. (05862), and ask for 2.

Bloemfontein: Johan Brits Caravan Park, PO Box 3704, Bloemfontein 9300, Tel. (051) 405-8488; Fax: (051) 30-4573. Maselpoort Resort, Private Bag 20519, Bloemfontein 9300, Tel. (051) 41-7848. Tom's Place, situated on N1 at the Tierpoort Dam; PO Box 7660, Bloemfontein 9300, Tel. (05215) 680.

Bothaville: Doring Park caravan park, situated on the banks of the Vaal River; PO Box 12, Bothaville 9600, Tel. (01414) 2017.

Brandfort: Andries Pretorius caravan park, PO Box 13, Brandfort 9400, Tel. (05222) 221.

Clarens: Steunmekaar caravan park, PO Box 24, Clocolan 9735, Tel. (05652) 24; Fax: (same) 24.

Clocolan: Ikebana guest farm, PO Box 365, Clocolan 9735, Tel. (05652) 3604; beautifully situated near Maluti mountains; 40 caravan/tent stands; 20 tent stands.

Deneysville: Rus-'n-Bietjie resort, PO Box 145, Deneysville 1932, Tel. (01618) 578; near Vaal dam and yacht club; caravan/camping (50 stands).

Ficksburg: Thom caravan park, PO Box 116, Ficksburg 9730, Tel. (0563) 2122.

Fouriesburg: Meiringskloof Nature Park, PO Box 101, Fouriesburg 9725, Tel. (014332) 115.

Frankfort: Dorpoewerpark, PO Box 2, Frankfort 9830, Tel. (01613) 3-1610.

Golden Gate: Golden Gate Highlands National Park, situated in the foothills of the Maluti mountains. Bookings: National Parks Board, PO Box 787, Pretoria 0001, Tel. (012) 343-1991.

Harrismith: Mount Everest Game Reserve, PO Box 471, Harrismith 9880, Tel. (01436) 2-3493; Fax: (same). President Brand caravan park, PO Box 43, Harrismith 9880, Tel. (01436) 2-1061.

Ladybrand: Leliehoek Pleasure Resort, Private Bag X11, Ladybrand 9745, Tel. (0561) 4-0654.

Odendaalsrus: Mimosa caravan park, PO Box 21, Odendaalsrus 9480, Tel. (0171) 41940.

Parys: Feesgrond caravan park, PO box 359, Parys 9585, Tel. (01601) 2131.

Reitz: Municipal caravan park, PO Box 26, Reitz 9810, Tel. (01434) 3-2811 (no tents allowed).

Sasolburg: Abrahamsrust Recreation Resort, situated on the Vaal River, PO Box 60, Sasolburg 9570, Tel. (016) 71-2222. Westvaal caravan park, PO Box 1031, Sasolburg 9570, Tel. (01601) 4008.

Trompsburg: Municipal caravan park, PO Box 23, Trompsburg 9913, Tel. (05812) 23.

Ventersburg: Willem Pretorius Game Reserve Resort, situated on the Allemanskraal dam in the reserve. Post Office Ventersburg 9451, Tel. (01734) 4229.

Welkom: Circle caravan park, PO Box 1034, Welkom 9460, Tel. (0171) 5-3987. Flamingo Lake Estate, PO Box 998, Welkom 9460, Tel. (0171) 3-2296/7. Municipal caravan park, PO Box 30, Welkom 9460, Tel. (0171) 2-1455.

Winburg: Municipal caravan park, PO Box 26, Winburg 9420, Tel. (05242), and ask for 3.

Zastron: Municipal caravan park, PO Box 20, Zastron 9950, Tel. (05542) 397.

USEFUL ADDRESSES AND TELEPHONE NUMBERS

Bethlehem Publicity Office, Civic Centre, Muller Street; PO Box 551, Bethlehem 9700; Tel. (01431) 3-5732; after hours: (01431) 3-1795.

Bloemfontein Publicity Office, Hoffman Square (between Maitland and St Andrew's streets), PO Box 639, Bloemfontein 9300; Tel. (051) 47-3859.

Clarens tourist information, Tel. (014326) 605.

Harrismith tourist information, Tel. (01436) 2-1061.

Kroonstad tourist information, Tel. (01411) 2-2231.

OFS Angling Association, PO Box 377, Welkom 9460; Tel. (0171) 5-1431.

OFS Hunters' and Conservation Association, PO Box 428, Bloemfontein 9300; Tel. (051) 30-5398.

Parys tourist information, Tel. (01601) 2131.

Qwaqwa Tourism and Nature Conservation Board, Private Bag X814, Witsieshoek 9870; Tel. (01432) 5886.

Satour, Second Floor, Penbel Bldg, 29 Elizabeth Street; PO Box 3517, Bloemfontein 9300; Tel. (051) 47-1362; Telex: 26-7919.

Sasolburg tourist information, Tel. (016) 76-0029.

Welkom Publicity Association, Clock Tower, Stateway; PO Box 2030, Welkom 9460; Tel. (0171) 2-9244.

ANNUAL EVENTS

Bloemfontein Agricultural Show: March/April □Rose Festival: October □Bethlehem Show: March □Corn Festival: October □Ficksburg Cherry Festival, November.

DURBAN, THE EAST COAST AND ZULULAND

Kwazulu-Natal – known as plain Natal until 1994 – arguably the most beautiful of South Africa's provinces, a well-watered, fertile region of rolling hills and a magnificent Indian Ocean coastline stretching from the Transkei in the south to Kosi Bay and the Mozambique border in the north. Extending elegantly over the northern coastal plain and the lush, north-eastern interior is the historic territory known as Zululand.

Inland, the country rises to the foothills and then, precipitously, to the massive heights of the Great Escarpment, called here the Drakensberg and, in Lesotho farther to the west, the Maluti Mountains.

It is a green and pleasant land, its soils rich, its climate benevolent: subtropical for the most part, temperate for the rest. The rains are generous during the summer months, the seaboard areas receiving something over 1 300 mm a year, the hills of the hinterland rather more. In summer the air along the coast is hot and humid, oppressively so in the weeks around Christmas. In the often misty higher ground, though, temperatures generally remain within comfortable limits.

Coal is the province's principal mineral: about 10 million tons of black gold are extracted annually from the northern fields, of which Newcastle is the main centre. Iscor operates a giant iron and steel plant in the area.

KwaZulu-Natal's rural economy is based on sugar-cane, a crop pioneered in the 1850s. Today the vast plantations, sited mainly along and close to the coast, yield some 20 million tons of cane a year, ranking South Africa among the world's top five sugar-producing nations. Other major commercial commodities include timber, tropical and subtropical fruit (pineapples and, especially, bananas), dairy products. Peasant (subsistence) farmers grow maize and keep cattle, but the modest amount

Durban's busy waterfront. The harbour – enclosed within a huge, almost landlocked bay – is one of the southern hemisphere's finest; the dockyards handle some 30 million tons of cargo each year.

of land allocated them under the now-obsolete race laws is overcrowded, overworked and becoming less and less capable of sustaining an expanding population, so families are migrating, in increasing numbers, to the cities.

The majority of KwaZulu-Natal's people – about three-quarters – are blacks of Nguni stock, collectively and rather loosely referred to as Zulu. Under the apartheid system they were concentrated in scattered tribal areas that, together, made up the KwaZulu homeland, the most populous of the so-called 'semi-independent national states' (see page 120). The second largest ethnic grouping, if one may still speak in these terms, is the nearly million-strong Indian. Whites account for just one-tenth of the provincial population, and they tend to be rather English in their manner and outlook: KwaZulu-Natal was for decades one of the Crown's loyalist colonies, luring gentleman farmers, second sons, aristocratic remittance men and thousands of ordinary Victorian Britons to its sunny shores.

Pietermaritzburg, set in the hills some 90 km from the sea, is the provincial capital, but by far the biggest urban concentration is in and around Durban, South Africa's third city, leading seaport and premier holiday destination.

DURBAN

The town grew up around a natural harbour so splendidly spacious that the early Portuguese navigators believed it to be a lagoon at the mouth of a large river, and which, because the coastline had first been sighted (by Vasco da Gama) on the Christmas Day of 1497, they called Rio de Natal. More than three hundred years were to elapse, though, before white men made any serious attempt to colonize what had for long been Nguni territory and which, by the second decade of the 19th century, had become an offshoot of Shaka's new and rapidly expanding Zulu kingdom.

In 1824 two small groups of men, under the leadership of Lieutenant Francis Farewell of the Royal Navy sloop *Julia* and of his deputy, the young and enterprising Henry Fynn, came ashore at the bay intent on opening up a potentially lucrative trade in ivory and skins. They cleared a site, built Port Natal's first rudimentary dwellings and within weeks had managed to extract a generous (though vague) land concession from Shaka. A decade later the settlers – still only 30 or so strong – proclaimed a township, which they named in honour of Sir Benjamin D'Urban, then governor of the Cape.

Durban began to develop in earnest around mid-century. In 1845 Natal was annexed to the Cape Colony, and a steady stream of immigrants began to make the three-month mail-packet voyage from Britain: by 1854 the town's population stood at just over 1 200; on 15 May of that year the settlement was formally declared a 'borough', one of the few such municipal titles granted in South Africa. A railway, South Africa's first, was completed in 1860, and by the end of the century, after decades of dredging and costly effort to remove the bay's notorious sandbar, the harbour had been opened to oceangoing steamers.

With these improvements came rapid expansion of the economic base. There was sugar, of course, and fruit (the stimulus for large-scale food processing enterprises), but also soap-manufacturing, textiles, printing and paper board; later on, shipbuilding and oil-refining and, always, the marine service industries: bunkering and chandling, warehousing and forwarding. Today Durban is a major industrial and commercial centre, and one of the world's busier trade outlets. Each year some 30 million tons of cargo – sugar, fruit, maize, coal, anthracite, manganese, manufactured goods – pass through its harbour.

The city, 300 km² in extent, sprawls along the coast to the south and across the Umgeni River to the north, and, inland, up the Berea, a ridge of hills overlooking the business district, the beachfront and the harbour.

At the top of the ridge is the Durban campus of the University of Natal, a prominent landmark and, for orientation purposes, a useful point of reference. The city's most distinctive topographical feature, though, is the bay itself: it is vast, virtually landlocked, its southern waters bounded by a 8 km-long, 250 m-high wooded headland known as the Bluff, its northern by a narrower lower-lying sandy spit called the Point. Within the bay is Salisbury Island, which is joined to the Bluff by a causeway carrying both a road and a railway. Beyond the

Berea ridge, to the west, is suburbia, and beyond that a plateau that rises some 500 m above sea level, high enough for the inhabitants of its fashionable residential areas – Kloof, Hillcrest, Gillitts, Westville – to escape the worst of the summer heat and humidity.

Durban-Pinetown is said to be the world's fastest-growing conurbation, its population expanding faster than those of Calcutta and Mexico City – but expanding for much the same reason. The armies of the poor are leaving a countryside that can no longer meet their minimum needs, and are congregating in their thousands around Ntujuma, Umlazi and Embumbula and other ramshackle settlements on the western city fringes. Their integration into the urban mainstream, the provision of houses, schools, clinics, the creation of jobs – these constitute Durban's real priority, and the contrast between that reality and the image the city projects – that of a playground for the privileged – is marked indeed. But then, when one comes down to it, it is only by exploiting its considerable natural assets to the full – by offering the ultimate in frivolous pleasure – that Durban can remain prosperous enough to cope with the future.

Greater Durban is also home to large numbers of Indian people, some of them direct descendants of the indentured labourers brought in during the 1860s to work the sugar plantations of the region. The communities have cherished their cultural heritage, retained their religions, languages and customs, their music, dress, food, and they add character to the city scene.

The Golden Mile

Durban's beachfront has served as a fun-in-the-sun mecca for millions of vacationers since just after the turn of the century, when land-locked Transvalers first began heading south in large numbers to take their annual holidays beside the warm waters of the Indian Ocean. By the 1960s, though, it had begun to look its age – a tired, tatty, congested area desperately in need of a facelift – and the City Fathers, after a great deal of acrimonious debate, decided on a massive redevelopment programme.

Conceived by Cape Town architect Revel Fox (leading international town planners Lord Holford and Leon Kantorowich had originally been commissioned, but their grand design would have bankrupted the city), the scheme has proved a brilliant success: the transformation process is by no means complete, but the Golden Mile now sprawls along a full 6 km of shoreline, from Rutherford Street in the south to North Beach's Playfair Road (it also includes the streets immediately behind Marine Parade) and it contains just about everything the heart of the hedonist could wish for, a pleasure-seeker's extravaganza of sound and light, of amusement parks, pavilions, piers and pools, round-the-clock eateries and nightspots, glittering entertainment centres and emporiums and colourful markets, wide white beaches, emerald lawns, fountains, graceful walkways and broad thoroughfares that lead past some of the world's most elegant hotels, among them the Elangeni and the Edward, the Tropicana and the famed Maharani.

Among the Golden Mile's points of special interest are:

SEAWORLD, the renowned aquarium and dolphinarium at the bottom of West Street. On display are tropical fish in great number and of exquisite variety, stingrays and turtles, dolphins, seals, penguins, an impressive collection of sharks and a colourful fantasia of live corals, anemones, seashells, octopus, lobsters. Divers enter the main 800 000-litre tank to hand-feed its residents; the sharks are fed three times a week (Mondays, Wednesdays and Fridays); daily highlights are the fascinating dolphin, seal and penguin shows.

Behind the popular displays, though, is serious intent: Seaworld is part of the South African Association for Marine Biological Research, a non-profit organization devoted to the study, preservation and intelligent use of marine resources; numbered among the Durban research institute's major (and so far most successful) projects are dolphin, seal and penguin breeding programmes and an ongoing campaign to rescue, treat and rehabilitate injured marine mammals. Entrance fees contribute to this excellent work. Seaworld is open each day of the week from nine in the morning to nine at night.

THE FITZSIMONS SNAKE PARK, on the Snell Parade opposite North Beach, houses about 80 of South Africa's 157 species of snake, and an intriguing variety of other reptiles – crocodiles, leguaans (iguanas), tortoises, terrapins and so forth. There are also some exotic species, which are kept in thermostatically controlled cages. Demonstrations are held four times a day during the tourist season; snakes are fed on Saturdays and Sundays; the crocs on Sunday afternoons.

THE AMPHITHEATRE, on Marine Parade opposite the Elangeni Hotel, is a most pleasant retreat from the noise and bustle, a sunken area graced by lawns and flowers, fountains and pools, footbridges and summer-houses. A rather splendid fleamarket is held here each Sunday; and there are 'international theme' days on which traditional dancing is performed and exotic food served.

THE WHEEL, Durban's newest and perhaps most lively shopping and entertainment complex, a kaleidoscope of speciality shops (about 140 of them), restaurants, bars and cinemas (a round dozen of these) that opened its doors in Gillespie Street and Point Road at the end of 1989. The place takes its name from a colossal revolving Ferris wheel ringed by Indian howdah gondolas and mounted on the building's façade above a garish, jewel-encrusted elephant's head. The Oriental theme is carried through into the interior, some of which (the second floor) makes out as a casbah, though for the most part the mood is nautical – flags, rigging, spars and lifeboats are everywhere; ship's railings separate the shops; the floor is a planked deck, the walls are bulkheads.

THE RICKSHAS, parked outside the Tropicana Hotel on Marine Parade, have been a familiar sight to generations of locals and visitors. The lightly-built man-pulled carts originated in Japan and were introduced to Natal by the sugar magnate Sir Marshall Campbell in the 1890s. They proved an immediate success: by 1903 a full thousand and more of them were plying Durban's streets, with many more in Pietermaritzburg, Cape Town, Pretoria and even Rhodesia (now Zimbabwe). The early ones were plain-looking, functional affairs, but with the passage of time and increasing competition for custom they and their handsome Zulu 'drivers' took on a much more decorative look: man and carriage were elaborately decked out with beadwork, furs and streamers. Only in Durban, though, did they survive the onslaught of petrol engine and electric trolley, and only as a tourist attraction. Just twenty or so are left, and even these are likely to disappear before long, so ride while you may.

Mainly for children:

☆ Minitown, on Snell Parade, is a beautifully constructed miniature city, complete with replicas of some of Durban's better-known buildings, ships and the harbour, trains and station, aircraft and airport, streets and cars. The transport moves around, its authenticity reinforced by the appropriate sound effects. In the evenings there's a working funfair and a mini drive-in cinema. Open Tuesdays to Sundays.

☆ Waterland, between Snell Parade and Battery Beach Road: kamikaze chutes and river-rides; also swimming, beautifully landscaped gardens, fast foods. Entrance fee covers the full day and an unlimited number of turns on the slides and rapids.

☆ Funworld, an all-age amusement park, on Marine Parade, that offers tilt 'n whirl dodgems and go-carts, boat rides and gut-wrenching aerial cableway flights, pool and miniature railway. Open daytime and evenings.

☆ Little Top, a red-and-white striped alfresco theatre on South Beach: concerts, music hall, puppet shows in peak season; the audience participates enthusiastically.

☆ Children's Ed-u-fun farm, on Battery Beach Road, enables city children to see piglets, goats, bantams; ride ponies; feed lambs; milk cows, Tel. (031) 32-1674.

Durban's beachfront, part of the Golden Mile

ACCESS Durban's Golden Mile is chock-full of people and cars during the holiday months and parking spaces, at all times except the small hours of the morning, are only for the lucky. Best way to get there from city centre and surrounds is by Mynah minibus (see page 148). Alternatively, park some distance from the beachfront and take a stroll.

Oriental Durban

Wander a short way south of Durban's central business district and you'll find yourself in a different world, in a colourful, vibrant, exotic and wonderfully attractive environment fashioned by the city's Indian community. Here, the air is aromatic, filled with the pungent scents of spice and sandalwood, incense and rose, noisy with the semi-tonal sounds of the tanpura and the beat of Eastern drums, and with the languages of Bombay and Calcutta, Delhi and Madras. The streets and alleyways are crowded; bright saris mingle with the more prosaic styles of the west. In Grey Street stands the southern hemisphere's largest mosque, an imposing affair of golden domes that catch and reflect the sunlight and, next door, the Madressa Arcade, a place of bargains and barter and of shops crammed to their low ceilings with both the ornamental and the functional: ceramic, ivory, bronze, brass (a great deal of this), silver, wood; sumptuous silks and satins; exquisite jewellery; craftware and curios; bangles, beads, baubles; fabrics and foods, shoes, shirts, shampoos.

Focal point of this enticing part of Durban, though, is the Victoria Street market, an extensive area bounded by Victoria, Russell and Queen streets and by Cemetery Lane.

The old Indian Market, one of the city's prime tourist attractions for 63 years, burnt down in 1973 and the large fraternity of traders – the place provided a living for about 10 000 families, many of whom lost their all in the massive blaze – eventually moved to 'temporary' and rather nondescript premises in Warwick Avenue, where it remained for eleven years before moving into the new building in July 1990. Here, modern though the place is, they have been able to recreate much of the enchantment of the past.

Some 80 stallholders sell spices, herbs, curries and other products on the spacious ground floor; above them are 50 shops and a number

The ornate Grey Street mosque

of inviting restaurants; a walkway leads you to the separate 'wet' meat and fish markets. There's underground parking in the basement area; the whole domed complex (it has eleven domes, each recalling a notable building in India) is a marvellous kaleidoscope of sounds, smells and clashing colours, and an absolute must for the visitor.

There is, of course, a great deal more to Durban's Indian cultural heritage, much of it devotional, sacrosanct and hidden from outsiders. But not all: accessible and of special significance are:

THE MOSQUE mentioned above; in Grey Street; tours by arrangement; contact the Islamic Propagation Centre, Tel. 306-0026.

HINDU TEMPLES Foremost among these is the Hare Krishna Temple of Understanding, at the Chatsworth Centre, south of Durban: a striking mix of eastern and western architectural styles, the marble-floored building is noted for its splendidly golden interior, its soaring towers, its surrounding moat and lovely gardens. It was designed and built by the International Society of Krishna Consciousness. Open daily (remove shoes before entering); guided tours; audio-visual presentation; gift shop; restaurant, Tel. (031) 43-5815/43-3384. Other temples, in which intricate religious festivals are celebrated, include:

✫ Durban Hindu Temple, Somtseu Road: significance of shrines, statuary and rituals are explained by the resident priest.
✫ Shree Shiva Subrahmanya Alayam, in Sirdar Road, Clairwood: an especially well-patronized temple complex.

RAMAKRISHNA CENTRE, north of Durban (take the Mount Edgecombe turn-off) is a non-denominational spiritual retreat; open daily.
    Phoenix Settlement, next to Kwa Mashu township (off the N2), is a centre for quiet prayer, an ascetic place containing relics and reminders of Mohandas Gandhi, the father of modern India and, in his early career, a dedicated campaigner for Indian rights in South Africa. Now better known as the Mahatma ('Great Soul'), Gandhi arrived in Natal in 1893 on a private legal brief but stayed on to lead a political struggle that involved strikes, massive marches and the refinement of his philosophy of passive resistance, or *satyagraha*, which held that nothing is achieved through violence, that love and truth eventually prevail. He founded the farm at Phoenix in 1903.

Museums, exhibitions, landmarks

For a young and often brash-seeming city Durban has a surprising amount to offer in terms of serious interest. It has a particularly fine public library (at the City Hall; special arrangements for visitors); excellent theatre, ballet, opera, orchestral music (see page 151), a modest sprinkling of monuments and statuary (the equestrian sculpture of Dick King, 'Natal's Paul Revere', is probably the most impressive; it stands at the bay end of Gardiner Street, Victoria Embankment) and a varied selection of museums, galleries and exhibition centres, most prominent of which are:

NATURAL HISTORY MUSEUM, on the first floor of the City Hall: rich displays of indigenous birds, mammals, reptile, insect life; fish; an impressive dinosaur model; a geological collection; an Egyptian mummy (with an X-ray of its skeleton), and the skeleton of a dodo, the flightless, turkey-sized Indian Ocean island bird that became extinct before the turn of the 19th century (the last one was seen on Rodrigues in 1790). Guided tours and film shows by request, Tel. (031) 30-40111.

LOCAL HISTORY MUSEUM, in the Old Court House, Aliwal Street: an intriguing insight into former Natal's often turbulent past, into old Durban (the Durban Room houses re-creations of early trader and settler life) and a splendid array of period costumes. There's also a museum shop which sells curios.

KILLIE CAMPBELL MUSEUM, housed in Muck-leneuk, the original home of sugar magnate Sir Marshall Campbell at the corner of Essenwood and Marriott roads, has three major compo-nents: the Africana library (rare books, pictures, maps, manuscripts); the William Campbell fur-niture collection, and the outstanding Mashu collection of Zulu art and craft, together with 400 'ethnic' (mainly costume and regalia) paintings by Barbara Tyrrell, who spent 20 years travelling and studying in search of the authentic.

Lovely bougainvillea grace the grounds of Muckleneuk. Open daily except Sundays; guided tours by appointment.

OLD HOUSE MUSEUM, 31 St Andrew's Street: once the home of Sir John Robinson, Natal's first prime minister, now restored and fur-nished (dining room, kitchen, bedroom) in mid-Victorian period style; also paintings of early Durban, and a remarkable early French clock with an elaborate system of dials giving the time, date, day, phases of the moon, equi-noxes, air pressure and much else. Open daily.

PORT NATAL MARITIME MUSEUM, comprising the classic tugboat *JR More* and the naval minesweeper SAS *Durban*, berthed at the small crafts basin: an intriguing insight into the sea-faring past; the museum's land components include the small tug *Ulundi* and Sea View Cottage, re-created early settler home (with souvenir shop). Open Tuesday to Friday, and on Sundays.

WARRIORS' GATE (Old Fort Road): relics of the many battlefields of the region; medals, badges and other pieces of militaria; open Sunday to Friday, Tel. (031) 32-9619.

ADDINGTON HOSPITAL CENTENARY MUSEUM (entrance from Nuns' Old Home, Hospital Road): medical, surgical and nursing his-tory,Tel. (031) 32-2111 ext 314.

WHYSALL'S CAMERA MUSEUM, at 33 Brickhill Road: splendid displays tell the story of photo-graphy from 1841; 3 800 exhibits; open daily.

DURBAN ART MUSEUM, City Hall (second floor): permanent exhibition of South African con-temporary and overseas works, including paintings by Utrillo, Corot, Lely, Constable, sculptures by Rodin and Dalou. Also modern graphics, Oriental art, numerous objets d'art; visiting exhibitions. Closed on Thursdays and Sundays.

Other galleries include: Big Ben (Argyle Rd/7th Avenue) ☆ Grassroots (works of indigenous ar-tists; ethnic beadwork, basketwork, pottery, weaving etc., 119a Jan Hofmeyr Rd, Westville) ☆ Dawn Connell (Anstey's Beach, Bluff) ☆ Hilton Hotel (Midlands Meander pottery & craft) ☆ Elizabeth Gordon (18 Windermere Rd) ☆ Graham Gallery (16 Fenton Rd) ☆ Morgan-Davies Gallery (Granada Centre, Umhlanga Rocks) ☆ Living Art (Shop 11, Broadwalk) ☆ NSA Gallery (Overport City) ☆ Orient gallery (109 Field St) ☆ Pieter von Blommestein (Elangeni Hotel) ☆ Portfolio (Overport Drive) ☆ Rennie Johnson (150 West St & Maharani Hotel) ☆ Sylvia Hanefy (Malibu Hotel) ☆ Tom Hamil-ton Studios (Escoval House, Smith St) ☆ Visuals (Musgrave Centre & Overport City).

DURBAN EXHIBITION CENTRE, conveniently central, accessible from both Aliwal Street and Walnut Road: an extensive (11 000 m^2 of halls and 15 000 m^2 of open-air display space, mak-ing it the second largest in South Africa): a new and rather splendid exhibition complex and arena, and a busy and flexible venue for a wide range of shows, exhibitions, sports, special (in-door and outdoor) events, including the famed Durban Tattoo (in October), the Careers Expo (March), the Easter Fiesta, Tourism Focus (May), Comrades Experience (May), Durban Arts Festival (June), Transport Exhibition (June), House & Garden Show (July), Compu-tex (August), Zest for Life (August), Wildlife Show (September) and many smaller happen-ings. The arena (boxing, show-jumping, fashion shows) can accommodate up to 7 000; permanent exhibitions, in hall four, include the audio-visual 'Durban Experience' presenta-tion (every hour on the hour). The open-air South Plaza hosts a lively Sunday fleamarket. Restaurants, bars, plenty of parking.

ESKOM VISITORS' CENTRE, ground floor, BP Centre (corner of West and Aliwal streets): technically sophisticated and entertaining displays depicting the realm of electrical energy; working models and visitor participation. Open weekdays, Tel. (031) 360-2111.

Gardens, parks and reserves

Despite the pressures of rapid population growth and urban development Durban has been able to maintain a remarkable number and variety of green spaces, small reserves and other conservation areas. And there are more to come: fully 13 new reserves have been earmarked for development in the Greater Durban area. All in all, it's an impressive environmental success story, for which a lot of the credit is due the Metropolitan Open Space System (Moss). Among the more prominent venues are:

ALBERT PARK, St Andrew's Street: ideal for jogging; also a feature playground; open-air chess board (no charge); restaurant.

BEACHWOOD MANGROVES NATURE RESERVE (north of Durban, access via Leo Boyd Highway). One of the last of the area's mangrove swamps. The term 'mangrove' is a loose but convenient group name for trees which are able to thrive in the salty or brackish fringes of tropical bays and river estuaries. Worldwide there are some 60 species of mangrove, belonging to 22 genera of a number of mostly unrelated plant families (many of which, in fact, cannot abide life in a swamp). Eight species occur along the KwaZulu-Natal coast, in swamps that are ecologically valuable: they serve as nursery areas for commercially important fish, and as self-renewing barriers against tropical storms that would otherwise destroy the fragile estuarine ecosystems. The 76-ha Beachwood swamp and its evergreen trees also protect a number of marine and estuarine species unique to the area, including the mudskipper (an amphibious fish), crabs and molluscs. Open at all times; guided tours may be arranged through the Wildlife Society (see Advisory).

BLUFF NATURE RESERVE (Tara Road, Jacobs). One of the Durban area's best bird-watching spots: a 45-ha expanse of coastal forest, shrub, grassland and vlei (wetland) in which there are hides and a network of pathways. Open sunrise to sunset.

BOTANIC GARDENS (Lower Berea; the information centre is next to the Sydenham Road car park). The gardens were founded, as an agricultural station, in 1849. Indigenous flowering trees, tropical plants, birds; special features include an orchid house, a herbarium, a fine cycad collection, a garden for the blind. There's a pleasant tea-garden and waterlily pond. Guided tours on the last Sunday of each month (at 10h30, starting from the information centre; booking advisable; Tel. (031) 21-1303).

BURMAN BUSH NATURE RESERVE (Morningside). A most pleasant place for rambling and bird-watching (it comprises 45 ha of indigenous woodland; trees bear their National Tree List numbers). There are also troops of vervet monkeys to be seen. Information centre; picnic spots; open daily.

JAPANESE GARDENS (Tinsley Road, Virginia). Charmingly designed area of arched wooden bridges, winding pathways, Torii gateways, stone lanterns.

KENNETH STAINBANK NATURE RESERVE (Yellowwood Park), proclaimed to conserve the coastal forest and grassland of the Little Mhlatuzana; contains some game species (rhino, giraffe, zebra, bushbuck, nyala, impala, reedbuck, blue and red duiker). Self-guided trails and picnic spots have been established; open six to six throughout the year.

MITCHELL PARK, Berea. A restfully shady and colourful area; pleasant for children: playgrounds, bird and animal displays (open-air pens of rabbits, tortoises and so forth); occasional Sunday brass-band performances; open-air restaurant.

PALMIET NATURE RESERVE (Morningside). A sanctuary for trees (150 species) and birds (145 species); the 60 ha comprise thick riverine forest, grassland and mixed scrub, crisscrossed by a number of short nature walks. Picnic and barbecue spots; guided trails by arrangement with the Wildlife Society (see Advisory).

PIGEON VALLEY PARK (between King George V and Princess Alice avenues, Bulwer): A patch of remnant forest of indigenous trees, among which are some rare Natal white stinkwoods;

also rare is the spotted thrush, seen in wintertime; generally excellent bird-watching.

ROOSFONTEIN NATURE RESERVE (Westville). A 50-ha strip of grassland along the Umbilo Valley, and a major haven for birds. The reserve is being expanded; trails and other facilities are being developed.

SEATON PARK (Park Hill). A small, 6-ha expanse of woodland, 3,5 ha of which protect remnant coastal forest containing fully 90 different tree species, each bearing its National Tree List number. Attractive birdlife, including the African goshawk; observation posts have been established. Lovely for walking.

SILVERGLEN NATURE RESERVE (Clearwater Dam, Silverglen). A fairly substantial (220 ha) area of beautifully preserved indigenous coastal grassland and bush which serves as home to forest fever berry, Natal camwood, velvet bushwillow and other trees, and to some 145 bird species. Some of the plants in the reserve are much sought after, for their real and supposed medicinal properties, by African traditional healers, and a protective nursery has been established to minimize the threat. Trails, picnic spots, information centre; angling, sailing and boardsailing on the reservoir; open from sunrise to sunset.

UMGENI RIVER BIRD PARK (access from Marine Parade via the Umgeni River Bridge). The Umgeni is, apparently, rated the third finest of the world's bird parks: a world of waterfalls, pools, enormous walk-through aviaries built into the cliff-face and filled with macaws, parrots, cockatoos, lorikeets, great Asian hornbills, rare pheasants, toucans, flamingos, cranes and so on – altogether, about 300 exotic and local species, many with magnificent plumage. Home-made refreshments and light lunches in pleasant surrounds; open each day between 09h00 and 17h00, Tel. (031) 83-1733.

VIRGINIA BUSH NATURE RESERVE (Kensington Drive, Virginia): A small (38-ha) patch of coastal terrain threatened by alien encroachment, but attractive enough, especially for bird enthusiasts (bush shrike; crested guinea-fowl). There are also some buck species, a short trail and an information centre.

A number of fairly major and attractive sanctuaries have been established in the semi-suburban and rather lovely inland areas west of Durban, accessible from the rising highway (the N3) that leads to Pietermaritzburg. Among the more prominent are:

KRANTZKLOOF NATURE RESERVE (north-west of the city; turn off the N3 at Kloof): A 535-ha area eminently worthwhile visiting for its deep gorge, its lovely forest, streams and waterfalls and for its wildlife, which includes some rare plant and bird species (cycads, crowned eagles) and buck, bushpig and vervet monkey. There are some 20 km of pathways, a pleasant picnic site, and an interpretive centre.

SPRINGSIDE NATURE RESERVE (lies in the Hillcrest area west of Pinetown): A charming little haven noted for its indigenous forest (among the trees are wild pomegranate and waterberry), its tree ferns and its varied birdlife. Self-guided walks.

NEW GERMANY NATURE RESERVE Unusually rich in plants (122 species of tree), birds (184 species, including eleven types of shrike) and mammals (nyala, duiker, reedbuck, bushbuck, impala, monkey and a remarkable number of small mammals). To get there, turn right off the N3 at Pinetown and head into the hilly and scenically enchanting countryside around the town of New Germany (founded in 1848 by a party of 183 German immigrants).

Villagers of the Valley of 1 000 Hills

The seafront near Umhlanga Rocks

AROUND DURBAN

In 1828 the great Zulu warrior-king Shaka led an impi down the south coast in a raid against the Pondo people, rested for a while on the lower reaches of a river, drank its cool water, and remarked appreciatively: *Kanti! amanzi a mtoti.* The words mean 'So, the water is sweet', and from them were derived the modern names of both the river and the settlement that grew up on its banks.

Amanzimtoti

The settlement, some 25 km south of Durban and a substantial town in its own right (though for practical purposes the two can be grouped together: many of its residents are city commuters), is now one of the most popular of KwaZulu-Natal's coastal resort areas. Among its attractions: superb beaches, a lagoon (easy-to-handle boats for hire); safe swimming (shark nets provide protection), surfing, sun-worshipping, rock- and beach-angling, entertainment, fun in the sun, hotels, bars and plenty of good holiday accommodation.

Each May the country's biggest Highland Gathering takes place in the town's attractive Hutchinson Park.

ILANDA WILDS, a few minutes' drive from the centre of town, is a beautiful and richly varied 14-ha riverine haven for over 160 species of birds, 120 kinds of tree and shrub. There are several popular nature trails along the river banks and picnic sites.

JAPANESE-STYLE GARDENS, along Fynn Road, are a joy; one can laze on a sundeck overlooking the pond and watch the birds. The gardens are open at all times.

UMDONI BIRD SANCTUARY, a smallish expanse of indigenous forest, is home to a wide variety of bird species, including giant and pygmy kingfishers, green-backed herons and, in a special section, exotic and indigenous species, many of them waterfowl; the peacocks are a feature; many of the trees and plants are labelled for identification. Bird-watching hides, one short trail, information centre, cream teas at weekends.

Umhlanga Rocks

The North Coast counterpart of Amanzimtoti, though rather nearer (18 km from city centre) and rather smaller (15 000 permanent residents) and especially noted for its four luxury (one five-star) hotels, three large resort complexes, apartment blocks, holiday homes, and the upmarket residential suburb of La Lucia. It has a fine beach; swimmers, surfers, paddle-surfers and ski-boaters are protected by shark nets (but only in the waters north of the distinctive red-and-white lighthouse), and the Natal Sharks Board maintains its headquarters on a low hill overlooking the town (lectures, demonstrations, audio-visuals are regularly presented; booking advisable). Excellent shopping facilities; 30 restaurants to choose from.

UMHLANGA LAGOON NATURE RESERVE This small (26-ha) patch of river-mouth, now rare dune forest and lagoon attracts a large number and attractive variety of birds (among them the fish eagle and the crested guinea-fowl), as does the adjacent, larger and privately owned Hawaan Bush. Buck species include blue and red duiker and bushbuck. Both reserves can be explored: the former by way of an established nature trail, the latter by arrangement with the Wildlife Society; Tel. (031) 21-3126.

Valley of a Thousand Hills

Probably the region's most striking natural feature, the majestic valley follows the course of the Umgeni River for some 65 km, from a flat-topped sandstone hill to the east of Pietermaritzburg called Natal Table Mountain, to the Indian Ocean in the east.

The mountain is 960 m high, its plateau-like summit graced by a profusion of wild flowers, and those who climb to the top (best route up begins on the Pietermaritzburg side) are rewarded with breathtaking views stretching to the sea on one side and the distant Drakensberg on the other. At the base of the massif is the Nagle Dam, one of Durban's more important sources of water. The dam is set in charming parkland countryside; facilities include a tea-room and picnic area.

The valley itself is incredibly hot in summer, heavily populated in parts (it is home to the Debe people, many of whom live in traditional beehive huts and some of whom still wear traditional dress), ruggedly wild in others, and everywhere luxuriant with lilies (arum, fire and snake), red-hot pokers, Mexican sunflowers and flowering aloes. One can drive along much of the southern rim of the valley. Two of South Africa's most exhausting sporting events take place in the area: the Dusi Canoe Marathon follows the turbulent course of the Umgeni; part of the famed Comrades Marathon leads along the Old Main Road above the river.

To get there from Durban takes a pleasant 30 minutes; follow the N3 to Hillcrest and turn right; there are farm and craft stalls and tea-gardens along the way. Points of interest within the valley include the unusual, capacious, vaguely Tudor-style Rob Roy Hotel (delicious cream teas and carvery lunches eaten on the terrace) and slices of 'authentic' Africa tailor-made for tourists:

PHEZULU The word means 'high up', the place comprises a Zulu village featuring Zulu life-styles, Zulu dancing (a superbly pulsating spectacle), bone-throwing witchdoctors, demonstrations of African cooking, thatching, spear-making and beading, an art gallery and shop (baskets, clay pottery, beadwork, carvings), a nature trail, tea-room and sundeck (light meals), Tel. (031) 777-1405. Somewhat similar to this Zulu village is:

ASSAGAY SAFARI PARK On offer: crocodiles (about 400 of them), snakes, a Zulu village (resident performers are the Gaza Zulu Dancers), a natural history museum, a botanic garden, a colonial-style restaurant, picnic areas, curio shop and, for the children, a treasure-trove, Tel. (031) 777-1205.

Getting around

Central Durban is symmetrically laid out; its main thoroughfares – notably Pine, West and Smith Streets and, along the Bay, Victoria Embankment – are broad, busy and they run west to east, towards the Indian Ocean. Much of the Golden Mile is within pleasant walking distance of the central area, though not, perhaps, in the ferocious humidity of high summer (December to March).

BUSES The Durban Transport Management Board (DTMB) provides an adequate service. There's no central terminal, but timetables and information are available from the DTMB's ticket office at the corner of West and Gardiner streets, Tel. (031) 309-4126.

Many visitors make use of the excellent Mynah minibus shuttle service, which links the central area with South and North beaches (Golden Mile). The enjoyable Tuk-Tuk three-wheeler service takes you through the city and to points along the beachfront.

TAXIS These are available but, in common with those of all other South African centres, Durban's cabs don't rove the streets on the lookout for fares. One must either locate the nearest rank or, more usually, telephone. Taxi companies are listed in the Yellow Pages.

CAR HIRE Most of the internationally-known companies – Avis, Hertz, Budget and so forth – have offices in the city, as do a number of competitive local operators. Information: Yellow Pages, Durban Publicity Association (see Advisory, page 173) or hotel reception.

PARKING On-street parking is difficult in season. The more accommodating parkades are the Albany (behind the Playhouse theatre); the Pine (Pine St/Commercial Rd); at the Workshop shopping centre; at the Beachview mall, and at Game City.

Walks and hikes

Durban Publicity Association organizes a number of city walks. Each is led by a knowledgeable courier and lasts just under three hours (09h45 to 12h30). The options:
✫ The Oriental Walkabout covers the Victoria Street market (page 142), the Indian area (jewellery and fabric shops, craft factory; refresh-

ments include Indian delicacies); Emmanuel Cathedral; Jumma Mosque (page 143).

☆ Durban Experience: Natal Playhouse (page 151), Local History Museum (page 144); City Hall.

☆ Feel of Durban Walkabout: Central Park, Old Fort, St Peter's-in-Chains (once the powder magazine, now an attractive miniature chapel), Warriors' Gate Museum (page 144), the 'Coast-of-Dreams' audio-visual (a superb multi-screen presentation laid on for groups of ten or more; smaller parties are taken to the informative Eskom visitors' centre: page 145), The Workshop (page 150).

☆ Historical Walkabout: St Paul's (Anglican) Church, the old Durban station (South Africa's first railway linked city and Point), Post Office, (the original City hall), Francis Farewell Square and Cenotaph, City Hall, Local History Museum and, along the Victoria Embankment, the John Ross statue, the Da Gama clock (impressively intricate, it commemorates the first European sighting of Natal, on Christmas Day 1487) and the Dick King statue.

☆ Architectural Meander: a stroll taking in some of Durban's older and historically more significant buildings.

NATURE WALKS The Durban department of Parks, Recreation and Beaches has established a number of attractive short walks and rambles through the city's green areas; each trail is mapped and described in a brochure, available from either the Department (PO Box 3740, Durban 4000; Tel. (031) 21-1303 or from the Durban Publicity Association (see Advisory, page 173). The areas, which are profiled on pages 145 and 146 include:

☆ Burman Bush nature reserve: Hadeda trail, 180 m; Pithi trail, 500 m; Umgeni trail, 1 km.

☆ Pigeon Valley Park: Elm trail, 500 m.

☆ Seaton Park: Yellowwood trail, 300 m; Bamboo trail, 200 m; Boundary path, 500 m.

☆ Silverglen nature reserve: Silverglen trail, 3 to 5 km.

☆ Virginia Bush nature reserve: Virginia Bush trail, 1,5 km.

Other rewarding walks have been developed in Beachwood Mangroves nature reserve; the Paradise Valley nature reserve; the Palmiet nature reserve; the New Germany nature reserve; the Kranzkloof nature reserve; the Hawaan Bush, and the Umhlanga Lagoon nature reserve, all of which are also described on pages

145 and 146; and in the Ilanda Wilds nature reserve at Amanzimtoti (page 147).

Rather special are the six (30- or 60-minute) self-guided trails, the two-hour circular walk and the 600-m trail for the physically handicapped in the Kenneth Stainbank nature reserve (page 145).

The Ingweni trail is a 25-km, two- to three-day hike which takes a horseshoe-shaped route through gorges, grassland and sandstone escarpment in the Pinetown-Kloof-Gillitts area; attractions include three lovely waterfalls and splendid views, tree ferns and wild poplar. The trail is a part of private initiative, developed by local schoolchildren in association with the Wildlife Society and the Lions Club. Information: Metropolitan Open Space System, Private Bag 9038, Pietermaritzburg 3200; Tel. (031) 21-3126, (0331) 3-3371/5-8041.

Local Tours

The visitor to Durban is exceptionally well looked after by tour operators. Some of the highlights include:

☆ The Durban Transport Management Board (DTMB) offers a wide selection of coach trips – around the city's Oriental areas, scenic drives around the gardens and nature reserves and to the Valley of a Thousand Hills (see page 147); cruises around the bay and harbour. Longer excursions include a ride down the southern shoreline to Transkei's Wild Coast Sun (see page 219). Information and bookings: the DTMB Coach Tours office is on the beachfront; call in, or telephone (031) 368-2848, or contact the Durban Publicity Association (see Advisory, page 173).

☆ 1000 Hills Tours (Tel. (031) 83-2302/ 866831) take in the Valley of a Thousand Hills (see page 142), either as a specific destination or as part of one of several attractive country drives. For more information contact DTMB, Tel. (031) 368-2848.

☆ Sarie Marais Cruises (Gardiner Street Jetty; Tel. 305-4022/2844) offer deep sea, harbour and educational cruises, and its launches are available for private charter (champagne, luncheon, sundowner and night excursions).

☆ Court Helicopters (Tel. (031) 83-9513): fun rides and scenic flips over city and coast.

☆ For railway enthusiasts and joyriders, there's the Strelitzia express, a Class 24 steam locomotive that takes you on a half-day's run down the

South Coast each Sunday morning (bar lunch or barbecue *en route*); and the Umgeni Steam railway regularly puffs its way between New Germany and Sarnia, Tel. (031) 86-1904 or contact the Durban Publicity Association.

☆ The sugar industry (Huletts) welcomes visitors to its giant Durban terminal on Mayden Wharf (bulk silos; audio-visual presentation) on Tuesdays, Thursdays and Fridays, and to its Illovo (south of Durban) and Maidstone (north of Durban) mills on Tuesdays, Wednesdays and Thursdays. Information and bookings: Tel. 301-0331 (terminal); 96-3310 (Illovo); (0322) 2-4551 (Maidstone).

Shopping

Among the bigger malls and shopping complexes are the Victoria Street market (mainly but not exclusively Indian, and a mandatory port of call for visitors to Durban: see page 142), the enterprising Game City (Stamford Hill Road, guaranteed lowest prices), La Lucia Mall (William Campbell Dr, La Lucia) and:

THE WORKSHOP in Pine Street, an enormous Victorian building that once served as a railway workshop and now transformed, at a costly sum of about R45 million, into a lively shopping/ browsing/eating/entertainment/fun showpiece and 'theme centre'. It houses something over 120 speciality shops, many of them replicas of, or at least reminiscent of, British-Natal colonial houses, complete with olde worlde fanlights, wrought-ironwork and brass trimmings; Victorian-type barrow stalls do business in the central ground floor area, which has been planted with fully-grown trees; some of the shop assistants are kitted out in period costume; one of the restaurants serves meals in the old Port Natal stationmaster's house (rebuilt on its new site) and serves drinks in its 19th century railway pub. Open seven days a week; extended shopping hours.

FLEAMARKETS do a brisk trade in the vicinity of The Workshop, in the Amphitheatre (see above, page 141), on the South Plaza of the Durban Exhibition Centre (page 144) and on the beachfront on the second and last Sundays of each month. Under development is the Pinelands Junction craft market, a venue that will re-create the art, craft and lifestyles of the past.

THE ARCADE, opposite the Pine Parkade and fronting on West, Field and Pine streets, houses about three dozen upmarket speciality shops.

THE AFRICAN ARTS CENTRE, in the Guildhall Arcade off Gardiner Street, is, according to the Transvaal institute of architects, 'one of the real treasures of Durban'. It's a non-profit enterprise (initiated by the Institute of Race Relations as a self-help project), a part-gallery part-shop that caters for discerning collectors of Zulu arts and crafts (bead-, wood- and grasswork, pottery, sculpture, fabrics, graphics). Well worth a visit.

The centre isn't, of course, the only such venue: Durban and its surrounds offer an attractive variety of craft and curio shops. There are for instance outlets on the way to and in the Valley of a Thousand Hills (page 147) and on the coast just south of the city, at:

SHELL ULTRA CITY (Umnini), on the N2, where some 500 Amatuli traders invite you to browse among stalls that display tropical fruits and a great many original goods, including some fine crochet and needlework, basketware, carvings, leatherwork. Adjoining the market is a service station and restaurant complex.

A craft market south of Durban

The Natal Playhouse complex, major venue for theatre and music

AFRICAN CURIO MARKETS A large roadside bazaar farther south along the coast road, between Umgababa and Umkomaas. Zulu women display a wide range of crafted items on the beachfront.

Theatre, music and entertainment

The scene is lively and, in its nature, very changeable: consult the Durban Publicity Association or watch the newspapers for specifics.

Focal point of Durban's performing arts is the stylish and historic:

NATAL PLAYHOUSE complex in Smith Street. Once a brace of cinemas, one Tudor-type and the other elaborately Moorish (this was the old and much-loved Colosseum), the building has been converted to provide five venues – used variously for drama, intimate theatre, orchestral music, ballet, opera – in which performances are given by, among others, the Natal Philharmonic Orchestra and the Natal Performing Arts Council. The foyers and wood panelling of the cinemas have been retained; everything else is very modern.

Supplementaries include lunchtime concerts, art and other exhibitions, and theatrical souvenirs from The Playhouse Shop. Informative guided tours are conducted on Tuesdays, Thursdays and Saturdays.

MUSIC Choral, orchestral, jazz and pop performances and the popular Sunday afternoon concerts are presented at the City hall (watch the press for notices as concerts are irregular); brass-band music in some of the Durban's parks on Sunday afternoons; musical soirées, chamber and jazz recitals at the Little Abbey Theatre; and there's a wide range of musical offerings from the universities of Natal (celebrity and lunchtime recitals) and Durban-Westville (the acclaimed Oudemeester Master Concerts, featuring visiting artists).

OTHER PERFORMING ARTS VENUES, include
☆ The Alhambra Theatre, central Durban
☆ Asoka Theatre, University of Durban-Westville (intimate theatre; local, experimental and classic drama)
☆ Elizabeth Sneddon Theatre, University of Natal (a very mixed calendar)
☆ The Hermit Theatre (fringe; indigenous drama)
☆ The Little Abbey Theatre (music: see above; also drama in an intimate atmosphere)
☆ The Nederburg Theatre, an elegant building attached to Stellenbosch Farmers' Winery at New Germany (soirées and individual recitals).

Wining and dining

The Durban area is a gourmet's delight, full of outstanding eateries, and it's difficult to present a fair selection in such limited space. A select list of restaurants appears on pages 171-173.

Dinner dancing

Plenty on offer in the way of nightclubs, discos, dinner-dancing, cabaret; venues include ☆ The Barn, Athlone Hotel Durban North (Irish sing-along) ☆ Break for the Border, Palm Beach Hotel (theme pub) ☆ The Cellar (theatrical review/ cabaret) P Causerie, Edward Hotel (dinner-dancing) ☆ Copacabana, Beverly Hill Hotel (dinner-dancing) ☆ Fingers, Blue Waters Hotel (dine-disco) ☆ Knight's Nite Club (cabaret) ☆ Lara's, Elangeni Hotel (dinner-dancing) ☆ Memories (dinner-dancing) ☆ Millionaire Club, Palm Beach Hotel (cabaret) ☆ Oyster Box Hotel. Grill Room (Saturday dinner-dancing) and Pearl Room (nightly dinner-dancing) ☆ Pieces of Eight (live entertainment) ☆ Raffles, Maharani Hotel (disco) ☆ Ruby Tuesday, Beach Hotel (cabaret) ☆ Selby's (live entertainment) ☆ Sir Benjamin's, Holiday Inn Marine Parade (cabaret) ☆ Smuggler's Inn (late-night action) ☆ The Grape Vine, Edward Hotel (cabaret) ☆ Top o' the Royal, Royal Hotel (dinner-dancing).

But it's a changing scene, so consult the newspapers or the Durban Publicity Association (see Advisory, page 173) for the current specifics.

SPORT AND RECREATION

Durban is world-famed for its wide white beaches, and especially for those along the Golden Mile (see above, page 140). Sunbathers, swimmers and surfers flock to them in their tens of thousands during the long hot summer.

Durban's Golden Mile can become uncomfortably crowded, especially during the Transvaal school holidays around Christmas, when the beautiful and far less congested stretches to the south and north beckon. Some of these are:

South of the city

☆ Ansteys's Beach, along Marine Drive and then Foreshore Drive; tidal pool; shark nets, good for surfing.
☆ Brighton, a little farther to the south; shark nets; good surfing; pleasant facilities.
☆ Amanzimtoti, 26 km along the N2 (see page 147). Two superb beaches; plenty of facilities.
☆ Kingsburgh area, farther on: two excellent stretches; tidal pools; shark-protected; good surfing and angling.

☆ Karridene and Umgababa, 37 km from along the N2; good for bathing, surfing, fishing, camping/caravanning.
☆ Umkomaas, 8 km farther on; tidal pool, no sea-swimming.
☆ Scottburgh, 55 km from Durban: lawns, nice beach, pool; good bathing and surfing; excellent facilities.

North of the city

☆ Umhlanga Rocks, 17 km from Durban (see page 147): safe bathing to the north of the lighthouse, dangerous elsewhere; popular among surfers; plenty of facilities.
☆ Umdloti and nearby Selection beaches, 25 km from Durban; relatively unspoilt; tidal pool.
☆ Tongaat, 10 km farther on, also unspoilt.
☆ Ballito, 10 km farther on: a series of pleasant beaches stretches north from here; good fishing, swimming, surfing.
☆ Shaka's Rock area, 52 km north of Durban: shark-protected spots; fine for picnicking. Beyond is Salt Rock, a tranquil resort with a tidal pool; fishermen are well served by specially constructed piers; full recreational amenities are offered by the country club.

BIRD-WATCHING
Human encroachment has limited the opportunities, but there's still prolific and attractive birdlife in the forest patches of the various nature reserves (see pages 145 and 146); at the wading ponds at Sea Cow Lake (African jacana, Egyptian goose, hamerkop, various ducks, various herons, and the pink-backed pelican); and around the Umgeni River estuary (plovers, fisheagle, sandpipers, osprey). Offshore birds, which can be seen on short (30-km) ocean trips to the east, include albatross, skua, petrel, and the sooty shearwater. Information: Durban Museum of Natural History, Tel. 300-6211; Natal Bird Club, Tel. (031) 23-0843 and the Wildlife Society Tel. (031) 21-3126.

BOWLS The Greater Durban area supports nearly 40 bowling clubs; visiting registered bowlers welcome; non-registered bowlers may take to the beach greens (at Victoria Park or South Beach). Contact: the Port Natal Bowling Association, Tel.(031) 21-1189.

CRICKET AND RUGBY The provincial (and international) grounds are the Old Kingsmead and

King's Park respectively. Natalians play both sports with equal flair, if not always with success; watch the press for details.

FISHING Popular areas are the harbour mouth, The Country Club, Snake Park piers, Blue Lagoon, but there are numerous other beach- and rock-angling spots north and south of Durban. Opportunities for deep-sea game fishing are also excellent; several charter companies offer well-equipped skiboat fishing forays: consult Durban Publicity Association (see Advisory, page 173); Yellow Pages, or telephone 304-8956.

GOLF Some excellent courses in the area; the Windsor Park municipal one is near the beachfront, the Athlone course is near the city. Elsewhere, visitors are generally most welcome, though some clubs ask for a letter of introduction. Putting practice at Blue Lagoon outdoor course and at the Durban Indoor Sports Centre, Brickhill Rd (36 holes). Contact: the Natal Golf Union, Tel. (031) 22-3877.

HEALTH AND FITNESS STUDIOS Durban has several of these; very well appointed and equipped; consult the Yellow Pages or Durban Publicity Association (see Advisory, page 173).

WALKING AND HIKING This is covered on pages 148 and 149. The Durban Ramblers' Club welcomes visitors, Tel. (031) 23-5895.

HORSES Principal equestrian venues are the Summerveld Training Establishment; the Turf Club Training Centre; the South African Jockey Academy (horses are paced at dawn – a magnificent sight), and the Equestrian Sports Centre (which trains polo ponies). For details of equestrian events, held mainly in the Shongweni-Hillcrest area, contact the Natal Horse Society, Tel. (0331) 3-4378.

RACING AT GREYVILLE High point of a fine winter season (May to mid-August; meetings held on Wednesdays and Saturdays), and the main event on the national racing calendar, is the Rothmans July Handicap, which takes place on the first Saturday of July. Other races include the SA Guineas and the Jockey Brand Gold Cup. Greyville has superb facilities, among them the Durban View Room (restaurant; closed-circuit TV at each table). There are

also regular meetings at the excellent Clairwood course, off the southern freeway.

ICE SKATING At the Ocean City rink in Sol Harris Crescent; gear may be hired; colourful ice extravaganzas during the holiday season.

SAILING Limitless options. Leading bodies are the Point Yacht Club (Tel. 301-4787); The Royal Natal Yacht Club (Tel. 301-5425), and the Mainstay Sailing Academy's sailing school (Tel. 6-5726).

SQUASH Numerous courts at sports clubs (visitors welcome), health and fitness studios. Major venues include the Disc Squash Centre, Brickhill Rd; La Lucia Mall; Royal Hotel; Akals Athletikon, Pinetown.

SWIMMING This can be enjoyed in the sea, of course (see page 147); beaches from Addington to Blue Lagoon are protected against sharks and patrolled by lifeguards.

Swimming also at the Rachel Finlayson seawater pool on Lower Marine Parade, North Beach; at Water Wonderland, Snell Parade (see page 142), and in the splendid Olympic-standard freshwater pool on NMR Avenue, King's Park (parking for 2 000 cars).

SURFING There are superb opportunities, especially in the Bay of Plenty, which hosts the annual international Gunston 500. Morning surfing reports on Radio Port Natal.

DIVING The clear waters of the Natal coasts are ideal for scuba and snorkel; contact the Northern Natal Underwater Union, (after hours) Tel. (031) 72-5730/74-2757; SADF Spearfishing Club, Tel. (031) 466-1521.

WATER WONDERLAND Fun for the young and young at heart: an enticing complex of pools, 'lakes', water slides and an enormous supertube; situated on the Golden Mile's Snell Parade.

THE SOUTH COAST
A balmy tropical climate, lovely wide expanses of beach, the warm, intensely blue waters of the Indian Ocean, a lushly evergreen hinterland, fine hotels, a score and more of sunlit towns, villages and hamlets, each with its own, distinctive personality and its own attractions –

The tree-fringed Uvongo beach

these are the ingredients that combine to create one of the southern hemisphere's most entrancing holiday regions.

The southern shoreline is divided into two segments (an arbitrary division really, since there's no essential difference between them, but those who promote and write about the region find it a useful distinction): the stretch from Amanzimtoti – 26 km from Durban and covered above (page 147) – to Mtwalume is known as the Sunshine Coast; that from Hibberdene to Port Edward on the Eastern Cape border as the Hibiscus Coast. Most prominent town along the former stretch is Scottburgh, most prominent along the latter is Margate.

The Sunshine Coast
From Amanzimtoti the main N2 highway leads through:

KINGSBURGH, an 8-km-long municipality encompassing five seaside resorts – Doonside, Warner Beach, Winkelspruit, Illovo Beach and Karridene – which are popular for their white sands and shark-protected offshore waters. Warner Beach is an especially pleasant little village (bathing and boating in the lagoon); Winkelspruit's shores are tree-fringed and there are some lovely walks in the woods beyond; good fishing at Illovo, around which there are lush fields of sugar-cane; Karridene has a charming lagoon.

UMKOMAAS, 14 km farther south, boasts a championship golf course, an indigenous tree park, and a floodlit tidal pool.

SCOTTBURGH is a substantial and very pleasant town, and one of the Sunshine Coast's most popular resorts. Scott Bay is the main beach, a charming expanse of sand overlooked by lawned terraces at the mouth of the Mpambanyani River (which translates as 'confusion of birds', a reference to its twisty course). Scottburgh's attractions include safe bathing and excellent angling, a fine golf course, bowling greens, a huge saltwater pool (with supertube), the renowned miniature railway and, 4 km to the north, Crocworld. This last comprises a wildlife museum, a snake pit and 'snake tunnel', nature trails, a Zulu village (Zulu dancing on Sunday afternoons) and, of course, crocodiles. Well worth a visit.

Inland from Park Rynie, a lively little village just south of Scottburgh, is Umzinto and, just beyond and to the right, the:

VERNON CROOKES NATURE RESERVE, a lushly hilly, 2 190-ha sanctuary for various antelope species. The reserve offers nature trails and drives, picnic sites and, if you're sleeping over, accommodation in four-bed rustic huts.

Back on the N2 and continuing south, one passes through the tranquil little seaside resorts of Kelso, Pennington (picnic lawns by the beach; chalets, tidal pool), Umdoni Park, Ifafa Beach (fishing, water-skiing, canoeing on the lagoon and for some distance upstream) and Mtwalume, whose rocky shores attract the more discerning angler.

The Hibiscus Coast
The 80-km shoreline from Mtwalume to Port Edward is studded with small resorts, not easily distinguishable from each other at first glance – they all offer sun, sea and sand in abundant degree – but, as the locals and regulars will tell you, highly individual places once you get to know them. To mention a few:
☆ Hibberdene: lovely beaches fringed by woodland; an 80-m long tidal pool, bowling green, picnic spots, boating on the lagoon; hotels, retirement homes, plenty of self-catering accommodation; an amusement park, an airfield for private aircraft.
☆ Umzumbe: quiet; excellent family hotel (the

Pumula); rock and surf angling.

☆ Banana Beach: safe bathing and surfing from sands fringed by banana plantations and attractive indigenous bush.

☆ Bendigo: a complex of four seaside resorts, all with their chalets, shops, restaurants, angling and swimming spots. Southport has two bowling greens.

☆ Umtentweni: secluded, largely residential but ideal for the quieter type of holiday. A few kilometres farther south is:

PORT SHEPSTONE, sited at the mouth of the Umzimkulu River, largest of southern KwaZulu-Natal's watercourses, navigable by small craft for 8 km upstream. Its estuary was wide enough to take the coasters that, before the coming of the railway, provided the town (which, curiously enough, had originally been developed by Norwegian immigrants) with its links to the outside world. Local industry is centred on sugar, marble and the limeworks, timber and subtropical fruits. For holiday-makers, there are bowling greens, an 18-hole golf course that ranks among South Africa's finest, part of the Country Club (which plays amiable host to visitors), lovely tree-shaded parks, beaches and tidal pools, watersports at the river-mouth and, once a year, a fiercely contested tube race down the river itself.

A little over 20 km inland from Port Shepstone, just off the N2 highway (this now makes its way westwards, through Harding and the Kokstad area, before turning south-east again to round the Transkei; the Hibiscus Coast road becomes the R61) is the:

ORIBI GORGE NATURE RESERVE, a 1 837-ha expanse of magnificently rugged hill and deep valley, stream, waterfall, forest and emerald-green grassland and, its most striking feature, the hugely spectacular canyon carved from the sandstone layers by the Umzimkulwana River. The gorge is 24 km long, 5 km wide, 366 m deep, and the vistas, including that from the extraordinary overhang called Hanging Rock, are unforgettable.

Other viewing points are in the Fairacres Lake (private, but visitors welcome), Echo Vallev, The Pulpit, Ola's Nose, Lehr's Falls, Baboon's Castle, Horseshoe Bend and Oribi Heads. Set aside at least a morning for the scenic drive through the gorge.

The reserve's wildlife comprises some 40 mammal species, including baboons and the shy samango monkey; various antelope, though not the graceful and now quite rare oribi, from which gorge and reserve take their name. Nearly 270 species of bird have been recorded in the area; of special note are the raptors (jackal buzzard; crowned, long-crested and black eagles).

There are trails, picnic sites, fishing spots (permits required) and, for overnight visitors, a hotel, and a hutted camp run by the Natal Parks Board. Information and bookings: Tel. (0331) 5-1514.

Oribi Gorge: a magnificent spectacle

Among notable ports of call as you carry on down the coast are:

☆ Shelly Beach, until fairly recently the quietest of hideaways but now a bustling seaside centre that boasts the region's largest shopping complex. It's also the venue for the country's biggest ski-boat club.

☆ St Michaels-on-Sea, whose river and lagoon are popular among boardsailers, its sea much favoured by surfers. Among the other attractions are a nine-hole golf course and a good hotel (the St Michaels Sands).

☆ Uvongo, also a lively resort, graced by a 23-m waterfall on the Vungu River. The river's estuary is one of the country's deepest. Bowling greens, tennis and squash courts, restaurant and shops (and a hotel) at next-door Manaba Beach. Pleasant walking between Uvongo and St Michaels and in Thure Lilliecrona Park above the falls (the park is also known as the Uvongo nature reserve: a peaceful 28-ha patch of still-unspoilt forest that contains fully a hundred bird species and a rich plant life); good fishing at Shad Bay and from Orange Rocks, La Crete Point and Beacon Rocks.

MARGATE Named after and in many ways much like the popular English seaside town, Margate – large, lively and crowded – is the 'capital' of the Hibiscus Coast, presenting all the standard holiday attractions but with a flair, with an uninhibited *joie de vivre,* that lifts it far above the ordinary. Among its tourist assets: lovely beaches, good fishing, safe bathing, an Olympic-standard pool, 18-hole golf course, bowling greens; an amusement park; hotel, apartment and self-catering complexes; shops and super-markets, speciality restaurants, discos. It is also a residential town with a substantial business base and an airport (Natal's second largest).

RAMSGATE, 4 km farther along the coast, is renowned for its magnificent Mbezane lagoon, a mecca for wind-surfers, and for its long beach, which it shares with the next-door and rather exclusive community of Southbroom (the private 'holiday cottages' here tend to be large and luxurious). The Frederika nature reserve, which protects the coastal forest, separates the beach from the short (but demanding), rather splendid and very busy 18-hole golf course.

Among Ramsgate's drawcards is the Crayfish Inn, which serves marvellous seafood and is crammed with seafaring relics of one sort and another; and the antique, craft and other 'browsing' shops that line the main street.

Between Ramsgate and Port Edward are:

☆ Marina Beach, a fast-developing resort noted for its man-made (and impressive) lagoon, for the San Lameer holiday estate (bowls, horse-riding, wind-surfing, golf, trim-park) and for its grand new hotel. Between the lagoon and the Mpenjati River, to the south, are the fossilized trees and the Yengele forest of the Trafalgar marine reserve.

☆ The Munster area, comprising a series of lovely little bays, beaches and coves, each with its scatter of chalets. Glenmore has a most attractive lagoon; Leisure Crest and Leisure Bay, the southernmost of the series, are especially tranquil: the emphasis here is on conservation, and commercial development is strictly limited.

PORT EDWARD is the last stop before you reach the Umtamvuna River (the Eastern Cape border), across which is the famed Wild Coast casino complex (see page 219).

Port Edward's pleasant beach is overlooked by the wooded slopes of Tragedy Hill, site of the 1831 massacre, by the Zulu, of a party of whites. The victims – of what was later acknowledged to have been a tragic misunderstanding – were mostly the family and followers of Henry Francis Fynn, well-known pioneer and founder of the Port Natal settlement that later became known as Durban.

To the south is the Umtamvuna nature reserve, a place of forest, gorge, steep hill, rich plant life (over 700 floral species, among them 35 types of orchid) and great scenic beauty. Among the birds to be seen are the rare peregrine falcon, the crowned eagle, Gurney's sugarbird, and a breeding colony of Cape vultures. Self-guided trails; no accommodation (though there's plenty just along the coast, of course).

THE NORTH COAST

The Dolphin Coast, stretching 100 km north from Durban to the Tugela River mouth, is noted for its seaside resorts – not as numerous as those along the South Coast but just as pleasant in their own, rather quieter way: small clusters of holiday homes, hotels, luxury apartment blocks built beside river-mouth lagoons and overlooking the warm and generally kindly Indian Ocean. The sands are broad and white, the shoreline tropical, graced by lala palms, Madagascar casuarinas, hibiscus, bougainvillea and other strikingly colourful flowering shrubs and trees. The coastal highway – the N2 – is called Shaka's Way, and it provides a splendid scenic drive from Durban. An alternative route is:

The old north coast road

Running a few kilometres inland and parallel to the N2, this follows the old trade route, once used by the hunters of elephant and traffickers in ivory and skins, and by the Zulu impis on their way south to do battle with the Pondo. It now serves the vast sugar-cane plantations and 'sugar towns' of the region, and is often busy with the passage of cane trucks. The estates and mills welcome visitors (tour arrangements can be made through the local offices). Largest of the centres is:

TONGAAT, a substantial town with a large Indian population and an attractively tropical feel about it: avenues and gardens are embowered with jacaranda and poinsettia and bamboo; street stalls sell luscious fruits (the litchis are especially inviting). Bordering the town is the headquarters of the giant (and very forward-thinking) Tongaat sugar group, whose office buildings are designed in Cape Dutch style and are quite beautifully furnished with antiques. The river from which the place takes its name (*thongathi* is the Zulu word for the *Strychnos mackenii* trees that line its banks) runs into the ocean at:

TONGAAT BEACH, a particularly lovely stretch of sand; the quiet little resort comprises seaside cottages in a setting of casuarinas, two hotels, a large tidal pool, and shark nets to protect those who prefer to bathe in the sea. A little way upriver is:

CROCODILE CREEK, a ranch devoted to the breeding and conservation of the Nile crocodile. On offer are guided tours, a curio shop, open-air restaurant; feeding times are on Wednesdays (14h00), Saturdays and Sundays (11h00 to 15h00).

STANGER, much farther north on the old road

and 8 km inland from the sea, is the main centre of another extensive sugar-producing district. It was established as a colonial town in 1873, on the site on which Shaka Zulu built his maze-like capital Dakuza (the word translates, roughly, as 'the place of the lost person') and where he was murdered, in 1828, by his half-brothers Dingane and Mhlangana. In the centre of town, marking the exact spot (occupied at the time by a grain pit, into which the king's body was thrown) is a small memorial garden. Of historical interest, too, is the Natal North Coast Museum, housed in a former railways cottage in Gledhow Mill Street.

Ballito to the Tugela mouth

The N2 links a series of resorts along this beautiful stretch of coast; all of them offer sun, sea, sand and quiet enjoyment. Prominent among them are:

BALLITOVILLE, a popular though still-tranquil holiday centre 40,5 km north of Durban; shark-protected bathing; tidal pool; hotel; caravan/camping ground; shops. Next door is the older and even quieter Willard Beach.

SHAKA'S ROCK, also peaceful; secluded and very lovely beaches; hotel; cottages and flats. The rocky headland is thought to have been used as a viewing point by Shaka Zulu. Close by is:

SALT ROCK Here the shoreline is wooded and attractively rugged; the Umhlali resort is just across the river, which has a profusion of monkey orange trees growing along its banks. Hotel and caravan park; good fishing from the jetties; bowling, tennis and swimming at the Country Club; golf a little way inland.

The coast from Salt Rock to the Tugela river-mouth is scenically superb; there are worthwhile digressions down to Sheffield Beach, Blythedale Beach and Zinkwazi Beach.

HAROLD JOHNSON NATURE RESERVE, a 104-ha sanctuary situated on the steep south bank of the Tugela, preserves a patch of coastal forest, some attractive orchid species, and relics of brutal Anglo-Zulu conflict, including Fort Pearson and the Ultimatum Tree. An intriguing excursion is the Remedies and Rituals trail (one of three self-guided walks), which introduces you to trees that are significant in traditional

ZULU HERITAGE

In traditional Zulu society the women cultivated the land, cared for the children, saw to the family's water, food and firewood needs; the young boys herded cattle; the men hunted and made war. Zulu homes were beehive-shaped and positioned around a central cattle-kraal, which was considered a sacred place, accessible only to the daughters of the house. Cattle served as the measure of wealth, and on marriage were used for the bride-price (called *lobola*), which the groom's family paid.

The customary clothing materials were hides and pelts, adorned in various ways by the fighting men to distinguish each of the age-graded regiments, the regimental 'uniform' completed by plumes and patterned oxhide shields. When the first white traders came onto the scene in the early 19th century they found a ready market among the Zulu for their coloured beads. These were stitched together in intricately ornamental designs, each colour taking on symbolic significance. The principal Zulu musical instrument was the cowhide drum – and the human voice, used with magnificent effect on ceremonial occasions, and as a prelude to battle. The Zulu language is complex, subtle, expressive, full of imagery, and punctuated by 'click' sounds borrowed from Bushman (San) speech.

The Zulu were intensely conscious of the spirits in the world around them. Animistic belief credited a rock, a pool, a tree, a river with a personality of its own, and it was held that a super-powerful force, called Nkulukulu ('great, great one') watched over the people. It was the ancestral spirits, however, who were responsible for the day-to-day welfare of their descendants.

The fourth element in the body of traditional Zulu belief are the diviners, or *sangomas*, who act as intermediaries between the ancestral spirits and their living descendants, and are able to predict, divine and heal a multitude of ills, usually psychological and social. They are recruited to their calling by the ancestors, and receive rigorous training under an already qualified diviner.

Today the majority of Zulu are both Westernized and urbanized, most belong to the Christian faith (though traditional convictions are still influential), and the old ways are fast dying. Ancient custom and ritual are at their most evident in the more remote rural areas.

A young Zulu couple in traditional garb. The old ways, though, are fast disappearing.

(and white settler) medical and spiritual belief. Booklet available in the reserve, which has a caravan/camp site and picnic spots.

KINGDOM OF THE ZULU

The territory extending from the Tugela River north to the frontiers of Swaziland and Mozambique is known as Zululand – a historical rather than a formal name that had a more precise meaning in the 19th century. Under the apartheid regime part of it fell within the scatter of territories that made up the 'homeland' of KwaZulu. The far northern subsection, a beautiful region of misty hills and sandy wetlands, is called Maputaland and, occasionally (the name is archaic), Tongaland.

All very confusing, but that's South Africa. A brief note on the history of the region may make things a little clearer:

Zulu 'beehive' and rondavel homes

RISE AND DECLINE Zululand had been home to the eastern Nguni – a linguistic and cultural group made up of some 800 different tribes and clans, of which the Zulu were a minor segment – since the beginning of the 17th century.

In 1816 Shaka succeeded to the Zulu chieftainship – not the most promising of positions, since his people numbered a bare 1 500 at the time. But his genius, and the ruthless discipline he imposed, immediately transformed the character, and the power, of the Zulu.

Shaka's first priority was the reorganization of his small army, its weapons and its fighting methods. He replaced the ineffectual throwing spear with the long-bladed, short-handled stabbing assegai, which forced warriors into close combat.

He also refined the age-graded regimental system (the *Amabutho*) which other Nguni groups to the north had introduced with success – warriors now lived with men of their own age, in their own quarters, and each regiment had its own markings and regalia.

Finally, Shaka developed the famed Zulu battle tactics to a fine science. The regiments on the field – collectively known as the *impi* – were split into four groups. The most powerful (the 'chest') clashed head-on with the enemy while the second and third groups (the 'horns') flanked and encircled them. The fourth remained in reserve.

And Shaka fought, not just to win, but to exterminate – a new approach to warfare

which, until then, had often amounted to virtually bloodless encounters, the weaker forces retiring quickly from the field after a token exchange of throwing-spears.

Before the end of 1816 the Zulu army had grown fourfold, and it swiftly overcame the small neighbouring clans, including the Langeni who, during Shaka's childhood, had inflicted bitter humiliation on him and his mother (his particular Langeni enemies were impaled on the stakes of their own kraal fences). The impis went on to conquer the powerful Ndwandwe and Qwabe people, and then the confederation of Nguni clans to the south. Their lands were devastated, villages put to the torch, the survivors to flight. Shaka's legendary military exploits were largely confined to the eastern coastal plain, but they had a ripple-like effect that spread with savagely disruptive force throughout the northern subcontinent – a hugely destructive domino sequence known as the Difaqane.

Zulu pre-eminence, though, was to prove short-lived. The first white colonists had arrived in 1824, established the Port Natal trading outpost (see page 139) and were tolerated because they were small in number and peaceful by inclination. Far more threatening were the Voortrekkers who came, in the late 1830s, intent on large-scale settlement. Against these, Shaka's successor Dingane fought a bloody, courageous but in the end unsuccessful war, suffering a devastating defeat at the battle of

Blood River in 1838. Shortly afterwards, Dingane's half-brother Mpande invaded the Zulu kingdom and, with Boer help, established himself as paramount chief. He ruled for 32 years, during which period the Zulu, now confined to the regions north of the Tugela River – contemporary Zululand – lost much of their power, and more of their territory, to the encroaching white colonists.

The decline became a rout during the latter part of the 19th century. In 1879 the British, determined on creating an Imperial confederation in southern Africa and conscious of the threat posed to their comfortable political schemes by an independent, still-powerful Zulu nation, invaded the country and, after suffering humiliating defeat at Isandlwana (where an entire force was wiped out), crushed the Zulu army at Ulundi. They then divided Zululand into 13 fragments and, in the decades that followed, systematically reduced the Zulu to impotence.

Zululand was annexed to Britain in 1887, and incorporated into Natal ten years later. In 1906 a section of the people rose in revolt, but the episode – the so-called Bambata Rebellion – was only a flicker of the flame that once burned so brightly. It was swiftly extinguished.

During the last two decades of the apartheid era much of Zululand, together with part of the central region and a small segment of what is now Eastern Transvaal, comprised the homeland or 'national state' of KwaZulu.

THE LAND TODAY The Zulu – or, more accurately, the Eastern Nguni people – number something over seven million, the majority of whom live in KwaZulu-Natal, though a significant percentage has settled permanently in the country's industrial northern areas.

The northern section of the province – Zululand – is a region of lovely hills and valleys, fringed in the east by flattish coastal terraces that for most of the year are heat-hazed and tropically humid. The higher ground of the interior, though, is cooled by the rising sea air and moistened by the mists it brings, and by good rains that enrich the grasslands and sustain the perennial rivers.

It is a luxuriant land, one that nurtures a marvellous proliferation of wildlife.

Indeed the northern KwaZulu-Natal conservation areas are among some of the most impressive in the world: warmth, moisture and lush vegetation provide ideal habitats for an astonishing variety of animals and birds. The Hluhluwe section of the Hluhluwe-Umfolozi Park, for instance, is little more than one-twentieth the size of the Kruger National Park but contains almost 70% of the total number of the Kruger's species. Other sanctuaries are in their way as notable.

Among the other and many attractions this lovely country has to offer are splendid walks and wilderness trails, bathing and skin-diving (though be careful to stick to the safe areas: sharks are a problem along much of the coast); superb opportunities for photography, hunting, fishing.

Eshowe

Established in 1860 by the Zulu king-in-waiting Cetshwayo on a ridge of hills some 36 km inland and 75 km north-west of the Tugela river-mouth, Eshowe was burnt to the ground (by the retreating Zulu; the huge royal 'residence' has been reconstructed, and a cultural centre and museum established, at Ondini near Ulundi) in the war of 1879 and then resurrected by the British to become the capital of Zululand in 1887, a status fairly recently transferred to Ulundi. It's an attractive little town, notable for Vukani (in Main Street: Zulu arts and crafts), for its romantic-looking colonial fort, for the Zululand Historical Museum it contains, and for the :

DLINZA FOREST NATURE RESERVE A 200-ha patch of indigenous woodland that occupies the centre of town. Dlinza's fauna includes a rich birdlife, vervet monkeys, wild pig, blue and red duiker, bushbuck. There are half-a-dozen pleasant picnic spots, a central clearing known as Bishop Seat (venue for church services and the occasional nativity play), and a network of short trails. Accommodation: hotels and a camping ground in Eshowe. Nearby is the:

OCEAN VIEW GAME PARK, sanctuary for blue wildebeest, kudu, impala, reedbuck and a fine variety and number of birds.

ENTUMENI NATURE RESERVE, 16 km from Eshowe, is a smallish (393-ha) expanse of mist-belt forest in sugar-cane country. Among the attractions: colourful birds (narina trogon; Knysna lourie; starred robin) and, especially, a fascinating array of plants and insects.

Nkwaleni Valley, along the road between Eshowe and Melmoth, is the location for three excellent and increasingly popular Zulu 'living museums' that offer visitors day-long and overnight 'kraal experiences'. Biggest is Shakaland, which featured in the TV epic *Shaka Zulu* and now comprises a hotel, a kraal of 120 beehive huts (with en-suite bathrooms); specialities include Zulu delicacies, dancing, praise-singing; displays by spirit mediums (sangomas) and herbalists, and of basket-weaving, pot-making, hut-building. Information and bookings: PO Box 103, Eshowe 3815; Tel.(0354) 655/648, (011) 484-1717 or toll-free 0100134.

Nearby are Stewarts Farm and KwaBhekitunga, offering similar but less ambitious insights into Zulu lifestyles.

Richards Bay-Empangeni area

Richards Bay is a relatively new deep-water port – it came on stream in 1976 – and, although its harbour isn't the biggest in the country (that ranking belongs to Durban), it's the busiest in terms of cargo volume handled: about 50 million tons a year during the 1980s. Most of the throughput comprises such bulk materials as coal, phosphates and fertilizers, pig-iron, ferro-alloys, granite and other minerals, timber and paper products. The coal terminal is the world's largest, with an annual export capacity of 44 million tons.

The port can at present service vessels of up to 150 000 tons deadweight but the harbour has been so designed that, with further dredging, ships of a formidable 250 000 tons will be able to use the quays.

Richards Bay was created principally to serve the giant enterprises of the Gauteng province (to which it is of course linked by rail) and is the port of the future. Local industrial development has been rapid: among other installations are an oil pipeline, a massive fertilizer plant and an aluminium smelter. Titanium is extensively mined in the area.

This all sounds rather industrial and unattractive, but in fact Richards Bay and, especially, the coast and countryside around have a fair amount to offer. Recreation facilities are outstanding; the lagoon of the Mhlatuze River, around which the town has grown, is a conservation area, as are some 400 ha of shore. The beaches are being developed for tourism (the area has the only officially-approved safe bathing beach in Zululand); of interest to visitors is the Kaffrarian Museum, particularly for its exhibit of Huberta the Hippo, an enterprising animal that went on a three-year, 2 000-km walkabout (at one point she turned up in the streets of Durban) during the 1930s.

Some 20 km inland (take the R34 and cross the N2 national highway) is Empangeni, a thriving centre for the sugar, cotton, timber and cattle industries.

Easily accessible from both these towns are a number of fine conservation areas, of which the more prominent are:

ENSELENI NATURE RESERVE, a small (293 ha) but lushly varied tropical sanctuary for zebra, wildebeest, various antelope, hippo and croc (in the Nseleni River); and for an impressive bird population (including some interesting water-related species). Recommended is the self-guided Swamp trail, which leads you for 5 km through mangrove and papyrus and forests of fig and water myrtle. Enseleni is about 13 km north-west of Empangeni. Information: Natal Parks Board (see Advisory, page 173).

UMLALAZI NATURE RESERVE, on the coast 35 km south of Empangeni. A popular venue: the adjacent and lovely beaches and the sea are magnets to sunbathers, anglers, sailors, water-skiiers. The reserve comprises just over a thousand hectares of mangrove swamp and sand-dune woodland and is inhabited by intriguing populations of crabs and mudskipper fish (who live on land for most of their lives), birds, butterflies and monkeys. There's a trail, picnic spots, 5-bed log cabins, a camping ground. Information and bookings: The Natal Parks Board (see Advisory, page 173).

WINDY RIDGE GAME PARK, in the Nseleni River valley about 30 km west of Empangeni: a 1 300ha woodland and riverine reserve notable for its larger game: white rhino, giraffe, leopard, kudu, nyala, impala, bushbuck, crocodile. It has a splendid bird population. There are two pleasant rest-camps comprising huts with basic facilities (including kitchens); game-viewing roads; guided drives; guided walks. Information and bookings: PO Heatonville 3881; Tel. (0351) 2-3465.

The St Lucia complex

One of Africa's biggest and most remarkable marine wilderness areas, the complex comprises a number of separate but closely inter-related components, among them river estuary, lake/lagoon, lily-covered pan, game reserve, forest, high dune (the highest in the world) and, of course, the sea.

Central feature, though, is the 36 000-ha lake formed 60 million years ago, when the ocean receded to leave a sandy flatland, parts of which were low enough to retain both sea- and fresh water. The lake and its immediate surrounds are a proclaimed game park. A scheme to consolidate and extend the land under protection – to create a 275 000-ha Greater St Lucia Conservation Area – was announced in March 1990 (a response to, among other things, public outrage over proposals to mine the St Lucia dunes).

THE LAKE is in fact a cluster of lagoons extending up from the estuary and is at its widest (20 km) in the north, where its eastern portion is known as False Bay (25 km long, 3 km wide). The waters are shallow (average 1 m), and home to some 600 hippos (most often seen grazing around the estuary), to crocodiles (common throughout the area) and to large numbers of fish, crustaceans, insects and other nutritious creatures that attract vast numbers of birds. Among the latter are a breeding community of fish eagles, thousands of white pelicans, twelve species of heron, flamingos, saddlebills, spoonbills, Caspian terns and many others.

Near St Lucia village in the south is the fascinating and informative Crocodile Centre.

ST LUCIA PARK is a narrow (about 1 km) belt running along most of the lake's shores and covering, altogether, something over 12 500 ha of reedbed, woodland and grassland. Plenty of birds; mammals include nyala, reedbuck, bushbuck, grey and red duiker, the shy suni, steenbok, bush-pig, vervet monkey.

CAPE VIDAL RESORT AND STATE FOREST This covers some 12 000 ha of sand-dune forest and marshy grassland to the north-east of Lake St Lucia. Here there is wonderful bird-watching; game includes black rhino, kudu, buffalo,

waterbuck. To the south of and attached to the Cape Vidal area (and lying between lake and sea) is the:

EASTERN SHORES NATURE RESERVE, comprising about 14 000 ha. Wildlife here includes brown hyena, side-striped jackal and huge numbers of reedbuck (Africa's largest concentration). In 1989 Richards Bay Minerals revealed plans to mine titanium in the reserve; these were shelved following a public outcry and the submission of a million-signature petition to the minister responsible.

ST LUCIA AND MAPUTALAND MARINE RESERVES These extend over 88 000 coastal ha, from Cape Vidal to the Mozambique border – the largest marine reserve in Africa. Offshore coral reefs in the south (these are the world's southernmost); splendid game-fishing; turtles nest in the northern parts.

DUKUDUKU FOREST RESERVE, a huge 6 000-ha woodland expanse, lies to the south and east of Lake St Lucia, and is severely threatened by human encroachment. Attractions (for the time being): floral wealth, lovely butterflies. Red duiker hover around the picnic spot; beware the gaboon viper.

FALSE BAY PARK covers over 2 000 ha of dune forest, woodland and bush to the west of False Bay. Here there is good camping; picnicking; bird-watching (150 species, including the pink-backed pelican); among the game are red and common duiker, bushpig, warthog, bushbuck,

Boating and fishing at St Lucia

Trail donkeys on the Black Umfolozi River

reedbuck, nyala and the elusive suni; of special interest are the immensely ancient fossil beds at Lister Point.

ST LUCIA'S AMENITIES The area offers splendid game- and bird-viewing; walks and trails; angling and big-game fishing; outdoor living, all of which are made easy and enjoyable for you.

ST LUCIA VILLAGE Private hotels, holiday apartments, self-contained accommodation (prices vary, but some units are incredibly good value, especially in the off-season), time-share; shops, garages, eateries; water-slide, swimming beach, tennis, boat-hire; the Monzi Country Club welcomes visitors; worth calling in at is the mNandi arts and crafts centre in the main street; guided tours to Hluhluwe and neighbouring reserves; holiday-makers with four-wheel-drive vehicles can drive for about 7 km along the broad white beach. The Natal Parks Board runs a large and popular public resort at the village: three caravan-camping grounds; boat tours; small game park.

IN THE PARK Log cabins and caravan/camp site, walking, bird-watching, surf fishing, ski-boating at Mapelane resort camp; cottage, rest-huts and caravan/camp site, reed-covered island, fishing, picnicking, hiking through the

forest, hippo, crocs at Fanie's Island; cottage, rest-huts, swimming pool, self-guided trail, launch tours, petrol at Charters Creek.

CAPE VIDAL Five- and eight-bed log cabins, bush camp, caravan-camp site, ski-boating and skin-diving, guided five-day trails in winter.

DUKUDUKU Picnic ground; trails.

EASTERN SHORES Three-day Mziki trail; picnicking at Mission Rocks.

FALSE BAY PARK Caravan/camp site; the Dugondlovu trail (overnight huts), shorter trails and walks; boat-hire, launch tours; petrol and groceries at Hluhluwe village.

PRECAUTIONS Malaria mosquitoes in St Lucia lake and park: be careful of the crocs and hippos and the occasional shark.

INFORMATION AND BOOKINGS Contact the Natal Parks Board (see Advisory, page 173).

Umfolozi game reserve

This and its lovely companion Hluhluwe (see further on) are the oldest of South Africa's sanctuaries; both were proclaimed in April 1897 – a year before the Kruger National Park began life as the Sabie reserve.

One of the Umfolozi's thriving white rhino

The Umfolozi extends over 47 753 ha of rolling hill and floodplain between central Zululand's White and Black Mfolozi rivers. The name in Zulu means (roughly) 'zigzag', a reference to the convoluted course it takes through the hills before dividing into its two colourful offsprings. The area – warm, well-watered, lush, sweetly grassed savanna – was home to teeming game populations long before the encroachment of man. Much of the game, though, disappeared during the years after 1921, when the authorities launched a sustained, misguided and in the event disastrous game extermination programme designed to eradicate the tsetse fly that plagued the surrounding ranchlands. Altogether, some 100 000 animals were slaughtered before finally, in 1945, the killings were abandoned in favour of chemical control.

The Umfolozi made an excellent recovery and today serves as a haven for white rhino, of which there are about 1 000 in the reserve – a surprisingly healthy figure, because the species faced almost certain extinction until the Natal Parks Board launched an ambitious and deservedly-publicized programme (it captured world headlines) in the 1960s. Still endangered elsewhere, it breeds exceptionally well here: surplus animals are regularly translocated to areas throughout and beyond South Africa.

Now its smaller black cousin is in similar decline, the victim of horn-hunting poachers. Two decades ago, the continent-wide population of black rhino stood at over 60 000; by the mid-1980s fewer than 4 500 remained, of which 400 were to be found in Natal. The Umfolozi is one of the keys to its survival.

Among the reserve's other game species are buffalo, giraffe, elephant, leopard, blue wildebeest, zebra, waterbuck, steenbok, mountain reedbuck, kudu, impala, nyala, spotted hyena, wild dog, black-backed jackal, warthog. Cheetah have been introduced. The lion population numbers something over 40, which in many respects is quite remarkable: these predators, prime targets of the 19th century white hunters, had been regionally extinct for nearly six decades until a lone male made its erratic and elusive way from Mozambique to Umfolozi (a distance of about 400 km) in the late 1950s, to be joined later, by a small group of females (of unknown origin) and the resultant prides flourished.

Birdlife: about 400 species have been recorded, among them Wahlberg's eagle, night heron, wood stork, black-bellied korhaan, Temminck's courser.

Umfolozi is well geared for visitors: accommodation at the hutted camp and the two bush camps ranges from the fairly luxurious to the basic; there's a wilderness trail, an auto-trail, several established walks, an extensive system of game-viewing roads; a shop (no groceries; bring your own food) and petrol filling facilities.

Hluhluwe game reserve

Umfolozi's near neighbour, and similar in many ways. Indeed the two are linked by a corridor of land along which the animals move at will, and tentative plans have been announced to combine the reserves. If these materialize, the Umfolozi/Hluhluwe complex will become the Kruger of Natal.

Hluhluwe, 23 067 ha in extent, is stunningly beautiful: a rich land of sometimes misty mountain forest, grass-covered slope, dense thicket, enchanting river (the Hluhluwe which takes its name from the lianas, or monkey ropes, that festoon the riverine forest) and of an incredible diversity of plant and animal life. Included among the 84 different mammals are white and black rhino, elephant, giraffe, buffalo, blue wildebeest, Burchell's zebra, nyala, lion and cheetah (though both these are elusive, especially in summer), samango monkey, baboon, wild dog, spotted hyena, waterbuck, bushbuck, kudu. There are crocodile, hippo and leguaan in the riverine areas. Bird species number about 425, and include the bateleur, the marabou stork and the white-backed vulture.

Best times to visit both the Hluhluwe and the Umfolozi are the drier and cooler months (April to October), when the game is at its most visible.

Accommodation comprises a luxury lodge, cottages and huts at Hilltop camp. There are walking and auto-trails, nearly 90 km of game-viewing roads, viewing hides, a Zulu village museum, a shop (but no groceries), and petrol filling pump. Information and bookings: Natal Parks Board (see Advisory, page 173).

Mkuzi game reserve

A large sanctuary, extending over 35 000 ha of savanna parkland and riverine and sycamore forest to the east of the Lebombo Mountains in the north-eastern region. The reserve is bisected by the Mkhuze River and its Nsumu Pan, home to the ghostly fever tree, to crocodile and hippo, and to a splendid number and variety of water-related birds – wild geese and duck, pink-backed pelican, fish eagle and squacco heron, the hamerkop and the wooolly-necked stork. Other birds to be seen include African jacana, purple gallinule, Natal francolin, white-backed vulture, crested guinea-fowl, black cuckoo, white-fronted bee-eater.

Among the mammals: white and black rhino, giraffe, blue wildebeest, mountain reedbuck, kudu, eland, nyala, waterbuck, bushbuck.

Mkuzi's amenities are especially attractive: there's a pleasant rest-camp (choice of cottages, bungalows, rest-huts; cooks and helpers make life comfortable); caravan/camping ground; thatched hides beside pan and waterholes; game-viewing drives, trails (including a 57-km auto-trail), shop (no groceries), petrol. Information and bookings: Natal Parks Board (see Advisory, page 173).

Ndumu game reserve

A smallish (10 000-ha) area of Tongaland, north-east of Mkuzi, renowned for the superb richness of its riverine life: the reserve lies on the floodplain of the Pongolo River, and the watercourse and the pans sustain a great many water-related birds (altogether, 416 species have been recorded, among them Pel's fishing owl and the southern banded snake eagle) as well as bream and barbel, tiger-fish and tilapia, hippo and crocodile. The last-mentioned had once been reduced to the point of local extinction by the depredations of hunters and by the proliferation of barbel (which destroyed the croc's food source) but now, thanks to the hatcheries, they're fully restored in number and condition.

Ndumu has a pleasant little rest-camp of two-bed cottages (cooks and helpers in attendance); game-viewing roads; hides. Guided tours, in open vehicles, are available. Information and bookings: KwaZulu Bureau of Natural Resources (see Advisory, page 173).

Sodwana Bay national park

A very popular resort among water sportsmen, skiboat fishermen and beach-lovers. The park comprises just over 400 ha of lake, marsh and forested sand-dune on the Tongaland coast and, crowded though it sometimes is, the land remains in fairly pristine condition. Small mammals abound; there are pleasant walks along the shores; short trails; log cabins, chalets, very extensive caravan/camping facilities; boat storage; shop; petrol. Information and bookings: Officer-in-Charge, Private Bag 310, Mbazwana 3974; Tel. (0356) 572.

The privately-run Sodwana Bay Lodge, on the shores of Lake Shazibe, offers more luxurious accommodation in self-contained chalets and time-share units; central restaurant; private pub (the Crowned Eagle), swimming pool, boma-braai areas, dive-pool (the place specializes in diving and big-game fishing: leisure resort has two full-time diving instructors, and a 6,6-m Acecat angling and diving boat). Also bird-watching, nature trails (to the turtle breeding grounds). Information and bookings: Tel. (031) 29-0972.

Lake Sibaya

The country's largest freshwater lake, Sibaya – nearly 30 m deep, intensely blue and crystal clear – extends over 70 km^2 of coastal plain north of Sodwana Bay, the eastern shores separated from the Indian Ocean by a high belt of wooded dunes. Attractions: crocs, hippo, reedbuck, side-striped jackal, birds (280 species; hides have been established); boating (craft available for hire); walking trails; tranquillity. Basic accommodation at Camp Baya (bring your own food); no other facilities. Information and bookings: KwaZulu Bureau of Natural Resources (see Advisory, page 173).

Kosi Bay nature reserve

This, the northernmost of the parks, comprises 11 000 ha of lakes and mangrove swamps which, like Sibaya (see above), are separated from the sea by dunes. Turtles – the famed loggerheads and leatherbacks – breed in the area; the lake supports hippo and crocodile. Accommodation: luxury lodges (well-appointed, fully staffed), caravan-camp site. Attractions: game trails, turtle-viewing trips, fishing. Information and bookings: KwaZulu Bureau of Natural Resources (see Advisory, page 173).

Itala game reserve

Not generically related to the other Zululand reserves, and rather off the beaten track: its

Exploring the pristine coral reefs off Sodwana Bay

30 000 ha lie along the Pongolo River (which here forms the provincial border) and is reached via Vryheid. Some 75 species of mammal inhabit the hilly grasslands and bushveld, among them white and black rhino, giraffe, zebra, cheetah, brown hyena and numerous antelope (including eland, kudu, the rare roan). Basic accommodation in the bush camp and at the caravan/camp site; there are trails and a guided day-walk. The sophisticated Ntshondwe restcamp, comprising luxury lodge, self-contained thatched chalets, shop, restaurant, swimming pool, conference venue, is one of KwaZulu-Natal's showpieces.

Information and bookings: Officer-in-Charge, PO Box 42, Louwsburg 3150, Tel. (03882) 7-5239, and the Natal Parks Board (see Advisory, page 173).

Private game lodges

A number of privately-run game ranches have been established in various parts of northern Zululand. Accommodation and board vary from the economical self-contained to all-found luxury comparable to the best on offer from the Eastern Transvaal private reserves (see page 93). Obvious attractions include excellent game-viewing opportunities, walking, bird-watching, personalized service, sociable camplife. Some of them concentrate on trophy-hunting during the winter months. Located in the Hluhluwe area are:

BONAMANZI GAME PARK Especially attractive accommodation in A-frame tree-houses (rather isolated), in the conventional thatched-hut camp and luxury lodge. Guests are encouraged to walk the free-ranging wilderness trails and strolls. Information and bookings: P.O. Box 48, Hluhluwe 3960; Tel. (03562), and ask for 3530.

BUSHLANDS GAME LODGE Air-conditioned, self-contained log cabins raised above the ground, connected by elevated wooden walkways; full-service restaurant (venison a speciality); guided game drives around Hluhluwe, Umfolozi, Mkuze, St Lucia. Information and bookings: P.O. Box 79, Hluhluwe 3960; Tel. (03562), ask for 144.

PHINDA RESOURCE RESERVE, a 15 000 ha expanse of recently stocked land between the Mkuzi game reserve and Sodwana state forest, is an upmarket 'eco-tourism' showpiece being developed with two aims in mind: to provide visitors (mainly from overseas) with a wilderness experience without parallel, and to share its considerable resources with the local rural communities – an integrated approach that benefits everyone. For the guests, there are superb guided game-drives through widely differing ecosystems (savannah, bushveld, palm veld, rare sand forest, wetland) and exploratory forays farther afield to take in the varied land, lake and marine splendours (including the lovely coral reefs) of Maputaland; bird-watching (360 recorded species) and luxury accommodation (main lodge, rock chalets and bush suites). Information and reservations: P.O. Box 1211, Sunninghill Park 2157; Tel. (011) 803-8421/8616; Fax. (011) 803-1810.

UBIZANE GAME RANCH Luxury forest camp accommodation (overlooking the fever trees); four-wheel-drive viewing and photographic safaris (day and night) in the main game reserves. Exclusive. Information and bookings: P.O. Box 102, Hluhluwe 3960; Tel. (03562) 3602.

GETTING AROUND
The north coast and Zululand regions are wonderful walking and driving country. You'll need a good map and a detailed regional guide.

Day drives
The scenically outstanding coastal route from Durban to Richards Bay provides a most pleasant outing (see brief details of the 'sugar circuit' further on). There are, though, a great many other options, among them:

✰ St Lucia to Hluhluwe (see pages 162-164): Take the R620 from St Lucia to Mtubatuba, then travel along the R618 to and through the Hluhluwe game reserve. Continue 14 km eastward to the N2 highway and return south.

✰ Round trip: Start from the Richards Bay-Empangeni area (see page 161) and follow the route (the R34; the R34/68 and the R66) to Ulundi via Melmoth. Visit the Zulu cultural museum at Ondini and continue eastward to and through the Umfolozi game reserve's western (Cengeni) gate, where a game-viewing road map is available. Explore the reserve. Leave via the Manbene (eastern) gate; take the R618 to join the N2 highway and continue south to the Enseleni nature reserve (page 161), before returning to Richards Bay-Empangeni.

✰ Sugar circuit (see page 150). From Durban: follow the N2 highway northward for 11,3 km

and take the R102 exit, continuing through Verulam to Tongaat, Shaka's Kraal and Stanger. Continue on the R74 to rejoin the N2 and drive south, digressing left to one or two of the very pleasant north-coast resort areas covered on pages 157-159.

Walks and hikes
Pleasant informal rambles along the mangrove-fringed shores all the way up the coast. Trails, long and short, have been established in the game reserves and conservation areas covered on pages 160-166; among the more notable of the serious hikes are the 40-km, 3-day Msiki trail through the Eastern Shores forest and St Lucia complex; the 3-day Umfolozi Wilderness and Primitive trails; the Umfolozi's 5-day White Rhino trail, and the 57-km, 3-day Mkuzi Bushveld trail.

Full information on these and the many other hikes and walks is available from the relevant authorities in charge, principal of which are the Natal Parks Board and the KwaZulu Bureau of Natural Resources (see Advisory, page 173).

On the Umfolozi hiking trail

ADVISORY: DURBAN, THE EAST COAST AND ZULULAND

CLIMATE

Kind to holiday-makers throughout the year, though the humidity can be ferocious in high summer (between January and March), especially in the northern coastal areas. Summer rainfall area; some winter rainfall: Durban January average 109 mm, July average 28 mm, annual average 1 008 mm. Durban average temperatures: January maximum 27,2 °C; January minimum 20,5 °C; July maximum 22,0 °C; July minimum 10,9 °C.

MAIN ATTRACTIONS

Durban: Sun, sea and sand □ The kaleidoscopic Golden Mile (see pages 140-142) □ Day-drive distance from Natal's renowned game parks and nature reserves □ Fine hotels, restaurants, shops, tourist amenities generally □ Excellent sporting facilities (see pages 152-153), especially swimming, fishing, golf.

South Coast: Sun, sea and sand □ Angling, skin-diving, golf □ The Oribi Gorge and nature reserve.

North Coast and Zululand: Splendid game and nature reserves □ Sun, sea and sand □ Angling □ Zulu history and culture.

TRAVEL

Road. Durban is 79 km from Pietermaritzburg, 608 km from Johannesburg, 640 km from Bloemfontein, 655 km from East London, 664 km from Pretoria, 764 km from Kimberley, 901 km from Port Elizabeth, 1 654 km from Cape Town.

National highways, generally in excellent condition, link Durban with all major South African centres. The N2 leads south and then east through Port Elizabeth to Cape Town; the N3 takes you northwest through Pietermaritzburg and Harrismith to Johannesburg.

KwaZulu-Natal's provincial roads have been maintained at a high standard but are now under pressure; reports in 1990 indicated that, without a major rebuilding and maintenance programme, the network could begin to deteriorate seriously in the next two to three years.

Coach travel Coach services link Durban with major centres. Contact Greyhound: Johannesburg (011) 834-3692, or Durban (031) 37-6478; Citiliner: 368-2848, 37-6478, or through Computicket (see page 173); Translux: 302-2921 or 302-3365; Golden Wheels Intercity (between Durban and Johannesburg): (031) 29-2894, or Johannesburg (011) 852-1423 (all hours).

A daily bus service operates between Durban railway station and Pietermaritzburg; Tel. 302-2989.
Scheduled bus services operate between Durban (and Pinetown) and the Wild Coast Sun; contact Durban Publicity Association (see page 173) for information.
A bus service connects Durban city centre with Umhlanga Rocks via La Lucia Mall; Tel. 561-1101.

Rail. There is a rail service to the south coast, as far as Port Shepstone. Inter-city railway passenger services connect Durban with all major centres. Information (arrivals and departures): Tel. (031) 31-0609. The main railway station is on the Umgeni Road, some way to the north of city centre.

Air. Scheduled airline services connect Durban with major centres. Durban airport is situated off the Southern Freeway (the South Coast road), about 15 minutes drive from city centre; a bus service operates between the terminal (corner of Smith and Aliwal streets) and the airport. Flight information: Tel. (031) 42-6156 or 42-6111; bookings: 305-6491.

Helicopter: Court Helicopters, Tel. 83-9513.

TRAVEL WITHIN AND AROUND DURBAN

City bus and taxi services are adequate; the Mynah minibus service excellent; local tour operators offer a wide choice of sightseeing trips; major car-hire companies have offices in the city, as do local car-, camper- and caravan-hire firms. Fuller coverage of city travel appears in Getting Around, page 148.

South Coast: Linked to Durban by the N2 highway as far as Port Shepstone, thereafter by the R61; both in good condition. Inland roads can be a bit rough.

North Coast and Zululand: Main road is also the N2, parallel to but out of sight of the coast to the general vicinity of Richards Bay (about two-and-a-half hours' drive from Durban) and then sweeping inland to the Swaziland border. Excellent condition. Major Zululand roads are tarred; most minor ones (including those in the reserves) are gravelled.

Air: Daily City Air flights from Durban, and Comair flights from Johannesburg to Richards Bay.

ACCOMMODATION

Durban and the South Coast are South Africa's principal leisure areas; visitors have a very wide choice of good hotels, guest houses, holiday apartments, resort accommodation and caravan/camping grounds. Book well in advance for the summer months, and especially for the period of the Transvaal school holidays.

Select hotels

DURBAN CITY CENTRE

Albany ★★★ 72 rooms; conference facilities for 200. 252 Smith Street, Durban 4001; Tel. 304-4381.

Royal ★★★★★ Smith St. One of South Africa's oldest, most famous and best. 250 rooms, 18 suites; conference facilities. PO Box 1041, Durban 4000; Tel. 304-0331; Fax: 307-6884.

GOLDEN MILE

Beach ★★★ Large, good value. 400 rooms, conference facilities. PO Box 10305, Marine Parade 4056; Tel. 37-5511; Telex: 62-2381.

Blue Waters ★★★ Snell Parade. 262 rooms; conference facilities. PO Box 10201, Marine Parade 4056; Tel. 32-4272.

Edward ★★★★ Marine Parade. Elegant accommodation. 90 rooms, 12 suites; conference facilities. PO Box 105, Durban 4000; Tel. 37-3681; Fax: 32-1692.

Elangeni ★★★★ Snell Parade. Large and luxurious. PO Box 4094, Durban 4000; Tel. 37-1321; Fax: 32-5527; Telex: 62-0133.

Four Seasons ★★★ Gillespie St. 200 rooms; conference facilities for 140. PO Box 10200, Marine Parade 4056; Tel. 37-3381.

Maharani ★★★★★ Snell Parade. Large and luxurious; conference facilities for 600. PO Box 10592, Marine Parade 4056; Tel. 32-7361; Telex: 62-2485.

Malibu ★★★ Marine Parade. 380 rooms, 8 suites; conference facilities. PO Box 10199, Marine Parade 4056; Tel. 37-2231; Telex: 62-0235.

Marine Parade Holiday Inn ★★★. 336 rooms; conference facilities for 300. PO Box 10809, Marine Parade 4056; Tel. 37-3341; Telex: 62-1448.

Ocean City Holiday Inn ★★★ Sol Harris Crescent. 265 rooms, 3 suites; conference facilities for 350. PO Box 10222, Marine Parade 4056; Tel. 37-1211; Telex: 62-0387.

Tropicana ★★★★. PO Box 10305, Marine Parade 4056; Tel. 368-1511; Fax: 37-2621; Telex: 62-2381.

GREATER DURBAN

Rob Roy ★★★ Rob Roy Crescent, Botha's Hill. 34 rooms, 3 suites; conference facilities for 120. PO Box 10, Botha's Hill 3660; Tel. (031) 777-1305; Telex: 62-5226.

UMHLANGA ROCKS

Beverly Hills ★★★★★. 74 rooms, 4 suites; conference facilities. PO Box 71, Umhlanga Rocks 4320; Tel. (031) 561-2211; Telex: 62- 2073.

Cabana Beach ★★★ Lagoon Drive. Huge hotel. 1 200 rooms; conference facilities. PO Box 10, Umhlanga Rocks 4320; Tel. (031) 561- 2371; Fax: 561 2371; Telex: 62-0165.

Oyster Box ★★★ 90 rooms; 7 suites; conference facilities for 80. PO Box 22, Umhlanga Rocks 4320; Tel. (031) 561- 2233; Telex: 62-3433.

Umhlanga Sands ★★★ 237 self-contained suites; conference facilities for 150; 3 restaurants. PO Box 223, Umhlanga Rocks 4320; Tel. (031) 561-2323.

SOUTH COAST

Bedford Inn ★★ Port Shepstone. Small (10 rooms); conference facilities for 100. 64 Colley St, Port Shepstone 4240; Tel. (0391) 2-1085.

Blue Marlin ★★ Scottburgh. 92 rooms; conference facilities. PO Box 24, Scottburgh 4180; Tel. (03231) 2-1214, or Johannesburg (011) 78-8669; Telex: 62-2896.

Crayfish Inn ★★★ Ramsgate. 14 rooms; conference facilities for 30. PO Box 7, Ramsgate 4285; Tel. (03931) 4410/1.

Cutty Sark ★★ Scottburgh. 55 rooms, 1 suite; conference facilities. PO Box 3, Scottburgh 4180; Tel. (03231) 2-1230; Telex: 62-8331.

Golf Inn ★★ Scottburgh. 33 rooms; conference facilities for 40. PO Box 456, Scottburgh 4180; Tel. (03231) 2-0913; Telex: 62-0300.

La Crete ★★ Uvongo. 100 rooms; conference facilities for 60. PO Box 1, Uvongo 4270; Tel. (03931) 5-1301.

Lido ★★ Umkomaas. 36 rooms. PO Box 24, Umkomaas 4170; Tel. (03231) 3-1002; Telex: 65-0172.

Margate Hotel ★★ Marine Drive Margate. 70 rooms; conference facilities for 600. PO Box 4, Margate 4275; Tel. (03931) 2-1410.

Marina Beach ★ 26 rooms; conference facilities for 100. PO Box 9, Marina Beach 4281; Tel. (03931) 3-0022.

Oribi Gorge Hotel ★★ 12 rooms; small conference facilities. PO Box 575, Port Shepstone 4240; Tel. (0397) 9-1753.

St Michael Sands ★★ PO Box 45, St Michaels-on-Sea 4265; Tel. (03931) 5-1230.

Sunlawns ★★ Margate. 30 rooms. PO Box 100, Margate 4275; Tel. (03931) 2-1078.

NORTH COAST AND ZULULAND

Chaka's Rock Hotel ★★ On sea-front cliff, wonderful views, Shaka's Rock. 38 rooms with bath or shower. PO Box 121, Umhlali 4390; Tel. (0322) 5015/6.

Forest Inn ★★ Mtunzini, in forest setting 45 km from Richards Bay. 42 en-suite rooms. PO Box 44, Mtunzini 3867; Tel. (0353) 40-1431.

Ghost Mountain Inn ★★ In the foothills of the Lebombo Mountains; 31 en-suite rooms; conference facilities for 35. PO Box 18, Mkuze 3965; Tel. (035662), and ask for Mkuze 18/29.

Hluhluwe Protea ★★ Near the major reserves; 62 en-suite rooms; conference facilities for 120. PO Box 92, Hluhluwe 3960; Tel. (03562), and ask for 46/47.

Hotel Luthando ★★ Stanger. 14 en-suite rooms; conference facilities for 200. PO Box 502, Stanger 4450; Tel. (0324) 2- 2208/9.

Karos Bayshore Inn ★★ Richards Bay; 103 en-suite rooms; conference facilities. PO Box 51, Richards Bay 3900; Tel. (0351) 3- 1246/3-2411.

Karos Richards ★★★ Central Richards Bay; 97 en-suite rooms, 2 suites; full room service; conference facilities for 170. PO Box 242, Richards Bay 3900; Tel. (0351) 3-1301.

Karridene Holiday Resort ★★★ Illovo Beach. Complex comprises hotel, flats and caravan park. Hotel: 23 rooms, 2 suites. PO Box 20, Illovo Beach 4155; Tel. (031) 96-3332.

Salt Rock Hotel ★★ 69 en-suite rooms; conference facilities for 200. P.O. Salt Rock 4391; Tel. (0322) 5025/29/36.

Trade Winds ★★ Near Mtunzini and the Umlalazi reserve. 17 en-suite rooms; conference facilities for 30. PO Box 100, Mtunzini 3867; Tel. (035322), and ask for Mtunzini 40-1411.

Umdloti Strand ★★ 50 en-suite rooms; conference facilities for 40. PO Box 1, Umdloti Beach 4350; Tel. (031) 568-1611.

Westbrook Beach ★★ Tongaat Beach. 24 en-suite rooms; à la carte restaurant (seafood specialities). PO Box 48, Tongaat Beach 4400; Tel. (0322) 4-2021.

Zululand Safari Lodge ★★★ In game ranch; full guest programme; 41 en-suite rooms; à la carte restaurant; bush breakfasts; conference facilities for 40. PO Box 116, Hluhluwe 3960; Tel. (03562), and ask for 63/64.

Game reserves

ZULULAND

Information and bookings for the major reserves: contact the Natal Parks Board or the KwaZulu Bureau of Natural Resources: see Useful Addresses on page 173.

Private lodges

Information from your travel agent. Addresses and contact numbers for some of the lodges appear on page 166. The Pongola Tourism Association (see Useful Addresses page 173) is a useful source of information on bush camps, ranging from the rustic to the luxurious, in the Pongola-Mkuze River regions.

Ungraded accommodation

There are numerous one-star and ungraded hotels, resorts and caravan/camping facilities in the Durban and coastal regions: contact Club Caraville Natal Experience, PO Box 139, Sarnia 3615; Tel. Durban (031) 701-4156; Johannesburg (011) 622-4628/9; or enquire at the Durban Publicity Association (see Useful Addresses on page 173) or your travel agent about the wider options, within Durban and its coastal regions.

Contact Bed and Breakfast: Johannesburg (011) 482-2206 (central reservations); (031) 306-3755 (Durban and district); (03931) 2- 2322 (South Coast); (035) 550-1207 (North Coast and Zululand).

Caravan/camping and self-catering accommodation

DURBAN AND SOUTH COAST

Durban: Ansteys caravan park (Brighton Beach, Bluff), Tel. (031) 47-4061.

Anerley: Marlon Holiday Resort, PO Box 112, Anerley 4230, Tel. (0391) 3596 (offers caravans for hire, caravan sites and self-catering accommodation). Prairie Park Holiday Resort (10 km from Port Shepstone), PO Box 51, Anerley 4230, Tel. (0391) 81-2013 (caravan sites and self-catering accommodation).

Banana Beach: Bendigo caravan resort, PO Box 91, Anerley 4230, Tel. (0391) 3451 (caravan sites and self-catering accommodation).

Bazley Beach: Mac Nicols' Bazley Beach caravan resort, PO Box 398, Scottburgh 4180, Tel. (03239) 9-8863/79.

Board-sailing off Durban beach

Hibberdene: Carousel Holiday Resort, PO Box 41, Hibberdene 4220, Tel. (0399) 2406 (caravans, no tents allowed, self-catering accommodation). Hibberdene caravan park, PO Box 143, Hibberdene 4220, Tel. 2308.

Illovo Beach: Karridene Holiday Resort, PO Box 19, Illovo Beach 4155, Tel. (031) 96-3321 (hotel, flats and caravan park).

Leisure Bay: Leisure View caravan park, PO Box 16, Voortrekkerstrand 4279, Tel. (03938) 9-2367.

Margate: Constantia park, PO Box 9, Margate 4275, Tel. (03931) 20-0482. De Wet caravan park, PO Box 71, Margate 4275, Tel. (03931) 2-1022. Margate caravan park, PO Box 228, Margate 4275, Tel. (03931) 2-0852.

Munster: Mittenwald caravan park (8 km from Port Edward), PO Munster 4278, Tel. (03938) 9-2347.

Scottburgh: Charles Hoffe caravan park. Bookings: PO Box 7551, Johannesburg 2000, Tel. (011) 725-5112. Happy Wanderers caravan park, Abrams Dr, Scottburgh. PO Kelso 4183, Tel. (03231) 5-1104; Fax: (03231) 5-1220 (caravan/camping and self-catering accommodation). Municipal caravan park, PO Box 19, Scottburgh 4180, Tel. (03231) 2-0291/2-1202.

Umtentweni: Caravan Resort, PO Box 44, Sea Park 4241, Tel. (0391) 5-0531 (caravan/camping and self-catering accommodation).

NORTH COAST AND ZULULAND

Ballito: Dolphin caravan park, PO Box 6, Ballito 4420, Tel. (0322) 6-2187.

Blythedale Beach: La Mouette caravan park, PO Box 3090, Stanger 4450, Tel. (0324) 2-2547.

Mtubatuba: Monzi caravan park, PO Box 142, Mtubatuba 3935, Tel. (035) 1704.

Mtunzini: The Forest Inn, PO Box 44, Mtunzini 3867, Tel. (0353) 40-1431; Fax: (0353) 40-1363.

St Lucia area: Eastern Shores (Cape Vidal) Nature Reserve, Natal Parks Board (see Advisory page 173), Bookings: Camp Manager, PO St Lucia 3936, Tel. (03592), and ask for 1104 (campsites and self-catering accommodation). St Lucia Park, Natal Parks Board (see Advisory page 173), Bookings: Fanie's Island: Camp Manager, PO Box 201, Mtubatuba 3935, Tel. (03552), and ask for 1431. Mapelane and St Lucia Resort: Private Bag, St Lucia Estuary 3936, Tel. (03592), and ask for 20/47. Travel Lodge and caravan park, PO Box 4, St Lucia 3936, Tel. (03592), and ask for 36.

Umhlanga Rocks: Umhlanga caravan park, PO Box 22, Umhlanga Rocks 4320, Tel. (031) 561-3217; Fax: (031) 561-4072.

Zinkwazi Beach: Zinkwazi Holiday Resort, PO Box 8, Darnall 4480, Tel. (0324) 3344/96; Fax: (0324) 3340.

SELECT RESTAURANTS

DURBAN CITY

Api Taki, 320 West Street. Tel. 305-4451. Indonesian, Chinese & Polynesian menus; delicious.

British Middle East Indian Sporting & Dining Club, 16 Stamford Hill Rd, Greyville. Tel. 309-4017. Durban's oldest pub; Indian & Middle Eastern fare, but the place is most notable for its grandly colonial character.

Chatters, Hermitage St. Tel. 306-1896. An 'in' place; imaginative fare in an intimate setting. Take your own wine.

Colony, The Oceanic, Sol Harris Crescent. Tel. 368-2789. Victorian-style décor and largesse; splendid meat and venison dishes.

Elarish, Grosvenor Shopping Centre, Bluff. Tel. 466 2086. Superb Indian restaurant.

Greek Taverna, 213 Musgrave Rd, Berea. Tel. 21-5433. Informal, Greek, excellent. Remember to take your own wine

La Mafia, Kearsney Rd. Tel. 32-0519. Unpretentious; Chicago pictures; exquisite Italian food. Take your own wine.

Landau's, Avonmore Centre, Ninth Avenue. Tel. 23-9135. Nouvelle but not aggressively so.

Leipoldt's of Port Natal, and Fat Frank's, The Workshop. Tel. 304- 6643. The old stationmaster's home, now attractively renovated; two restaurants: South African (Leipoldt's) downstairs; lively American (southern) upstairs.

Le Montmartre, BP Centre, West Street. Tel. 32-6548/32-3887. French Provincial in bistro-type atmosphere.

Maitre Per's, Mona Rd. Tel. 32-8866. Small and popular; superb meat dishes in Continental style.

Nataraja, The Workshop, Commercial Rd. Tel. 305-3143. Marvellous curries.

O Cacador, Point Rd. Tel. 301-6476. Portuguese; excellent.

O Pescador, Albany Grove. Tel. 304-4138. Also Portuguese and excellent; take your own wine.

Playhouse Legends, Natal Playhouse complex. Tel. 304-3297. Theatrical atmosphere and clientele; good food.

RJ's, Gardiner St. Tel. 304-8685. Cozy; excellent steaks and seafoods.

Roma Revolving Restaurant, John Ross House, Victoria Embankment. Tel. 37-6707. Panoramic vistas from the turning top; quality fare.

Royal Grill, Royal Hotel, Smith St. Tel. 304-0331. Colonial; impeccable cuisine and service; has been awarded the blazon of the Chaîne des Rôtisseurs.

Saint Geran, Aliwal St. Tel. 304-7509. Sociable, clubby, popular with business people; excellent seafood.

Squire's Loft, Florida Rd, Berea. Tel. 303-1110. Sophisticated steakhouse; à la carte and value-for-money set menu.

Tong Lok, Point Rd. Tel. 37-4537. Authentic and marvellous Cantonese food.

Ulundi, Royal Hotel, Smith St. Tel. 304-0331. The Royal, and its Ulundi restaurant, recall the Raj at its elegant best.

Wolfgang's, Florida Road. Tel. 23-2861. Delicate food (nouvelle) and décor. Take your own wine.

Woodcutter's Charcoal Restaurant, Several branches. Tel. 75-1038. Honest-to-goodness steakhouse cuisine; family atmospshere.

GOLDEN MILE

Cloud 9, Malibu Hotel, Marine Parade. Tel. 37-

2231. Noted for its seafood and venison dishes; décor has a novel (airliner cabin) theme.

Coimbra, Gillespie St. Tel. 32-7876). Portuguese; modest; very good.

Garfunkel's, Marine Parade. Tel. 37-2083. Popular, cool atmosphere and cool music.

Grapevine, Edward Hotel, Marine Parade. Tel. 37-3681. French cuisine; delightful décor.

Les Saisons, Maharani Hotel, Marine Parade. Tel. 32-7361. The very best of classical cuisine; subdued setting.

Papadum, Maharani Hotel, Snell Parade. Tel. 32-7361. Indian curries and traditional English dishes.

Punchinello's, Elangeni Hotel, Snell Parade. Tel. 37-1321. What you'd expect at this excellent hotel; seafood specialities

Scalini's, Marine Parade. Tel. 32-2804. Italian; full of personality.

Sir Benjamin's, Marine Parade Holiday Inn. Tel. 37-3341. Quietly elegant décor; classic cuisine; awarded the blazon of the Chaîne des Rôtisseurs and, of course, highly recommended.

Stax, Marine Parade. Tel. 32-5291. Steakhouse; also seafood; magnificent salad bar.

Sukihama of Japan, Elangeni Hotel, Snell Parade. Tel. 37-1321. Japanese cuisine, with American overtones.

Villa d'Este, Gillespie St. Tel. 37-0264. Italian and seafood dishes eaten in a lovely courtyard.

SOUTH OF DURBAN

Razzmatazz, Beach Road, Amanzimtoti. Tel. 903-4131. Very unpretentious, but superb food (go for the specials and game dishes).

NORTH OF DURBAN

Bailey's on the Rocks, Granada Centre, Umhlanga. Tel. 561-4190. Informal; curries and seafood; excellent value.

The Cabin, Beverly Hills Hotel, Umhlanga. Tel. 561-2211. Superb seafood; quiet atmosphere.

La Provence, Beverly Hills Hotel, Umhlanga. Tel. 561-2211. Classic cuisine; large menu; pleasant sea-facing aspect.

Pablo's, Cabana Beach Hotel, Umhlanga. Tel. 561-2371. Adventurous menu; beachfront position.

INLAND

Black Forest, Pinetown Arcade, Pinetown. Tel. 72-2908. Cozy, welcoming, German. Take own wine.

Coltranes, Hill Street Arcade, Pinetown. Tel. 72-8173. Enormously varied menu; jazz at weekends.

La Brasserie, Pine City Centre, Pinetown. Tel. 701-1656/5580. Honest German dishes; good beer and cheer.

Le Troquet, Old Main Rd, Cowés Hill. Tel. 86-5388. French Provincial fare; appropriately Gallic décor; try the specials. Popular.

Michael's Cuisine, Waterfall Centre, Waterfall (between Hillcrest and Inanda). Tel. 763-3429. Dishes from several parts of the world, prepared with superb flair. Take your own wine.

Seasons, St Hellier, near Hillcrest. Tel. 75-1518. Country-style fare in a country atmosphere; friendly and thoughtful service.

Meeting places

Petit Suisse, The Workshop. Tel. 304-0226. Sustaining breakfasts; excellent coffee and cakes; light lunches.

Press Club, Salisbury Centre. Tel. 304-9747. Breakfast and lunches, opens at 06h00.

Selwyn's, Fedlife Building. Tel. 304-2984. Racy atmosphere; breakfasts and light meals; opens at 06h00.

USEFUL ADDRESSES AND TELEPHONE NUMBERS

Durban

Addington Hospital, Tel. 32-2111.

Alcoholics Anonymous, Tel. 301-4959.

Amanzimtoti Visitors' Bureau, Inyoni Beach Complex, 95 Beach Rd, PO Box 26, Amanzimtoti 4125; Tel. 903-2121.

Automobile Association (breakdown service), Tel. (031) 305-1324

Computicket, Tel. 304-2753.

Durban Publicity Association, Church House, Church Square, PO Box 1044, Durban 4000; Tel. (031) 304-4934/304-4981/2/3; Fax: 304-6196. The Visitor's Bureau is in Church Square, next to the post office. The Beach Information Office is on Marine Parade, Tel. (031) 32-2595/32-2608.

Emergency numbers: *Ambulance* 48-5252; *National Ambulance Number* 10-177. *Fire Brigade* 309-3333. *Police* 32-2322 (charge office); *Police flying squad* 1-0111. *Life Line* (equivalent to British Samaritans) 23-2323. *Sea Rescue* 37-2011.

Satour (South African Tourism Board): Suite 520, 5th Floor, Southern Life Centre, 320 West Street, PO Box 2516, Durban 4000; Tel. (031) 304-7144; Fax: 305-6693; Telex: 62-1205.

Teletourist (a 24-hour information service): Tel. (031) 305-3877 (English-language); 305-2723 (Afrikaans).

Game reserves

KwaZulu Bureau of Natural Resources, Private Bag X23, Ulundi 3838; Tel. (0358) 907-5061.

Natal Parks Board, PO Box 662, Pietermaritzburg 3200; Tel. (0331) 47-1981.

South Coast

Margate Publicity Association, Margate beachfront, PO Box 25, Margate 4275; Tel. (03931) 2-2322.

North Coast and Zululand

Dolphin Coast Publicity Association, PO Box 534, Ballito 4420; Tel. (0322) 6-1997. The Association runs an information office on the link road from the N2 to Ballito (next to the BP garage).

Eshowe Publicity Association, PO Box 25, Eshowe 3815; Tel. (0354) 4-1796.

Pongola Tourism Association, c/o Tolbos, PO Box 116, Pongola; Tel. (03841) 3-1251.

St Lucia Publicity Association, PO Box 80, St Lucia 3936; Tel. (03592), and ask for 217.

Zululand Publicity Association, PO Box 1265, Richards Bay 3900; Tel. (0351) 4-2243.

ANNUAL EVENTS

Dusi Canoe Marathon: second week in January □Durban International Film Festival: April/May □Comrades Marathon: 31 May □ Virginia Air Show: July □Durban Tattoo: July □Rothmans July Handicap: July □Gunston 500 Surfing Contest: July □Champion of Champions Zulu Dancing: July.

KWAZULU-NATAL INTERIOR AND THE DRAKENSBERG

Lovely red-brick Victorian buildings; cast-iron railings and store-fronts; luxuriant parks and gardens bright with roses and azaleas; antique shops and bookstores, and an ambience that draws much from a very colonial past – this is Pietermaritzburg, KwaZulu-Natal's capital (see page 19) and second city (population: around 200 000 and still growing), nestling among green and sometimes misty hills just under 100 km west of Durban and a place which, to quote the traveller and writer H V Morton, 'wears its air of grace and quality with becoming ease'.

Pietermaritzburg has a lot to offer the discerning visitor: it is an ideal base from which to explore the KwaZulu-Natal interior.

The roads north – the national route for those in a hurry; the old and scenically charming R103 for the leisurely traveller – lead you past and through pleasant and hospitable towns, each with its own, distinctive character and its modest array of attractions. Those in the far northern parts – Newcastle, Dundee, Ladysmith, Vryheid – tend to be rather industrial, but they have a special place in the annals: it was on the great grassland plains of the region that Boer, Briton and Zulu played out the bloody dramas of the 19th century, and military enthusiasts come from afar to wander the killing fields, and to reconstruct the battles.

To the west is the immensity of the Drakensberg, towering 2 000 m and more above foothills that beckon the hiker and the rambler.

PIETERMARITZBURG

The eastern prong of the Voortrekkers founded Pietermaritzburg in 1838, just prior to their victory over Dingane's Zulu army at Blood River, as their fledgling Republic of Natalia's seat of government, naming the place in honour of two of their leaders – Gert Maritz, and the ill-fated Piet Retief, done to death on Kwa-

The rolling foothills of the Drakensberg, here overlooked by The Ampitheatre, part of the Mont-aux-Sources massif. The area is well served by rest-camps, caravan and camping grounds and, especially, by the so-called 'resort hotels', of which there are about a score.

Matiwane, the bloody 'hill of execution', earlier that year. The republic, though, lasted only until 1843, when the British annexed the territory and built Fort Napier to reinforce the new authority. The Crown Colony of Natal was granted responsible government in 1893, at which time a fine new assembly was added to Pietermaritzburg's already graceful skyline.

Landmarks

Much of Pietermaritzburg's heritage, Trekker as well as colonial, has been proudly preserved, justifying its ranking as 'one of the most important high-character cities in Africa'. Visitors are introduced to its history-laden charm via the self-guided Town Trail (brochures and maps from Publicity House, next door to City Hall). Among places of interest that you will find *en route* are:

CHURCH OF THE VOW Shortly before the battle of Blood River the Boers promised that should the Almighty see fit to grant them victory they would build a church as a memorial for future generations, and that the date – 16 December – would be observed as a Sabbath, day of thanksgiving. All of which came to pass: though the Boer forces totalled just 470 (including some British settlers and mixed-descent employees), numbers proved no match for the white man's guns. The Zulu impi was forced to retire, with 3 000 dead. Trekker casualties amounted to just three men wounded.

The church was duly built, a small, white, gabled building that now serves as the Voortrekker Museum. Among various Trekker relics on display are an ox-wagon and an ironwood chair carved for Dingane. Next door is the Modern Memorial Church (statues of Retief and Maritz) and the house of Andries Pretorius, victor of Blood River. They are open weekdays and Saturdays; closed Sundays and religious holidays.

CITY HALL, across the square, was built in 1893 and is the southern hemisphere's largest all-brick building, an impressive affair of domes, stained glass and clock tower.

CENTRAL LANES This charming network of narrow pedestrian alleys – bounded by Longmarket, Timber and Church streets and Commercial Road – was once the city's financial and legal centre: it encompassed four different stock exchanges between 1888 and 1931 and, because of its proximity to the Old Supreme Court, a number of lawyers' chambers. Of special interest to visitors are the small speciality shops and the elegantly Edwardian Harwin's Arcade.

THE HINDU TEMPLE in Longmarket Street, venue of the annual Firewalking Festival (held on Good Friday).

FORT NAPIER and its garrison church, sited on a hill overlooking the city, are national monuments. On display in the grounds are some interesting artillery pieces; in the church are reminders of the British colonial presence. Open Wednesday afternoons.

Museums and galleries
Among the recommended ports of call are:

THE CITY'S OLDEST HOUSE is a beautifully renovated Voortrekker home on Boom Street; open weekdays and Saturday mornings.

THE NATAL MUSEUM, in the city centre and very well worth visiting, houses a fascinating number and variety of natural history exhibits, and has sections devoted to geology, paleontology and ethnology. The Hall of Natal History features Victorian Pietermaritzburg; among the displays is a reconstruction of an early street scene. Open daily.

MACRORIE HOUSE MUSEUM, on the corner of Loop and Pine streets, also houses some splendid Victoriana. Open Tuesday, Wednesday, Thursday and Sunday mornings.

THE NATAL ARCHIVES, in Pietermaritz Street; records and relics of, among other things, the founding of the republic and of the colony.

ST PETER'S CHURCH, Church Street. Partly a museum (religious artifacts, stained glass). The building served as John Colenso's cathedral in the latter part of the 19th century. Colenso, a controversial churchman and first Bishop of Natal, provoked a religious schism when he challenged a number of fundamentals of Anglican belief. He was tried for heresy and deposed, but was reinstated in 1865 by a Privy Council decision. He also affronted white opinion by defending the Zulu king Cetshwayo and condemning the Anglo-Zulu War of 1879.

TATHAM ART GALLERY, old Supreme Court. On display are works by European artists (Picasso, Degas, Renoir, Sisley, Corot, Chagall, Henry Moore, and the Bloomsbury Group) and by some leading local painters.

COMRADES MARATHON HOUSE, found in Connaught Road is a meticulously restored Victorian home honouring the intrepid runners who covered the 90 or so gruelling kilometres between Pietermaritzburg and Durban since Arthur Newton inaugurated South Africa's premier ultra-long-distance event in 1921. Newton entered and won the second race, in 1922, maintaining such a pace that officials at the finish line were entirely unprepared to receive him – and this despite his short break *en route* for a sustaining glass of brandy at the Star and Garter Hotel. The Comrades has been dominated in recent years by the phenomenal Bruce Fordyce; oldest successful entrant is former world record holder Wally Hayward, who first won the race in 1930 and completed the run in 1988 at the age of 79 – and went on to repeat the feat two years later. On display are photographs, trophies, fascinating race memorabilia.

Gardens, parks, reserves
Pietermaritzburg is known as the 'city of flowers', and deservedly so. It is at its best in springtime; the annual flower show is held in September.

Green Belt walking trails, each clearly marked and involving a gentle two-hour walk, enable visitors to enjoy some of the lovely countryside that fringes the city. Attractions are the wild flowers, at their spectacular best during spring and early summer. There are three major routes: the World's View (which follows a portion of the Voortrekkers' road); the Ferncliffe (indigenous and exotic vegetation) and the Dorpspruit (historical). Seven other trails lead walkers to superb viewpoints.

The trails complement the city-centre Town

Trails (see page 175); brochures and maps are available from the Publicity Association, Pietermaritzburg, City Centre.

BOTANIC GARDENS A must for visitors: the 22-ha international section' is devoted to exotics, and is famed for its spring displays of azaleas and camellias, and for its lovely mature trees (Moreton Bay fig, swamp cypress, and one truly impressive camphor). The magnolias and the plane avenue are also notable features. The 24-ha Indigenous Garden contains many Natal mist-belt specimens. There's also a peaceful lake, and a tearoom.

ALEXANDRA PARK, along Park Drive, is a 65-ha oasis of rock garden (wonderful in wintertime) and azalea, scatters of yellowwood, jacaranda, Cape chestnut; aloes and bougainvillea, and an avenue of stately plane trees. Also a charming pagoda-style pavilion, bandstand, and Mayor's Garden of formal beddings, rose section, conservatory. The grounds are used for a grand art exhibition held each May. Open daily.

BIRD SANCTUARY, worth visiting for its many and fascinating species, and in the evenings for its roosting egrets.

GARDEN OF REMEMBRANCE, at the end of Commercial Road, commemorates the fallen of two world wars, and is especially notable for the Weeping Cross of Delville Wood. The battle, fought in mid-July 1916, involved the 3 032-strong South African Brigade of the 9th Division; only five of the Brigade's officers and 750 of its men survived unwounded. The Cross, according to eyewitnesses, 'weeps' on each anniversary of the battle.

QUEEN ELIZABETH PARK, 8 km north-west of the city, is 93 ha in extent and serves as the Natal Parks Board's headquarters. Aloes, proteas, some game animals (including white rhino), snake-pits, aviaries, self-guided and conducted walks, picnic spots; also monthly wildlife film shows, a curio shop, and a nursery that sells indigenous plants.

DOREEN CLARK NATURE RESERVE, a   small (only 5 ha) but charming patch of evergreen forest; attractions include its picnic spots and the varied birdlife.

WYLIE PARK, on the Howick Road: proteas and other South African flora, including Cape fynbos and azaleas. Pleasant.

CEDARA STATE FOREST, extending over 670 ha, has been planted with an attractive variety of exotic trees (part of an experiment launched in 1903) and includes species from the Himalayas, China, the Mediterranean, Northern Europe, North Africa, Australia, Japan, Mexico, and the United States. There's a picnic and barbecue area, fishing in the dams, and a lovely forest trail.

Around Pietermaritzburg

There's plenty to see and do in the general area; especially worth exploring are:

NATAL LION AND GAME PARK, 22 km from the city just off the N3 highway to Durban. On view are lion, white rhino, giraffe, ostrich and other species. Orang-utans are entertaining residents of the Zoological Gardens opposite the park. There's also a curio shop that stocks hides, skins and souvenirs.

SAFARIWORLD, just over 20 km from Pietermaritzburg, is a superb, privately-owned wildlife complex that combines conservation and fun-filled family entertainment with extraordinary success.

The enterprise is the brainchild of James Meyer, a young Natalian with a mission. Meyer bought the neglected Karkloof Falls nature reserve just over a decade ago and, after the catastrophic floods of 1987, decided to revitalize the area, which he did with the expert help of the Natal Parks Board, painstakingly restoring the 1 000-ha valley's lovely indigenous forest and grasslands to their original pristine condition.

The reserve lies within three distinct climatic zones (rainfall ranges from 500 mm a year in some sections to 1 500 mm in others) and is unusual if not unique in the number of different habitats – and the consequent variety of animal and plant life – it encompasses. Among the many game species introduced are white rhino, giraffe, roan, the endangered sable (now successfully breeding; an important conservation breakthrough) and Cape buffalo (the country's largest herd). There are designated sections for lions, hippos, crocodiles.

Attractions: game drives in canopied vehicles; foot trails; Waterworld; Petworld and Playland for the kids; and a Pioneer Village containing a licensed restaurant, shops, boutiques, amphitheatre (African dancing, wildlife demonstrations, etc), picnic and barbecue spots. A luxury game lodge has recently been opened; for more information contact SafariWorld, PO Box 3180, Pietermaritzburg 3200; Tel. (03393) 787/797/800; Fax: (03393) 795.

MIDMAR PUBLIC RESORT AND NATURE RESERVE
This popular resort, 24 km from Pietermaritzburg, 7 km from the town of Howick and a favourite among water-sportsmen, has been established around the 1 822-ha Midmar Dam. For visitors the range of recreational attractions includes tennis and squash courts; bathing in the dam (the water is bilharzia-free) and swimming pool; fishing (carp, bass); boat-hire; shop; camping ground, and the Midmar Historical Village, which features among other attractions: a Zulu homestead, a wood-and-iron Hindu temple, blacksmith's shop, and the retired steam-tug *J E Eaglesham*, now moored in the dam's fresh water after a long and honourable working life in Durban harbour. Information: Officer-in-Charge, Private Bag, Howick

3290; Tel. (0332) 30-2067; or Reservations Officer, Natal Parks Board, PO Box 662, Pietermaritzburg 3200; Tel. (0331) 47-1981.

The adjacent reserve is home to white rhino, zebra, wildebeest, a variety of buck and prolific birdlife (of note are the waterfowl, and the kingfishers, which include both the giant and the pygmy species); facilities include chalets; game-viewing trails. Information and bookings: Natal Parks Board (see Advisory, page 193). About 3 km from Midmar are the:

HOWICK FALLS, plunging some 95 m into the Mgeni River, are much photographed. Other cascades in the area are the Shelter and the 105-m Karkloof. Close by is the town of:

HOWICK, named by Earl Grey, the eminent 19th century statesman and Colonial Secretary, after his stately home in Northumberland. It's a bustling, friendly, attractive place, unusually well geared to receive visitors; among its welcoming hostelries is the Howick Falls Hotel, built in 1872 and one-time host to distinguished Americans Mark Twain and the newsman-explorer Henry Morton Stanley of 'Dr Livingstone-I-presume' fame. A charming old Victorian house serves as the Howick Museum.

Pietermaritzburg street scene

The splendid Howick falls

The Tugela River on its way to and through the Natal midlands

UMGENI VALLEY NATURE RESERVE, situated below the falls just east of Howick, is a noted conservation education centre, its 656 ha comprising a variety of habitats. Wildlife includes giraffe, a variety of antelope and over 200 bird species. There are self-guided and conducted (by the Wildlife Society) trails, and some lovely picnic spots.

THE ALBERT FALLS, also on the Mgeni River, are 22 km from the city on the Greytown Road and are worth visiting more for the lake and the luxuriant beauty of the surrounding country-side than for the cascades themselves, which are a modest 7 m high. The lake is a popular fishing and boating venue; the 3 000-ha nature reserve in which it is set is a pleasant place for bird-watching and picnicking. Accommodation: chalets and rondavels, caravan/camp site; facilities: picnic sites, pool, game-viewing drives and walks. Information and bookings: Natal Parks Board (see Advisory, page 193).

THE ROAD NORTH

The highway that leads from Pietermaritzburg northward through Howick, Nottingham Road, Mooi River, Estcourt, Frere, Colenso and across the Tugela to Ladysmith takes you through the Natal Midlands, the country that lies between the extremes of humid coastal woodlands to the east and the monumentally craggy, often ice-capped heights of the Drakensberg to the west. It is a lovely, misty land of deep river valleys, hill upon rolling hill and sweet green grasses that once sustained great herds of migrating antelope.

The beauty and the peace, though, are deceptive: for a hundred years this region served as southern Africa's great battleground. It was here, in 1818, that Shaka's armies erupted in all their disciplined magnificence to spread fire, sword and famine among the neighbouring peoples; here that the eastern Voortrekkers fought and sometimes lost to the impis – at Bloukrans, Bushmans River, Italeni – before breaking the power (though not the pride) of the Zulu at Blood River.

Thereafter, for the next three decades, black and white men managed to coexist in tolerable harmony until, in 1879, British Imperial ambition provoked new warfare and Isandlwana, Rorke's Drift and Ulundi took their places in the bloody annals of Natal. And here, too, along and near the banks of the Tugela, were fought some of the most bitter battles of the South African (Anglo-Boer) War, when, in the early months of the hostilities, the parade-ground British regiments were cut to ribbons by General Louis Botha's well-armed, well-entrenched Boer riflemen.

In a word, the midlands have a great deal to offer those with a military interest (see Day-drives, page 188).

For the rest, the countryside has gentler enticements.

THE MIDLANDS MEANDER, between the villages of Nottingham Road and Lidgetton the R103, connects with a number of other roads to form a most absorbing arts-and-crafts route. Enterprises that open their doors to the public include Andy and Helen Shuttleworth's weaving studio (carpets, shawls; garments of pure wool, mohair and cotton); Ian and Kalli's Dargle Valley pottery; Lindsay Scott's Hillfold pottery (unusual techniques, dramatically attractive results) and Jane Buckle's Caversham Mill (woollen products; Jane's husband runs a small gallery, and restores old maps and documents). Check open days with the publicity associations in Howick or Pietermaritzburg (see Advisory, page 193).

MOOI RIVER, a small and attractive town noted for its crisp climate, for the willow trees and trout of the watercourse, and for the Craigie Burn resort and nature reserves, some 30 km to the east, on the road to Greytown (picnicking, angling, boating, camping, bird-watching).

GREYTOWN, set on the banks of the Mvoti River 70 km east of Mooi River in the coolness of the Natal mist-belt, is the centre of a thriving and most attractive forestry area. The wattles were originally (around 1890) cultivated for the tannic acid in their bark, but timber is the principal industry today. The town has a fine little museum. A few km to the south is the farm on

which Louis Botha, military genius and the Union of South Africa's first prime minister, was born. Some way farther south is the Umvoti Vlei nature reserve (267 ha of water, swamp, reed-beds and a fascinating array of waterfowl).

At Muden, 23 km from Greytown, is an orange winery that's well worth a visit, as is the Mhlopeni nature reserve. Just 20 years ago this was a barren, much-abused 1 000 ha of land, but it's been beautifully rehabilitated by the SA Council for Conservation and Anti-Pollution and now well matches its Zulu name, which translates as 'peaceful valley of white rocks'. One can walk here at will to enjoy the flora (aloes, euphorbias, white stinkwood, thorn-bush varieties) and fauna (zebra, and numbers of antelope) and to explore the area for Stone and Iron Age sites. Mhlopeni is privately owned and largely devoted to educational programmes. Accommodation: thatched huts and rondavels; information: Mr R Alcock, PO Box 381, Greytown 3500; Tel. (03346) 722.

Back on the main highway north:

ESTCOURT is a fairly substantial industrial town on the Bushmans River. Good fishing in the river, and at the Wagendrift resort (camping and caravanning) and reserve some 4 km away. The Moor Park nature reserve at the head of the Wagendrift dam has antelope (kudu, blesbok, wildebeest, impala), a self-guided trail and a picnic spot.

COLENSO, on the Tugela River, was named after the controversial Bishop of Natal (see St Peter's Church, page 176) but is better known for its place in military history. One of the major and several minor battles of the South African War were fought in the vicinity; it was here that Winston Churchill was captured, following the Boer ambush of an armoured train, in 1899; nearby is the Bloukrans monument commemorating Voortrekker casualties of the Boer-Zulu conflict of 1838. There are superb views of river and battlefields from the Tugela Drift nature reserve, 6 km north of town.

WEENEN, just over 30 km to the east of Colenso (take the R74) means 'weeping' in Dutch, and was so named in memory of the Trekkers who fell before the Zulu assegais at Bushmans River in 1838. Of interest is the town's museum, and the Weenen nature reserve, a 3 325-ha stretch of scrub and grassland that sustains a variety of game species, including the white and the rare black rhino, buffalo, giraffe, eland, kudu, mountain reedbuck and steenbok. Also: caravan/camp site, picnic and barbecue sites; trails, and a curio shop.

LADYSMITH Of the three garrison towns invested by the Boers in the early months of the South African War, Ladysmith suffered the most: many of the British troops, deprived of food and medical supplies, died during the 115-day siege. The museum recalls those grim but sometimes glorious days. Other military sites in the area include Wagon Hill, Caesar's Camp, Umbulwana Hill and Lombards Kop.

Spioenkop, the hill over which Boer and Briton fought so furiously in January 1900 (and so pointlessly: it had no real strategic importance; over 2 000 troops were killed or wounded on the bloody slopes before the British, inexplicably, retired) is to the south-west; a resident historian shows visitors over the killing ground. Of more recent vintage is the Spioenkop resort, nature reserve and dam, popular among water-sportsmen. The adjacent 400-ha game park is home to white rhino, wildebeest, eland, kudu, giraffe, zebra and other species. For visitors: game-viewing walks, horse-riding, boating, picnicking; chalets, camping ground at the resort; and a small war museum. Information and bookings: Reserve: Natal Parks Board (see Advisory, page 193); Resort: The Camp Superintendent, PO Box 140, Winterton 3340; Tel. (03682), and ask for 78.

The main N3 highway now carries on north-west past the Drakensberg resort area (see page 183), and Harrismith to Johannesburg; the R23 due north to:

NEWCASTLE, a large industrial centre, revolves around its steelworks which visitors may tour by arrangement. The town boasts good hotels, a new 500-seat convention centre, a small airport (daily flights to Durban and Johannesburg), and an impressive colonial-style Town Hall. The Carnegie Library houses an art gallery; several factory shops, associated with the town's half-dozen textile plants, invite bargain-hunters, as do the Ozisweni Handicraft Centre (woven goods; basketry), the Mother Earth pottery, and The Weavery. For information and

guidance, call in at the Publicity Association's office in the Town Hall (Scott Street).

Plenty of military history unfolded in the area, notably during the brief Anglo-Transvaal conflict of 1880-81 (the British lost): the Majuba, Laing's Nek and Ingogo battle sites are within short driving distance of town.

Less aggressive distractions include the lovely Ncandu River waterfall (16 km on the Mullers Pass road; picnic spots, horse-riding facilities) and the Chelmsford resort and nature reserve to the south-west of town. This pleasant recreational area offers chalets, camping facilities; boating, fishing in the 6 000-ha dam; game-viewing (white rhino; various antelope), bird-watching (Spurwing goose, Egyptian goose). Information and bookings: Reserve: Natal Parks Board (see Advisory, page 193); resort: Officer-in-Charge, PO Box 3, Ballengeich 2942; Tel. (03431) 7715.

Branching right from the R23 north of Ladysmith (take the R621), one arrives at Glencoe and then:

DUNDEE, focal point of the giant Natal coalfields. Well worth visiting is the Talana Museum, built on the site of the South African War's first battle. It's an impressive collection of red-brick, Victorian-style buildings set in park-like surrounds; on display are some fascinating military exhibits. There are also sections devoted to coal-mining, glass-manufacturing and brick-making. Operating from the museum is the local Publicity Association, whose staff will advise you on points of interest in the area, which include:
☆ The MOTH Museum, which has an impressive collection of Anglo-Zulu War (1879) relics and memorabilia.
☆ The Tactile Carpet Enterprise, which turns out fine and increasingly sought-after mohair and karakul ware.
☆ The Maria Ratschitz Mission, originally a Trappist hideaway; the church is graced by lovely stained glass and murals.
☆ The various South African War memorials around Dundee. Indeed, for battle sites the area can hardly be surpassed: to the south are Isandlwana and Rorke's Drift (Anglo-Zulu War; an art and craft centre has been established on the site: see page 189)); to the north-east is Blood River (Trekker-Zulu War). Here, the original 64-wagon Boer laager has been reconstructed,

impressively and perhaps controversially, in bronze. Blood River is just over halfway between Dundee and:

VRYHEID, once the capital of the New Republic, a Boer mini-state founded in 1884 on land granted to some 500 white mercenaries (including Louis Botha, later prime minister of South Africa) by the Zulu king Dinuzulu. The old Raadsaal is now a museum. Today Vryhied is a largish centre of the coal-mining and ranching industries.

Features of interest include the Knabbelhuisie home industries enterprise in President Street (handmade products, preserves and so forth) and, on a farm outside town, the Creative Hands weaving complex.

Vryhied's 720-ha nature reserve is a pleasant place for walking, game-viewing (antelope; zebra) and bird-watching.

To the north of Vryhied is Paulpietersburg; between the two towns (16 km south of the latter) is the Natal Spa Country Resort: hot and cold natural springs and pool; pleasant accommodation; Tel. (03852), and ask for 4, or make reservations through The Rob Roy hotel, Valley of a Thousand Hills; Tel. (031) 903-7917. The impressive Itala game reserve lies some 70 km to the east of Vryhied: see Zululand, page 159.

THE DRAKENSBERG AND ITS FOOTHILLS

The formidable range of mountains called the Drakensberg is part – the loftiest and most splendid part – of the Great Escarpment which, rather like a gigantic horseshoe, runs down, across and then up the southern Africa's U-shaped perimeter, dividing the relatively narrow coastal plain (or, more technically, the 'marginal zone') from the great plateau of the interior. The range is at its highest in Lesotho, where it is known as the Maluti Mountains, but in visual terms is at its most spectacular in the east, where the heights fall almost sheer for a full 2 000 m down to the green and pleasant uplands of KwaZulu-Natal.

The range is, geologically speaking, a young one, formed about 150 million years ago by seismic convulsions that deposited stupendous quantities of basalt lava onto the sandstone plains. The 'wall' so created – 4 000 m above sea level, 200 km wide – was then, over the aeons, eroded by rain and river, elements that carved the deep ravines and sculpted the Drakensberg's extraordinary fantasia of cliff, buttress and dragon-tooth ridge, cave, ledge and balancing rock. The massifs and their peaks have evocative names: The Sentinel, The Amphitheatre, Mont-aux-Sources, The Organ

The beauty of the 'Berg. The mountains in the distance soar 2 000 m above sea level.

Pipes, Champagne Castle. To climbers, they represent a profound challenge; for everyone else, they are grand beyond description, a joy to behold.

The 'Berg' has a great deal to offer the visitor. Those drawn to the uplands come, not for the more sophisticated pleasures (though these are available) but for the unparalleled scenic beauty, for the fresh, clean mountain air; for the rambles and the horseback trails, the hikes and climbs; for the trout in the streams, the animals and birds of the reserves; for undemanding relaxation in a casual atmosphere.

CLIMATE To people who have only heard of the Drakensberg, the region conjures up intimidating images of frozen peaks and snowbound isolation. And the high country can indeed be a formidable environment, beset in winter by blinding blizzards that descend in a matter of minutes, literally out of the blue, and in summer by stupendous thunderstorms. But the places one actually stays at – the resort hotels – enjoy a remarkably benevolent climate. They're on the much lower, much gentler slopes, where summer nights are pleasantly cool, the days warm, sometimes hot, subject to morning mists and early-evening thunderstorms. Winter days are generally mild, the nights cold and occasionally bitter, best enjoyed with family or friendly company in the warmth of a scented log fire.

GETTING YOUR BEARINGS If you look at the map, you'll see that there are three fairly distinct areas of tourism development: in the Mont-aux-Sources area in the north; around Cathedral Peak and Champagne Castle in the north-central section; and, thirdly, below Sani Pass in the south. The last named, 3 200 m above sea level, accommodates the only roadway (restricted to four-wheel-drive vehicles) over this 250-km stretch of the Natal Drakensberg. Between Cathedral Peak and Sani are a number of important conservation areas, most notable of which is probably the Giant's Castle game reserve.

The northern and north-central segments are served by the attractive little centres of Bergville and Winterton, from which roads radiate in all directions; the southern region is served by the even more appealing ones of Himeville and Underberg.

Hikers in the Royal Natal National Park

As the crow flies, the three areas aren't very far apart, but the connecting roadways are rather rugged and to travel comfortably from one to the other involves a loop route, east to the N3 highway and west again towards the mountains.

WHERE TO STAY There are excellent facilities for caravanning and camping throughout the region, and pleasant self-contained accommodation in the various game parks and nature reserves. Especially popular, though, are the so-called 'resort hotels', of which there are a score and more scattered around the lower slopes of the 'Berg. Many of them are old-established, unpretentious places catering for families and the more casual vacationer, though some are decidedly upmarket (Drakensberg Sun; Cayley Guest Lodge: see below) and others are making efforts to upgrade themselves. A representative cross section (see Advisory, page 192, for addresses) would be:

✩ Cayley Guest Lodge: Scottish country house atmosphere; secluded, with the emphasis on quiet quality and personal service. Imaginative country-style cuisine. The buildings look over to a 'loch'.

✩ Cathedral Peak Hotel: set beneath the grandeur of The Bell, the Inner and Outer Horns and the spire of Cathedral Peak itself. Owner-managed; largish and very sociable; lovely gardens; an ideal base for climbing, hiking, walking: there are 17 recommended and mapped routes from the hotel, that to the Tseketseke Blue Pool is a joy; the 'champagne breakfast ride' is also rather special.

✩ Champagne Castle: one of the 'Berg's highest hotels; charmingly old-fashioned, lovely grounds. The hotel is especially popular among mountaineers; golf just down the hill.

✩ Drakensberg Sun: new, large and in a different category, a four-star Southern Sun luxury hotel.

✩ Little Switzerland: also biggish and busy; very sociable. The hotel offers luxury and executive suites as well as standard accommodation. Horse-riding, walks through the forest to view fine Bushman art.

✩ Mont-aux-Sources Hotel: more sophisticated; meticulously managed; magnificent view of the Amphitheatre below which it nestles. The hotel's bowling green, fringed by citrus orchards and a glorious bank of azaleas, is particularly attractive.

✩ Royal Natal National Park Hotel: a biggish, busy place, especially geared for outdoor enjoyment: it's within the park of the same name. A resident ranger is in attendance; pleasant hikes to the Tugela gorge, and a strenuous clamber up to the Amphitheatre's summit.

✩ The Nest: informal, friendly and highly popular among bowlers: it has three championship greens and is the venue of some major tournaments.

Mont-aux-Sources area

The lofty geological formation known as Mont-aux-Sources acquired its name from two adventurous French missionaries who trekked in from the west, across the hugely hostile 'Roof of Africa' – the Lesotho highlands – in the early 1830s. Towards the precipitous eastern side they observed the rising of an unusual number of rivers and streams, and called it the 'mountain of springs'.

Included among these watercourses are the Elands and the Tugela. The latter initially follows a spectacular course on its 322-km journey from the Drakensberg and across Natal to the Indian Ocean: it rises at the western end of the Mont-aux-Sources plateau, finds its way to and then plunges over the Amphitheatre's rim in an 850-m-long series of dramatic cascades and falls, one of which drops a sheer 183 m (which makes it the country's highest waterfall). In mid-winter the uppermost cascade freezes to a stalactite-like sheet of ice. The Elands, a smaller river, runs northwards, falling 1 200 m to join the Vaal, tributary of the westward-flowing Orange. Five other rivers are born on Mont-aux-Sources.

Prominent among the peaks are The Sentinel (3 165 m, and difficult to climb); The Eastern Buttress (3 009 m) and Devil's Tooth (3 282 m), a jagged feature attempted by only the most experienced of mountaineers.

THE ROYAL NATAL NATIONAL PARK This is an 8 000-ha sanctuary for various antelopes and some 200 species of bird, including the rare black eagle, the Cape vulture and the lammergeier, or bearded vulture.

Botanists come from afar, especially to investigate the lichens of the area. There are at least four easily accessible Bushman sites; the paintings are impressive.

The park, though, is popular principally for the scenic magnificence of its mountains, cliffs and rolling grasslands, and for its outdoor attractions: there are over 30 recommended walks and hikes ranging from the gentle 3-km Otto trail to the 46-km route that takes you to the Mont-aux-Sources plateau, the last stretch involving a chain-ladder ascent up the sheer eastern face. But it's worth it when you reach the top: the vistas are quite breathtaking.

There are rewarding excursions, too, to the Tugela falls (see opposite page), to the river's pools and, if you're a fisherman, to its dam. The park's trout hatchery is KwaZulu-Natal's largest.

Accommodation: at the Mont-aux-Sources Hotel on the eastern boundary; and at the hotel within the park (see page 192); or at one of the two camps, which offer bungalows, cottages and, at Tendele, a luxury lodge. There's a campsite at Mahai, in a setting of trees and splendid sandstone hills. The Rugged Glen nature reserve, virtually part of the park, has a caravan/camping ground and riding stables.

Cathedral Peak area

The peak, rising 3 004 m above sea level, is one of a complex of pinnacles, much favoured by mountaineers, that includes the Bell (2 918 m), which is one of the country's most challenging climbs, the Pyramid (2 914 m) and the Column (2 926 m), detached from the main buttress and also difficult; Cleft Peak (3 281 m) and the Organ Pipes or alternatively Qolo la maSoja, meaning 'ridge of soldiers'. To climb Cathedral Peak itself does not demand great experience, though the ascent, which takes a full day, is rather strenuous.

Lesser features are the curiously-formed Mitre and Chessmen and, further down and worth making a journey to, the Rainbow Gorge, Mushroom Rock, the Doreen, Albert and Ribbon falls, and the deeply green and mysterious Oqalweni fern forest. There are many delightful picnic spots in the area.

To walk from the Cathedral Peak ridge (or, more correctly, the Mponjwana ridge) to:

CHAMPAGNE CASTLE, to the south, involves a two- or three-day hike along the foot of the high escarpment, through quite splendid countryside.

Champagne Castle was named by two very British Victorian officers who took a bottle of good bubbly on their climb, found it half empty when they stopped to rest and, rather than accuse each other, politely laid the blame on the mountain itself. The Castle is one of the Drakensberg's easier climbs; its slopes are crisscrossed by an inviting network of foot- and bridle-paths.

Other peaks are more striking and present greater mountaineering challenges. Most prominent among them is undoubtedly the 3 194-m Cathkin, detached from the main formation and looming majestically over dense forest plantations. Here the Sterkspruit rises to descend to a wide and fertile valley, its middle reaches distinguished by an especially fine waterfall and by some attractive pools.

On the slopes below Cathkin Peak is the renowned:

DRAKENSBERG BOYS' CHOIR SCHOOL , founded in the 1960s with a complement of just 20 pupils, now over 100 strong, divided into three choirs that have acquired a reputation for excellence well beyond South Africa's borders. They perform for the public on Wednesday afternoons.

The land between Cathedral Peak and Champagne Castle is protected within the extensive Mlambonja and Mdedelelo wilderness areas. In these lie the:

NDEDEMA GORGE, the name meaning 'place of rolling thunder', which is apt enough, since some of the 'Berg's noisier storms occur in the area. The gorge, though, is more famed for the 150 or so caves and rock shelters that were once haven to the long-vanished Bushman (San) people of the region. These gentle folk, the greatest of the prehistoric artists and among the finest of all time, found protection in the deep, cavern-studded ravine, both from the elements and from the depredations of their more aggressive fellow-men.

Ndedema and its surrounds are the location for 17 'galleries' holding over 4 000 paintings in all, many of superb quality. One cave alone, the Sebaaieni, holds over 1 000 individual subjects; in another, the Elands Cave in the nearby Mhlwazini valley, there are over 1 600.

Great numbers of paintings may also be found in the Giant's Castle region to the south (see below); together, the two areas hold about 40 % of all known southern African rock art.

There are about 15 000 art sites in the subcontinent, ranging in age from 27 000 years (this is pre- or at least proto-San) to a very recent 200. Most of them are less than 1 000 years old; all show the remarkably advanced foreshortening technique associated with the culture: a three-dimensional approach that gives vibrant reality to the animals, to the hunt and the ritual and dance depicted. Movement, flow, power are all there in the leap of an antelope, in the surge of a buffalo. The colours, too, are striking, their essence the mineral oxides of the earth: manganese for black; zinc for white, iron to produce the deep browns, the reds and yellows.

Sadly, many of the paintings have suffered grievously from the passage of time, damaged over the centuries by seepage, and by soot from the cave fires of the Bushman's less creative successors – and by the downright vandalism of the moderns. Nevertheless, a great deal of the beauty remains.

Giant's Castle and other reserves

Originally established to provide sanctuary for eland, the mountainous, beautiful 35 000-ha reserve now holds a round dozen species of antelope – together with an impressive variety of birds. The raptors here include the lappet-faced, hooded, white-backed, Cape, Egyptian and bearded vulture (lammergeier); the martial, black, crowned and the two types of snake eagle. There is a special hide – the only one in the world – from which the lammergeier may be observed.

A large proportion of the Drakensberg's 800 species of flowering plant ocurs in the area.

A jackal buzzard makes its landfall in the Giant's Castle reserve. The area is famed for its raptors, and for its flowering plants.

The Devil's Tooth peak, climbed for the first time in 1950 and still one of the Drakensberg's toughest mountaineering challenges.

The Drakensberg region is a floral wonderland; these cosmos grace the Giant's Castle reserve

The reserve's southern parts are dominated by the enormous dark basalt wall of the Giant's Castle buttress; the north-western by the high Injesuthi geological complex (the Njesuthi Dome rises a full 3 410 m above sea level) that offers a hutted camp as well as some magnificent views of the south-eastern slopes of Champagne Castle, Monk's Cowl and Cathkin Peak and, to the west, of the formidable bulk of Njesuthi Buttress.

For the rest, the reserve offers a comprehensive network of hiking trails (the crest of the Giant's Castle formation can be reached fairly easily); guided horse-trails; three- and four-day mountain rides (for the experienced); fishing for brown trout in the Bushmans and Little Tugela Rivers.

As we've noted, the area is famed for its proliferation of Bushman art; there are two site museums within the reserve's boundaries. Accommodation is available in three camps and includes lodges, bungalows, cabins, rustic huts, camping sites, and in rather isolated mountain huts. Information and bookings: Natal Parks Board (see Advisory, page 193).

To the south of Giant's Castle are three other conservation areas:

KAMBERG NATURE RESERVE, consisting of 2 230 ha of grassy hill, set against a backdrop of imposing mountain. Very attractive. Fauna includes antelope species; the flora is interesting (tree ferns, yellowwoods). There are 13 km of trout-angling waters and good fishing in dams; the hatchery welcomes visitors; the 4-km Mooi River self-guided trail is worth following: laid out on level ground, it's one of the few in the country planned to accommodate the physically handicapped. Accommodation: cottages, rest-huts, and 'Stillerust', a 10-bed farmhouse. Information and bookings: Natal Parks Board (see Advisory, page 193).

LOTENI NATURE RESERVE, a scenically outstanding 4 000 ha in what is known as the Little Berg. Here there is superb birdlife, including eagle and stork species; fine trout-fishing in the lower reaches of the Loteni River; and a Settler's Museum exhibiting 19th century furniture and implements. Horse-riding, swimming, the self-guided, circular Eagle trail; accommodation in 6-bed cottages, 3-bed bungalows, 10-bed rustic cottage, and at the campsite. Information and bookings available from: Natal Parks Board (see Advisory, page 193).

VERGELEGEN NATURE RESERVE, very similar to Loteni but smaller (just over 1 100 ha). From here, you can observe Thabana Ntlenyana, towering 3 482 m above sea level (this is southern Africa's highest mountain). Trails; trout-fishing; accommodation comprises two small cottages. Information and bookings: Natal Parks Board (see Advisory, page 193).

Southern Drakensberg

The sole route breaching the Drakensberg to link KwaZulu-Natal and the mile-high Kingdom of Lesotho runs over the Sani ('Bushman') Pass, a rugged road that follows the course of the Mkhomazana ('Little Mkomazi') River along the cascades and tumbling rapids of its upper reaches.

The mountain-and-valley scenery of the Sani is breathtaking; the dizzy hairpin and switch-back ascent – and certainly the final stretch – really too steep for anything but four-wheel-drive vehicles and the pack-mules and donkeys of the Sotho transport riders. There's a police post halfway up. At the top: a customs post (passports are needed for entry into Lesotho) and the Mountaineers Chalet, a small hostelry (licensed, but one does one's own cooking); at the bottom: the Mzimkulwana reserve (22 751 ha; antelope, and some fine raptors) and the Sani Pass Hotel, a largish, rambling, nicely-appointed, rather colonial cluster of buildings set in spaciously attractive grounds (golf course; spa complex) beneath the Twelve Apostles, Hodsons Peak and Giant's Cup.

Access to Sani Pass is via:

HIMEVILLE, a charming place, notable for the old jail, which started life as a stockade and now serves as a fascinating little museum; for its superb hotel (13 rooms and a pub for connoisseurs), and for the 105-ha:

HIMEVILLE NATURE RESERVE, something of a paradise for trout fishermen: it has two lakes, and there are boats for hire. Also waterfowl, some antelope, and a camping ground.

Beyond Himeville, back along the route towards Loteni, the foothills have large numbers of beautiful trees, most of them exotics: cypress and birch, oak and maple, ash and poplar, tulip and crab apple. They were planted by Kenneth and Mona Lund, a farming couple and passionate lovers of nature (they also created an en-

chanting little reserve of artificial lake and selected tree species on their property which they call Hazelmere).

Just off the road that leads south-eastwards to Pevensey is:

THE SWAMP NATURE RESERVE, a small, 220-ha expanse, of which about a quarter is given over to wetland to serve as home to waterfowl. Of special note is the rare wattled crane.

To the south of and twinned with the village of Himeville is:

UNDERBERG, a slightly larger place that hugs the grassy slopes beneath the high Hlogoma ('place of echoes'). At one time there was a lot of quarrelsome and unforgiving rivalry between the two settlements, but eventually the Lunds (see above) healed the wounds by giving oaks to anyone who agreed to plant a few along the linking road, and the avenue of stately trees became an attractive and enduring monument to renewed friendship. Underberg, too, is a favourite among trout fishermen.

COLEFORD NATURE RESERVE, 22 km to the south of Underberg, is a 1 300-ha area bisected by the Ngwangwana and Ndawana rivers, and anglers come from afar for the rainbow trout. Other attractions: antelope (including wildebeest and oribi); game-viewing hide; splendid upland scenery; walking and riding trails; rest-huts and cottages. Information and bookings: Natal Parks Board (see Advisory, page 193).

Back on the route connecting Himeville with Pietermaritzburg (the R617) one passes Lundy's Hill and Bulwer, with its welcoming Tavern Inn and its all-timber Holy Trinity Yellowwood Church, and some quite spectacular countryside; the pleasant valley of the Mkhomazi River, the lovely Rainbow Falls; the deep-green magic of the Orchid Forest; Devil's Cavern, and the tiny yellowwood and mural-decorated church of the Reichman Mission.

GETTING AROUND

Day drives

There's a wide and inviting choice of routes and destinations throughout the Natal midlands and Drakensberg regions. The southern Zululand reserves are also within comfortable driving distance of Pietermaritzburg. It's worthwhile investing in a good map and a detailed regional guide. Meanwhile, some pointers:

An excursion that would appeal to motorists with a sense of history, and an interest in matters military, takes in the:

☆ *Battlefields of Natal.* Follow the N3 to Ladysmith (siege memorabilia from the South African War of 1899-1902) and west to Spioenkop (South African War; 24/1/1900; Boer victory; see page 181), or, alternatively, before you arrive in Ladysmith, call in at the Tugela Drift nature reserve (page 180), north of Colenso, where the trail guide will tell you all about the SA War engagements in the area, including the fairly minor battle of Colenso (December 1899; Boer victory).

Travel north from Ladysmith on the R23, digressing to Elandslaagte (SA War; second battle, 21/10/1899, British victory). Take the R621 to Glencoe, Dundee and the Talana Hill battlefield (SA War, first battle, 20/10/1899, British victory, but costly).

From Dundee take the R33 north, digressing south-east to Blood River (Trekker-Zulu War, 16/12/1838; Trekker victory; see page 175). Travel back to Dundee and south-east on the R33, digressing left for Rorke's Drift (Anglo-Zulu War, 22/1/1879, skirmish: the British defence of the post yielded no less than 11 Victoria Crosses); the far more important battlefield of Isandlwana lies to the east.

Worth mentioning is the noted craft centre at Rorke's Drift (hand-woven rugs and tapestries; hand-printed fabrics; pottery). A pleasant place to stay in the area is Fugitives' Drift, a cluster of well-appointed cottages close to both battlefields (Tel. (03425) 843). Continue on the R33 to Greytown and beyond.

Note: A specialist guidebook is probably essential if you intend covering the battlefields instructively and without losing your way. A 'Battlefields Route' – extending from Colenso in the south to Utrecht in the north and taking in Ladysmith, Newcastle, Dundee and Vryheid – was inaugurated in 1990. Details from the Pietermaritzburg Publicity Association; Tel (0331) 5-1348. Alternatively, contact: the Talana Museum in Dundee; Tel. (0341) 2-2121 extension 264.

☆ Towards the southern 'Berg: travel from Pietermaritzburg to Howick, and on to the R617, continuing west through Bulwer to Underberg, Himeville and the Sani Pass Hotel, where transport can be arranged, given some advance warning, to the top. Return to the Himeville area and north-east on an extension of the R617 to Nottingham Road and via the old road (R103) to rejoin the N3 just north of Howick.

☆ Towards the northern 'Berg: take the old highway, the R103, from just north of Howick, through Nottingham Road, Mooi River and Estcourt to Frere. There is an optional arts-and-crafts and scenic digression: the Midlands Meander (see page 180). After Frere, take the R615 north-west through Winterton and Bergville to the Mont-aux-Sources area, and then back down the R615, digressing westwards at will – towards Cathedral Peak, Champagne Castle and so forth. Most of the roads are good gravel, and very well signposted. Rejoin the R103. These areas are covered on pages 179-182 and 184-188.

Walks and hikes

The Natal midlands and the Drakensberg foothills are superb walking country.

Each of the game reserves (GR), nature reserves (NR) and wilderness areas (WA) covered in this chapter has its own network of trails – the Royal Natal's, for instance, extends over a healthy 130 km; Giant's Castle's over 50 km.

Jaynee Levy gives detailed information on the many options in her *Complete Guide to Walks and Trails in Southern Africa.* Alternatively, consult the various authorities, such as:

☆ Natal Parks Board (see Advisory, page 193): Royal Natal National Park; Spioenkop NR; Giant's Castle GR; Kamberg NR; Loteni NR; Vergelegen NR; Coleford NR; Weenen NR.

☆ Wildlife Society, Umgeni River Valley Project, PO Box 394, Howick 3290; Tel. (0332) 30-3723.

☆ Natal Forest Region, Forestry Branch, Department of Environment Affairs, Private Bag X9029, Pietermaritzburg 3200; Tel. (0331) 42-8108; Forest Technicon, CSIR, Tel. (012) 841-2911; Cathedral Peak Research Station, Tel. (0364) 38-1021; Mlambonja WA; Mdedelelo WA; Loteni Hiking Trail; Mkomazi WA; Mzimkulu WA; Mzimkulwana NR; Drakensberg Hiking Trail, Giant's Cup Section; Dargle River Trail; Cedara State Forest, Pietermaritzburg.

☆ Pietermaritzburg Publicity Association (see Advisory, page 193): Ferncliffe Forest walks; Green Belt trails; Pietermaritzburg town trails.

ADVISORY: KWAZULU-NATAL INTERIOR AND DRAKENSBERG

CLIMATE

Equable throughout except in the high Drakensberg, where climbers have to be wary of winter blizzards and sudden summer thunderstorms. In the higher areas - the escarpment's foothills - summer days are warm, nights cool; winter days are sunny, the nights crisp, often chilly, occasionally very cold. The mountain air has a champagne quality.

This is a summer rainfall region; the upland areas are prone to mist. Pietermaritzburg average rainfall: January 241 mm, July 14 mm, yearly average 928 mm, highest daily recorded 214 mm. Pietermaritzburg temperatures: average daily maximum January 27,1 °C, July 21,2 °C, extreme 40 °C, average daily minimum January 16,6 °C, July 6,0 °C, extreme 1,0 °C.

MAIN ATTRACTIONS

Pietermaritzburg: Charming Victorian buildings □ Museums □ Lovely parks and gardens □ Modern city amenities □ Convenient base for exploring midlands, Drakensberg, Zululand.

Midlands: Charming countryside □ Historic sites □ Game and nature reserves.

Drakensberg: Spectacular scenery □ Game and nature reserves □ Walking, climbing, fishing, horse-riding.

TRAVEL

Road. Pietermaritzburg is 79 km from Durban; 529 km from Johannesburg; 585 km from Pretoria; 1 595 km from Cape Town; 842 km from Port Elizabeth; 561 km from Bloemfontein; 596 km from East London.

The N3 national highway links the city with Durban to the east and Johannesburg to the north-west. More scenically interesting is what used to be the old main road, the R103, which runs parallel to the N3, taking in Nottingham Road and Estcourt before becoming the R615 near Frere. The R615 is the northern Drakensberg's principal access route.

KwaZulu-Natal's provincial roadways have been well maintained in the past but are reported to be under severe pressure. It has been indicated that, failing a major rebuilding and maintenance programme, the network could begin to deteriorate seriously before the mid-1990s.

Coach travel Scheduled services link Pietermaritzburg with Durban (City Hopper, Tel. (0331) 42-0266) and Johannesburg (and points between). The terminus is on Church St, between the City Hall and the library. Translux, Tel. (0331) 55-2525; Intercity Greyhound, Tel. (0331) 42-3026.

Car hire Facilities available in Pietermaritzburg and major midland and northern centres.

Rail. Passenger services link major centres and many of the minor towns. The Pietermaritzburg railway station is at the top end of Church St. Rail reservations, Tel. (0331) 55-2191.

The Mzimkulu River near Underberg, in the southern foothills of the Drakensberg.

Air. Scheduled daily flights connect Pietermaritzburg with Johannesburg international airport. See also air services to and from Durban, page 168. Comair operates to and from Margate; Tel. (03931) 2-1365/2-2060.

Newcastle has a small airport; daily scheduled flights to and from Johannesburg and Durban, Tel. (03431) 2-2602.

ACCOMMODATION

Select hotels

PIETERMARITZBURG

Camden ★★★ City centre. 50 rooms; 2 restaurants; conference facilities for 200. PO Box 2460, Pietermaritzburg 3200; Tel. (0331) 42-8921.

Imperial ★★ City centre. 50 en suite rooms; 3 restaurants; conference facilities for 2 000. PO Box 140, Pietermaritzburg 3200; Tel. (0331) 42-6551.

Karos Capital Towers ★★★ City centre; busy (4 cinema studios). 108 rooms; à la carte restaurant, carvery, action bar; conference facilities for 250. PO Box 198, Pietermaritzburg 3200; Tel. (0331) 94-2761.

Royal ★★ 25 rooms, 1 suite; conference facilities for 200. PO Box 202, Pietermaritzburg 3200; Tel. (0331) 42-8555.

CENTRAL AND NORTHERN NATAL

Capricorna ★★ Newcastle. Central; 17 rooms; conference facilities for 200. PO Box 2440, Newcastle 2940; Tel. (03431) 2-7021.

Crown ★★ Ladysmith. 61 rooms; à la carte restaurant, carvery, steakhouse, 3 bars; conference facilities for 400. PO Box 9, Ladysmith 3370; Tel. (0361) 2-2266.

El Mpati ★★ Dundee; 41 rooms; conference facilities for 75. PO Box 15, Dundee 3000; Tel. (0341) 2-1155.

Etna ★★ Dundee; 30 rooms. PO Box 586, Dundee 3000; Tel. (0341) 2-4191.

Granny Mouse's Country House ★★★ Balgowan. Superbly appointed; 19 rooms. PO Box 22, Balgowan 3275; Tel. (03324) 4071/4532.

Hartford Country House ★★★ Mooi River. Elegant stately home, lovely grounds; just 8 rooms. PO Box 31, Mooi River 3300; Tel. (0333) 3-1081.

Hilton Hotel ★★★ Hilton, near Pietermaritzburg. Tudor-style; elegant; 41 rooms; conference facilities for 300. PO Box 35, Hilton 3245; Tel. (0331) 3-3311.

Holiday Inn ★★★ Newcastle; central. 168 rooms; conference facilities for 250. PO Box 778, Newcastle 2940; Tel. (03431) 2-8151.

The elaborate Victorian bandstand in Pietermaritzburg's Alexandra Park

Lucey's Plough Hotel ★★ Estcourt. 24 rooms; conference facilities for 60. 86 Harding St, Estcourt 3310; Tel. (03631) 2-3040/1.

Mount West Inn ★★★ On the national highway, 7 km from Nottingham Road. 30 rooms; conference facilities for 60. PO Box 61, Nottingham Road 3280; Tel. (0333) 3-6266.

Rawdons ★★★ Nottingham Road. Gracious country house; superb setting. 19 rooms, 3 suites, cottage; conference facilities for 50. PO Box 7, Nottingham Road 3280; Tel. (0333) 3-6044.

Stilwater Motel ★★ Vryheid; about 5 km south of town. 80 rooms; conference facilities for 100. Private Bag X9332, Vryheid 3100; Tel. (0381) 6181.

Royal ★★ Ladysmith. 74 rooms, à la carte restaurant, 2 bars; conference facilities for 300. Murchison St, Ladysmith 3370; Tel. (0361) 2-2176.

Status Hotel ★★ Newcastle; 31 rooms; conference facilities for 150. PO Box 273, Newcastle 2940; Tel. (03431) 2-7064.

Wartburger Hof ★★★ Wartburg, about 30 km from Pietermaritzburg. German-style decor and hospitality. 13 rooms, 1 suite; conference facilities for 60. PO Box 147, Wartburg 3450; Tel. (033532), ask for 268.

NORTHERN DRAKENSBERG

Cathedral Peak Hotel ★★ Largish family hotel; beautiful setting; 86 rooms. PO Winterton 3340; Tel. (0364) 38-1381.

Cathkin Park ★★ Family hotel; 45 rooms; conference facilities for 200. Private Bag X12, Winterton 3340; Tel. (036) 38-1091/2, 468-1091/2.

Cayley Guest Lodge (grading pending). Pleasant blend of homeliness and sophistication; unusual but effective architectural designs; 18 double, 6 'superior' rooms. PO Box 241, Winterton 3340; Tel. (036) 468-1222.

Champagne Castle Hotel ★★ Old-fashioned country hospitality. 49 rooms. Private Bag X8, Winterton 3340; Tel. (0364) 468-1063.

Drakensberg Sun ★★★★ Southern Sun excellence, in Cathkin Park area. 148 rooms; conference facilities. PO Box 335, Winterton 3340; Tel. (036) 468-1000.

Karos Mont-aux-Sources ★★★ Excellent all-round hotel; spectacular setting beneath Amphitheatre. 86 rooms; 3 conference venues; lovely bowling green. Private Bag 1, Mont-aux-Sources 3353; Tel. (036) 438-6230.

Little Switzerland ★★ Mont-aux-Sources area; approx. 50 rooms and suites. Private Bag X1661, Bergville 3350; Tel. (036) 38-1175.

Royal Natal National Park Hotel ★★ Mont-aux-Sources area; situated within the Royal Natal National Park; family-orientated; swimming pool; tennis and bowls; 65 rooms. Private Bag 4, Mont-aux-Sources 3353; Tel. (036) 438-6200.

Sandford Park Lodge ★★ Near Bergville; 28 cottages. PO Box 7, Bergville 3350; Tel. (0364) 38-1001.

The Nest ★★ Renowned for its bowling greens. 60 rooms. Private Bag X14, Winterton 3340; Tel. (036) 468-1068

SOUTHERN DRAKENSBERG

Drakensberg Garden ★★ Lovely setting; 80 rooms. PO Box 10305, Marine Parade 4056, Tel. (031) 37-4222; or Tel. (0020), ask for Drakensberg Garden 1.

Himeville Hotel ★★ Homely and welcoming; 13 rooms. PO Box 105, Himeville 4585; Tel. (033722), ask for 5.

Sani Pass Hotel ★★★ Rambling country estate; golf course. 66 rooms, 3 suites; conference facilities for 150. PO Himeville 4585; Tel. (033722), and ask for 29.

Ungraded accommodation

Club Caraville: Excellent chalet, lodge and caravan/camping facilities available through Club Caraville. Contact Club Caraville Natal Experience, PO Box 139, Sarnia 3615; Tel. Durban (031) 701-4156; Johannesburg (011) 622-4628/9.

Northern Natal: (Bed and breakfast) contact Mrs Margie Vogt, PO Box 1327, Pietermaritzburg 3200, Tel. (0332) 30-2175 (w) or 30-3343 (h); Mrs Jackie White, PO Box 1, Newcastle 2940, Tel. (03431) 5-1915.

Durban and District: (Bed and breakfast) contact Mr Mike Moore, PO Box 88, Durban 4000, Tel. (031) 306-3755.

Caravan/camping and self-catering accommodation

Colenso: Municipal caravan park, PO Box 22, Colenso 3360, Tel. (03622) 2112.

Drakensberg area: Drakensberg Garden caravan park (no tents allowed), PO Underberg 4590, Tel. (0020), and ask for Drakensberg Gardens 1; Giant's Castle Game Reserve (caravan/camping and self-catering accommodation), Bookings: Natal Parks Board, Tel. (0331) 47-1981/Camp Manager, Hillside, PO Box 228, Estcourt 3310, Tel. (03631) 2-4435/(0020), and ask for Loskop 1311; Kelvin Grove caravan park (on a farm between Champagne Castle and Cathedral Peak), PO Box 31, Winterton 3340, Tel. (03682), and ask for 2502; Loteni Nature Reserve (caravan/camping and self-catering accommodation), Bookings: Natal Parks Board, Tel. (0331) 47-1981/Camp Manager, PO Box 14, Himeville 4585, Tel. (033722), and ask for 1540; Rosetta: Glengarry Park, Highmoor Rd, Kamberg, PO Box 39, Rosetta, Tel. (0333) 3-7225 (80 caravan/camp sites). Spioenkop public resort and nature reserve: bookings through the Natal Parks Board (see next column and page 181); Royal Natal National Park (caravan/camping and self-catering accommodation), PO Mont-aux-Sources 3353, Tel. (0364) 38-1803. Winterton: Dragon Peaks holiday resort (caravan/camping and self-catering accommodation), PO Winterton 3340, Tel. (036) 468-1031.

Dundee: Municipal caravan park, Union Street, PO Box 76, Dundee 3000, Tel. (0341) 2-2121/2-2607.

Estcourt: Municipal caravan park, PO Box 15, Estcourt 3310, Tel. (0363) 2-3000 ext 238; Fax: (0363) 33-5829; Wagendrift Public Resort Nature Reserve, (camp sites and youth centre), Natal Parks Board, Tel. (0331) 47-1981; White Mountain resort, PO Box 609, Estcourt 3310, Tel. (03631) 2-4437; Fax (same).

Himeville: Cobham camping site (caravans/tents), PO Box 116, Himeville 4585, Tel. (033722) 1831; Fax (same).

Howick: Municipal caravan park, PO Box 5, Howick 3290, Tel. (0332) 30-6124; Fax: (0332) 30-4183.

Mooi River: Craigie Burn Public Resort Nature Reserve, Bookings: Natal Parks Board, Tel. (0331) 47-1981.

Newcastle: Chelmsford Public Resort Nature Reserve (caravan/camping and self-catering accommodation), Bookings: Camp Manager, PO Box 3, Ballengeich 2942, Tel. (03431) 7715.

Pietermaritzburg: Municipal caravan park, Cleland Road, Tel. (0331) 6-5342.

Vryheid: Klipfontein Dam caravan park, PO Box 1774, Vryheid 3100, Tel. (0381) 4383; Fax: (same); Vryheid caravan park, PO Box 57, Vryheid 3100, Tel. (0381) 81-2133; Fax: (0381) 80-9637.

Weenen: Weenen nature reserve, Bookings: Camp Manager, PO Box 122, Weenen 3325, Tel. (0363) 4-1809.

USEFUL ADDRESSES AND TELEPHONE NUMBERS

Drakensberg Publicity Association, PO Box 1608, Estcourt 3310; Tel. (03631) 2 4186. Information offices are located near Durban (Shell Ultra City) and at the municipal buildings in Bergville and Winterton.

Dundee Publicity Association, Private Bag 2024, Dundee 3000; Tel. (0341) 22121 Extension 264, Talana Museum; Tel. (0341) 2-2654/2-2677.

Howick Tourism Association, PO Box 881, Howick 3290; Tel. (0332) 305-305.

Ladysmith Publicity Association, PO Box 1307, Ladysmith 3370: Tel. (0361) 2-2992.

Mountain Club, contact the Ramblers Club; Tel. (0331)42-8874.

Natal Parks Board, PO Box 662, Pietermaritzburg 3200; Tel. (0331 47-1981; Fax: (0331) 47-1980.

Newcastle Publicity Association, Private Bag X6621, Newcastle 2940; Tel. (03431) 2-7211/5-3318/5-3212.

Pietermaritzburg Publicity Association, PO Box 25, Pietermaritzburg 3200; Tel. (0331) 45-1348; visitor information: Publicity House, 177 Commercial Rd; Fax: (0331) 94-3535.

Satour (South African Tourism Board): Suite 520, 5th Floor, Southern Life Centre, 320 West Street, PO Box 2516, Durban 4001; Tel. (031) 304-7144. Fax: (031) 305-6693.

The Regional Director, Natal Forest Region, Forestry Branch, Department of Environment Affairs, Private Bag 9029, Pietermaritzburg 3200; Tel. (0331) 42-8101.

Wildlife Society of SA; Tel. (0332) 30-3931, Pietermaritzburg Wildlife Club, contact Mrs Pringle; Tel. (0331) 94-7286.

ANNUAL EVENTS

Pietermaritzburg: Dusi Canoe Marathon: January □Camps Drift Regatta and Carnival: April □ Royal Agricultural Show; Comrades Marathon: May □Art in the Park: June □Heritage Week: July □Food and Wine Fair: August □ Garden Show: September □SA Invitation Stakes at Scottsville: November.

THE EASTERN CAPE

The region, for the purposes of this chapter, extends eastwards along the Indian Ocean from Cape St Francis through Algoa Bay (Port Elizabeth) and beyond, along the lovely 'Wild Coast' shoreline to the KwaZulu-Natal border. Inland, it covers the country stretching northwards from Port Elizabeth, and westwards from the Transkei area, to the Drakensberg foothills and the semi-arid edges of the Great Karoo.

It is a vast expanse of terrain, multi-faceted, a kaleidoscope of contrasts, the local areas strikingly different in climate and character and in the nature of their attractions. In fact probably the only unifying element is to be found in the colonial past: this was frontier territory until the later years of the 19th century, often violently disputed, an arena in which white settler and black clansman fought bitterly for possession of the land.

Inevitably, the better-equipped whites prevailed, the process of conquest and organized territorial expansion beginning in earnest with the importation of shiploads of British immigrants in 1820.

These families – 4 000 people in all – landed at Algoa Bay (location of the future Port Elizabeth), were immediately dispatched inland to occupy the newly-created Albany border district, and in due course they and those who followed managed to 'pacify' the countryside. Many of the Eastern Cape's towns and villages began their lives as garrisoned outposts and fortified settlements, sited and designed to defend the isolated communities against hostile Xhosa, and their origins – part farming, part military – are still discernible.

The Xhosa, for their part, were progressively pushed back into the eastern seaboard region and its hinterland between the Great Fish and Mtamvuna rivers, a region divided into two distinct 'homelands': Ciskei and Transkei, separated from each other by a narrowish strip of 'white' territory still known as Border country. The latter's principal centre is the small river-port city of East London.

Ciskei and Transkei have been regarded as the historic territories of the Xhosa peoples

East London, the Eastern Cape's second city and South Africa's only major river-port

since the twilight years of British colonial rule, but it was much later – during the apartheid era – that for a brief period they achieved a modicum of genuine (if generally unrecognized) autonomy.

PORT ELIZABETH

South Africa's fifth city and third largest port, Greater Port Elizabeth (encompassing nearby Uitenhage) is the economic heart of the Eastern Cape, a conurbation with 800 factories, a population of some 800 000 and a preoccupation with motor manufacturing: Ford established the country's first assembly plant here in the mid-1920s (in Grahamstown Road: it employed 70 people and turned out 12 Tin Lizzies a day); General Motors set up shop two years later, and until recently the city, commonly referred to as the 'Detroit of South Africa' served as the more-or-less exclusive home of the vehicle industry.

Port Elizabeth, set along the shores of Algoa Bay, is a major tourist centre, and in this guise likes to be known as the 'Friendly City' (yet another, and less flattering, soubriquet is 'Windy City', but in fact it's no gustier here than along any other part of the Cape coast). Its principal attractions are its wide, open beaches, oceanarium and snake park, historic buildings, fine shops, sophisticated hotels, restaurants and strategic position as a base for exploring the coastline and hinterland.

Historic places

The city owes its origins to the 4 000 or so British settlers who landed on the shores of Algoa Bay in 1820 (though the colonial authorities had built a fort there 20 years earlier). Sir Rufane Donkin, acting governor of the Cape, arrived to welcome the disembarking newcomers personally, and decreed the establishment of a township, which he named Port Elizabeth in memory of his young wife, who had died of fever in India two years before.

Growth was slow but steady, the impetus provided, initially, by the increasingly prosperous farms of the hinterland: the port served as an essential outlet for the region's beef, butter, mutton and above all for the products of the merino sheep and angora goat.

By mid-century the town's population numbered about 5 000; an impressive Commercial Hall had made its appearance; work on a new breakwater began in 1855 (this wasn't a complete success: the splendid artificial dock-basin that exists today came into operation only in 1938); the foundation stone of a grand Town Hall was laid in 1858, and by 1861, when Port Elizabeth received full municipal status, substantial buildings and elegant homes graced the thoroughfares, the style of many reflecting the early settlers' rural British origins. Some of this past has survived: it can be seen in Regency-type houses in Cora Terrace, in the early Victorian balustrades and verandahs along Donkin Street and elsewhere, and in the gracious villas around St George's Park.

Of particular note are:

FORT FREDERICK, in Belmont Terrace, overlooking the Baakens River estuary; built in 1799, four years after the first British occupation of the Cape, and named after the grand old Duke of York. The fortress was designed for a garrison of 350 men and eight 12-pounder guns so placed to defend the bay (and more specifically the estuary) against attack from either sea or land, but it never fired a shot in anger, and by the time the 1820 immigrants made their landfall the outpost had been reduced to a mere handful of officers and men. Open to the public on weekdays.

THE CAMPANILE, in Jetty Street at the entrance to the docks: the site of the 1820 landing and inaugurated in 1923 in memory of the British immigrants. Its 204-step spiral staircase leads you up to a platform (good views of the city); the 23-bell carillon rings changes on ten bells three times a day. Open weekdays and Saturday mornings.

DONKIN RESERVE, an open area from which one can survey the bay, was created by Sir Rufane as a shrine to his dead wife; its pyramid bears a moving inscription to 'One of the most perfect human beings, who has given her name to the city below' and mourned by 'the husband whose heart is still wrung by undiminished grief'. Next door is an old lighthouse which now serves as a military museum (badges, medals and other militaria of local interest). Open daily.

NO 7 CASTLE HILL Period furniture, household items and an attractive collection of antique dolls, housed in the city's oldest dwelling. Open daily.

CITY HALL AND SURROUNDS The Market Square where wagons assembled for the journey inland, and where farmers sold their wares. The City Hall is notable for the replica of the *padrão* (cross) erected by Bartolomeu Dias in 1488, on the headland (Kwaaihoek) on which he landed – the first European foot to be set on what is today South Africa.

HORSE MEMORIAL Fewer than a third of the more than half-million horses in service with the British forces during the South African (Anglo-Boer) War of 1899-1902 survived; a British general told the Royal Commission afterwards that he had 'never seen such shameful abuse of horseflesh in my life'. At the junction of Port Elizabeth's Russell and Cape streets there's a fine memorial to these hard-used animals, erected by public subscription in 1905 and one of only two such monuments in the world.

PORT ELIZABETH'S STATION The station building dates from 1875, when the first line, started by the Port Elizabeth and Uitenhage Railway Company and completed by the Cape government, came into operation. Part of the terminus has been carefully restored; the cast-iron roof supports are of Victorian vintage.

For railway enthusiasts: the Humerail Museum houses some fascinating exhibits – narrow-gauge equipment, steam engines, early passenger coaches and so on. The busy railway repair workshop welcomes visitors.

Steam locomotive excursions are a popular feature of the tourist scene: see Apple and Dias expresses, page 198.

Museum Complex
On the seafront at Humewood and a prime tourist drawcard: it comprises an extensive collection of indoor and outdoor areas whose multiplicity of enticements include:

THE OCEANARIUM, noted for its dolphins, caught in Algoa Bay and trained to play to the gallery, which they do quite delightfully twice a day in the huge (nearly 5-million litre) pool. Cape fur seals also get into the act. Jackass penguins, and a proliferation of other marine life – sharks, rays turtles and fish of all kinds – are on display in two large tanks.

THE SNAKE PARK: one of the country's leading reptile repositories and research centres.

On view (behind glass) are some 80 snake species of both southern African and exotic origin; also a host of crocodiles, alligators, leguaans, lizards, tortoises, otters, meercats and even brightly coloured parrots. Also incorporated into the park is:

The Tropical House, an imaginative and very modern exhibition concept: the building encloses a sculpted landscape of jungle-like vegetation, pool, stream, waterfall, artificial 'mountain'; the resident wildlife includes some lovely birds.

The 'Reptile Rotunda' is an educational centre that regularly hosts thematic exhibitions and video shows.

THE MAIN MUSEUM features cultural as well as natural history exhibits; among the various components are a costume gallery (fashionable clothing from the Edwardian era to the 1940s); a bird hall; a maritime hall (shipwrecks). Early humanoids (Boskop Man) and other fossils, and Algoa Bay's marine life, are also on display.

THE CHILDREN'S MUSEUM Open wildlife displays, intelligently grouped according to type. Youngsters may touch as well as look.

KING GEORGE V1 ART GALLERY A complex of three halls at the Cenotaph, St George's Park, the gallery is noted for its permanent collections of British (19th and 20th century) and South African art, its modern graphics and its fine Oriental porcelain and miniatures. Consult the local newspaper for details of special exhibitions, lectures and so forth. The gallery is open daily.

Gardens, parks, reserves

The city has some most attractive open areas, three of the more prominent of which are:

ST GEORGE'S PARK 73 ha in extent, headquarters of the country's first cricket club and venue of provincial matches (and, in normal years, the occasional Test). Worth visiting for its outstanding floral displays of orchids and other plants is the adjacent Pearson Conservatory. Elsewhere in the park is a 28-ha garden that is noted for its massed annuals and perennials and its mature trees, some of them rare. The monthly 'Art in the Park' market offers a wide variety of goods for purchase.

SETTLERS' PARK NATURE RESERVE, on How Avenue: a beautifully preserved 54-ha expanse of indigenous fynbos (heath), coastal forest, grassland and Karoo vegetation. The park is bisected by the Baakens River, which meanders through a cliff-lined valley; there are broad stretches of lawn, riverside walks, water features, some exotic woodland, colourful cultivated displays (best time to visit: November) and a resident buck population – all within shouting distance of the city centre.

HAPPY VALLEY A delightful recreational area at Humewood Beach, popular for its gardens, including some designed for young visitors (they have nursery-rhyme themes), lawns (for picnickers), ponds, a river (the Shark), riverside footpaths, palm trees, and for its giant open-air chess board. The gardens are illuminated, in colour, on summer nights.

The section of beachfront from the Elizabeth Sun to Happy Valley is to be revamped in the 1990s, which will increase the attractions of this popular area.

GETTING AROUND

Port Elizabeth's public transport system maintains adequate standards, though bus services came under strain in 1990. The bus station is beneath the Norwich Union Centre on Market Square; central city services (the Circle service) run every 20 minutes or so and inter-connect the main shopping areas; the bus from Platform 5 takes you to the beach and Museum Complex (Oceanarium and so forth; see opposite page). Information: Tel. (041) 56-1356/7.

TAXIS Cabs do not roam the streets in search of fares. Consult the Yellow Pages or your hotel reception for telephone numbers. Taxi ranks can be located at the railway station, Victoria Quay, Fleming Street, the Commercial Centre, Cawood Street and at the airport.

Street and speciality maps are available from the Publicity Association's tourist information desk (see Advisory, page 229).

Port Elizabeth, and some of its historic terraced houses, seen from the Donkin reserve

RAIL EXCURSIONS The age of steam survives and flourishes in and around Port Elizabeth; of special interest to visitors are:

THE APPLE EXPRESS A diminutive, apple-green, squeaky-clean steam loco pulls the Express on the 283-km narrow-gauge (61 cm) line between the city and the fruit-growing centre of Loerie in the Long Kloof. The line has been operating since 1906. *En route* the train passes through charming mountain and forest country, and over the 125-metre-high Van Stadens River Gorge bridge (highest of the world's narrow-gauge bridges). Tourist excursions are conducted on scheduled Saturdays; information and bookings at the mainline ticket office, Tel. 520-2260.

THE DIAS EXPRESS Another delightful steam-pulled narrow-gauge train, but on a much shorter route: this one plies between the Campanile and King's Beach, calling in at the fascinating Humerail railway museum on the way (see page 196). Enquiries: Tel. 520-2400.

The local and very hospitable Steam Enthusiasts Society welcomes like-minded visitors; the organization is contactable through the Publicity Association (see Advisory, page 229).

Walks and hikes

Detailed information on some 20 recommended walking routes in the Port Elizabeth, Uitenhage, Seaview, Van Stadens, Zuurberg and Port Alfred areas is available from the Publicity Association (see Advisory, page 229).

One of Port Elizabeth's major hiking trails is the day-long Bushbuck, which leads you for 16 km through the Island State Forest, located some 36 km from the city on the Seaview road. There are also shorter, one- and two-hour walks through the pleasant woodlands. Information and maps from the Publicity Association (see Advisory, page 229).

Day drives

One of the finest scenic routes in the general region is that which follows the 150-km-long ravine of the Baviaanskloof to the west. The route proper starts at Patensie, nearly 100 km from Port Elizabeth, and penetrates three splendid mountain ranges before emerging into the Karoo. The road is lonely; the drive will take a full day.

Some suggested shorter excursions:

✫ To Jeffrey's Bay (see page 203) and beyond to the Seekoei River lagoon and its bird sanctuary, off the Aston Bay road. Aston Bay, further on, is 80 km from Port Elizabeth and has lovely broad beaches.

✫ To the Van Stadens area (see page 202).

✫ To the beautiful Longmore and Loerie forest plantations, about 60 km from Port Elizabeth (call in at the Longmore forester's residence for a permit).

✫ To the Gamtoos River valley, on the way to Patensie and the Baviaanskloof. Turn right at

Patensie, left after 26 km to the Paul Sauer dam, a 29-km-long expanse of water.
✰ Along the Elands River: a superb scenic drive through the mountain-fringed valley, with views of the Tygerhoekberg and the towering (1 789 m) Cockscomb peaks.

Tours
Full details of what the touring companies offer are available from the Port Elizabeth Publicity Association (see Advisory, page 229).
Tour & Trail (Tel. 52-2814) run excursions around Port Elizabeth and Uitenhage and, farther afield, trips to the Addo Elephant National Park, Grahamstown and environs; to lovely Plettenberg Bay on the southern Cape coast (see page 232); along the Garden Route (pages 231-237) and to the Fish River Sun hotel-casino complex in Ciskei (see page 210).

CITY LIFE
Port Elizabeth has modern shops, good restaurants, excellent sporting and recreational facilities, and a lively if rather limited theatre, music and entertainment scene.

Shopping
Principal shopping area in the central business district is Market Square and Main Street; along the western parts of Main are several buildings with upstairs malls; Traduna Mall lies off Market Square; there are inviting speciality shops in Rink Street, Parliament Street and at Walmer Park. Suburban Greenacres is the third-largest roofed centre in the country, the busiest in the city (bus from Market Square station platform 7).
The Publicity Association (see Advisory, page 229) provides details of the various craft, cottage-industry and street markets that are held in the city. Prominent among them are the Agricultural Society's mini-shows; the Small Business Development Corporation's 'Hive of Industries'; Operation Hunger's African craft outlets, and the carnival-like Market Faire.

Theatre and music
Principal venue is the splendid, 690-seat, two-level Opera House in Donkin Street (it dates from 1892, has been nicely renovated, and is a national monument). Concerts, opera, ballet and drama are staged by the Cape Performing Arts Board (Capab), and by touring professional and talented local amateur companies.

Other venues include:
✰ The Feathermarket Hall, near Market Square. Built in 1882 as auction premises and storage facility for the ostrich-feather industry, it now serves as an auditorium for Music Society celebrity performances and an exhibition centre.
✰ The Mannville open-air theatre, in St George's Park, stages Shakespearean productions; the annual festival is very well supported.
✰ The Savoy Club: Gilbert and Sullivan, of course, but also classical operetta and modern musicals.
✰ Ford Little Theatre: shows presented by the Port Elizabeth Musical and Dramatic Society.
✰ St Mary's Collegiate Church, Main Street: the choir presents some beautiful sacred music.

Wining and dining
There's a varied selection of eating houses, both classic and ethnic, to choose from; the seafood dishes are generally quite excellent. Some specific suggestions appear on page 228.

SPORT AND RECREATION
Beaches and watersport feature strongly. The coasts in both directions are distinguished by wonderful stretches of golden sand; the waters of the Indian Ocean are warm (22 °C in summer); the bathing is safe; the rollers, in many places, ideal for both casual and competitive surfing; scuba divers and snorkellers revel in the clear waters; Algoa Bay is sometimes storm-tossed but more often calm enough to attract yachtsmen and anglers. There's also good angling from rock and surf, and game-fishing in the open sea.
For the rest, there is the standard range of sports on offer; clubs welcome visitors; details from the P E Publicity Association (see Advisory, page 229).

BEACHES Port Elizabeth has four main ones: they're all north-facing and spacious:
✰ King's, between the harbour and Humewood (this is a 1,6-km stretch); relatively free of current and backwash; lifeguards nevertheless keep an eye on bathers. Among the supplementary attractions are an entertainment amphitheatre; waterslides; pools (including the McArthur Bath freshwater and tidal complex), putt-putt, a 'supertube', a miniature railway and some fast-food outlets.
✰ Humewood: popular; sheltered by its promenade, and linked with the pleasant Happy Valley recreational area (see page 197).

☆ Hobie and Pollock beaches, close to Summerstrand, are also attractive to bathers and sun-lovers. The former is notable for the Hobie Cats (of the PE Yacht Club) that sail the waters. Nearby Pollock Beach is frequented by surfers.

Farther down the west coast are The Willows seaside resort (rocky bay, tidal pool, chalets); Skoenmakerskop (24 km from the city; rock pools, attractive marine life) and Sardinia Bay (beautiful beach, and the waters are favoured by experienced snorkellers, but the bathing isn't all that safe).

Up the north-east coast, on the broad sweep of Algoa Bay, is the Swartkops River estuary, a favourite venue of fishermen, boating enthusiasts and bird-watchers (see opposite page). Between the city and Swartkops stretches the huge expanse of sand known as the Northern Beaches; beyond the estuary are the inviting Bluewater Bay Beach, St George's Strand, Jooste Park and, 44 km from the city, the Sundays River resort.

DIVING Superb dive-sites along the coasts either side of Port Elizabeth. Ocean Divers International, a chain of diving schools started by expatriate Israeli David Cohen, is based in the city, and offers the full range of training and equipment-hire facilities, Tel. 55-2723.

Wreck-diving is an increasingly popular pastime in the area (the Eastern Cape coasts are the graveyard of literally hundreds of ships). For details of expeditions, contact the P E Publicity Association (see Advisory, page 229); for information on underwater sports generally, contact the Algoa Bay Diving School, Tel. 55-3367.

SWIMMING Swimmers can enjoy themselves at St George's Park (pool, steam baths, massage, gymnasium, tearoom; open throughout the year), and in the Olympic-standard pool at Newton Park (separate diving and children's pools; the No. 66 bus from Market Square will get you there).

FISHING Excellent opportunities for surf, rock, river and deep-sea anglers; catches include steenbras, galjoen, elf, musselcracker, poenskop, blacktail, hottentot, tiger, kob, leervis; among the best places are Humewood, Marine Drive, Summerstrand, Cape Recife, Skoenmakerskop, Flat Rocks, Sardinia Bay, Seaview, the Swartkops, Sundays and Gamtoos rivers, and the Maitland river-mouth.

For details of deep-sea fishing expeditions, phone 52-4138, or Owen Charsley on 33-2124, or the PE Publicity Association (see Advisory, page 229).

Trout-fishing Contact the Eastern Province Freshwater Angling Society, L5 Dumant Park, Summerstrand 6001; Tel. (041) 54-7131, ask for Mr Pitt.

GOLF The major clubs make visitors feel at home; contact telephone numbers: Humewood Golf Club 53-2137/8; Port Elizabeth Golf Club 34-3140; Wedgewood Country Club 72-1212; Walmer Country Club 51-4211.

Putting practice can be enjoyed at the Greenacres entertainment centre in Rink Street (36-hole course).

TENPIN BOWLING Also at Greenacres (16 lanes).

AROUND PORT ELIZABETH

Uitenhage

Nearby neighbour to and closely associated with Port Elizabeth is Uitenhage, the eastern Cape's oldest town: it was founded in 1804 on the banks of the Swartkops River beneath the high Winterhoek mountains by General Jacob Abraham Uitenhage de Mist, the Cape representative of the Batavian (Dutch) government.

Uitenhage is 37 km north of Port Elizabeth (an excellent freeway, a weekday bus service and a train service link the two). It is now an industrial centre concerned with motor assembly, vehicle component and tyre manufacturing, textiles and railways (the workshops are extensive and ultra-modern), but despite all this it has managed to preserve at least a part of its heritage.

Features of interest include:

CUYLER MANOR CULTURAL MUSEUM A pleasant Cape Dutch homestead on the outskirts of town and dating to 1814. Among the exhibits are old farm implements, a mill (in working order) and a charming herb garden. The adjacent Mohair Demonstration Farm is an added attraction. Open weekdays.

OLD DROSTDY AFRICANA MUSEUM Caledon St: houses some interesting local-history displays, including early furniture, utensils, clothing. Open weekdays.

RAILWAY STATION MUSEUM Transport relics in the old terminus, built in 1875. Open weekdays.

SPRINGS RECREATION PARK AND RESERVE

Beautifully clear water from the three springs, or 'eyes', of the area; picnic spot; two swimming pools; restaurant; a circular nature trail, and a longer hike that takes you through the Upper Swartkops valley. Bird-watching around the springs; the aloes are magnificent between June and August.

Addo Elephant National Park

This 8 595-ha reserve, in the rugged bush country 72 km north-east of Port Elizabeth, was established in 1931 to preserve the last, tiny remnant of the once-prolific herds of Cape elephant.

A decade earlier the elephants had almost been wiped out: they were causing havoc in the cultivated lands of the region and the farmers, losing patience, hired a professional hunter to exterminate them. Between 90 and 100 of the animals were shot before the survivors – just 16 of them (and later reduced to 11) – escaped into the almost impenetrable tree-and-creeper tangle of the Addo bush and there, in what was described as 'a hunter's hell', they were protected from further persecution by the difficult terrain, and by outraged public opinion. They now number a healthy 185.

The Addo bush consists largely of spekboom (*Portulacaria afra*) and other woody plants that elephants find sustaining – so much so, indeed, that the park is able to support a population three times denser than any other reserve in Africa. That said, however, the Addo pachyderms are genetically identical to those of the Kruger park, though only the males have tusks, and these tend to be rather short.

The Addo is also home to black rhino, buffalo, eland, kudu and a number of other bovids, and to some 170 species of bird. The latter tend to be rather elusive (much of the vegetation is too thick for good visibility) but an observation point has been established and this helps. The elephant and other large game are a lot easier to locate and study: there are game-viewing roads, and viewpoints at the watering places.

Accommodation in the park comprises self-contained two-bed (plus bunk) rondavels, some 6-bed family cottages and a caravan-camp site. There's also a licensed restaurant, shop, petrol pump. Information: Tel. (0426) 40-0556; bookings: National Parks Board, PO Box 787, Pretoria 0001; Tel. Pretoria (012) 343-1991, or Cape Town (021) 419-5365.

Zuurberg National Park

The Zuurberg reserve, in the Winterhoek mountain range 12 km north of the Addo and until recently a state forest, has been proclaimed a 20 777-ha park to preserve the region's three types of transitional vegetation: the macchia of the dry uplands (species include the cushion bush, the mountain cedar, buchu, and the Zuurberg cycad); Alexandra forest (ironwood, yellowood, assegai, white stinkwood) and the Addo-type spekboom mentioned above. The mountain scenery is spectacular; the prolific birdlife notable for its black eagles. The park is being restocked with game; elephant and buffalo will be reintroduced in future.

The Zuurberg is a place for the hiker, the backpacker, the lover of peace. Accommodation: there is none in the park (facilities are still being developed) but the nearby Zuurberg Inn is a pleasant place from which to explore (it also offers horse-riding, swimming, tennis, bowls, croquet, Tel. (0426) 40-0581).

Sundays and Swartkops rivers

The broad alluvial valley of the Sundays River, extending from the shores of Algoa Bay through Kirkwood to Lake Mentz some 100 km to the north, is wonderfully fertile, especially along the middle reaches, and produces about two-thirds of the country's citrus fruit, together with a huge volume of fruit juices. To drive up the valley from Port Elizabeth in October, when the trees are in blossom and the air heavy with their scent, is a delight indeed. Flowering plants – bougainvillea, frangipani, poinsettia, poinciana – are everywhere.

The Pearson Park resort (caravan/camping grounds; water-skiing, canoeing, river and surf fishing) is situated at the river-mouth; Tel. (041) 68-0040.

Much closer to the city (10 km away) is the Swartkops estuary. There are some splendid beaches in the area; the river is navigable for 18 km upstream, and the waters attract yachtsmen, windsurfers and canoeists. There are three river-side resorts:

SWARTKOPS Hosts a yacht club and the Swartkops Rod Club. Excellent facilities for sailing (two slipways) and angling.

REDHOUSE Higher up than Swartkops, also has a yacht club; weekly regattas in summer.

AMSTERDAMHOEK A charming little hamlet on a creek at the river-mouth and a popular angling venue. Attractions include Dufour Park (picnicking) and the aloe reserve on the Tippers Creek road.

West of Port Elizabeth

Well worth exploring is the coastal region on either side of the national highway (the N2) that leads to Cape Town. Of note:

ST FRANCIS BAY Extending from Cape Recife (near Port Elizabeth) in the east to Cape St Francis in the west, St Francis Bay is distinguished by its sandy beaches and by a number of attractive resorts, including Skoenmakerskop, Seaview, Sardinia Bay, Aston Bay and Paradise Beach. The Gamtoos River discharges into the bay 50 km from Port Elizabeth, and its estuary offers good fishing (kob, grunter, silvie). The waters off Cape St Francis are greatly favoured by anglers for their large (22 kg) yellowtail.

Proclaimed reserves along or close to the 100 km of the bay's shoreline include:

☆ Cape Recife nature reserve: 336 ha of vulnerable shoreline and dune next to the popular beaches of Summerstrand (page 200). Sea, shore, bush and areas of fresh water attract numerous birds (notable are the waders); marine life is especially rich.

☆ Maitland nature reserve, at the mouth of the Maitland River, 17 km west of Port Elizabeth: a pleasant 127-ha expanse of forest and bush; caravan/camping site at the estuary; self-guided trail; picnic areas.

☆ Seaview game park, some 25 km west of the city, is a 40-ha farm that hosts a variety of wildlife – including lion, giraffe, zebra, kudu and various other buck species – and bird sanctuary. There's a nature trail, picnic area, campsite. Next door to the park is a chinchilla farm (visitors are welcome to tour the breeding buildings).

☆ Van Stadens wild flower reserve: see opposite column for details.

☆ Seekoei River nature reserve, just north-west of Aston Bay, is a 66-ha bird sanctuary around the common estuary of the Swart and Seekoei rivers. Waterbirds include red-knobbed coot, little egret and a number of tern species.

☆ Cape St Francis nature reserve: a tiny (36-ha) patch of fragile dune and heath close to the hamlet of Cape St Francis. Attractive birdlife.

THE VAN STADENS RIVER AREA Just over half an hour's drive from Port Elizabeth, this region is famed for its scenic splendour, and for the large, dune-enclosed lagoon at the estuary. The river is navigable (to small boats; good fishing for musselcracker and steenbras) up to the gorge, which is crossed by a 350-m-long bridge. Motorists look down a drop of no less than 125 m to the river below.

You reach the bridge and gorge via the spectacular and very lovely Van Stadens River Pass, just before which is a signpost directing you to the wild flower reserve, a 500-ha area (60 ha under cultivation) that protects an unspoilt countryside of heath and Alexandra forest. The flowers (erica, protea, watsonia) are attractive between April and September, and especially so at the height of spring. Facilities include a network of paths, picnic spots, and an information centre.

Holiday homes on St Francis Bay

JEFFREYS BAY On the shores of St Francis Bay some 45 minutes from Port Elizabeth, and one of the world's most notable surfing areas: the rollers off a number of beaches within easy walking distance of the town attract international competitors as well as large numbers of local sportsmen.

As renowned are the seashells found along a 3 km stretch of sand: huge numbers of tropical Indo-Pacific and temperate Cape species that attract collectors from afar. Searching the tideline is a favourite (and rewarding) pastime among holiday-makers; a museum in town houses unusual and enchanting shell displays.

Jeffreys Bay has excellent visitor facilities: self-contained cottages; caravan/camping grounds; hotels (including the Savoy; farther down the coast is the St Francis Bay Protea). The magnificent new Marina Martinique Bay is being developed on the Aston Bay segment of St Francis Bay (among its features are 3,5 km of canals, an inner harbour, a lake, a drawbridge, an electrically controlled mechanical lock system, a plaza, shops, entertainment venues, a floating paddle-boat restaurant).

The quiet dignity of Grahamstown

SETTLER COUNTRY

This is the name by which most white South Africans know the territory that stretches from Port Elizabeth east to the Great Fish River and inland up the valley of that river: a countryside more or less permanently occupied by the Xhosa (together with a handful of hardy Boer frontier families) until the arrival of 4 000 British immigrants in 1820.

The influx represented a major chapter in the politically (and morally) complicated story of colonial expansion in the eastern Cape, a saga that properly began with the eruption of the first Frontier War in 1779. Altogether there would be eight more major confrontations over the next hundred years (a tragic clash of cultures that saw many of the black clans dispossessed, and the Cape Colony's border moved progressively eastwards), the most significant of which was probably the fifth, in 1819, when the 9 000-strong Xhosa army mounted a direct attack on the military outpost of Grahamstown. This was repulsed, but the event convinced Lord Charles Somerset, the strong-willed Cape governor of the day, that only massive white immigration – from Britain, since 'anglicization' was part of official

policy – could bring a semblance of stability to the border areas. Hence the landings at Algoa Bay in the following year.

Initially the success of Somerset's scheme was in some doubt: the newcomers suffered hardship and bitter disappointment; many had no experience of farming, and their farms, in any event, were too small to be viable; there were locust plagues and droughts, and endemic conflict with the Xhosa. Most of them gave up the unequal struggle and drifted into the villages, nearly all of which had, like Grahamstown, started life as frontier garrisons. Life on the land improved, though; in the decade after 1825, a period during which government restrictions were relaxed, the settlers' allotments were enlarged, and the fledgling sheep-farming industry took solid root and began to flourish.

Such, very briefly, are the origins of 'Settler Country': a region of historic little towns, many with Settler connections and rather British in character, surrounded by a countryside of pleasant hills and valleys graced by aloe and euphorbia, and by farmlands which still yield the products of the merino sheep (though today much else as well – wheat and lucerne, beef, milk, butter, cheese, fruit, timber).

GRAHAMSTOWN

An elegant place of some 20 000 inhabitants, situated 60 km from the coast and set among green hills 535 m above sea level, Grahamstown is known both as the 'Settler City' and, because of the number of churches within its bounds (around 40 places of worship in all), as the 'City of Saints'. It's also a leading academic and cultural centre, home to Rhodes University, St Paul's Theological College, a number of fine schools, and the 1820 Foundation and the National Festival of the Arts.

Grahamstown's past is attractively discernible in the original Settler homes that have been preserved and in the rather more imposing Victorian edifices erected during the later and more prosperous years of the 19th century.

Memorials, museums, landmarks

The early British immigrants (and other English-speaking people who followed) are commemorated by the grandly modern 1820 Settlers Memorial, situated on Gunfire Hill above the city. The monument, built in 1974, consists of exhibition halls, a 900-seat conference centre, a splendid 920-seat auditorium, function rooms, entertainment and recreation areas and so forth. Among its showpieces is the Memorial Court, a place full of symbols representing the British contribution to South Africa's cultural heritage. Of special note is the series of 24 panels, created by the artist Cecil Skotnes, portraying the story of the Settlers.

The auditorium is used for, among other things, the annual (winter) festival, during which an imaginative programme of drama is staged, music heard, dance performed, paintings and sculpture displayed. The buildings, though, are in full use throughout the year: consult the local press, or the Grahamstown Publicity Association (see Advisory, page 229) for details.

THE SETTLERS WILD FLOWER RESERVE covers most of Gunfire Hill: it's a 61-ha expanse of ground stretching from the university to the monument and enclosing the town's former botanic gardens. Features include a pleasant stone-walled lily pond, flora indigenous to the areas of early British settlement and other local species (proteas, cycads, and a great many aloes), and the Old Provost, a military prison. Altogether a most attractive place.

FORT SELWYN, just below the memorial complex, was built in 1836 and served as a signalling (semaphore) point linking Grahamstown, through a series of towers, to other fortified settlements, and as a military barracks until 1870. Of interest are its three naval nine-pounder guns. The Fort is part of the:

ALBANY MUSEUM, which focuses on Settler history, of course, (see below) but more prominently – in its main building on Somerset Street – on natural history, ethnology and anthropology: the history of man, African artefacts and musical instruments, exhibitions of traditional Xhosa lifestyles.

There's also a wildlife gallery for children. The museum is open daily.

THE 1820 MEMORIAL MUSEUM, also in Somerset Street (below the Monument) and part of the Albany complex, houses a fine collection of Settler family treasures (jewellery, silver, porcelain); firearms and military memorabilia; furniture and implements; costumes and accessories, and a photographic essay on Grahamstown's growth. Open daily.

OBSERVATORY MUSEUM, Bathurst Street, is significant for its place in the story of South Africa's diamond industry: it was here that Dr William Atherstone identified Hopetown's 'Eureka' stone in 1867, so prompting the first great rush (he was also noted for his medical work: he pioneered the use of ether as an anaesthetic, founded the Albany Hospital in 1858, the Grahamstown lunatic asylum in 1875 and South Africa's first medical research laboratory, the Colonial Bacteriological Institute, in 1891). Other features of the museum include its Victorian furniture, its attractive herb garden, its Meridian Room (where astronomical time was calculated) and the country's only camera obscura – a darkened chamber into which coloured images were projected from the outside by an ingenious system of lenses and mirrors (a novelty much enjoyed by wealthy Victorians in the age of nascent photography). Open daily.

NATIONAL ENGLISH LITERARY MUSEUM, an impressive resource centre housing manuscripts and published works by and memorabilia relating to South Africa's English-speaking writers. Open Monday to Friday.

JLB SMITH INSTITUTE OF ICHTHYOLOGY, houses marine exhibits, including several connected with the thought-to-be-extinct coelacanth, the first specimen of which was identified by Professor Smith (see page 213). The Institute is one of the country's leading research centres. Open weekdays.

RHODES UNIVERSITY MUSEUM, though originally (1886) a chapel, it is now devoted to scientific exhibits and historical photographs.

ARTIFICERS' SQUARE, around the junction of Cross and Bartholomew streets; distinguished by its charming early Settler homes (now privately owned).

PLACES OF WORSHIP A great many, as mentioned. Among the more noteworthy are:
✩ Anglican Cathedral of St Michael and St George, an imposing building whose bells, lectern, pulpit, rood screen and organ hold special interest, and whose spire rises almost 50 m over a town square fringed on the southern side by pleasant Victorian façades (all are now national monuments).
✩ The Baptist Chapel (Bartholomew Street), South Africa's first such: it was completed in 1823.
✩ The Wesleyan Chapel in Market Street (completed 1832) contains the eastern Cape's earliest pipe-organ.
✩ St Patrick's (Roman Catholic) church, built in 1839 by the 28th Inniskilling Regiment: its military origins (and those of the town) are evident in its exterior architecture.

HISTORIC HOTELS Two are of note: the Cathcart Arms welcomed its first guests in 1825 (the original deed of sale is displayed); the Grand, in High Street, has been the site of a hostelry for the past century and now boasts the country's largest private wine cellar (open weekdays and Saturdays; tastings on Saturday mornings).

AROUND GRAHAMSTOWN

Within easy driving distance of the city are some pleasant nature reserves and a number of small and very attractive rural centres, most of them with close Settler associations. To the south, at the mouth of the Kowie River on what is known as the Sunshine Coast, is one of the Eastern Cape's fastest-growing resorts:

Port Alfred

The river is navigable for 21 km upstream, and at one time – in the mid-19th century – costly efforts were made to develop the harbour, but there were technical difficulties and, when the railway line between big-brother Port Elizabeth and Grahamstown was completed in 1881, the project was abandoned.

Port Alfred is now a residential and holiday town, noted for its 18-hole golf course (one of the country's finest); its proximity to the lively Fish River Sun hotel-casino complex (28 km away, in the Ciskei region: see page 210), and for its pleasant beaches and their seashells (1 800 different kinds have been found, including some rare species). There's safe bathing and excellent fishing (deep-sea, surf, rock, freshwater) in the area; bathing, canoeing and other watersports in and on the river. Among the special attractions are the two-day Kowie canoe trail along the spectacular valley (information: Tel. (0464) 4-1140) and the 8-km hiking trail through the 174-ha Kowie nature reserve (birdlife includes the fish eagle).

In town there's the Kowie historical museum, which contains detailed Settler family records, much used by genealogists, and the small Settler church, built by Methodists in 1826.

Along the coast, 24 km to the west, are Kenton-on-Sea and Bushman's River Mouth, two smaller estuary resorts with plenty to offer the boating enthusiast, angler and beach-lover.

Bathurst

Situated on the road between Port Alfred and Grahamstown: a charming place embowered by giant wild figs and coral trees and set in a countryside renowned for its splendid pineapple harvests. Among the many features of interest are:
✩ Summerhill farm, which boasts the world's largest 'pineapple', a traditional Xhosa village, mini-farm, tractor rides, walks, restaurant and charming pub.
✩ The two-pulpit St John's (Anglican) church, which served as a fortified Settler sanctuary during the 19th century frontier conflicts.
✩ The Pig and Whistle pub, which started life in 1821 as a blacksmith's forge and an inn, survived the troubles (it was looted, burned and then rebuilt) and still plays amiable host to the thirsty.
✩ The Agricultural Museum: implements and so forth; closed on Wednesdays and Saturdays.

✩ The toposcope, built on the spot from where the first of the British Settlers were directed to their lands. Bronze plates (57 of them) record names, farms, directions and distances.

✩ Bradshaw's Mill, thought to be the country's first textile factory; built in the 1820s, it heralded the establishment of the region's thriving wool industry. It is signposted on the road to:

✩ Horseshoe Bend nature reserve, 7 km west of Bathurst and so named for the remarkably convoluted course of the Kowie River. The area is graced by some lovely trees and flowering plants, among them aloes, crane flowers, gazanias, euphorbias, mesembryanthemums, crassulas. There are panoramic views of the bend, the countryside around and the distant Sunshine Coast from the Thornridge vantage point, just 2 km from town.

Salem

An attractively preserved village, 13 km from Grahamstown on the road to Port Elizabeth. It was founded by the largest (344-strong) of the Settler groups; of interest is the fortified Wesleyan chapel, and some of the surviving early houses, double-storeyed and designed for defence. A plaque on a nearby hill commemorates the courage of Richard Gush, a Quaker whose soft words turned away a Xhosa war party. The name of Salem is derived from the Hebrew word for peace (Psalm 76); cricket has been played on the village green since 1844.

THOMAS BAINES NATURE RESERVE Some 15 km from Grahamstown on the Port Elizabeth road and to the north of Salem, this is a 1 013-ha sanctuary for 42 mammal species, including white rhino, buffalo, eland, black wildebeest, bontebok, mountain reedbuck; 171 different types of bird and 24 of reptile. Within the reserve, which is bisected by the Palmiet River, is part of the extensive Settlers Dam, Tel. (0461) 2-8262 for information.

ANDRIES VOSLOO KUDU RESERVE Situated in the Great Fish River valley between Grahamstown and Fort Beaufort to the north (take the R67), the reserve was originally a smallish haven for kudu but was recently expanded with the addition of the Sam Knott reserve which, with adjoining Double Drift (formerly the LL Sebe) game reserve, brings the conservation area up to 45 000 ha and more.

Wildlife includes the kudu, of course, but also white rhino, Cape buffalo, eland, steenbok, springbok, and 184 bird species (checklist available at the gate). Of note is the dense, 2-m-high semi-succulent vegetation (known as Fish River Valley Bushveld) which covers large parts of the terrain, and a euphorbia 'forest'. Accommodation has been confined to a tented camp and a camping area (at Double Drift); facilities are being developed. Other features: game-viewing roads, walks, observation hides, picnic and fishing spots, reception centre. Information: Tel. (0461) 2-7909.

ECCA NATURE RESERVE Located 16 km north of Grahamstown, this small (134-ha) expanse of broken country is notable for the interesting, and scientifically important, saurian fossils it yields, among them those of the early reptile Mesosaurus. Kudu, bushbuck and other bovids can be seen; there's a game trail, and a pleasant picnic area.

A Xhosa horseman

The Fish River passes through the Vosloo reserve on its way to the sea

THE NORTHERN AREAS

Longer excursions from Port Elizabeth and Grahamstown lead you across the Great Fish River valley, towards and through the rugged Winterberg range of mountains and beyond, through increasingly dry country to the fringes of the Great Karoo.

The Winterberg runs east to west for some 200 km north of the small country-towns of Fort Beaufort, Adelaide and Bedford, the mountains rising 900 m above the surrounding countryside, on average 1 800 m above sea level and at one point – the Great Winterberg peak – to an impressive 2 371 m.

The heights are often snow-clad in winter; the major pass in the east is the Katberg. The range marks the outer limits of 'Settler Country'; the lands to the north and east are part of a region known as the Eastern Cape midlands.

Fort Beaufort

A substantial and pleasant town on the banks of the Kat River and a major centre of the citrus-farming industry. Fort Beaufort was founded as a military post in 1822; successfully resisted a Xhosa onslaught in 1851; its Military Museum, once the garrison officers' mess, and its Martello Tower house some intriguing militaria. Open daily.

In Durban Street is the Historical Museum, devoted to items of less aggressive origin: early household implements, documents, and some paintings of local interest by Frederick I'Ons and the prolific (and much underrated) Thomas Baines. Open Mondays-Saturdays.

Adelaide

A centre for the wool, mohair, citrus and grain industries, situated in 'Scottish Settler Country' on the banks of the Koonap River. Adelaide's attractions include the Our Heritage Museum and its lovely Ash Collection of antique porcelain, glass and silver. To the north is the quite beautiful Mankazana Valley, and there are some fine examples of Settler fortified houses in the surrounding farmlands.

The town of Bedford, below the wooded Kagaberg a short distance to the west of Adelaide, is noted for its close associations with the Settler leader, poet and philanthropist Thomas Pringle, and for its annual gymkhana, a premier event on the country's equestrian calandar.

Somerset East

Situated beyond Settler Country, at the foot of the attractive Bosberg, in a fertile, well-watered area of streams and waterfalls, fully 16 of which are visible from the town. The Glen Avon falls are especially worth visiting (permission required); recommended is the 10-km Auret mountain drive and the pleasant wood-and-ravine walks.

The town itself, a fairly substantial one that started life as a military farm in 1815, is noted for its attractive gardens, its excellent 18-hole golf course, and the elegant campus of Gill College. Among its other points of interest are:

☆ The museum, housed in a Georgian parsonage: artifacts date back to 1770; the emphasis is on church history, though there are displays devoted to early wedding gowns and to some exquisite period dolls. The museum's rose garden is outstanding.

☆ The Walter Battiss art gallery contains works of this fine South African artist, born in Somerset East in 1906.

☆ The Bosberg nature reserve covers just over 2 000 ha of dense grassland on the southern slopes of the range; residents include mountain zebra, mountain reedbuck, steenbok, baboon, vervet monkey; among the trees are Outeniqua yellowwood, wild peach, white stinkwood. For visitors: the 15-km circular Bosberg hiking and bridle trail; hiking hut (high up, affording superb views of the Besterhoek Valley); a caravan/camping ground. Other accommodation is available in town (three hotels) and on the area's guest-farms. For information, contact the municipality, Tel. (0424) 3-1333/3-2681.

Cradock

Originally yet another military outpost, established in 1813 on the upper reaches of the Great Fish River 260 km north of Port Elizabeth, and now a largish and fairly attractive Karoo town – though the fertile Fish River Valley countryside, with its orchards and pastures and fields of lucerne, is quite unlike the Karoo proper. Of interest to visitors:

THE GREAT FISH RIVER MUSEUM, local history (Voortrekker, Victorian), with the emphasis on 1825-1925 domestic lifestyles.

HISTORIC BUILDINGS, which include the splendid Dutch Reformed mother church, a replica of London's famed St Martins-in-the-Fields; and the (restored) cottage of the noted author and feminist Olive Schreiner, who wrote her best-known book, *The Story of an African Farm*, while working as a governess in the area. Books

that belonged to Schreiner and her politician husband are housed in the town library, which is the country's second oldest and contains a fine collection of Africana.

FLORAL FEATURES The Van Riebeeck Karoo Garden in town (next to the Dutch Reformed church) is worth visiting for its tranquillity and its indigenous plants. In Dundas Street are the Ilex oak trees, planted in 1850 and thought to be the largest of the species in the world.

KAROO SULPHUR SPRINGS, just outside town on the R32, are medicinal and well patronized: there are chalets, rondavels, a caravan/camping ground and walking trails.

Mountain Zebra National Park

This fine wilderness area, 24 km south-west of Cradock in a great amphitheatre of the Bankberg range, was established in 1937 to preserve the last small remnant of the once-numerous Cape mountain zebra (which are quite distinct from the familiar Burchell's variety). The exercise proved highly successful: about 200 of the animals now graze on the hillsides of the 6 500-ha reserve, which is about the optimum number for the area. Surplus animals are translocated to other sanctuaries.

The park is home to 57 other types of mammals, including eland, black wildebeest, mountain reedbuck, springbok, African wildcat, black-footed cat, black-backed jackal, Cape fox, bat-eared fox, aardwolf. Dassies (rock rabbits) are a common sight. Over 200 bird species have been recorded, among them some of the more notable raptors (black, martial and booted eagles, the splendid Cape eagle owl and the chanting goshawk).

For visitors, there is luxurious, but remarkably inexpensive, accommodation in 18 two-bedroomed chalets (bathroom, living room, fully equipped kitchen, barbecue facilities) and in the lovingly restored Victorian Karoo farmhouse 'Doornhoek'. There's also a caravan/camping ground, and two trail-huts. Amenities include a conference centre for 40 people, à la carte restaurant, shop (groceries, fresh meat), petrol pump, pool, riding stables, picnic areas and, for the energetic, the three-day Mountain Zebra hiking trail. Information: Tel. (0481) 2427/86; bookings: National Parks Board (see Addo, page 201).

THE CISKEI REGION

The wedge-shaped Ciskei area, now an integral part of the Eastern Cape province, lies between the Great Fish River in the west and the Great Kei River in the east (the name, given it by the early white colonists, means 'this side of the Kei', to distinguish it from nearby Transkei). The 8 500-km² region is home to more than a million people, most of whom are of Xhosa stock though there are substantial Mfengu and Thembu minorities. All three belong to the Nguni group.

It's a poor territory, over-crowded, its soils leached over the decades by over-cultivation and over-stocking. The main economic activity is subsistence farming (maize, of course, but also wheat and subtropical fruits). The region is notably lacking in minerals; the commercial infrastructure is generally unsophisticated. Most of the regional income is derived from money earned by migrant and commuting workers – and from tourism.

The region has a lot of tourist potential, its most enticing assets the superb scenery, pleasant climate and 65 km of warm Indian Ocean shoreline whose golden, gently-shelving beaches, estuaries and lagoons remain largely unspoilt. Inland there are forest-clad mountains that served as natural strongholds for the often embattled Xhosa of yesteryear. You'll also find some impressive game and nature reserves, challenging hiking trails and a sprinkling of excellent lodges, hotels and resorts.

Many of the traditional ways have survived in the rural areas. Xhosa boys still whiten their bodies and don reed costumes in preparation for initiation into manhood; many adults smoke long, carved pipes in the manner of their forefathers; the women dress according to the dictates of clan custom and personal status, and the beadwork is intricate, much of it quite beautiful. Visitors with cameras should observe the courtesies: ask permission before you take photographs and, as a token of goodwill, offer cash or a small gift in return.

Travelling conditions: Altogether, the countryside is traversed by some 800 km of surfaced and 3 000 km of gravelled roads. Drive carefully: cattle and other animals tend to stray on the roadways. The major N2 highway bisects the region, connecting Grahamstown with King William's Town, East London and Durban; the R72 runs along the coast from Port Alfred to East London. Minor and rather rough roads south from the N2 to the various coastal centres and resorts. Bisho has an international airport.

The towns

BISHO, on the northern outskirts of King William's Town, is Ciskei's capital, developed largely as a dormitory city during the racially restrictive years to accommodate tens of thousands of commuters.

It has, besides the sprawl of high-density and largely impoverished housing sections, a legislative building, supreme court, modern business and shopping centre, an airport, and Sun International's 83-room Amatola Sun hotel-casino complex. Guests enjoy views of the distant Amatola Mountains, the slots and roulette tables, sundowners on the terrace, sauna and massage in the health spa, golf, tennis. The conference centre seats up to 300. Information and bookings: see Advisory, page 226.

ZWELITSHA, another large commuter area, is to the south of King William's Town.

MDANTSANE, next door to East London, has a population of 200 000 and is Ciskei's largest urban area.

DIMBAZA, 20 km west of King William's Town, is an industrial (mainly textiles) centre: the hand-woven karakul and woollen rugs are rustically attractive.

ALICE, on the western side of Ciskei, near Fort Beaufort, founded in 1847 and named after Queen Victoria's daughter. Places of interest include the politically important Lovedale Mission (founded more than 20 years earlier than the town) and the University of Fort Hare, which has educated many of southern Africa's black leaders; the FS Malan Museum (ethnology, African arts and crafts, traditional costumes and medicines), and the University's art gallery (contemporary African art).

PEDDIE, in the south-west, started out as a frontier wars garrison town. It's now a fairly substantial trading centre; the early mission and its Ayliff House are interesting.

WESLEY, a tiny place just inland from the coast, is noted for its hand-woven Kei carpets.

The Mpekweni Sun marine resort, on the attractive Ciskei coast

The coast

The Fish River mouth is distinguished by its extraordinary geological formations – the maze of caves, tunnels and blowholes sculpted out of the headlands by wind and wave – and by its birdlife: the estuary and lagoon teem with waders and waterfowl, among them Egyptian and spurwing geese, yellow-billed ducks, stilts and wimbrells and breeding pairs of Cape teal.

This is the start of the popular and exceptionally rewarding Shipwreck Trail, a 64-km route along sand and rocky shoreline to the mouth of the Ncera River, which can be walked, by anyone who is reasonably fit, in three to four days. Attractions along the way include the wrecks themselves of course (over the centuries this part of the southern African coast has functioned as something of a marine graveyard), and the stretches of lovely golden beach (though there's the occasional military zone, prohibited to the public), the dense coastal bush, the prolific birdlife and, for those lovers of the outdoors who camp out near one of the resorts (you're allowed to make camp anywhere along the beach for a small fee), angling, spearfishing and scuba diving, boardsailing, surfing and canoeing.

The Bira River mouth, about 25 km east of the Fish River, is an especially attractive spot. Farther along, the estuaries of the Gqutywa and Keiskamma rivers are noted for their bird populations – breeding pairs of white-fronted sandplovers and oystercatchers, among others, can be seen. The shoreline between the Keiskamma and the Chalumna is magically wild: dune-forested and a paradise for shell-collectors.

The more prominent resort centres include:

FISH RIVER SUN A fairly recent and largish (300-bed) addition to the well-patronized Sun International hotel-casino empire; the amenities are predictably varied and excellent: Polynesian-style buildings, casino, à la carte restaurant, cocktail bars, 18-hole golf course (designed by Gary Player), lovely pool, squash, tennis and other sports. Information and bookings: see Advisory, page 226.

MPEKWENI SUN MARINE RESORT, another Sun International enterprise, on the beachfront, overlooking the lagoon (safe swimming) just along the coast. Caters for the luxury-loving family; the emphasis is on watersports; also river-cruises, bowls, tennis, squash. Information: see Advisory, page 226.

BIRA COASTAL RESORT, a holiday 'township', also rather upmarket; lagoon, lovely surrounds, much favoured by bird-watchers and water-sportsmen. Information: Ciskei Department of Tourism and Aviation (see Advisory, page 229).

HAMBURG Founded by ex-soldiers of the British German Legion in 1857 at the mouth of the Keiskamma River, Hamburg didn't develop as a town but has done so as a resort village. Its African name, Emthonjeni, means 'place of the waters', and it is renowned for its fishing grounds (galjoen, musselcracker, blacktail, leervis, kob, together with estuarine and river species). Holidaying revolves around the most comfortable Hamburg Hotel, Tel. (0403) 61-1501), the Angler's Inn chalets and caravan ground, Tel. (0403) 61-3201) and the Hamburg caravan park, Tel. (0403) 61-3201.

XHOSA HERITAGE

Of Nguni stock, the Xhosa comprise a diversity of eastern Cape (Ciskei and Transkei) clans, the main groups being the Gcaleka, Ngika, Ndlambe, Dushane, Qayi, Ntinde and, of Khoisan (Bushman and Hottentot) origin, the Gqunkhwebe. The language contains three types of click sound, borrowed from the Khoisan tongues when the southward-migrating Xhosa began to settle the region sometime before the 17th century.

The Xhosa were, and still are, known for the magnificence and variety of their beadwork. Traditionally, their garments and ornamentation reflected the stages of a woman's life: a certain headdress was worn by a newly-married girl; a different style by one who had given birth to her first child, and so on. Marriages – the Xhosa are polygamous (though today only the wealthier men have more than one wife) – involved protracted negotiations between the families of bride and groom over the payment of the bride-price ('lobola'). The Xhosa man fulfilled the roles of warrior, hunter and stockman; the woman looked after the land and the growing of crops.

A clan comprised a number of groups, each led by a chief, or Inkosi, who owed his position to his mother's status (the society, however, was a patriarchal one in which women weren't formally accorded political authority). The land was communally held; and great emphasis placed on giving according to need: everything was shared, in bad times as well as good; Xhosa families still routinely help one another with such tasks as hut-building and the tilling of the soil.

The body of Xhosa lore has much in common with that of the other Nguni peoples (see Zulu, page 158); animism, and recognition of the presence and power of ancestral spirits and of a supreme authority, are basic elements of belief. Misfortune and illness are attributed to unnatural or supernatural influences (such as the 'tokoloshe', a hairy and potentially malevolent goblin); other prominent figures are the huge lightning bird ('impundulu'), and the gentle 'aBantu bomlambo', human-like beings believed to live in rivers and the sea, and who accept into their family those who drown.

Initiation rites differ markedly between the various African peoples; some groups have abandoned circumcision altogether. Among the Xhosa, the youths whiten their bodies, and wear a white blanket or sheepskin to ward off evil; during the ceremonies, enlivened by energetic dances, they wear costumes made from reeds, and at the end of the lengthy initiation period – spent in isolation from the rest of the community – the specially built huts in which the young men have been living are ceremoniously burned.

A rural settlement in the remoteness of the Transkei hinterland

The inland areas

Prime attraction for nature-lovers are the three forest reserves – the Cata, Mnyameni and Zingcuka – on the slopes of the lofty and lovely Amatola range in the north, the Ciskei's and the far-eastern Cape's principal coastal-belt rampart. The mountains have an average height of 1 800 m above sea level; highest points are Gaikaskop (1 962 m) and the Hog's Back (1 938 m; see below). The indigenous forests are dense, distinguished by their yellowwoods, white stinkwoods and Cape chestnuts. There are also plantations, and patches of high macchia and grasslands decorated with wild flowers. Birdlife includes the Cape parrot and the Knysna lourie; the emerald shores of Mnyameni dam are worth a visit.

Winding a 104-km course through these forest areas is the outstanding Amatola trail, attractive both to hikers and climbers. Information and bookings (well in advance): Ciskei Department of Tourism and Aviation (see Advisory, page 229).

To the west, bordering on and overlapping into Settler Country (see page 203), is the Katberg range of grass-covered hills, and equally popular for its walks, its horse trails and its clear mountain air.

HOGSBACK, on the northern edge of the Ciskei region, and accessible via either Stutterheim or the Ciskei centres of Bisho and Alice, is a resort area comprising a scatter of permanent homes, three hotels (Hogsback Inn is recommended), holiday bungalows, a caravan park, and an exquisitely shaded camping ground, all set in the loveliest countryside imaginable. Hikers and ramblers along the country lanes and fern-fringed woodland paths enjoy breathtaking views (of four peaks, including the Hog's Back), waterfalls (notable are The Madonna and Child, The Swallowtail, The Kettle Spout and The Bridal Veil). One of the more pleasant strolls leads to the Oak Avenue site, where open-air services are held at Christmas and Easter. Nearby is St Patrick's-on-the-Hill, one of southern Africa's smallest churches.

SANDILE DAM, the region's largest stretch of inland water, is the site of the Sandile Dam mountain resort. The setting, at the confluence of the Keiskamma and Wolf rivers on the slopes of the Amatola, is unsurpassed. The resort is in its infancy; accommodation, a game reserve, and camping, boating, fishing, hiking and picnicking facilities are being developed.

TSOLWANA GAME PARK, south of Tafelberg and abutting the Swart (black) Kei River in the northern area, is a quite magnificent, 17 000-ha mountain reserve run (unusually) with both conservation and 'resource management' in mind: the local inhabitants benefit from cheap fresh meat and from the jobs on offer, so poaching and other habitat-damaging practices – fence- and tree-cutting, for instance – are kept to the minimum. There are lessons here for other southern African conservationists.

Principal features of the park are the river-valley, the Tsolwana mountains, and the region's mix of Karoo scrub and temperate-zone vegetation. On view: white rhino, giraffe and a large number and variety of bovids. Several exotic species have been introduced, including Barbary and mouflon sheep, fallow deer and Himalayan tahr.

Tsolwana caters well for the hunting fraternity (both rifle and – again unusual – bow); professional guides are available; trophy-seekers tend to go for the exotics.

There are guided walking and pony trails, game-viewing roads (vehicles may be hired), trout-fishing spots (rods are also available for hire), winter-time hunting safaris. Accommodation: self-catering lodges, luxury hunting-lodge, caravan/camping site. Information and bookings: The Manager, Tsolwana Game Park, PO Box 1424, Queenstown 5320; Tel. (04582), and ask for Thibet Park 5402.

DOUBLE DRIFT GAME RESERVE (formerly the L L Sebe game reserve) is joined to the Andries Vosloo kudu reserve (see page 206) to cover an extensive portion of the rugged Fish River Valley. On offer: game viewing, hunting, the Double Drift hiking trail, and the Mbabala Lodge self-catering unit. The area is being developed for tourism. Information and bookings: The Warden, PO Box 408, Alice 5700; Tel. (0404), and ask for Alice 1403 or 1421.

KATBERG STATE FOREST, to the south of Tsolwana, lies in lovely mountainous countryside traversed by one- to four-hour nature trails. For naturalists: antelope and a variety of small mammals; prolific birdlife, ranging from the crowned eagle at one extreme to the chorister robin at the other.

Accommodation is available at the Katberg Hotel, Tel. (04049) and ask for 3, and at the Highlands-Katberg Holiday Resort (rondavels, chalets, caravan and camping sites): shop and petrol; other amenities include horse riding, bowls, tennis, swimming. Information and bookings: The Manager, Highlands Holiday Resort, PO Balfour 5740; Tel. Balfour (040452) 1002/1022.

The Mpofu game reserve extends over 12 000 ha south from the Katberg to the Kat River. There are guided trails and hunting facilities; other amenities are being developed.

EAST LONDON

The territory stretching from the far-Eastern Cape seaboard inland, through the narrow corridor between the Keiskamma and Kei rivers (between, that is, the Ciskei and Transkei regions) to Queenstown and beyond is known as Border, a hangover from the colonial and rather turbulent past: the region, for long occupied by the Xhosa, lay at the extreme limits of white encroachment until the mid-1800s, when East London was founded and immigrants – many of them German – brought a degree of stability and permanence to the tentatively-settled land. The Xhosa were in due course confined to their 'homelands' across the two rivers.

The Border area has its devotees among the holiday-going public. Along the coast there are some quite splendid beaches, bays, lagoons, estuaries and secluded coves; the waters are warm, the surf challenging in places, the fishing excellent.

East London is a fairly substantial city and South Africa's only major river-port: it's situated at the mouth of the Buffalo, which rises in the high Amatola Mountains to the north-west. The estuary is not naturally suitable as a harbour, and was slow to develop as such: it wasn't until 1937, when the C W Malan Turning Basin was completed, that liner passengers could disembark directly onto the quayside (previously they had to be lifted, by means of wicker baskets, onto lighters). The docks now boast 2 600 m of quayage, a tanker berth, a container handling facility and a grain elevator with a storage capacity of 76 000 tons. The port, which handles some three million tons of cargo each year, serves the

Eastern Cape and, increasingly, the giant Free State goldfields, and is a major wool-exporting outlet; auctions are held at the city's Wool Exchange from May to September.

The resident population totals some 170 000; about the same number of people travel in each working day from the dormitory town of Mdantsane, 17 km away.

East London's attractions are of the quiet, undemanding, family-orientated kind: it has fine beaches, pleasant parks and gardens, good hotels and restaurants, and some fairly entertaining nightlife in the summer months along the seafront. The climate is equable (there are an average 7,5 hours of sunshine a day throughout the year); the waters of the Indian Ocean warm (temperatures range from 17 °C to 23 °C). As its publicists say, the place 'combines the charm of a relatively small community with all the essential amenities of a large city'.

The principal thoroughfare is Oxford Street, along which you'll find modern shops and office blocks (though glitzy high-rises are conspicuous by their absence), the post office and the City Hall. Satour, and the air terminal, are in nearby Terminus Street.

Memorials, museums, galleries

The East London Museum, in Oxford Street, houses the first coelacanth – a primitive fish (*Latimeria chalumnae*) that lived in the Mesozoic period some 250 million years in the past and was thought to have become extinct 60 million years ago – to have been caught in modern times. The unusual mauve-blue fish was landed near East London in 1938 and shown to Professor JLB Smith of Rhodes University, Grahamstown, who described it as a 'living fossil'. The museum also boasts the world's only known dodo's egg (the last of these large, flightless birds, once common on Mauritius, died in about 1680, though related species survived on other Indian Ocean islands until the 1790s).

Other more general displays are devoted to ethnology, prehistory and local history (with the focus on the German immigrants); of special note is the fine collection of Karoo reptile fossils; the exhibition of Xhosa beadwork and other items traditional to African ornamentation, custom and belief; and the maritime exhibits, which tell the story of East London harbour. Other places of interest include:

GATELY HOUSE In Queen's Street, one of the East Bank's first private homes and now part of the Museum complex. It's furnished with its original Victorian contents and serves as a fine period museum. John Gately 'Father of East London', was the town's first mayor.

THE ANN BRYANT GALLERY An imposing mansion off Oxford Street (between St Mark's and St Luke's roads) exhibits some fine local paintings (Battiss, Pierneef) and sculpture (notably pieces of sporting significance).

THE GERMAN SETTLERS' MEMORIAL An impressive work on the Esplanade commemorating the arrival of 3 150 German immigrants in 1858. Most of them were ex-Legionnaire veterans of the Crimean War, and single; later that year 153 Irish colleens were brought in as prospective brides.

AQUARIUM On the Esplanade; smallish, but its 400 marine species are well chosen and well displayed. Also in residence are penguins and seals (seal shows are held twice daily and are very popular, especially with children) and a number of oil-polluted and otherwise injured sea creatures that are being nursed back to health. Open daily.

Gardens, parks, reserves

The Queen's Park botanical gardens, along Settlers' Way and Beaconsfield roads (that is, between city centre and river) display some attractive indigenous flora (among them the crane flower, *Strelitzia reginae*, which is common in the area); among the 1 000 animals resident at the park's zoo is an endearing bear called Jackie; the children's zoo features pony-rides. Other green areas are:

☆ Marina Glen: a favourite for family outings (picnic spots; miniature railway); craft market on Sundays.

☆ Settlers' Park, on Union Avenue: displays of the region's flora.

☆ James Pearce Park, off Gleneagles Road, contains splendid nursery gardens and is the venue for dog shows and obedience classes.

☆ Bridle Drift dam and nature reserve: a popular 300-ha recreation area 25 km from the city on the Mount Coke road: bird-watching (a hide has been established), sailing, boating, canoeing (boats for hire), watersports, nature trail (overnight hut), picnic spots.

☆ The Amalinda nature reserve, on the N2 to King William's Town, features a fish hatchery; also on view are bushbuck, southern reedbuck and other bovids, and a great many birds and reptiles. Pleasant picnic and fishing spots.

Gonubie Mouth, 25 km north of East London. Nearby is an enchanting bird sanctuary.

Xhosa youngsters mind the family street-stall

Beaches and resorts

East London's three beaches are renowned. Orient is the nearest to the city and most popular; bounded by the 2-km Esplanade, its attractions include the promenade pier, Orient Theatre (plays and reviews), restaurant. Nahoon and Eastern beaches are also wide and golden, and ideal for safe surfing (the former is a venue for international contests). East London has two freshwater swimming pools.

Along what is known as the Romantic Coast to the south-west and north-east of the city are a number of inviting resorts offering the full range of outdoor recreation, and accommodation from the rudimentary rondavel to the fairly sophisticated hotel. Among the prominent places are:

☆ Kidds Beach, at the mouth of the Mcantsi River abutting the Ciskei region, is well patronized. There are holiday cottages and three caravan parks; bowling green, tennis courts and a splendid expanse of sand. Fishermen favour nearby Kayser's Beach, Christmas Rock and Chalumna Mouth. The local blacksmith's and wheelwright's shop is worth a visit – by appointment

only: Tel. (04323) 780 – for its collections of wagons and tools of the trade, and its early-model caravan.

On the same shores are Cave Rock and Rockclyffe, Fuller's Bay (tidal pool) and Hickman's River, all offering good fishing, bathing, sun-worshipping, caravanning and camping. To the north-east of East London, on the rather longer stretch of coastline that extends to the Kei river-mouth and the Transkei region, you'll find:

☆ Beacon Bay and next-door Bonza Bay, a pleasant little residential town on the Quinera estuary: beach, lagoon, palm-fringed seafront, and two nature reserves especially notable for their birdlife.

☆ Gonubie Mouth, 25 km from East London, has first-class tourist amenities and an enchanting bird sanctuary. The tiny (8-ha) Gonubie nature reserve, proclaimed as a waterfowl haven, hosts more than 130 different bird species, including summer-nesting cranes. Among the visitor facilities are observation points, footpaths and an information centre. Within the reserve is a garden of medicinal plants used by black herbalists.

☆ Haga Haga and Morgan's Bay, quite a bit farther up the coast, are noted for their especially fine sands, and for their seashells. Pleasant walks in the Morgan's Bay lagoon area. Kei Mouth, an especially attractive spot, is popular among rock-fishermen. There are three nature reserves in the vicinity:

☆ Bosbokstrand, a 205-ha private resort area of forest, beach, estuary and a rich birdlife; mammals include eland, bushbuck, impala, blesbok. Fully equipped chalets; caravan/camp site, shops, nature walks, the Strandloper hiking trail, fishing (bait available). Tel. (04372), and ask for Mooiplaas 4512; bookings: Johannesburg (011) 696-1442.

☆ Cape Henderson, a rugged 240-ha patch of coastline favoured by walkers and bird-watchers (among the many species are the blue-mantled flycatcher and the collared sunbird); flora includes milkwood, candlewood, wild banana.

☆ Ocean View guest farm and reserve, a 260-ha working farm noted for the number and variety of its raptors (breeding pairs of long-crested and crowned eagles among them). There are also some antelope species. Accommodation in 2- and 5-bed rondavels, caravan/camping site; Tel. (04372) and ask for 2603.

Sport and recreation

There are a number of rewarding day-walks and hikes in and around East London; the Pineapple Trail tour takes visitors to places of interest (the delicious pineapple-wine cocktail known as a 'fizzannana' can be sampled *en route*). Details from the Greater East London Publicity Association (see Advisory, page 229). Sport and recreation opportunities include:

☆Underwater sports: well catered for; wreck-diving is becoming increasingly popular, and expeditions regularly set out for the more interesting sites.

☆Deep-sea fishing facilities are excellent.

☆ Golf: some fine courses; visitors are made welcome at the East London Golf Club, Tel. 35-1356; Alexander Country Club, Tel. 46-3646; and West Bank Golf Club, Tel. 31-1523.

☆ Yachting and sailing on the Buffalo River; regattas are held regularly.

☆ Performing arts: the Guild Theatre, next to the Museum on Oxford Street, is a pleasantly intimate venue for drama, opera, ballet and musical performances, sometimes staged by the Cape Performing Arts Board (Capab). There's also the Orient Theatre on the beachfront. Consult the local press for details.

Travel

RAIL The railway station (built in 1877; the waiting room has served variously as meeting hall and church; on view is a 1903 steam locomotive) is at the junction of Fleet and Station streets, Tel. 34-2126.

COACH TRAVEL Scheduled luxury coach services to and from East London, and some inviting coach tours of the area, Tel. 58-9401.

AIR East London airport is 12 km from the city; there are daily scheduled flights linking East London with the major centres; the terminal is on Terminus Street.

CAR RENTAL The major hire companies are well represented; consult the Yellow Pages or your hotel reception.

BORDER HINTERLAND

The inland areas of the Border region are less well-known, certainly to tourists and holiday-makers, than East London and its flanking coasts. The countryside, though, is green and pleasant, worth exploring for the attractiveness of its forested hills, its rich farmlands, its nature reserves and for small towns that offer history and hospitality.

King William's Town

Set on the banks of the Buffalo River some 50 km west of East London, King William's Town started life as a mission station in 1825. The town is steeped in military and political history: it became the capital of the short-lived Province of Queen Adelaide (1835-36: the area was settled by 'loyal' Xhosa to act as a 'buffer zone' between their more hostile cousins and the whites), was destroyed in 1836 and resurrected in 1847 to serve as the 'capital' of British Kaffraria, another but stronger buffer zone.

King William's Town is now a fairly substantial farming and manufacturing centre of some 26 000 people. Among its attractions are:

KAFFRARIAN MUSEUM One of the best in the country. It was founded in 1884 by the Natural History Society and is now the repository of more than 25 000 African mammal specimens. Of less academic interest are the mounted remains of Huberta, the itinerant hippo that enchanted the public during her 1 000-km wanderings between 1928 and 1931, when she was accidentally shot. Other displays focus on Xhosa culture and ornamentation, and on German and English immigrant lifestyles, costumes, militaria. Open daily.

THE RESIDENCY On Reserve Road. Sir Harry Smith's headquarters during the inauguration of British Kaffraria, now excellently restored. Open daily.

SOUTH AFRICAN MISSIONARY MUSEUM King William's Town was founded by the London Missionary Society; the museum features mission illustrations, printing presses, household items. Open weekdays.

ROOIKRANS DAM Two kilometres from town and popular among yachtsmen and watersportsmen; brown-trout hatchery nearby.

STUTTERHEIM Some way to the north of King William's Town in the foothills of the Amatola range and a most pleasant area to visit. Specific places of interest include the Forest Resort, on the Keiskammahoek road (walking, riding, swimming, trout fishing, conference venue); Tel. (04362) 324; the Kologha and Kubusie forests, along the same road (lovely waterfalls; picnic spots), and Gubu Dam (sailing, watersports, trout-fishing). The Kologha hiking trail (35 km; two days) winds through the countryside. Information: Tel. (0346) 3-1100.

Queenstown

On the Komani River and not strictly speaking Border country (it's technically part of the Eastern Cape midlands). The town, whose name honours Queen Victoria, was founded in 1853 and laid out around a hexagonal centre from which the streets radiate (the authorities insisted that the townspeople be responsible for their own defence; the hexagon arrangement served as both a laager and a means of rapid egress). It's a fairly large railways, cattle- and sheep-farming and educational centre of some 42 000 people, and is famed for the roses that are grown in its gardens.

MEMORIALS, MUSEUMS, GALLERIES The old Queenstown and Frontier Museum (in Shepstone Street, and part of the Cultural Centre) is an eclectic repository for items ranging from an early steam locomotive (built in 1921; transported the Royal Family in 1947), settler cottage; drinking fountain. Open daily. Also recommended to visitors are:
☆ The Queenstown Art Gallery is in Ebden Street and displays works by South African artists. Nearby is the Penny Lane Gallery, the home of artist Dale Elliott.
☆ The Abbott Collection in Reservoir Road has a mechanical emphasis. On display are clocks, car badges and an impressive number and variety of early telephones. View by appointment; Tel. (0451) 4008.
☆ Ruth Lock Shell Art Collection of intriguing seashell ornamentation. In Lamont Street; open during office hours.

GARDENS, PARKS, RESERVES The main road from East London enters Queenstown through the Walter Everitt sunken garden, a charmingly landscaped place of lawns, ornamental trees, ponds, water-birds, picnic spots. On the slopes of Madeira Mountain just north of town is the J de Lange nature reserve, crossed by a superb scenic drive. Among the game animals are

springbok; flora includes acacia species, aloes, cycads; the reserve's red- and yellow-blossomed tamboekie thorn, *Erythrina acanthocarpa*, is found nowhere else. There are some pleasant picnic spots.

FOR SHOPPERS: The Xhosa Carpet Factory lies just across the Transkei border. Its Persian-style rugs are very attractive; Tel. (0451) 3131.

The North-eastern areas

The region north of Queenstown, beyond the rugged Stormberg range, fringes the Karoo on the one hand and the lovely foothills of the western Drakensberg on the other. The countryside in the west is dry, the horizons far, the few towns and villages isolated. Those in the east, in the uplands close to the Transkei region, are much favoured by hikers, winter-sportsmen and seekers after tranquillity. Principal centre is:

ALIWAL NORTH, on the south bank of the Orange River, was named by the energetic Sir Harry Smith to remind posterity of his victory over the Sikhs at Aliwal, in India, in 1846. The 'North' was an afterthought, appended to avoid confusion with Mossel Bay's originally-conceived name. The town's tree-graced Juana Square honours Sir Harry's Spanish-born wife (other South African towns similarly connected include Harrismith in the Free State and Ladysmith in Natal). Aliwal North is particularly renowned for its:
☆ Curative mineral springs. The health spa, on De Wet Avenue, offers rhuematics, arthritics and baskers a main indoor spring-filled pool (water-temperature is a constant 35 °C; the flow is two million litres a day); four outdoor pools (plus two specially for children), and a 'bio-kinetic centre' (staffed by experts). The grounds are attractively landscaped. Tel. (0551) 2951.
☆ Buffelspruit game reserve covers nearly 1 000 ha along the Kraai River to the east of town. The grassland and Karoo-scrub area is being developed for visitors; on view are eland, gemsbok and other antelope. One can enjoy a fine view of the reserve from the Garden of Remembrance on Barkly Street. Of interest is the garden's Anglo-Boer War blockhouse. Information: The Town Clerk, Tel. (0551) 2441.
☆ Among other places to visit are the Bushman art sites in the region (tours available; Tel. (0551) 2123); the wheat mill, and the cheese factory (one of largest in the country).

ELLIOT, a small town set against a backdrop of the high Drakensberg – a scenically lovely area. The Twelve Apostles – a series of weird sandstone formations – should be viewed in the dramatic light of dawn or early evening. The longest-known 'gallery' of Bushman paintings may be viewed on the farm Denorbin, off the R58 from town: by arrangement; Tel. (045312) 1322; from the R56 road to Ugie one can see the extraordinary, cyclops-like Gatberg geological feature.

MACLEAR lies beneath the Drakensberg peaks; from the village a road takes you up southern Africa's highest pass (Naude's Nek, 2 623 m; the wintertime slopes attract skiers); another road – that to Transkei – leads you to the magnificent Tsitsa waterfall.

RHODES is a cluster of cottages, many occupied by artists, others by holiday-makers who come for the skiing (Ben MacDhui, at 3 001 m, is the area's highest peak), for the trout-fishing, game-bird shooting (partridge in season), horse-riding, and to walk in the champagne-like mountain air. The village's Victorian hotel offers cosy home-style hospitality.

Pipe-smoking is part of Xhosa tradition

BARKLY EAST, situated in the western Drakensberg foothills, 1 813 m above sea level, the area is popular among trout-fishermen (the annual trout festival is held in March). The Barkly Pass linking the town with Elliot is scenically stunning, the rail service rather acrobatic: trains have to negotiate eight 'reverses' on their run down the steep gradient (this is thought to be a world record). Special runs for railway enthusiasts can be arranged. Information: Tel. Aliwal North (0551) 2362.

BURGERSDORP, in the west, is the region's oldest town (founded 1846), and displays minor but fascinating collections in its museum and in the Jan Lion-Cachet Parsonage. The place featured prominently in the Afrikaans Language Movement.

THE GARIEP DAM (formerly Hendrik Verwoerd), more than 100 km long by 15 km wide, lies north-west of Burgersdorp, on the Northern Cape-Free State provincial border. Its tourist attractions are covered on pages 131-132.

THE TRANSKEI REGION

The territory, situated between the Great Kei and Mtamvuna rivers, is the traditional home of sections of the southern Nguni peoples, who speak dialects of the Xhosa tongue *(isiXhosa)*, though different groups – the Gcaleka in the south, the Pondo, Mpondomise, Cele and Xesibe in the north and the Thembu and Bovana in the central parts – preserve their own customs, clothing and ornamentation. The old ways, however, are in decline, even in the remoter rural areas (see page 211).

Transkei was the first of the 'national states' to be granted full independence (in 1976), though its republican status was never recognized outside southern Africa. It has an area of 42 000 km^2; a population of something over three million, and its principal town is Umtata, a pleasant little town on the N2 and astride the Mtata River. It is a largely agricultural region of rolling grass-covered uplands dotted with homesteads (most of them of the rondavel type and many, curiously, built with their doors facing east) and bounded in the south-east by a magnificently rugged coastline, its principal tourist drawcard. Among the inland attractions are the Hluleka and Dwesa nature reserves.

A terraced section of the luxurious Wild Coast Sun hotel and casino complex

CLIMATE Warm and sometimes hot in summer; cool but seldom cold in winter. The rains fall mainly in summer (October to March).

Motoring: the N2 national highway, connecting Port Elizabeth and Durban, runs north-eastwards through the region. Gravel feeder roads lead from the N2 to the coastal resorts. Drive carefully as the lesser roadways tend to be convoluted, and cattle and goats regard them as their own domain.

The Wild Coast

Transkei's 280 km of beautiful (but sometimes treacherous) Indian Ocean shoreline is a holiday-maker's and hiker's paradise, an unsurpassed stretch of unspoilt wilderness famed for its scenic variety. Here there are sandy bays, lagoons and estuaries, imposing cliffs and rocky reefs that probe, finger-like, out to sea, the immediate hinterland, green hills and dense woodlands.

Over the centuries the reefs, offshore currents and periodic storms led to many shipwrecks. Some are still to be located and explored.

The coast has been developed – but by no means over-developed – for the leisure-bent visitor: for the fisherman, sailor and golfer, the swimmer, surfer and skin-diver and the lazer in the sun – and for the gambler. The largest of the seaside villages are Port St Johns and Coffee Bay; the most prominent holiday complex the superb Wild Coast Sun. Other much smaller and generally charming beach and river-mouth resorts dot the shoreline.

WILD COAST SUN One of southern Africa's premier hotel, casino and resort complexes is set beside a tranquil lagoon on the northernmost portion of Transkei's splendid shoreline. On offer is the full range of sporting and recreational facilities (superb golf course; bowls, tennis, squash; rock, surf and deep-sea angling; ski-boating; freshwater and sea bathing; water-skiing, canoeing and sailing at Waterworld); gaming rooms; excellent restaurants (the Commodore is among the country's best); a theatre that hosts international entertainers, and two explosively live show bars.

Not too far away is the Umtamvuna River and its fine waterfall, and the Mzamba river mouth where, at low tide, petrified trees and other fossil remains can be seen. The nearest town is Bizana, known for the herbalists that do brisk pavement business; the hillsides around are aflame with aloes in June.

Farther south along the coast, between the Msikaba and Mtentu rivers, is the:

MKAMBATI NATURE RESERVE A pleasant expanse of grassland and subtropical countryside sliced through by perennial streams and by the beautifully forested ravines of the Msikaba and Mtentu rivers. The Mkambati has been stocked with eland, hartebeest, blesbok, gemsbok and blue wildebeest; birdlife is prolific (recommended for the more energetic ornithologist is a canoe trip up the Msikaba River: Cape vultures nest on the gorge's sheer cliffs).

Of interest to botanists are the Pondoland palms, or the mkambati coconuts, which are unique to the area.

Facilities include cottages and rondavels, a main lodge (five double rooms, guest lounge, table d'hôte restaurant), and the Club House à la carte restaurant (delicious venison and seafood specialities). A network of pathways takes you along the spectacular shoreline and through stretches of inland countryside graced by some exquisite wild flowers (watsonias, gladioli, ground orchids and daisies in grassland; wild frangipani and arum lilies in swamp forest).

Information: Transkei Department of Agriculture and Forestry (see Advisory, page 229); reservations: Mkambati Nature Reserve, PO Box 574, Kokstad; Tel. (0372) 3101 or (0471) 2-2176.

PORT GROSVENOR Little now remains of a 19th century attempt to create a harbour on this rugged part of the Pondoland coast. The 'port' was named after the ill-fated *Grosvenor*, a treasure-ship that came to grief on the rocky shore in August 1782. Only 15 of the 123 people on board were drowned but most of the survivors, lacking food, weapons and trading goods, either perished or simply disappeared (some were absorbed, it is thought, into the black communities) on the long trek west to Cape Town. The *Grosvenor* had been laden with gold, jewels, plate, coins and other precious cargo (including treasure associated with the legend-

ary Peacock Throne of Persia); ambitious and ingenious recovery schemes have been launched by a number of salvage companies, and a great many individual divers have explored the turbulent wreck-site, but, although some fascinating and quite valuable odds and ends have been found, the principal prize remains buried beneath the sands of the sea-bed.

More than two centuries earlier, in 1552, another fine ship, the Portuguese vessel *St John*, ran onto the rocks some way farther down the coast, and the survivors – 440 men (some of them of noble rank), women and children – set out on what was to become one of the most tragic odysseys of the pre-colonial era. Their route took them northwards, to Lourenço Marques and from there on to the island of Mozambique, an incredible 1 600 km from the scene of the wreck and, again, most died along the way. Just eight Portuguese and 17 slaves finally staggered to safety.

PORT ST JOHNS The settlement, which takes its name from the renowned wreck, lies at the Umzimvubu river-mouth in a stunning setting of majestic headland, forest, golden sand and blue sea, and it is perhaps the most pleasant of the Wild Coast's holiday areas.

The river, navigable for some 10 km, is ideal for boating. Its valley nurtures lush plantings of subtropical fruits and pathways lead through dense woodland to some exquisite beauty spots. There are three splendid beaches, two good hotels, the excellent Second Beach 'cottage colony' resort, clusters of holiday bungalows, caravan/camping sites, a nine-hole golf course, bowling greens, tennis courts, and, in town, a small museum, a public library, several garages and general dealers and nine purveyors of patent medicines. Roadside stalls sell bananas, lychees, pawpaws, mangoes, avocados and an attractive array of rugs and basketware. The climate is superb, the sea safe and warm enough even for mid-winter bathing. Quite a few artists, writers and discerning refugees from the concrete jungle have made their home in Port St Johns.

For further information and holiday reservations, contact the Port St Johns Municipality, PO Box 2, Port St Johns, Transkei; Tel. (04752), and ask for 31; or the Second Beach Holiday Resort, PO Box 18, Port St Johns Transkei; Tel. (04752), and ask for 61.

Just to the south is the small and enchanting Silaka nature reserve, set in a wooded valley and haven for blue wildebeest, zebra, blesbok, for some elusive forest animals and birds, and for a kaleidoscopic variety of orchids, lilies, mosses, lichens and red-hot pokers. The shoreline is rugged and rocky, though there is a small beach at the mouth of the Gxwaleni River. Accommodation comprises self-catering four-bed chalets.

Information: Transkei Department of Agriculture and Forestry (see Advisory, page 229).

UMNGAZI RIVER A most pleasant family resort of thatched cottages overlooks the river's estuary, the lagoon and the sea. Many of the guests are serious anglers who come for the fine fishing from boat, rock and surf and river-bank; marine catches include the hammerhead shark. The countryside around is a stunning blend of hill, valley and river; beaches, coves, cliffs and a mangrove forest, at the Umngazana river-mouth, are features of the shoreline. The resort has the standard recreational amenities; the restaurant offers a table d'hôte menu (seafood is a prominent item). The informal bar specializes in an imaginative concoction called a Fluffy Duck. Information: Umngazi River Bungalows, PO Box 75, Port St Johns, Transkei; Tel. (0020), and ask for Umngazi Mouth 1/3.

HLULEKA NATURE RESERVE A small, especially attractive expanse of countryside some 30 km south of Port St Johns, noted for its patches of evergreen forest, its prolific birdlife, for the antelope and zebra that browse on the grassland reaches of the Hluleka River, and for its rocky coastline, a paradise for fishermen (catches include kob, blacktail and shad). Accommodation comprises a dozen or so 6-bed chalets; other facilities are as yet minimal.

Information and bookings: Transkei Department of Agriculture and Forestry (see Advisory, page 229).

COFFEE BAY Somewhat similar to Port St Johns in the magnificence of its cliff and mountain setting, the bay's name is also associated with a shipwreck, though this one held far less drama: the vessel in question was carrying a cargo of coffee beans, some of which were washed ashore to take root and flourish in the area. Coffee Bay, situated between the estuaries of the Nenga and Mbomvu rivers, is a tranquil little holiday village that has two comfortable hotels (one of which overlooks the kilometre-long beach, the other the adjoining lagoon), two caravan/camping sites, excellent fishing and surfing, safe bathing and, for light aircraft owners, a 750-m landing strip. A pleasant walk along the coast will take you to the famed:

HOLE IN THE WALL Probably the most distinctive – and certainly the most photographed – of the Wild Coast's natural features is a massive detached cliff that stands island-like in the sea, and through whose huge arched opening the surf thunders. Its flat top, extensive enough to accommodate several football fields, is mantled in greenery. The extraordinary structure is known to the locals as esiKhaleni, which means 'place of the noise'.

Two kilometres away, situated above a small bay, is the Hole in the Wall hotel and holiday village (en suite rooms, comfortable family chalets, cottages set in landscaped gardens, restaurant, bar; information and reservations: see Advisory, page 226).

DWESA AND CWEBE NATURE RESERVES These two adjoining wilderness areas, separated by the Mbashe River, are of similar character – an attractive mix of evergreen forest and open grassland that sustains a wide variety of birds and small mammals, and of rocky shorelines interspersed by mangrove communities, secluded bays and long stretches of golden sand. Shell collectors find the area enchanting.

Dwesa, 3 900 ha in extent, is home to a number of introduced and re-introduced species (red hartebeest, blesbok, blue wildebeest; crocodile, buffalo, eland, warthog, samango monkey, tree dassie), to a flourishing birdlife that includes the mangrove kingfisher and narina trogon, and, in the rock pools, to a fascinating variety of east-coast marine creatures. Facilities: four- and five-bed chalets (with stoves and gas refrigerators), caravan/camping site; self-guided trails, fishing spots. Private holiday homes, erected on stilts, have been built just behind the beach near the mouth of the Ingomana River.

The newer 2 150-ha Cwebe reserve, still under development (self-catering units and a caravan/camping ground are being established), boasts a splendid waterfall – on the Mbanyana

River – and an especially beautiful lagoon, home to the Cape clawless otter, to the fish eagle and to many other waterbirds. Best fishing spot is from a rocky outcrop known as Shark's Island; Cwebe's seashells are particularly numerous and attractive. Within the reserve is The Haven resort hotel, known for the quiet comfort of its bungalows, its views of sea and forest, and for its seafood dishes and poolside barbecues (information and reservations: see Advisory, page 226).

QORA MOUTH The small resort at the Qora River estuary, near the town of Willowvale, offers a fine beach, a lagoon that is ideal for bathing and boating, and some excellent rock, surf and freshwater fishing spots, all within easy walking distance of the Kob Inn (cottage-style bungalows, family rooms, airstrip, marvellous seafood dishes, and a bar set on the edge of the rocks; information and reservations: see Advisory, page 226). There is good fishing for kob (kabeljou) throughout the year; anglers come from afar to take part in the annual (July/August) 'pignose grunter run'. This is ideal walking country: inland there are evergreen forests, river valleys, deep gorges; much of the shoreline is heavily wooded; especially rewarding is the hike from Qora Mouth to:

Searching for oysters at Coffee Bay

MAZEPPA BAY Here there are three broad, palm-fringed beaches and an excellent resort hotel (its seafood is famed) linked to its own island by a small suspension bridge. All in all, a most pleasant place for rambling through coastal dune and forest; bathing, snorkelling, scuba-diving and fishing in the sea. Especially fishing: the area's hammerhead sharks, some weighing an impressive 450 kg and more, present a splendid challenge to serious anglers. Other catches include barracuda, galjoen, bronze bream, blacktail, kob, yellowtail, shad, garrick, musselcracker, mackerel, queenfish.

QOLORA MOUTH Another small estuary resort with a fine beach, three hotels (including the well-known Trennery's; see Advisory, page 226) and excellent caravan/camping facilities. In the general area is the wreck of the *Jacaranda*, which foundered on the rocks in 1971; and, historically more significant, the lovely pool of Nongqawuse, the young Xhosa prophetess who, in 1857, claimed to have seen a great vision. This vision, as interpreted by her ambitious uncle Mhlakaza, foretold that a powerful wind would spring up, bringing with it ancestral spirits who would drive the white colonists into the sea. But before this could happen, Mhlakaza said, the Xhosa must first destroy all their grain and slaughter their cattle, after which 'cleansing' the fields would again stand ready for reaping, the byres would be full, illness and old age would disappear, and the white settlers would be no more. The events that followed represent perhaps the most tragic chapter in the story of southern Africa: over 200 000 head of cattle and most of the grain and garden harvests were destroyed, leading to wholesale starvation, to a huge decline in population, and to the demise of the Xhosa nation as a military power.

WILD COAST HIKING TRAIL One can explore the sandy beaches, lagoons and estuaries, cliffs, coves and caves, rock-pools and wrecks, forests and mangrove swamps of this most dramatic 280-km coast via the established trail. The full course, marked by white footprints, takes between 14 and 25 days to complete (duration is a matter of personal preference and capability) and is divided into five 3- to 6-day sections. Bookings through and brochures and maps available from the Transkei Department of Agriculture and Forestry (see Advisory, page 229).

Back-packers make their way across the lovely Transkei countryside

Inland centres

UMTATA, the region's principal town, was founded in the late 1860s on the banks of the Mtata River (the name means 'to take', a reference either to the number of its flood victims or to the local burial rituals, which involved the incantation 'Take him, Father') as a buffer separating the warring Pondo and Thembu groups. It is now a sizeable and fairly pleasant town of some 50 000 people. Its modest range of assets includes the University of Transkei, the *Bunga* (parliament of the quasi-independent republic), several schools, two public libraries, a museum, hotels, shops, churches, a newspaper and a broadcasting station (Capital Radio). Of greater interest to visitors are:

☆ The Matiwane mountain range nearby, where there are forests, lakes, trout-stocked streams and secluded picnic spots.

☆ The Nduli nature reserve within the city's limits, and the Luchaba nature reserve flanking the Umtata dam. Both are stocked with game; the latter is haven to an impressive variety of birds, and there's fishing in the adjacent recreational area.

☆ Izandla Pottery, whose artists (some of them extremely talented) work with a special clay that is fired, at about 1 350 °C, to produce immensely hard stoneware. Among the products are complete dinner services.

☆ Transkei Hillmond Weavers turn out a highly attractive range of hand-woven mohair products, including wall hangings, curtaining and table cloths.

Worth a mention among Transkei's other, smaller centres, are:

LUSIKISIKI Biggest town in the the Pondoland region, Lusikisiki (the name represents the sound of the wind in the marsh reeds of the area) has a busy main street, a hotel and a pub that is much favoured by treasure-hunters on their way to the shipwrecks of the Wild Coast.

BUTTERWORTH The oldest town, Butterworth began life in 1827 as a Wesleyan mission school, and is now one of the territory's foremost growth points. It boasts some 50 industries, a population of 40 000, a large hospital, the Butterworth campus of the University of Transkei, and a country club.

Nearby are the splendid, 85-m-high Butterworth River Cascades and the even-higher (110-m) Bawa Falls. The latter are also known as the High Executioner (criminals were once hurled to their death from the rim of the falls).

ADVISORY: THE EASTERN CAPE

CLIMATE

The Eastern Cape is in the transitional zone between the 'Mediterranean' winter-rainfall and the subtropical summer-rainfall regions: it becomes warmer, and the summers are wetter, the further north-eastwards one travels. Cold, clear winter days in the north-eastern Cape interior; hotter and drier towards the west.

Port Elizabeth enjoys a daily average 7,5 hours of sunshine throughout the year. Temperatures: average daily maximum January 25,4 °C, July 19,5 °C; minumum January 16,3 °C, July 7,1 °C; extremes 40 °C and -0,3 °C. Rainfall: average monthly January 30 mm, July 51 mm; highest daily recorded 103 mm.

East London temperatures: average daily maximum January 25,2 °C, July 21 °C; minimum January 17,9 °C, July 10,2 °C; extremes 41,3 °C and 2,8 °C. Rainfall: average monthly January 73 mm, July 35 mm; highest daily recorded 152 mm.

Wild Coast temperatures: average daily maximum January 28 °C, July 21 °C; minimum January 17 °C, July 8 °C.

MAIN ATTRACTIONS

Port Elizabeth: □ Incorporates all the amenities of a modern city □ Museums and places of historical interest □ Sun, sea and sand □ The Oceanarium and its famed dolphins □ Sailing and watersports on the blue waters of Algoa Bay □ Fishing and surfing along the coasts to either side □ Steam train trips to the scenically lovely Long Kloof □ Proximity to the Addo Elephant National Park.

Settler Country: □ The charm of Grahamstown □ Historic villages, many of which began life as military garrisons. □ Scenic drives.

East London: □ Similar assets to those of Port Elizabeth, though on a smaller scale □ Broad beaches and, along the shoreline, inviting resorts.
The north-eastern areas: □ Medicinal springs (at Aliwal North) □ Bushman art □ Splendid scenery, delightful little upland villages and clear mountain air in the east.
The Ciskei and Transkei regions: □ Magnificent stretches of coastline □ The Wild Coast Sun pleasure-palace □ Pleasant resort hotels □ Bathing, fishing, hiking, birding.

TRAVEL

Road. Distances from Port Elizabeth in kilometres: Jeffreys Bay 79, Grahamstown 124; Somerset East 152; East London 310; Bloemfontein 680; Cape Town 785; Durban 952; Johannesburg 1 115.

National highways and main roads, in good condition, link Port Elizabeth and East London with all major SA centres; the N2 leads to Cape Town (west) and Durban (north-east); the R32 regional highway links Port Elizabeth with Cradock. Ciskei and Transkei coastal resorts are accessible via subsidiary (gravel) roads leading off the N2. Beware potholes, hairpin bends and stray animals.

Coach travel Transnet operates 37 routes within the region. Luxury travel includes: Leopard Express (Port Elizabeth/Grahamstown); Copper Rose (Port Elizabeth/East London); Whippet Express (Port Elizabeth/Graaff-Reinet); Translux services (Cape Town/Port Elizabeth/Durban); Trans City (Cape Town/Port Elizabeth); Inter Cape (Cape Town/Port Elizabeth). Various coach tours of the region are laid on by Plusbus, Springbok Atlas, Garden Route Tours, Algoa Tours, Tour and Travel. Information: Tel. Port Elizabeth (041) 56-1357/51; 51-2699; 52- 2814; East London (0431) 58-9401; Johannesburg (011) 218-3581; Cape Town (021) 218-3581.

Car hire Major rental companies are well represented in Port Elizabeth, East London, Bisho, Umtata and other eastern Cape centres; consult the Yellow Pages or your hotel reception.

Rail. Port Elizabeth's Apple Express for steam enthusiasts (see page 198). Passenger services link the city with major centres; the P E railway station is at the harbour entrance; passenger services information: Tel. (041) 520-2975. East London: passenger services link the city with major centres; the station is at the corner of Fleet and Station streets; for information telephone (0431) 44-2020.

Air. Daily scheduled flights connect Port Elizabeth and East London with major centres; Port Elizabeth's terminal is in North Union St; Port Elizabeth airport is 10 km from city centre; Tel. (041) 504-4201 for information; reservations (041) 34-4444. Private airlines also operate scheduled services. National Airways Corporation runs charter flights to the region's smaller airfields. East London airport is 12 km from the city centre; the terminal is in Terminus St; information and reservations: Tel. (0431) 46-1400; 44-2535/6.

ACCOMMODATION

Select hotels

The following is a representative but by no means exhaustive list of hotels. Most of those in Ciskei and Transkei do not subscribe to the grading system.

PORT ELIZABETH

Algoa Protea ★★★ Central; just 10 rooms, designer-styled; conference facilities for 120; excellent restaurant. Lutman Street, Port Elizabeth 6001; Tel. (041) 55-1558.

Beach Hotel ★★★ Marine Drive, Humewood (near Oceanarium); 63 rooms; conference facilities for 100. PO Box 319, Port Elizabeth 6000; Tel. (041) 53-2161.

Edward ★★ Adjacent Donkin reserve; 132 rooms; conference facilties for 500; carvery restaurant and 2 coctail bars. PO Box 319, Port Elizabeth 6000; Tel. (041) 56-2056.

Elizabeth Sun ★★★★ On King's Beach; Southern Sun excellence; 210 rooms, 18 suites; conference facilities for 750. PO Box 13100, Humewood 6013; Tel. (041) 52-3720.

Holiday Inn ★★★ In Summerstrand; 230 rooms, 7 suites; conference facilities for 250; superb restaurant. Marine Drive, Summerstrand 6001; Tel. (041) 52-3131.

Humewood Hotel ★★ Beachfront; 69 rooms; à la carte restaurant. PO Box 13023, Port Elizabeth 6013; Tel. (041) 55 8961.

Hunter's Retreat ★★ On the Old Cape Road, 12 km from city; 17 rooms, 2 suites; à la carte restaurant. PO Box 7044, Newton Park 6055; Tel. (041) 30-1244.

Marine Protea ★★★ On the Summerstrand beachfront; 73 rooms; à la carte restaurant, buffet. PO Box 501, Port Elizabeth 6000; Tel. (041) 53-2101.

Walmer Gardens ★★ Garden setting, near airport. 26 rooms; à la carte restaurant, 2 cocktail bars. PO Box 5108, Walmer 6065; Tel. (041) 51-4322.

EAST LONDON

Esplanade ★★ Overlooks beach; 75 rooms; conference facilities for 25. Beachfront, East London 5201; Tel. (0431) 2-2518.

Holiday Inn ★★★ Central; 173 rooms, 2 suites; conference facilities. Cnr John Bailie and Moore streets, East London 5201; Tel. (0431) 2-7260.

Hotel Osner ★★ On beachfront; 98 rooms, 14 suites; conference facilities for 300; à la carte restaurant, 2 cocktail bars. PO Box 334, East London 5200; Tel. (0431) 43-3433.

Kennaway Protea ★★★ On beachfront; 84 rooms, 4 suites; conference facilities for 140; excellent restaurant. PO Box 583, East London 5200; Tel. (0431) 2-5531.

GRAHAMSTOWN

Cathcart Arms ★★ Cape's oldest licensed premises (see page 205); just 14 rooms; conference facilities for 25; à la carte restaurant. PO Box 143, Grahamstown 6140; Tel. (0461) 2-7111.

Graham ★★ Central; 37 rooms; conference facilities for 30; à la carte restaurant. 123 High Street, Grahamstown 6140; Tel. (0461) 2-2324.

Grand ★★ Early settler's home; in business for a century (see page 205); 50 rooms; conference facilities for 50; 2 restaurants. PO Box 23, Grahamstown 6140; Tel. (0461) 2-7012.

Settlers Inn ★★ Close to Monument; 52 rooms; conference facilities for 50; à la carte restaurant. PO Box 219, Grahamstown 6140; Tel. (0461) 2-7313.

FORT BEAUFORT

Savoy ★★ 21 rooms; conference facilities for 30; swimming pool; à la carte restaurant, 2 bars. PO Box 46, Fort Beaufort 5720; Tel. (0435) 3-1146.

Yellowwoods ★★ Set in a lovely green parkland estate; just 7 rooms; conference facilities for 20. PO Box 432, Fort Beaufort 5720; Tel. (04662) 1131.

CRADOCK

New Masonic ★★ 26 rooms; conference facilities for 100; à la carte restaurant, beergarten. PO Box 44, Cradock 5880; Tel. (0481) 3115.

ALIWAL NORTH

Juana Maria Hotel ★★ 17 rooms; conference facilities. PO Box 34, Aliwal North 5530; Tel. (0551) 2475/3092.

Umtali Motel ★★ 33 rooms; PO Box 102, Aliwal North 5530; Tel. (0551) 2400.

QUEENSTOWN

Hexagon Hotel ★★ Central; 50 rooms; conference facilities for 200; à la carte restaurant. PO Box 116, Queenstown 5320; Tel. (0451) 3015.

J'Eantel Hotel ★★ 25 rcoms; conference facilities for 50; swimming pool; à la carte restaurant. PO Box 116, Queenstown 5320; Tel. (0451) 3016.

EASTERN CAPE COAST

Glengariff, Gonubie ★ 27 km north-east of East London; 18 rooms; traditional Cape restaurant. PO Box 538, Gonubie 5256; Tel. (0431) 38-3006.

Hotel Victoria, Port Alfred ★★ 24 rooms; à la carte and table d'hôte; PO Box 2, Port Alfred 6170; Tel. (0464) 4-1133/4.

Kidd's Beach Hotel ★ South-west of East London; 11 rooms. Main Road, Kidd's Beach 5264; Tel. (0432) 81-1715/81-1603.

Kowie Grand ★★ 24 rooms; conference facilities for 35; PO Box 1, Kowie West 6171; Tel. (0464) 4-1150/1.

St Francis Protea ★★ 29 rooms; conference facilities for 40; continental restaurant. PO Box 152, St Francis Bay 6312; Tel. (04231) 94-0304.

Savoy Hotel, Jeffreys Bay ★★ 37 rooms; PO Box 36, Jeffreys Bay 6330; Tel. (0423) 93-1106.

EASTERN CAPE: INLAND RURAL

Eagle's Ridge Forest Resort, Stutterheim ★ In Amatola Mountains; 24 rooms; conference facilities for 30; table d'hôte menu. PO Box 127, Stutterheim 4930; Tel. (0436) 3-1200.

Hogsback Inn ★ In business since the 1850s; 28 rooms; conference facilities for 55; table d'hôte menu. Main Road, Hogsback 5312; Tel. (0020), and ask for Hogsback 6.

Hogsback Mountain Lodge (Arminel) ★ 19 rooms; swimming pool. PO Box 67, Hogsback 5312; Tel. (0020), and ask for Hogsback 5.

King's Lodge, Hogsback ★ Forest setting; 24 rooms; conference facilities for 50; table d'hôte menu. PO Hogsback 5312; Tel. (0020), and ask for Hogsback 24.

Mountain Shadows, Elliot ★ 17 rooms; à la carte restaurant. PO Box 136, Elliot 5460; Tel. (0020), and ask for Barkly Pass 3.

Pig and Whistle, Bathurst ★ Built in the 1830s (see page 205); 10 rooms, 4 en-suite. PO Box 123, Bathurst 6166; Tel. (0464) 25-0673.

Rhodes Hotel ★ The hotel is a restored Victorian hostelry; 12 rooms; traditional Cape restaurant. PO Box 21, Rhodes 5582; Tel. (04542), and ask for Rhodes 21.

CISKEI

Amatola Sun, Bisho, Standard Southern Sun professionalism; 59 rooms, 2 suites; several restaurants and cocktail bars, casino, live entertainment. PO Box 1274, King William's Town 5600; Tel. (0401) 9-1111.

Fish River Sun, ★★★★★ (see page 210) 120 rooms; conference facilities for 200; casino, cinema, 18-hole golf course, full range of sporting and recreational activities. PO Box 323, Port Alfred 6170; Tel. (0403) 61-2101.

King William's Town Protea, ★★ Market square, 19 rooms, 2 suites. PO Box 84, King William's Town 5600; Tel. (0433) 2-1440.

Mpekweni Marine Resort, (see page 210) overlooking Mpekweni lagoon, near Fish River Sun. 100 rooms, 1 suite; à la carte restaurant (seafood specialities); conference facilities. PO Box 2060, Port Alfred 6170; Tel. (0403) 61-3126 ext 113.

TRANSKEI

Cape Hermes Hotel, Port St Johns, at mouth of Mzimvubu River; 58 rooms; conference facilities for 100. PO Box 10, Port St Johns, Transkei; Tel. (04752) 35.

Hole in the Wall Hotel and Holiday Village, near Coffee Bay (see page 221). 22 en-suite rooms, several family chalets and thatched cottages. PO Box 54, Umtata, Transkei; Tel. (031) 25-8263 or (0431) 5-8003.

Kob Inn, Qolora Mouth, on coast 35 km from Willowvale; 33 rooms; conference facilities for 30; private airstrip; table d'hôte restaurant. PO Box 20, Willowvale, Transkei; Tel. (0474) 4421.

Mazeppa Bay Hotel, 41 rooms; conference facilities for 40; table d'hôte (seafood buffet Friday and Saturday). Private Bag 3014, Butterworth, Transkei; Tel. (0474) 3278.

Ocean View, Coffee Bay, 34 rooms. PO Coffee Bay, Transkei; Tel (04732) ask for 50.

Seagulls Beach Hotel, 40 en-suite double rooms; table d'hôte restaurant, bar; pool, tennis courts, horse-riding; private airstrip. PO Box 436, Butterworth, Transkei; Tel. (04341) 3287.

The Haven, Cwebe nature reserve, thatched bungalows with en-suite bathrooms; pool, tennis courts, golf course, shop. Private Bag X5028, Umtata, Transkei; Tel. (0471) 2-5344.

Trennery's Hotel, Qolora Mouth, 65 rooms; 11-hole golf course; table d'hôte restaurant. Private Bag 3011, Butterworth, Transkei; Tel : (04341) 3293.

Umtata Holiday Inn, 113 rooms, 4 suites; golf, bowls, tennis, swimming pool. PO Box 334, Umtata, Transkei; Tel. (0471) 2-2181.

Wavecrest Hotel, Nxaxo river-mouth, island-style bungalows (en-suite bathrooms) overlook river and sea; squash court, cocktail bar, airstrip. PO Box 81, Butterworth, Transkei; Tel. (04341) 3273.

Wild Coast Sun, Mzamba, superb hotel-casino complex (see page 219); 399 rooms; extensive con-

The Wild Coast Sun's 18-hole course is one of the country's most attractive

ference facilities; 3 restaurants, theatre, cinema, gaming rooms, health centre, bank, shops. PO Box 23, Port Edward 4295; Tel. (0471) 512/519.

Ungraded accommodation

Bed and Breakfast: Port Elizabeth/Eastern Cape, Tel. (041) 55-3080. East London/Border, Tel. (0431) 5-2192.

Port Elizabeth: Richley House: Family accommodation, Tel. (041) 33-7995. Bliss Apartments, Marine Drive, Tel. (041) 53-2171/4. Langerry Apartments, Beach Rd, Tel.(041) 55-2654.

East London: Accommodation Agency, Box 64, East London 5200, Tel. (0431) 43-7933. Airport Lodge, New Settlers Way, Tel. (0431) 46-2201. Craighall Guest House, 18 Currie Street, Tel. (0431) 2-1580. Nordic Guest House, 28 Currie Street, Tel. (0431) 2-2159. Salisbury House, 17 Rhodes St, Tel. (0431) 2-6520.

Grahamstown: Contact the Publicity Association (see page 229) for an extensive list.

Caravan/camping and self-catering accommodation

Addo Elephant National Park, Bookings: National Parks Board, PO Box 787, Pretoria 0001, Tel. (012) 343-1991.

Aston Bay, Caravan Park, PO Box 50, Jeffreys Bay 6330, Tel. (04231) 92-0202.

Bathurst, Newman Walker Timm caravan park, PO Box 20, Kowie West 6171, Tel. (0464) 4-1651.

Cape St Francis, caravan park, also has bungalows. Tel. (04231) 94-0420.

Cathcart, Moth caravan park, PO Box 35, Cathcart 5310, Tel. (04562) 22.

Cradock, Municipal caravan park, PO Box 24, Cradock 5880, Tel. (0481) 71-1007.

East London and district, Club Areena Riverside Resort. 26 km from city on Kwelega tidal river; Tel. (0431) 95-1459. Pirate's Creek Holiday Resort, at Quinera Lagoon 10 km north of city. Tel (0431) 47-1160. Quinera Lagoon Holiday Resort, Tel. (0431) 38-1462. On lagoon; excellent site for bird-watching. Lagoon Valley, Tel. (0431) 46-1080. Ocean View Guest Farm and Caravan Park, Tel (04372) 2603; 65 km from city. Cefani Mouth Holiday Resort, Tel. (0431) 38-5027. Gonubie Caravan Park, Tel. (0431) 40-2021.

Fort Beaufort: Municipal caravan park, PO Box 36, Fort Beaufort 5720, Tel. (0435) 3-1136.

Grahamstown, Municipal caravan park, Tel (0461) 2-9112 ext. 256. Self-catering accommodation as well as caravan stands.

Jeffreys Bay, Municipal caravan park, PO Box 21, Jeffreys Bay 6330, Tel. (04231) 3-1111.

Kei Mouth, Municipal caravan park, Tel. (043272)/ (0020), and ask for Kei Mouth 4. Situated on the Transkei border.

Kenton-on-Sea, Cannon Rocks caravan park (also has caravans for hire), Tel. (0464) 81208; 15 km from sea.

Kidd's Beach, Aqualea caravan park, PO Box 571, East London 5200, Tel. (04323) 811858.

King William's Town, Municipal caravan park, PO Box 33, King William's Town 5600, Tel. (0433) 2-3160.

Port Alfred, The Halyards, Royal Alfred Marina, Port Alfred: luxury accommodation; restaurants, shops, watersports. Contact the Royal Alfred Marina Club Hotel, PO Box 208, Port Alfred 6170; Tel. (0464) 4-2410. Riverside caravan park, Tel. (0464) 4-2230. On banks of Kowie River; caravan/camping and self-catering accommodation. Medolino caravan park, Tel. (0464) 4-1651.

Port Elizabeth, Algoa RSC resorts, PO Box 13368, Humewood 6013, Tel. (041) 74-1884. Humewood Recreation Club, PO Box 402, Port Elizabeth 6000, Tel. (041) 55-4013. Sea Acres Holiday Resort, Tel. (041) 53-3095; (caravan/camping and self-catering accommodation). Willow Grove, Tel. (041) 36-1697. Willows, Tel. (041) 36-1717/34, or write to Algoa RSC, PO Box 13368, Humewood 6013. Van Stadens River Mouth, Tel. (0422) 5990.

Queenstown, Municipal caravan park, PO Box 122, Queenstown 5320, Tel. (0451) 3131.

Somerset East, Linci caravan park, PO Box 307, Somerset East 5850, Tel. (0424) 3-1376.

Uitenhage, Springs Pleasure Resort, 6 km from Uitenhage (rondavels, chalets, caravan park), Tel. (0422) 966-1161.

TRANSKEI

Port St Johns, First Beach Holiday Camp, PO Box 2, Port St Johns, Tel. (04752) 75. Second Beach Holiday Camp, P O Box 18, Port St Johns, Tel. (04752) 61.

SELECT RESTAURANTS

PORT ELIZABETH

The Bell, Beach Hotel, Marine Drive, Tel. 53-2161. Fine all-round menu, classic cuisine; favoured by businessmen.

Bella Napoli, Hartman St, Tel. 55-3819. Unpretentious, very good Italian fare; Sunday buffet lunches are rather special. Take your own wine.

Boodles, Holiday Inn, Tel 53-3131. Sophisticated; small but beautifully chosen menu; seafood something of a speciality.

The Coachman, Lawrence St, Tel. 52-2511. Excellent steakhouse, family-run. Try the gargantuan 'prime cut' if you're really hungry.

El Cid, a brace of restaurants in Parliament St, Tel. 55-5664. Spanish-type steakhouse and Seafood Boulevard respectively. Imaginative menus and excellent service.

It's Country, Evatt St, Tel. 52-3835. Friendly and unpretentious; all-purpose menu; open early to late. Take your own wine.

La Fontaine, Rink St, Tel. 55-9029. Elegant Italian cuisine and setting.

La Vigie, Mount Rd, Tel. 54-4066. Charmingly small restaurant, varied menu, classic cuisine.

Margot's, Evatt St, Tel. 52-3352. French, and quite superb.

Nelson's Arm, Trinder Square, Tel. 55-9049. Early naval-wardroom décor, seafood specialities.

Oasis, Swartkops Riviera Hotel, Grahamstown Rd, Tel. 66-7882. Fine seafood and pasta dishes.

Old Austria, Uitenhage Rd, Tel. 54-1204. Continental and charming.

Ranch House of Steaks, Russell and Rose streets, Tel. 55-9684. What its name suggests: splendid meat dishes, served in attractive surrounds.

Rumours, Burgess and Zareba streets, Tel. 33-8216. Old-style hospitality; cosy atmosphere; imaginative menu.

Sabatinos, Westbourne Rd, Tel. 33-1707. Italian, informal, excellent.

Saucy Mermaid, Algoa Protea Hotel, Union St, Tel. 55-1558. Smallish but careful menu, pleasant décor.

Sir Rufane Donkin Rooms, George St, Tel. 55-5534. Homely menu, deliciously prepared food.

Tivoli, Pamela Arcade, 2nd Avenue, Tel. 35-2096. Italian, and very good. Take your own wine.

For late-night dining and entertainment, try Limelight Supper Club and Discothèque, The Corner House, Evatt Street, Tel. 56-2686.

EAST LONDON

Collette, Kennaway Protea Hotel, Tel. 2-5531. Extensive menu; beautifully restful décor.

Guido's, of which there are two establishments: in Pearce St (take your own wine) Tel. 5-8103 and on Major Square, Beacon Bay Tel. 47-3995. Both serve marvellous Italian food in an exceptionally friendly atmosphere.

Le petit, Beach Rd, Nahoon, Tel. 35-3685. Emphasis is on French-Swiss cuisine; sophisticated; dancing as well as dining.

USEFUL ADDRESSES AND TELEPHONE NUMBERS

Adelaide Municipality, Tel (04662) ask for 34.

Aliwal North Information Office, Public Library, Somerset Street, Aliwal North 5530; Tel. (0551) 2362.

Automobile Association, Port Elizabeth, AA House, Granville Rd (tourist information) (041) 34-1313 (breakdown services) (041) 34-1313 (o/h) 34-1424 (a/h).

Bathurst Municipality, PO Box 128, Bathurst 6166; Tel. (0464) 25-0639.

Burgersdorp Municipality, PO Box 13, Burgersdorp 5520; Tel. (0553) 3-1753.

Ciskei Department of Tourism and Aviation, Private Bag X1006, Bisho, Ciskei; Tel. (0401) 9-1131/2/3.

Ciskei Tourism Board, PO Box 56, Bisho, Ciskei; Tel. (0401) 9-2171.

Cradock Municipality, PO Box 24, Cradock 5880; Tel. (0481) 2108.

Emergency numbers, Port Elizabeth code (041): *Ambulance* 34-2233. *Hospital* Provincial: 33-7811. Livingstone: 405-9111. Dora Nginza 42-1061. *Fire brigade* Municipal: 55-1555. Regional Services Council 31-1177, (0422) 2-2222. *Police headquarters* 33-8281, 33-5811. *Police flying squad* 10-111. *After-hours pharmacy* 13 Lower Mount Rd, 54-3838. Cape Rd Newton Park, 31-3240. *Lifeline* 52-3456, 55-8565, 36-1258. *Sea rescue* 520-2716.

Fort Beaufort Municipality, Tel. (0435) 3-1136.

Grahamstown Publicity Association, Church Square, Grahamstown 6140; Tel. (0461) 2-3241.

Greater East London Publicity Association, Old Library Building, Argyle Street; PO Box 533, East London 5200; Tel. (0431) 2-6015.

Jeffreys Bay Municipality, Da Gama Street, PO Box 21, Jeffreys Bay 6630; Tel. (0423) 93-1111.

Port Alfred Publicity Association, PO Box 63, Port Alfred 6170; Tel. (0464) 4-1235.

Port Elizabeth Publicity Association, Market Square, Port Elizabeth 6000; Tel. (041) 52-1315.

Queenstown Municipality, PO Box 22, Queenstown 5320; Tel. (0451) 3131.

Satour (South African Tourism Board), Port Elizabeth: 21-23 Donkin Street; PO Box 1161, Port Elizabeth 6000; Tel. (041) 55-7731. East London: Fourth Floor, NBS Building, Terminus Street, PO Box 1794, East London 5200; Tel. (0431) 43-5571.

Somerset East Municipality, PO Box 21, Somerset East 5850; Tel. (0424) 3-1333.

Stutterheim Municipality, Tel. (0436) 3-1100.

Theatre and other bookings, Port Elizabeth. Computicket Information Kiosk, Greenacres Centre: Tel. (041) 34-4550/1.

Transkei Department of Agriculture and Forestry, Private Bag 5002, Umtata, Transkei; Tel. (0471) 2-4322/24-9309.

Transkei Department of Commerce, Industry and Tourism, Private Bag X5029, Umtata, Transkei; Tel. (0471) 2-6685.

Transkei Central Reservations, Private Bag X5028, Umtata, Transkei; Tel. (0471) 2-5344/5/6.

Uitenhage Municipality, Town Hall; PO Box 45, Uitenhage 5850; Tel. (0422) 992-6011.

ANNUAL EVENTS

Grahamstown. National Festival of the Arts; National Schools English Festival: June/July.

East London. Mayfair: April/May □ East London Expo; Pineapple Beauty Queen Contest: September □ Oktoberfest: October □ Marina Rush; Oxford Street Carnival; Potjiekos Competition: December.

Port Alfred. Deepsea Angling Competition: Easter and Christmas □ Annual Waterskiing Championships: December.

Port Elizabeth. Picardi Summer Horse Show: January □ Eastern Province Angling Week; Port Elizabeth Shakespearean Festival: February □ Herald Cycle Tour: March □ Agricultural, Commercial and Industrial Show; Rose Exhibition (Walmer): April □ Index Industrial Exhibition: April/May □ Algoa Bay Week; Bon Appetit Food Fair; Habitat Home Exhibition: May □ Hobbies Fair; Oratorio Festival: June □ Great Train Race (runners compete against the Apple Express); Orchid Show; Festival of the Sea (Lions St Croix); Sundays River Valley Citrus Carnival; Hang Ten Longboard Surfing Competition: September □ Harbour Festival; Texan Paddle Ski Marathon, Port Elizabeth-East London: December.

THE SOUTHERN SEABOARD AND THE LITTLE KAROO

The Cape Fold Mountains are a series of sandstone formations that stretch along the beautiful southern Cape coast, from an area some way east of Port Elizabeth to False Bay's Cape Hangklip, near Cape Town in the west (and beyond: the series includes the Cederberg, Olifants River and Drakenstein ranges: see page 327). At no point do the heights quite reach the shoreline: uplands and sea are for the most part separated by a narrow, lushly fertile plain hugely rich in plant species.

Most prominent of southernmost mountains are the Outeniqua range and its extension, the Tsitsikamma, thickly forested hills blessed with generous rains and the many perennial streams they create. To the west, running 50 km from the Worcester area, past the historic town of Swellendam – and dominating a loosely defined region known as the Overberg – is the Langeberg range.

To the north is the Swartberg, an imposing 800-km-long chain of mountains lying between the Great and Little Karoos.

The coast and its immediate hinterland – especially the 230 lovely kilometres known as the Garden Route – are prime holiday areas.

THE GARDEN ROUTE

This scenically stunning segment of the coastal belt extends from Storms River to Mossel Bay. On one side is the Indian Ocean, its shores a delightful compound of rocky cliff, cove, broad embayment and beach, navigable river estuary, lagoon and lake; on the other are the wooded slopes of the Tsitsikamma and Outeniqua mountains; between the two is the coastal terrace, the aptly named 'garden' of which a scholarly French traveller of the 1780s wrote: 'The flowers that grow there in millions, the mixture of pleasant scents which arise from them, the pure and fresh air one breathes there, all make one stop and think Nature has made an enchanted abode of this beautiful place.'

The Wilderness shoreline. The coastal belt is famed for its entrancing Garden Route, and for the splendour of the backing mountains.

François le Vaillant's words are as descriptive today as they were two centuries ago.

For the modern visitor, the attractions are many, various and mostly gentle. There's the charm of the green and pleasant countryside of course; and the kindly climate: plenty of sunshine; rains that fall throughout the year (and, happily, mostly at night-time); modest extremes of heat and cold. There are excellent hotels, resorts, caravan and camping grounds; attractive marinas; good restaurants. The clear blue waters of the ocean are warm in summer, and they invite the bather and surfer, the sailor, the rock angler and the deep-sea fisherman. Marine life is prolific and brilliantly coloured.

Inland there are forests, deep valleys, spectacular mountain passes, rivers, waterfalls and secluded, ever-moist kloofs to explore. Wild flowers are everywhere, among them arum and watsonia, iris and, in places, the exquisite George lily.

The Tsitsikamma area

The name is derived from the Khoikhoi (Hottentot) word for the sound of running water, and it's apt enough: the region, extending across the 160 km of coastal countryside between Humansdorp and Knysna, is notable for its high rainfall and for the numerous perennial streams that tumble down the slopes of the Tsitsikamma Mountains. The latter are an eastward extension of the Outeniqua range, with their highest point 1 677 m above sea level.

STORMS RIVER This rises in these mountains, and flows through the lovely indigenous and exotic forests of the uplands to reach the sea at the eastern end of the Tsitsikamma National Park (see page 232). Motorists starting off on (or, if they're travelling in the reverse direction, ending their journey along) the Garden Route cross the river's precipitous gorge by means of the 192-m-long Paul Sauer bridge. The bridge, a dizzy 139 m high, is an impressive piece of civil engineering; photographs of its construction can be seen in the nearby restaurant.

TSITSIKAMMA STATE FOREST RESERVE This 500-ha patch of upland was proclaimed to preserve a remnant of the once-vast natural forests of the southern seaboard: dense woodlands of yellowwood and stinkwood, white alder, candlewood, ironwood, assegai and other handsome tree species. The giants among them are the Outeniqua yellowwoods, growing to 50 m and more in height (the famed 'Big Tree' is estimated to be more than 800 years old). Among the rather secretive forest residents are bushbuck and duiker, bushpig, baboon and some brilliantly colourful birds, including the narina trogon and the Knysna lourie. Accommodation and amenities: there's a caravan/camping ground, shop, restaurant and petrol filling station at Storms River; good hotels in the general vicinity. Information: The Regional Director, Tsitsikamma Forest Region, Private Bag X537, Humansdorp 6300; Tel. (04231) 5-1180.

TSITSIKAMMA NATIONAL PARK This lovely park comprises an 80 km strip of narrow coastal plateau extending from the Groot River near Humansdorp to a point near the Keurbooms River and embracing the sea for a distance of 5 km from the rocky shoreline. The waters of the many rivers and streams that enter the ocean within the park are brown (from the slow decay of vegetation); the land area is richly endowed with a plant life that includes fynbos (heath), forest, ferns, wild orchids and a fine array of lilies; among the land animals are the Cape clawless otter, baboon, bushbuck, blue duiker, Cape grysbok. About 280 bird species have been recorded in the area. The rock pools teem with marine life – anemones, sponges, starfish – and whales and dolphins can often be seen sporting beyond the breakers.

Accommodation consists of fully equipped cottages, 'oceanettes' and a pleasant caravan/camping ground at Storms River Mouth; caravan-camping ground at Nature's Valley. Information and bookings: National Parks Board (see Advisory, page 253).

Within the coastal park there are underwater trails for swimmers and divers (only qualified scuba divers may do the trail as such but snorkellers are always welcome); short land trails, and 30 km of alternative pathways in the De Vasselot area.

The park is also traversed by the:

OTTER TRAIL The country's first organized hiking route and still a great favourite among walking enthusiasts, this trail leads from Storms River Mouth through 41 km of unsurpassed coastal scenery to the Groot River estuary at Nature's Valley; en route there are lovely patches of natural forest, streams and waterfalls and, of course, the ocean. Longest day's walk is 14 km; there is time to amble, study the flora and birdlife, take a dip in the sea, snorkel in the tidal pools. Information and bookings: National Parks Board (see Advisory, page 253).

NATURE'S VALLEY A small village and reserve at the bottom of the Groot River Pass (from the top of which there are stunning views of the valley), in a charming setting of mountain, forest, lagoon and sea. The valley is surrounded on three sides by the Tsitsikamma National Park and provides a splendid place for rambling, walking (short routes of up to 4 km have been established) and bird-watching (species such as Cape gannet, fish eagle, giant kingfisher, black oystercatcher among many others). There's a caravan/camping ground within the park.

The Plettenberg Bay Area

The town of Plettenberg Bay is probably the most fashionable of the coastal resort centres. It's a charming little place just to the west of Nature's Valley, modern and sophisticated for the most part though it does have its history: the bay was known to European seafarers from the earliest days of maritime exploration (and given several names before Cape governor Joachim van Plettenberg visited the area in 1778). Its first 'settlers' were sailors from the *Sao Gonçalo*, which came to grief off the coast in 1630, and from which some fine Ming pottery was recovered. The pieces, now known as the Jerling Collection, are on display in the municipal buildings.

The bay and its surrounds are spectacularly beautiful; the area is blessed with 320 days of virtually uninterrupted sunshine each year; there are three superb beaches in the vicinity; Beacon Island (linked to the shore by a causeway) supports a fine hotel and time-share complex; 'Plett time' gives visitors an extra hour of daylight from December to April to enjoy the amenities, which include golf, bowls, tennis, horse-riding, angling (there's a thriving local club; Tel. (04457) 3-1325), scuba diving (Tel. (04457) 3-1120); boating (the World Hobie Championships are held off Central Beach) and water-skiing (on the Keurbooms River).

ROBBERG NATURE RESERVE This reserve extends over a red-sandstone promontory that juts 4 km into the Indian Ocean to the southwest of town. The headland ends in a point called Cape Seal; to the north there are almost-sheer cliffs; the southern slopes are gentler. White-breasted cormorants, southern black-backed gulls and black oystercatchers breed in the area, and the sea around is a marine reserve. Signs of primitive Khoikhoi 'Strandloper' habitation can be seen in the Nelson Bay cave. A marina for yachts and deep-sea fishing boats is being developed nearby.

KEURBOOMS RIVER NATURE RESERVE, situated some 8 km north-east of Plettenberg Bay, is a pleasant 760-ha expanse of river-bank and forest adjoining the larger (3 500 ha) Whiskey Creek reserve. Attractions include some lovely rambles; fishing (the Plettenberg Bay Angling Club is based here) and bird-watching (among the recorded species are African finfoot and breeding pairs of Caspian terns). The Keurbooms River Resort offers a hotel, fully equipped family cottages, a caravan/camping park and an attractive stretch of beach.

RECOMMENDED PICNIC SPOTS The beautifully forested Kranshoek area near Harkerville, 12 km from Plettenberg Bay (cliff-top views, nature walks), and, secondly, the Garden of Eden, 14 km from Plettenberg Bay on the Knysna road. Many of the Garden's splendid trees are labelled.

The Knysna area

Also a most attractive and highly popular resort town, but bigger than Plettenberg Bay (it has a population of around 40 000). Knysna's motto is 'This fair land is the gift of God', a fitting testament to the beauty of lagoon, forest and coastal countryside. The local (independent) Mitchell's brewery, which welcomes visitors, produces superb draught ale. Knysna is also famed for its honey, cheese, ham (from Dormehl Farm), trout, oysters (see Lagoon, below) and furniture (excellent pieces, made from local indigenous timber; the fashionable Furni-

ture Manufacturers Auction is held, in association with the Nederburg wine estate, each December). The town's station is one of the terminals of the Outeniqua 'Choo-tjoe' steam train service (see under George, page 235).

Knysna was home from 1803 until his death in 1839 of the legendary George Rex, said to be the son of England's King George III. Rex lived – with two common-law wives (though not concurrently) – the life of a country squire, lavishly entertaining a string of distinguished visitors on his extensive estate.

Rex's property now forms part of the Knysna National Lake Area that encompasses the town, the lagoon, its two distinctive rocky promontories and its backing of evergreen forest. Though it isn't a proclaimed reserve in the orthodox sense of the term, the area is monitored by the National Parks Board, who ensure that an intelligent balance is maintained between conservation and tourist development.

KNYSNA LAGOON The sea entrance to this magnificent 17-km-long expanse of water is guarded by two steep sandstone cliffs known as 'The Heads', the eastern one of which affords splendid views of Knysna and Leisure Island. The western one accommodates the Featherbed Bay private nature reserve, which is open to the public (approachable only by boat; the ferry service is free; there are guided nature trails along the lovely Bushbuck walk, and gourmet meals – oysters and champagne breakfasts, for example – in the forest restaurant; Tel. (0445) 2-1233).

The lagoon is a popular arena for sailing, boating (cabin cruisers may be hired), canoeing, water-skiing and fishing. It's also one of nature's treasure-houses, noted for its superb oysters (the hatchery supplies restaurants throughout the country), for the variety of its fish, birds, crabs, prawns, for its 'pansy shells', and for the rare sea-horse *Hippocampus capensis*.

Two local boating companies offer a holiday with a difference: you live aboard one of their cabin cruisers (the crafts sleep between two and eight people); cruise wherever the fancy takes you; cook your meals in the galley or tie up for a braai at one of the lagoon's many secluded spots. The *John Benn* floating entertainment centre – an attractive, locally-built 20 ton boat – departs from the jetty each morning (wining, dining, sightseeing).

Plettenberg Bay's distinctive Beacon Island (see page 251)

KNYSNA FOREST When combined with the Tsitsikamma, this forms the largest expanse of indigenous high forest in South Africa, a 36 400-ha home to the stately yellowwood and ironwood, the kammasie (Knysna boxwood), the stinkwood, the white alder and the blackwood. In its deep-green depths live the last, tiny and almost certainly doomed remnant of the once-great herds of Cape bush elephant.

Forest hikes include the Elephant Walk, a six-hour trek (there are shorter alternative rambles) that starts from the Diepwalle forestry station, just over a kilometre away from which is King Edward's Tree, a yellowwood whose circumference measures an impressive 7 m.

MILLWOOD Site of South Africa's first gold mine, situated in the heart of the Goudveld state forest some 25 km north-west of Knysna. There are some most inviting walks and picnic spots among the trees; a yellowwood house built at the original diggings has been re-erected in Knysna, where it serves as a museum (local history; George Rex memorabilia).

The Royal Hotel is rather special. Its original licensee, Master-Mariner Thomas Horn, settled in Knysna in 1847, and during the next century and more the establishment played caring host to an unusually distinguished clientele (early guests included Prince Alfred; later ones George Bernard Shaw, who spent some weeks here writing his play 'A Black Girl in Search of God').

YSTERNEK NATURE RESERVE covers about 1 200 ha of fynbos and natural forest some 25 km north of Knysna. There are several rare species among the flora; the birdlife is interesting; the reserves' mammals (leopard, bushbuck, bushpig) tend to be elusive; the views from the observation point are splendid.

OTHER ATTRACTIONS in this generally spectacular area include:
☆ Bracken Hill Falls, on the Noetzie River 10 km from Knysna (forest, waterfall, picnic spots).
☆ Brenton-on-Sea: a resort village with an interesting church, a good hotel (see Advisory, page 251), and some fine views of Knysna lagoon along the way.
☆ Noetzie: an expansive beach east of Knysna (to get there, you'll either have to walk or take a four-wheel-drive vehicle).

Wilderness

This enchanting resort is set around a lagoon at the mouth of the Touw River, 40 km west of Knysna and the first in a chain of lakes that lie between the two towns. Again, the area falls under the auspices of the National Parks Board, which helps co-ordinate development.

Oddly enough, although the Wilderness lakes are very close together they were not all formed by the same process. Swartvlei is really a drowned river-valley originally filled by the rising seas of a post ice-age era; Rondvlei is known as a 'deflation basin', created by the scouring action of wind and later filled with water; Langvlei, like Rondvlei, has no direct connection with rivers – it's a low-lying area drowned by rising water levels. Groenvlei, although separated from the sea by just a single tier of dunes, is a freshwater lake. Other largish expanses of water are Island Lake (Eilandvlei) and the Serpentine. The lakes in their present form are barely 2 000 years old; the backing dune system to the north is a great deal older, established about three million years ago when the coastline between Wilderness and the Goukamma River was a large and fairly shallow bay.

A variety of aquatic plants and the sedge and reedbeds provide food and shelter for fish, and for about 200 bird species, including some 80 types of waterfowl. There is a bird-watching hide. Mammals include bushbuck, common duiker, Cape grysbok, the golden mole and the Cape clawless otter.

The Wilderness area has excellent tourist facilities, among them some good hotels (one of which is quite outstanding: see Advisory, page 251), Parks Board chalets, caravan/camping sites. Swartvlei and Eilandvlei are favoured by water-sportsmen, the entire region by hikers and nature-lovers.

GOUKAMMA NATURE RESERVE This is a 2 230-ha area east of Wilderness that takes in Groenvlei and the lower reaches of the Goukamma River, its estuary, and the rocks, dunes and beaches along 14 km of coastline. The offshore marine reserve protects most species, but one may fish from the sands. Among the residents are bontebok, common and blue duiker, Cape grysbok, vervet monkey and around 210 bird species, including the African finfoot (this is the western limit of its range). There are 35 km of pathways; picnic and barbecue sites around the estuary. Canoeing, boating and boardsailing are among the popular watersports.

BUFFELS BAY One of the more inviting holiday spots; a magnificent beach stretches from the bay eastwards to Brenton-on-Sea.

SEDGEFIELD Another favourite among vacationers, this charming village is set on the Swartvlei lagoon.

George

A largish, most pleasant town at the foot of the high Outeniqua Mountains, named after England's King George III and distinguished by its broad, oak-lined streets. The general area is as attractive now as it was in the 1780s, when

The Outeniqua Choo-Tjoe on its way from Knysna to George

the traveller François le Vaillant (see also page 231) recalled that 'here we were privileged to see the most beautiful land in the universe. In the distance we spied the mountain range covered in proud forests, that had cut off our horizon .... Below us lay the extensive valley, decorated by shapely hills alternating with countless undulating forms down to the sea'.

The town is the Garden Route's principal urban centre, a fast-developing place of some 75 000 people; the surrounding countryside is devoted to general farming, forestry and the cultivation of hops, used in the brewing of beer (this is the world's southernmost, and technically most advanced, hop-growing area).

George is linked to Knysna by the main Garden Route highway; by the Old Passes Road, which runs through an enchanting countryside of fern forest and woodland (fine views *en route*: on one side is the 'Map of Africa'; on the other the blue Indian Ocean); and by the:

OUTENIQUA CHOO-TJOE This old (Class 24) narrow-gauge steam train will take you on a memorable day-trip. Essentially a working freight train, its starts its journey from George at 08h10 and puffs into Knysna at 11h30, giving you time to browse around briefly and perhaps have a pub lunch before starting the return trip at 12h55. Tickets may be bought at the George railway station.

GEORGE MUSEUM Housed in the Old Drostdy (magistrate's court and residence, established in 1813), this museum is noted for its fine array of antique musical instruments (it boasts the country's largest collection of early gramophones). Also on display are exhibits relating to local history and to the timber industry. Open Monday to Saturday.

CHURCHES George's St Mark's, consecrated by the distinguished Bishop Gray in 1850, is South Africa's smallest cathedral (it also has lovely stained-glass windows); the Dutch Reformed church, completed in 1842, has a fine stinkwood pulpit and yellowwood pillars, ceiling and dome; St Peter and St Paul (1843) is the country's oldest Roman Catholic church.

THE CROCODILE PARK Situated 2 km from town centre; visitors are conducted on tours; open daily.

RECREATION Outeniqua Park is the town's main sporting venue. The Garden Route dam, 2 km away, is worth a visit for its beautiful mountain and forest setting. Visitors are welcomed by the local 18-hole golf course; Tel. (0441) 6160, and bowling club; Tel. (0441) 74-3183. Witfontein, just outside town, is the starting point of the renowned Outeniqua trail, a 140 km, 8 day, rather strenuous hike, initially through fynbos country and then through forests (optional walks, shorter and circular, have been established *en route*). The pleasant Groenweide nature trail meanders around the George and Wilderness areas.

COASTAL RESORTS Those near George (the town is 8 km from the nearest shore) include Herold's Bay, attractively set in a sheltered cove (tidal pool, good fishing, safe bathing; surfing prohibited during the December holiday period); and, a little farther west, Glentana.

The Mossel Bay area

The bay, for centuries home to the less-advanced Khoikhoi 'Strandlopers' (their staple diet comprised the mussels after which the place was eventually named) was known to the earliest of the white seafarers. In 1501 the Portuguese admiral Joao da Nova camped out on the shores, staying long enough to construct a small chapel, the first European-type stone building erected in South Africa (nothing remains of the edifice). Bartolomeu Dias, Vasco da Gama and other navigators replenished their freshwater supplies from the perennial spring. In 1500 one of the Portuguese captains placed his report in the trunk of a large milkwood tree, for collection by the next fleet that passed by; other sailors got into the habit of using the tree for mail delivery, so establishing the country's first 'post office'.

Mossel Bay is a fairly large town: the 1985 census pegged its population at a modest 37 000, but with the later discovery and current exploitation of offshore oil deposits, the numbers have increased quite dramatically, threatening to transform what was once a quiet fishing village and holiday resort into a busy little industrial and commercial centre. Mossgas, the controlling authority, is expected to be in full production by 1992.

Still, the local beaches are as inviting as ever, the mussels as delicious, the sea as kind to yachtsmen, windsurfers and bathers. The resort's hotels, chalets and caravan/camping grounds tend to be crowded during the peak summer holiday period; summer social life (barbecues feature prominently) is spirited.

THE BARTOLOMEU DIAS MUSEUM This complex was established in 1988 to commemorate the 500th anniversary of the great navigator's visit; among its components are a maritime museum, an arts-and-crafts centre (housed in Munro's Cottages), the original Post Office Tree (see above), and a replica of a *padrão* (the stone cross erected by Portuguese explorers at various points along the southern African coastline).

MOSSGAS The oil exploration organization; runs an information centre in town. Slide shows brief visitors on exploration techniques and drilling progress.

SEAL ISLAND Home to around 2 000 of these marine mammals. The island may be visited; cruises start from the harbour.

HARTENBOS A seaside and river resort situated nearby and popular among Afrikaans-speaking holiday-makers. Among its excellent amenities is a 10 000-seat stadium (folk festivals, religious services, sports); a heated swimming pool, a skating rink, bowling green, tennis courts; post office, shops, restaurants; modern accommodation and caravan/camp sites, and a museum that houses an intriguing array of Voortrekker exhibits. Information: Tel. (04441) 5481.

LITTLE BRAK RIVER Farther along the coast, on the George road, a resort area of sea, lagoon and river set among hills bright with winter-flowering aloes. The place is popular among anglers, and among those who appreciate peace. Its companion is:

GREAT BRAK RIVER A larger coastal village to the east, which nestles in a lovely setting of estuary and sea. Among its features are a wide beach, an informative little local history museum (open late mornings, Mon. Wed. and Sat.), and a shoe factory. The Spanish-style church is worth a visit.

THE GOURITS RIVER The southern Cape's biggest watercourse, the Gourits, flows into the ocean to the west of Mossel Bay; motorists travelling to or from Cape Town cross over an aloe-festooned gorge measuring 75 m across and 65 m in depth. At the river-mouth is a small resort that offers safe bathing (there's a tidal pool), excellent fishing and boating.

Mountain passes

Tsitsikamma: access from the main road to the Groot River and Bloukrans passes, and to the magnificent vistas they afford, is via the turn-off at Coldstream. The Bloukrans River bridge, where Satour and the National Parks Board provide a useful information service, is much favoured by campers and picnickers.

Farther afield, scenically superb passes lead off the Garden Route to cross the Tsitsikamma, Outeniqua and Langeberg and into the Long Kloof and the Little Karoo. Among them are Prince Alfred's (between the Long Kloof and Knysna); the Montagu (George and Herold's Bay), the Outeniqua (George and Oudtshoorn), the Robinson (Mossel Bay and Oudtshoorn) and Garcia's (Riversdale and Ladismith).

THE LITTLE KAROO

This distinctive and, in places, ruggedly beautiful region, about 250 km long and 70 km wide, lies between the southern coastal rampart (the Outeniqua and Langeberg) and the Swartberg uplands to the north.

There can be few more impressive ranges than the Swartberg, a spectacular chain of mountain heights sliced through by precipitous passes and deep, tangled kloofs. The wild flowers here – the painted ladies, the fire lilies and many more – are quite lovely; the air sweet and clear, the vistas magnificent.

The plain below is part of the Karoo System, but it has its own personality, distinctive and very different from the Great Karoo, its big brother in the north (see page 255). Although rainfall averages a low 150 mm a year, the countryside isn't dry: there is good water from the perennial streams that flow down from the mountains to join the Olifants River, bringing rich deposits of soil southwards (the Olifants becomes the Gourits before it enters the sea; see page 237). The countryside around the Olifants is fertile; each of the smaller watercourses has its lush valley.

The Little Karoo is renowned for its flocks of ostriches, a species that prefers a dry climate and thrives on the emerald-green lucerne that is grown in the area. During the fashion-led ostrich feather boom of the late 19th and early 20th centuries these big birds were the mainstay of the local economy, and indeed they still contribute to the region's wealth. Today, though, farming is a lot more diverse: in addition to the lucerne, the land yields fine crops of wheat, tobacco, walnuts and grapes.

The Little Karoo's principal town is:

Oudtshoorn

Set along the banks of the Grobbelaars River south of the Swartberg range, Oudtshoorn (population: 60 000) was founded in 1847 and named after Baron Pieter van Rheede van Oudtshoorn, governor-designate of the Cape, who died in 1773 on his way to take up the appointment. The town is popularly known as the world's 'feather capital', a reference to its preeminent position as the centre of the late-Victorian and Edwardian ostrich-feather industry.

During those years the bigger farms of the area each accommodated around 600 birds; a bird would earn its owner up to £6 a year; a breeding pair could fetch £1 000 on the market;

Ostrich-riding near Oudtshoorn

London buyers paid up to £112 for a pound of prime white plumes – and some of the local farmers and businessmen made fabulous fortunes. The richest built themselves marble-floored farmhouses, or moved into town and constructed mansions that came to be known as 'feather palaces', hugely ostentatious multiroomed extravaganzas of turrets and gables and cast-iron trimmings. A little of this lively past has been preserved, and is perhaps seen at its most evocative in the:

CP NEL MUSEUM (High Street). The museum's period-furnished annexe is one of the original feather palaces; the façade of the main building, green-domed, constructed of sandstone, and formerly the Boys' High School, is considered the most splendid example of stonemasonry in South Africa. Display exhibits include those in the Ostrich Room, which features the bird and the industry in all its aspects; feather-boom fashions; a fine collection of firearms; and local antiques. Open Monday-Saturday. Other 'Feather palaces' that have survived include Dorphuis (Adderley Street), Pinehurst (now part of the local teachers' college), Greystones and Welgeluk.

ARBEIDSGENOT This house in Jan van Riebeeck Road was the home of C J Langenhoven (1873-1932), lawyer, politician, champion of the Afrikaans language, lyrical poet and prolific author. The house is now a museum; exhibits include personal memorabilia and the wood carvings of the central character (an elephant) in his endearing *Herrie op die ou Tremspoor* ('Harry on the old Tramcar', published in 1925). Open Monday-Saturday.

DE OUDE PASTORIE A shop in Baron van Rheede Street that offers an interestingly eclectic range of goods, including antique furniture, dried fruit, hand-woven wear, locally made pottery and an art gallery, and refreshments in the garden.

OSTRICH FARMS Still very much a feature of the area (the demand is steady; Oudtshoorn is the only place in the world where feathers are still sold at regular auctions). Apart from the feathers – used mainly in the manufacture of fashion accessories and household dusters – the bird is valuable for its meat (ostrich steak

Stalactites in Cango One. Largest of the 28 chambers is over 100 m in length

and biltong), its egg (equal, in terms of an omelette, to 24 hen's eggs), and skin (handbags, wallets and shoes). Show farms – those that are open to the public – include Safari and Highgate (open daily; two-hour guided tours; 'ostrich derbies').

The homestead on Safari, 'Welgeluk', is one of the most splendid of the 'feather palaces'.

CANGO CROCODILE RANCH AND CHEETAHLAND This complex, just outside town, is home to about 300 of these giant reptiles; among other features of interest are a crocodile museum, snake park, children's farmyard, tame animals (including Twinkle the otter, Winston the warthog, Claude the camel, and some endearing miniature horses), curio shop, tearoom. Cheetahland, a complex within the ranch, has a 200 m raised walkway that meanders across the bushveld, enabling visitors to observe and photograph these graceful big cats (as well as lions and jaguars) in their natural environment. There are conducted tours by expert and efficient guides.

GREYSTONE GAME PARK This is well worth calling in at for its cheetahs, confined to enclo-

sures but some tame enough for visitors to enter and be photographed with the big cats. Other residents include springbok, red duiker, mountain reedbuck, bushbuck, rhebok, gemsbok, blesbok, zebra, wildebeest, baboon, bat-eared fox, lynx, caracal, spotted hyena. Many of the animals wander freely. There are walking trails; and a rewarding stroll to the top of Tafelkop, from which especially fine views can be enjoyed. Open daily.

A little over 40 km from Oudtshoorn is the:

RUST-EN-VREDE ('rest and peace') waterfall. A lovely series of cascades that drop 74 m into the pool below. The rock-faces are curiously coloured; the wild flowers are enchanting, as are some of the picnic spots in the vicinity.

Cango Caves

This limestone labyrinth of multi-coloured stalagmites and stalactites, situated in the Swartberg range 26 km north of Oudtshoorn, is ranked among the most splendid of Africa's natural wonders. About 200 000 people visit the complex each year.

The caves were 'discovered' and tentatively explored by a white farmer named Van Zyl in

1780. He gained access to the first and one of the most impressive caverns, the 98-m-long chamber now called Van Zyl's Hall. Stone implements and Bushman (San) wall-paintings later found near the entrance to the complex indicated that the site was occupied by man as early as the Middle Stone Age (8 000 to 2 700 BC). The caves were also home to countless generations of bats: their petrified skeletons, litter an area known as the 'bats' graveyard'.

The 28 chambers are linked by 2,4 km of passages, and they're quite remarkable for the variety of their calcified formations, the whole combining to produce a wonderful array of colours and weirdly sculpted shapes. The largest chamber is the Grand Hall, 107 m across and 16 m high; Botha's Hall contains a column fully 12,5 m high. The temperature in the caves remains at a constant 18,3 °C.

In 1970 Cango Two (the Wonder Cave), a beautiful 270 m extension of the original system, was discovered; Cango Three, a sequence stretching for 1 600 m, was first explored in 1975. Cango Four, beyond and at a lower level than the others, is still being investigated by the experts. There are several other cave systems in the area, at least two of which are larger than the Cango, but difficult access and potentially dangerous passages keep them closed to the public.

Open daily; conducted tours (once an hour on the hour in peak season; every two hours at other times); restaurant; curio shop; crèche.

West of Oudtshoorn

A number of small centres on the R62 highway that leads, eventually, to Montagu on the fringes of the Cape winelands (see page 307) are of passing interest:

CALITZDORP Situated on the plains of the Little Karoo and also a centre of the ostrich-farming industry: the birds can be seen wandering freely among the lucerne fields. The village, which has a great deal of old-fashioned charm, overlooks the lovely Gamka River valley; the local church, built in Renaissance-Byzantine style and capable of seating a congregation of 1 500, is worth visiting.

The area is also noted for its wheat, tobacco, deciduous fruit – and for its vineyards. The Calitzdorp Wine Route takes in the Boplaas Estate (cheese lunches), Die Krans Estate (which has

its own 'vineyard route') and the Calitzdorp Fruit and Wine Cellar.

Calitzdorp Spa, on the banks of the Olifants River just over 20 km from the town, is a renowned health resort centred on thermal springs whose waters emerge at a constant temperature of 51 °C.

The place is especially popular in winter; facilities include swimming pools (here the temperatures are around 35 °C), sauna, restaurant, entertainment complex, fully equipped, attractively sited chalets and a caravan/camping ground. Information: The Town Clerk, Voortrekker Street, Calitzdorp 6660; Tel. (04437) 312.

Calitzdorp is an up-and-coming wine-producing area and has its own wine route (two estate cellars, one co-operative). The grapes have a high sugar content. During your tour you can also sample and enjoy the region's excellent sun-dried fruit.

LADISMITH Overlooked by the Swartberg's 2 203 m twin Toorkop (or Towerkop) peaks some 45 km west of Calitzdorp, Ladismith is famed for its marvellously scenic setting. The village has some pleasant Victorian houses (wrought iron-work is a feature); the farmlands are given over to ostrich and sheep, lucerne and fruit; the Towerkop cheese factory turns out an especially fine product.

BARRYDALE On the R62 about 80 km southwest of Ladismith, this is a tranquil little village, centre of a thriving apple, peach, apricot, grape and brandy producing area. The local mesembryanthemums ('vygies') are lovely; the Anna Roux Wildflower Garden, a little way outside town, is an inviting port of call. Back along the R62, at the foot of the Warmwatersberg, there's a hot spring (40 °C) and pleasant spa complex.

Nature reserves

The Little Karoo region isn't especially well endowed with these; and those that have been established tend, in tourism terms, to be underdeveloped. Three, however, are certainly worth a mention:

GAMKA MOUNTAIN NATURE RESERVE A rugged, ravine-sliced 9 500-ha area 35 km north-west of Oudtshoorn proclaimed in 1970 specifically to protect the Cape mountain zebra, though it's perhaps better known for its rare plants. Vegetation comprises false macchia, succulent mountain scrub, Karoo flora; some attractive proteas and ericas may be seen. Hikers like the area because it's entirely unspoilt; there's a two-day guided educational trail and half-a-dozen shorter walks. Nearest accommodation is at the Calitzdorp Spa, 10 km away (see page 240). Information: Officer-in-Charge, Private Bag X21, Oudtshoorn 6620; Tel. (04437) 371.

NIETGENAAMD NATURE RESERVE East of Oudtshoorn (take the R341), this covers about 1 500 ha of Karoo shrubs, succulents and fynbos. There are hot springs near the entrance, around which are clustered huts and cottages; attractions include walking trails and tractor trips. Information: Officer-in-Charge, PO Box 81, Uniondale 6460; Tel. (04462), ask for 1912.

GAMKAPOORT NATURE RESERVE Reached via the Swartberg Pass to the north-west of Oudtshoorn. Among the features of this quite spectacular mountain area are the Gamkapoort dam and the splendid gorge below its wall. Attractions: fishing, boating, picnicking.

Day drives

There are some magnificent routes through the Swartberg and other Little Karoo mountain ranges. Some suggestions:

ROBINSON PASS This breaches the Langeberg and is the direct route between Oudtshoorn and Mossel Bay. There are fine views from its 860 m summit; the countryside *en route* is scenically lovely, mantled in heath and wild flowers. The road is excellent, the distance between the two points can be covered in an hour.

SEVEN WEEKS POORT (Seweweekspoort). A truly lovely river pass through the Swartberg north of the road connecting Calitzdorp and Ladismith. Towering over the pass is the 2 326 m Seven Weeks Poort Mountain, the Swartberg's highest. The origin of the name is obscure: it may be derived from the length of time it took the old brandy-smugglers to complete their evasive route, or from the everlasting 'seven-weeks' wild flower that graces the hillsides. There are picnic sites and a caravan/camping ground *en route*.

OUTENIQUA PASS This links the southern Cape town of George (see page 235) with the Little Karoo. The modern pass, 16 km long and a fine piece of engineering (Italian prisoners-of-war contributed their skills) cuts through the Outeniqua range, rising from 210 m to 800 m above sea level. Splendid views all along, but especially from the summit; there's a toposcope 51 km from Oudtshoorn.

SWARTBERG PASS One of the finest of South Africa's passes, this was constructed by the ubiquitous and talented 19th-century road builder Thomas Bain (son of the famous Andrew Geddes Bain) with the help of convict labour between 1881 and 1888 and was, for the time, a quite remarkable feat of engineering. It links Oudtshoorn and the Little Karoo with the village of Prince Albert on the southern fringes of the Great Karoo (see page 255). There are stunning views all the way up and down the other side, though the gradients along its 24 km length are unremittingly steep and the curves endless.

The summit is 1 585 m above sea level; the mountain slopes are covered with proteas and watsonias in summer and with snow in winter.

From a point close to the summit a road branches off to:

GAMKASKLOOF Formerly known as 'The Hell' (or Die Hel), this is a deep, 20-km-long gorge through which the Gamka River flows. The valley, rich in soil and water and beautiful in its winter clothing of aloes, served as refuge for a reclusive 19th century farming community, people who deliberately shut themselves off from civilization.

Something of the same isolationist spirit still pervades the valley, though its residents are amiable enough. They grow wheat, raisin grapes, figs and vegetables, and keep cattle, goats and bees (and make a powerful mead-brew from the honey).

Meiringspoort, the third of the passes through the Swartberg, follows the main highway from Little to Great Karoo (the R29 from De Rust north to Beaufort West). Once again, splendid vistas unfold along the route; the road, which crosses the Groot River fully 26 times, is flanked by precipitous and often strangely eroded sandstone cliffs. The cleft of Meiringspoort is especially dramatic.

Cape Agulhas, southernmost point of Africa. The continental shelf here is wide, the waters rich in fish.

THE OVERBERG

The word translates as 'the other side of the mountain', and was used by early Capetonians to describe the lands beyond the Hottentots Holland range. For the purposes of this chapter the Overberg covers the region from Still Bay and the inland centre of Riversdale in the east to the foothills of the Hottentots Holland, Cape Hangklip and Betty's Bay in the west: a narrow coastal strip bisected by the N2 national highway, its shoreline lapped, for the most part, by the waters of the Indian Ocean.

This segment of the southern coast is known for its wild flowers, for the gentleness of its countryside, for its rich wheat and barley fields, its green pastures and its forest plantations. The ocean, too, can be gentle, but is not always so: it has claimed a great many ships over the centuries, and their wrecks, some of them visible, most of them hidden beneath the shallow seas of the Agulhas Bank, testify to the ferocity of the storms that sometimes lash the shores. But most summer days are balmy, the water warm, placid, playing host to holiday-makers, fishermen, sailors, surfers and skiers.

If you look at the map, you'll see that the marine resorts – and these are the areas that attract the majority of holiday-makers – tend to be rather isolated from each other. There isn't a major, continuous coastal route and, generally speaking, in order to reach them one takes the N1 route, turning south at the appropriate inland town. This is the course we shall be following here, starting in the east with:

The Riversdale area

The town itself, on the N2 some 80 km west of Mossel Bay, is a small farming centre of only modest distinction. Worth a visit is the Julius Gordon Africana Museum in Versveld House (paintings by, among others, South Africans Irma Stern, Thomas Bowler and local landscape artist Jan Volschenk; antique furniture; porcelain); the Jurisch Park wild flower garden (aloes, mesembryanthemums), and the Werner Frehse nature reserve, a 270-ha expanse of fynbos (heath) vegetation. Among its game species are black wildebeest, gemsbok, eland and bontebok. The road to the north of Riversdale (the R323) will take you over the mountains to the Little Karoo (see pages 237-242). It slices through the Langeberg range via:

GARCIA'S PASS Built by the prolific 19th century road engineer Thomas Bain, this is a rewarding scenic drive: there are some lovely flowering plants along the route. The old Tollhouse at the top is a national monument. To the north-west of the pass is the:

GARCIA STATE FOREST This 12 000-ha reserve was proclaimed principally to protect the water catchment area and the mountain vegetation. This is good hiking country; 62 km of trails and footpaths have been established; bird-watchers will find the walk along the wooded banks of the Meul River especially rewarding; bird species recorded include black eagle, rock kestrel, malachite and orange-breasted sunbird. Nearest accommodation is in Riversdale, 10 km away. South of Riversdale (take the R323) is:

The Still Bay area

The bay itself, and especially the banks and mouth of the Kafferkuils River, has been pleas-

antly if rather informally developed for tourism and recreation. The area is popular among local farming folk; it's crowded in the summer-holiday season, almost deserted during the rest of the year; the sea is safe for bathing, the beach wide and sandy; there's good fishing in both the ocean (rock, surf, deep-sea) and estuary; the river is navigable for 12 km, and its eels are famous: many weigh up to an impressive 7,5 kg and, curiously, they tend to be quite tame.

Beachcombers find delight in the unusual quantity and variety of shells, marine seeds and, occasionally, prehistoric (Still Bay Culture) relics found along the shores. Still Bay has a small harbour; there's a generous range of accommodation on offer. Many of the holiday cottages are built on stilts to cope with the strong spring tides. Nearby is the:

PAULINE BOHNEN NATURE RESERVE A small sanctuary for bushbuck, duiker, Cape grysbok

Fishing boats at Struisbaai ('straw bay', so named for the village's thatched cottages)

and a variety of birds, this area is being developed for the public.

GEELKRANS NATURE RESERVE A small (170 ha) area to the east of the Still Bay resort, worth visiting for the summer-flowering fynbos flora. Residents include a variety of buck species and some interesting birds (red-necked francolin, southern tchagra).

Next stop on the national route is:

HEIDELBERG Set on the banks of the Duivenhoks ('dovecote') River, this is a centre for the thriving wheatlands of the area. There are pleasant picnic spots along the water's edge; the Dutch Reformed church towers over town centre; the small Anglican church is notable for its lovely rose windows and wood sculptures. Also worth visiting is the Heidelberg wild flower garden, established to preserve the local and now rare renosterveld vegetation.

The road south (the R322) leads to:

The St Sebastian Bay area

A fisherman's paradise: some superb catches have been recorded from both bay and Breede River estuary, where the popular little resort of Witsand has been established. There's also a small fishing harbour; the area is renowned for its oysters and other shellfish. The river is navigable for 35 km; a little way upstream is:

PORT BEAUFORT Once a thriving little harbour, this place has long since been given over to a more relaxed lifestyle. The old customs house still stands, though (it serves as a hotel). The thatched church, built in 1849, is now a national monument.

MALGAS Situated at the end of the navigable stretch of river, this was also a port of sorts: before the coming of the railway it was used as an outlet for wheat and wool and for the ostrich feathers of the Little Karoo (see page 238). Much of the quaintness of the past remains, most obviously discernible in the workings of the vehicle pont, powered by two men and the last such working contraption in South Africa.

DE HOOP NATURE RESERVE To the west of St Sebastian Bay, beyond Cape Infanta, this is one of the Cape's most important sanctuaries: it protects the most extensive remaining expanse of coastal fynbos (heath) vegetation, of which nearly 90% has been destroyed by encroaching cultivation. The reserve contains some 1 500 plant species, 50 of which grow only in this particular place, over 70 of which are classed as either endangered or rare.

The proclaimed area, which includes the adjacent marine reserve, extends over some 60 000 ha; among the residents are about 70 mammal species (bontebok, Cape mountain zebra, Cape clawless otter, various buck). Of the 13 marine mammals to visit the reserve, the southern right whale is perhaps the most distinguished. An impressive 230 bird species have been recorded.

Visitor amenities include game-viewing roads, trails (guided and self-conducted), picnic and barbecue spots and fairly simple accommodation (4-bed rondavels, communal facilities).

SKIPSKOP This is a tiny and most attractive cluster of cottages 6 km from the entrance to De Hoop. The local farm is rather special: the home is a national monument; bontebok, black wildebeest and pink flamingo may be seen in the area.

North again, to:

The Swellendam area

The country's third-oldest white settlement (after Cape Town and Stellenbosch), Swellendam was founded in 1746 and named after Cape governor Hendrik Swellengrebel and his wife, Helena ten Damme. Fifty years later, when it was still very much a frontier outpost, its burghers, complaining that they had 'for long enough been under the yoke of slavery', declared themselves independent of Dutch East India Company authority (ironically, though, many of the rebels were slave-owners themselves). The Swellendam Republic lasted only a few months before submitting, in 1796, to the newly-ensconced British regime.

One enters Swellendam from the east, along a lovely avenue of stately oak trees. Beyond the town are the Langeberg's Clock Peaks (the twelve o' clock is the closest), a series of heights whose summits cast shadows from which one can tell the approximate time of day.

For walkers and sightseers, the Publicity Association (see Advisory, page 253) has prepared useful little sheets entitled 'Short kloof outings near Swellendam' and 'Swellendam Treasures'.

The latter profiles historic sites of significance, of which Swellendam has many. They include:

✩ The Drostdy complex (Swellengrebel Street), completed to accommodate the landdrost (magistrate) in 1747. A splendid building, which now houses a museum exhibiting period furniture, old household items, animal-drawn vehicles, and an interesting collection of early paper money.

Opposite is a cluster of re-created craftsmen's premises: blacksmith, cobbler, charcoal burner, coppersmith, miller, cooper and so forth. A watermill grinds flour (which is available to visitors on the premises). Within the complex is Zanddrift, an 18th century house which now serves as a pleasant restaurant.

✩ The old jailhouse, and the thatched-roofed post office next door (the goaler also functioned as postmaster).

✩ The Cottage, an impressive example of Cape architecture of the middle period (it dates from the early 1830s).

✩ The Auld House, once home to the commercially distinguished Barry family.

✩ The Oefeningshuis, a meeting house used by the early burghers; and the Heemraadenhuis (council office).

✩ Farther afield, on the way to the scenically outstanding Tradouw Pass and Oudtshoorn, is Zuurbraak, a 19th century mission station that now turns out cane sturdy cane furniture. The 'Zuurbraak Chairbodgers' use traditional craftsmen's methods.

MARLOTH NATURE RESERVE Situated just to the north of Swellendam, in the ruggedly beautiful hills of the Langeberg, this is an impressive 11 300-ha area of high peaks, deep ravines and refreshing streams.

Wildlife includes buck and some interesting birds (black eagles may be spotted in the area), but this is primarily a place for the hiker: the six-day Swellendam trail crosses the reserve. Walkers stay in overnight huts; the nearest conventional accommodation is in Swellendam (the hotels are adequate, one is very good: see Advisory, page 252). The Marloth Flower Reserve covers 430 ha of fynbos terrain (visitors require a permit from the forester).

BONTEBOK NATIONAL PARK This reserve, 7 km south of Swellendam, has had a chequered and in some ways remarkable history. In the early 1830s a group of Cape farmers had the foresight to keep the few remaining bontebok in safety on their lands, so sparing the antelope the fate that overtook the bluebuck, a species that once roamed the plains of the southern Cape in huge numbers. A century later the first Bontebok National Park, containing a breeding herd of just 17 animals, was proclaimed in the Bredasdorp district; 30 years later the reserve was moved to its present location. By then, the bontebok had grown to 84 in number.

The park, through which the Breede River passes, sustains some 500 plant species, many of them rare; yellowwood, wild olive and milkwood line the river-banks; the climate is temperate; most of the rain falls in winter; in spring wild flowers carpet the ground. Apart from the bontebok, the antelope population includes grysbok, grey rhebok, steenbok and duiker. About 200 bird species have been recorded.

Facilities include game-viewing roads, walking trails, picnic areas, a caravan-camping site; a shop, information centre, petrol pump. Fishing and swimming are permitted (in the Breede River); caravans can be hired at the camping area. For information, contact: The Warden, PO Box 149, Swellendam 6740; Tel. (0291) 4-2735; bookings: National Parks Board (see Advisory, page 253).

The Cape Agulhas area
The Cape is the southernmost point of the African continent, its name derived from the Portuguese word for needles – the early navigators found that here their compasses weren't affected by magnetic deviation, 'bearing directly upon the true poles of the earth'.

Apart from that, though, the area has little of immediate interest to offer. The cape itself is the southern part of a substantial inland plain which, after the mild interruption of a small range of hills, slips quietly under the sea to become the vast, shallow Agulhas Bank, the most extensive part of southern Africa's continental shelf. The shallow waters of the 250 km-wide Bank, warmed by the westward-flowing Mozambique-Agulhas Current, are among the southern hemisphere's richest fishing grounds, sustaining huge numbers of sole, kabeljou (kob) and other bottom-dwellers. A lighthouse (18 million candlepower), built in 1848, stands at the cape; close by is the tiny village and beach resort of L'Agulhas, but the nearest town of any substance is:

BREDASDORP Centre of a prosperous farming region (wool, grain, dairy products), 24 km north of Agulhas. The town's Maritime Museum will occupy a fascinating hour of your time: it exhibits relics of many of the vessels wrecked along the rocky, gale-swept coast over the centuries. Of these, the most celebrated is the HMS *Birkenhead*, which came to grief off Danger Point, 70 km or so to the west, in 1852 (see page 249). Also of note is the Cape Gothic-style, oak-ceilinged Dutch Reformed church.

BREDASDORP MOUNTAIN RESERVE Just to the south of town, this extends over 800 ha of coastal bush and mountain fynbos. There are fine views from its highest point (360 m); and some interesting plants in its 86-ha cultivated area (ericas, giant proteas and the red Bredasdorp lily). Walking trails have been established. A wild flower show is held each August.

ELIM A Moravian mission station 37 km to the south-west of Bredasdorp, founded in 1824. It is a picturesque little place of beautifully thatched, whitewashed cottages, fruit trees and wild flowers (notably the great mass of everlastings that decorate the countryside). Elim's German-made church clock first started ticking in 1764 and still keeps good time; the town's watermill (1828) is a national monument.

STRUIS BAY Next door to Agulhas, this is a popular resort boasting a splendid 16 km beach and a small harbour. Some charming straw-roofed fishermen's cottages at nearby Hotaglerklip have been lovingly restored. Excellent fishing, safe bathing, good surfing.

ARNISTON Also known by its more official name, Waenhuiskrans, this is an enchanting little fishing village of thatched and lime-washed cottages farther along the coast, to the east. The two names given the place have their interest: the *Arniston* was a British troopship wrecked in the area, with the loss of 372 lives in 1815; Waenhuiskrans translates as 'wagon house cliff', a reference to the huge sea-cavern nearby.

Of interest here and along the coast are the giant pods of the *Entada gigas* sea-bean, and a

A terrace of cottages in the historic hamlet of Elim, founded as a mission station in 1824

The beach at Arniston, a picturesque village boasting an especially fine hotel

number of stone fish-traps built by the 'Strand-loper' ('beachranger') people in prehistoric times. The local hotel is deservedly renowned (see Advisory, page 252).

Between Struis Bay and Arniston is the:

DE MOND NATURE RESERVE, a tranquil and utterly unspoilt 300-ha area of dunes, heath, milkwood, mountain cypress and other in-digenous forest patches, kloofs, rock pools and ecologically important river estuary. Birdlife is prolific (the uncommon Knysna woodpecker and the martial eagle have been recorded). Among the various charted walks is the 30 km, scenically outstanding Grootberg-Horingberg trail. No accommodation.

The Greyton area

West of Swellendam on the N2 is the small town of Riviersonderend which takes its name from the local river: it rises in the Hottentots Holland mountains and flows eastward, seem-ingly (to the early settlers) 'without end'. The area is noted for its natural forests. A minor road (the R406) will take you along the south-ern slopes of the attractive Riviersonderend range of hills to:

GREYTON, one of the region's most peaceful and charming villages (though press and pub-lic 'discovered' it fairly recently; it's becoming fashionable among weekenders and its charac-ter could be threatened). The village's main street is pleasantly oak-lined; the surrounding countryside is scenically pleasing; the Greyton nature reserve comprises 2 220 ha of quite spectacular terrain at altitudes ranging from 240 to 1 465 m above sea level. A fine place for walking (especially in springtime, when the wild flowers are in bloom), Greyton boasts three hotels. One of them, the renowned Post House, was built in 1860 in English-country style (antiques, log fires, rose garden) and bills itself as 'purveyors of food and lodging to the gentry' (see Advisory, page 252).

GENADENDAL This charming settlement, whose name means 'valley of grace', is a little to the west of Greyton. It was South Africa's first mission station, founded by Georg Schmidt, the 'Apostle of the Hottentots', at which time it was known as Baviaanskloof (cleft of the baboon); it was later taken over by the Moravian missionaries. The place is frozen in the past; of note are the church and its old bell, the parsonage, the early school building and the neat little thatched cottages.

The Caledon area

The town of Caledon was established (its orig-ins go back to 1709) to take advantage of the area's most prominent asset: the six superb hot springs, (and one cold one) whose radioactive waters are said to have real curative properties.

The springs still yield over two million litres a day, at a constant temperature of 49 °C. In the decades before the Second World War the place ranked as one of the southern hemisphere's most fashionable spas, boasting pools, a sanatorium and a fine hotel, but the complex was destroyed by fire.

Many people still 'take the waters'; a caravan/camping park provided most of the accommodation until 1990, when the splendid Overberger Hotel opened its hospitable doors for the first time (see page 252).

CALEDON MUSEUM In Krige Street, this is a complex of two small buildings (one a farmstead, the other a townhouse) containing some fascinating historical exhibits covering the years 1840 to 1900. It also features an interesting section devoted to textiles. Open Monday to Saturday.

CALEDON NATURE RESERVE AND WILD FLOWER GARDEN More officially known as Victoria Park, the garden is widely renowned for its magnificent displays of springtime flowers, among which are fully 135 species of proteaceae. The reserve covers 214 ha of Swartberg hillside; within it there is a 56-ha cultivated section, a masterpiece of landscaping distinguished by its indigenous trees and shrubs and colourful fynbos species (including the lovely Caledon bluebell, *Gladiolus spathaceus*), its scenically charming pathways, wooden bridges, picnic spots, and its curious 'Window' rock formation. A 10 km trail traverses the reserve. The Caledon Wild Flower Show is an annual event (it's held in mid-September) that attracts thousands of visitors.

SALMONSDAM NATURE RESERVE A little over 50 km to the south-east of Caledon, near the village of Stanford, this reserve is noted for its spectacular scenery, its streams, kloofs and waterfalls. Wildlife includes springbok, klipspringer and a number of other buck, and some 130 bird species.

The 850-ha area is much favoured by hikers and nature-lovers; picnic spots and shortish (3- to 8-km) trails have been established. Accommodation is unpretentious but very adequate (6-bed cottages and 4-bed huts, appointed with the basics).

The highway from Caledon eastwards to the Hottentots Holland mountains and the Cape winelands (and Cape Town) beyond is a beguiling route: travellers by road – and by rail – make their way through the wheatlands of the Overberg to and past the splendid apple, pear and peach orchards of the Elgin and Grabouw areas (see page 312).

Recommended overnight stops include the historic Houw Hoek Inn (built, at the foot of the pass, in 1794) well-known for its rustic atmosphere; Windermere Lodge (English country-house atmosphere, home-style cuisine), and Wilderkrantz, a Cape Dutch farmstead (one does one's own cooking here; the kitchen is well equipped).

Caledon and Houw Hoek are a little over 20 km from the south coast's Walker Bay and:

The Hermanus area
Greatly favoured by weekending Capetonians, and indeed by vacationers from much farther afield, and by well-off retirees. Hermanus itself is a fairly substantial centre and the Overberg's premier resort, attractively set between mountain and blue ocean and a paradise for fishermen (magnificent catches have been recorded), crayfish and perlemoen divers, sailors and water-sportsmen.

There are some quite splendid beaches in the area; the sea is safe for bathing and surfing; the popular Kleinriviersvlei lagoon is a longish inviting stretch of placid water that hosts the local yacht club.

The walk along the top of the cliffs, from the harbour to the lagoon at De Mond (see page 247) yields fine views of the rocky shoreline and its secluded coves; even grander vistas unfold along the Rotary Mountain Way, a scenic drive that cuts through the overlooking uplands. Golf (18-hole course) tennis and bowls are available to visitors.

Other recommendations: the nearby Hamilton Russell vineyards are Africa's southernmost. Tim Hamilton Russell's stated and ambitious aim is 'to produce South Africa's best red and white wines'; he's making excellent progress. His tasting room, originally stables, faces into the Hermanus marketplace. For dining, try the next-door Burgundy restaurant (Cape-style cuisine; voted one of the western Cape's ten best eating houses by a leading magazine). For coffee or a light lunch: Mallards in Mitchell Street.

OLD HARBOUR For over a century Hermanus served as the centre of a thriving fishing (and whaling) industry. The old harbour has been preserved as a museum (and a national monument); on view are reconstructed buildings and vintage fishing boats. The fine new harbour accommodates modern craft used by both commercial and sporting fishermen; some of the boats can be hired for deep-sea tunny and marlin expeditions.

FERNKLOOF NATURE RESERVE Situated on the saddle between Lemoenskop and Olifantsberg in the Kleinrivier mountains to the north of Hermanus, this is a 1 500-ha expanse of coastal and montane fynbos rising abruptly from 60 to nearly 900 m above sea level. A pleasant place for walking (there are 35 km of trails); the wild flowers are attractive, some of them exquisite.

Also in the mountains above Hermanus is the Orothamnus reserve, a 12-ha patch proclaimed specifically to protect the rare marsh rose *Orothamnus zeyheri*. Grafting experiments have proved successful, and the plant can now be propagated in nurseries.

Across Walker Bay to the south-east of Hermanus is:

GANSBAAI, a tranquil little fishing village whose name means 'Goose bay'. Freshly caught fish are sold at the harbour. Nearby is the well-named Danger Point, off which the British troopship the HMS *Birkenhead* came to grief in February 1852 with the loss of 445 lives. Most of the dead were soldiers bound for the eastern Cape frontier, and they died heroes to a man, standing to rigid attention as the vessel foundered, so allowing the civilians to clamber aboard the three serviceable lifeboats. Their courage, exemplified by the phrase 'women and children first', is honoured both in the annals and in the language: the 'Birkenhead Drill' became descriptive of unyielding discipline in the face of disaster.

Today a lighthouse (which welcomes visitors) guides shipping around the point; nearby is a remarkable 'blowhole' through which the sea jets to heights of 10 m and more.

Just to the north is Die Kelders, a sequence of caves through which an underground stream flows. One may swim in the clear pools within the labyrinth; entry tickets are available from the hotel situated on the cliffs above from which there are splendid views of the broad sweep of Walker Bay and its rolling white dunes. In early summer one can often see whales spouting in the blue waters.

North of Gansbaai is the small village of:

STANFORD, notable for the Evans pottery and local craft centre. Apart from its sturdy glazed-clay products, it turns out copperware, hand-spun jerseys, wooden toys, and traditional rawhide whips.

On the other (western) side of Hermanus are the hamlets of Onrus River (a peaceful place at the entrance to the lagoon; the Onrus Kitchen, according to the *Cape Times*, 'just has to be one of the best restaurants in the country'), Vermont, Hawston and:

KLEINMOND, a pretty little resort at the mouth of the Bot River. Nearby are the Palmiet River lagoon and Sandown Bay (where the fishing is good but the swimming hazardous). Water birds in their thousands congregate on the Bot River marshes.

The Kleinmond coastal and mountain reserve covers 600 ha of the area, through which there are short walking trails. Picnic/barbecue sites have been laid out at Fairy Glen. The reserve's marshland is a haven for 1 500 plant species, a variety of buck and birds, and for the rare and endearingly tiny micro frog.

BETTY'S BAY A little to the west of Kleinmond, this is yet another quiet resort area, popular among anglers, lazers-in-the-sun and, especially, among nature-lovers. Its 190-ha Harold Porter botanic garden is renowned for the wealth and beauty of its wild flowers, among which the ericas feature prominently. Many of the plants are rare; most charming floral resident is the red disa (*Disa uniflora*) also known as 'Pride of Table Mountain'. One may picnic near the enchanting waterfall.

CAPE HANGKLIP The southern extremity of the Hottentots Holland mountains and the easterly limit of False Bay (see Cape Town and the Peninsula, page 285). A lonely place, once a refuge for runaway slaves and cattle-rustlers and now the location of a lighthouse (automatic) and a scatter of cottages. Pringle Bay, tranquil and unspoilt, lies to the north.

ADVISORY: SOUTHERN SEA-BOARD AND LITTLE KAROO

CLIMATE

Transitional but mainly summer-rainfall region. The uplands enjoy good rains; the Little Karoo has a generally hot, dry climate, though the land is well watered by the streams that flow down from the mountains. Winter nights can be cold. Strong summer winds sporadically assault the coastal areas.

Coastal region. Cape Agulhas temperatures: January average daily maximum 23,5 °C, daily minimum 17,2 °C; July average daily maximum 16,4 °C, daily minimum 10,0 °C; extremes 36,1 °C and 3,9 °C. Rainfall: January average monthly 20mm, July 54 mm; highest recorded daily rainfall 126 mm.

Little Karoo. Oudtshoorn temperatures: January average daily maximum 32,2 °C, daily minimum 15,3 °C; July average daily maximum 18,9 °C, daily minimum 3,4 °C; extremes 44,2 °C and -3,3 °C; Rainfall: January average monthly 10 mm, July 16 mm; highest recorded daily rainfall 51 mm.

MAIN ATTRACTIONS

Garden Route: Scenic variety and beauty □ Forest, mountain and ocean □ Pleasantly developed coastal resorts □ Sun, sea and sand □ The lakes and lagoons of the Knysna-Wilderness area.

Little Karoo: Scenic drives through the Swartberg and other spectacular ranges □ The Cango Caves □ Ostrich farms.

TRAVEL

Road. The main N2 national highway runs from east-west along the coastal belt from Port Elizabeth to Cape Town; its 230-km middle stretch, which hugs the shoreline, is the famed Garden Route; from Mossel Bay it follows an inland course to the Strand-Somerset west area. From the latter stretch, subsidiary routes take you south to the Overberg coastal resorts. Generally good roads lead over the often spectacular mountain passes to the Little Karoo (see page 241).

Car hire: Facilities are available in Knysna, George, Oudtshoorn and other major centres described in this chapter.

Coach travel: An inter-city express coach service operates between Cape Town and Port Elizabeth via the Garden Route and Oudtshoorn; Tel. Cape Town (021) 931-8000; or Port Elizabeth (041) 53-3184; or Johannesburg (011) 774-4128. Spoornet coaches also serve the region; Tel. Cape Town (021) 218-3581; or Port Elizabeth (041) 529-2400; or Johannesburg (011) 774-4128. Tour operators cover the region extensively: consult your travel agent. South African Airways, in association with a regional airline, undertake tours of the Garden Route; Tel. George (0441) 76-9215, or SAA in Johannesburg (011) 773-6618.

Rail. Spoornet passenger services connect centres between Cape Town and Port Elizabeth; Tel. Cape Town (021) 218-2991 or Port Elizabeth (041) 520-2975. A steam passenger train runs between George and Knysna (see page 236).

Air. George airport, 10 km from town, served by national and regional airlines; Plettenberg Bay and Oudtshoorn by regional airlines.

The high Bloukrans River bridge, part of the Garden Route (see page 231)

ACCOMMODATION

Select hotels

Garden Route

GEORGE

Fancourt Hotel (grading pending). Built in 1860, now a national monument; supremely elegant; 5 km from airport; 30 luxurious rooms, 5 executive suites, 2 presidential suites. PO Box 2266, George 6530; Tel. (0441) 70-8282.

Far Hills Protea ★★ On the N2 highway; 49 en-suite rooms; conference facilities. PO Box 10, George 6530; Tel. (0441) 4941.

Hawthorndene ★★ 34 en-suite rooms; conference facilities. PO Box 1, George 6530; Tel. (0441) 74-4160.

KNYSNA-WILDERNESS

Brenton-on-Sea Hotel ★★ About 15 km from Knysna; 30 en-suite rooms; conference facilities. PO Box 36, Knysna 6570; Tel. (0445) 81-0081.

Fairy Knowe Hotel ★★ On banks of Touw River; 42 en-suite rooms; conference facilities for 60; table d'hôte; pool. PO Box 28, Wilderness 6560; Tel. (0441) 9-1100.

Karos Wilderness Hotel ★★★ Widely known for its quality; close to lakes and lagoon; 160 rooms; conference facilities for 400; à la carte restaurant, carvery, 2 cocktail bars; swimming pools, bowls, tennis, squash. PO Box 6, Wilderness 6560; Tel. (0441) 9-1110.

Knysna Protea ★★★ Near lagoon; 50 rooms, 1 suite; conference facilities for 200; à la carte restaurant; pool. PO Box 33, Knysna 6570; Tel. (0445) 2-2127.

Leisure Isle ★★ 38 rooms, 2 suites; PO Box 19, Knysna 6570; Tel. (0445) 2-3143.

Wilderness Holiday Inn ★★★ Superb setting on beachfront; 149 rooms; conference facilities for 100; à la carte restaurant, carvery, action bar; pool, tennis courts. PO Box 26, Wilderness 6560; Tel. (0441) 9-1104.

MOSSEL BAY

Eight Bells Mountain Inn ★★★ Lovely setting below Robinson Pass, 35 km from Mossel Bay; 10 rooms, 8 family suites, 5 Swiss-style chalets; table d'hôte; pool, bowling greens, tennis and squash courts, horse-riding. PO Box 436, Mossel Bay 6500; Tel. (0444) 95-1544/5.

The southern coast is an angler's paradise

Golden Rendezvous ★★ 55 double rooms; conference facilities. PO Box 380, Mossel Bay 6500; Tel. (0444) 93-0040.

Santos Protea ★★★ A pleasant hotel on the beachfront; 58 rooms; pool. PO Box 203, Mossel Bay 6500; Tel. (0444) 7103.

PLETTENBERG BAY

The Arches ★★ Set on a hill overlooking lagoon; 20 en-suite rooms; conference facilities for 150; à la carte restaurant, 2 disco bars. PO Box 155, Plettenberg Bay 6600; Tel. (04457) 3-2118.

Beacon Island ★★★ Unique setting; 189 rooms, 8 suites; conference facilities for 250; à la carte (seafood specialities) and table d'hôte; several bars; pool, sauna, floodlit tennis. Private Bag 1001, Plettenberg Bay 6600; Tel. (04457) 3-1120.

Formosa Inn ★★ Old-established (1870); 38 rooms (chalets in garden setting); conference facilities for 50; à la carte restaurant, carvery, disco. PO Box 121, Plettenberg Bay 6600; Tel. (04457) 3-2060.

Hunter's Country House (grading pending). Elegantly appointed; 10 thatched cottages; conference facilities; pool. PO Box 454, Plettenberg Bay 6600; Tel. (04457) 7818/7858.

SEDGEFIELD

Lake Pleasant Hotel ★★ 17 en-suite rooms; pool and tennis courts. PO Box 2, Sedgefield 6573; Tel. (04455) 3-1313.

STORMS RIVER

Tzitzikama Forest Inn ★★ 34 en-suite rooms; conference facilities for 60; table d'hôte. PO Storms River 6308; Tel. (04237) 711.

Little Karoo

OUDTSHOORN

Holiday Inn ★★★ 30 km from Cango Caves; 120 rooms; conference facilities for 85; à la carte restaurant, 2 cocktail bars; pool, tennis court. PO Box 52, Oudtshoorn 6620; Tel. (04431) 2201.

Kango Protea Hotel ★★★ Close to town centre; 40 rooms in thatched chalets; conference facilities for 120; à la carte restaurant and carvery; pool. PO Box 370, Oudtshoorn 6620; Tel. (04431) 6161.

Queens ★★ Central; 70 en-suite rooms, 2 suites; conference facilities for 100; à la carte restaurant; pool. PO Box 19, Oudtshoorn 6620; Tel. (04431) 2101.

The Overberg

ALBERTINIA

Albertinia Hotel ★★ 16 en-suite rooms; conference facilities for 30; table d'hôte. Main Street, Albertinia 6795; Tel. (02952), ask for 30.

ARNISTON (WAENHUISKRANS)

Arniston Hotel ★★ Long a favourite among discerning holidaymakers; recently renovated. 23 en-suite rooms; conference facilities for 20; à la carte (lunch only) and table d'hôte; pool. PO Box 126, Bredasdorp 7280; Tel. (02847) 5-9000.

BREDASDORP

Victoria ★★ 29 rooms (most en-suite); PO Box 11, Bredasdorp 7280; Tel. (02841) 4-1159.

CALEDON

Alexandra ★★ 10 en-suite rooms; conference facilities for 120; à la carte restaurant, 2 cocktail bars; pool. PO Box 3, Caledon 7230; Tel. (0281) 2-1007.

De Overberger (grading pending). 99 rooms, conference and convention centre, hot spa, health centre. PO Box 480, Caledon 7230. Tel. (0281) 4-1271.

GREYTON

Post House. Built in 1860; served as the village post office; a charming place of roughly-hewn yellowwood ceilings, fireplaces, traditional English pub; 14 en-suite Beatrix Potter bedrooms. Main Road, Greyton 7233; Tel. (02822) 9995.

HERMANUS

Marine ★★ Excellent hotel; lovely views of Walker Bay; 41 rooms, 14 suites; conference facilities for 80; table d'hôte; outdoor and indoor pools, whirlpool. PO Box 9, Hermanus 7200; Tel. (0283) 2-1112.

KLEINMOND

Beach House Hotel ★★ On Sandown Bay beachfront; has excellent reputation; 23 rooms; conference facilities for 30; à la carte restaurant (seafood specialities). PO Box 199, Kleinmond 7195; Tel. (02823) 3130.

RIVERSDALE

Hotel President ★★ 22 en-suite rooms, 1 suite; conference facilities for 50; à la carte restaurant. PO Box 1, Riversdale 6770; Tel. (02933) 3-2473

Royal ★★★ 12 en-suite rooms; à la carte and table d'hôte; pool and sauna. PO Box 5, Riversdale 6770; Tel. (02933) 3-2470.

SWELLENDAM

Swellengrebel ★★ 51 en-suite rooms, 1 suite; conference facilities for 50; à la carte restaurant. PO Box 9, Swellendam 6740; Tel. (0291) 4-1144/5/6/7/8.

Ungraded accommodation

Farm holidays: contact the Garden Route Holiday Farm Association in Plettenberg Bay (Bed and Breakfast; self-catering cottages and chalets; town cottages and flats), PO Box 37, The Crags 6602; Tel. (04457) 8657.

Caravan/camping and self-catering accommodation

Agulhas/Struisbaai: Struisbaai caravan park, c/o Overberg Regional Services Council, PO Box 35, Bredasdorp 7280, Tel. (01841) 4-1126. A few kilometres from Cape Agulhas; offers self-catering accommodation, camping and caravan facilities on the beach-front.

Agulhas Caravan Park, address and telephone number as above; close to sea and Agulhas lighthouse; offers camping and caravan facilities close to tidal pool.

Arniston: Seaside cottages (self-catering), Bookings: PO Box 27, Bergvliet 7864, Tel. (021) 72-2000.

George: Brigadoon Park – 6 km outside town, PO Box 1397, George 6530, Tel. (0441) 74-1179. Caravan/camping facilities; self-catering accommodation. George Tourist Camp, York Street, PO Box 772, George 6530, Tel. (0441) 74-5205.

Hermanus area: Salmonsdam Nature Reserve has caravan/camping facilities and self-catering huts. Cape Department of Nature and Environmental Conservation, PO Box 5, Stanford 7210, Tel. (02834) 30-0789. Paradise Park Holiday Camp, PO Box 567, Hermanus, Tel. (0283) 6-1007. In village of Onrus, about 7 km from Hermanus.

Kleinmond: Municipal caravan park, PO Box 3, Kleinmond 7195, Tel. (02823) 4051 has 217 stands. Palmiet caravan park, address as above, Tel. (02823) 4050 has 207 stands.

Knysna/Wilderness: Lakes Holiday Resort, PO Box 38, Wilderness 6560, Tel. (0441) 9-1101. Wilderness National Park, PO Box 35, Wilderness 6560, Tel (0441) 9-1197. Caravan/camping, caravans for hire. Island Lake Holiday Resort, PO Wilderness 6560, Tel (0441) 9-1194. Self-catering accommodation, caravan/camping facilities; on the shore of Eilandvlei.

Brenton Holiday Resort, PO Box 235, Knysna 6570, Tel. (0445) 81-0060. On the lagoon; self-catering accommodation, caravan and camping facilities. Woodbourne Holiday Farm, PO Box 78, Knysna 6570, Tel. (0445) 2-3223; Self-catering accommodation, caravan/camping facilities.

Oudtshoorn: Kleinplaas Holiday Resort, Baron van Rheede St, PO Box 24, Oudtshoorn 6620, Tel. (04431) 5811. Cango Mountain Resort, PO Box 255, Oudtshoorn 6620, Tel. (04431) 22-4506. Calitzdorp Spa, PO Box 1266, Oudtshoorn 6620, Tel. (04437) 371.

Plettenberg Bay: Robberg Holiday Resort, PO Box 81, Plettenberg Bay 6600, Tel. (04457) 3-2571. Caravan/camping facilities; self-catering accommodation. Dune Park Holiday Resort, PO Box 658, Plettenberg Bay 6600, Tel. (04457) 9606. Keurbooms River Public Resort, Tel. (04457) 9309.

Sedgefield: Landfall Resort, Kingfisher Drive, Tel. (04455) 3-1840. Jooris Park, PO Box 22, Sedgefield 6573, Tel. (04455) 3-1905. On Swartvlei Lagoon.

Swellendam: Die Stroom (municipal caravan park) PO Box 20, Swellendam 6740, Tel. (0291) 4-2705.

Tsitsikamma: National Park Camp, Storms River Mouth, PO Storms River 6308, Tel. (04237) 607. Cottages, oceanettes, camping.

USEFUL ADDRESSES AND TELEPHONE NUMBERS

Ambulance, George (0441) 74-4000, after hours 73-3343; Knysna (0445) 2-1770; Mossel Bay (0444) 91-1911; Oudtshoorn (04431) 22-2241, a/h 4361/3457; Swellendam (0291) 4-2500; Riversdale (02933) 3-2418, a/h 3-1177 or 3-2291; Hermanus (0281) 2-1120 or 2-1607 a/h.

Car hire, at PW Botha Airport, George. Tel. (0441) 76- 9314, 76-9216. George town: 73-6295/73-6442. Mossel Bay (0444) 91-1541; Plettenberg Bay (04457) 3-3176, 3-2197.

George Publicity Association, PO Box 1109, George 6530; Tel. (0441) 74-4240.

Hermanus Tourist Information Bureau, Main Road, Hermanus 7200; Tel. (0283) 2-2629.

Knysna Publicity Association, PO Box 87, Knysna 6501; Tel. (0445) 2-1610.

Mossel Bay Tourist Information, The Town Clerk, PO Box 25, Mossel Bay 6500; Tel. (0444) 91-2215.

National Parks Board, PO Box 787, Pretoria 0001; Tel. (012) 343-9770. Cape Town: PO Box 7400, Roggebaai 8012: Tel. (021) 419 5365 or 418-5010.

Oudtshoorn Publicity Association, PO Box 256, Oudtshoorn 6620; Tel. (04431) 22-2221/22-2228.

Plettenberg Bay Angling Club, Tel. (04457) 9740.

Plettenberg Bay Publicity Association, PO Box 26, Plettenberg Bay 6600; Tel. (04457) 3-4065/6.

Satour (South African Tourism Board), 124 York Street; PO Box 312, George 6530; Tel. (0441) 73-5228; Telex: 5-24646 SA.

Swellendam Publicity Association, PO Box 369, Swellendam 6740; Tel. (0291) 4-2770.

ANNUAL EVENTS

Wilderness Rubber Power Boat Competition: New year weekend □ Uniondale Show: January □Cango Caves Marathon, Oudtshoorn area □Hermanus Festival of the Sea: March □Knysna Festival: June □ East-West Hobie Challenge, Mossel Bay: July □Caledon Wild Flower Show; Caledon Beer and Bread Festival: September □Little Karoo Agricultural Show; Outeniqua Agricultural Show; □Bredasdorp Foot of Africa Marathon: October □Wilderness New Year Regatta; Zwartvlei New Year Regatta: December.

THE GREAT INTERIOR

The Great Karoo covers some 400 000 km² of the Western and Northern Cape (and some of the Free State) – about one-third of the area of South Africa. Its boundaries can't be precisely defined because it is the product of a number of different elements: the nature of its soil and rocks, topography, vegetation and climate. Generally speaking, though, it extends from the southern rim of the Great Escarpment – the mountain ranges of the Cape hinterland – northwards to the Orange River.

It is a huge, semi-arid country whose name, derived from the Khoisan word for 'thirst', is apt indeed. There are few villages, and even fewer towns; those that have been established are isolated from each other and remote from the country's major centres, though the roads are generally good, and straight, enabling one to travel quickly.

To the north, beyond the wide reaches of the Orange, are the great diamond fields of the Northern Cape, their focus the historic city of Kimberley. West of these lies the Gordonia region, also vast and dry, whose principal town is Upington. Its northern limit is the Kalahari Desert and Botswana, its western the newly independent country of Namibia. To the north and west of Upington are two tourist showcases: the Kalahari Gemsbok National Park and the magnificent Augrabies Falls.

In the remote wilderness far south of Upington are some of the world's largest 'pans', enormous shallow depressions from which the rare rainwater has evaporated to leave hard sediments of mineral salts – whitish surfaces that reflect the intense sunlight, disturbing the atmosphere to create shimmering mirages and violent little whirlwinds called 'dust devils'. Grootvloer ('great floor'), 40 km by 60 km, is the most extensive of these dry 'lakes'; Verneukpan ('deception pan') the best known: it was selected by Sir Malcolm Campbell in 1929 for his near-successful assault on the world land speed record.

The Great Karoo, a region of bone-dry air, of intense sunshine and a haunting beauty of its own. The rains are rare, but underground water sustains huge flocks of sheep.

THE GREAT KAROO

Geologically, the region is part of what is known as the Karoo System, which extends over a very much wider area. The shale and sandstone strata are horizontal, and large parts of the countryside are flat and featureless, though elsewhere the monotony is relieved by dolerite formations – dykes (or ridges) and sills (kopjes, or rocky outcrops) – thrust up by millennia of volcanic action and weathered by periodic floods into stark and often bizarre shapes. Perhaps the most scenically remarkable example of this broken Karoo country is the aptly-named Valley of Desolation, near the town of Graaff-Reinet.

It is a region of far horizons; of the occasional, lonely farmstead, girded by its windmill and by the green of gumtree and willow, a brave splash of colour in the huge bleakness; of clear and bone-dry air, intense sunshine, blistering days and, in winter, bitter nights – and of low rainfall, varying from 375 mm a year in the eastern areas to under 50 mm in the desolate west. Predictably, plant cover is sparse, but special in the way it has evolved and adapted to the harsh conditions: the Karoo's succulents – aloes, mesembryanthemums, crassulas, euphorbias and stapelias – are unique, surviving because they are able to store water in their thick leaves or root systems.

And then there are the desert ephemerals, wild flowers whose seeds remain dormant for years, only germinating and briefly blossoming when the rare rains come.

But there is plenty of underground water in much of the Karoo – a precious resource that is tapped by thousands of wind-pumped boreholes – and this, together with the sweet grasses of the eastern areas, sustains enormous flocks of sheep.

Bisecting the Karoo is the N1 national highway, the Great North Road, that links Cape Town with Johannesburg, Pretoria and points far beyond. About a quarter of the way along it (travelling from the Cape, that is) is Beaufort West, the 'capital' of the region; halfway point is the town of Colesberg; between the two, at Three Sisters, one turns off onto the R29 to Kimberley. For the unhurried visitor, the first port of call is:

Matjiesfontein

A lovely little Victorian village that takes its name from a reed (matjiesgoed) found in the area that is used in the manufacture of matting. Its small cluster of buildings and its railway station are situated in a hollow just off the main highway (there's a scenic view of the place from the road) 250 km from Cape Town.

The place was built (around the station) in the 1880s by ex-railwayman James Douglas Logan, an entrepreneur with flair, impeccable taste and a nagging chest complaint, as a dry-air health resort. Soon enough it attracted a fashionable clientele which included, among many others, Lord Randolph Churchill, the Sultan of Zanzibar and the writer Olive Schreiner. It was also, incidentally, the first village in the country to be serviced with electricity and waterborne sewerage.

Matjiesfontein hosted 12 000 British soldiers during the South African (Anglo-Boer) War (1899-1902); its hotel, the Lord Milner, was used as a military hospital and the hotel turret as a lookout. When the gutsy commander of the Highland Brigade, General 'Andy' Wauchope, fell at the battle of Magersfontein, outside Kimberley far to the north, and was buried there, Logan felt that his distinguished fellow-Scot should have a memorial closer to civilization, and had the body reinterred at Matjiesfontein.

The village, Victorian down to the street lampposts that the 'Laird of Matjiesfontein' imported, has been preserved in its entirety by hotelier David Rawdon as a 'living museum'. Features of particular interest are Schreiner's cottage; the tiny museum, crammed to its low eaves with a fascinating array of trivia ranging from weapons to porcelain to household utensils; the village store and coffee shop; the post office; and the Lord Milner, a superbly elegant hostelry that was adjudged South Africa's best country hotel in 1990 (see Advisory, page 268).

Beaufort West

The largest town (population 29 000) on the Karoo section of the Great North Road, Beaufort West was founded in 1818 and, 20 years later, became the first municipality to be proclaimed in South Africa (under the new elective laws). It is noted for its pleasant pear-tree-lined streets, and as the birthplace of famed heart surgeon Chris Barnard, many of whose awards

and medals are on display in the local museum. Its newspaper, *The Courier*, has been published without interruption since 1869. Just north of the town is the:

KAROO NATIONAL PARK, a 33 000-ha expanse of flattish terrain proclaimed in 1979 to preserve the local vegetation, mainly dwarf shrubs, scatters of sweet-thorn trees and, along the invariably dry riverbeds, a variety of other hardy flora. Reintroduced game includes Cape mountain zebra (the 120-strong herd is the country's second largest; see also page 208), black wildebeest, springbok, mountain reedbuck, gemsbok, steenbok, klipspringer, kudu and duiker, and some leopard. About 170 bird species have been spotted in the area.

The park is still being developed; at the moment there are some 100 km of game-viewing roads; self-guided trails, picnic and viewing points, the three-day Springbok hiking trail and a main camp comprising fully equipped chalets, a restaurant, a shop, an information centre and provision for business conferences. There's also a camping ground. Information: the Park Warden, PO Box 316, Beaufort West 6970; Reservations: National Parks Board (see Advisory, page 269). Well to the east of the Beaufort West area (take the R61 for approximately 200 km) is:

Graaff-Reinet

Named after Governor Cornelis Jacob van der Graaff (1785-91) and his wife Cornelia Reynet, Graaff-Reinet is the oldest town in the eastern Cape, and the third oldest in the entire Cape region. Known as the 'Gem of the Karoo', Graaff-Reinet was founded in what was then the rugged frontier region – at the limits of white settlement – in 1786, and had a stormy childhood: less than ten years after its birth, its citizenry was in open revolt against the authority exercised from Cape Town by the Dutch East India Company. The tiny republic was forced to capitulate with the installation of the new British regime in 1796, but rebelled again – on three occasions.

Graaff-Reinet nestles in a loop of the Sundays River beneath the double-domed summit of Spandau Kop. It's a neat, well-ordered place of great historical interest. Unlike so many other South African towns that grew in haphazard fashion, it was laid out according to a sensible plan; much of the early construction work was carried out by talented craftsmen; over 200 of its early buildings, ranging from rudimentary, flat-roofed Karoo-style homes to imposing Cape Dutch and Victorian houses, have been restored and declared national monuments. Parsonage Street, between the Drostdy and Reinet House, is being restored in its entirety. Of particular interest:

THE DROSTDY, in Church Street; completed in 1806 as the residence and office of the early landdrost (magistrate), one of the finest examples of French architect Louis Thibault's work. Its interior has been carefully restored and the building, together with a mall of 13 renovated old cottages, now forms a rather unusual and very beautiful hotel complex (see Advisory, page 268).

REINET HOUSE, in Parsonage Street. A classic H-plan, thatched and gabled Cape Dutch residence, built in 1812 as the Dutch Reformed church's pastorie and now a splendid period-house museum (yellowwood ceilings; handsome 18th and 19th century furniture). In its garden is what was, until recently (and may indeed still be) the world's largest grapevine: before it was pruned in 1983, it had a girth of about 3 m and extended over 123 m^2 in area. Other features include a wagon house and the Mill House. Open daily.

THE REINET MUSEUM (Church and Somerset streets) is a multi-faceted repository, well worth visiting for its various and contrasting collections. These include permanent displays of clothing dating from 1800; the William Roe exhibition featuring the work of an early (1860) and talented local photographer; some superb reproductions of Bushman art, and a collection of reptile fossils dating back 230 million years. The Karoo shales form one of the world's most prolific sources of saurian remains; the Beaufort Series has yielded especially significant, and interesting, specimens: too many to enumerate, but they include the massive, thick-skulled reptile Tapinocephalus, one of the oldest of the 'fearful-heads' (the Dinocephalians); and a numerous Dicynodonts ('double dog-toothed' creatures with smallish bodies and huge heads). The museum houses the information office of the Graaff-Reinet Publicity Association.

HESTER RUPERT ART MUSEUM (Church Street). A restored and converted mission church housing some excellent contemporary South African works. Open daily.

THE RESIDENCY, a gracious building in Parsonage Street, is used as a museum which contains, among other objects, a superb collection of sporting rifles. Open daily.

THE GROOT KERK, an imposing building at the northern end of Church Street, is modelled on Salisbury Cathedral in England, and houses an unusually fine collection of ecclesiastical silver (on view during office hours).

THE GRAAFF-REINET PHARMACY Opened in 1870 and still going strong.

THE JAN RUPERT CENTRE (Middle Street) was inaugurated in the early 1980s as a labour-intensive (unemployment-relief) project specializing in spinning and weaving. Local materials (Karoo bush dye; merino wool) are used in the manufacture of some most attractive items of clothing, furnishings, tableware. Open during working hours. Almost entirely surrounding the town is the:

KAROO NATURE RESERVE A 16 000-ha wilderness area proclaimed in 1975, and developed by the South African Nature Foundation primarily to preserve the indigenous vegetation: succulents, Karoo scrub, spekboom. Game includes naturally occurring kudu, mountain reedbuck and other antelope, and reintroduced Cape mountain zebra, black wildebeest, eland, blesbok, springbok, red hartebeest. There are self-guided and longer overnight walks, picnic spots, the large Vanrhyneveld's Pass dam (boating, with permission) and, near the dam, bird-watching hides. Accommodation: in nearby Graaff-Reinet. Much of the terrain is ruggedly hilly; impressive natural features include Spandau Kop, and the famed:

VALLEY OF DESOLATION A remarkable fantasia of wind-eroded and strangely shaped dolerite peaks, pillars and balancing rocks that loom over Graaff-Reinet. There are fine views of the Plains of Camdeboo to the south and of the surrounding countryside. The valley is easily accessible from town.

NIEU BETHESDA is a tiny, charming hamlet in the foothills of the Compassberg 50 km north of Graaff-Reinet. A place of simple shuttered homes and lovely gardens, and of the Owl House, home of the late and eccentric Helen Martins. Ms Martins was a sculptor who specialized in bizarre figures – largely but not exclusively of owls; the sculptures are on display in the back garden. A private collection of prehistoric Karoo fossils may be viewed nearby.

Other Karoo towns

Travellers passing through these great spaces on the long, and for the most part lonely, highway between Cape Town and Johannesburg – the 'Cape-to-Cairo' road – have a choice of fewer than half a dozen places at which to break their journey in comfort. Some of the larger centres, most offering good or at least adequate hotel accommodation, are:

COLESBERG, an historic place at the halfway mark between the two cities. It was founded in 1829, named after Cape governor Sir G Lowry Cole, and was the original home of several leaders of the Great Trek. Nearby is the 1 707-m-high, flat-topped, distinctively symmetrical Coleskop mountain. This is sheep-farming country; the local mutton is said to be the country's tastiest.

LAINGSBURG, 274 km from Cape Town by road and about half the size of Colesberg. A centre of the wool industry, and of wheatlands, it was devastated by a flash flood in January 1981.

TOUWS RIVER is the last town you arrive at on the drive southwards, that is, before reaching the mountains that mark the Karoo's southern limit. A rather ordinary railway centre, most notable as the final resting place of some splendid steam locomotives.

PRINCE ALBERT lies 42 km south of the N1 (take the turn-off at Prince Albert Road), a scenically outstanding route that takes you to and through the Swartberg range. It is distinguished by its charming and historic buildings, ranging in style from Cape Dutch to Victorian and Edwardian. The Fransie Pienaar Museum is worth a visit; the hotel, the Swartberg Protea, is excellent. On the alternative north-south route (the R29 through Kimberley) is:

VICTORIA WEST, another wool town (population: 10 500), and rather attractive in a old-fashioned way. Features of note include the veteran and vintage cars on a nearby farm, and the Victoria West nature reserve, a 430-ha area of scrubby vegetation that sustains zebra, black wildebeest, eland, gemsbok and springbok.

CALVINIA, set beneath the Hantam range in the north-western Karoo, was named after the ascetic Protestant churchman John Calvin and is the centre of the second largest wool-producing district in the country (after Harrismith in the Orange Free State). A pleasant if somewhat austere place with an interesting museum. Four kilometres away, at the foot of the mountains, is the Akkerendam nature reserve, whose vegetation (mostly Karoo scrub) contains ten plant species unique to the Hantamsberg. The sunsets here are quite magnificent. The Tankwa-Karoo National Park, a 27 000-ha expanse of succulent vegetation, lies 90 km south of Calvinia. It's a new reserve, and has little to offer the visitor at the moment.

CARNARVON, (population: 9 100) in the very remote northern Karoo, suffers some of the country's chilliest winter weather. Sheep-farming is the principal industry; there are some rare corbelled houses (early and rather primitive Boer homes, circular and – because the region lacks trees – built entirely of stone) on the nearby Stuurmansfontein property. The Carnarvon nature reserve contains zebra and a variety of antelope on its 760 ha.

PRIESKA, on the Orange River at the Karoo's northern limit, is a largish copper-mining and livestock breeding centre of about 21 000 people. The area is famed for its superb tiger's eye (crocidolite) and other semi-precious stones – indeed, the British Anglo-Boer war stone fort, on the crest of Prieska Koppie (from which there are fine views) is built of tiger's eye. Of note in and around town are the Ria Huisamen aloe garden; the Schumann rock collection (at the municipal offices); and the Die Bos nature reserve (interesting birdlife; rondavel accommodation; Tel. (0594) 5). Along the Rock Garden route, which follows the Orange River towards Viooolsdrif, are strange *halfmens* (or 'half-human') quiver trees and floral species found nowhere else in the world.

Matjiesfontein's renowned Lord Milner hotel

DIAMOND COUNTRY

South Africa's first notable diamond was found by 15-year-old Erasmus Jacobs in 1866, near Hopetown on the banks of the Orange River in a region called Griqualand West. He gave it to a neighbouring farmer, Schalk van Niekerk, and in due course it reached Dr William Atherstone, Grahamstown's leading medical practitioner. Atherstone identified what was to be known as the 'Eureka' stone (21,77 carats, valued at R500 at the time).

Three years later, Van Niekerk produced another find: an 84-carat stone given him by a Griqua shepherd in exchange for 10 oxen, 500 sheep and a horse. This was the renowned 'Star of South Africa'; the new El Dorado, it was now thought, lay well north of Hopetown; and the rush was on: diggers poured into Griqualand West and by the end of 1869, some 10 000 claims had been pegged along several miles of the Vaal River in the vicinity of Klipdrift, later renamed Barkly West.

All this, though, paled to insignificance when several diamond-rich kimberlite 'pipes' were discovered, four of them clustered within an 8 km² patch of arid countryside about 30 km south of Klipdrift, in an area which included the farms Bultfontein and a 9-m-high hill called Colesberg Kopje.

The kopje lay on the farm Vooruitzicht, owned by the brothers De Beer; it had been discovered in July 1871 by a party of prospectors led by one Fleetwood Rawstone, and it was full of diamonds. It was soon to disappear beneath the picks and shovels of what was to become Kimberley's world-famed Big Hole.

Kimberley's mined-out Big Hole

Kimberley

By 1872, when the young Cecil Rhodes arrived on the scene, a huge tent-town had spread across the arid veld; 50 000 miners had congregated; at any given time 30 000 could be found working together cheek by jowl in the ever-deepening Big Hole. Instant fortunes were made (and lost); money and champagne flowed like water.

At this stage some 3 600 claims were being worked, each about 9 m², most of them divided and subdivided into even smaller plots. As the men dug deeper into the 'blue ground' many of the paths that crisscrossed the Big Hole collapsed, so an elaborate and confusing network of aerial ropeways made its appearance, and mining conditions became increasingly chaotic. Syndicates and a few small mining companies were formed, but by 1885 there were still nearly 100 separate operators, and the confusion grew worse as mining costs escalated and the diamond selling prices fluctuated wildly.

Rhodes decided to consolidate the fields and began buying up claims held by the De Beers company. By 1887 he owned the enterprise outright, and then turned his attention to the even richer Kimberley Mine, owned by the flamboyant Jewish Londoner, Barney Barnato. In his year-long struggle for possession of the diggings, Rhodes was backed by the immensely wealthy and internationally connected Rothschild family, and in 1888 Barnato came to terms, accepting a cheque for £5 338 650 – an almost unheard-of sum in those days.

Thereafter De Beers, in total control, managed to stabilize the industry, and Kimberley settled into a more orderly, and more respectable way of life, though its peace was briefly and explosively shattered during the South African (Anglo Boer) War: from November 1899 until February 1900 its residents (Rhodes among them) were besieged by Boer forces, suffering bombardment and a degree of deprivation. The siege had especially tragic consequences for the town's black people.

Today four of the area's diamond 'pipes' are still active; several other minerals (iron, gypsum, salt) are mined in the area; and the town (population: 150 000) serves as the principal centre for the cattle ranches and irrigated farmlands of the region.

The original diggings – long since mined out – are now part of a number of historical sites and exhibits that combine to form the:

KIMBERLEY MINE MUSEUM The museum's centrepiece is the Big Hole, until recently the world's largest man-made crater: by 1914, when it closed down, it had reached a depth of 1 097,6 m and yielded three tons of diamonds.

Beside the partly-filled Big Hole, and providing an evocative and pretty comprehensive insight into the Kimberley's lively past, is a re-creation of part of the early town: lining the cobbled street are shops and cottages, a diggers' pub, Barney Barnato's boxing academy, the private railway coach used by the De Beers directors, and much else. Nearby is the old mining headgear; other components of the museum include:

☆ The De Beers Hall, which houses diamond displays, among them finished jewellery, stones of various and attractive colours ('fancies'), the world's largest uncut diamond (616 carats) and the'Eureka' diamond which young Jacob Erasmus picked up near Hopetown (see page 259).

☆ The Transport Hall, which holds some splendid Victorian vehicles.
☆ The Art Galley, which profiles the various and fascinating faces of 19th century adolescent Kimberley.

The museum is open daily; there's a tearoom and gift shop (which sells diamonds, among other things). For information, telephone Kimberley (0531) 3-1557/8/9 or Johannesburg (011) 638-5126.

DUGGAN-CRONIN GALLERY (Egerton Road). The noted ethnologist and pioneer photographer, Alfred Duggan-Cronin, settled in Kimberley in 1897, developed a deep interest in the peoples of the area and in the San (Bushman) culture, and later (in 1919) embarked on a systematic, 20-year photographic survey. The results were outstanding in terms of both artistic merit and ethnological value.

The gallery's photographic collection includes some non-ethnic subjects; rock engravings and African crafts are also on display. Open daily. Next door is the:

MCGREGOR MUSEUM This started life in 1897 as a sanatorium (Cecil Rhodes was keen to promote Kimberley as a health resort), and now contains a diverse variety of displays. Of note are the rooms, furnished in period style, that Rhodes occupied during the South African War siege; the lavishly imposing entrance hall; the Hall of Religions (exhibits focus on five major faiths) and the Environment Hall (regional ecology). Open daily.

THE OLD MUSEUM, in Chapel Street, features a wide range of geological and mineral exhibits. Open daily.

KIMBERLEY'S PERIOD HOMES include Rudd House (in Loch Road), which belonged to Charles Rudd, Rhodes's associate and agent, and is now being restored to its original plushness; Dunluce, a stately 19th century residence in Lodge Road, Belgravia (viewing by appointment; Tel. (0531) 3-2645/6); and the Africana Library (Du Toitspan Road), a Victorian 'gentleman's retreat'.

WILLIAM HUMPHREYS ART GALLERY, Civic Centre, houses excellent collections of South African and European paintings, sculpture, furniture and objets d'art. The gallery's garden wall holds the controversial Moses Kottler sculptural work, banished by the prudes of Pretoria in the late 1950s: it comprises two semi-nude figures, one of which appears to have wandering hands.

MEMORIALS Kimberley has a fairly impressive selection that tends to focus on mining and war, though they include the:
☆ Sister Henrietta Stockdale Chapel, built in 1887 and now part of the provincial hospital. Sister Henrietta, an Anglican nun and former pupil of Florence Nightingale, arrived in Kimberley in 1876, worked among the miners as a district nurse and later became matron of the town's Carnarvon hospital, where she established a progressive nurses' school. She was largely responsible for the official recognition, in 1891, of nursing as a profession: the Cape Parliament was the first of the world's legislatures to make provision for formal registration. A statue of Sister Henrietta stands in front of St Cyprian's Cathedral. Among the city's other memorials are:
☆ The fine equestrian statue of Cecil Rhodes, on Du Toitspan Road near the cathedral. The latter, incidentally, boasts the largest nave in South Africa.
☆ Honoured Dead Memorial (Dalham Road, south of the city), the work of the noted architect Herbert Baker, erected to commemorate those who died during the siege. Featured is 'Long Cecil', the huge siege gun, named after Cecil Rhodes, designed by American mining engineer George Labram and manufactured in the De Beers Kimberley workshops. In reply, the Boers brought up their 'Long Tom' French Creusot long-range, large-calibre artillery piece (it fired 42-kg shells over a distance of 9 000 m). Tragically, and ironically, Labram was killed by one of Long Tom's salvos while resting in his hotel room.
☆ The Diggers Fountain, in the Oppenheimer Memorial Gardens, is an impressive piece of statuary honouring the thousands of miners past and present who helped create the Diamond City.

DIAMOND DEALERS These include The Jewel Box (diamonds available ex factory; a goldsmith works while you watch; in Long Street, Tel.(0531) 2-1731); Kimberley Jewellers (video

presentation and goldsmith; in Jones Street, Tel. (0531) 2-5522 or 2-5101), and V E de Smidt Jewellers (Jones Street; Tel. (0531) 2-3862). The curio shop at the Mine Museum also sells diamonds; Tel. (0531) 3-1557.

DRIVE-IN PUBS Only two are believed to exist anywhere in the world, and they're both in Kimberley.
The Halfway House Hotel, at the corner of Du Toitspan and Egerton roads, is a hangover – if one may use the word – from the days when patrons arrived, and stayed for a drink or two, on horseback. The Kimberlite Hotel has a similar amiable facility.

TRAMS, TRAINS AND TOURS A veteran (1913) tram plies between the City Hall and the Big Hole several times a day. For railway enthusiasts, there's a daily steam passenger/freight service between Kimberley and De Aar; Tel. (0531) 288-1111; steam locomotives are on view at Witput station, and the steam locomotive shunting yards at Beaconsfield may be visited; Tel. (0531) 288-2061.
Local tours (historical, cultural, diamond) and visits farther afield – to the Magersfontein battlefield (see page 262), the Kalahari Gemsbok National Park (see page 264) and the Augrabies Falls (see page 265) – are available.
For information on these, and on hunting safaris in the northern Cape, telephone (0531) 3-1581 or 2-5842.

Around Kimberley

The semi-arid countryside of the region offers few natural features of immediate interest to the visitor, though it has considerable botanical significance: it's a transitional zone between Karoo, Kalahari and grassland vegetation. Some 16 km north-west of Kimberley, on the banks of the Vaal River (take the R31), is the small town of:

RIVERTON This attractive pleasure resort offers fully-equipped luxury chalets, and villas, rondavels and caravan/camping sites; swimming pool; boating on the river (navigable for 25 km); angling, horse-riding, recreation hall, tennis, playgrounds, mini-zoo.
The international barefoot water-skiing championships are held here each year (March/April); Tel. (0531) 2-2241.

The far horizons of the Cape interior

BARKLY WEST Originally named Klipdrift, it was the frenetic scene of South Africa's first diamond diggings, and of the 'diggers' rebellion', a comic-opera affair which created a very short-lived Klip Drift Republic. This functioned, after a fashion and under the presidency of the reprehensible Stafford Parker, for a few months in 1870.

The gravels along the Vaal are invitingly rich in diamonds and gemstones, and numbers of prospectors are still drawn to the area in the dry months between June and September: about 70 of them are licensed to search the alluvial fields, and each Saturday morning they bring their finds – sometimes quite impressive ones – into Barkly West, where they bargain with the local diamond-dealers (and, if sales are good, fill the pubs).

Worth visiting in town is the Canteen Kopje nature reserve and open-air archeological museum (geological exhibits, fossils). The Mining Commissioner's Museum houses some interesting Stone Age artifacts, most of them unearthed by the miners.

VAALBOS NATIONAL PARK, off the R64 west of Kimberley, is still under development and, at the time of writing, offered few visitor facilities. However, it's potentially one of the country's more intriguing wilderness areas: it lies in the transitional zone mentioned above (Karoo, Kalahari, grassland), has recently been enlarged to 20 000 ha, and has two extensive stretches of Vaal River frontage and many seasonal pans. The vegetation must be allowed to recover fully before a major restocking programme can be launched; wildlife currently in residence includes giraffe, kudu, eland, springbok and red hartebeest; scheduled for reintroduction are rhino and buffalo. Vaalbos, incidentally, is the common Afrikaans name for the camphor bush, *Tarchonanthus camphoratus.* Information: National Parks Board (see Advisory, page 269).

MAGERSFONTEIN Some of the Anglo-Boer War's earlier and most bitterly contested battles were fought in the Kimberley area, the most notable perhaps that at Magersfontein, 32 km to the south. Here, on the Modder River during the British 'Black Week' of December 1899, the brilliant Koos de la Rey's burgher forces halted Lord Methuen's advance with murderous Mauser fire delivered from a network of trenches – a novel defensive technique that was to be developed and used with devastating effect in the Great War of 1914-18. There's a small museum and a tearoom on site; other monuments along the Modder River honour specific military units.

The Diamond Route

This follows a path between Victoria West (see page 258) through Hopetown, Kimberley and Warrenton to Potchefstroom to the west of Johannesburg. At the entrance to each town there's a notice board briefing travellers on local sites of interest.

HOPETOWN, about 130 km south-west of Kimberley, an isolated, pleasant little place close to the Gazella game reserve (gemsbok, eland, kudu, springbok) and not too far from the extensive Vanderkloof Dam. In the vicinity of Witput Station a local farmer has established some rewarding one- and two-day trails along the Orange River; hikers enjoy good game-viewing and bird-watching (fish eagle, black eagle, bustard, waterfowl); Tel. (05392) 122.

WARRENTON, situated beside the Vaal River to the north of Kimberley on the R29 road, is the supply artery to the Vaalharts irrigation scheme, the southern hemisphere's largest: it covers about 40 000 ha. The countryside is refreshingly lush; diamond mining is still a preoccupation; the semi-precious stone processing factory welcomes visitors; the Warrenton nature reserve, rich in succulents, is worth calling in at (best time: May-June). Far to the north-west of Kimberley – 310 km along the R31 – is the small centre of:

Kuruman

Site of one of Africa's most important mission stations, and the base from which many pioneering expeditions, both religious and adventurous, set out in Victorian times. Robert Moffat of the London Missionary Society established his headquarters here in 1824 (his predecessors were Johannes Kok, murdered in 1808; and the LMS's Robert Hamilton), baptized the first Tswana converts, built a church for 800 people, and gave his daughter Mary in marriage to explorer David Livingstone (the trunk of the almond tree under which Livingstone proposed still stands). The church and mission buildings are a functioning complex; the grounds are overgrown, shaded by syringa and fig trees, pears and pomegranates, and they're quite lovely.

Nearby, below a small range of hills, is the source of the local river, a spring that yields 20 million litres of sparkling water each day. This is the famous 'eye' of Kuruman: it supplies the town, and around it a most pleasant little park has been created (there are restful picnic spots beneath the willow trees; the fat fish of the river expect to be fed). Restful too is the 850-ha Kuruman nature reserve, sanctuary for rhino, zebra and a number of antelope species.

SISHEN AND KATHU South-west of Kuruman on the long road (the R27) to Upington, is the giant Iscor mine at Sishen, site of the earth's largest known iron-ore deposits. The open-cast mining methods used are claimed to be the most advanced in the world; a specially constructed 861 km railway carries the ore to Saldanha Bay on the Cape's lower west coast (see page 336) in ore-trains up to two kilometres long: a system geared to handle a phenomenal 33 million tons a year. Sishen's residential area

is Kathu, a surpisingly attractive, neat, lively town of modern buildings. The Kathu game reserve's 2 300 ha are home to 16 larger game species (among them are white rhino, black wildebeest and kudu). Next door is a resort area (caravan/camping; fishing; picnicking).

THE NORTH-WESTERN AREAS

Most of the region comprises Gordonia, named after one-time Cape prime minister Sir Gordon Sprigg (he held office four times between 1878 and 1902) and the country's largest magisterial district: it covers nearly 55 000 km² of dry scrubland, semi-desert and, in the Kalahari region to the north, pure desert.

A vast, lonely country, sparsely populated, dry, seemingly barren for the most part – but bountiful nevertheless: Gordonia is bisected by the Orange River, whose waters irrigate fields and plantations that yield marvellous harvests of lucerne and wheat, raisins and sultanas, cotton, vegetable seeds, grapes. Beyond the irrigated areas are huge salt pans, and ranchlands that nurture hardy cattle and karakul sheep.

Upington

A pleasant, fairly substantial, isolated town set on the north bank of the Orange, founded as a mission station in 1871 and named after Thomas Upington, prime minister of the Cape Colony from 1884 to 1886. The early missionary Christian Schroder established an irrigation scheme that, over the decades, has been hugely expanded and now stretches either side of the river from the Boegoeberg down as far as the Augrabies area; the fertile islands of the Orange are also intensively cultivated; palm trees grow especially well in the region and dates are a prominent crop.

Upington is a major railhead (the line reaches town via a 1 067-m bridge) and has a modern airport, whose 5,5-km runway is the southern hemisphere's longest. The town is 588 km from Bloemfontein, 796 km from Johannesburg, 894 km from Cape Town and 1 236 km from Durban, and it's a convenient stopover on your way to Augrabies or the Kalahari. Incidentally, motorists journeying between Johannesburg and Cape Town would do well to consider the alternative Kimberley-Upington-Namaqua route: it's about 200 km longer than the N1 through the Karoo but the road is good and relatively free of traffic.

The countryside is semi-desert; the summers (October-March) are blistering, winter days warm, winter nights cool and sometimes very cold. The sun shines brightly all year round. The terrain tends to be rather featureless, but has its special attractions: diamonds and semi-precious stones (amethyst, beryl, agate, jasper, rose quartz, tourmaline, tiger's eye, ruby) attract fossickers from afar.

UPINGTON'S MUSEUM, housed in an early mission church, displays interesting exhibits relating to the town's history and to that of the Lower Orange River.

LOCAL PRODUCTS Visitors are welcomed by the Karakul Research Station (contact the Upington Tourist Information Office: see Advisory, page 269); by the South African Dried Fruit Co-operative, the world's second largest; Tel. (054) 2-2167; and by the Oranjerivier Wine Co-operative, the country's most northerly and, again, the world's second largest (tours by arrangement; Tel. (054) 2-5651/2/3).

OLYVENHOUTSDRIFT is an island resort in the middle of the Orange River – a pleasantly refreshing place of lawns, a 1 041-m avenue of date palms (longest in the world), bowling greens, tennis courts, pool, chalets, caravan/camping ground and facilities for watersports and angling (carp, moddervis, yellowfish). Information: Eiland Holiday Resort, Tel. (054) 2-5211.

KANONEILAND, one of the bigger, better-known and most developed of the river's islands, lies about 25 km downstream of Upington and is worth visiting to see how crops are grown under irrigation, and for its place in military history. The densely wooded islands were once home to sections of the warlike Korana people, river-pirates and rustlers whose raiding forays in the 1860s provoked three colonial punitive expeditions, the second of which was directed specifically at the river strongholds. There's a camping ground on Kanoneiland.

SPITSKOP NATURE RESERVE, 13 km north of Upington, is a 2 740-ha haven for zebra, ostrich, eland, gemsbok and a number of other game species. There are 30 km of game-viewing roads and a viewing point (with telescope).

TIERBERG NATURE RESERVE, south-west of town and near the small centre of Keimoes, is a modest (160 ha) area noted for its winter-flowering aloes (most prominent of which is the Gariep aloe) and its springbok population. Superb views of the surrounding and refreshingly fertile countryside from the crest of the 'berg itself.

KEIMOES AND KAKAMAS These two villages are on the banks of the Orange River to the west of Upington (on the way to Augrabies Falls; take the R64: see page 265). They're both attractive little places set among green farmlands, and both areas are noted for their giant water wheels – Victorian relics that still function efficiently. Kakamas, surrounded by vineyards and fields of lucerne and cotton, has a surprisingly fine hotel (see Advisory, page 269). Features of the countryside are the pear trees, and the deposits of beautiful rose quartz, tourmaline and amethyst.

THE ROARING SANDS This is a unique feature of the region – an extraordinary, 9-km-long, 2-km-wide 'island' of white dunes set among the red-sand country off the R32, near the village of Groblershoop some 120 km southeast of Upington. The dunes are about 100 m high and in dry weather the sands, when disturbed (even slightly, by for instance running your hand through them) emit an eerie moaning sound that occasionally rises to a muted roar. The phenomenon has something to do with the white sand's granular texture and loose composition, elements that prevent it mixing with the more compacted red sands. Best places to hear the noise are on the southerly faces. Fulgurites – sand fused into threads and tube-shaped lengths by the action of lightning – are sold by the locals as souvenirs. Visitor facilities in the area include hutted accommodation and a camping site.

Kalahari Gemsbok National Park

The Kalahari, 1,2 million km² in area, extends over the eastern parts of Namibia, most of Botswana, a large portion of Zimbabwe, some of Angola and a small segment of South Africa north of the Orange River. Although termed a desert – because of its porous, sandy soils and lack of surface water – much of the region is in fact wilderness, its great plains covered by sparse but sweet grasses that sustain enormous herds of game animals.

This immense, parched-looking and hauntingly beautiful country is the last refuge of the traditional Bushmen (San), only a few clans of whom remain relatively untouched by Western culture (see box, page 266).

The Kalahari Gemsbok National Park is a 9 590-km^2 wedge of sandy territory sprawling between the borders of Namibia and Botswana. Combined with the adjoining Gemsbok National Park in Botswana (there are no fences; game animals are free to trek, which they do *en masse* – an unforgettable spectacle), the conservation area extends over 2 046 103 ha, or 79 000 km^2, which is somewhat larger than the Republic of Ireland and seven times the size of Lebanon. Much of the countryside between the invariably bone-dry riverbeds of the Auob and the Nossob (the latter 'watercourse' flows about once a century) is rolling red duneland, scantily clad with grasses. Plant life, more profuse near the river courses, includes camel-thorn, blackthorn and other acacia species. Summer temperatures often exceed 40 °C; winter nights can be freezing.

The park was proclaimed in 1931 to put an end to the indiscriminate slaughter of the gemsbok and springbok herds. About 80 wind-powered boreholes have been sunk to tap the underground water, and dams and waterholes attract large numbers of game. Many of the park's animals, though, obtain their moisture from the hardy and ingeniously adapted desert succulents, notable among which are the tsamma melon (*Citrullus lanatus*) and the wild cucumber (*Acanthosicyos naudinianus*).

The park serves as sanctuary for blue wildebeest, eland, steenbok, red hartebeest, duiker and many smaller mammals – and, of course, for gemsbok and springbok. Among the carnivores are lion, leopard, cheetah, wild dog, spotted hyena and the rare brown hyena; avian life (215 species have been recorded) includes the secretary bird, bateleur, martial eagle, tawny eagle and two types of snake eagle.

Visitors to the Kalahari Gemsbok have a choice of three camps: Twee Rivieren, near the confluence of the Auob and Nossob; Mata Mata, on the Auob to the west, and the Nossob, near the Botswana border. All have fully equipped four- and six-bed huts and cottages (kitchen, bathroom; Twee Rivieren's are air-conditioned) and caravan/camp sites. Groceries and fuel are available; Twee Rivieren offers fresh food (but no bread or milk), a swimming pool, a 'lapa' where informal meals are served, and a landing strip (Avis car-hire available). The game-viewing road network is extensive. Information and reservations: National Parks Board (see Advisory, page 269).

Augrabies Falls

About 120 km west of Upington, in a desolate land of sand, scrub and rock, the Orange River plunges through a massive canyon in a dramatic sequence of rapids and cascades. In exceptional seasons and at flood peak the flow rises to 400 million litres a minute, the waters descending through the ravine to breach the rim of the main gorge. Here, 19 separate waterfalls drop, sheer at first and then in a misty tumble of cataracts, to the turbulent, rock-enclosed pool 200 m below. At times of medium flood the flow is confined to a single fall.

The Augrabies – the name is derived from the Korana word for 'big waters' – are ranked among the world's six largest waterfalls. The gorge is 18 km long, 250 m deep in places, and all along its length there are towering, starkly eroded granite cliffs. The suspension bridge was washed away in the 1988 floods.

THE AUGRABIES FALLS NATIONAL PARK This was proclaimed in 1966 to conserve just under 10 000 ha of river landscape along both banks of the Orange, and was recently – and greatly – enlarged with the addition of a 70 000-ha expanse known as the Riemvasmaak. The expansion will enable the area to be restocked with the larger game species. Currently in residence are black rhinoceros, eland, springbok, klipspringer and steenbok, leopard, caracal, black-backed jackal and bat-eared fox, baboon and monkey, and about 160 species of bird (among them the martial and black eagles).

Visitor amenities include accommodation in fully equipped cottages and huts (kitchen, bathroom, air-conditioning), camping site, restaurant, shop, petrol pump, information centre. There are picnic spots, game-viewing roads, walking trails, and the Klipspringer hiking trail (April to October; overnight huts *en route*). Information: The Warden, PO Box 10, Augrabies 8874; bookings: National Parks Board (see Advisory, page 269).

THE BUSHMEN OF THE KALAHARI

By tradition the Bushmen (or San) people are hunter-gatherers, subsisting largely on game, honey and the roots and fruits of plants. They lived – and in the Kalahari a few still live – in total harmony with nature, posing no threat to either wildlife or vegetation, their semi-nomadic routines governed by the seasons and by the movement of the animals.

That the Bushmen once inhabited most of southern Africa is evident from their wonderfully animated paintings on rocks and cave walls, their 'galleries' still to be seen as far afield as the Drakensberg and the southern Cape. But from about 2 000 years ago pastoral peoples began to encroach on the ancient hunting grounds. Some Bushmen clans were assimilated by the newcomers (who incorporated two or three of the San 'click' sounds into their own Nguni languages); others moved on west and north until they found land where they could live freely – which, in effect, confined them to areas that were too inhospitable for peoples who were less skilled in the ways of the wild: to the remote wilderness regions of the northwestern Cape, the Kalahari, Namibia and Botswana.

Today, most Bushmen groups have abandoned the nomadic lifestyle in favour of a more settled, sometimes even pastoral existence.

The true desert people live much as their ancestors did, moving in small clans, each with its clearly defined territory. The women gather roots and edible berries and wild melons such as the tsamma, a source of both food and water. The men hunt with a wooden bow strung with sinew, and arrows which they carry in a skin or bark quiver (they also use clubs or spears if the occasion demands). The arrowheads are tipped with a poison made from insect grubs, a toxin which acts slowly on the prey's nervous system, and the hunters may have to pursue the animal for enormous distances before it finally drops.

When the kill is made, the whole group joins in the feast, singing and dancing in a trance-like ritual around the fire. Bushman music is based on an atonal scale and is as unique to these people as their clan language. When game is scarce, the group splits up into smaller parties to glean food (snakes, lizards and even scorpions are included in the diet); during severe, prolonged droughts the women chew the bark of a particular tree: this prevents conception, so limiting the number of mouths to feed.

In especially dry areas, and in times of drought, the Bushmen store water in ostrich shells, which they bury deep below the sandy surface of the desert. These they recover with uncanny accuracy, even when no signs of the cache are visible. Ostrich shells are also used for making beads; clothing consists of skin karosses, loincloths and aprons. Possessions are very simple, and few: nothing can be owned which cannot be carried. Shelters are rudimentary, comprising structures of sticks which form two-thirds of a 150-cm-high circle. Some of the southern clans cover the sticks with mats woven from reeds.

Making a home among the red sands of the Kalahari

ADVISORY: GREAT INTERIOR

CLIMATE

The Cape interior extends over a large part of the great central plateau. It's a summer-rainfall region, but the rains tend to be infrequent; summer days can be extremely hot, nights much less so; winter days are blessed by long hours of intense sunshine, nights can be bitterly cold.

Karoo. Beaufort West temperatures: January average daily maximum 32,5 °C, daily minimum 16,2 °C; July daily maximum 18,1 °C, daily minimum 4,9 °C; extremes 41,9 °C and -5,6 °C. Rainfall: January average monthly 23 mm; July 8 mm; highest recorded daily rainfall 104 mm.

North-western areas. Upington temperatures: January average daily maximum 35,2 °C, daily minimum 19,7 °C; July average daily maximum 20,0 °C, daily minimum 4,8 °C; extremes 42,1 °C and -4,7 °C. Rainfall: January average monthly 16 mm, July 2 mm; highest recorded daily rainfall 119 mm.

MAIN ATTRACTIONS

Karoo: □ Starkly beautiful landscapes, at their best at dawn and sunset □ Historic Matjiesfontein and Graaff-Reinet. Northern Cape: □ The Diamond City of Kimberley. North-western Cape: □ Kalahari Gemsbok National Park □ The Augrabies Falls.

TRAVEL

Road. Kimberley is 175 km from Bloemfontein, 484 km from Johannesburg, 540 km from Pretoria, 764 km from Durban and 965 km from Cape Town. Upington is 402 km to the west; for distances from Upington, see page 00.

The main highways of the Karoo and the northern and north-western regions are in good condition.
Alternative routes between Johannesburg and Cape Town are: □ The R29 via Kimberley, which joins the national highway (N1) at Three Sisters in the Karoo, between Richmond and Beaufort West; or □ The R29 to Kimberley, west on the R64 and R32 to Upington, west again on the R64 to Springbok in Namaqualand and then south along the N7 to Cape Town. This is 200 km longer than the direct route, but the roads are relatively free of traffic.

Rail. Kimberley's railway station is on Florence Street; Tel. (0531) 288-2060 (arrivals and departures); 288-2631 (reservations).
Coach tours, local and regional: Tel. (0531) 3-1581 or 2-5842 (see also page 261).

Air. Kimberley and Uppington have air and rail links with major centres.

Kimberley: Regular SAA flights connect Kimberley airport (12 km from city centre; no bus, but taxi, car hire and hotel transport facilities are available). Information: (0531) 2-6572; 288-2176; 288-2276, or 2-2431.

Upington: With the exception of Saturdays, there are daily SAA flights in and out of Upington airport (7 km from town centre; no buses, but two car-hire firms have offices in Upington). Daily private airline flights between Johannesburg's Lanseria airport and the Namaqualand centre of Aggeneys and Springbok stop over on request. Air travel information: Tel. (054) 2-4611 and Civil Aviation, Tel. (054) 2-5656.
Coach tours: available from Upington include trips to Augrabies Falls and Kalahari Gemsbok National Park (4 days); also self-drive packages from Upington to major attractions; Connex Travel, Tel. (054) 2-5131/2-5746.
There is a coach service between Cape Town and Upington four days a week; Tel. (021) 218-6814 for details. Also contact Inter Cape, Tel. (054) 2-7091; Spoornet, Tel. (054) 28-2224, 28-2203; Mainliner (Upington to Johannesburg), Tel. (054) 2-5131.

The magnificent Augrabies Gorge (see page 265)

Graaff-Reinet: The Garden Route Inter-City coach service between Johannesburg and Mossel Bay passes through Graaff-Reinet; information and reservations: Tel. George (0441) 74-1509 or Graaff-Reinet (0491) 22-2222. Whippet Express minibuses run between Graaff-Reinet and Port Elizabeth; Tel. Port Elizabeth (041) 54-2683, or Graaff-Reinet (0491) 2-4151.

Kuruman: Coach tours from Kuruman take in the Kalahari Gemsbok National Park and the Roaring Sands; Tel. (01471) 2-1252.

ACCOMMODATION

Select hotels

Karoo

BEAUFORT WEST

Oasis ★★ Central; 49 rooms, 3 bars. PO Box 115, Beaufort West 6970; Tel. (0201) 3221/2/3/4.

COLESBERG

Central ★★ Convenient halfway-house between Johannesburg and Cape Town; 63 rooms; conference facilities. PO Box 58, Colesberg 5980; Tel. (05852) 90.

Merino Inn Motel ★★ Convenient halfway house between Johannesburg and Cape Town; 54 rooms; conference facilities for 100; à la carte restaurant. PO Box 10, Colesberg 5890; Tel. (05852) 265.

GRAAFF-REINET

Drostdy ★★ Atmospheric (see page 257); one of SA's best country hotels; 45 rooms; conference facilities for 80; swimming pool. PO Box 400, Graaff-Reinet 6280; Tel. (0491) 2-2161.

Graaff-Reinet Hotel ★★ Market St; 21 rooms; à la carte restaurant. PO Box 43, Graaff-Reinet 6280; Tel. (0491) 2-4191/2/3.

Panorama Protea ★★ On Magazine Hill overlooking town; 48 rooms; conference facilities for 300; à la carte, buffet and traditional Cape restaurants. PO Box 314, Graaff-Reinet 6280; Tel. (0491) 2-2233.

LAINGSBURG

Laingsburg Hotel ★★ On N1; 13 en-suite rooms; à la carte restaurant, pool. PO Box 53, Laingsburg 6900; Tel. (02372), ask for 9 or 185.

MATJIESFONTEIN

Lord Milner ★★ Historic (see page 256); one of SA's best country hotels; 33 rooms; pool; table d'hôte. PO Matjiesfontein 6901; Tel. (0020), ask for Matjiesfontein 3.

PRINCE ALBERT

Swartberg Protea ★★ Charming surrounds; 20 rooms; pool; PO Box 6, Prince Albert 6930; Tel. (04436) 332.

Northern Cape

BARKLY WEST

Queens ★ 13 en-suite rooms; restaurant. PO Box 17, Barkly West 8375; Tel. (05352), ask for 85.

HOPETOWN

Radnor ★★ 13 en-suite rooms; PO Box 25, Hopetown 8750; Tel. (05392), ask for 15.

KIMBERLEY

Colinton ★★ In Thompson St; just 10 double rooms. PO Box 400, Kimberley 8300; Tel. (0531) 3-1471.

Halfway House ★ Historic; 12 en-suite rooms; drive-in pub (see page 261). PO Box 650, Kimberley 8300; Tel. (0531) 2-5151.

Horseshoe Motel ★★ Central; 56 rooms; conference facilities for 300; à la carte restaurant, pool. PO Box 67, Kimberley 8300; Tel. (0531) 2-5267.

Kimberlite ★★ 30 rooms; drive-in pub (see page 261). 162 George St, Kimberley 8300; Tel. (0531) 81-1967.

Kimberley Sun ★★★★ Garden setting, 3 km from Big Hole; standard Southern Sun quality; 107 rooms, 8 suites; conference facilities for 300; 2 restaurants, pool. PO Box 635, Kimberley 8300; Tel. (0531) 3-1751.

Savoy ★★★★ Central; 43 rooms, 2 suites; conference facilities for 200. PO Box 231, Kimberley 8300; Tel. (0531) 2-6211.

North-western Cape

KAKAMAS

Waterwiel Protea ★★★ 25 rooms; conference facilities for 100; pool, tennis courts. PO Box 250, Kakamas 8870; Tel. (05442) 250/363.

KURUMAN

Eldorado Motel ★★ 62 en-suite rooms; conference facilities for 200; à la carte restaurant. PO Box 313, Kuruman 8460; Tel. (01471) 2-2191.

UPINGTON

Oranje ★★ 78 rooms; conference facilities. PO Box 100, Upington 8800; Tel. (054) 2-4177/8.

Upington Protea Inn ★★★ On banks of Orange River; 44 rooms, 13 suites; conference facilities for 100. PO Box 13, Upington 8800; Tel. (054) 2-5414.

Caravan/camping and self-catering accommodation:

Beaufort West: Beaufort West caravan park (caravans available for hire), PO Box 352, Beaufort West 6970, Tel. (0201) 2800.

Calvinia: Municipal caravan park, PO Box 28, Calvinia 8190, Tel. (02772) 11.

Colesberg: Karoo Tuishuise, PO Box 169, Colesberg 5980, Tel. (05852) 135. Restored historical cottages; ideal overnight stop. Vergenoeg Ruskamers, PO Box 72, Colesberg 5980, Tel. (05852) 72. Van Zylsvlei Motel has caravans for hire; PO Box 50, Colesberg 5980, Tel. (05852), and ask for 153.

Graaff-Reinet: Urquhart Park (municipal resort; has caravans/camping and self-catering accommodation), PO Box 71, Graaff-Reinet 6280, Tel. (0491) 2-2121. Karoo Park Guesthouse, PO Box 388, Graaff-Reinet 6280, Tel. (0491) 2-2557. Camdeboo Cottages, 16 Parliament St, Graaff-Reinet 6280, Tel. (0491) 2-3180; restored historic cottages, fully serviced.

Kimberley: Langleg and Riverton resorts (both administered by the municipality) Private Bag X5030 Kimberley 8300, Tel. (0531) 2-1703. On the Vaal River; has caravan/camping facilities and self-catering accommodation.

Kuruman: Municipal caravan park, PO Box 4, Kuruman 8460, Tel. (01471) 2-1479. Near the famous 'Eye'; also has overnight accommodation.

Laingsburg: Sit en Rus Caravan Park, Voortrekker Road, Tel. (02372) 93.

Somerset East: Somerset Cottages, Swartfontein Street; PO Box 123, Somerset East, Tel. (0424) 3-3512.

Touws River: Loots Caravan Camp, PO Box 8, Touws River 6880, Tel. (02382) 49. Also has overnight accommodation.

Upington: Die Eiland Resort, Private Bag X6003, Upington 8800, Tel. (054) 2-6911 ext 2236 or 2-5211.

Vryburg: Swartfontein resort, PO Box 35, Vryburg 8600, Tel. (01451) 4461. In a nature reserve 8 km

outside town. Offers caravan/camping facilities and self-catering chalets.

USEFUL ADDRESSES AND TELEPHONE NUMBERS

National Parks Board

Head Office, PO Box 787, Pretoria 0001; Tel. (012) 343-9770.

Southern Cape, PO Box 774, George 6530; Tel. (0441) 74-6924/5.

South-western Cape, PO Box 7400, Roggebaai 8012; Tel. (021) 419-5365.

KIMBERLEY

Automobile Association, Cor Main and Craven streets, Kimberley 8300; Tel. (0531) 2-5207 or (emergencies) 81-1960.

Car hire, major rental firms represented at airport and in city; consult local directory or hotel reception.

Emergency numbers, *Ambulance* Tel. (0531) 2-9561/2 or 81-1955. *Hospital casualty* Lyndhurst Road; (0531) Tel. 80-2911. *Fire brigade* 24-2111. *Police headquarters* 81-2310. *Police flying squad* 1-0111. *All-night pharmacy* The Piet Muller Pharmacy, Old Main Rd (opp Post Office); Tel. (0531) 2-8981.

Kimberley Municipal Publicity Office, City Hall, Market Square, Kimberley 8300; Tel. (0531) 2-2241; 2-2264/5/6; Tourist Information Office, Tel. (0531) 80-6264/5. There's also an information kiosk at the Big Hole, Tel. (0531) 2-6883.

Satour (South African Tourism Board), Louverdis Building, 1 Market Square; Private Bag X5017, Kimberley 8300; Tel. (0531) 3-1434 or 2-2657.

Tour Guide Services, Tel. (0531) 2-5842.

OTHER CENTRES

Graaff-Reinet Publicity Association, PO Box 153, Graaff-Reinet 6280; Tel. (0491) 2-2479 (chairman's residence).

Upington Tourist Information Office, Public Library Building, Town Square, Upington 8800; Tel. (054) 2-6911.

CAPE TOWN AND THE PENINSULA

The Cape Peninsula is a slender, 75-km-long, 460 km² promontory curving into the sea at the extreme south-western corner of the African continent. Popular belief has it that it is the dividing line between the Atlantic and Indian oceans, but the technical separation occurs farther to the east, at Cape Agulhas, Africa's most southerly point.

The confusion, though, is understandable: the waters off the Peninsula's western coast are markedly cooler than than those that lap the eastern shores, and when you stand atop Cape Point, the massively impressive buttress at the southern end, you can actually see the interaction of two great ocean currents – the tropically warm Agulhas and Antarctic-chilled Benguela (see Introduction to South Africa, page 12).

The Peninsula stretches from the Cape of Good Hope and Cape Point northward to Table Bay and the city of Cape Town. It comprises, for the most part, a strikingly beautiful mountain plateau that achieves its loftiest and most spectacular heights in the famed Table Mountain massif overlooking bay and city. Its western and eastern shorelines are graced by attractive little (and some not so little) residential and resort centres that are a magnet for holiday-makers, boating enthusiasts, scuba-divers, surfers, sunworshippers.

To the north are the Cape Flats, a region that once – 60 million years ago – lay beneath the sea, so separating what is now the Peninsula from the mainland. Over the millenia the waters receded to expose a low, sandy, flat area known to the early Dutch colonists as 'Die Groote Woeste Vlakte' (the Great Desolate Plain) – a nightmare of drifting dunes. Eventually, during the 19th century, the sands were stabilized by planting out hardy hakeas and wattles and, most of all, Port Jackson willows. These last, imported from Australia, served their purpose only too well: in due course the tenacious plants spread throughout the region

The city and its mountain, viewed from Table Bay. Beyond, probing finger-like 80 km into the Atlantic Ocean, is the Cape Peninsula.

and are now regarded as thoroughgoing pests.

Today the northern plain is intensively culti-vated in some parts (wheat, vegetables, straw-berries) and dense with suburbia in others.

CLIMATE This is a winter-rainfall region, its climate classed as Mediterranean.

Summers are cloudless, bright and dry, the days generally hot but seldom uncomfortably so: temperatures are modified by the prevailing south-easter, a strong, blustery and sometimes destructive wind that often blows for days at a stretch and which, when it comes to one's enjoyment of the outdoors, can be thoroughly disruptive.

Without it, though, Cape Town would be as steamily enervating as Rangoon. Its freshness is said to cleanse the city of sickness (this may well have been so in earlier and less sanitary days), and for this reason it is known to locals as the 'Cape Doctor'.

Winter is the green season. Periods of driving rain, brought in by moist air from the north-west, are interspersed by crisp, sunlit days of magical quality.

FLORA The Peninsula is part of the Cape Floral Kingdom, a zone that extends over the winter-rainfall belt running along the country's south-western and southern coasts and botanically quite remarkable: occupying just 0,04% of the earth's total land area, it nevertheless enjoys equal status with the great Boreal Kingdom that extends over North America and most of Europe and Asia.

The Cape Floral Kingdom includes almost 8 600 species; of the 989 genera occurring, fully 193 are unique to a particular area; as many as 121 different species have been found growing within a single 10-m² patch. Collectively, this floral wealth is known as 'fynbos', and for the most part comprises such tough, low-growing, small-leafed, evergreen shrubs as the lovely ericas (600 species of them); the proteas (368 species; the king protea is South Africa's national flower); the almost leafless, reed-like restio and a great number and variety of bulbous and cormous plants.

The tallest and one of the most attractively distinctive members of the protea family is the silver tree (*Leucadendron argenteum*), growing 10 m and occasionally 16 m tall, its large, delicate leaves green but with a silver sheen imparted by a dense covering of long, silky hairs. The sheen is at its most noticeable and most entrancing when the leaves quiver in the strong wind. Legend has it that the silver tree will only flourish within sight of Table Mountain, but in fact it is found as far away as Stellenbosch and Paarl Mountain, and it has even been successfully cultivated in Europe.

Some 3 000 fynbos species – rather more than a third of the total – occur on the Peninsula itself. But the numbers are declining, the plants steadily falling victim to human encroachment and pollution, competitive alien flora, too-frequent fires and the predations of the flower industry. In the mid-1980s it was estimated that 1 250 species were threatened with total extinction (though not all were formally classified as such).

CITY AND SUBURB Cape Town is a place of contrasts, two of which strike visitors immediately on the drive in from Cape Town airport. In the distance there's the spectacular, distinctively flat-topped bulk of the Mountain towering over a city that seems as remote from the Third World as Brussels, Bristol or Boston. It's a clean, neat, bustling little metropolis of handsome buildings, gracious thoroughfares, glittering shops and a general ambience that has more of Europe in it than of Africa.

Along either side of the airport road, though, the picture is very different. Here, on some of the stretches, the buildings are small, shabby, occupied by people who look poor and are poor. Beyond, on the sand-blown Cape Flats to the east, there are densely packed townships and 'squatter' areas of rudimentary houses, and of row upon row of shelters thrown together with corrugated iron and plastic sheeting.

These are the two Cape Towns. The first beckons the visitor with a smile, entertains him royally and sends him away replete with pleasant memories. The second barely intrudes: the poverty and deprivation are there, but for the most part they are silent and go unnoticed.

Greater Cape Town has a population of about two million, a figure that will rise by a further million and more during the next ten years if the present pattern of 'urban drift' continues. Most of the newcomers will be black families who find it increasingly difficult to survive in the traditional Xhosa 'homelands' of Ciskei and Transkei in the east, territories plagued by overcrowding, soil erosion and a grievous shortage of skills and development funds.

The massive influx has created an urgent and continuing need for more land, for houses, schools, clinics, roads and other services, and the burden on the public exchequer is heavy. But the City Fathers and private enterprise are doing their best with the limited resources at their disposal. One of their major recent projects is Khayelitsha, a brand-new suburb well south of the airport, close to the shores of False Bay and linked by rail to the central area. The township has a huge, modern shopping centre, an industrial complex with provision for 100 factories, and is intended to accommodate around 250 000 people in decent comfort. Cape Town needs several more Khayelitshas if it is to survive the century with honour. However, from the general to the particular:

Cape Town is the legislative capital of and fourth largest city in South Africa, and by far the oldest of the country's urban centres: it was established in 1652 by Commander Jan van Riebeeck and his small party of settlers as a replenishment station for the fleets of Holland's great maritime empire.

The metropolitan area fills the amphitheatre formed by Table Mountain and its flanking peaks, sprawls northwards over the Cape Flats, and stretches on either side of the Peninsula and inland, the suburbs hugging the lower slopes of the mountain range and extending southwards along the line of rail (these are the oldest of the residential areas outside the city proper, founded as farms by the first of the 'free-burghers' in the later 1650s). The central area is comparatively small, its potential for expansion restricted by sea and mountain.

Popularly termed the 'Tavern of the Seas', Cape Town owed its prominence and prosperity over three centuries and more to its strategic position astride the ocean lanes, and to its harbour. And it is, still, an exceptional harbour – in all respects but one: maritime traffic has declined dramatically over the past few years; outlets closer to the Witwatersrand, the Republic's industrial heartland, have siphoned off all but a trickle of trade.

Nevertheless, Cape Town remains a substantial port city: the harbour is South Africa's fifth busiest and, after Durban, its second biggest; the pre-cooling stores are among the world's most extensive; ship repair is a major industry (the dry dock, well used by tankers in need of maintenance, is the largest in the southern hemisphere). And there are imaginative plans to revitalize the unused portions of the harbour area (see page 281).

Other significant economic activity in and around Cape Town includes marine fishing and fish processing, petroleum refining, cement production, chemical and fertilizer processing, plastics, textiles, clothing, footwear, light engineering and high-tech manufacturing, printing and publishing, banking and insurance. And tourism.

CITY CENTRE

Cape Town's main thoroughfare is the Heerengracht, which starts at the harbour and runs straight as an arrow towards the mountain, changing its name to Adderley Street at about the halfway mark. To stroll from one end to the other takes a pleasant half-hour.

In its broad lower reaches the thoroughfare is flanked by rather stately office blocks; the central island section supports lawns, palm trees, an ornamental fountain and pond and some quite impressive statuary (the war memorial; Jan van Riebeeck and his wife, Maria de la Queillerie). This area is part of what is called the Foreshore, a 145-ha expanse of land reclaimed from the sea, some of it during the 19th century and the rest in the 1930s and 1940s. The enterprise was a spin-off from harbour construction work – the dredging operations produced enormous quantities of sand that had to be disposed of, and the new ground was a bonus.

If you position yourself on the busy intersection of Lower Adderley and Strand Street, facing south, you'll see on your left the mosaic-walled railway station; across the road is the massive Golden Acre office and shopping complex; beyond, farther away to the left, are the Castle of Good Hope, the Grand Parade and City Hall. Diagonally opposite you, on Strand Street, is the five-star and futuristic Cape Sun Hotel. At the top, where Adderley sweeps around to become Wale Street, there is St George's (Anglican) Cathedral and the public gardens.

The Castle

A massively pentagonal fortress and the oldest occupied building in South Africa: its construction began in 1666 and, after some delays, ended during the brief governorship of Johann Bax (1676), at which time it comprised 'five polygons with their gate, sally port, outworks, two ravelins with their counter-scarps and those of the outworks'. The bastions were named after the various titles of the Prince of Orange: Nassau, Oranje, Leerdam, Buren and Catzenellenbogen.

Eight years later Commander Simon van der Stel decided that the sea entrance might present a danger in the event of a naval attack and had it closed up, constructing in its place the present entry-way. This incorporates a bell-tower, the carved coats of arms of the six chamber-cities of the Dutch East India Company (Amsterdam, Rotterdam, Delft, Hoorn, Enkhuizen and Zeeland), the monogram of the VOC (Vereenigde Oost-Indische Compagnie) and, surmounting all, the crest of the Netherlands. The bell, the country's oldest, is still rung on occasion.

Originally, the Castle's interior was a single large courtyard, but this was later divided in two by a defensive cross-wall, or 'Kat', on which additional cannon were mounted. Later still the wall was used as support for the Kat balcony, an elegantly-balustraded feature fronting the large reception room, which became the focal point of the Cape governor's splendidly attractive official residence and of Cape Town's aristocratic social life.

Part of the Castle has served as the headquarters of the Western Cape military command; elsewhere it functions as a museum. On display are furniture, carpets, porcelain, objets d'art and the principal paintings of the noted William Fehr collection.

Extensive renovations on the Castle are in progress and are planned to reach completion by 1993.

New attractions will be a reconstruction of the original moat and wooden bridge, and the Good Hope Collection, consisting of a house, a military and a restoration museum (containing artefacts found during renovations which date to the Dutch, British and French occupations of the Castle). A Ceremony of Keys is also to be introduced. There are other imaginative plans to develop its tourist potential.

Street musician in St George's Mall

Adderley Street

Named in honour of Sir Charles Adderley, a mid-19th century British politician who helped prevent the establishment of a convict colony at the Cape.

On the left as you walk up toward the mountain are the famous flower-sellers: raucous, good-humoured, offering exquisite blooms at low prices. Other points of interest on Adderley Street include the:

RAILWAY STATION On display is South Africa's first steam locomotive, imported in pieces from Scotland for local assembly in 1859. One of the city's livelier flea markets operates on the paved section just outside the main concourse. The coach terminal is part of the station area. The air terminal has moved to Thibault Square.

The Dolphin Pool in front of the 'Het Bakhuys' was 'rediscovered' and officially opened in September 1990. Daily tours are conducted; the entrance is on Castle Street.

Strand Street

This runs down from the slopes of Signal Hill and through the city centre. Principal points of interest are:

KOOPMANS-DE WET HOUSE, once the home of Maria Koopmans-De Wet (1834-1906), a noted patron of the arts, philanthropist, socialite and passionate Afrikaner (she was placed under house arrest during the South African War for her republican leanings and for her efforts to help the women and children of the concentration camps).

Originally built in 1701, the house was enlarged several times by different owners. Today, with its façade attributed to Louis Thibault and Anton Anreith, it stands as a classic example of late 18th century Cape domestic architecture. After the death of the last of the Koopmans-De Wet family it was acquired for the nation. On display: a priceless collection of Cape and European furniture, Delft ware and objets d'art. Open Monday to Saturday. Close by is the:

LUTHERAN CHURCH, with its splendid pulpit (carved by Anreith). Next to the church is Martin Melck House, once the parsonage and also designed by Anreith. Beautifully restored; secluded walled garden. Open Monday to Saturday.

GOLDEN ACRE A vast and glittering complex of department stores and speciality shops, coffee shops and restaurants, cinemas and offices, and part of an even more extensive underground concourse running beneath Adderley and adjoining streets.

The area is believed to be the site of Jan van Riebeeck's first earth-and-timber fort (1652). During excavations for the Golden Acre's foundations a dam, or reservoir, built by Van Riebeeck's successor, (Zacharias Wagenaer) was discovered. The architects redrew their plans in order to retain the relics *in situ*, and they're now on display, behind glass.

Among points linked by the concourse are two tourist information offices, the Cape Sun Hotel, two large public parking garages and the railway station.

Flower-seller, Greenmarket Square

The Groote Kerk, Adderley Street

GROOTE KERK This splendid Dutch Reformed Church (NGK) building stands at the upper end of Adderley, though it also fronts onto Church Square (a place lined with historic buildings and also worth a leisurely look-over). The first stone of the original Kerk was laid in 1678, but the project was abandoned until 1700, when Governor WA van der Stel ceremonially laid the foundation stone. The church was formally consecrated in 1704. Of this building, only the soaring steeple remains.

The second Groote Kerk was consecrated in 1841 and is notable for a number of architectural and sculptured features, including its pulpit, resting on a pedestal of carved lions. This, the work of Anreith and the wood-carver Jan Jacob Graaff, is a lot older than the present building. Also notable are the teak-and-pine timbered roofing and vast roof-span, and the old gravestones, some of which have been incorporated as paving stones, others into the walls.

CULTURAL HISTORY MUSEUM in Upper Adderley Street. Originally the Dutch East India Company's slave lodge (and brothel), the building was converted into government offices between 1809 and 1815, in the early years of the second British occupation, and in 1810 served as the Supreme Court. Parts of it (notably the fine Assembly Room, the Court Room and the judges' chambers) were masterfully designed by Louis Thibault. When you're there, take special note of the pediment on the rear façade: yet another creation of the ever-present and mischievous Anreith, it features a carica-

The Rose Window in St George's Cathedral

ture of the Royal coat of arms, with the Unicorn showing shocked revulsion for an old and degenerate British Lion. The museum has an interesting archeological section (Egyptian, Greek, Roman); other displays include furniture, glassware, weaponry, musical instruments and exhibits relating to the country's postal and currency history. Open Monday to Saturday.

ST GEORGE'S CATHEDRAL, in Wale Street, round the corner from Adderley. The church became a cathedral when Robert Gray was appointed Cape Town's first Anglican bishop in 1848. Later Victorians condemned the building as too 'pagan' in concept, and architects Herbert Baker and Francis Masey were commissioned to produce a more respectable 'new Gothic' edifice. The lovely classical spire and portico were lost in the process; the most recent extensions, completed in the 1980s, are functional and unremarkable. Of note, though, are the Rose Window (by Francis Spear), the Lord Mountbatten memorial window, and stained glass work by Gabriel Lore of Chartres. The cathedral has been the venue for some no-nonsense 'political' sermons by Nobel laureate Archbishop Desmond Tutu; the meeting place for protest against injustice, and starting point of the first legal mass peace march in recent years. On a gentler note, the choir, led by Barry Smith, sing like angels.

City centre stroll

Cape Town is one of the few South African cities (two others that come to mind are Pietermaritzburg and Grahamstown) whose central areas are best explored on foot. A great deal of what there is to see is concentrated and within ambling distance. In fact the City Council has published a series of booklets entitled *Cape Town Historical Walks*, which include two city pedestrian routes (together with, among others, a harbour route). The publications are available at a small charge from Captour and other outlets. The city walks last a little over two hours, longer if you linger. Alternatively, try an even easier and perhaps less earnestly educational stroll taking in:

ST GEORGE'S MALL This used to be a six-block traffic-congested city street until closed off for the near-exclusive use of pedestrians. The excellent St George's Hotel is at the bottom end; shops and arcades run up on either side; there are kiosks and umbrella-shaded bistros along the central pavement area. Buskers (to date not very talented ones) entertain passers-by.

GREENMARKET SQUARE, one of the prettiest plazas in Africa, and usually filled to the limits by street-traders' stalls. There are invariably some intriguing buys and occasionally a genuine antique among the bric-a-brac. A colourful, cheerful place, girded around by graceful buildings, including:

☆ The Inn on the Square: a good, standard city hotel with an inviting terrace.

☆ The Old Town House: an elegant late-1750s Cape Baroque structure once used by the Burgher Senate and the Burgher Watch, the city's first police force. It's now a gallery housing some fine works of art, including the 96 Dutch and Flemish masters donated in total from 1913 by Rand financier Sir Max Michaelis (who also funded the noted Michaelis School of Fine Art). Open daily between 10h00 and 17h00.

☆ The Metropolitan Methodist Church, round the corner in Burg Street: a fulsome Gothic building regarded by the Victorians as the country's most splendid place of worship.

LONG STREET, once the vibrant centre of city life. It is now a bit seedy, but lively enough with its inviting antique shops; well-stocked second hand bookstores (the best is probably Clarke's: if they don't have what you're looking for they can almost certainly obtain it for you) and, especially at the top end, a number of charmingly filigreed Victorian façades.

Of note and of curiosity interest are buildings in Orphanage Lane; the Blue Lodge (beautifully preserved exterior); the Palm Tree mosque, the city's only complete surviving 18th century house; the Dorp Street mosque; Carnival Court and the nearby building No. 203; and the Sendinggestig.

A church museum and one of Cape Town's most elegant edifices, the Sendinggestig was built in 1804, eventually to become the mother church of Dutch Reformed missionary activity. Most of its congregation was 'coloured' until the early 1970s, when the crudities of the Group Areas Act led to wholesale 'relocation', and the building was sold – and would have been demolished but for the efforts of the preservationists. It now houses, among other things, valuable documents relating to the early churchmen (London Missionary Society as well as Dutch Reformed) and their work. Open Monday to Friday; open Saturday during December.

The Gardens area

The humble vegetable patch that the first white colonists planted in the autumn and winter of 1652 (see page 22) still flourishes, though over the centuries it has changed beyond recognition, both in appearance and function. It is now one of the world's more attractive, and botanically most interesting, city parks.

During the 1680s a pleasure lodge made its appearance (later to be rebuilt and eventually to become Tuynhuys: see further on) and tall oak trees were planted to give shade. Simon van der Stel added more beauty to the area, allocating part of it to rare plants; his son established a menagerie at the mountain end. A hundred years later, at the close of the 18th century, the Garden measured 370 m by 900 m and was bisected by a main avenue lined with lemon and orange trees; bordering the lesser avenues were pomegranates, quinces, pears, apricots and apples.

Since then the Garden's extent has been greatly reduced by the splendid encroachment, on the east side (Government Avenue) of the Houses of Parliament, Tuynhuys, the National Gallery, the Old and Great Synagogues and Cape Town High School, and on the west by the South African Museum and the buildings of the former South African College. The South African Library, St George's Cathedral (see page 275) and the former Grammar School buildings are on the north side.

For visitors, and especially those with a botanical interest, the gardens are a must: over 8 000 varieties of tree, shrub, flower and other plant – most of them exotic – can be seen in the grounds. The large conservatory at its upper (mountain) end is known for its fine palm and orchid species; nearby is an attractive aviary and a tea-garden.

HOUSES OF PARLIAMENT Originally built in 1884, the handsome buildings that initially housed the Cape colonial legislature were enlarged at Union in 1910, extended several times in the decades that followed and were remodelled, in 1988, to include the debating chambers of the controversial tricameral system and a new assembly hall with seating capacity for 350 parliamentarians and 750 members of the public. Apart from the banqueting hall, caucus and committee rooms and so forth, two of the complex's more notable features are:
☆ The Library of Parliament of over 200 000 reference books, among which is the magnificent 50 000-volume Mendelssohn collection of Africana. The library is open to students and researchers.
☆ The Parliamentary museum, which contains the Gallery Hall housing portraits, busts, and relics of the Cape and Union parliaments (in-

cluding the Black Rod and mace, and the Speakers' chairs), and a wealth of historical documents.
There is public access to the parliamentary gallery during sessions; tickets are available from Room 12; overseas visitors need to show their passports. Guided tours during recess periods (usually July to January).

TUYNHUYS, just off Government Avenue and adjacent to the Houses of Parliament. Not open to the public, but can be viewed from the outside. It originally served as a pleasure lodge, later as the Dutch East India Company's guest house, and finally, in the early 1800s, extended in delightful Colonial Regency style eventually to become the state president's town residence.

STAL PLEIN, the open space in front of Tuynhuys, contains an impressive equestrian statue of Louis Botha, the Union of South Africa's first prime minister (1910-19); the Anton Anreith gateway to the Lodge de Goede Hoop (the country's first Masonic lodge); and the Flame of Remembrance, which honours those who died in their country's service. The presidential guard changes every two hours.

SOUTH AFRICAN NATIONAL GALLERY, off Government Avenue. The gallery holds over 6 500 works of art; the main hall is used for, among other things, a frequently changed exhibition of modern South African art. Open daily. Details of exhibitions, film shows, lectures are given in *What's On* and the daily press. There's also a Touch gallery for the blind. The gallery reopens in September 1991 after extensive renovations.

BERTRAM HOUSE, Government Avenue: a fine example of late-Georgian architecture (brick-built, with beautifully proportioned lines). Inside: an attractive display of period furniture, ceramics and other objets d'art, of which the Anna Lidderdale collection is the focus.

GREAT SYNAGOGUE, Government Avenue. An impressive Baroque building, domed and twin-towered, consecrated in 1905. Next door is the Old Synagogue, the first to be built in South Africa, now housing the historical and ceremonial treasures of the Jewish Museum. Open Tuesdays and Thurdays. The Old Syna-

Bertie's Landing, part of the imaginative new waterfront scheme (see page 281)

gogue, the Egyptian Building further up the avenue and the Gymnasium at Paarl are the only major edifices in the country designed in the Egyptian Revival style.

SOUTH AFRICAN MUSEUM, Queen Victoria St, offers a range of displays, in the spheres of natural history (marine life, birds), geology, ethnology, archeology and printing. Of special interest are the plaster casts of San (Bushman) people, created from living subjects by the artist James Drury in the early years of the 20th century; the San rock art exhibits, and dioramas of the fossil-rich Karoo and its reptiles of 200 million years ago. The forecourt serves as, among other things, an 'educational centre'. Open daily. Next door is the:

PLANETARIUM, Queen Victoria St: completed in 1987 as part of the R20 million extension to the South African Museum. Its projectors are able to reproduce the day or night sky over Cape Town at any stage during a 26 000-year period – 13 000 years on either side of the present time (the particular instrument that does this is an improved version of the Minolta Series Four star-projector, similar to those used by NASA astronauts during training). The equipment is capable of simulating panoramic terrestrial landscapes as well as celestial subjects; sound effects complement the visuals. The shows are changed every three months; Tel. 24-3330 for details.

SOUTH AFRICAN LIBRARY, Queen Victoria St. A graceful building in the Classical tradition, its design (1860) based on that of the FitzWilliam Museum in Cambridge, England. Founded in 1852, the SA Library was one of the world's first free libraries and is now a leading reference repository containing, *inter alia*, the 4 500 volumes bequeathed by Joachim von Dessin in 1761 'to serve as the foundation of a public library for the advantage of the community'. It also houses the Grey Collection of rare books and documents and a great many valuable Africana works. The library is open from Monday to Saturday.

RUST-EN-VREUGD, Buitenkant Street. Not part of the Gardens area (it is some way to the east) but worth a digression: the 18th century house contains the bulk of the noted William Fehr collection of Africana and watercolour paintings (the rest of the collection is housed in the Castle). Guided tours Monday to Friday.

ISLAMIC CAPE TOWN

Although relatively few in number, Muslims contributed a great deal to the early development of the Cape. The first to arrive were slaves from Java, the Celebes, Bali and Timor and other Indonesian islands and regions, who were immediately valued for their skills as craftsmen – and for their exotic cuisine, from which such traditional Cape foods as bobotie, bredie and blatjang developed. The slaves were soon joined by high-born political exiles, men such as Sheik Yusuf and the Rajah of Tambora, who had rebelled against the often-harsh authority of the Dutch East India Company in Java and Ceylon (Sri Lanka), and who brought their families and some of their followers with them.

For almost 50 years, from 1715 onwards, slaves arrived from the East in an almost continuous stream until the community had grown from a handful to several thousand. Many who were not originally of the Islamic faith were converted after their arrival. Among them were skilled silversmiths, tailors, coopers, wainwrights and builders (the famed Cape Dutch gable did not in fact originate in the Netherlands but in the East). With the abolition of slavery in the 1830s, many of these highly-respected people settled on the slopes of Cape Town's Signal Hill, in the picturesque Bo-Kaap ('Above-Cape', sometimes but wrongly called the Malay Quarter).

The customs and traditions which the community has maintained include the Chalifa (Khalifa), originally a sword dance that was part of Islamic religious ceremony. It was performed under a kind of hypnosis, or self-induced trance, during which youths and men pierced their flesh with swords and other sharp metal instruments. These did not draw blood, nor was there any sign of a wound when they were withdrawn. Today the dance lacks much of its religious significance and many imams (spiritual leaders) disapprove of the ritual, though it is still performed as a spectacle.

There was little intermarriage with other groups and the community is still very much integrated (though it hasn't confined itself to the Bo-Kaap area) and devoutly Muslim. Its members regularly attend their mosques and many make pilgrimages, not only to the Holy City of Mecca (as is required of every Muslim if he can afford it) but also to the local kramats – the tombs of holy men. The oldest and most important of these kramats is that of Sheik Yusuf near Faure, a town 13,5 km from Kuilsrivier, which is 38,5 km from Cape Town at the junction on the main road from Cape Town to Stellenbosch. This is one of five such places on or near the Peninsula and one on Robben island which, together, form a 'holy circle'.

A street of flat-roofed 18th-century houses typical of the Bo-Kaap area

TABLE MOUNTAIN

Flanked by Devil's Peak and Lion's Head, moody and changeable, majestically dominating the Peninsula's northern skyline, the mountain is without doubt South Africa's best-known landmark and premier tourist attraction. Sculpted from sandstone, it rises 1 086 m above the bay; its flat summit measures nearly 3 km from end to end and, on clear days, it can be discerned about 200 km out to sea.

Very often, though, the heights are hidden from view. The clouds that billow across its rim to tumble down the massively precipitous northern faces are known as the 'tablecloth', and are the product of the south-easter. The wind, which collects moisture as it blows around False Bay, collides with the mountain barrier and rises, cooling as it does so, the moisture condensing to form a thick cloud cover which then cascades down, dissipating as it reaches the warmer levels. It is a continuous and spectacular process, and a source of endless fascination to watchers in the city below.

Almost every one of the Peninsula's nearly 3 000 species of indigenous flora is found on the slopes and on the mountain's heavily-watered central plateau, among them the silver tree and the lovely wild orchid *Disa uniflora*. Hunters long ago exterminated the bigger game, but the uplands and heights are now a protected area and they still sustain baboon, duiker, grysbok, grey rhebok, civet cat, lynx, rock-rabbit (dassie), porcupine, tortoise, and an exotic animal called the Himalayan tahr, which is reminiscent of a goat. The tahrs, descendants of a pair that escaped from Groote Schuur in the 1930s, are a menace to the environment and their numbers have to be controlled.

More than two million people ascend the mountain each year, most of whom take the:

CABLEWAY, which provides easy, comfortable and safe access. The trip takes about five minutes, and in over 50 years of operation there has never been a serious accident.

The cableway is operative throughout the year (including public holidays – but always subject, of course, to favourable weather conditions); from 08h00 to 22h00 in summer (December through April) and from 08h30 to 18h00 in winter (May through November).

Until recently visitors had to stand in line for a place on the cable car, sometimes for hours.

It is now both possible and preferable to book in advance (see Advisory, page 305).

The departure station is at the top of Kloof Nek. Either drive there, take a taxi, or board the bus that leaves from Adderley Street (outside OK Bazaars) in the city centre.

ON THE SUMMIT There are splendid viewing points, a restaurant, a souvenir shop from which letters bearing the Table Mountain post-mark can be sent, a fax machine and three wall plaques that describe the Table Mountain nature reserve, the short walks that may be taken from the cable station, and the flora that may be seen in the different seasons. Best time of the day to make the ascent is probably late afternoon, to catch the sunset and the deepening colours of sky and land. Table Mountain is a proclaimed national monument, and is flood-lit at night for much of the year.

CLIMBING UP There are more than 350 charted paths to the plateau summit, (see Walks and trails, page 293), some fairly undemanding, others exceptionally difficult – and it's only too easy to lose your way, which can prove disastrous if the mountain's treacherous weather suddenly takes a turn for the worse.

The heights regularly and tragically exact their toll of human life. Arm yourself with a good map and guide-book, available from most local bookshops; choose a route that's well within your physical capacity, and make the climb in company with someone who knows the route. Other safety hints:

☆ Wear or carry warm clothing: sunshine can give way to the bitter chill of mist and cloud within less than an hour. In fact, it is suggested you go even further and purchase a cheap thermal emergency blanket, one that folds up into a pocket-sized package.

☆ Before setting out, leave word of your intended routes, both up and down, with a responsible person.

☆ Never stray from defined paths.

☆ If you do get lost, don't embark on a random downward course, but instead backtrack and look for the path. If visibility is really poor, or if you cannot find your way before nightfall, stay where you are.

☆ Members of the Mountain Club of South Africa are on call 24 hours a day, Tel. (021) 45-3412.

LION'S HEAD is the unusual sugar-loaf feature to the right of Table Mountain as you look from the city. The two are connected by the saddle of land known as Kloof Nek.

Lion's Head and its attendant ridge, which ends in the 'rump' of Signal Hill, is said to resemble that animal when viewed from certain angles. One may climb (chain-ladders help you to negotiate the most difficult stretches) to the 669-m peak of the Head, from which there are lovely views of the mountain and, to the south, the massive buttresses of the Twelve Apostles, and of Robben Island, sea and city.

Signal Hill was once used as a semaphore post for communication with ships at sea, and it is from here that the noon gun is fired each day. One can drive to the top, from where the vistas are also impressive.

DEVIL'S PEAK guards Table Mountain's eastern flank. It too is just over 1 000 m high; on its slopes there are three small blockhouses, complete with cannon, built by the nervous British during their first occupation of the Cape (1795-1803). The actual peak is accessible only to experienced climbers.

ON THE WATERFRONT

The Victoria and Alfred basins are the oldest part of the harbour. And they were, until about fifty years ago, intimately connected with Cape Town and its people; a part of their daily lives. But then, with land reclamation and motorway construction and the dwindling volume of maritime traffic, the links were broken. The leisure beach, the charming old pier and much else disappeared, eventually to be replaced by a wasteland of functional dockyard, ugly buildings, oil storage tanks, fences and a raised highway that stands as a monument to bad planning and bad taste.

Now, if the new planners have their way, sea and city will again be joined, brought together in happy reunion by the hugely ambitious and imaginative Victoria and Alfred Waterfront (VAW) scheme.

The multi-billion rand venture (a private, not a government one) draws its inspiration from highly successful harbour redevelopment projects elsewhere – from Boston's Quincy Market and from San Francisco, the fish market of Granville Island, the traffic-free waterfronts of St Tropez and Antibes, from Sydney, Van-

couver and New York's South Seaport – but it is tailored to suit Cape Town's own needs and distinctive character. Some of the elements are:
☆ The removal of the oil storage tanks, fences, customs offices and so forth. The more colourful of the old buildings are being converted, and quite a number of new ones built, to serve as hotels, museums, restaurants, fish markets, cinemas, shops, recreation and entertainment centres. Focal point will be the Pier Head retail complex, erected on an R85 million 'speciality waterfront' and comprising 80 or more shops, 10 cinemas, 15 restaurants, a flea market, a huge fish market and parking for approximately 2 500 cars. Pier Head is scheduled for completion in 1992.
☆ A new jetty, basin for yachts and a sophisticated marina.
☆ Open quaysides, promenades, public squares, a walkway and possibly a waterway leading to the city.
☆ A world-class oceanarium with underwater tunnels, made of a transparent material, will give visitors the sensation of 'walking on the ocean floor'.
☆ The Waterfront is basically but by no means exclusively a tourist enterprise: it will function as a worked-in, lived-in area as well as a fun place. The Robinson Graving Dock will continue to operate; fishing boats will still use the basin; there are plans for office premises, and for a residential section, and there's the possibility of another new suburb to the east, near Mouille Point.

Much of this is still in the future, but the transformation is proceeding apace, the process starting early in 1990 and modestly enough with a 68-bedroom three-star hotel (the old North Quay warehouse with a new personality); Bertie's Landing tavern and restaurant, (international yachtsman Bertie Reed is part-owner) and the commissioning of the South African Maritime Museum with its 4 000 m² of display area. Two of the museum's historic ships can be seen in Alfred basin.

A lot will have happened down on the docks by the time this book appears. The waterfront is developing, as moving spirit David Jack says, into 'a place people will come to; it will indeed be full of festival and delight', and it is well worth exploring. Obtain information from Captour or Satour (see Advisory, page 305), and pay it a visit.

Sea Point's graceful ocean frontage

PENINSULA: WEST COAST

The western, or 'Atlantic', shoreline is characterized by rocky indentations, one beautiful stretch of wide beach and charming bays around which cluster some of the Peninsula's more affluent suburbs and villages. The route – Beach Road, which turns into Victoria Drive, or the M6 – begins at Green Point and Sea Point on the city's western fringes and winds its way, ultimately as Chapman's Peak Drive, to Scarborough, some 54 km to the south. The scenery along the way is always attractive, sometimes breathtaking.

The western strip is a prime holiday area. Many sunworshippers prefer this side of the Peninsula to the east: the water is cold, but the beaches are sheltered from the prevailing summer south-easter.

Green Point

A sought-after residential suburb of apartment blocks rising above scattered Victorian houses. Green Point Common is a well-used recreational area with a pleasant 18-hole golf course, The Point Health and Racquet Club, sportsfields and a multi-purpose stadium. The lighthouse is the oldest in the country and a national monument: it dates from 1824, when it beamed a modest light from its two oil lanterns; it now has an 850 000-candlepower lamp that can be seen 23 km out to sea, and a foghorn that keeps residents awake at night. Worth visiting are:

THE CAPE MEDICAL MUSEUM at New Somerset Hospital, corner of Beach and Portswood roads: surgical instruments and other relics of modern medicine's pioneering days; a reconstructed dentist's surgery, and a variety of visuals, including a picture of Dr James Barry, who in 1818 performed South Africa's first Caesarian section. Barry was something of an enigma: an energetic and excellent doctor (he eventually became Inspector-General of Britain's army hospitals), his effeminate appearance was cause for comment and it was said that after his death in 1865 'he' was found to be a woman. The claim has never been verified.

HERRING BEQUEST INSTITUTE in Antrim Rd: musical instruments, furniture, objets d'art, and practice rooms available to members of the public for a small fee; the Steinway Grand costs a little more to hire than the other pianos.

FORT WYNYARD, the naval museum in Fort Wynyard Road, just off Portsmouth Road; special emphasis on the history of coastal defence.

Sea Point

A busy, vibrant, crowded, cosmopolitan seaside suburb and the nearest thing Cape Town has to a holiday playground. Parts of it are shabby but luxurious apartment buildings line the elegant, palm-graced beachfront and time-share is much in evidence, hotels, delis, restaurants, discos and other nightspots are everywhere. A bright, glitzy, often noisy place, and full of fun if you're in the mood.

If you're driving into Sea Point, take Beach Road, which (obviously) runs along the shore. Main Road is where all the shops are and it may be the more direct route, but it is invariably congested. The five-star President Hotel is at the end (drinks on the terrace, overlooking the sea, can fill a pleasant hour); along the front are lawns, children's playgrounds, a putt-putt course, and a very large and well-patronized outdoor swimming pool. The beach isn't special and most places are too rocky for comfortable swimming.

Clifton

The area is renowned for its magnificently wide white beaches – four of them – sheltered from the wind by the bulky mass of Lion's Head and much favoured by the beautiful people. The backing slopes support expensive-looking holiday cottages, houses and small luxury apartment blocks.

On your left, for several kilometres as you drive south, are the Twelve Apostles, a series of imposing, often cloud-wreathed peaks that form part of the Table Mountain range.

Camps Bay

Similar to Clifton (both places have withstood commercial inroads, and retain their dignity) but larger and perhaps even richer: some quite stunning houses have been built into the cliffs. There are shops, a lovely beach, a large tidal pool and a new and imaginatively conceived hotel called The Bay. Kloof Road, which leads up the mountainside, will take you to the Round House (an early 19th century shooting lodge; now an excellent restaurant) and the Glen, a picnic area with fine views of suburb, bay and the sea beyond.

Llandudno

After a winding and dramatically scenic 15-km drive along a by-now virtually deserted coastline you reach this small, exclusive seaside village. It has a quite spectacular setting, hugging the precipitous slopes beneath a peak called Little Lion's Head. From the viewing spot on Victoria Drive the place looks like Toy Town, and is much photographed.

Hout Bay

An enchanting town and fishing harbour nestling in a wide, green, hill-flanked valley. In translation the name means 'Wood Bay', derived from its value as a source of timber in the earliest colonial days. Tourism and fisheries are now its main industries.

Hout Bay is the headquarters of the Peninsula's crayfishing fleet, though crayfish aren't the only sea harvest: in June and July vast quantities of snoek are caught offshore and sold on the quayside; the annual and very popular Snoek Festival is held during this period. Tourist attractions include:

THE HARBOUR, full of fishing boats and yachts in a picturesque setting of sea and mountain. From here one may embark on launch trips around the coast; on the quayside is Mariner's Wharf, an emporium modelled on its namesake in San Francisco (fresh fish and live lobster, nautical gifts and curios, and an atmospheric seafood bistro/restaurant). There are imaginative schemes for further waterfront development; a five-star 'low profile' hotel is planned for the beachfront.

HOUT BAY MUSEUM in Andrews Road: natural and cultural history of the area from prehistoric times to the growth of the modern fishing industry.

Leisure-time in Hout Bay harbour

KRONENDAL, a Cape Dutch H-plan homestead on Main road, built in 1800 and now a national monument, housing an excellent restaurant (see page 304) and The Rialto Gallery where exclusive gifts can be bought.

THE WORLD OF BIRDS, in Hout Bay valley. This is the country's largest bird park, attracting upwards of 100 000 visitors a year. The aviaries are beautifully landscaped to simulate natural habitat; you walk through them while the inmates (over 3 000, belonging to some 450 different species) carry on with their busy lives as if you weren't there.

The marine drive from Hout Bay then continues, in a dramatic 10-km stretch, over:

Chapman's Peak Drive

Here, the road cuts through different strata of granite and sandstone and the rock faces are attractively multi-coloured, red and yellow predominating. At its highest point the drive skirts cliffs that plunge almost sheer to the sea 600 m below, and there are magnificent views, from the picnic sites and look-out points, of Chapman's Bay and its wide expanse of beach, and of Hout Bay and its distinctive Sentinel peak.

You then descend into the flat, low, marshy plain of Noordhoek, until recently a relatively isolated rural settlement but now a fast-developing suburb. The beach here is broad, long, windy, excellent for surfing but not recommended for casual swimming.

The main coastal road loops inland just before you reach Noordhoek. At the first major junction you can either continue on the M6 to Fish Hoek on the east coast (see page 286), or turn left on the M64 and back towards the city, or right on the M65 to rejoin the shoreline at Kommetjie, a pretty little seaside centre where there's good surfing, angling and sunbathing and rather cold swimming.

Final port of call on the west-coast route is Scarborough, a tiny cluster of holiday cottages set in wild heath-type countryside. Here, you turn inland to reach the entrance to the:

Cape of Good Hope nature reserve

In fact, although the western approach is scenically attractive and full of interest, the quicker, more direct route from town to the reserve and Cape Point is via the M4 or M5 to Muizenberg and then along the eastern, or False Bay, coastal road. This is described further on.

The reserve, about 70 km from Cape Town city centre, covers an area of 7 750 ha, with a coastline of about 40 km, and is noted more for its floral diversity – indigenous fynbos, with some annoying and in places seriously threatening alien encroachment – than for its fauna. In springtime (September and October) the wild flowers are a delight. About 1 200 plant species have been identified on the ridge of hills that runs down the False Bay side, from Smitswinkel Bay to Cape Point, and on the undulating plain to the west. But there are also animals to be seen, including bontebok (a type of antelope once threatened with extinction; see page 245), Cape mountain zebra, springbok, steenbok, Cape grysbok, grey rhebok, red hartebeest, eland, duiker, Cape fox, caracal and chacma baboon, of which there are four troops.

These baboons are thought to be unique within the primate world – if, that is, we exclude man himself – in that their diet consists largely of marine foods, which they garner at low tide. They also feed on tourist handouts, which poses something of a problem: they have become too familiar with and dependent on visitors. If thwarted they can be annoyingly persistent and even aggressive (in which case they simply have to be put down). The troop near Cape Point is adept at raiding cars. Please don't feed these animals, and make sure you lock your vehicle.

Over 160 species of bird have been recorded in the reserve, ranging from the reintroduced ostrich down to minuscule sunbirds. Marine life is especially interesting: species found along the western coast differ markedly from those of the eastern waters.

Within the reserve, which is open throughout the year, there is an extensive network of roads; picnic spots with barbecue facilities; viewsites; some pleasant walks and trails, and a restaurant (the Homestead, an old farmhouse now restored) and gift shop. Swimming at Venus Pool and in the Bordjiesdrif and Buffels Bay tidal pools. Buffels Bay also offers beach bathing and a slipway for small boats. Fishing is permitted along certain sections of the coast.

Cape Point

Cape Point itself is the finest of viewsites: one either climbs the steps (which is hard-going) or takes the shuttle bus to the top. The vistas, from the base of the old lighthouse, are unforgettable. Albatross, gannet, petrel and gull wheel over and around the Point; the cliffs fall sheer to the sea, and one can often spot whale, dolphin and seal, and shoals of tunny and snoek, in the blue depths far below.

It is off Cape Point that the *Flying Dutchman*, the phantom ship with its broken mast and tattered sails, is destined to sail the seas until the end of time. The legend originated in the 17th century, when the Dutch captain Hendrik van der Decken, his storm-tossed ship foundering, swore to round the Cape of Good Hope even if it took him until Doomsday to do so. Providence took him at his word, and many 'sightings' have been recorded, most notably that by the future King George V while he was serving as a Royal Navy midshipman.

PENINSULA: EAST COAST

The eastern shoreline is lapped by the warm (summer average 22 °C), sparklingly blue and often wind-blown waters of False Bay, which stretches in a wide arc from Cape Point northward and then eastward to the Hottentots-Holland mountains, a range which projects into the sea at Cape Hangklip. The bay is so named because early navigators, bound for Table Bay, often mistook the Point for Hangklip – a costly error: wind and current are perverse, and over the centuries there have been a great many shipwrecks.

The bay is one of the country's principal angling, surfing and boating areas (and, incidentally, a treasure-house for marine biologists). It is fringed by a 35-km, almost continuous stretch of beach; on its southern shores are a scatter of seaside towns and resort villages linked by rail and by the coastal road. From the city one drives out on the M4 or M5 (or takes the train), through the southern suburbs to Muizenberg and then follows the shoreline through St James, Kalk Bay, the fairly large residential centre of Fish Hoek and on to Simon's Town and the entrance to the Cape of Good Hope Nature Reserve (see page 284).

On the other (eastern) side of Muizenberg are some of the widest and finest of the beaches. In terms of tourism, this section of the coast has remained relatively undeveloped, though recreational amenities along Baden-Powell and Marine drives are improving, especially around Strandfontein.

Muizenberg

A rather old-fashioned town, notable for its turn-of-the-century villas, boarding houses and (converted) fishermen's cottages, and until fairly recent times one of the southern hemisphere's best-known seaside resorts. Rudyard Kipling loved the place ('white as the sands of Muizenberg,' he wrote, 'spun before the gale'); so did the Victorian and Edwardian gentry, and Cecil John Rhodes and the rest of the holidaying multi-millionaires of the Rand.

Indeed Rhodes spent his last years in Barkly Cottage (now called Rhodes Cottage), on Main Road between Muizenberg and St James. The house, which contains personal relics (photographs, memorabilia) of the controversial politician and financier, is now a museum. Just above the cottage is Rust en Vrede, which Rhodes planned in collaboration with the architect Herbert Baker, and sited 'on a great high terrace-wall, designed so that from the house and stoep the public road would be hidden, and there would be seen through white columns the fullest sweep of the blue sea, and the rhythm of the blue surf, and the two far-off mountain promontories ...'. Rhodes died not long afterwards and it was Sir Abe Bailey who put the finishing touches to this lovely, red-roofed, gabled country mansion. Among other features of interest around Muizenberg are:

DE POST HUYS, Main Road: built in 1673 as an observation post and small fort, and today the oldest habitable building in South Africa.

NATALE LABIA MUSEUM, Main Road: a branch of the National Gallery and named in honour of Prince Natale Labia (1877-1936) and his wife Princess Ida Louise (1879-1960). Fine furniture, works of art; open Tuesday to Sunday.

SANDVLEI ('sand marsh'): an attractive, shallow stretch of water just to the north of town. An unusual waterfront suburb, Marina da Gama, has been developed on its eastern shores; in the centre of the 'lake' is Park Island, a recreational area.

MUIZENBERG BEACH: a wide, gently sloping expanse of sand; no rock, few pebbles, safe bathing. The Muizenberg walkway is a 15-minute stroll all along the coast to St James, starting out after the Muizenberg Pavilion.

ST JAMES, directly south of Muizenberg overlooking False Bay. The hillside village has a pleasant beach and excellent hotel, and is favoured by the quieter type of holiday-maker and by overseas visitors.

KALK BAY means lime bay, and is so named after the kilns where shells were burnt to produce lime for painting buildings. This pretty little fishing centre and resort is much visited and photographed by holiday-makers. It's especially busy during the snoek season (June and July). Fresh fish sales are a feature of harbour life.

THE KALKBAAIBERG hills that rise behind the shoreline between Kalk Bay and Muizenberg are popular among hikers, ramblers, naturalists and those who like exploring caves, of which there is a profusion in this wild and rocky area. Some are substantial networks of underground chambers, most have intriguing names: Boomslang Cave, Rest-a-Bit, Light and Gloom, Moss and Diamonds, Drip-Drop, Mirth Parlour, Creepy Corridor, Dolly's Doorway, Ronan's Well (an extensive complex) and so on.

Simon's Town's dignified main street

Fish Hoek

A solidly middle-class seaside town set in a valley that runs across the Peninsula to Chapman's Bay in the west (see page 284). About halfway along the valley is Peer's Cave, a large rock shelter and site of important archeological finds (of Fish Hoek Man, who lived about 15 000 years ago). The cave's walls are decorated with prehistoric paintings.

Fish Hoek is southern Africa's only 'dry' town: no liquor may be sold within the municipal limits (under the original title deed granted by Lord Charles Somerset in 1818 the sale of liquor was prohibited. The town is situated close to the naval base of Simon's Town and he feared that the area would become a den of iniquity). It has a good beach, and the bathing is safe. Recommended is the Jager Walk, along the rocks at the water's edge.

Simon's Town

The town, terminus of the Peninsula railway line, was named in honour of Simon van der Stel, the early and accomplished Dutch governor of the Cape, who explored the bay in 1687 and recommended it as a winter anchor-

age. It served as the Royal Navy's principal South Atlantic base from 1810 to 1957, when the dockyards were taken over by the South African Navy. There are many fine beaches and walking trails in the area. Specific features of interest in and around town include:

SIMON'S TOWN MUSEUM (formerly The Residency) in Court Road features naval and local history displays. Open Tuesday to Friday; guided tours for groups (by arrangement).

MARTELLO TOWER museum: built in 1796 and the earliest surviving British structure in the country. British and South African naval history; intriguing dioramas of town and docks. Open daily.

JUBILEE SQUARE, in which stands the statue of Able Seaman Just Nuisance, a gregarious Great Dane dog who befriended, and was much loved by, British sailors during the Second World War. He was formally attested into the Royal Navy, and on his death received a military funeral.

THE STEMPASTORIE, the original Dutch Reformed parsonage, now a museum. Among the displays are those telling the story of South Africa's national emblems (anthem, coats of arms, flag – officially flown for the first time in Cuba, of all places).

TOPSTONES, off the Red Hill Road leading to the west coast, is a large gemstone factory. Visitors are introduced to the manufacturing and polishing processes, and are allowed to fossick in the 'scratch-patch', a dump containing many beautiful gemstone fragments. What you find you may keep, providing you buy a container from the factory.

THE BOULDERS, a rocky stretch of coastline south of Simon's Town. Here there are numerous inlets, pools and secluded little beaches.

MILLER'S POINT, the last port of call on the drive to Cape Point. A popular holiday spot: it has a caravan park, a restaurant, picnic and barbecue sites, a tidal swimming pool, safe bathing and a wealth of (unusually tame) marine life.

PENINSULA: INLAND

The central portions of the Cape Peninsula are heavily residential along the suburban line of rail but in many other parts, and especially on the mountain slopes, quite beautifully treed. The woodland mantles are at their most attractive around Constantiaberg and Tokai and in the Silvermine nature reserve.

The nearest 'suburb' to the city is Zonnebloem, a largely deserted, grass-covered area better known by the colloquial and historic name of:

District Six

Once described as 'the soul of Cape Town', and until 1966 a vibrant town of 55 000 'coloured' people, District Six became the focus of national and international attention in the mid-1960s, when the government declared it 'white' under the apartheid laws and began moving its residents to Mitchell's Plain, 30 km away, and to other townships on the desolate Cape Flats.

Officialdom argued that the removals were part of a genuine upliftment programme, that District Six had become untenable in terms of the Public Health Act and the Slums Act. And indeed the place was overcrowded and unsanitary, its buildings dilapidated, its warren-like streets crime-ridden. But it had colour, and charm, and above all a powerful perception of community. Remembers one resident: 'When we were evicted, we lost more than our home. We lost neighbours and friends whom we could rely on in times of sickness and other misfortune. The government gave us another home; it couldn't give us a sense of belonging.'

District Six is prime residential land, yet the developers did not move in. It remained a wasteland, mute reminder of a tragic exercise in what its apologists called 'social engineering', and of a heartless system that only recently began to crumble.

Rosebank

A small suburb on the city side of Rondebosch, notable for the Baxter Theatre complex (see page 296). Also in Rosebank, in the house called 'The Firs', is the Irma Stern Museum, devoted largely to the works of this renowned South African artist but also displaying some superb antique furniture, objets d'art and African artifacts. Open daily except Monday.

Rondebosch

Site of the Dutch colony's first wheat-growing experiment, launched in 1656 near a distinctively round grove of trees (the area was known as 't Ronde Doorn Bosjen at the time). Now a

Mostert's Mill, built in 1796

major suburb containing a number of leading schools (Bishops, Rustenberg, Rondebosch Boys' High) and hospitals (Red Cross Children's, William Slater).

The famed Groote Schuur Estate, bequeathed to the nation by Cecil Rhodes on his death in 1902, sprawls over the western segment of Rondebosch, on the lower slopes of Table Mountain. Prominent elements of the estate are:

THE UNIVERSITY OF CAPE TOWN and its teaching hospital, Groote Schuur, where the world's first heart transplant operation was performed – by Prof Chris Barnard and his cardiac team, in 1967. The university is the country's oldest (it started life as the South African College in 1829) and probably the most attractive: the splendid heights of Devil's Peak provide its backdrop; the campus's stately, ivy-covered buildings provide a view across to Milnerton on the coastal plain and Table Bay beyond. Student enrolment is about 12 000.

GROOTE SCHUUR, or 'Great Barn': the mansion was originally a 17th century granary, later converted into a house (which burned down) and finally reconstructed for Rhodes by his friend and 'personal architect' Herbert Baker to create a grand, but essentially simple, home that now serves as the state president's official residence. Close by, set in the estate's lovely tree-shaded grounds, are two other houses of note: Westbrooke, a state guesthouse, and The Woolsack, built in the 1890s and used as a summer home by another of Rhodes's friends and admirers, Rudyard Kipling (it is now a campus residence).

RHODES MEMORIAL, an impressively imperialistic, classical-style 'temple' set some distance up Devil's Peak. The memorial incorporates GF Watts's fine statue, 'Physical Energy', and a large bust of Rhodes beneath which is inscribed part of Kipling's moving tribute to a man who, whatever his faults – and they were many – was undeniably a powerful force in the shaping of the subcontinent during the latter part of the 19th century: 'The immense and brooding spirit shall quicken and control. Living he was the land, and dead, his soul shall be her soul.'

It is a pleasant walk to the memorial, from which there are fine views over the suburbs towards the Hottentots-Holland mountains.

GROOTE SCHUUR PADDOCKS, along the city side of Devil's Peak, provide grazing for eland, wildebeest, zebra, bontebok and for a number of more exotic animals, including Chinese deer, Himalayan tahrs and American grey squirrels. The last two are regarded as pests.

MOSTERT'S MILL, on De Waal Drive, just below the university campus, is one of Cape Town's best-known landmarks.

Built in 1796 as a 'horse' mill, it was restored with the help of the Netherlands government in 1936. It is not functional, though there are plans in the pipeline to make it so.

Newlands

A large, fashionable and mostly attractive suburb 9,5 km from the city centre, noted among other things for its exceptionally high rainfall (over 1 500 mm a year), for the beautiful homestead that once belonged to the social commentator and letter-writer Lady Anne Barnard and which is now the Vineyard Hotel, and for its famed rugby and cricket grounds, venues for both provincial and international matches.

THE JOSEPHINE WATERMILL stands at the entrance to the rugby stadium. Built in 1840, named after the Queen of Sweden and powered by the Liesbeeck River, the building and its massive waterwheel have been meticulously restored (by university students and the Historical Society) and is in excellent working order.

There are daily milling demonstrations and a permanent blacksmithing exhibit. Open Monday to Friday. Tours at 10h00 and 14h00. The mill's first floor serves as the:

NEWLANDS RUGBY MUSEUM, the largest of its kind in the world, housing a fascinating collection of exhibits and mementos dating back to 1891, when South Africa first entered the international rugby arena (the visiting British team, captained by WE Maclagan, conceded just one try in the 19 matches played against local sides). Open daily on weekdays and on those Saturdays for which big matches have been scheduled. Nearby is:

OHLSSON'S BREWERY, South Africa's oldest. Tours on Tuesday and Thursday afternoons (book first).

NEWLANDS FOREST The main road past the university (De Waal Drive, which changes to Rhodes Drive, which in turn becomes Union Avenue) is a scenic joy: there are lovely trees everywhere along the route and on the hillsides that rise grandly above, and the verges and centre islands support a profusion of flowering plants. To your right, driving away from the city, is Newlands forest, a favourite among picnickers, walkers and joggers.

Claremont

Still affectionately called 'The Village' – a reference to its once-separate status – but now one of the fastest-growing residential and commercial areas in the country. Excellent speciality shopping in Cavendish Square (see page 296).

Claremont's gardens are well worth a visit. They were part of a 19th century estate called The Hill on which the owner, Ralph Arderne, planted a great many splendid trees (cypresses, Norfolk Island pines, cedars) and, around a spring, a delicate Japanese garden.

Constantia

Not so much a suburb as an extensive area of attractive wooded parkland, valley and hill on the northern uplands of the Table Mountain range. Constantia homes tend to be spacious, luxurious and secluded.

If you turn right at the intersection of Union and Rhodes avenues (see Newlands Forest, above) and follow the route for 2 km you'll see, on your right, the entrance to:

KIRSTENBOSCH, one of the world's leading botanic gardens and headquarters of South Africa's National Botanic Gardens network. It was established in 1913 on yet another parcel of land bequeathed to the nation by Cecil Rhodes: 560 ha of lush terrain extending over the mountain slopes to Maclear's Beacon. Here, some 9 000 of the country's 18 000 indigenous flowering plant species are cultivated – mesembryanthemums, pelargoniums, proteas, ericas, ferns, cycads and many others. The Compton Herbarium, within the grounds, has over 200 000 plant specimens. The attractive birdlife includes dusky and paradise flycatchers, sunbirds, sugarbirds, Klaas's cuckoo, bulbuls, pigeons and the Cape batis.

Part of Jan van Riebeeck's hedge of wild almond, which enclosed the first Dutch settlement, can still be seen on the property. Also of interest is the spring, lined with Batavian bricks and shaped like a bird, which is popularly but incorrectly known as Lady Anne Barnard's bath. There are delightful walks along the many pathways; expert guides are available to conduct parties; for the blind, a perfume garden and the Braille walk have been laid out. There's a pleasant restaurant within the grounds. Open daily.

From the T-junction just beyond Kirstenbosch, Rhodes Drive bears right and winds its way up the slopes to Constantia Nek – a magnificent scenic drive. Above the road is:

CECILIA FOREST, an entrancing place for communing with nature, for picnicking and for walking. There are many winding tracks and paths; the Cecilia waterfall is worth finding your way to. At the top of Rhodes Drive is the Constantia Nek restaurant, and here the route divides, the road to your right leading down to Hout Bay valley (see page 283), that to your left taking you through the lush and long-renowned wine-producing countryside of Constantia, and to Groot Constantia, its most notable farmstead (see panel, page 290).

From Constantia valley a short and pleasant drive north-eastwards will bring you to:

Tokai, Retreat and beyond

Much of this area is taken up by run-of-the-mill suburban development, but by no means all. Among its attractions are:

TOKAI FOREST, which extends up the slopes of Constantiaberg. A lot of the trees, of which there are many different and lovely kinds, were planted in the 1880s as part of an afforestation experiment. Pleasant walks and picnic sites. Visit the Elephant's Eye cave. The forest is open to the public, though, only during the winter months, when fires are less of a hazard. An entry permit is required.

THE TOKAI ARBORETUM is some distance away, near the Constantia Village Centre (where there's an enticing farm stall).

TOKAI MANOR HOUSE, dating from 1795 and described by one architectural writer as 'the most outstanding homestead in the Peninsula', stands just outside the forest reserve.

CONSTANTIA'S GRACEFUL HOMESTEADS

Groot Constantia, stateliest of the Cape's historic mansions, was originally designed and built, with loving care, by Simon van der Stel, the outstanding early Cape governor and a man of impeccable taste. He lived there until his death in 1712. Later, in 1778, the estate was taken over by Hendrik Cloete, who added a fine cellar and developed the vineyards to produce wine of legendary quality, sweet and rich vintages that found their way to the royal tables of Europe and whose praises were sung by poets. The Cloete wine-making secrets did not survive the passing of the estate's vintners, but the Constantia valley still produces fine reds, some of them awarded the rare 'Superior' accolade. Constantia wines generally are much sought after and in short supply (see also page 292).

The farmstead, now owned by the government and a national monument, was burned down in 1925 but has been superlatively restored. It is notable for its architecture, its splendid period furniture, its Chinese, Japanese, Rhenish and Delft porcelain, and for its two-storeyed cellar, designed by the French architect Louis Thibault. The cellar's exquisite cherub-adorned pediment is the work of Anton Anreith. The adjacent museum tells the story of wine and wine-making through the centuries. From the homestead an oak-lined avenue leads to an ornamental pool in which the Augustan owners and their guests once bathed, and where the smiling, berobed ghost of Van der Stel is reported to have been seen. House, museum and cellar are open daily.

Groot Constantia is one of three functioning wine farms in the valley. As attractive in their own, slightly more modest way are Klein Constantia, a lovely old (1796) farmstead rescued from urban assault, neglect and decay by Cape Town businessman Douglas Jooste, who has renovated it quite beautifully; and Buitenverwachting, also resurrected, the gabled house, stables, cellars and slave quarters faultlessly restored. Buitenverwachting has an especially inviting restaurant.

For details of the Constantia wine route, see page 292.

The historic Groot Constantia, a much-favoured venue for Sunday outings

SILVERMINE NATURE RESERVE lies to the north of Tokai forest and is accessible via the scenically enchanting Ou Kaapseweg ('Old Cape Road'). An unspoilt wilderness area that extends from Muizenberg and Kalk Bay on the east coast to Noordhoek Peak in the west, the reserve is very popular among picnickers and ramblers. The walk to the heights above the reservoir gives you a grand view over woodland and heath to Hout Bay in the distance.

RONDEVLEI NATURE RESERVE, to the east, is an important waterfowl wetland and ornithological research station, haven to about 220 bird species, 70 of which breed within its 137-ha area. The reserve comprises a shallow lake (or vlei), marshland and indigenous bush, a pleasant picnic area and interesting small museum, and a number of observation points and waterside hides. A mecca for bird-watchers. Open daily; the best months to visit are January to April.

GETTING AROUND

Public transport in the Greater Cape Town area is of an adaquately high standard but, in common with services throughout the country, is coming under increasing pressure from a rapidly growing urban population.

BUSES Regular services link the city with all the major suburbs. The main bus terminal is situated behind the Golden Acre, between the Parade and Strand Street; supplementary departure points are in Adderley Street, outside OK Bazaars (for Kloof Nek/Table Mountain cable station, and Hout Bay) and in Lower Plein Street, opposite the Post Office (for Durbanville and Bellville).

The Silvermine reserve: ideal walking country

TAXIS Taxi-cabs of the standard, meter-fitted kind do not roam the streets in search of fares. They are to be found in the three designated city ranks (two in Adderley Street and one in Plein Street, behind the post office) and at several but not all suburban railway stations. Normally your best course would be to telephone for a cab (taxi firms are listed in the telephone directory and in the Yellow Pages) or ask your hotel reception to do so for you.

Travel by taxi is expensive: if your journey is anything more than a cross-city hop, ask the driver for an estimate of the cost. Moreover, make quite sure that he can precisely locate your destination: Cape Town cabbies do not match the standards set by their counterparts in London and New York, and some of them are surprisingly unfamiliar with their own city and its suburbs.

Black taxis: about 5 000 of these minibuses ply the busier Peninsula routes. They have undesignated but customary stopping points, and will stop if you hail them. They are a cheap, quick, sociable means of transport, but they do not have a reassuring safety record.

TRAINS Good, fast, electrified rail services connect Cape Town city with the major southern and east-coast suburbs and towns, and with those of the Cape Flats and northern areas. The Peninsula's west coast and southern interior (Sea Point to Hout Bay and beyond, Constantia) have no rail service.

CAR HIRE The major, internationally-known hire companies – Avis, Hertz and so on – have offices at the airport, in the city and at other points throughout the region. In addition, a number of smaller local firms offer their services, some of them at healthily competitive rates. Consult the Yellow Pages.

PARKING Finding on-street parking in the city can be a frustrating business, as of course it is in most of the world's major centres. The peripheral areas are more accommodating, and there's usually (but by no means always) space in one or other of the open squares (for instance, adjacent to the Railway Station and the Civic Centre, and at various 'Pay and Display' areas) and vacant building sites, which charge a daily rate.

Covered (underground and multi-storeyed) parking is available at ☆ The BP Centre, Hans Strijdom Avenue ☆ City Park, Loop Street ☆ Civic Centre, Hertzog Boulevard ☆ The Golden Acre, Castle Street ☆ Medipark, DF Malan Street ☆ The Nico Malan theatre complex, DF Malan Street ☆ The Parkade, Strand Street ☆ Pleinpark, Plein Street ☆ Thibault Square ☆ Riebeeck Square, Shortmarket Street ☆ Picbel Parkade, Strand Street. For more details, consult a city street-plan.

Select drives and routes

The western Cape is scenically outstanding: pretty well every part of the Peninsula, and of the winelands to the north (see pages 307-325), is worth driving to and through. These are just three suggestions (specific attractions *en route* are described between pages 282 and 291):

THE LONGER CIRCULAR ROUTE The scenic anti-clockwise trip around the Peninsula will take you from city to Sea Point (Beach Road); along the western shoreline (Victoria Drive) to Hout Bay. Look in at the harbour and the World of Birds before lunching at Kronendal. Continue over Chapman's Peak (Chapman's Peak Drive)

and through Noordhoek to Scarborough, turning inland for entry into the Cape of Good Hope Nature Reserve. Catch the shuttle bus up to the high crest of Cape Point. Return to Cape Town via the eastern coastal route through Simon's Town, Fish Hoek and Muizenberg, and then inland through the southern suburbs (M4). Total distance: 139 km; numerous optional variations and digressions. The clockwise route (up the east coast, back along the west) is of course just as pleasant.

THE SHORTER CIRCULAR ROUTE A truncated version of the round trip will lead you from Hout Bay up the M63 to Constantia Nek. Bear left at the top, into Rhodes Drive (still the M63) and along the winding valley route to Kirstenbosch Botanic Gardens, after which you turn left again onto Union (M3) and so back to the city. Total distance: about 21 km from Hout Bay; 46 km round trip.

Alternatively, you may continue straight on from Constantia Nek (M41) to Constantia Village Centre and then bear left onto Simon van der Stel freeway (M3), which will take you back to town.

THE WINE ROUTE around the Constantia homesteads can either be incorporated into the shorter circular drive or undertaken as a separate journey. In the latter case take De Waal Drive (M3, becoming Union) past the University and Newlands forest on your right to the intersection with Rhodes; turn right, continue past Kirstenbosch Botanical Gardens to Constantia Nek; turn left onto the M41 and, after 2 km, right into Schoenstatt and right again into Groot Constantia Road. Follow the signs for Groot Constantia, Klein Constantia and Buitenverwachting.

☆ Groot Constantia: guided tours through the cellars, hourly between 10h00 and 16h00; daily wine sales, 10h00 to 17h00; gentle walks along the Estate's footpaths; two restaurants: the Jonkershuis (traditional Cape lunches and teas) and the Tavern (buffet meals) or, as the management suggests, simply pack a picnic basket and relax on the shady lawns behind the cellars. Tel. 794- 5178/9

☆ Buitenverwachting: excellent restaurant; gabled and thatched cellar; maiden vintage from the new vines appeared in 1985 and the wines have since won international awards.

Cellar tours, by appointment (Tel. 794-5191), Monday to Friday 11h00 to 15h00; wine sales and tastings weekdays 09h00 to 17h00, Saturday 09h00 to 13h00.

✩ Klein Constantia: beautiful homestead, rather more private than the other two; no restaurant. After a 49-year break the estate's first wine, the 1986 Sauvignon blanc, was adjudged best white at the SA Wine Show; the new cellars have won design awards. Cellar tours by appointment (Tel. 794-5188); wine sales: weekdays 09h00 to 13h00 and 14h00 to 17h00, Saturdays 09h00 to 13h00.

FARTHER AFIELD The wine routes of the Western Cape are renowned, and deservedly so. Those most convenient to Cape Town are the Constantia (see page 292), the Stellenbosch, the Paarl and the Vignerons de Franschhoek (see page 320).

However, there's a lot more to the region than its lovely vineyards, and an impressive number of other thematic routes have been established, giving the visitor a balanced choice of general and specialist interests. They include the Fruit Routes (see page 321), the Cheese Route (page 321), the Crayfish Route along the west coast, the Wool Route of the southern Cape, the Afrikaanse Taal (Language) Route, the French Huguenot Farms Route, the Arts and Crafts Route of the Peninsula and the Cape Winelands (maps available from Captour and Satour), the Antique Route of the Peninsula, Somerset West, Stellenbosch and Paarl, the Wreck Route along the south and west coasts, the Whale Route along False and Walker bays ... and so on.

Advice, brochures and maps are available from Captour's Visitors' Information Centre, Strand Concourse.

Walks and trails

As we've seen, the best way to explore the city is to wander the streets on foot: practically everything that's worth seeing is within gentle walking distance. One recommended route is described on page 276, but if you'd like a fuller and firmer itinerary, ask Captour for information on city walks or obtain a copy of Maxwell Leigh's *Pocket Guide to Cape Town*.

However, a word of caution: there's a lot of poverty in and around Cape Town, the incidence of violent crime is high, and the unwary risk muggings. Take the basic precautions: the main streets and open spaces of the city and of most suburbs are quite safe during the busy daylight hours; at other times it's generally wise to take your urban ramble in company, preferably in a group.

Prime (and safe) walking and hiking areas are along stretches of the west and east coasts; in the Cape of Good Hope Nature Reserve; inland around Fish Hoek, Hout Bay and Constantia, and of course on the many slopes of Table Mountain. Useful publications on the subject include Tim Anderson's *Day Walks in and around Cape Town*. A few suggestions:

✩ Table Mountain (page 280): numerous possible walks and climbs; useful literature includes Shirley Brossy's *A Walking Guide for Table Mountain* and the Mountain Club of South Africa's *Table Mountain Guide: Walks and Easy Climbs*. Two of the more popular routes are the Pipe Track, and the path from the cable station along the high plateau to Maclear's Beacon (follow the yellow klipspringer signs).

✩ Lion's Head (page 281): a 670-m, difficult, one-hour (or less, depending on how fit you are) climb to the top. Fixed chains help you up the steeper parts; fine views of Table Mountain, Robben Island, the sea and city. Literature: as for Table Mountain.

✩ Newlands Forest (page 289): a most pleasant place in which to stroll (though keep to the paths). A longer and tougher walk is through the forest, up to Newlands Ravine and the Saddle linking Devil's Peak with Table Mountain. Literature: as for Table Mountain.

✩ Kirstenbosch National Botanic Gardens (page 289): footpaths, forest walks, mountain streams; guides available if required; brochures and booklets, including a trail guide entitled *Two Easy Routes*, are obtainable at the kiosk.

✩ Constantia Nek to the lovely Cecilia Forest (page 289), and then follow the path up to Constantia Ridge.

✩ Tokai forest trails (page 289): six routes have been laid out, covering 37 km of mountainside woodland. Literature includes the Western Cape Forestry Branch's two detailed publications, *Teacher's Guide to Tokai* and the *Tokai Nature Trail*.

✩ Hout Bay (page 283): beautiful hiking and rambling country. Literature available includes Shirley Brossy's detailed *A walking guide for the Hout Bay to Simon's Town Mountains* and

Jogging in the Newlands area

Mike Lundy's *Twenty Walks around Hout Bay*. One of the more difficult routes – it's a 12-km scramble rather than a walk – is that from the north-shore part of the village to Llandudno via the lower slopes of the Sentinel and Karbonkelberg peaks.
✰ Silvermine Nature Reserve (page 291): a variety of routes ranging from a brief stroll to a half-day hike. Literature: a brochure and map, obtainable in the reserve, describes seven trails.
✰ Rondevlei Nature Reserve (page 291): several trails; a bird-watcher's paradise.
✰ Cape of Good Hope Nature Reserve (page 284): there are relatively few formal trails here; you wander freely. A brochure is available at the entrance; even more helpful would be a detailed map of the area, and a copy of Odden & Lee's *Cape Point*.

For information on the various options, contact the National Hiking Way Board, 7th Floor, Foretrust Building, Hammerschlag Way, Foreshore; Tel. 402-3093. Among other useful sources are:
✰ The Trails Club of South Africa; Tel. 72-9189 or 797-1906 (day and weekend trails).
✰ Wanderlust Walks; Annette Mason, Tel. 438-1948 (guided walks, on Thursdays, in the Peninsula mountains; day-packs provided)
✰ Cape Natural History Club; Tel. 24-6967.
✰ For guided walks on Table Mountain: the Mountain Club; Tel. 45-3412, or contact Lou Robertson on (0224) 2-3269.

Local tours

A great many coach, minibus and microbus half- and full-day trips are on offer. Most tour operators cover the west and east coasts of the Peninsula, Cape Point, Constantia and Kirstenbosch, mountain, bay and harbour, and places farther afield – the Winelands and beyond (see pages 307-325).

BUS AND COACH City Tramways has introduced a special 'Sunshine Rover Ticket', which enables visitors to reach, via the scheduled bus routes, virtually all the Cape's more popular attractions.

Other variations from the standard sightseeing fare: several firms cover scenic Cape Town and then take you to dinner at Bloubergstrand (see Advisory, page 305), from where you can enjoy unparalleled views of Table Mountain. Sun Tours advertises a 'Kiddies Tour', taking the children off your hands for a day filled with fun and adventure (including visits to the World of Birds, page 284; Chapman's Peak, page 284; Topstones, page 287; and Sleepy Hollow Farmyard). Safari Escape includes Duiker Island, off Hout Bay and home to a seal colony, in its Cape Point round-trip. Pat's Adventures concludes one tour with a champagne cruise out of the Royal Cape Yacht Club and another with a sociable beach barbecue.

For full details, call in at Captour's Visitor's Information Centre in the Strand Concourse, or contact individual tour companies, some of the more prominent of which are:
✰ Plusbus Touring, Tel. 218-2191/2/3 ✰ Tales of Africa Tours, Tel. (0282) 2-3702 ✰ Top Tours, Tel. 551-2904 ✰ Pat's Adventures, Tel. 794-4140 (all hours), 683-3311 (alternative); day or evening yacht charter (skipper and hostess included) also available ✰ Safari esCape, Tel. 794-4832 ✰ Sealink, Tel. 25-4480; also offers boat cruises and charter, helicopter trips and charter; minibus hire and chauffeur-driven cars ✰ Springbok Atlas, Tel. 45-5468 or 417-6545 (business hours), 461-9263 (after hours) ✰ Hylton Ross, Tel. 438-1500 ✰ Rodeon Tours, Tel. 419-6150/1 ✰ City Tramways, Tel. 934-0540 (all hours) ✰ Welcome Tours & Safaris, Tel. 434-3890, 434-1954 ✰ Sun Tours, Tel. 689-1232 ✰ Specialized Tours, Tel. 25-3259.

Tours operators with a difference include: ✰ Township Tours, Tel. 96-8182; visits to Crossroads 'squatter' community (how the people live; the 'informal' business sector).

STEAM TRAIN TRIPS The Cape Western Railway Preservation Trust organizes a number of runs, the shortest on a train called 'Pug', along the Paarden Eiland industrial line; longer ones to the winelands (Franschhoek, Ceres, Caledon, Worcester) and, in spring, to the wildflower areas of the western coastal region. For information and bookings, consult Captour.

SEA CRUISES AND BOAT CHARTER Charters, Tel. 21-4000 ☆ Sealink (see also Bus and Coach, page 294) ☆ Ocean Star Yacht Charters, Tel. 75-1706, sightseeing by luxury yacht ☆ Condor Charters, Tel. 417-5612, business-seminar cruises a speciality ☆ Falcon Charters, Tel. 790-3619 or 790-5624, local cruises, offshore tuna-fishing trips ☆ Warren Marine, Tel. 790-1040, *Circe* launch trips from Hout Bay ☆ The schooner *Laura Rose* is available for special charters and parties, Tel. 438-9208.

AIR AND HELICOPTER TOURS AND CHARTER: ☆ Peninsula Air Services, Tel. 934-8952 (all hours), coastal trips and general tours, one-hour to full day ☆ Sealink (see page 294) ☆Fisante Kraal Air Services, Tel. 96-1691; air tours of the Peninsula and winelands in a six- or four-seater ☆ Flying Eye Aerial Photography, Tel. 434-4513 (low-level photographic trips) ☆ Court Helicopters, Tel. 25-2965, operating out of Table Bay docks; short flips, Peninsula tours, Stellenbosch winelands (including a delicious estate lunch), and farther afield, to the 'ostrich country' of the southern Cape, with lunch at Oudtshoorn ☆ Cape Helicopter Services, Tel. Somerset West (02231) 901-254/900-234, offers pre-arranged helicopter package tours, including half- and one-day wine route, two-day Garden Route, and 24-hour Bush Camp tour to the Breede River (accommodation, barbecue, optional boating, walking, bird-watching).

CITY LIFE

Shopping

The city's principal retail area is the Golden Acre and its adjacent Strand Concourse network (see page 274), Adderley Street, St George's Street Mall, and the Old Mutual Centre in nearby Exchange Place. On the city's southern perimeter is the pleasant Gardens Centre.

BUYING CHEAP If you're bargain-hunting for standard items, you could do a lot worse that go straight to the manufacturer. Pam Black's *A-Z of Factory Shops* is a useful guide. Otherwise, try the Pick 'n Pay Hypermarket in Ottery – it stocks just about everything you could possibly need or want, at competitive prices.

After the rains: a suburban view of Devil's Peak

MARKETS For fun shopping, there are three permanent city open-air markets, situated in Greenmarket Square, on the Parade and at the railway station. They offer a great deal of junk, some good buys and a few real bargains.

Similar markets are held sporadically at a number of other venues, mostly over weekends and public holidays and mostly under the auspices of the Cape Crafters' Association. Biggest of the dozen or so is the Cape Craft and Expo, held in the Constantia area, with 300 exhibitors. Again, a lot of the handwork is fairly ordinary, but if you take your time and look carefully you'll find both the unusual and the exquisite. Captour has the full details.

SPECIALITY SHOPPING Three of the more rewarding venues are Claremont's Cavendish Square (90 speciality shops, restaurants and bistros, art exhibitions, demonstrations, concerts; open till late; the adjacent Link complex houses 48 shops) and the huge and all-purpose Tyger Valley centre between Durbanville and Bellville (150 outlets, large and small).

ANTIQUES There's plenty to explore in this field, but beware tourist traps. Available at most hotels and from Captour is Shirley Kelner's booklet on the 'Antique Route'.

Long Street (page 276) is a good place to start. Best of the open-air antique fairs is that held each Friday on Church Street's pedestrian mall.

AFRICANA Try Clarke's Bookshop (Long Street, Tel. 23-5739; see page 276); Jeffrey Sharpe's Rare Books (Victoria and Alfred Basin, Tel. 438-5010).

GEMSTONES Outlets include: Afrogem (Mercantile Centre, Bree Street; Tel. 24-8048); Topstones (near Simon's Town, Tel. 86-2020; see page 287); Hout Bay Mining Company (Beach Crescent, Hout Bay; Tel. 790-5637).

ARTS, CRAFTS, CURIOS The choice is wide; some of the more interesting outlets are: Kottler's of Cape Town (branches in Adderley Street and at the Mount Nelson Hotel, Gardens); The Sun Art Gallery (Cape Sun Hotel, Strand Street); Bundu Art and Curios (Picbel Parkade, Strand Street); Zimbabwe Curios (St George's Street Mall); Images of Africa (Shortmarket Street, on Greenmarket Square); Gra-

ham Ivy's African Bazaar (Adderley Street); African Market (Pearl House, Heerengracht); The Cape Gallery (Church Street); Ikapa Gallery (Strand Street); The Sheep Shop (a job-creation project, 37A Somerset Road, Green Point); The Rialto Gallery (Kronendal, Hout Bay).

Theatre and music

Cape Town's two principal performing arts venues are the Nico Malan and the Baxter theatre complexes.

THE NICO MALAN (DF Malan Street, Foreshore, Tel. 21-5470). Three auditoriums: the Opera House (1 200 seats), the Theatre (550 seats) and the Arena (120 seats). Opera and drama, of course, but also some outstanding ballet and oratorio, and lighter presentations (operetta and modern musicals), mostly staged under the auspices of the Cape Performing Arts Board (Capab), which has a resident orchestra. Restaurant; undercover parking. Bookings: Computicket.

THE BAXTER (Main Road, Rondebosch; Tel. 685-7880). An integral part of the University of Cape Town; 657-seat theatre; 100-seat studio/workshop; 640-seat concert hall. Popular theatre and music but also local and, occasionally, experimental drama. Students of the university's School of Music perform in the concert hall between 13h45 and 14h30 each Wednesday during term-time. Restaurant. Bookings: Computicket.

SMALLER VENUES There are several of these, including the Herschel in Claremont, the Masque in Muizenberg, and the Little Theatre and UCT Arena in Orange Street, Gardens. The leading privately run venue is the Theatre on the Bay, in Camps Bay, which puts on excellent (professional) shows in its pleasant 400-seat auditorium. Bookings: Computicket.

THE CAPE TOWN SYMPHONY ORCHESTRA gives regular concerts (on Thursdays and Sundays) in the City Hall. Recess from 20 December until 10 January and 1st week in June until 2nd week in July. The programmes are suitably varied to cater for most tastes in classical music. Programmes are published well in advance, and are available from Captour. Bookings: Computicket or Tel. 462-1250.

JAZZ can be enjoyed at, among other places, The Jazz Den (88 Shortmarket Street); Tattler's (The Don Hotel, Sea Point); The Fire Escape (Buitengracht Street); The Green Dolphin, harbour, and at the Cape Sun Hotel. The jazz scene, though, changes all the time: consult the entertainment sections of the newspapers.

Wining and dining

City and Peninsula have a lot to offer the lover of fine food. Captour brings out an annual *Restaurant Guide*, and there are several intelligently opinionated books on the shelves, including Peter Devereux's *The South African Good Food Guide*. Also contact Raymond Davis of Cape Liaison, Tel. 557-8069. He suggests restaurants, makes bookings on your behalf, organizes office functions.

A select list of Cape Town restaurants appears on pages 302-305.

Live entertainment Popular night-spots include Abigail's (Main Road, Rondebosch) ✰ After Hours (Wale St, City) ✰ Arties (Riebeeck St, City) ✰ The Base (Shortmarket St, City) ✰ Brass Bell (Kalk Bay) ✰ Café Royal (Church St, City) ✰ Cesar's (Long St, City) ✰ Galaxy (Cine 400 Complex, College Rd, Athlone) ✰ Hardrock Café (Beach Rd, Sea Point, and Main R, Rondebosch) ✰ Idols Nightclub (Loop St, City) ✰ Josephine's (Main Rd, Claremont) ✰ Pranks (Regent/Queens, Sea Point) ✰ Smoke House (Loop St, City) ✰ Space Odyssey (Main Rd, Salt River) ✰ Tom's Cabin (Main Rd, Three Anchor Bay) ✰ Yellow Door (NY1, Guguletu).

Dinner dancing For a relaxed evening of dining, wining and dancing, try the ✰ Constantia Nek Restaurant (Constantia) ✰ The Innsbruck Inn (Queen's Road, Sea Point) ✰ Laurel's (Regency Hotel, Sea Point) ✰ Michel's (Beach Road, Bloubergstrand) ✰ The Villa dei Cesari (Cape Sun Hotel, City).

Cape Town's pubs City and suburbs are well served by English-style pubs, unusually so since they are something of an anomaly: licensing laws generally insist that drinking places also provide full meals and/or accommodation (that's to say, the great majority of South African bars are appendages to either restaurants or hotels, or both).

Cape Town's more atmospheric locals include Barristers Wine Tavern (Main St, Newlands and Beach Rd, Hout Bay), Bertie's Landing (Victoria Basin, Harbour), Ferryman's (Victoria and Albert Basin), The Fireman's Arms (Mechau Street), Forester's Arms (Newlands Ave), Oyster Bar (De Waal Sun Hotel), Perseverence, (Buitenkant Street). However, there are many others to choose from and each has its own clientele and character. For visitors with a healthy thirst and limited time to explore the possibilities, a useful buy is Mike Shay's *The Good Pub Guide of the South West Cape*, which features about 170 watering holes of all kinds.

Sport and recreation

SUN, SEA AND SAND The Peninsula has nearly 150 km of coastline, much of it ideal for beach leisure, bathing, boating, surfing, fishing. The western waters are chilly but many of the beaches are pleasantly sheltered from the south-easter and favoured by sunworshippers. Conversely, the eastern (False Bay) side tends to be windy but the sea is warm.

Currents, backwash and the odd rogue breaker put bathers at risk along some stretches. Warning notices will tell you which parts to avoid but, still, if you're a first-time visitor you'd be wise to seek advice from someone who knows. Generally, it's sensible to stick to the more popular areas – those monitored by lifesavers, and patrolled by beach constables.

Some of the Cape Peninsula's more pleasant beaches are:

Milnerton Closest to the city; 8 km of sands; safe bathing, canoeing and boating in the lagoon, strong surf elsewhere.

Bloubergstrand 10 km north of Milnerton; popular with bathers and photographers (for the views of Table Mountain).

Peninsula west coast (see pages 282-285) Clifton First, Second, Third (fashionable among the young) and Fourth (favoured by families) beaches are all excellent for sun and sand; also Maiden's Cove next door (tidal and paddling pool); Glen Beach (surfing and sunbathing); Camps Bay (for experienced swimmers only, and not well sheltered from the wind, but there's a tidal pool) and Bakoven (a charming cove; good for skin-diving). Farther along: attractive beaches at Llandudno (a pretty little cove, pleasant for picnic parties and sunset-watching; strong backwash); Sandy Bay (once a quiet 'nudist' beach, now spoilt by voyeurs in the high season) and Hout Bay. Beaches at Noordhoek, Kommetjie and Scarborough are not suitable for casual swimming, but the waters are popular among boating enthusiasts.

Cape Of Good Hope nature reserve Maclear beach is excellent for snorkelling/diving (clear water, enchanting underwater scenery; crayfish and perlemoen).

False Bay/Peninsula east coast Mnandi, Strandfontein and Sunrise beaches: lovely, wide stretches of sand, often windy. Strandfontein, until recently designated a 'coloured' beach, has a pavilion, large tidal pool and the African Reptile Park (snakes, lizards, crocodiles). Sunrise tends to be crowded near the car park, almost deserted farther away.

Muizenberg beach Safe bathing, broad white sands; popular, with plenty laid on (pavilion, putt-putt, boat-pond, kiosks, restaurant). Beaches farther south include St James (sheltered cove: tidal pool; good snorkelling); Fish Hoek (gentle surfing; popular boating and sailing venue; pleasant amenities); Boulders (sheltered; safe bathing); Froggy Pond and Miller's Point (both much favoured for family outings; safe bathing; picnic spots).

SWIMMING There are spacious public pools at Newlands (Olympic standard), the Sea Point Pavilion (sea-water; Empire Games standard) and at the top of Long Street (indoor; heated; Turkish baths).

SEA ANGLING Freely allowed from and off the Peninsula coasts except at Cape Town Harbour. Species include white steenbras, red roman, snoek, musselcracker, elf and kabeljou. Deep-sea anglers also catch marlin, swordfish and tunny (the waters off Cape Point are the only ones in the world in which all three tunny species are found).

At present, casual sea anglers do not need a permit, but there are strict catch limits. Crayfish (rock lobster), oysters and perlemoen (abalone) may not be taken out of season.

CHARTER BOATS are available from Big Game Fishing Safaris, Tel. 64-3837; Bluefin Charters, Tel. 83-1756; African Fishing Safaris, Tel. 72-1272; Falcon Charters (Hout Bay Boat Yard), Tel. 790-3619; 790-5624; Condor Charters, Tel. 47-0741 and Seaboard Yachting Ventures, Tel. 25-4292.

Radio Good Hope, the local station, broadcasts information on fishing conditions at 18h15 each day; local newspapers run informative angling columns. For detailed advice, contact the Department of Environmental Affairs: Sea Fisheries, Tel. 402-3911.

FRESHWATER ANGLING Catches are limited to 10 per person per day irrespective of fish species; there are also size restrictions; permits are required. Open season for trout is 1 September – 1 June.

Further information can be obtained from Mr Urs Schwarz, secretary of the WP Artificial Lure Society, Tel. 24-5613; and the Cape Piscatorial Society, Tel. 24-7725.

OTHER WATERSPORTS There are virtually limitless opportunities for boating, yachting, boardsailing, waterskiing, diving and so forth off the Peninsula's shores. Contact numbers include: WP Sailing Association, Tel. 64-2972; Cape Sailing Academy, Tel. 86-1640; Ocean Divers International (diving and snorkelling), Tel. 23-5898; Cape Peninsula Aquatic Club (waterskiing), Tel. 73-1150.

BIRD-WATCHING Over 300 bird species have been recorded on the Peninsula. Some of the more rewarding of the bird-spotting venues are the public gardens (see page 276); Kirstenbosch (page 289); Rietvlei, north of Milnerton (a major waterfowl breeding area; the coastal bird conservation council runs a sanctuary here for contaminated and injured seabirds); Rondevlei (page 291); the World of Birds in Hout Bay (page 284), and the Cape of Good Hope Nature Reserve (page 284).

Further information is obtainable from the Cape Bird Club, Tel. 686-6393 (afternoons); and Bird Safaris, Johannesburg, Tel. (011) 726-8095, who organize small-group (6-14 people), short-duration bird-watching excursions under expert guidance, including sea trips in search of albatross, skua, prior, petrel, fulmar and a number of other species.

A gentle ride on the wide white sands of Noordhoek (see page 284)

CYCLING A wonderful way to explore the Peninsula. The WP Pedal Power Association organizes recreational rides each Sunday throughout the year, Tel. 794-2268; excursions begin from Newlands pool; for the coming Sunday's route, contact 'Dial-a-Ride' 61-2415. There are numerous other organized weekend fun-rides on the calendar, including the hugely popular Argus Tour. A useful publication is *Cycling in and around Cape Town*, by Tim Anderson and Colin Dutkiewicz (Struik Timmins, 1990) which features 36 rides in the Peninsula and its hinterland.

Other contacts include Cycles In The Forest, in Plettenberg Bay, contact Ingrid Tel. (04457) 3-1961 (cycling expeditions to the Garden Route); Cape Cycle Ventures, Tel. 80-1353 (Cape of Good Hope Nature Reserve) and Blazing Saddles (rent bicycles), Tel. 80-1353.

WALKING AND HIKING: See Walks and trails, page 293.

HORSE-RIDING The Peninsula's riding schools and stables welcome visitors: contact Captour for a list and directions. Exploratory rides: contact Horse Trail Safaris, Tel. 73-4396; 73-1807. Vineyard Horse Trails, Tel. 981-2480. Milnerton Riding Club, Tel. 557-3032. Downs Riding Centre, Tel. 62-1414. The Cape Hunt and Polo Club at Durbanville, the southern hemisphere's oldest hunt, meets on Sundays (various venues) for a chase without blood-letting; Tel. 96-3968.

HORSE-RACING Regular meetings at the Ascot course (Milnerton); Durbanville and Kenilworth, where the prestigious Metropolitan Handicap concludes the summer season.

GOLF Peninsula golf clubs welcome visitors; excellent courses at Green Point, Milnerton, Mowbray, Rondebosch, Wynberg, Simon's Town, Westlake and Clovelly. Contact the WP Golf Union, Tel. 531-6728.

BOWLS Numerous clubs; contact the WP Bowling Association, Tel. 24-1919.

SQUASH A great many venues; contact the WP Squash Rackets Association, Tel. 461-4107.

HEALTH AND FITNESS The Peninsula generally and the city in particular are extremely well served by health studios. Among the more prominent are the Health and Racquet Club, Tel. 419-6600; Heerengracht Health and Fitness Centre, Tel. 25-2929; Capetonian Health Spa, Tel. 25-3163 or 21-1150; Turkish Steam Baths, Tel. 210-3302.

ADVISORY: CAPE TOWN AND THE PENINSULA

CLIMATE

Mediterranean; winter-rainfall region. Summers: warm to hot, but cooled by frequent and strong south-easterlies. Winters: cold and wet periods interspersed with warmer, sunny spells and, sometimes, by hot 'berg wind' conditions. Best weather: spring (September), autumn and early winter (March-June). For details, see page 271.

MAIN ATTRACTIONS

The mountain□Sun, sea and sand□The waterfront □The Constantia estates□Cape winelands□Botanical and public gardens□Historical Cape Town□ Fine hotels, restaurants, shops, tourist amenities generally.

TRAVEL

Road. Cape Town is 1 421 km from Johannesburg, 1 479 km from Pretoria, 1 776 km from Durban, 790 km from Port Elizabeth, 1 015 km from Bloemfontein, 1 500 km from Windhoek.

These cities, and others within southern Africa, are linked by a network of excellent national highways. The main route north to Johannesburg, Pretoria and the Zimbabwe border at Beit Bridge (this was originally the first section of Cecil Rhodes's overambitious Cape-to-Cairo highway) is the N1, which passes through the lovely Cape Winelands and, via the toll-gated Huguenot Tunnel, through the high Du Toits Kloof Mountains, before entering the arid vastness of the Great Karoo. Other major routes include the N2 eastwards (inland to Mossel Bay, coastal thereafter) to Port Elizabeth, Grahamstown and eventually, to Durban and beyond, to the Swaziland border; and the N7 that runs up through Namaqualand to Namibia (see pages 329-333).

    Coach travel: Inter-city semi-luxury bus services include Autonet's thrice-weekly run between Cape Town, Johannesburg and Pretoria, via Bloemfontein, and once-weekly run via Kimberley. Also contact Intercity Greyhound, Tel. (021) 419-2246; Connex coach tours, Tel. (021) 218-2191; Inter Cape, Tel. (021) 934-4400; Translux, Tel. (021) 218-3871.

Rail. Railway passenger services connect Cape Town with all major centres in South Africa, Namibia, Botswana and Zimbabwe. Enquiries: station information desk, or Tel. (021) 940-2667/8/9; mainline reservations: Tel. (021) 940-2033; rail tours, Satour: Tel. (021) 21-6274; Blue Train: Tel. (021) 218-2672.

Air. Cape Town airport is 22 km from city centre, off the N2 highway. Regular services connect all major centres; twice a week direct flight operates between Cape Town and London's Heathrow airport (leaves SA on Wednesdays and Fridays and leaves London on Thursdays and Saturdays). Passenger services/information: Tel. (021) 93-6223. SAA International enquiries, Tel. (021) 418-1525; SAA Domestic enquiries, Tel. (021) 25-4610. There is bus transport between city terminal and the airport. Tel. Inter-Cape (021) 934-4400.

Travel within Cape Town and Peninsula

City and Peninsula rail, bus and taxi services are adequate. Major international car-hire companies have offices in the region, as do local car-, camper- and caravan-hire firms. Tour operators offer a wide choice of one-day and half-day scenic coach (and to a lesser extent air and sea) trips. Fuller coverage of local travel options appears in *Getting Around*, pages 291-295. For detailed information, contact Captour.

ACCOMMODATION

The Peninsula is a prime tourist area; visitors have a wide choice of good hotels, guesthouses, holiday apartments and hideaways. Book well in advance for December and January (and especially for the period of the Transvaal school holidays). These are the prime vacation months, during which many hoteliers and landlords increase their rates.

The following is a representative but by no means exhaustive selection of graded hotels. Full details of all types of accommodation on offer can be obtained from Captour and Satour (which publishes a comprehensive booklet entitled *Where to Stay in the Cape Province*) or from your travel agent.

Select hotels

CITY AND FRINGES

Cape Swiss Hotel ★★★ South of city centre, on lower slopes of mountain. 80 rooms, 4 suites. PO Box 21516, Cape Town 8008; Tel. (021) 23-8190; Fax: (021) 26-1795; Telex: 52-4235.

Capetonian Protea ★★★★ Conveniently situated just off the Heerengracht, close to harbour and city centre; Galley restaurant specializes in seafood. 125 rooms; conference facilities for 100. PO Box 6856, Roggebaai 8012; Tel. (021) 21-1150; Fax: (021) 25-2215; Telex: 52-0000.

Cape Sun ★★★★★ City-centre (Strand St) skyscraper; glitzy; six service lifts afford superb views; three restaurants (Riempies serves traditional Cape dishes; Tastevin is renowned for its cuisine). 342 rooms, 20 suites; conference facilities for 750. PO Box 4532, Cape Town 8000; Tel. (021) 23-8844; Fax: (021) 23-8875; Telex: -52-2453.

De Waal Sun ★★★★ In the Gardens area, on the mountain side of the city. Attractive grounds, views; known for its Chinese restaurant and Oyster Bar. 127 rooms, 3 suites; conference facilities for 150; swimming pool; tennis and squash courts nearby. PO Box 2793, Cape Town 8000; Tel. (021) 45-1311; Fax: (021) 461-6648; Telex: 52-0653.

Holiday Inn ★★★ In Woodstock, five minutes up the hill from city centre. 290 rooms, 2 suites; conference facilities for 900; swimming pool; á la carte restaurant. PO Box 2979, Cape Town 8000; Tel. (021) 47-4060; Fax: (021) 47-8338; Telex: 52-0576.

Inn on the Square ★★★ Charmingly positioned in Greenmarket Square. Nice coffee-shop and terrace. 170 rooms. PO Box 3775, Cape Town 8000; Tel. (021) 23-2040; Fax: (021) 23-3664; Telex: 52-1050.

Metropole ★★★ In Long Street, near city centre. Small, long-established, slightly old-fashioned and very hospitable; restaurant renowned for its seafood. 39 rooms. PO Box 3086, Cape Town 8000; Tel. (021) 23-6363; Fax: (021) 23-6370; Telex: 52-0295.

Mount Nelson ★★★★★ In the Gardens area, on the mountain side of the city; one of the world's most elegant hotels, recently renovated but retains much of its graceful past. Old-style personal service, exquisite cuisine. 131 rooms; conference facilities: 5 venues, 500 people. PO Box 2608, Cape Town 8000; Tel. (021) 23 1000; Fax: (021) 247-472; Telex: 52-7804.

Park Avenue★★★ The old Gardens Village hotel, renovated and renamed. 32 rooms; conference facilities for 150. Union Street, Gardens, Cape Town 8001; Tel. (021)24-1460.

St George's ★★★★ Centrally situated in St George's St. Prides itself on personal service; excellent La Brasserie restaurant. 135 rooms, 2 suites. PO Box 5616, Cape Town 8000; Tel. (021) 419-0808; Fax: (021) 419-7010; Telex: 52-1533.

Town House ★★★★ On fringes of city centre; quietly tasteful; excellent restaurant; health and squash club on premises. 104 rooms. PO Box 5053, Cape Town 8000; Tel. (021) 45-7050; Fax: (021) 45-3891; Telex: 52-0890.

Tulbagh Hotel ★★★ A quiet place located in an attractively secluded central city square. 48 rooms, 6 suites, conference facilities, à la carte restaurant. Tulbagh Square, Cape Town, 8001. Tel. (021) 21-5140.

RIVIERA

Ambassador by the Sea ★★★ Overlooks the ocean (magnificent views from the very good restaurant). 64 rooms; conference facilities. 34 Victoria Road, Bantry Bay, Cape Town 8001; Tel. (021) 439-6170; Fax: (021) 439-6336; Telex: 52-0721.

Karos Arthur's Seat ★★★ Sea Point, near front. Recently renovated, stylish. 115 rooms, 4 suites; conference facilities. Arthur's Road, Sea Point, Cape Town 8001; Tel. (021) 434-3344; Fax: (021) 439-9768; Telex: 52-7310.

Peninsula (not yet graded). Luxurious all-suite hotel at the end of the Beach Road; 112 suites. PO Box 17188, Regent Road, Sea Point 8060; Tel. (021) 462-4444; Fax: (021) 462-4593.

President ★★★★★ On Sea Point seafront, but away from the crowds. One of Cape Town's oldest and most distinguished hotels; its Finch's restaurant is highly regarded. 127 rooms, 26 suites; conference facilities for 300. PO Box 62, Sea Point, Cape Town 8060; Tel. (021) 434-1121; Fax: (021) 439-2919; Telex: 52-6620.

Ritz Protea ★★★★ Sea Point, but not on front. Tall building, noted for its revolving restaurant and views. 216 rooms; excellent conference facilities (13 venues, 400 people). PO Box 27224, Rhine Road, Sea Point 8060; Tel. (021) 439-6010; Fax: (021) 434-0809; Telex: 52-0682.

The Bay (not yet graded). New and ultra-elegant hotel overlooking the sea at Camps Bay. Classy colonial-style restaurant. 65 rooms, 5 suites, all with balconies. PO Box 21, Camps Bay 8040. Tel. (021) 438-4444; Fax: (021) 438-4455.

Winchester Mansions ★★★ Old-style family hotel overlooking sea. 20 rooms, 21 suites. 221 Beach Rd, Sea Point, Cape Town 8001; Tel. (021) 434-2351; Fax: (021) 434-0215; Telex: 52-7479.

SOUTHERN SUBURBS

Alphen ★★★ An historic and beautiful Constantia Valley homestead and wine estate. Antiques everywhere; excellent restaurant; also pleasant lunches under the oaks. Some of the 39 suites and rooms open out onto courtyards. PO Box 35, Constantia 7848, Cape; Tel. (021) 794-5011; Fax: (021) 794-5710; Telex: 52-6195.

Newlands Sun ★★★★ Standard luxury hotel, close to Newlands rugby/cricket grounds and Kenilworth racecourse. Coach House restaurant specializes in traditional English food. 139 rooms, 5 suites; conference facilities for 350. Main Road, Newlands 7700; Tel. (021) 61-1105; Fax: (021) 64-1241; Telex: 52-0686.

The Vineyard ★★★ Historic country house in Newlands area, built in 1799 and now one of South

Africa's finest hotels. Lovely grounds; tastefully imaginative décor; splendid restaurant. 113 rooms. PO Box 151, Newlands 7725; Tel. (021) 64-2107; Fax: (021) 683-3365.

FALSE BAY

Lord Nelson Inn (grading pending). Situated on Simon's Town's main street, overlooking harbour. Historic building, recently renovated; old-style hospitality; *haute cuisine*; décor: colonial with naval theme. 58 St George's Street, Simon's Town 7995; Tel. (021) 86-1386; Fax: (021) 86-1009.

Shrimpton Manor ★★ Muizenberg, on the False Bay coast. Small, exclusive, hospitable; excellent restaurant. 19 rooms. 19 Alexander Road, Muizenberg 7951; Tel. (021) 88-5225; Fax: (021) 88-1129.

Ungraded accommodation

For information on and reservation of ungraded accommodation, contact:

Bed and Breakfast, 17 Talana Rd, Claremont, 7700; Tel. (021) 61-6543, 697-4662.

Holiday Booking Service, PO Box 5514, Cape Town 8000; Tel. (South Africa 021) 24-3693, or (United Kingdom 041) 554-1713. Guesthouses, self-contained flats and cottages; beachfront apartments; country houses.

Caravan/camping and self-catering accommodation

False Bay coast: Fish Hoek Beach caravan park, Tel. (021) 82-5503; Miller's Point park, Tel. (021) 86-1142; Oatlands Holiday Village, Simon's Town, Tel. 86-1410 (facilities for caravanners/campers as well as chalets and camping rondavels); Sunny Acres park, Fish Hoek, Tel. (021) 85-1070; Zandvlei caravan park, Muizenberg, Tel. (021) 88-5215.

Southern suburbs: Allandale Bungalows and caravan park, Tokai, Tel. (021) 75-3320; Fax (021) 72-9744.

Peninsula west coast: Imhoff park, Kommetjie, Tel. (021) 83-1634.

SELECT RESTAURANTS

In 1990, six Peninsula restaurants had been awarded the blazon of the *Confrèrie de la Chaine des Rôtisseurs*, the international society of gourmets. Rosenfontein has since closed; the others are:

Champers, Deer Park Drive, City (Tel. 45-4335). Low-key, friendly but rather formal; *cuisine moderne* with classic undertones; superlative salads.

Finch's, President Hotel, Sea Point (Tel. 434-1121). *Haute cuisine* in Regency-style surrounds.

Tastevin, Cape Sun Hotel, City (Tel. 23-8844). Imaginative menu, excellent wine-list.

Truffles, Heathfield, southern suburbs (Tel. 72-6161). A small restaurant serving superb food in a delightful atmosphere.

The Vineyard, Vineyard Hotel, Newlands (Tel. 64-2107). Outstanding menu, beautiful dining room.

Other eating houses with a reputation for excellence are:

CITY AND FRINGES

Alibi, Upper Waterkant Street (Tel. 25-2497). Italian perfectionism; take your own wine.

Anatoli, Napier St (Tel. 419-2501). Excellent Turkish food in dramatic Middle Eastern surrounds. Take your own wine.

Biesmiellah, Wale St, Bo-Kaap (Tel. 23-0850). The real Cape Malay fare, eaten with fingers. No alcohol allowed.

Floris Smit Huijs, Church Street (Tel. 23-3414). Modern and unusual décor; fine food.

Freda's, Kloof Street, Gardens (Tel. 23-8653). Simple, lightish, but innovative food, a mix of local and Mediterranean. Nice wine-list.

The Grill Room, Mount Nelson Hotel, Gardens (Tel. 23-1000). Cape Town's most famous hostelry, now impressively restyled. Continental classic-type food in modern setting; light music for dancing. The Garden Room next door is baronial and graceful, and offers an attractively conservative menu. Service is impeccable throughout.

The Hildebrand, Strand Concourse (Tel. 25-3385). Popular for business lunches; busy in the evening as well; Continental cuisine, extensive menu; altogether rather sophisticated.

Kaapse Tafel, Queen Victoria St, Gardens (Tel. 23-1651). Authentic Cape home cooking of the highest order. Take your own wine.

La Brasserie, The St George's Hotel, St George's Street (Tel. 419-0808). Varied menu, including French Provincial specialities; cheerfully modern setting.

Leinster Hall, Gardens (Tel. 24-1836). Charming manor-house type surrounds; solid and unpretentious; excellent food.

Maria's, Barnett St (Tel. 45-2096). Tiny restaurant serving delicious Greek fare; casual and atmospheric. Take your own wine.

Nelson's Eye, Hof Street, Gardens (Tel. 23-2601). Cosy, nautical-pub atmosphere; seafood and delicious meat dishes, charmingly served. Take your own wine.

No 10, Kloof Nek Road, Tamboerskloof (Tel. 24-3838). Imaginative and varied menu, nice ambience. Take your own wine.

Old Colonial, Barnett Street, Gardens (Tel. 45-4909). Exceptionally hospitable; restfully old-fashioned décor; varied menu, though there are German and Cape traditional undertones. Altogether quite excellent.

Rozenhof, Kloof Street, Gardens (Tel. 24-1968). A quiet and dignified place that serves you the very best.

Taiwan City, Darling and Plein streets (Tel. 461-1414). Oriental fare in unpretentious setting.

34 Napier Street (Tel. 25-1557). Quiet, tasteful décor, *cordon bleu* cuisine. Take your own wine.

The Tent, Vredehoek (Tel. 45-3840). Commercial Middle Eastern (belly-dancer performs on certain nights); good food and a fun place.

Townhouse Restaurant, Townhouse Hotel, Corporation Street (Tel. 45-7050). Standard large menu, beautifully prepared dishes; extensive wine-list.

Zeestraat, Strand St (Tel. 25-3732). Continental cuisine, seafoods a speciality. Take your own wine.

RIVIERA

Andy's Bistro, Sea Point (Tel. 439-2470). Just what it sounds like: cheerful, fresh, friendly – and good. Take your own wine.

The Beachcomber, Camps Bay (Tel. 438-1213). Large menu, imaginative dishes; informal and friendly. Take your own wine.

Blues, Camps Bay (Tel. 438-2040). Varied menu, quality fare superlatively served.

Europa, Sea Point (Tel. 439-2820). An elegantly converted old house; seafood specialities.

Kamakura, Sea Point (Tel. 434-2228). Sophisticated Japanese dishes, prepared by a regiment of imported chefs. Take your own wine.

La Galiote, Sea Point (Tel. 44-4510). French Provincial specialities; Continental atmosphere. Stylish.

La Perla, Sea Point (Tel. 44-2471). Very popular; huge menu.

Mykonos Souvlaki, Main Rd, Sea Point (Tel. 439-2106). Traditional and very good Greek fare; family-run. Take your own wine.

The Round House, the Glen, Camps Bay (Tel. 438-7193 or 438-2320). Stylish, imaginative fare; lovely leafy setting.

Street markets are a prominent feature of the Cape Town scene (see page 296)

San Marco, Sea Point (Tel. 439-2758). Popular; true Italian cuisine; beautiful tableware.

Stones, Main Rd, Sea Point (Tel. 439 6747). Turquoise and mauve décor, youthful clientele, interesting food. Take your own wine.

Tandoori, 3 Holmfirth Rd, Sea Point (Tel. 439-1429). Traditional Indian food and décor; atmospheric. Take your own wine.

Tarkaris, 305 Main Rd, Sea Point (Tel. 434-4266). Indian food at its best; rich décor. Take your own wine.

Ticino, Beach Rd, Sea Point (Tel. 434 9969). Stylishly Continental, large menu, seafood specialities.

Time Out, The Point Health and Leisure Club, Green Point (Tel. 434-0780). French and Italian influences discernible. Upmarket.

Top of the Ritz, Ritz Protea Hotel, Sea Point (Tel. 439-6010). Imaginative *haute cuisine*, enjoyed in sky-scraping, revolving room.

SOUTHERN SUBURBS

Almondbury, Lakeside (Tel. 88-5789). Unspecialized, unpretentious, top quality. Take your own wine.

Barristers, Newlands (Tel. 64-1792). Standard range of dishes, beautifully prepared and served; popular and often crowded.

Belvedere House, Claremont (Tel. 61-8513). Fairly limited menu, carefully contrived; quality fare; intelligent wine-list.

Clementine's, Wynberg (Tel. 797-6168). Popular, with a youngish clientele; innovative menu. Take your own wine.

Farthings, Kenilworth (Tel. 61-8235). Patronized by those who know food; classic fare in a converted cottage. Take your own wine.

Fisherman's Cottage, Plumstead (Tel. 797-6341). Careful menu, honest food exquisitely prepared. Take your own wine.

Jake's, Kenilworth (Tel. 797-0366). A friendly place with an innovative menu. Take your own wine.

Josephine's Supper Club, Claremont (Tel. 64-4379). Modern; à la carte menu, a dinner/dance restaurant, cocktail bar and live entertainer.

La Scala, Cavendish Square, Claremont (Tel. 61-3252; 61-2394). Bistro-type Italian eating; lively atmosphere; super food.

La Vita, Newlands (Tel. 685-2051). Very popular; Continental cuisine.

Pancho's Mexican Kitchen, Lower Main Rd, Observatory (Tel. 47-4854). Mexican menu; casual, inexpensive, youthful customers, fun. Take your own wine.

Truffles, Main Road, Heathfield (Tel. 72-6161). Original dishes, reverently prepared; gorgeous desserts, deservedly very popular venue.

SOUTHERN PENINSULA

Alphen Restaurant, Alphen Hotel, Constantia (Tel. 794-5011). Formal, gracious, quiet; classic menu.

Black Marlin, Miller's Point, near Simon's Town (Tel. 86-1621). Enterprising à la carte in charming Victorian house; on the way to Cape Point. Seafood a speciality.

Brass Bell, Waterfront, Kalk Bay (Tel. 88-5456). Casual, a favourite among surfing fraternity; seafood features prominently; braais on the terrace.

Bressay Bank, Hout Bay (Tel. 790-1140). Dinner with a difference – aboard a moored yacht; seafood specialities.

Buitenverwachting, Constantia (Tel. 794-3522). Stately home overlooking the Constantia valley (see page 289). Opulent restaurant, superlative cuisine.

Camel Rock, Scarborough (Tel. 80-1122). Small, modest, informal, charming; menu chalked on blackboard; excellent fare, mostly seafood. Take your own wine.

Jonkershuis, Groot Constantia estate (Tel. 794-6255). Superb Cape cuisine in a 300-year-old setting.

Kronendal, Hout Bay (Tel. 790-1970). Elegant Cape Dutch homestead, modern dining room; smallish menu, classic dishes.

Restaurante Don Pepe, Muizenberg (Tel. 88-8459). Honest and delicious Portuguese food. Take your own wine.

Shrimpton's, Muizenberg (88-5225; 88-1128). Emphasis mainly but not exclusively on seafood; luscious sauces, delicious. Take your own wine.

Tavern, Groot Constantia estate (Tel. 794-1144). Lunches: boisterous, Germanic atmosphere, bench-seating, crowded, noisy, and a great deal of fun.

Wharfside Grill, the Harbour, Hout Bay (Tel. 790-2130). Seafood in atmospheric setting.

NORTHERN AREAS

Bellinzona, Table View (Tel. 557-6151). Famed for its view of Table Mountain; conservative, classic menu; superbly prepared food.

Blue Peter, Blue Peter Hotel, Bloubergstrand (Tel. 56-1956) Fine food, French influence, eaten overlooking sea. Dinner dances Fri. and Sat.

La Camargue, Table View-Bloubergstrand (Tel. 56-1973). French-style cuisine; lovely view of the mountain.

Le Chalet, Pinelands (Tel. 531-1628). Continental-style food in most pleasant surrounds, appealingly served. Take your own wine.

Ons Huisie, Bloubergstrand (Tel. 56-1553). Early 19th century fisherman's cottage; seafood specialities; simple and excellent.

On the Rocks, Bloubergstrand (Tel. 56-1988). Continental cuisine, enjoyed in a shoreline setting with spectacular views of Table Mountain.

CITY LUNCHES

Squares, Stuttaford's Town Square, St George's Street Mall (Tel. 24-0224). Upmarket, very inviting venue for breakfasts, teas, lunches.

Upper Crust, Long Street (Tel. 419-1940). Appealingly cosy; imaginative cuisine; lunches only.

USEFUL ADDRESSES AND TELEPHONE NUMBERS

Automobile Association Tel. 21-1550 (general); 419-4378 (breakdown service); 21-1550 (touring information); Fax: (021) 419-6032.

Captour Head Office (021) 462-2040; Visitor's Information Bureau, Strand Concourse, Adderley St, Tel. (021) 25-3320; Johannesburg office, Tel. (011) 331-8494; Western Cape Tourism Association, Shop 11, Tygervalley Centre, Tel. (021) 948-4993.
   Captour offers an accommodation booking service for those who find themselves stranded in the Peninsula; Tel. 419-1961. The Bureau also handles tour bookings (coach, sea, air) and car-hire reservations, and produces a number of very useful booklets and brochures (covering accommodation, restaurants, shopping, the Winelands, special-interest routes) and the Cape Town *What's On.* Street and other maps are available from the Visitor's Information Bureau.

Satour (SA Tourism Board) Shop 16, Piazza level 3, Sanlam Golden Acre, Adderley Street, Tel. (021) 21-6274.

Theatre and other bookings Through Computicket. No telephonic reservations, but ring 21-4715; 21-4205 for information/enquiries. Fax: (021) 418-3409. Computicket offices are at Strand Gallery in the Concourse; Golden Acre Cine in the Golden Acre; Nico Malan theatre complex on the Foreshore; Garlicks in Claremont; Accent in the Constantia Village shopping centre; AP Jones on Main Road, Fish Hoek; at the Gardens shopping centre, Gardens; Centrepoint in Pinelands; the Baxter theatre complex in Rosebank, and at the Adelphi Centre in Sea Point.

Table Mountain and cableway The Kloofnek bus departs from Adderley Street, outside OK Bazaars. Change buses at Kloofnek terminus for the lower cable station. Bookings for cableway and guides: Tel. 24-5148.

Embassies and Consulates, telephone numbers Australia 419-5425; Austria 21-1440; Belgium 61-7376; Canada 23-5240; Denmark 25-1025; Finland 23-7240; France 21-5617; Germany 24-2410; Greece 23-1354 (Embassy), 24-8161 (Consulate); Israel 45-7207; Italy 23-5157 (Embassy), 24-1256 (Consulate); Japan 25-1695; Netherlands 21-5660; Norway 25-1687; Portugal 21-4560 (Embassy), 24-1454 (Consulate-General); Spain 25-1468; Switzerland 25-4838 (Embassy), 21-7633 (Consulate); Taiwan (Republic of China) 21-1993 (Embassy), 21-4267 (Consulate-General); United Kingdom 461-7220 (Embassy), 25-3670 (Consulate passport section), 25-3670 (commercial section); United States 21-4280 (Embassy and Consulate).

Emergency numbers *Ambulance* 1-0177; *Groote Schuur Hospital* 404-9111; *casualty departments*: Somerset Hospital (Green Point) 21-3311; Groote Schuur Hospital (Observatory) 47-3311; Conradie Hospital (Pinelands) 531-1311; Red Cross Children's Hospital (Rondebosch) 685-5011; Victoria Hospital (Wynberg) 797-8131; *poisoning centre*: Red Cross Children's Hospital (Rondebosch) 689-5227, or Tygerberg Hospital (northern areas) 931-6129; *fire brigade* (Cape Town) 461-5555; 461-4141; *police headquarters* 461-4326, 461-4370; *police flying squad* 1-0111; *after-hours pharmacy* 461-8040; 82-1101; *Lifeline* (local equivalent of Samaritans) 461-1111; *mountain rescue* 1-0111; *sea rescue* 218-3500.

ANNUAL EVENTS

Minstrel (Coon) Carnival: early January □ Metropolitan Handicap: 3rd Saturday in January □ Cape Festival: variable in recent years; usually April, for two weeks □ Spring Wild Flower Show, Kirstenbosch: September □ Rothman's Sailing Week: December □ Two Oceans Marathon: Easter Sunday □ Hout Bay Snoek Derby: July/August.

THE CAPE WINELANDS

Splendid mountain ranges, green and fertile valleys, historic towns and villages, gracious homesteads, orchards and vineyards heavy with fruit – these, in brief, are the physical elements that distinguish the Cape's winelands, a loosely defined region that stretches, very approximately, north-east from Cape Town to the Hex River valley and the edge of the arid Karoo, and from Tulbagh and Ceres in the north-west to Robertson in the east.

Not that the wine industry is confined within these limits. On the contrary, the Peninsula's Constantia valley (see page 289) is renowned for its superb vintages, and the newer growing areas – the Swartland, Olifantsrivier and Piketberg, and the lands extending to and including the Little Karoo far to the east – are rapidly gaining a reputation for the quality of their table wines and, in the latter instance, for their fortified wines and brandies. In recent years, too, vineyards have been established as far north as the Transvaal.

But it is the winter-rainfall areas of the Western Cape, and most notably the rolling foothills around Stellenbosch, Franschhoek and Paarl and the rich alluvial soils of the Breede River valley that consistently produce the best: the vineyards average between eight and twelve tons of grapes a hectare, and from the pressings come reds and whites, sherries and ports and brandies that find their way to the most discerning of tables, both in South Africa and, increasingly, abroad.

These were the first country areas to be settled by the white colonists: prompted by the need to feed an expanding Cape Town, they began infiltrating the traditional Khoisan lands of the interior during the 1660s. Stellenbosch, 41 km from Cape Town, was founded as an agricultural settlement in 1679, a venture that, in terms of food production, proved so successful that farmers soon began to turn their energy and surplus resources to the growing of vines.

Thereafter, river valley after river valley was occupied, the land turned over to pasture, to

Part of the lovely Boschendal estate near Franschhoek. In the distance are the Groot Drakenstein mountains.

wheat – and to grapes. By 1687 an impressive 400 000 vines had been planted and were flourishing, and the arrival, in the following year, of a small group of French Huguenots – skilled people, some of them well versed in the sciences of viticulture and wine-making – lent impetus to an industry that was already burgeoning.

And as the farms prospered, so their owners extended their sturdy but modest two- and three-roomed homes. They added wings, built cellars, stables, coach-houses, slaves' quarters, a *jonkerhuis* (a house for the eldest son), laid courtyards encircled by whitewashed walls, steepened the pitch of the roofs to allow for a gabled loft, and a distinctive architectural form began to emerge during the last years of the 17th century. It was a style that drew from medieval Holland, from the France of the Huguenots and the islands of Indonesia, but which developed in unique fashion to become known, and admired, as Cape Dutch.

Some lovely Cape Dutch country houses grace the winelands. Most are gabled, a few are truly grand, nearly all are beautiful – and accessible to the ordinary tourist by way of the various wine routes that have been established.

THE STELLENBOSCH AREA

The town of Stellenbosch, founded in the green and fertile valley of the Eerste River and overlooked by the forested heights of the Papegaaiberg (Parrot Mountain), grew gracefully, in keeping with the charm of its setting: the early settlers planted oak trees that were to reach splendid maturity, created open spaces, built churches and schools and thick-walled, limewashed homes with thatched roofs and timberwork of stinkwood and yellowwood, and it's all been beautifully preserved. One can see it at its best, perhaps, along Dorp Street, which has the longest row of historic buildings in the country, and around Die Braak, the village green once used for military parades and for festivals, feasting and games and still fringed by the quaintness of the past.

Stellenbosch has been an important educational centre for over a century, home to such notable places of learning as the Rhenish Institute for Girls, Bloemhof School, the Paul

Roos Gymnasium and the famed University, principal academic breeding ground for generations of Afrikaner prime ministers, politicians and leaders in various fields. Campus and town are nicely integrated.

Wine is of course a major industry, but by no means the only one. On the outskirts of town is the Techno Park, South Africa's fast-growing 'silicon valley', Tel. (02231) 9-8509.

THE VILLAGE MUSEUM (Ryneveld Street) is a magnificent collection of historic houses dating from a number of eras, meticulously restored and furnished in period style, the gardens planted with the flowers, shrubs and trees that would have graced the original homes. The Schreuderhuis (1709), a smallish cottage, is believed to be the country's oldest surviving town house. Other buildings include the gabled Blettermanhuis (1760-90); Grosvenor House (1800-30), and the House of OM Bergh (1840-70). Open daily.

DIE BRAAK (Bird Street). On and around the town square are the pretty thatched-roof Anglican Church of St Mary (1852); the Rhenish Mission; the old Burgerhuis (1797) and the VOC-Kruithuis, or Dutch East India Company powder-house (1777), now a national monument housing a small military museum.

D'OUWE WERF (Church Street) is one of the country's earliest boarding houses. Built in 1710, on the foundations of an earlier church, it's been restored and still does noble service as a lovely little hotel. If you're not staying over, do at least visit the coffee shop.

THE UNIVERSITY boasts some fine buildings, an art gallery (at the corner of Dorp and Bird streets; open daily but closed between exhibitions) and fine botanical gardens noted for their displays of indigenous succulents, cycads, orchids, ferns, bonsai, and the strange Welwitschia species that grows in the harshness of the Namib desert. The gardens are open Sunday to Friday, closed on Saturday, and are in Neethling Street.

LIBERTAS PARVA (corner of Old Strand Road and Dorp Street). An elegant, gabled mansion that incorporates both the Rembrandt van Rijn art gallery (works by leading 20th century artists, including Pierneef, Van Wouw and Irma Stern) and, in its cellar, the Stellenryck wine museum (huge old vats, Cape furniture, brassware). Both museums are open Monday to Saturday and on Sunday afternoons.

And if it's wine you're interested in – in its history and the way it is made today – make a point, too, of visiting the:

OUDE MEESTER BRANDY MUSEUM (Old Strand Road). Relics of a fascinating past (stills, bottles, glassware) and an insight into the present. Open Monday to Saturday and on Sunday afternoons.

THE BERGKELDER (on the Papegaaiberg, next to the railway station). The 'mountain cellars' have been hollowed out of the hillside; they contain some extraordinarily large and impressive vats, and they offer tours and tastings (Monday through Saturday).

THE OUDE LIBERTAS CENTRE (opposite Stellenbosch Farmers' Winery), is an enchanting venue for open-air Sunday shows – music, drama, ballet, opera. Performances are held in the Amphitheatre; Sunday concerts in the season (December through March) are enormously popular: you bring a picnic basket and sip wine in the evening sunshine as the music washes over you. Tours of the winery by appointment.

THE LANZERAC HOTEL (Jonkershoek Road) is a stately Cape Dutch mansion with excellent restaurants, a splendidly stocked wine-cellar, an art gallery (the Tinus de Jongh Memorial) and a museum (early Cape furniture).

OOM SAMIE SE WINKEL (Dorp Street). For local colour, an absolute must. Oom Samie was one of the town's very first general dealers, and his shop's been rebuilt in period style, declared a national monument and crammed with traditional home-made preserves, bric-a-brac, curios and other goods. On the corner is De Akker, a well-known pub with a wine library and an information service.

AROUND STELLENBOSCH

Some of the most attractive of the western Cape's vineyards, estates and homesteads are concentrated in the area, over 20 of them on the Stellenbosch wine route (see page 320) and each worth visiting for its cellar tours and tastings; for the good lunches provided by many of them, and for the beauty of the surrounding countryside. To mention, briefly, a few by name:

☆ Avontuur, on the Stellenbosch-Somerset West road. Splendid thoroughbred horses roam the farm.

☆ Blaauwklippen, 4 km along the Strand Road. The charming, gabled house was built in 1789. Traditional 'Cape Malay' preserves and relishes on sale; coachman's lunch.

☆ Delaire, at the top of Helshoogte Pass (see page 310). Stunning views.

☆ Delheim, on the high slopes of the Simonsberg and described as a 'touristic jewel and photographer's paradise'. Serves a vintner's platter during the summer months (October through April) and country soup in winter.

☆ Hartenberg (in the beautiful Devon Valley) and Morgenhof (in the south-western foothills of the Simonsberg) both serve excellent vintner's lunches.

☆ Saxenburg, on the hills above Kuilsriver. Under development is a farm museum and small restaurant.

☆ Spier, on the R310 to Cape Town. Renowned for its two charming restaurants; the original wine cellar has been converted into the Ou Kelder art gallery.

THE VAN RYN BRANDY CELLAR, near Vlottenberg on the R310 to Cape Town, offers weekly tours of one of the country's largest distilleries (Viceroy, Royal Oak, Van Ryn's Rare Cabinet). It also runs brandy courses, and musical evenings (a recital in the cellars followed by cooperage demonstration, audio-visual presentation, cocktails and dinner). A fun 'brandy breakfast' (train journey from Cape Town, brandy cocktails, brunch) happens three times a year.

THE JEAN CRAIG POTTERY, on the Devon Valley road (off the R310 to Cape Town). Here, one stands in a central viewing area to watch the various and fascinating processes – throwing, glazing and so forth.

The range of products is wide, the styles vary from the charmingly homely to the sophisticated, the quality is good. There's a shop on the premises.

ANIMALS ON VIEW Tygerberg Zoo lies 15 km north of Stellenbosch (take the R304, cross the N1, first left). It's billed as 'the zoo for everyone', though it's really not everyone's scene (there's something depressing about wildlife in confinement, especially in Africa). On show are primates, big and small cats, kangaroos and wallabies, antelope, snakes, parrots, eagles, vultures, giant tortoises, and a children's farmyard.

Also north of town (12 km along the R44) is Wiesenhof game park: free-roaming animals (feeding time is between 11h00 and 12h00 each day); picnic and barbecue sites; lake (for boating); coffee bar and light refreshments; roller skating rink.

Somewhat similar is the Safariland game park (take the R310 north-east, right onto the R45, left onto R303; or take the N1 from Cape Town and turn right onto the R303).

JONKERSHOEK VALLEY, to the east of Stellenbosch, is a scenic joy. The Eerste River rises in the area, and in one place cascades in a magnificent waterfall; to the north are spectacular peaks known as The Twins, to the south the Stellenboschberg and Haelkop (1 490 m).

Within the valley are the famed and very lovely Lanzerac and Oude Nektar estates, and the Jonkershoek state forest, which contains the hatcheries of the Fisheries research station and the Assegaaibosch nature reserve, a 168-ha stretch of montane fynbos (heath) and sanctuary for rare proteas, small buck and some interesting bird species. The Assegaaibosch is also noted for its wildflower garden, and there are picnic and barbecue sites and short nature trails. Larger paths and trails criss-cross the state forest, which is accessible to the public during the daylight hours of the wet season (May through September).

Farther to the east is the Hottentots Holland nature reserve, a 22 569-ha mountain preserve of rugged cliff and peak (the Victoria, at 1 589 m above sea level, is the highest), tumbling river and gorge and deep green woodland. Access is by foot (the nearest point one can get to by car is the Jonkershoek state forest: see above). Many watercourses rise in the area, draining in all directions but mostly south-eastwards. The rugged Boland hiking trail, from which there are short optional digressions, runs through the area.

Alfresco fare at Boschendal

HELSHOOGTE PASS The name translates, aptly, as 'steep heights': the pass climbs at a gradient of 1 in 10, and the traveller is treated to marvellous views of the Simonsberg and the Wemmershoek mountains before he descends in the Drakenstein valley, setting for some of the Cape's most notable homesteads.

Franschhoek

A small commercial centre serving the wine and fruit farmers of the area, Franschhoek ('French glen') was founded in 1688 on land given to Protestant Huguenot refugees who had fled a Europe torn by religious strife.

Though of fiercely independent disposition, the Huguenots were not permitted to form a separate community in the Cape hinterland but were mixed in with the resident Dutch and German free burghers, and within three or four decades little remained of their cultural heritage: French was no longer spoken, and assimilation was complete. The settlers did, however, have a powerful influence on the development of the wine industry, and on the gracious rural architecture of the period. Their national origins can still be discerned in a number of common Afrikaans family names, among them De Villiers, Le Roux, Du Preez, Fouché, Marais,

Rousseau, Malan, Du Plessis, Theron and Du Toit. And in the names of many of the homesteads and splendid vineyards of the Franschhoek and Groot Drakenstein region: La Provence and Haute Provence, La Bris, La Motte, Le Chênes, L'Ormarins, Mouton-Excelsior and so on.

Of note in Franschhoek itself is the large but delicately graceful Huguenot Memorial and the adjacent Huguenot Museum complex. This includes Saasveld, a Cape Dutch home removed from its original site in Kloof Street, Cape Town, and rebuilt here during the 1960s.

HOMESTEADS Although the Vignerons de Franschhoek is classed as a wine route, some of the wine estates belonging to it are not open to the general public (see page 320). Some of the cellars are, though, and others can be visited by appointment. Of special note are:

☆ Bellingham (3 km beyond the Dwars River bridge on the Franschhoek road). The original grant for this farm dates back to 1693. The estate declined sadly during the earlier part of the 20th century but has risen, phoenix-like, during the past few decades and the cellars are now famed for their excellent dry white wines. A different kind of drawcard is its natural amphitheatre, which seats an audience of about 90 and in which musical and other performances are periodically staged.

☆ Haute Provence (before entering the Franschhoek village, cross the railway line and turn right). A pleasant homestead whose owners, Michael and Norma Guassardo, are talented potters. Their work is on show, and for sale, at their studio on the estate.

☆ Boschendal (before reaching Groot Drakenstein station, on the right of the road). One of the best-known farms, the quintessence of country elegance and popular with visitors from Cape Town. The Cape Flemish-style manor house, dating from 1812 and for long the property of the De Villiers family, fell into decay in the latter part of the 19th century but has been beautifully restored and is now a museum as well as the centrepiece of a splendid wine farm. The Waenhuis now serves as a gift shop; the Taphuis as a winery and tasting room. Boschendal's restaurant is famed for its buffet lunches; picnic baskets are provided in summer for those who prefer to eat in the shady grounds. Open from 11h00 daily.

THE DRAKENSTEIN VALLEY, overlooked on the west by the Groot Drakenstein mountains, is noted not only for its vineyards but also for its fine deciduous fruit orchards and its crops of table grapes. Indeed, the area was the birthplace of South Africa's thriving export fruit industry.

Somerset West

South of Stellenbosch, 48 km east of Cape Town and twinned with the adjacent Strand municipality, Somerset West is an attractive and fast-growing residential centre set delightfully between the Hottentots Holland mountains and the waters of False Bay. Many of its residents commute to work to and from Cape Town and Stellenbosch. Worth visiting are the Ou Pastorie, the historic NG Kerk (Dutch Reformed Church; 1820); the Country Craft Market (120 stalls; some quite excellent hand-crafted goods on display and sale) and, on the north-western edge of town, the:

HELDERBERG NATURE RESERVE, a lovely 400-ha stretch of pleasant countryside set against a backdrop of the high Helderberg peak. Principal attractions are the spectacular scenery, the area's wealth of proteas and other indigenous flora and its rich birdlife, which includes species unique to the region (among others, the protea seed-eater, Victorin's scrub warbler, and three types of red-crested fluff-tail).

The reserve is also home to a variety of antelope, and there's an oak-shaded picnic spot, lily ponds, a duck pond, a herbarium, an arboretum and a small and delightful patch of natural forest (stinkwoods, yellowwoods, rooi els). The path to the Disa Gorge and the mountain road are much favoured by discerning walkers; the cliffs a challenge to climbers. Gentle trails beckon the rambler.

GORDON'S BAY, just along the coast east of Somerset West, is a charming resort village and fishing harbour, popular among vacationing families (there are three resorts in the area) and among Capetonian weekenders for the sailing, fishing, swimming, sunbathing, hiking and walking that the area offers. There are also some lovely coastal scenic drives.

The main highway – the N2, which follows an inland course until it reaches Mossel Bay (350 km from Gordon's Bay) and the start of the Garden Route (see page 231), which ends in Humansdorp – climbs over the spectacular:

The Cape Dutch elegance of L'Ormarins

SIR LOWRY'S PASS that cuts through the Hottentots Holland range above Somerset West. From the heights there are quite stunning views of the mountains, the plains far down below and, in the distance, Table Mountain and the Peninsula. Once over the pass, one descends in rather less precipitous fashion to the small centres of:

ELGIN AND GRABOUW, headquarters of the country's apple-growing industry. Elgin in fact comprises little more than a railway siding, but there are two large packing houses in the immediate vicinity (visitors are welcome, though there are no formal tours during the busy season). Pears and peaches are also cultivated in the area; Grabouw has a small museum devoted to the story of the apple; the Orchard Elgin Country Market (signposted from the Grabouw turn-off on the N2) is billed as 'a fresh new concept in country shopping' and offers local produce, preserves, handicrafts, 'haute deli', a continental bakery, and excellent breakfasts and luncheons. There are pleasant scenic drives in this rich farming region.

THE PAARL AREA

This is a region of impressive scenic splendour. Five passes lead you over majestic mountain ranges that are often snow-capped in winter; below, the Berg River winds its way through lush countryside on its way to the Atlantic Ocean 200 km away, bringing sustenance to the vineyards and orchards of what was for long known as the Pêrelvallei ('vale of pearls').

In fact, the name applies not to the general beauty of the area but derives from a dome-shaped buttress that soars high over the river – Paarl Mountain and its three attendant features, one of which, Paarl Rock, caught the eye of an early Dutch explorer, reminding him of a 'diamandt-ende perelberg' ('diamond and pearl hill') when seen at dawn, with the sunlit dew glistening on its mica-studded surface.

The Rock overlooks the town of Paarl. To the east are the Klein Drakenstein mountains, breached by the precipitous Du Toit's Kloof pass (now, with the completion of the Huguenot road tunnel through the hills, this stretch of the main Cape-Transvaal highway is a lot easier for motorists, although a lot less spectacular). To the north is the attractive and substantial town of Wellington.

Paarl

An historic town, and the biggest of the Western Cape's inland centres, founded in 1720 as a farming and wagon-building settlement, later developing its economic base to include quarrying (for building stone), canning (fruit, vegetables) and manufacturing (jam, cigarettes, eau de Cologne).

Among Paarl's claims to notability are its unusually long oak- and jacaranda-shaded main street, which runs a full 10 km from end to end; its lovely suburban gardens; its prominence in the powerful and ultimately successful Afrikaans Language Movement; its fine buildings, and its intimate associations with the wine industry.

Paarl has its wine route (see page 320), and serves as the headquarters of the giant Co-operative Wine Growers' Association (KWV); the famed Nederburg wine auctions are held each year just outside town.

THE KWV (the Association's original Dutch name, Ko-operatieve Wijnbouwers Vereniging) is the world's largest wine co-operative. Formed in 1918, it now controls the South African wine and spirit industry at producer level, regulating sales, fixing the minimum prices paid to growers and handling some 70% of the country's wine exports. Its offices are in La Concorde, an imposing neo-classical building on Main Street. KWV's enormous wine and brandy cellar complex, in Kohler Street, is open to the public on weekdays for tours, tastings, lectures.

KWV also runs Laborie, a gracious old manor house and model wine estate nestling at the foot of Paarl Mountain. Visits by arrangement (Tel. (02211) 63-1001). Its adjuncts include an excellent restaurant, which is housed in a restored wine-cellar and which offers a range of delectable traditional dishes.

WAGONMAKERS MUSEUM, recently established and still developing, is well worth a visit for the fascinating relics of this once-flourishing trade on display: wagons, carts, craftsman's tools and equipment.

OUDE PASTORIE (Old Parsonage) is an architectural gem. It was built in 1786 beneath the imposing Tower Church and is now a museum featuring fine collections of Cape Dutch furniture, Cape silver and copperware and relics of

Huguenot and early Dutch-Afrikaner culture. Open weekdays.

Other attractive religious buildings include the Holy Trinity (Anglican) Church in Main Street; the old Zion Church in Church Street; the old Bethel (Apostolic) Church in Rose Street (Bethel House, its namesake in Mill Street, is the oldest building in town) and the:

STROOIDAKKERK, or 'thatched church'. A simple, dignified building designed by noted French architect Louis Thibault, completed in 1805 and now one of the oldest still-used places of worship in the country. Intriguing features of the graveyard are its gabled burial vaults.

THE AFRIKAANS LANGUAGE MONUMENT (Taalmonument) stands on the slopes of Paarl Mountain: a splendid structure of three linked columns, a soaring spire and a fountain, each element symbolizing a debt owed by the language – to the western world, to Africa, to the Cape people of eastern origin.

In town, on Pastorie Avenue, is the Gideon Malherbe House (named after one of the eight original pioneers of the Afrikaans language), which now serves as a museum housing, among other relics, the press on which the first Afrikaans newspaper, *Di Patriot*, was printed. Open daily.

PAARL MOUNTAIN The area's most distinctive feature – a cluster of three peaks named Britannia Rock, Gordon Rock and, as mentioned, Paarl Rock.

To get to Paarl Mountain one takes the Jan Philips road from town – a circular and scenically attractive route along which there's a picnic site and the Mill Stream Wild Flower Garden. The area around the mountain has been proclaimed as the:

PAARLBERG NATURE RESERVE, a pleasant 1 910- ha expanse of fynbos (heath) countryside dominated by the trio of peaks and graced by a variety of protea species, wild olive, aloes, bastard saffron, wild currant; by groves of natural forest, among them (an unusual feature) a patch of woodland containing the delicate silver tree (see page 272). Birds to be seen include the Cape bunting, the redwinged starling, the Cape robin, black eagle, sugarbird, sunbird. There are numerous paths and picnic/barbecue areas, and several dams in which anglers fish for black bass that are said to be the largest in the country.

LA BONHEUR CROCODILE FARM, in Suider (southern) Paarl, has over a thousand of these giant reptiles in its dams. The gift shop stocks a wide variety of hand-worked goods including, of course, crocodile-leather handbags.

Estates and wineries

There are numerous wine farms and estates in the area, many of which are on the Paarl wine route (see page 320). The more notable are:

✰ Backsberg, on the lower slopes of the Simonsberg, has an especially pleasant tasting parlour; self-guided tours of the cellars (complemented by closed-circuit TV demonstrations) and a small wine museum.

✰ Fairview, just south of Paarl Mountain, offers a variety of cheeses made from the estate's own goat's milk. At nearby Landskroon there's a splendid choice of Jersey-milk cheeses, and a vintner's platter lunch, on offer.

✰ De Leuwen Jagt, on the south-western slopes of Paarl Mountain. Has beautifully restored dwellings, and remarkable views towards far-off Cape Town.

✰ Villiera, south-west on the Old Paarl Road. Delicious 'tapas-style' lunch on the terrace, under the oaks.

✰ Rhebokskloof, just north of Paarl Mountain, has a traditional Cape restaurant; 45-minute estate tours in a 4-wheel drive vehicle.

✰ Paarl Rock brandy cellar, in the northern part of town. Apparently the only one in the country where you can view the entire brandy-production flow-line.

✰ Nederburg, perhaps the best-known of all the estates. Its origins and reputation for fine wines date back to 1792; the H-shaped gabled and quite enchanting homestead, set in a wide sweep of countryside mantled by vines, has been lovingly preserved. The renowned annual Nederburg wine auction, held around mid-April, is one of the most important wine events, and social occasions, on the South African calendar: merchants, collectors, investors, private buyers and others with good (or plausible) reasons for being there come from afar to enjoy the sales and the carnival atmosphere. There are food and wine stalls, tastings, and a fashion parade.

Wellington

This attractive little town, set on the Berg River a few kilometres to the north of Paarl, is the headquarters of South Africa's dried fruit industry, and of a prosperous wine-producing area. Its vineyards form part of the Paarl wine route (see page 320). Notable features of the town include the Old Blockhouse, southernmost of the nearly 8 000 small forts built by General Sir Horatio Kitchener to contain the elusive Boer guerrilla commandos during the South African War of 1899-1902; and Twistniet, the original homestead of the farm Champagne, on which the town was laid out in 1840. Among other historic farms of the area are Hexenberg, De Fortuin and Leewen Vallei.

BAIN'S KLOOF PASS, which carries the R303 road north-eastward from Wellington, is one of the scenic wonders of the region.

Built in the 1850s by Andrew Geddes Bain, southern Africa's foremost road engineer of the pioneering Victorian era and a geologist of note, the pass is 30 km in length, and it affords magnificent views towards Paarl and Wellington and the distant Swartland. At the summit there's a picnic spot set in pleasant woodland surrounds, after which you descend over the northern slopes of the mountain range, through a deep ravine, to a land of river, rapid and waterfall. Here, at the Bainskloof forestry station, is the start of a circular walk through the Wolvenkloof ('hyena's pass'), an area noted for its rock formations and lovely wild flowers.

THE BREEDE RIVER VALLEY

The Breede (or Breë) River valley is the largest and probably loveliest of the south-western region's three wine- and fruit-producing valleys. The river rises in the high Ceres basin, a region whose mountains are often white with enough snow to attract skiers and whose main centre is the town of Ceres, named after the Roman goddess of agriculture, or fertility.

The Breede gathers momentum through the narrow and strikingly rugged Michell's Pass, plunges down between the Witsenberg and Elandskloofberg ranges and then flows south-eastwards through a lush countryside of orchards and vineyards and into the Robertson area. Of its many tributaries, the 40-km-long Hex River is the most notable, its valley both stunningly beautiful and hugely productive.

The rugged grandeur of the Bains Kloof area

Tulbagh

Earthquakes are a rare occurrence in southern Africa, and when they do happen they're usually mild, but on 29 September 1969 a tremor measuring 6,5 on the Richter scale shook the Tulbagh-Ceres area. Nine people died and many buildings were destroyed, among them some of Tulbagh's, and the country's, finest historic houses.

Tulbagh began life as a tiny frontier settlement during the first years of the 18th century, later growing (around the Old Church, built in 1743) into a tranquil, charmingly picturesque country town. After the earthquake its old buildings were carefully restored to their pristine 18th century condition, and those on Church Street – 32 of them in all – now comprise the largest single group of national monuments in South Africa.

OUDE KERK VOLKSMUSEUM is in fact a small network of four buildings that, together, give the visitor an intriguing insight into the town's past. They are:

☆ The Old Church Museum (in Church Street): Victorian furniture; works by the once much under-estimated Thomas Baines. Open Monday to Saturday.

✩ The Old Drostdy (Van der Stel Street): Drostdys served as both the administrative office and the residence of the landdrost, or magistrate, at the Cape between 1685 and 1828. Of those still in existence, that at Swellendam is the oldest (see page 244), and Graaff-Reinet's (page 256) probably the finest, though the Tulbagh Drostdy, designed by Louis Thibault, comes a close second. It's now both a museum (early Cape furniture and household utensils) and the headquarters of a leading wine company, a hospitable firm which treats visitors to an excellent glass of sherry (or to Drostdy Hof wine) while they view works by local artists. The museum is open Monday to Saturday; the Drostdy Wine Cellar offers daily tours, film shows, tastings, Monday to Sunday 11h00 to 15h00.

✩ Monbijou (Church Street): A building dating from 1815, and also designed by Thibault: antiques; works of art; tours by appointment.

✩ The Victorian House (Van der Stel Street): period furniture and décor; open Monday to Friday (Saturdays during school holidays).

Ceres

An enchanting little town set among the mountains of the Witsenberg, the Hex River and the Skurweberg ranges.

The basin in which Ceres nestles is one of South Africa's most bountiful (and scenically most outstanding) fruit-growing areas, yielding fine crops of apples, pears, peaches, nectarines (and vast quantities of potatoes as well). Ceres boasts the southern hemisphere's largest fruit-packing enterprise.

The Dwars River runs through the town, inviting visitors to relax at its picnic spots and to fish and swim in its waters. There are trout in the mountain streams higher up; skiers come in the winter-time; the upland air can be crisp (even in summer), especially in the early mornings and at dusk, but it is clear and invigorating. A prime holiday area, serviced by good hotels and family resorts (The Pine Forest; The Island). Specific attractions include:

TRANSPORT RIDERS' MUSEUM (Orange Street): wagons and carts, and a fascinating array of the equipment and utensils that the self-sufficient early traders took with them in their houses-on-wheels. Open weekdays and Saturday mornings.

CERES NATURE RESERVE A 6 800-ha sprawl of upland countryside to the south and west of town, established to protect the mountain fynbos (heath) vegetation, which includes rare floral species. A good place for walking; trails are being developed; some fine Bushman paintings can be seen.

South-west of Ceres is the small town of Wolseley (fruit-canning and packing), situated at the entrance to the dramatic Michell's Pass, a cleft in the high and otherwise impenetrable mountains that both man and migrating animals used long before Andrew Bain built the first modern throughway in 1846.

To the north of Ceres is the pretty little centre of Prince Alfred Hamlet, a terminus from which the fruits and vegetables of the region are railed. To the east are the:

HEX RIVER MOUNTAINS AND VALLEY One of the world's most dramatic railway passes cuts through the heights: a tortuous route that twists up to almost 1 000 m above sea level. The line carries the main south-north rail traffic; passengers on the Blue Train and the Trans-Karoo, both of which negotiate the mountains in daylight, enjoy breathtaking vistas.

The mountains and valley of the Hex River

The sandstone Hex River range, whose cliffs and ravines are a magnet to mountaineers, runs south-west to north-east, rising to between 1 200 and 1 800 m above sea level. Highest of the many pinnacles and peaks are the Matroosberg (2 251 m) and the Buffelshoek (2 070 m). Winter snows and high average rainfall (over 1 500 mm a year) create the many seasonal streams of this spectacularly attractive region. Some of the mountain slopes are suitable for ski runs; the Cape Town Ski Club maintains a base, or hut, on the Matroosberg; there are other runs, lifts and huts on the Waaihoek peak and the Brandwagberg.

As impressive and as much a delight to the eye is the valley below: fringed by grand mountains, wide and immensely fertile, its summer greens turning to lovely muted shades in the autumn and early winter, heavily irrigated and intensively cultivated, the Hex River valley sustains nearly 200 farms that, together, produce most of the late-maturing grapes that are exported from the country. At the entrance to the Hex River valley is:

Worcester

Founded in 1818, this is a thriving commercial and industrial centre and the Breede River valley's largest town. It's on the main Cape Town-Johannesburg road route, and serves as a convenient and most pleasant stopover. The countryside is fertile, the farms prosperous: grapes are a major crop, grown in enormous quantities; the area supports 17 wine co-operatives and a number of brandy distilleries (see wine routes, page 320). Among specific features of interest:

WORCESTER MUSEUM, which has three distinctive parts:
✩ The Afrikaner Museum (Church Street): intriguing displays include a fully-equipped turn-of-the-century doctor's surgery, dentist's surgery and a lawyer's office. Open Monday to Saturday.
✩ Beck House (Baring Street): this incorporates both the Afrikaner Museum and Stofberg House. Late 19th century furnishings and documents of local historical note.
✩ Hugo Naude House (Russel Street): devoted to the works of this talented artist, who began, in the early 1900s, as an impressionist but later adopted a more representational style. Naude's

landscapes are especially evocative, capturing the elusive quality of South African sunlight as few other painters have managed to do. Open Monday to Saturday.

KLEINPLASIE OPEN-AIR MUSEUM, just outside town, depicts the life and times of the early Dutch farmer. Replicas of huts and cottages, ovens, a butchery, kitchen, kiln, tobacco shed, milk room, soap kitchen, horse mill; daily demonstrations include bread-baking, wheat-milling, tobacco-rolling, candle-making, blacksmithing; seasonal programmes focus on spinning, weaving, threshing, sheep-shearing, raisin-making and brandy-distilling. The museum's cafeteria serves delicious traditional Cape food.

Open Monday to Saturday; information: Worcester Agricultural Society, PO Box 59, Worcester 6850; Tel. (0231) 7-0091. Nearby about 30 local wine-producers display their wares and invite you to taste them – a kind of mini wine route. Other stalls show and sell local preserves, cheeses, honey, confectionery and so forth. On view are shire horses of noble stock; amenities include restaurant and self-catering cottages.

THE PIONEER SCHOOL and workshop in Church Street is an outlet for products hand-crafted by blind people. Open during normal shopping hours.

KAROO NATIONAL BOTANIC GARDEN, 3 km off the national highway (N1). The Worcester area is on the western edge of the Little Karoo (see page 237); the 154-ha garden conserves and displays the flora of what is called the Karoo broken veld – mainly succulents, with some trees (the International Organization for Succulents recognizes the reserve as one of the world's five authentic succulent gardens). Ten hectares are under cultivation, the plants logically grouped according to climate, region and type, and there are a number of special displays (succulents, carrion flowers, bulbous species). The flowers are at their most attractive in the winter and spring. There are short walks, and a picnic area. The botanic garden is open daily, sunrise to sunset.

From Worcester, the R60 highway leads south-eastwards, for 46 km through the Breede River valley, to:

Robertson

A fairly substantial, very pleasant town set against the high Langeberg, 160 km from Cape Town on the railway line between that city and Port Elizabeth far to the east.

The area is notable for its fine wines, brandies, sherries and jeropicos (fortified, high-sugar, high-alcohol wines) and for the sweet and musk-flavoured muscatel grapes grown in its extensive vineyards. There are six estates and nine co-operatives in the region (see wine routes, page 320), one of which produces the magnificent Mont Blois Superior muscatel label.

It's also one of the country's foremost horse-breeding areas: there are 14 thoroughbred stud farms, boasting between them some 700 brood mares, within a 30-km radius of Robertson; the industry is sustained by lime-rich soils, superb pasturage and an excellent climate. The region hosts the annual South Cape Spring Show (saw-dust track; wine garden).

A short distance outside town is Sheilam, a farm on which cacti and succulents are culti-vated – 3 000 varieties in all. Farther away (23 km from Robertson) is Robertson Ostrich Farm, where Tienke and Heléne Rabie breed ostriches. Visitors are most welcome; the drive out, past orchards and vineyards and pastures where splendid horses graze, is a joy.

ROBERTSON MUSEUM (Paul Kruger Street) houses various intriguing displays, including a superb collection of lace. Open Monday to Saturday.

THE KWV (Co-operative Wine Growers' Asso-ciation) has established South Africa's largest brandy distillery (it boasts about 130 stills) in Robertson. KWV also operates Branewynsdraai, a taphouse and excellent restaurant serving traditional Cape food.

SILWERSTRAND, on the Breede River 2 km from Robertson, is an above-average family holiday resort. The water here is deep, the stretch is straight and magnificent for swim-ming, boating and other watersports. There's also golf and squash, a restaurant, and some pleasant self-contained chalets.

VROLIJKHEID, on the road to McGregor, is a 2 000-ha conservation centre. Open Monday to Friday. Tel. (0231) 621.

Just outside Robertson (about 4 km) on the Ashton road is the splendid:

NORMANDY FARM-STALL and restaurant: local produce, arts and crafts, stud-farm tour, wine-tasting; information: (0234) 5-1590.

Montagu

Some 20 km east of Robertson, Montagu is set on the edge of the Little Karoo (see page 237) in a region of prosperous fruit-farms and vine-yards that produce, among other things, the richly flavoured muscatel and fortified wines. The town hosts the annual Muscatel Festival.

North of Montagu is what is known as the Koo, a scenically rugged area graced by lovely orchards of apple and pear, apricot and peach trees, and by delightful displays of wild flowers. The Koo is a fine place for walking, and some excellent trails have been established. For the less energetic, there's a tractor-drawn trailer trip from the Koo valley to the top of the high Langeberg.

Montagu itself is both attractive and historic. Of Long Street's houses, fully 14 have been officially designated as national monuments (there are also nine other proclaimed buildings in town). And of course there's the famed:

MONTAGU SPA White travellers stumbled upon the mineral spring about 200 years ago and it has since drawn generations of visitors to its warm (a constant 43 °C) and soothing waters. The spa is now served by an excellent three-star hotel, and by time-share apartments and holiday cottages. There's another hot spring, on the farm Baden, about 4 km away.

MONTAGU MUSEUM (Long Street). Once a church, the building now houses displays fea-turing the Little Karoo region in the early days of white settlement. Joubert House, oldest of the town's dwellings, is part of the complex. The museum also offers a fairly unusual service: it supplies a wide selection of natural herbs that have been collected from the veld. Open daily (mornings only on Saturday and Sunday).

THE TOWN GARDENS boast the country's lar-gest collection of 'vygies' (mesembryanthe-mums). Each Tuesday morning from May through October the ladies of Montagu enter-tain visitors here with tea and cake.

MONTAGU MOUNTAIN RESERVE is a 1 200-ha sanctuary on the northern edge of the Langeberg range: superb upland countryside on which a number of hiking trails, ranging from 12 km to 15 km in length, have been established. One may, though, take gentler walks, and there's a picnic site and fireplace at Keurkloof, half-way up the Cogmanskloof, a spectacular 6-km-long pass. Fauna includes leopard and various buck species; among the flora are aloes and other succulents.

Worth visiting in the general region are a number of little centres, among them:

ASHTON, just south of Montagu, site of the southern hemisphere's largest cannery (fruit, jam, vegetables) and not an especially attractive town. Of more interest to visitors are the thoroughbred horses of the area and, especially, its lovely rose nurseries.

BONNIEVALE, farther south, is wine-farming, peach-growing and cheese-making country. Both the peaches and the cheeses are of superb quality. A rather special cheese shop does business in the eastern part of town.

GETTING AROUND

Walks and hikes

The Western Cape's dramatic sandstone mountain ranges and their foothills – the so-called 'berg interface' that descends to the coastal plain in the south – combine to provide wonderful walking country. The options are virtually limitless. A few suggestions:

✫ Paarlberg nature reserve (page 313). Main attractions: scenic splendour, birdlife and the three granite features. Paarl and Britannia rocks are fairly easy to climb (the latter has chain hand-holds); magnificent views. Information: Paarl Municipality, PO Box 2, Paarl 7622; Tel. (0221) 2-2141.

✫ Ceres Mountain Fynbos Reserve (page 315). Visitors may walk where they wish; formal hiking trails are being developed. Information: Ceres Municipality, PO Box 44, Ceres 6835; Tel. (0233) 2-1177.

✫ Hex River Mountains (page 315). Spectacularly rugged terrain; for experienced hikers only; much of the land is privately owned and permission to enter must be obtained from the local farmers.

The snow-capped Mostertshoek peaks in the Ceres region

EMBLEMS OF QUALITY

Many of the Cape's wines display a 'Wine of Origin' (WOS) seal on the neck of the bottle – a certification, awarded by the South African Wine and Spirits Board, authenticating the data given on the label (though the absence of such a seal does not indicate inferior quality: some very good wine-makers decline to apply for the guarantee).

The seal may show one-, two- or three-coloured bands, each imparting a particular piece of information, namely:

BLUE BAND, carrying the word 'Origin': confirms that 100% of the wine derives from the district specified on the label.

RED BAND, carrying the word 'Vintage': guarantees that at least 75% of the wine is made from grapes picked in the year specified.

GREEN BAND, carrying the word 'Cultivar': indicates that the bottle contains the required legal minimum percentage of the cultivar specified, and

that it is characteristic of the cultivar in taste, bouquet and appearance. The word 'Estate' also appears on the seal.

THREE BANDS (blue, red, green), carrying the appropriate words (see above), with the word 'Estate' appearing on the seal: a guarantee that the wine is made on the estate specified, from grapes grown there. It may, though, have been bottled elsewhere.

GOLD SEAL, with the three bands and the words 'Superieur' and 'Superior' prominently displayed: an assurance of the wine's exceptional quality at the time assessed by an expert panel. This is the only quality grading for a South African wine.

The seal and bands, however, are to be replaced in due course by a new system of indicators.

Recommended reading for travellers with more than a passing interest in the subject is *The Complete Book of South African Wine* by Kensch, Hands and Hughes (Struik, Cape Town).

✫ The Boland hiking trail (Limietberg section): a 37-km, 2-day hike through the mountains. The trail starts at the Hawequas state forest station near the high pass and finishes at the Tweede Tol camping site on the road to Wolseley. One need not, though, do the whole bit: among the popular day walks is that from Bain's Kloof to Du Toit's Kloof Traverse. Short hikes in the Hawequas state forest include the Krom River Waterfall walk (5 km); the Eland River Cave walk (6 km), and the Donkerkloof walk (6 km). Information: Western Cape Forest Region, Forestry Branch, Private Bag 9005, Cape Town 8000.

✫ Alternatively, the area around Tweede Tol itself is well worth exploring on foot; 30 km of mountain paths take you past and through pools, indigenous forest, wildflower displays. The round-trip Wolvenkloof Circle is a 3-hour walk. An especially pleasant hike starts from the tiny centre of Eerste Tol and ends at the waterfall on the Bobbejaan River. Information: The Foreman-in-Charge, Tweede Tol; Tel. (02324) 607.

✫ Karoo National Botanic Garden (page 316): pleasant and, for those interested in plants, most rewarding 10- to 60-minute strolls. Brochure, trail guide, map and bird-list available in the reserve. The 5-hour Quarry nature trail from the garden to the Hartbeest River is being developed. Information: Karoo National Bo-

tanic Garden, PO Box 152, Worcester 6850; Tel. (0231) 7- 0785.

Day drives

The whole of the region's winelands are a delight to the eye, and one doesn't really need to plan too meticulously; simply wandering where the mood and moment lead brings its rewards. However, some of the pleasant formal routes would include:

✫ The Hex River circular drive: Start from Ceres (see page 315); follow the R46 north-east for 60 km, turn right (signpost: Touws River) to remain on the R46 until it joins the N1 national highway. Turn right for De Doorns, Worcester and the Karoo National Botanic Garden (page 316), then to Rawsonville and Goudini on the secondary loop road. Rejoin the R43, past the Mostertshoek Twins, then turn right onto the R46 again and over Michell's Pass (page 315) and so back to Ceres.

✫ The Boland circular drive: Start from Paarl (page 312) and follow the R45, turning right onto the R303 for Wellington (page 314). Continue on the R303, turn right onto the R43 until it meets the N1 highway; turn right and then left for Worcester (page 316) and beyond, until it becomes the R321 to Villiersdorp. After Villiersdorp, rejoin the R45 for Franschhoek (page 310), turn right onto the R303 for the return to Paarl.

☆ The Four Passes circular drive: Start from Stellenbosch (page 307) and take the R310 over Helshoogte Pass (page 310). Turn right on the R45 for the Franschhoek Pass, Franschhoek (see page 310) and beyond, to Theewaterskloof dam. Turn right onto the R321, through Viljoen's Pass, then digress right through Grabouw (page 312); exit to join the N2 west over the precipitous Sir Lowry's pass (page 312) and on to Strand and Somerset West (page 311). Back to Stellenbosch on the R44.

The wine routes

There can be few more pleasant ways of exploring the south-western region's hinterland than to follow one or other of these routes – wineways inspired by the popular *Routes de Vin* of France and Germany's *Weinstrassen*. The concept was transplanted to the Cape in the early 1970s and has proved hugely successful.

For many, the routes (they are clearly signposted, the entrance to each farm, co-operative and estate marked by a roadside emblem) provide a good excuse to travel into the countryside for a day's or weekend's relaxation; others, more serious about wine, set out to add to their stock of favourite labels or to explore new areas, discover new tastes, perhaps picking up a bargain caseload along the way.

Whatever the motives, though, those with limited time at their disposal will be able to cover only a small fraction of the ground. There are literally hundreds of wineries and estates, and they produce between them something over 2 000 different wines. A visit to three, maybe four and at the most five different points along the route is probably the most one can expect to manage in a single outing.

The growers are proud of their farms, and of their wines, and the welcome they extend to visitors goes well beyond a simple quest for sales and profit. Most of the cellars offer tastings (there's no limit to the number of wines you're allowed to try, though many places charge a small fee per glass) and tours (these are at set times); some run excellent restaurants; at others you'll find a farm stall selling local specialities (produce, preserves and so on), a gift shop, perhaps a small private museum. Many of the beautiful homesteads are historic.

But whatever part of a particular route you select, it'll prove a pleasant experience indeed. You talk to people who know all the subtleties and secrets of wine-making, inspect the bottling and labelling machinery and the wooden casks tiered in coolness of a wine- and wood-scented cellar; sample the vintages at leisure, maybe buy a bottle or two, take luncheon on the terrace, and go on to the next farm. Nothing is hurried: there is time to absorb, assess, compare, savour, enjoy.

To date, nine routes have been created, though four of them – the Constantia (Cape Peninsula; see page 292), the Swartland and Olifantsrivier (west coast; page 339) and the Little Karoo (southern Cape; page 237) – do not, strictly speaking, fall into the winelands proper. The five within the parameters of this chapter are:

STELLENBOSCH The first to be established, this takes in 17 private cellars and five co-operative wineries, all located on four major roads within a 12-km radius of Stellenbosch and half-an-hour's drive from Cape Town. Some of the route's features are covered on page 309. Information: the route's offices are located in the Doornbosch buildings on Strand Road, Stellenbosch (open Monday to Friday). Call in, or contact the Wine Route Office, PO Box 204, Stellenbosch 7600; Tel. (02231) 4310, or the Information Bureau, Tel. (02231) 3584.

PAARL Within an hour's drive from Cape Town; smaller than the Stellenbosch route, covering just four estates and three co-operatives, some of which are discussed (see page 313). Nederburg and the KWV are in the area but are not part of the formal route. Information: Paarl Publicity Association, cnr Main and Auret streets, Paarl; Tel. (02211) 2-4842.

VIGNERONS DE FRANSCHHOEK Boschendal and Bellingham are probably the best known of the cellars on this 'route' which shouldn't really be classed as such since it's rather an exclusive association, formed to promote the fine wines of the Franschhoek valley generally (the wines are made centrally, on a co-operative basis) and as a commemorative tribute to the early Huguenot settlers. Not all the members of the Vignerons open their cellars to the public at set hours; several offer tastings and tours by appointment only. All their wines, however, may be sampled at the Franschhoek Vineyards Co-operative in town, Tel. (02212) 2086. Two of the estates (Bien Donné and La Provence) have stalls adjacent to the Co-operative; and Die Binnehof, a tasting shop, and Le Quartier Français, a rather lovely winehouse and restaurant (the dining room overlooks a flower and herb garden) are nearby.

WORCESTER A prolific wine-making area: about a quarter of the national grape harvest is produced in the general region (which includes Robertson: see below). The 22 co-operative wineries and three estates are known for their white wines, varying from dry to lusciously sweet muscatels and hanepoots. The route is very rural, not too sophisticated, and one enjoys country hospitality at its warmest. Information: Worcester Winelands Association, which maintains a permanent presence at the Kleinplasie open-air museum (see page 316). Call in, or contact the Association, PO Box 59, Worcester 6850; Tel. (0231) 7-1408.

ROBERTSON Also a hugely productive district; the KWV concentrate plant at Robertson is geared to process an annual 200 000 hectolitres of grape-juice. The Robertson Wine Trust comprises 11 co-operative cellars, nine estates and seven private producers. For enquiries, contact Robertson Information, Tel. (02351) 4437.

Other speciality routes

The Western Cape's wine-ways are renowned, attracting thousands of visitors each year. Not so well known are a number of other thematic itineraries – fruit, cheese, antiques, historic homes, museums and, farther afield, crayfish (west coast; see pages 327-338) and wool (southern Cape; pages 231-255).

THE FRUIT ROUTES Farms, co-operatives, farm stalls, packing houses and others have combined to provide a comprehensive and fascinating insight into the industry in all its guises. Typical is the Ceres Fruit Farm tours itinerary: bus trip from Cape Town, tea and scones, lunch at a farm or hotel, visits to orchards, a fruit-drying yard and nature reserve. Full information can be obtained from Captour (see Advisory, page 325).
☆ The Ceres route (see page 315): takes you through three of the deciduous fruit-growing regions: the Ceres Bokkeveld (including the Warm and Koue Bokkeveld), Tulbagh and Wolseley, the latter two in a lush valley named,

by the early white settlers, 'Het Land van Waveren'.
The region, though, began to be developed in earnest only after the completion of Michell's Pass in 1848.
If your tour is self-conducted, plan an itinerary that takes you through Du Toit's Kloof Pass, the Slanghoek valley and along the R431 between Worcester and Wolseley, then over Michell's Pass, gateway to the Bokkeveld. Alternatively you can go through Wellington, Bain's Kloof and then on to Ceres, again via Michell's Pass. The Koue Bokkeveld is beyond Prince Alfred Hamlet, and is reached via the spectacular Gydo Pass.
☆ The Four Passes fruit route: takes you 210 km through the superb countryside of the Elgin/Grabouw, Villiersdorp and Franschhoek areas: see page 312 and 310.

THE CHEESE ROUTE This will lead you to select dairy farms, all of which produce distinctive and splendid cheeses and some of which are also wine-producers. They include Zandam, Simonsberg, Fairview, Landskroon, Bloublommetjieskloof, Bonnievale, Eendekuil and Cape Dairy Co-operative. Captour has produced an informative little booklet which gives details of these, and of wine farms and other establishments that provide delicious cheese lunches (among them Blaauwklippen, Delheim, Eikendal, Hartenberg, Lanzerac, Neethlingshof, Spier, Villiera, Welmoed, Boschendal and Swiss Farm Excelsior).

The Champagne Express

This well-preserved steam-drawn passenger train (once part of the Union Express, predecessor of the Blue Train, and now finished in the elegant style of the old Orient Express) runs on the little-used 30-km line between Paarl and Franschhoek, through the scenic Franschhoek valley, stopping at wine farms and a newly-established art centre *en route*. The package, aimed at the more sophisticated end of the tourist market, includes luxury coach transport from Cape Town to Paarl, farmstead lunches and teas, and an optional stopover at a private guesthouse in Franschhoek, returning to Paarl by train the next day. Information: Tel. (02212) 3000; Paarl Publicity Association, Tel. (02211) 2-4842/2-3829; Franschhoek Publicity Association, Tel. (02212) 2055.

The autumnal glory of the Cape winelands

Tours

Most Cape Town tour operators offer day-long and longer trips to and through the Winelands. The packages include wine tastings and cellar visits, lunches, teas and sightseeing. A representative cross section:

✪ Plusbus (SAR Travel), Tel. (021) 218-2191/2/3. *Route*: Paarl, Nederburg, Franschhoek, Simonsig Estate; or Bloubergstrand, Paarl, KWV cellars, Stellenbosch, Neethlingshof (8,5 hours).

✪ Top Tours, Tel. (021) 551-2904. *Route*: Stellenbosch, two wine estates, Lanzerac (lunch), Franschhoek, Swiss Farm Excelsior (8 hours).

✪ Hylton Ross, Tel. (021) 438-1500. *Route*: Stellenbosch, Du Toits Kloof, Huguenot tunnel, Wellington, Paarl (9 hours).

✪ Safari esCape, Tel. (021) 794-4832. *Route*: Paarl, Stellenbosch, Van Ryn brandy cellar (about 9 hours); or Worcester, Tulbagh, Rie-

beeck West, Bloubergstrand (about 9 hours).

✪ Springbok Atlas, Tel. (021) 45-5468 (after hours: 461 9263). *Route*: Neethlingshof, Stellenbosch, Paarl (lunch at Rhebokskloof), Franschhoek (8,5 hours).

✪ Sea Link, Tel. (021) 25-4480. *Vineyards route*: Stellenbosch Farmer's Winery, Simonsig, Lanzerac, Stellenbosch (historical tour), Van Ryn brandy cellar (8 hours); *Four Passes route*: Sir Lowry's Pass, Viljoen's Pass, presentation by Fruit Board, Waenhuis coffee shop (lunch), Helshoogte, Stellenbosch Village.

✪ Sun Tours, Tel. (021) 689-1232/35. *Route*: Spier (museum, tastings), Stellenbosch (Dorp Street, Oom Samie se Winkel, Village Museum), Delheim, Fairview (tastings; goat's milk cheese), Paarl (8 hours).

✪ Rodeon, Tel. (021) 419-6150/1. *Route* includes three estates (tasting and lunch), Paarl, Franschhoek, Stellenbosch (7 hours).

ADVISORY: CAPE WINELANDS

CLIMATE

Winter-rainfall area. Hot summer periods are relieved by cool and sometimes very strong southeasterly winds; cold and wet winter spells are interspersed with warm, sunny periods. For more details, turn to the relevant sections of the previous chapter, Cape Town and the Peninsula, which covers a similar climatic area.

MAIN ATTRACTIONS

Scenic splendour □ Fine wines and foods □ Stately houses □ Recreation: sightseeing drives □ Walking □ Hiking □ Mountain-climbing □ Freshwater angling.

TRAVEL

Road. Excellent tarred roads connect the main centres with each other, with Cape Town, and with most of the wine-route venues. Distances from Cape Town: Stellenbosch 41 km; Franschhoek 57 km; Somerset West 48 km; Paarl 60 km; Ceres 130 km; Tulbagh 153 km; Worcester 157 km; Robertson 160 km; Wellington 72 km.

Car hire: Facilities available in Cape Town; see Cape Town and Peninsula, page 292.

Coach travel: Tour operators offer a variety of Winelands packages; see page 322.

Rail. Scheduled passenger train services connect Cape Town with Stellenbosch, and major centres in the western Cape and beyond.

Air. Light aircraft and helicopter tours available; for further information see Cape Town and Peninsula Advisory, page 300.

ACCOMMODATION

Select hotels

STELLENBOSCH AREA

D'Ouwe Werf ★★★ In town; loaded with charm. 26 en-suite rooms; small-group conference facilities. 30 Church Street, Stellenbosch 7600; Tel. (02231) 9-6120; Fax: (02231) 7-4626; Telex: 520 706.

Devon Valley Protea ★★ Good country hotel on Devon Valley Rd. 21 en-suite rooms; conference facilities for 20. PO Box 68, Stellenbosch 7600; Tel. (02231) 7-0211.

Lanzerac ★★★ On the Jonkershoek Rd; historic, atmospheric; excellent restaurant. 32 en-suite rooms, 5 suites; conference facilities. PO Box 4, Stellenbosch 7600; Tel. (02231) 7-1132.

Stellenbosch Hotel ★★★ In town; quite excellent. 20 en-suite rooms and suites. PO Box 500, Stellenbosch 7600. Tel. (02231) 7 3644; Telex: 527 172.

Wine Route Hotel ★★ Klapmuts Rd. 47 en-suite rooms; conference facilities. PO Box 431, Stellenbosch 7600; Tel. (02231) 9-5522; Fax: (02231) 9-5524/6/7.

FRANSCHHOEK

Swiss Farm Excelsior ★★ Outstanding country hotel. 40 en-suite rooms; conference facilities for 100. PO Box 54, Franschhoek 7690; Tel. (02212) 2071/2; Telex 542 942.

SOMERSET WEST AREA

La Cotte Inn ★ Lovely country hotel. Huguenot Rd, Franschoek 7690; Tel. (02212) 2081.

Lord Charles ★★★★★ One of SA best hotels; just outside town. 188 rooms, 10 suites; generous conference facilities. PO Box 5151, Helderberg 7135; Tel. (024) 51-2970.

Metropole ★★ On Strand's Beach Rd. 26 rooms, 2 suites; conference facilities. PO Box 21, Strand 7140; Tel. (024) 3-1501.

Van Riebeeck ★★★ First class hotel in the fishing and holiday village of Gordon's Bay. 68 rooms; conference facilities. PO Box 10, Gordon's Bay 7150. Tel. (024) 56-1411.

CERES

New Belmont ★★ Long-established and excellent. 40 rooms; conference facilities for 150. Address: Porters Street, Ceres 6835; Tel. (0233) 2-1150; Telex: 542 042.

WORCESTER

Cumberland ★★★ Solid comfort and value. 35 rooms, 2 suites; conference facilities. PO Box 8, Worcester 6850. Tel. (0231) 7-2641.

MONTAGU

Avalon ★★ 25 rooms, 2 suites. PO Box 110, Montagu 6720; Tel. (0234) 4-1122.

Avalon Springs ★★★ Sophisticated country hotel; 5 swimming pools. 12 rooms, 29 suites; conference facilities for 120. PO Box 110, Montagu 6720; Tel. (0234) 4-1150; Fax: (0234) 4-1906; Telex: 542 089.

Mimosa Lodge (ungraded). Edwardian charm and hospitality; superb cuisine. PO Box 323, Montagu 6720; Tel. (0234) 4-2351.

Ungraded accommodation

There are numerous small hotels, lodges and guest-farms in the Cape's Winelands, most of which may be classed as 'unsophisticated' but many of which offer warm country hospitality, personal service, comfort and value for money. Contact the local tourist and publicity offices, or Satour: see Useful Addresses and Telephone Numbers page 325.

Holiday Booking Service, PO Box 5514, Cape Town 8000; Tel. (South Africa 021) 24-3693 and (United Kingdom 041) 554-1713. Handle reservations for guesthouses, self-contained accommodation, country houses. International Home Exchange, PO Box 188, Claremont 7735, South Africa; Tel. (021) 61-4334. Among the recommended smaller places of the hideaway type are:

Arumwood Lodge, Lourensford Rd, Somerset West 7130; Tel. (024) 51-1970.

Goedemoed, Cecilia St, Paarl. Bed-and-breakfast; family hospitality in best Cape tradition. PO Box 331, Paarl 7620; Tel. (02211) 61-1020 (after hours: 2-6613).

Mountain Shadows, Paarl. Tranquil, family atmosphere. PO Box 2501, Paarl 7620; Tel. (02211) 62-3192.

Roggeland, Paarl. The house is a national monument, set in the heart of the Dal Josaphat valley; excellent cuisine. PO Box 7210, Noorder Paarl 7623; Tel. (02211) 62-7501.

Windermere Lodge, Elgin. Beautiful location; quietly luxurious. Viljoenshoop Rd, Elgin 7180; Tel. (024) 59-2503.

Caravan/camping and self-catering accommodation

Stellenbosch area: Bergplaas holiday ranch (cottages and rondavels), Tel. (02231) 7-5119. Mountain Breeze caravan park (50 stands; also self-catering accommodation), Tel. (02231) 90-0020.

Gordon's Bay (Somerset West area): Gordon's Bay Hydro (en-suite rooms), Tel. (024) 56-3356. Panorama caravan park (including self-catering rondavels), Tel. (024) 56-2135. Sea Breeze Club Caraville holiday resort (cottages), Tel. (024) 56-1400.

Paarl area: Berg River resort (cottages), Tel. (02211) 63-1650. Safariland holiday resort (cottages), Tel. (02211) 4-2110.

Ceres: Die Herberg guest-farm (very pleasant rondavels and rooms), Tel. (0233) 2-2325. Pine Forest public resort (rondavels), Tel. (0233) 2-1170/1.

Worcester area: Country Houses (cottages), Tel. (0231) 7-0200. Rustig holiday resort (cottages and rooms), Tel. (0231) 2-7245. Rondalia Goudini spa, Rawsonville (rondavels), Tel. (0231) 9-1100.

SELECT RESTAURANTS

Good food, much of it Cape traditional and often served in attractively historic surrounds, is one of the most pleasant features of this inviting region. Some suggestions:

STELLENBOSCH AREA

Decameron, Plein St. Tel. (02231) 3331. Popular among aficionados of Italian fare.

De Kelder, Dorp St. Tel. (02231) 3797 or 7-8358. Aristocratic Cape eating house (built 1790); everything out of the top drawer, including traditional dishes. Huge wine list.

De Volkskombuis, Old Strand Rd. Tel. (02231) 7-2121 or 7-5239. Cape cuisine in historic cluster of labourers' cottages. Popular, and deservedly so.

Doornbosch, Old Strand Rd. Tel. (02231) 7-5079/6163. A winehouse, and one of the Cape's finest restaurants. Classical cuisine, French undertones; superb wines.

D'Ouwe Werf, Church St. Tel. (02231) 7-4608. Renowned country inn, serving light, home-style and delicious food in ambient setting. The small vine-shaded courtyard is a joy.

Lanzerac, Jonkershoek Rd. Tel. (02231) 7-1132. Atmospheric: the hotel is steeped in history. Casual, lively; seafood a speciality.

Le Pommier, New Helshoogte Rd. Tel. (02231) 9-1269. Delicious Cape food in charming setting.

Lord Neethling, Neethlingshof Estate. Tel. (02231) 9-8964. Member of the *Confrérie de la Chaîne des Rôtisseurs*, which says it all. Several rooms, full of antiques; imaginative and varied menu.

Mamma Roma, Pick 'n Pay Centre, Merriman Av. Tel. (02231) 6064. Italian fare in cheerful atmosphere.

Oom Samie se Koffiekamer, Dorp St. Tel. (02231) 9-8964. Coffee shop attached to the old trading store (see page 308). Traditional Cape lunches.

Ralph's, Andringa St. Tel. (02231) 3532. Imaginative Continental-style menu, lavish helpings, striking décor. Take your own wine.

Spier Estate. Tel. (02231) 9-3832. Beautiful setting (see page 309); lightish meals (breakfast, tea, lunch).

FRANSCHHOEK AREA

Boschendal, Boschendal Estate, Groot Draken-stein: see page 310. Tel. (02211) 4-1252. Graceful-ness and exquisite taste the keynotes. Hot and cold buffet lunches.

La Petite Ferme, Franschhoek Pass. Tel. (02212) 3016. Dramatic mountain setting; unpretentious, friendly restaurant; all-purpose menu tending to country-style food; popular, so booking essential. Lunches only.

Le Quartier Français, Main Rd, Franschhoek. Tel. (02212) 2248. French-influenced Cape-style cook-ing; excellent. For lighter meals, try the coffee shop next door.

Train de la Cotte, Main St, Franschhoek. Tel. (02212) 3067. French-style food eaten in railway carriage: novel, and most pleasant. Good wines.

SOMERSET WEST

Chez Michel, Victoria Rd. Tel. (024) 51-6069. Un-assuming, Continental cuisine; a favourite with those who know food. Take your own wine.

The Garden Terrace, Lord Charles Hotel. Tel. (024) 51-2970. Enormous choice of delicious dishes (à la carte and buffet); highest standards; superb wine list.

PAARL

Troubadour, Main St. Tel. (02211) 63-3556. Con-tinental-style dishes, but you can also order an ex-cellent steak; pleasant atmosphere.

TULBAGH

Paddagang Wine House, Church St. Tel. (0236), 30-0242. Cape-style food in delightful setting. Lun-ches only; groups may book for evening functions and dinners.

WELLINGTON AREA

Onverwacht Wine House, Onverwacht Estate. Tel. (02211) 3-4315. Traditional Cape setting, varied menu, memorable food. Lunches only.

USEFUL ADDRESSES AND TELEPHONE NUMBERS

Automobile Association, Cape Town offices: (021) 21-1550 (general); (021) 419-4378 (break-down service); (021) 21-1550 (touring information).

Captour, Head Office (021) 462-2040; Visitor's In-formation Bureau, Strand Concourse, Adderley Street, Cape Town 8001; (021) 25-3320; Johannes-burg office (011) 331-8494; Western Cape Tourism Association (021) 93-2336. (See also Cape Town and Peninsula advisory, page 305.)

Ceres Information Bureau, Public Library, Voor-trekker St, Ceres 6835; Tel. (0233) 2-1177.

Franschhoek Tourism Association, La Provence, Franschhoek 7690; Tel. (02212) 2440.

Gordon's Bay Information Office, Hendon Park, Gordon's Bay 7150; Tel. (024) 56-2321.

Hottentots Holland Publicity Association, Municipal Bldgs, Main Rd, Strand 7140; Tel. (024) 51-4022.

Montagu Tourism Information Bureau, Bath St, Montagu 6720; Tel. (0234) 4-2471.

Paarl Publicity Association, 216 Main St, Paarl 7646; Tel. (02211) 2-4842.

Robertson tourist information, Town Clerk's office; Tel. (02351) 3112.

Satour (SA Tourism Board). Regional office: Shop 16, Piazza level, Golden Acre, Adderley Street, Cape Town 8001; Tel. (021) 21-6274.

Somerset West Information Bureau, 11 Victoria St, Somerset West 7130; Tel. (024) 51-4022.

Stellenbosch Publicity Association, De Witt House, 30 Plein St, Stellenbosch 7600; Tel. (02231) 3584. Wine Route Office, Tel. (02231) 4310.

Tulbagh Tourism Office, Old Church Museum, 14 Church St, Tulbagh 6820; Tel. (0236) 41.

Wellington Information Bureau, Jan van Rie-beeck St, Wellington 7655; Tel. (02211) 3-1121.

Worcester Publicity Association, 23 Baring St, Worcester 6850; Tel. (0231) 7-1408.

ANNUAL EVENTS

Worcester Agricultural Show: January □ University of Stellenbosch Carnival: March □ Paarl Vineyard Festival: mid-March □ Boland Agricultural Show: end April □ Worcester Wine and Food Festival: Au-gust □ Robertson Spring Show: September □ Tul-bagh Agricultural Show: September □ Villiersdorp Wild Flower Show: September/October □ Ceres Ag-ricultural and Wild Flower Show: 1st week in Oc-tober □ Van der Stel Festival, Stellenbosch: October □ Stellenbosch Food and Wine Festival: last week-end in October □ The renowned Nederburg Auc-tions, Paarl: mid-April.

THE WEST COAST
AND NAMAQUALAND

The Olifants is, by South African standards, a fairly large river, rising in the Great Winterhoek and Cold Bokkeveld mountains of the southern Karoo and flowing northwestwards, past the pleasant towns of Citrusdal, Clanwilliam and Vredendal before entering the Atlantic Ocean 250 km north of Cape Town. Its valley is fertile, sustaining fine crops of wheat and subtropical fruits, rooibos tea, tobacco, vegetables, wine and table grapes and, most notable of all, grove upon grove of delectable Washington and Navel oranges.

North of the Olifants is the region called Namaqualand, a 48 000-km^2 swathe of increasingly arid territory stretching to the lower reaches of the Orange River, and falling within the Northern Cape province. Beyond is the newly independent country of Namibia and the great dunes and drifts of the Namib desert.

Most of the coastal strip up to the Orange is what is known as the 'sandveld', narrow for the most part, up to 50 km wide in places, elevated above sea level and distinguished by 'raised beaches' – sandy terraces full of seashells and wave-eroded pebbles that are the legacy of the period in far-distant prehistory when the ocean's surface was about 100 m higher than it is today. To the east of the sandveld is the broken country of the Hardeveld, which has an average altitude of 900 m and is part of South Africa's Great Escarpment (see page 9). Farther eastward, beyond the Hardeveld, are the flattish, semi-arid inhospitable wastelands of Little Bushmanland.

Altogether a dry, bleak, sparsely populated land. Surface water is almost nonexistent, though the interaction of cool Benguela ocean current and warm desert air often produces dense mists. Rainfall varies between 250 mm and a low 50 mm a year, and at first sight the terrain seems relentlessly harsh, intimidating in its huge emptiness, incapable of sustaining

A quiver tree, or kokerboom (Aloe dichotoma) stands sentinel-like in a field of flowers near Springbok. The Khoikhoi made quivers for their arrows from the bark of the plant.

any but the simplest, least appealing forms of life. Yet Namaqualand, and especially the coastal sandveld, has an enormous profusion of succulents and flowering plants. After the winter rains – between August and October but most often during three weeks of September – the land is briefly and gloriously mantled by great carpets of wild flowers that stretch to the far horizons.

The region is home to about 4 000 floral species, most of which belong to the daisy (Compositae) and mesembryanthemum groups but also include perennial herbs, aloes, lilies and a host of other plant families. The small, low-growing plants are drought-resistant, the seeds lying dormant during the long dry months and then, after the rains and before the onset of the blistering desert breezes, when they sense a warming of the earth and the impending arrival of the pollinators, they burst into life, maturing in a matter of days to transform the countryside.

THE FAR NORTH

The largest town in Namaqualand proper, and at the centre of the spectacular springtime flower show, is:

Springbok

The place, about 80 km from the Atlantic coast, began its life when a copper mine began operating in the area in 1852. In fact the metal had featured much earlier on in the region's history: it was worked by the local Khoi centuries ago, and much sought after by the first Dutch settlers. Governor Simon van der Stel mounted an expedition to the 'copper mountains' of Namaqualand in 1685, and the shaft his men dug can still be seen near the town. Today there are fairly large-scale workings in the general area, at nearby Carolus, Okiep (which has historical associations with the miners of Cornwall; there are still some Cornish-style buildings in town) and Nababeep (the name means 'the water behind the little hill'; visitors may view the mining and smelting processes, and there's a museum).

Springbok is not too well geared for visitors. It has its airport, its hotels and caravan/camping ground and its local gemstones (on display and for sale at the Springbok Kafee), but the flower season is really too short to justify much in the way of sophisticated wining, dining and accommodation. Nevertheless people do flock there, during September, braving the long road from Cape Town or making forays from the better-endowed tourist areas farther down the Atlantic seaboard (see page 333) or as members of air or coach tour groups.

And the region has its devotees, especially among hikers and botanists. Near town (the entrance is 4 km beyond the airport), is the:

HESTER MALAN NATURE RESERVE, (soon to be known as the Goegab), a 15 000-ha expanse of stark countryside, some of it flat, most of it broken by enormous dome-like granite outcrops. Only part of the reserve is open to the public, but there is a game-viewing network of good gravel roads; three established walks, ranging from 4 to 7 km, and picnic spots with barbecue facilities. Wildlife includes eland, gemsbok, springbok, klipspringer and Hartmann's mountain zebra. Labelled samples of local flora – technically classified as Namaqualand Broken Veld vegetation – are displayed at the reserve's office. Open throughout the year; no accommodation.

The great, dry, harsh spaces beyond Springbok are known as:

THE RICHTERSVELD, a wilderness vastness bounded in the north by the curve of the Orange River, where the terrain is hilly, rugged, distinguished by weird, wind-sculpted rock pillars and spires and, except for the astonishingly lush greenness of irrigated land, brown and bone dry. A spectacular feature of the northern segment is Wondergat, a deep cave which holds deep religious significance for the local Nama people. The southern section comprises scrub-veld and scattered grassy plains.

Botanically, the Richtersveld is in a class of its own. Fully a third of all known mesembryanthemum species are found here; quiver trees and the bizarre *halfmens* plant are common sights; some of the flora has yet to be identified and classified.

Those who embark on back-packing hikes and horseback trails in this strange and lonely region

really do feel like pathfinders. You're strongly advised, though, not to venture forth into this wilderness without an experienced guide.

At the time of writing, plans to establish some 160 000 ha of the Richtersveld as a national park – South Africa's third largest – were well advanced. The authorities have been keen to proclaim the area for some years, but there were disputes involving the local stock herders (the land does, grudgingly, provide a modicum of grazing). Eventually the herders and conservationists reached agreement and the Richtersveld will soon become a 'contractual park'.

To the west, on the coast, are Port Nolloth and, farther up towards the Orange, Alexander Bay. Both are fishing ports and, more prominently, diamond towns.

Diamond country

In 1908 an ex-Kimberley labourer, Zacharius Lewala, recognized diamond chips in the sand he was shovelling at Kolmanskop, north of the Orange River and east of the now-Namibian town of Lüderitz. Within a few months thousands of hectares had been pegged.

Yet, although the alluvial potential of the river estuary itself and of the coastal belt to the south had long been suspected, it wasn't until 1925 that news broke of the first big find, made by a young Port Nolloth soldier (on leave from the Indian army) named Jack Carstens.

The rush was on: prospectors converged on the desolate 80-km 'diamond strip' between Port Nolloth and the Orange to unearth hitherto unimaginable riches; some were unlucky, others made a good living, a few became wealthy overnight. One of them – the renowned geologist Hans Merensky – picked up 487 diamonds from beneath a single flat rock and, during a 30-day period in 1926, collected a total of 2 762 precious stones near the town of Alexander Bay.

In some areas the actual process of finding the treasure was comparatively simple – it lay everywhere, on or just beneath the ground – but it was made even simpler by a curious scientific phenomenon: the diamonds occurred in gravels containing fossils of an extinct species, the warm-water oyster *Ostea prismatica*. The two elements – gemstones and shellfish – have nothing in common, but were linked to some major geological upheaval that, millennia before, had changed the ocean currents, killing the oysters and sweeping the diamonds ashore. The 'oyster line' was profitably used by the prospectors as a beacon to the fabulous wealth of the ancient beach gravels.

Today, the diggings are still among the world's most lucrative. Much of the area is state-controlled and you can enter only with a permit and by prior arrangement.

PORT NOLLOTH To get to the town from Springbok, follow the N7 north and then, at Steinkopf, turn west along the 93-km R382 road, through the dramatic Anenous pass, leaving the scrubland behind to enter the sandveld.

In some ways Port Nolloth is a surprising place: it's been there a long time (it was originally established to serve the copper mines) but there's still a rugged, frontier-like, transitory feel about it. Most of the concession divers working the offshore gravels aren't locals: they come, stay to search for a few months, and go away again, perhaps the richer, probably to return next year.

There's fairly ordinary accommodation at the hotel (the Scotia Inn; fresh crayfish a speciality), a camping ground, Mamma's Italian Trattoria, and that's just about the lot, though the people are friendly and sociable and their parties lively. The harbour still serves the trawlers and crayfishermen, and local canneries process the catch, but the industry is in something of a decline. For sportsmen: good line fishing. A little beyond the town is McDougall's Bay: holiday cottages; caravan park; fishing boats for hire.

ALEXANDER BAY, to the north, is a 'closed' place, accessible by permit and via the very rugged road from Port Nolloth. The town, centre for the largest of the alluvial (sea, beach and land) diggings, is in a high-security area; there's no tourist accommodation – but the mining interests tolerate and even encourage visitors, providing the tours are supervised. What you see is spellbinding: colossal earthmovers cutting away huge slices of ground with almost surgical efficiency; the trenches, some as much as 30 m deep and 100 m wide; the exposed gravels; the sifting and sweeping; the diamonds. It's all on a grand scale, and it's fascinating. For tour bookings, contact The Personnel Manager, Alexkor, Private Bag X5, Alexander Bay 8290; Tel. (0256) 330.

THE ROAD NORTH: INLAND

The springtime glory of wild flowers is by no means confined to Namaqualand proper – the sandveld region north of the Olifants. Patchwork profusions of daisies and vygies mingle with the proteas, ericas and pincushions of the Cape Floral Kingdom's fynbos vegetation, far to the south, gracing a region that has other, very distinctive attractions.

The main highway north from Cape Town is the N7; a wide, straight, good road that leads through Citrusdal and Clanwilliam, to Springbok and then across the Namibian border and through the sandy wastelands to Windhoek, capital of Namibia. Don't be fooled by the bare simplicity of the map, the apparent ease with which one can get to these places: the route may be direct but the distances are enormous. Springbok is 565 km from Cape Town; Windhoek a further 1 000 km.

For the first 150-km stretch you drive through the great wheatland expanses of what is known as the Swartland, or 'black country', so named for the rich darkness of its soil. Perhaps other colours, though, would be a great deal more appropriate for in spring the fields are bright green with the splendid harvests and in summer a ripe gold.

About a sixth of the national wheat crop is produced in the region, 'capital' of which is the small town of:

MALMESBURY, founded in 1743 in the shallow valley of the Diep River and at one time renowned for its curative mineral springs (now in sad disuse). Just south of town is the Kalbaskraal nature reserve. Other features of interest in the general (Riebeeck Valley) area are De Oude Kerk, the first church to be built in the region, and now a museum housing old farming implements, utensils, and church documents; a cartwright's museum, on the farm Spes Bona (wagons, wagon-building, blacksmithing), and the house in which the great Jan Christiaan Smuts was born. This has been lovingly restored, by the leading architect Gawie Fagan, and is open to the public.

Adjacent to the village of Riebeeck Kasteel is the Kasteelberg ('castle mountain') where a nature walk, or 'wandelpad', enables visitors to see baboons, black eagles and the fynbos vegetation of the area. The Swartland's other wheat centres include:

Wheatfields near Moorreesburg

MOORREESBURG AND PIKETBERG, both on the N7 north of Malmesbury. The former is modestly notable for its Wheat Industry Museum, one of only three such in the world; the latter for its fruit cooling and packaging complex (visitors welcome), for its Edwardian-style museum, and for its backcloth of imposing sandstone mountain.

Long ago the high places of the Piketberg gave sanctuary to groups of San (Bushmen), and some fine examples of their rock art can still be seen in the area. Later came the Cochoqua Khoikhoi (until recently referred to in history books as Hottentots) who, in the later 1700s, under their leader Gonnema, first traded with the white settlers and then fought them. The war lasted from 1674 to 1677, in which year a bloodied but unbowed Gonnema struck a mutually profitable deal with the colonists, lived in relative peace thereafter, and prospered. During the hostilities the Dutch established a military outpost, or 'piquet', on the mountain slopes and it was from this that the village's name was taken.

Citrusdal and Clanwilliam

These are pleasant little towns situated about 30 km apart off the N7. They nestle in fertile valleys – of the Olifants (the 'Golden Valley') and the Jan Dissels respectively – and each serves as the centre of a major farming industry.

CITRUSDAL is set among splendid orange groves which, collectively, comprise the third largest of South Africa's citrus-growing areas after the Northern Transvaal's giant Zebediela estates (see page 102) and the Eastern Cape's Sundays River Valley – but, because this is a frost-free winter rainfall region, it probably surpasses all in the quality of its oranges. And its estates are by far the oldest: the original orchards were planted from seedlings nurtured in Jan van Riebeeck's Cape Town garden – trees that bore their first fruits in 1661. One particular specimen, on the farm Hexrivier near Citrusdal, has yielded a seasonal bounty for the past 250 years and is now a proclaimed national monument.

Visitors may tour the estates. The Goede Hoop citrus co-operative operates one of the country's largest packing sheds, handling a massive 66 000 tons of oranges during the season; fresh fruit can be bought at the kiosk.

Some 30 km out of town are The Baths, a radioactive, warm (43 °C) medicinal spring rising in a pleasantly shady gorge. Visitors welcome; self-contained accommodation and caravan sites available. Also of interest are the area's wine cellars (see page 339), and the Vanmeerhoff farm stall (known as the 'Gateway to the Cederberg') – a large country store enticingly stocked with fruit, preserves and home-style foods and craft products. It has a restaurant attached, and is situated atop the

The Cederberg's Wolfberg Arch (see page 332)

Multi-coloured daisies carpet the springtime countryside near Clanwilliam

spectacular Piekenierskloof pass above the Olifants valley.

The Olifants River is popular among anglers – it sustains the largest variety of indigenous fish south of the Zambezi (including *Barbus capensis*, the yellowfish) – and among serious canoeists for its swirling currents and rapids. Some 50 km north of Citrusdal the waters have been dammed to supply the irrigated farmlands of the Hantam district and the needs of:

CLANWILLIAM, headquarters of the country's rooibos tea industry.

This needle-leafed tea shrub (*Aspalathus linearis*) is a wild plant that grows throughout the Western Cape but is especially prolific on the higher slopes of the Cederberg range that lies to the east of the Citrusdal-Clanwilliam axis (see further on). The tender tips of the young shoots have been used for centuries by the black peoples, and more recently prized for their medicinal properties by the rural white communities, though systematic cultivation began only in the early 1900s. There are a number of rooibos varieties, but most aficionados consider Northier the best. The tea does not contain caffeine and it has a low tannin content, so its popularity in this health-conscious age – both at home and abroad – is increasing by the year. There are guided tours through the tea-packing sheds at, Tel. (02682) 64 or 69.

The town is one of South Africa's ten oldest: farms were flourishing in the district as early as 1732. Its more noteworthy buildings include the drostdy (or magistrate's court), built in 1808; the old prison-cum-garrison; the Dutch Reformed church (1864), and the Anglican church, designed by the talented Sophy Gray. Sophy was a remarkable woman: an outstanding architect, an accomplished artist and married to Cape Town's first Anglican bishop, Robert Gray, she effectively administered her husband's new, vast and expanding diocese; helped him found now-famous schools (Bishops, St George's Grammar, St Cyprian's, Zonnebloem College), and designed over 50 splendid churches.

The area is almost as renowned for its wild flowers as for its rooibos, and is seen at its best in the springtime floral wonderland of the Biedouw Valley and the 125-ha Ramskop nature reserve, whose displays – a mix of coastal fynbos and Karoo succulents – are strikingly colourful between June and October. The reserve is crisscrossed by footpaths; on sale are bulbs and seeds; there's a pleasant roof-top tearoom and superb views of the Olifants River, Pakhuis Pass and the often snow-capped hills of the Cederberg (see below).

Worth noting, too, are the Boskloof and Kranskloof picnic/swimming spots; the Clanwilliam dam, 18 km long and reckoned by water-skiers to be the country's finest venue for their sport; the Bulshoek recreational dam; and Bulshoek, which is a river-bank bathing area. San rock paintings can be seen at their best in the Agter-Pakhuis vicinity.

In a remote valley some 75 km from Clanwilliam, and reached via the Pakhuis Pass, is the historic Rhenish Mission village of:

WUPPERTHAL, founded in 1830 and virtually unchanged since then – still a picturesque cluster of white-walled, black-thatched cottages (three terraces of them) and a winding street along which donkey-carts ply and where water flows in the furrows. The area is noted for its tobacco and rooibos tea, and for the *velskoene* – tough but comfortable walking shoes – that are made in the village. If by chance you're in the vicinity at Christmas, try very hard to attend the carol service at the mission: it's an occasion you'll remember.

The Cederberg Wilderness Area

The ruggedly beautiful mountain range, whose loftiest peak is the Sneeuberg (2 028 m), takes its name from the rare and at one time almost extinct Clanwilliam cedar (*Widdringtonia cedarbergensis*). These lovely trees suffered grievously from the axe and from uncontrolled burning during the early years of white settlement, but a few hardy specimens managed to cling to life on the upper slopes and these, now strictly protected, will hopefully prove to be the nucleus of new generations. Another, even rarer plant is the pure-white snow protea (*Protea cryophila*), which lives precariously above the Cederberg's snow line and occurs nowhere else in the world. For the rest, there's the rocket pincushion, the large red disa (*Disa uniflora*) and a myriad other endemic plants varying from spring annuals to fynbos and handsome indigenous forest species.

The Cederberg is a vast controlled area of stark and strangely eroded rock formations, of waterfalls, crystal streams and clear pools, of magnificent viewsites, of caverns, overhangs, peaks and ravines. It has 254 km of unmarked

but well defined footpaths, and it attracts hikers and backpackers, climbers, campers, photographers and nature-lovers from afar.

Rock features of special interest include the 20-m-high pillar named the Maltese Cross; the Wolfberg Arch and the 30-m cleft called the Wolfberg Cracks; the Tafelberg and its Spout. Wildlife: not prolific; some 30 mammal species are present, among them klipspringer, grey rhebok, steenbok, grysbok, caracal, bat-eared fox, wild cat, baboon. Sunbirds and orange-crested sugarbirds and a number of fine raptors – black eagle, jackal buzzard, rock kestrel – can be seen.

The Cederberg is a proclaimed wilderness area and you need a permit to enter. Entry is on foot, generally speaking – some visitors hire donkeys at the Algeria forest station (see below). One can also hire a guide at the Algeria. No cars; no fires allowed, for obvious reasons. You'll need to arm yourself with a forestry map showing the area's paths and overnight huts. There are some 15 resident snake species: watch out for the berg adder and the puff adder. Climate: heavy winter rainfall (up to 1 000 mm a year) but it can also rain in the summer months. Snowfalls occur from May to September.

To get to the Cederberg, turn right off the N7, 27 km north of Citrusdal; cross the Olifants River and drive (carefully) over the high Nieuwoudt Pass. From its summit there are fine views of the mountains; in the valley below lies the Algeria forestry station, principal starting point for excursions into the wilderness.

Algeria has a particularly fine camping ground and picnic site, and you can if you're feeling brave take a dip in the close-by Rondegat River (there's an enticing, clear natural pool there). Several farms in the region offer accommodation ranging from campsites to furnished chalets. For those who like their comforts, there is also the Citrusdal Protea Hotel (see Advisory, page 340).

Beyond Clanwilliam

On or just off the N7, as you progress northwards, are the modest towns of:

VANRHYNSDORP, halfway point between Cape Town and Springbok, and a convenient base for exploring the wild flower areas. Of interest: the Succulent Nursery (this includes some rare species) in Voortrekker Street. The local museum is being developed. Nearby is the country's biggest gypsum mine, and two marble mines. Sightseeing: Kobee and Gifberg gorges and the 125-m Ouberg waterfall.

VREDENDAL, situated 24 km east of Vanrhyns-dorp and centre of a 'Wine of Origin' area (five co-operatives; light table wines). The town's museum is worth a brief visit.

NIEUWOUDTVILLE, on the R27 to the east, reached via the grand 82-m Vanrhyns Pass. A major sheep-rearing region, silent and lonely. Renowned author Laurens van der Post wrote of 'farms hidden behind rare puritanical hills guarding secret water, so that [the land] appears totally unpeopled'. The village has some attractive, and unusual, sandstone buildings; worth visiting is its 115-ha wild flower reserve (bulbous plants are a feature). Nearby, on the Loeriesfontein road, is the splendid 100-m-high Nieuwoudtville waterfall.

Atlantic digression

There's not much for the tourist beyond Vanrhynsdorp – until you reach Springbok and the wild flower and diamond country of the far north (see page 328). Take the 64-km-long road west from Clanwilliam, however, and you'll arrive at:

LAMBERT'S BAY, a large fishing village with two mild claims to historical notability. The bay was Bartolomeu Dias's last landfall before he sailed south and then east to round the Cape (though he wasn't aware he had done so at the time) in 1487. And it was here that the only 'naval action' of the South African War was fought when, in 1901, a Boer guerrilla commando under General Barry Hertzog, later to become prime minister, opened fire on the Royal Navy ship *Sybille.*

This coastal area is something of a birdwatcher's paradise: the bay's Bird Island – a bit of a misnomer since you can walk to it, via the harbour wall – is haven to a huge colony of Cape gannets and to cormorants, penguins, seagulls and 'sterretjies'. Altogether, the islet plays host to more than 150 different seabird species. Then there's the Longvlei dam, about a dozen kilometres inland where, after good winter rains, the flamingos gather in their thousands. Down the coast at Elands Bay (a

48-km drive along the gravel road; good beach and quite excellent surfing when the south-easter blows, which is often) is the west coast's only large river estuary. In its upper reaches it is known as Verlore Vlei, or more commonly Voorvlei and here, too, great numbers of seabirds and waders congregate.

Lambert's Bay is tourist-conscious; amenities are casual but improving. People go there on family weekends (though the beach, like all the exposed west-coast venues, tends to be windswept, and the water is cold for swimming), for the birdlife and for the excellent sea-fishing. There's a museum; a caravan/camping ground; a good hotel (the Marine Protea), and an open-air, marvellously informal seafood eatery (see page 341). Visitors may venture on cray-fishing trips (arrangements through the hotel).

THE COASTAL ROUTE

An attractive alternative way north from Cape Town is the road that takes you up the rugged western shores to the Langebaan Lagoon and Saldanha Bay.

For much of the time you're in sight of the sea, and you'll find it a pleasant enough drive. It's a scenically uncluttered and even stark but in places remarkably beautiful coastline of heath, sandveld, jagged cliff and wide beach. The rains don't come very often, the sun can be fierce, and one is too often plagued by a high offshore wind that sweeps stinging flurries of sand into the air, but for all that the region is becoming increasingly popular among local holiday-makers, and the west-coast property and timeshare markets have been enjoying something approaching boom conditions. The journey, for the most part, will take you along the R27. You leave Cape Town at the wooden bridge at Milnerton, and bear left on the M14 to pass through:

BLOUBERGSTRAND ('blue mountain beach'). Have your camera ready: there are stunning views of Table Mountain from the shoreline here. Incidentally, this is becoming an increasingly sought-after residential and holiday-cottage area, and the village has one or two first-class restaurants (see page 305). If you're staying in Cape Town, an early-evening drive out followed by dinner at Ons Huisie, a restored fisherman's cottage and national monument, makes a most enjoyable outing.

Lambert's Bay is haven for 150 species of seabird, including these gannets and cormorants

MELKBOSSTRAND ('milkwood beach'), venue of large and energetic *Boeresport* get-togethers – traditional Afrikaner country sports gatherings – each New Year. Events include obstacle races (including mounted ones), various forms of tug-o-war and other contests. The futuristic Koeberg nuclear plant is close by; visits by appointment. For the rest, the area is popular among beach anglers and crayfishermen.

Back on the R27: the route is long, straight, passing through scrubland with glimpses of dunes and rocky promontories on your left, and there are turn-offs that lead down to wide beaches. Eventually (after 50 km) you'll arrive at the junction with the east-west R315 which, if you turn towards the coast, will lead you to the pretty little hamlet of:

YZERFONTEIN, notable for the great rollers that sweep inshore and reckoned to be one of South Africa's finest surfing spots. This, too, is an exposed, wind-blown area, but there's some shelter for both surfers and fishermen from the derelict jetty that probes 150 m into the ocean, relic of the ill-fated canning enterprise launched after the Second World War. There's a caravan/camping ground close by, and an open-air restaurant, Die Pan, that serves excellent seafood in a most sociable atmosphere.

The islet in the bay is known as Meeurots ('gull rock'), sanctuary to a large seagull colony.

The western isles

To the south-west lies Dassen, one of about 40 submerged mountains off southern Africa's south and west coasts whose summits, projecting above the waters, are large enough to be termed islands and inhabited by huge numbers of seabirds: gulls and gannets, penguins and cormorants. They are collectively known as the Guano Islands, a name derived from their enormous surface deposits of bird-manure – a valuable source of fertilizer that has been commercially exploited for centuries (at one period they were the focus of the so-called 'guano wars' between competing interests). Some of the more prominent western ones are Vogelsteen and Robbesteen off Bloubergstrand; Vanderling, Jutten, Malgas, Marcus, Schaapen, Meeu, Jacob's Rock and North-west Rocks, all in Saldanha Bay; Paternoster Island a little farther north; Bird Island in Lambert's Bay (see page 333), and Elephant Rock, near the Olifants River mouth.

Most are uninhabited, visited only by yachtsmen, conservation officials, naturalists and occasional tour parties. Dassen is an exception: it is 223 ha in extent (4,5 km long by 2 km wide) and, although it rises just 10 m above sea level at its highest point, boasts one or two buildings, including a lighthouse. It also supports a great many seabirds, serving as the main breeding ground of the Cape penguin (*Spheniscus demersus*), more commonly known as the jackass penguin for its harsh, braying call. Nearly 100 000 of these birds congregate in September, and again in February. Also among Dassen's residents are rock-rabbits, or dassies, which gave the island its name.

Jan van Riebeeck, who visited Dassen in the 1650s, thought very little of the place, describing it as 'not so much of an island, all sand and full of seals', but a modern scientist has termed it 'one of the naturalist's wonders of the world'.

Darling

Turn right along the R315 and, after 15 km, you'll arrive at this attractive small town, set in a countryside famed for its springtime flower shows, best exemplified perhaps in the nearby Tienie Versfeld Wild Flower Reserve, a 22-ha botanical sanctuary that preserves a typical fragment of sandveld environment. The reserve is open to visitors throughout the year, though it looks its best, around September. The farm Oudepost, in the Darling area, boasts the country's largest orchid nursery.

Darling itself is a prosperous agricultural centre; the surrounding farms diverse, producing wheat and wine-grapes, wool, peas, milk, cheese and butter (the town has a Butter Museum), and such unusual export commodities as lupins and the beautiful chincherinchee members of the lily family.

Langebaan Lagoon

Situated some 18,5 km north of Darling, 16 km long, 4,5 km at its widest and projecting southwards as an arm of Saldanha Bay, the lagoon is the focal point of a magnificent wetland wilderness area, and of the burgeoning west-coast tourist industry.

The lagoon is an ornithological treasure-house. Its waters are clear and shallow (maximum depth is 6 m) and they, and the salt marshes, the mud- and sand-banks and the rocky shores and islands of the bay are a magnet for tens of thousands of waders and other bird species. Among them are flamingos, cormorants, plovers, gulls, gannets, herons, sanderlings, knots, turnstones, and the sacred ibis – altogether, there are about 55 000 birds in residence during the hot summer months.

Curlew sandpipers account for about two-thirds of this number; they and others are migrants that leave their breeding grounds in Arctic and sub-Arctic regions for the long and often final flight to the sunny south. All are attracted to Langebaan by the shelter it provides and by the abundance of easily accessible food: marine algae, molluscs, crustaceans and other mud-loving organisms.

There are rich deposits of fossils at Langebaan – of their kind, the richest in the world: over 200 species belonging to the Pliocene era have

Langebaan Lagoon, wetland home to great numbers of birds and a popular water-sport venue

been discovered, opening a fascinating window into a world that disappeared four million years ago. The lagoon, too, once sustained vast colonies of oysters which, at some period, were killed off by changes in water temperature. None are left, but their remains – 30 million tons of shells – lie thick on the lagoon bed and are commercially exploited (by limeworks).

Langebaan, the islands and about 20 000 ha of the coastal zone form the recently proclaimed West Coast National Park, which is still being developed and likely to be larger once the private landowners of the area are tied into the general conservation scheme. The park encompasses the Postberg nature reserve, which has a modest game population.

The terrain is, in common with most parts of the west coast, virtually treeless, but the ground vegetation has its interest and, in spring, its beauty. It comprises succulents and succulent-type plants, low bushes, sedges, some coastal fynbos (heath) and, in their brief season, a glorious profusion of flowering annuals.

Where to stay

Langebaan Lodge is within, and serves as headquarters of and information centre for, the national park. There are conservation displays, short guided walks to the saltmarsh and driftsand areas; hiking and horse-back trails are planned – with overnight stops at Geelbek, an old farmstead now restored to its simple and dignified 1860 specifications (oddly enough the restoration was financed by, among others, two wealthy Arab sheikhs).

The Lodge is also a commercial hotel, and a very pleasant one too: tastefully appointed, with lovely views of Schaapen Island and the lagoon from its public rooms.

Just north of the lagoon mouth and outside the park's boundaries is Club Mykonos, a new, large, and expanding hotel, timeshare and resort complex drawing its design inspiration from the Greek isles. Your accommodation is a *kalifa* (a spacious, whitewashed, colourfully trimmed and simply furnished apartment with lounge, kitchen, bedrooms, bathroom, shade balcony and 'braai balcony'). When you emerge, you walk along cobbled alleys and through village squares. If it wasn't for the wind, and the obvious newness of everything, you could easily imagine yourself beneath an Aegean sky.

For the weekender, Club Mykonos has pretty well everything: gymnasium and sports complex (aerobics, weights, air baths, heated pools, squash and tennis courts), coffee houses, bars, bakeries, boutiques, delicatessens, snackeries. Mixing ethnic origins a little, there's also the Venetian Quarter, a waterfront cluster of shops, pubs, restaurants (the Ariadne serves wonderful Greek dishes) and a 140-berth marina graced by expensive-looking yachts. Sailing and boat cruises around the lagoon are favoured pastimes. It's all a bit contrived and, at the time of writing, unfinished and rather windswept, but the concept is imaginatively grand, and staying there is a lot of fun.

Smaller and more exclusive is the lovely Port Owen development, farther north, near Velddrif. Here there are white-painted, red-roofed, fully equipped cabanas for hire (or time-share, or sale, or indeed you can buy a plot of land and build); nearly 4 km of private waterways and 100 ha of private land, which the owners are doing their best to preserve in its attractive and pristine state, though human encroachment will inevitably have its impact. There's a marina, of course, a yacht club, a restaurant and, nearby, the Langebaan Country Club and its excellent golf course.

The Saldanha area

Beyond Langebaan Lagoon is the broad expanse of Saldanha Bay, one of Africa's finest natural harbours but, because the area is bone dry and drinking water scarce, little used until fairly recent times.

Today, though, Saldanha is both the main centre of the west coast's fishing industry and a deep-sea terminal for the export of iron ore, capable of accommodating the largest of bulk carrier vessels and geared to handle up to 33 million tons of ore a year. The iron is brought from Sishen in the northern Cape over a specially-built 861-km electrified railway line.

Local tourism has been slow to find its feet: Saldanha is a long way from Cape Town; the shores of the bay are dotted with fish-processing factories; the countryside around has few immediately appealing features. But the area does have its drawcards: it's becoming popular among sailors and other watersport enthusiasts, and the town is one of the stops on the so-called Crayfish Route. There are guided tours of the harbour and loading terminal (every

Wednesday). Crayfish Route Bookings: Lambert's Bay, Tel. (026732) 635; Specialized Tours, Tel. (021) 25-3259; Hylton Ross, Tel. (021) 438-1500 and Connex Travel, who offer an outstanding Crayfish Route Tour, Tel. (021) 218-2191.

North of Saldanha is St Helena Bay, 'discovered' by Vasco da Gama in November 1497 and now, too, largely given over to commercial fishing: the upwelling of the cool Benguela Current here provides the nutrients that sustain, among other fish species, vast shoals of pilchards, anchovies and mackerel.

Attractive fishing villages on this and adjacent coasts include:

VELDDRIF, at the mouth of the Berg River. The estuary attracts large numbers of flamingos, spoonbills, avocets and, sometimes, the otherwise seldom-seen glossy ibis. The annual and very rugged three-day Berg River canoe marathon, which starts from Paarl in the winelands north of Cape Town, completes its course at Velddrif.

PATERNOSTER is one of the more pleasant coastal hamlets, and well worth visiting for its attractiveness and for the crayfish and perlemoen taken from the waters.

GETTING AROUND

Day drives

The principal coastal and inland routes are covered in the main narrative (pages 329 to 337). If you have a day to spare and an urge to explore a region of far horizons, we recommend you obtain a good map and Maxwell Leigh's *Touring in South Africa*, which suggests some attractive itineraries, and which goes into a lot more detail than we have room for here.

Walks and hikes

The prime walking and climbing area is the Cederberg wilderness (see page 332), over which there's an extensive (254-km) network of unmarked but well-defined paths. Much of the land is privately owned; there are excellent camping facilities at the Algeria forest station; huts at Waenhuis and at Uitkyk forest refuge. Permits and information from The Forester, Cederberg State Forest, PO Citrusdal 7340, Tel. (02682) 3440.

Other, privately run accommodation facilities in the vicinity include the Sanddrif campsite (contact Nieuwoudt Brothers, Dwarsrivier, PO Cedarberg 7341); the Driehoek Farm campsite (contact the farm at PO Citrusdal 7340); and at the Cederberg Tourist Park, which offers furnished bungalows (contact A P C Nieuwoudt and Son, Kromrivier, PO Citrusdal 7340). Less demanding nature trails in the west-coast region include:

☆ Ramskop nature reserve, Clanwilliam (see page 331): attractive diversity of plant life; bulbs and seeds for sale; caravan/camping ground nearby; open only during the spring months.

☆ For bird-watchers, the Rocher Pan nature reserve near Velddrif: 150 species, including large numbers of waterfowl; hides, picnic sites. Best time to visit: spring; permits and information: The Reserve Manager, Private Bag, Velddrif 7365, Tel. (02288) 727.

☆ The Tienie Versfeld Wild Flower Reserve near Darling (page 335): footpaths; no amenities; worth visiting only during the springtime flowering season.

☆ Yzerfontein Sandveld trails, near Langebaan Lagoon: short and longer (up to 16,5 km) walks, none of them strenuous, have been established; flowers, birds and coastal scenery are the attractions; bungalow accommodation on Blombos Farm (contact Mrs Wrightman, 14 Higgo Crescent, Higgovale, Cape Town 8001).

☆ West Coast National Park (page 335): spring flowers, wonderful birdlife. Trails, including a beach walk, were being developed at the time of writing.

☆ Columbine nature reserve, in the Saldanha area: pleasant for strolling, rock-angling and crayfishing. Poster-map available from the municipality. More demanding are hikes in:

☆ The Great Winterhoek wilderness area, to the east of Porterville. A 20 000-ha expanse of rugged mountainous countryside (the Winterhoek peak itself rises to 2 078 m). Wintertime here is bitterly cold and wet, and snow often covers the higher ground. There are some 90 km of paths. Information and permits: The Forester, Great Winterhoek State Forest, PO Box 26, Porterville 6810; Tel. (02623) 2900.

☆ Farther north, in the remote Garies area, is the Namaqualand Coast trail, which leads 80 km from the Groen River north to the Spoeg River. The trail and its facilities were still under development at the time of writing.

Namaqualand's springtime glory draws tourists, hikers and cyclists from afar

Cycling

Trailblazers (PO Box 18692, Hillbrow, Johannesburg 2038, Tel. (011) 724-5198, offer the inviting Namaqualand Daisy Cycle Trail during the spring flowering season (August/September). It starts from Springbok and leads over the Komaggas mountains to the coast and its diamond diggings, turning inland again on the long route over the Spoeg River to Garies and Vanrhynsdorp. It's really not as strenuous as it sounds, though, and a back-up vehicle copes efficiently with any problems that may arise. You may take your own cycle (fat-tyre machines are preferred); everything else laid on; camp accommodation.

Tours

Several tour operators offer trips to and around Namaqualand during the spring wildflower season. Typical are:

☆ Plusbus's 'Crayfish Route' luxury coach tour, which starts from Cape Town and leads north to Citrusdal (page 330), west to Lambert's Bay (page 333), south to Langebaan (page 335) and includes a visit to Bird Island, some pleasant farm hospitality (traditional Cape meals are served) *en route* and, of course, the wild flower displays. The round trip takes three days. Twice as long is the Plusbus 'Road to Namibia' tour, which takes in the foregoing and Springbok, Keetmanshoop, Lüderitz, Kolmanskop (ghost town) and Windhoek.

☆ Rand Coach Tours' Namaqualand spring flower trip, which starts from Johannesburg and follows the road through Northern Cape diamond country (Kimberley) and the Karoo to Clanwilliam, Lambert's Bay and Citrusdal, Springbok, north to the Orange River and the Augrabies Falls (see page 265) and back via Kuruman in the far north.

Other firms offer roughly the same kind of packages. Particularly appealing are tours – advertised by Thompsons and Swan, among others – that combine a day's journey on the famed Blue Train (see page 71) to Cape Town followed by a coach expedition to points north – Tulbagh and Ceres in the winelands (see page 314), Citrusdal and through Namaqualand to the Augrabies Falls, returning to Johannesburg via the far north. Detailed information and bookings: contact your travel agent or the tour companies direct.

Altogether different and not strictly in the touring category are the various options on offer from Schaafsma Marine (PO Box 172, Vredenburg 7380; Tel. (02281) 3-1571). These include ocean trips (a two-week voyage to the Vema seamount, 500 nautical miles west of Lambert's Bay, for instance), deep-sea fishing expeditions, sailing camps, coastal hikes.

WINES OF THE WEST

Some very drinkable wines are produced in these western areas, in the Swartland and farther north, in the region stretching from Citrusdal up to Lutzville. The grape harvests are especially bountiful in the irrigated lands around the Clanwilliam and Bulshoek dams, where many of the vineyards are terraced and characterized by unusually extensive trellis-work (to allow plenty of 'active leaf surface'). Wine-grapes are also grown in the predominantly wheat-producing area stretching from the Berg River north-west to the Atlantic coast.

A number of the co-operatives and one estate – the renowned Allesverloren (by appointment with the Bergkelder) – are open to the public. Co-ops include the Swartland Wine Cellar in Malmesbury (a wide range of labels), the Riebeeck Wine Cellar (a special Late Harvest), the Mamreweg and Winkelshoek cellars, the Porterville to the west; Citrusdal Cellars (a pleasant Chianti-type wine, marketed under the Goue Vallei label), the Cederberg Cellars,

where you can buy, among other things, excellent wine produced on the Nieuwoudt family farm, and Vredendal, which offers a wide range of dessert labels and the local 'witblits', a fierce, pale, brandy-type brew.

Two wine routes have been established – the Swartland and, fairly recently, the Olifantsrivier – and there's a country-style welcome for tourists along the way: what the region lacks in hotels is more than made up for by the friendliness and hospitality of the local farmers. In the Swartland area alone, a total of nearly 150 of them host visitors in bungalows, cottages and guesthouses. Bookings for these and for day- and half-day tours may be made through Kontrei Farm Holidays in Cape Town, Tel. (021) 96-0146.

Advice and brochures on the wine routes are available from Captour (see Advisory, page 341) and from the Olifants River and West Coast Wine Trust, Tel. (02724) 6-1731/3.

Vineyards in the fertile valley of the Olifants River

ADVISORY: WEST COAST

CLIMATE

Winter-rainfall area, but the rains are infrequent and the countryside bone-dry for most of the year. Hot and windy in summer; winter nights and early mornings can be bitterly cold, the days generally cool to warm. Best time to visit: spring (September/October).

MAIN ATTRACTIONS

Viewing the spring wild flowers □ Scenic and sightseeing drives □ Camping and caravanning □ Hiking trails and nature walks (see page 337) □ Climbing (Cederberg, page 332) □ Bird-watching □ Sea-fishing; crayfish diving □ Sailing and boating. Generally speaking, the sea is too cold for enjoyable swimming.

TRAVEL

Road. Distances from Cape Town: Malmesbury 64 km; Clanwilliam 240 km; Langebaan via Malmesbury 124 km; Saldanha Bay 149 km; Springbok 559 km; Port Nolloth 704 km; Alexander Bay 784 km; Orange River (Namibian border) 824 km; Windhoek 1 500 km.

Main roads are excellent; minor roads can be rough. Inland route from Cape Town to Springbok and northern Namaqualand: take the N7, through Malmesbury, Citrusdal, Clanwilliam. At Steinkopf, north of Springbok, turn west on the R382 for Port Nolloth; coastal road (very rough) from Port Nolloth to Alexander Bay. Permits are needed to enter Alexander Bay.

Coastal route from Cape Town to Langebaan Lagoon and Saldanha Bay area: take the R27; follow map thereafter.

Coach travel: A coach service (Namaqualand Bus Service) operates between Cape Town and Springbok: contact (021) 21-6630, or (0251) 2-2061.

Air. National Airlines operates a scheduled weekly service between Cape Town and Springbok, serving Alexander Bay (and Upington and Aggeneys) *en route.* Information and bookings, Tel. (021) 931-4183/4 and (0251) 2-2061. There are also regular scheduled flights from Lanseria airport (near Johannesburg); for information and bookings, Tel. (011) 659-2750.

Sea. Intec Maritime, Cape Town, Tel.(021) 47-3070, offers sailing courses and travel up the West Coast. Yacht Master Ocean Services CC offer training and cruises on multi-hulls; for information and bookings, contact Mrs Bird; Tel. (021) 462-3413. Schaafsma Marine, Tel. (02281) 3-1571 also run boat/yacht trips.

ACCOMMODATION

Select hotels

CITRUSDAL

Cederberg Hotel ★★ Comfortable, unpretentious, hospitable. 57 Voortrekker Road, Citrusdal, Tel. (02662), and ask for 82.

CLANWILLIAM

Olifants Dam Motel ★ 7 km from Clanwilliam, within walking distance of the dam. 12 en-suite rooms; à la carte restaurant. PO Box 78, Clanwilliam 8135, Tel. (02682) ask for 284 or 342.

Hotel Clanwilliam ★ 27 rooms, 18 with en-suite bathrooms; conference facilities for 50; à la carte restaurant and cocktail bar. PO Box 4, Clanwilliam 8135, Tel. (02682) and ask for 61.

LAMBERT'S BAY

Marine Protea ★★★ Excellent holiday hotel, geared to crayfish and flower seasons; offers spectacular crayfish barbecues. Voortrekker Street, PO Box 1, Lambert's Bay 8130; Tel. (026732), and ask for 49.

SALDANHA

Hoedjiesbaai Hotel ★★ 16 rooms; swimming pool. PO Box 149, Saldanha 7395, Tel. (02281) 4-1271/2/3.

Saldanha Hotel ★★ 25 en-suite rooms. PO Box 2, Saldanha 7395, Tel. (02281) 4-1011.

SPRINGBOK

Masonic Hotel ★ 24 rooms (16 with bath). PO Box 9, Springbok 8240, Tel. (0251) 2-1505.

ST HELENA BAY

Steenberg's Cove Hotel ★ 12 rooms, 4 chalets, 4 units have en suite bathrooms. Main St. St Helena Bay 7390, Tel. (02283) 760.

Ungraded accommodation

Contact: Kontrei Farm Holidays, Tel. (021) 96-2118; Cape Holiday Estates (furnished flats & houses), Tel. (021) 52 1200.

Langebaan area: Langebaan Lodge (see page 336 for details). Within the West Coast National Park. PO Box 25, Langebaan 7357; Tel. (02287) 2144, or National Parks Board, PO Box 7400, Roggebaai 8012; Tel (021) 419-5365. Club Mykonos (see page 336 for details). Private Bag X2, Langebaan 7357; Tel. (02287) 2101; Fax: (02287) 2303; or through central reservations, Cape Town (021) 23-1070.

Caravan/camping and self-catering accommodation

Cederberg: Algeria, c/o forester, Private Bag 1, Citrusdal 7340, Tel. (02682) 3440. Cederberg Tourist Park, Private Bag Kromrivier, PO Citrusdal 7340, Tel. (02682) 1404, On a farm about 78 km from Citrusdal.

Lambert's Bay: Caravan park, Tel. (026732), ask for 588.

Langebaan: Municipal caravan parks (old and new), PO Box 11, Langebaan 7357, Tel. (02287) 2752. Leentjiesklip Park, PO Box 11, Langebaan 7357, Tel. (02287) 2752/2115/6/7.

Melkbosstrand: Ou Skip caravan park, Tel. (02224) 2058.

Port Nolloth area: McDougall's Bay caravan park, Tel. (0255) 8657.

Port Owen (see page 336), PO Box 117, Velddrif 7365; Tel. (02288) 3-1144; or Johannesburg (011) 484-1670.

Saldanha: Blouwaterbaai Holiday Resort, Tel. (02281) 4-2400. Saldanha Holiday Resort, situated on the seafront at Saldanha Bay. Private Bag X12, Vredenburg 7380, Tel. (02281) 4-2247 (caravan and self-catering accommodation). Tabakbaai Holiday resort, Private Bag X12, Vredenburg 7380, Tel. (02281) 4-2248.

Yzerfontein: Municipal caravan park, PO Box 1, Yzerfontein 7351, Tel. (02245) 258.

SELECT RESTAURANTS

There are some quite excellent restaurants in the Bloubergstrand area, near Cape Town (see page 336). Best bets in the remoter reaches are:

Citrusdal: Cederberg Hotel, Voortrekker Street, Tel. (02662), and ask for 82. Country-style fare in tasteful surrounds; welcoming pub.

Clanwilliam: Rheinholds, Clanwilliam Hotel, Main Street, Tel. (02682), and ask for 2 or 61. Stylish country-style cuisine, with some unusual dishes.

Club Mykonos: Langebaan (see page 336). One or two quality restaurants; information, Tel. (02287) 2101.

Lambert's Bay: Marine Restaurant, Marine Protea Hotel, Voortrekker Street, Tel. (026732), and ask for 49. Historic colonial-style building; seafood specialities (including crayfish cooked in a number of imaginative ways).

Lambert's Bay: Die Muisbosskerm, sea front, Tel. (026732), and ask for 17. Seafood in the open air; rough-and-ready, the food is great.

Langebaan: Langebaan Country Club, Tel. (02287) 2112/3.

Langebaan Beach: Franel's, Tel. (02287) 2734.

Paternoster: Paternoster Hotel, Tel. (02285) 703. Renowned for its seafood dishes.

St Helena Bay: Steenberg's Cove Hotel, Tel. (02283) 760. Seafood specialities.

Vredendal: Kliphuis, at nearby Koekenaap Village, Tel. Jack Wiggins (02725) 7-1788. Memorable 'boerekos' in open-air restaurant.

Yzerfontein: Die Pan, Tel. (02241) 2830. An open-air seafood eatery; good food, sociable atmosphere.

USEFUL ADDRESSES AND TELEPHONE NUMBERS

Automobile Association, Cape Town; Tel. (021) 21-1550 (general); 419-4378 (breakdown service); 21-1550 (touring).

Captour, Head Office; Tel. (021) 462-2040, Information, Tel. (021) 25-3320.

Langebaan Publicity Association, Bree Street, Langebaan; Tel. (02287) 2115.

Olifants River and West Coast Tourism Bureau, PO Box 31, Klawer 8145; Tel. (02724) 6-1731/3.

Satour (SA Tourism Board), regional office: Shop 16, Piazza Level, Golden Acre, Adderley St, Cape Town; Tel. (021) 21-6274.

Vredenburg-Saldanha Publicity Association, Berg Street, Vredenburg; Tel. (02281) 4-1276 or 3-2231.

West Coast Tourism Bureau, (026732) 516.

ANNUAL EVENTS

Saldanha Sailing Championships: Easter weekend □Lutzville Valley Carnival: April/May □Lambert's Bay Crayfish Carnival: May □Sandveld Potato Festival, Clanwilliam: August □ Vredendal Agricultural, Food and Wine Festival: August □Clanwilliam Wild Flower Show: last weekend in August □Citrusdal Citrus and Agricultural Festival: early September □Saldanha Harvest of the Sea Festival: 2nd Saturday in September □Darling Wild Flower Show: 3rd weekend in September □Clanwilliam Angling Festival: October/November □Olifantsrivier Young Wine Show, Vredendal: October.

PART THREE

VISITOR'S DIGEST

VISITOR'S DIGEST

Entering South Africa

VISAS AND PASSPORTS Most visitors need visas as well as valid passports to gain entry into the country. Holiday-makers from the United Kingdom, Eire, Germany and Lichtenstein, however, are exempt from the visa requirements, as are citizens of the neighbouring states of Lesotho, Swaziland and Botswana, providing their visit does not exceed 14 days.

Visas may be obtained free of charge from South African diplomatic and consular offices abroad (see page 352). If there is no South African mission in your country, or if the representative is an honorary one, write to the nearest such mission or to the Director General: Home Affairs, Private Bag X114, Pretoria 0001 for the relevant form. Applications should be made well in advance of the intended visit.

Urgent visa requests Forms may be requested from the Department of Home Affairs by cable (telegraphic address: INTERIOR PRETORIA) or telex (321 353 SA). The completed forms can then be submitted with a request that approval be given by cable or telex. The request should state the date and place of entry, and be accompanied by a fee to cover the cost of the reply. On arrival, present the cable or telex reply to the immigration officer in lieu of a visa.

Transit visas These are issued to travellers passing through South Africa on their way to or from neighbouring countries. Applicants must be able to produce a return ticket and a visa or other written authority from the country of destination.

Multiple-entry visa This may be granted if, for instance, your tour involves visits to, and re-entry into South Africa from neighbouring countries.

TEMPORARY RESIDENCE PERMIT Every visitor is issued with this document. You'll be given a form to fill in (airline passengers receive theirs on the aircraft). This specifies the length and purpose of the visit, and is submitted to the Passport Control Officer on arrival. He may require proof that you can support yourself while in South Africa, and if you don't have a return ticket you may have to show that you have the funds to buy one.

HEALTH REQUIREMENTS Visitors coming from, or passing through a place or port within, a yellow fever zone should be able to produce a valid International Certificate of Vaccination. The zone extends over much of tropical Africa and South America (Brazil is now regarded as a risk area).

Airline passengers – those whose aircraft land for refuelling in or are otherwise in transit through a yellow fever zone – do not need a vaccination certificate providing they do not leave the transit airport.

Note that cholera and smallpox vaccination certificates are no longer required. There are no screening procedures in force for Aids at present.

If you intend visiting the Transvaal Lowveld (the region encompasses the Kruger National Park) or northern Natal and Zululand, you are urged to begin a course of anti-malaria tablets before starting out (see page 355). The tablets are available without prescription from South African pharmacies.

CUSTOMS Personal effects (but not unopened packages) are admitted duty free. In addition, you are allowed to bring in R500 worth of other goods, together with limited quantities of alcoholic beverages, perfume, cigarettes and tobacco, free of duty. Further items to a value of R1 000 per person may be brought in at a flat-rate 20% duty plus General Sales Tax (currently 13%). Everything else (except motor vehicles: see Arrival by road, page 345) is dutiable.

Firearms: the required permits are available at points of entry. They are valid for 180 days, and may be renewed at South African police stations.

WHAT CLOTHING TO PACK South Africa enjoys long, hot summers; clothing is generally informal, though some formality (at least 'smart casual' wear) is often required after dark at theatres and other art/entertainment venues and by the more sophisticated hotels and restaurants. Beachwear is acceptable only on the beach. Very casual clothing is customary at resorts and in game parks.

For the summer months (approximately October-April), pack lightweight clothing but include a jacket or jersey for the cooler and occasionally chilly night. Most of the country is in the summer-rainfall region, so bring an umbrella or raincoat. For the winter months, pack warm clothing.

ARRIVAL BY AIR After years of partial isolation South Africa is now well served – increasingly so – by international flights.

South African Airways, the national carrier, operates a fleet of 15 Boeing 747 airliners over a network that spans most of the globe. The network is expanding as new landing rights are negotiated.

Other carriers that offer scheduled flights to and from South Africa include British Airways (London), Alitalia (Rome), KLM (Amsterdam), Lufthansa (Frankfurt), Sabena (Brussels), Swissair (Zurich), UTA (Paris), Varig (Rio de Janeiro), Luxavia (Luxembourg), El Al (Tel Aviv), Quantas (Sydney), Cathay Pacific (Hong Kong), Singapore Airlines, China Airlines, Egypt Air, Air Mauritius, Air Madagascar, Air Seychelles, and Kenya Airlines.

Airports The main points of entry are Johannesburg international airport, which serves both Johannesburg and Pretoria; as well as Durban and Cape Town international airports. Johannesburg is the busiest, and has not always coped well with the pressures: in 1990 an international airline journal awarded it the title of the world's most unfriendly airport, describing its immigration and customs amenities as 'halls of horror'. Improvements are under way.

Airport passenger facilities, currently being upgraded, include banks, currency exchange (a 24-hour service at Johannesburg), post offices, duty-free and other shops, restaurants, snack-bars and cocktail bars, car-hire, taxis, and bus transport to and from town. Major hotels provide courtesy transport.

Air fares SAA and other airlines offer the standard range of fares: first class (on most international flights), business class and economy class. There are special excursion fares for visits of between 14 and 45 days, with optional stopovers *en route*; and cheaper Apex (Advance Purchase Excursion) fares for visits of between 19 and 90 days. Apex prices vary with the season; fares do not include the stop-over option.

Increasing numbers of tour operators and special-interest concerns are advertising budget charter flights.

REGIONAL AIR SERVICES SAA operates scheduled services to and from other southern African countries, including Zimbabwe (Bulawayo, Harare, Victoria Falls), Mozambique (Maputo), Zambia (Lusaka), Malawi (Blantyre), Botswana (Gaborone) and Namibia (Windhoek). The airline inaugurated its Kenya (Nairobi) service at the end of 1990; other continental routes are planned.

Other regional services are provided by Air Botswana, Air Malawi, Air Zimbabwe, Air Lesotho, Linhas Aereas de Moçambique, Bop (Bophuthatswana) Air, Royal Swazi Air, Namib Air, Transkei Airways and Zambia Airways.

A comprehensive domestic air network links centres within South Africa (see page 349).

ARRIVAL BY SEA Several shipping lines offer a limited number of passenger berths on cargo vessels plying between European and southern African ports. Fare prices – generally rather high, but one is paying for what amounts to a three-week cruise as well as transport – vary according to the type and size of cabin. The main points of entry are Cape Town and Durban.

The St Helena shipping line's cargo/passenger vessel carries 125 passengers from Avonmouth (near Bristol) to the Canary Islands, Ascension, St Helena and Cape Town, normally returning by the same route. For details, contact St Helena Line (Pty) Ltd, 4th Floor, BP Centre, Cape Town 8001; Tel. (021) 25-1165; or, in the United Kingdom, Curnow Shipping Ltd, The Shipyard, Porthleven, Helston; Tel. (03265) 6-3434.

The Ellerman & Bucknall line reintroduced a refitted *City of Durban* to South African seas in 1991.

Cruise ships, including the noted *Achille Lauro* and the *Odysseus*, also call at South African ports. For details, contact TFC Tours, PO Box 10558, Johannesburg 2000; Tel. (011) 331-7281; Cape Town (021) 21-7400.

ARRIVAL BY RAIL Passenger services connect Harare and Bulawayo in Zimbabwe with Pretoria and Johannesburg. Passenger trains also run to and from other neighbouring countries.

ARRIVAL BY ROAD South Africa is bordered by Zimbabwe and Botswana in the north, by Namibia in the north-west and by Mozambique and Swaziland in the north-east. There are numerous border crossing points; most travellers from the north enter through Beitbridge, a small Zimbabwean town close to the Limpopo River, on both sides of which there are customs and immigration posts (open daily from 06h00 to 20h00). The routes from Harare and Bulawayo converge here to become, in South Africa, the N1 national highway leading to Pretoria and Johannesburg. Travellers crossing the bridge have been subject to long waits, but the situation is improving.

Opening times of the Botswana, Namibia, Lesotho, Swaziland and Mozambique border posts vary according to local requirements.

Travellers intending to bring their motor vehicles into the Common Customs Area that embraces South Africa, Namibia, Botswana, Lesotho and Swaziland must obtain the necessary documents – a triptyque or carnet authorizing temporary importation – from an internationally recognized motoring organization in their country of origin.

Money

CURRENCY The South African monetary unit is the rand (symbol: R), divided into 100 cents (symbol: c). Coins are issued in denominations of 1c, 2c, 5c, 10c, 20c, 50c, R1 and R2; notes in denominations of R5, R10, R20 and R50. The old R2 note may occasionally be encountered. Some of the lower denominations are to be phased out; beware the superficial similarity between the 20c and the R2,00 coins.

CURRENCY REGULATIONS The South African authorities impose no restrictions on the amount of foreign currency travellers may bring with them. Some countries, however, have set limits on the export of banknotes and, in these cases, visitors are advised to convert the bulk of their funds into travellers' cheques (see below). The importation of South African currency is limited to R500 per person.

Visitors can convert their foreign currency into rands at banks, bureaux de change and through such authorized exchange dealers as Thomas Cook and American Express.

BANKS The banking system is similar to and as sophisticated as those of the Western industrialized countries. Among the major local banking houses are First National (formerly Barclays), Nedbank, Standard Bank, Trust Bank and Volkskas. A number of foreign banks are represented in South Africa.

Normal banking hours in the major centres are from 09h00 to 15h30 on weekdays and from 08h30 (Standard), 09h00 (First National) to 11h00 on Saturdays.

There are banking facilities at the three international airports (see page 344) during normal hours. Special banking services (currency exchange, for instance) are available to passengers on incoming and outgoing international flights at other times.

TRAVELLERS' CHEQUES These may be cashed at any bank (provided the currency in which they are issued is acceptable in South Africa), and they are accepted by many hotels and shops.

CREDIT CARDS Most hotels, restaurants, shops, carriers and tour operators accept international credit cards, among which are American Express, Bank of America, Visa, Diners Club and MasterCharge.

Petrol cannot be purchased on a credit card. Some banks, however, issue a special 'petrocard'.

SERVICE CHARGES Hotels may not by law levy a charge for general services (though there is often a telephone service levy). Restaurants may levy a service charge; few do so.

TIPPING Providing the service is satisfactory, it is usual to tip porters, waiters and waitresses, taxi drivers, room attendants and golf caddies. Tipping petrol attendants is optional, though a window-wash and a cheerful smile do merit recognition.

Generally speaking, gratuities to waiters and taxi drivers should amount to around 10% of the cost of the service. For non-quantifiable services of a minor nature – portorage, for instance – it's usual to proffer a tip of between 50c and R2.

Accommodation

HOTELS The top South African establishments compare with the best in the world but, generally speaking, local hoteliers still have a lot to learn from their counterparts in Europe, North America and the more advanced Far Eastern countries.

The Hotel Board, a statutory but independent body, grades hotels within South Africa for the guidance of the travelling public, awarding from one to five stars according to the range and sophistication of their facilities, the quality of the service and the tariff.

A one-star hotel will be an unpretentious establishment offering modest amenities at reasonable rates – requirements for the grading include a dining room, a 16-hour floor service of light refreshments, and en-suite bathrooms or showers in at least a quarter of its accommodation units. Many one-star country hotels offer a great deal more than these minimum criteria suggest, but one-star city hotels are generally of a poorer quality, often functioning as little more than liquor outlets.

At the other end of the scale, a five-star establishment will be supremely comfortable, even luxurious, offering suites as well as rooms.

Hotels must display their grading prominently, together with symbols denoting the type of occupancy and liquor licence they enjoy, as follows:

T = Tourist: more than half the occupancy is transitory.

T/R = Between a quarter and half of the occupancy is transitory, the remainder residential.

R/T = Between half and three-quarters of the occupancy is residential.

R = More than three-quarters of the occupancy is residential.

YYY = These symbols, representing drinking glasses, indicate that the hotel is fully licensed.

YY = Licensed to sell only wine and beer.

Y = Licensed to sell wine and beer only with a meal.

HOTEL GROUPS Many of South Africa's better establishments are controlled by one or other of the half-dozen large hotel chains; most offer packages, special out-of-season and family rates and other inducements. The more prominent are:

☆ Southern Sun, nearly all of whose 40 or so four- and five-star establishments include the word 'Sun' in their names (Cape Sun, Johannesburg Sun and so forth), and their associated group:

☆ Holiday Inns, known throughout much of the world for professionalism and excellent value.

☆ Sun International, separate from though sharing common origins with Southern Sun. Sun International hotels are to be found in neighbouring countries and in the quasi-independent states of southern Africa, usually as parts of larger casino and resort complexes. Biggest of these is Sun City in Bophuthatswana (see page 117).

☆ Karos hotels, a relatively new, small but fast-growing group. One of its younger establishments is the imaginatively designed Kruger Lodge, on the border of the Kruger National Park near Skukuza.

☆ Protea Hotels. These are establishments which have a management arrangement with but are not owned by the Protea group, and thus tend to retain their individual character. They generally fall into the middle (two- and three-star) range; the Protea seal indicates quality.

MOTELS These cater for the practical needs of motorists and their families, and are to be found at strategic points along the main tourist routes. Tariffs are generally reasonable; many feature a swimming pool, and a restaurant of the steakhouse type. They are graded on the same basis as hotels.

COUNTRY GETAWAYS The eastern Transvaal and the Natal midlands are especially well endowed with secluded, restful little lodges and country houses tucked away among the forested hills. Most of them are supremely comfortable, some of them highly sophisticated in terms of appointments and cuisine, all of them informal and friendly.

Some, though by no means all, are classed as hotels and graded accordingly.

No comprehensive guide is available, but local tourist and publicity associations will have the details. Useful publications include *Weekends Away from Johannesburg & Pretoria* by Joyce & Learmont (Struik; available in Transvaal and Natal bookstores), *Weekends In and Around Cape Town* by Joyce & Johnson, and *Portfolio of Country Places*, which may be ordered by telephone: (011) 788-0287 or (021) 61-5856.

GAME LODGES Usually located in private game reserves and on game farms, these cater mainly for affluent people who like to live well while they explore the ways of the wild. Most lodges pride themselves on the degree of personal attention lavished on each guest, and on the skill of their rangers and trackers.

Some of the best, and most expensive, lodges are to be found in the large private reserves bordering the Kruger National Park (see page 350).

GAME PARKS AND NATURE RESERVES Many of the larger conservation areas offer accommodation: see individual coverage in Part 2, and on page 350.

SELF-CATERING ACCOMMODATION The spectrum is wide, ranging from the rudimentary and isolated overnight hiking hut to the well-appointed, even luxurious resort chalet.

The bigger resorts – invariably sited in areas noted for their natural attractions (lake, river, mountain, mineral spring, game park or nature reserve) – usually offer a selection of chalets, bungalows and cottages which may either be self-contained (kitchen, bathroom) or attached to communal cooking, eating and washing facilities. Other features will include a central restaurant, swimming pool, perhaps an entertainment centre and the full range of sporting and recreational activities. Some resorts incorporate a conventional hotel; nearly all make provision for caravans and campers.

Furnished holiday apartments and cottages in and around the coastal centres are a relatively cheap alternative to hotel accommodation: in many cases an entire family can be housed for the cost of a single hotel bed. Most apartments have a private bathroom, kitchen, fitted carpeting; the furnishings tend to be functional and durable; not all are serviced nor is bedding always provided. Again, however, the range is wide: some units are luxurious, and pricey. There is usually a refundable deposit. Publicity associations and local booking agencies will have the details.

Timeshare is becoming increasingly fashionable among South Africans. Here, one buys a portion of the title to a unit or complex of units, sharing ownership and use (on a rota basis) with the other part-owners. Part-owners may also take part in broader schemes that encompass timeshare ventures in other parts of the country and even other parts of the world, which creates many more holiday options. Game lodges, seaside apartment blocks and 'oceanettes' clustered around a marina are typical timeshare enterprises.

An attractive and economic alternative for prospective overseas visitors, and for South African travellers, is to swap homes and vacations with a local family for the holiday period. One or two agencies specialize in matching preferences; contact International and National Home Exchange, PO Box 188, Claremont 7735, Cape; Tel. (021) 61-4334.

GUEST FARMS These are ideal for low-cost, healthy family holidays. One stays in either the farmhouse or a chalet or cottage on the property, and takes part in the life of the farm, ranch or wine estate.

Satour and the local publicity associations will supply you with a select list or refer you to someone who can. Booking agencies include Kontrei Tours Farm Holidays, Oude Stallen, Huguenot Road, Franschhoek 7690; Tel. (02212) 3118.

CARAVAN PARKS Over 650 of these are scattered around the country and they enable a great many South Africans and not a few visitors to combine travel, accommodation and recreation in a remarkably cheap package.

Most holiday resorts, municipalities and the larger game parks and nature reserves incorporate caravan sites, which are generally well organized and well equipped. The better park will have hot and cold running water, a grocery store, restaurant, swimming pool and other leisure facilities. Caravans, campers and motorhomes may be hired in the major centres.

Consult Satour, the local publicity associations or the Yellow Pages for details of rental facilities. General advice on caravan touring is available from the Automobile Association (see the various Advisories in Part 2) and from the Caravan Club of Southern Africa, PO Box 50580, Randburg 2125; Tel. (011) 789-3202.

YOUTH HOSTELS These provide some of the cheapest accommodation available. There are hostels in Johannesburg, Kimberley, East London and two near Cape Town (at Camps Bay and Muizenberg). For information contact Satour, or The National Secretary, SA Youth Hostels Association, PO Box 4402, Cape Town 8000; Tel. (021) 419-1853.

YMCA AND YWCA Both these organizations offer budget accommodation to young travellers. Contacts: YMCA, 41 Beckett St, Johannesburg 2001; Tel. (011) 339-1285; and YWCA World Affiliated, Suite 603, MSOA Building, 41 Biccard Street, Johannesburg 2001; Tel. (011) 339-8212.

BED AND BREAKFAST The number of private homes offering this type of comfortable, convenient and comparatively cheap lodging is growing rapidly, especially in and around the Cape coastal centres. Contact: Bed 'n Breakfast, PO Box 31124, Braamfontein 2017; Tel. (011) 726-6915.

PETS Although some hotels allow guests to bring their dogs with them (and a few provide kenneling facilities), the practice is generally discouraged. Pets are not permitted in any national park, provincial game reserve or wilderness area.

Travel within South Africa

TRAVELLING BY ROAD This is perhaps the best way to get to know the country. The road network is extensive, comprising 200 000 km of national and provincial highways, 85 000 km of which are fully tarred. Surfaces are generally in good condition, though the going can be rough in some of the remoter and more hilly rural areas.

DRIVER'S LICENCE A foreign licence is valid in South Africa provided it carries the photograph and signature of the holder and is printed in English or, failing this, is accompanied by a certificate of authenticity (in English) issued by an embassy or other competent authority.

Alternatively, obtain an International Driving Permit before your departure. The application procedure is straightforward; the licence is valid for 36 months.

Zimbabwe, Mozambique, Namibia, Botswana, Lesotho and Swaziland licences are valid in South Africa.

PETROL Cities, towns and main highways are very well served by filling stations; the more remote areas less so. Many filling stations stay open 24 hours a day; others (usually) from 06h00 to 18h00, during which hours repair services are available. Pump attendants see to your fuel and other needs (self-service is in its infancy in South Africa); petrol is sold in litres.

MAPS AND BOOKS Excellent road maps are available from Satour and, especially, from the Automobile Association (see further on).

The major bookstores stock other publications useful to the motorist, including detailed street-maps of the major centres and some splendid touring guides. Among the latter are *The South African Touring Atlas* and *Off the Beaten Track*, both published by Reader's Digest, and Maxwell Leigh's *Touring in South Africa* (Struik, Cape Town)). A book that has no maps but which covers the country's roads (and places of interest *en route*) in meticulous and highly informative detail is TV Bulpin's *Discovering Southern Africa* (Treasury of Travel, Muizenberg, Cape).

ROAD SIGNS Visitors intending to drive should get hold of an inexpensive publication entitled *Pass Your Learners Easily* (available at most bookshops), which graphically illustrates South African traffic signs and the rules of the road.

THE ROUTE MARKER SYSTEM The country's main roads are identified by number rather than by name. National highways take the prefix 'N' followed by a number (the N1 is the principal south-north route leading from Cape Town to Johannesburg, Pretoria and beyond to the Zimbabwe border); regional highways the prefix 'R' followed by a number; metropolitan roads the prefix 'M' followed by a number and, very often, a letter indicating direction (N, S, E or W).

If the route marker has white lettering against a blue background, the road is a designated freeway: a multi-laned route which a vehicle can enter only via an on-ramp and exit via an off-ramp positioned to the left of the traffic flow.

All other route markers have white (sometimes yellow) lettering against a green background.

The system sounds complicated but is in practice simple and effective. Armed with a good map – one which incorporates the route markers – the visiting motorist shouldn't find it too difficult to find his way around city, town and country.

Parking Restrictions are indicated by encircled letters painted on the road surface; 'L' stands for a loading zone (goods vehicles only); 'B' for buses; 'T' for taxis; and 'FB' for firefighting equipment. A road sign showing an 'S' with a diagonal stripe means no stopping; a striped 'P' no parking.

Terminology and local peculiarities South Africa has two official languages; public notices and signs are expressed in both English and Afrikaans, which can be confusing for the first-time visitor.

Some of the more common Afrikaans road sign words you'll come across are:

Links (left); *Regs* (right); *Stad* (city); *Lughawe* (airport); *Straat* (street); *Weg* (road); *Rylaan* (Avenue); *Hou* (keep); *Slegs* (only); *Oop* (open); *Gesluit* (closed); *Gevaar* (beware; hazard); *Verbode* (forbidden); *Ompad* (detour); *Strand* (beach); *Hawe* (harbour).

In South Africa, a *Robot* is a set of traffic lights.

Some road rules Traffic keeps to the left-hand side of the road. Generally the speed limit on national highways, freeways and other major routes is 120 km/h (it may be lower; the roads are signposted accordingly). The general limit on rural roads is 100 km/h; that in built-up areas 60 km/h unless otherwise indicated. Keep an eye open for speed-limit signs at all times. The general rule is: Keep to the left, pass on the right, even on dual and multi-laned highways.

The traffic police officer is not a member of the South African Police, but belongs to a local force trained to control the flow of traffic, render assistance at accidents, and monitor road behaviour. He is especially strict on motorists who exceed the speed limit (the fines are heavy) and who drive while under the influence of alcohol.

AUTOMOBILE ASSOCIATION The AA of South Africa is the country's biggest motoring club, providing a wide range of services. These include advice on touring, caravanning, camping and places of interest, together with maps and brochures; help in preparing itineraries; insurance, car hire and accommodation reservation facilities; assistance with breakdowns and in other emergencies. Trained personnel patrol major centres and the more popular tourist routes and areas.

These services are offered to visitors who are able to produce the membership card of a motoring organization affiliated to the AA of SA through the AIT (Alliance Internationale de Tourisme) or FIA (Federation de l'Automobile).

The AA of SA's headquarters are in AA House, 66 Korte St, Braamfontein 2001; Tel. (011) 403-5700. For AA offices in other centres, consult the relevant Advisories in Part 2 of this book or the local telephone directory.

CAR HIRE A number of international firms, including Avis, Imperial (incorporating Hertz) and Budget, are well established in South Africa, serving all major centres, airports and some of the bigger game parks and nature reserves, including the Kruger National Park. Tariffs vary widely according to the type of vehicle, and a kilometre charge is levied. For one-way (city-to-city) rentals there are no 'drop-off' charges; delivery and pick-up services within a city are usually free of charge. Numerous local rental firms provide similar facilities. Other companies offer for hire caravans, campers and campmobiles (fully equipped with stoves, refrigerators, linen, kitchen utensils); four-wheel-drive vehicles, mini- and microbuses. For local addresses, contact Satour otherwise consult the Yellow Pages.

LONG-DISTANCE DRIVING Distances between towns in the interior and west-coast regions are sometimes vast, petrol filling stations few and far between. Plan your journey accordingly.

As a general rule, it is wiser not to stop for hitchhikers, though obviously one exercises on-the-spot discretion: it's easy enough to tell whether someone is genuinely stranded and in need of a good Samaritan. Uniformed servicemen going on or returning from leave use designated stopping points (usually located on the outskirts of a town) on some of the highways. There are roadside rest points on all major routes. These are developed and often shady areas equipped with a table or tables, benches and a refuse bin.

What to take on your overland trip depends on the particular circumstances (length and condition of route, frequency of garages, the condition of your car and so forth). For journeys through remote regions and over rough road surfaces, a basic checklist would comprise:

Route maps; a jack, wheelbrace and good set of tools; a spare wheel in good condition; tyre levers, a pump and tube; a spare fanbelt; spare fuses; a container of brake fluid; jump leads; a tow rope; electric torch; spare set of car keys; car instruction manual; 5-litre can of water; fire extinguisher, first-aid kit (and, for campers, a snakebite kit).

Really careful travellers would also carry an extended range of spares that includes a set of contact-breaker points and condenser; radiator hose and clips; tyre valves; insulating tape; insulated electric wire; 'in line' fuel filter, and a selection of nuts, bolts, washers and split pins.

And don't forget the basic documentation: identity card or passport, driver's licence, firearm licence if you're carrying a gun, rabies inoculation licence if you're carrying a pet, medical aid card or similar record of health insurance, traveller's cheques and a separate copy of the cheque numbers.

COACH TRAVEL Luxury coach services link major centres throughout South Africa; tour operators spread the network wider, taking in game parks, natural wonders, scenic attractions and other tourist areas. For details, consult a travel agent or Satour.

TRAVELLING BY RAIL Train travel within South Africa is a relatively cheap, reasonably comfortable, rather slow way of getting around.

Rail passenger services connect the major centres and many of the minor ones; the most prominent of the cross-country 'name' trains are the Orange Express, which plies once a week between Cape Town and Durban via Kimberley and Bloemfontein; the Trans-Natal Night Express, between Johannesburg and Durban, and the Trans-Karoo Express between Cape Town and Johannesburg. The word 'express' tends to flatter. Other even more leisurely long-distance services are known as 'milk trains'.

Pride of the railways is the celebrated Blue Train (see page 71), which travels between Pretoria, Johannesburg and Cape Town, offering its guests luxurious comfort, five-star cuisine and service amenities that include baths, showers, a lounge bar and a cocktail bar.

Ordinary long-distance trains have dining saloons and catering trolleys; sleeping berths in first and second class coupés (two or three passengers) and compartments (four or six passengers).

Discount fares are available for out-of-season travel. Transnet, the umbrella organization which incorporates Spoornet, the national railways, has offices in London (5th Floor, 266 Regent Street, London W1R5DA; Tel. (071) 29-5552) and New York (370 Lexington Avenue, New York 10017; Tel. (212) 370-9333; Toll Free 1800 223-1880).

The principal railways booking office in South Africa is Central Reservations, PO Box 1111, Johannesburg 2000; Tel. (011) 774-4504.

STEAM TRAINS South Africa is one of the last remaining countries to operate steam locomotives commercially, though even here they are now few in number. They attract railway romantics from all over the world. The most popular among tourists are the Outeniqua Choo-Tjoe (see page 236), the Dias Express (page 198), the Apple Express (page 198) and the Banana Express, which puffs along Natal's South Coast (see page 153).

Spoornet organizes special tours, enabling enthusiasts to travel the entire country by steam train. For information, contact The General Manager, Transnet, Private Bag X47, Johannesburg 2000; Tel. (011) 774-4128, or any Satour office.

TRAVELLING BY AIR In the past, SAA, the national carrier (see page 344), has enjoyed a virtual monopoly over the major internal routes, but with the general trend towards deregulation other domestic, hitherto 'feeder', airlines will offer an increasing number of scheduled services between the main centres.

Domestic points served by SAA are Bloemfontein, Cape Town, Durban, East London, George, Johannesburg, Kimberley, Port Elizabeth, Pretoria and Upington. In 1992, the feeder airlines serving the smaller centres included:

☆ Border Air: Port Elizabeth, East London, Umtata (Transkei).

☆ Citi Air: Durban, Bloemfontein, Ladysmith, Nelspruit, Newcastle, Pietermaritzburg, Richards Bay, Skukuza (Kruger National Park), Ulundi, Umtata and Vryheid. There was also a weekly return flight between Durban and Maputo (Mozambique).

☆ Commercial Airways (Comair): Johannesburg, Phalaborwa, Skukuza, Richards Bay, Margate, Pietermaritzburg, Manzini, Gaborone (Botswana).

☆ Giyani Airways: Johannesburg, Pietersburg, Tzaneen.

☆ Magnum Airlines: Johannesburg, Nelspruit, Pietersburg, Welkom, Bloemfontein, Newcastle, Ladysmith, Vryheid; also Durban to Nelspruit.

☆ National Airlines: Lanseria Airport (near Johannesburg), Aggeneys, Springbok, Alexander Bay, Sishen, Upington; linked to Namaqualand Airways, a regional service operating from Cape Town.

☆ Flitestar: a recently inaugurated regional airline with a fleet of 4 Airbus A320s which link Cape Town, Johannesburg and Durban. Smaller turbo-prop aircraft based in Cape Town serve centres along the west and south coasts including Alexander Bay, Walvis Bay, George and Oudtshoorn. Tel. (011) 333-8724.

AIR CHARTER SERVICES These are offered by all the airlines mentioned above, and by a number of other firms. Helicopters may also be chartered. Information: SA Air Charters (Pty Ltd), Main Terminal Building, Lanseria Airport, Transvaal; Tel. (011) 659-2770.

PUBLIC TRANSPORT IN THE CITIES Bus services in the major centres are adequate and reasonably cheap.

South African taxis do not cruise the streets in search of fares: they are found at designated ranks, at railway stations and at airports. Normally, your best course is to telephone for a cab (taxi firms are listed in the telephone directories and the Yellow Pages) or ask the hotel porter to do so for you.

Travel by taxi is expensive: if your journey is anything more than a cross-town hop, ask the driver for an estimate of the cost. Moreover, make quite sure that he can precisely locate your destination.

Less costly are the so-called 'black taxis' (locally known as Zola Budds and Mary Deckers) that ply the busier routes. These minibuses, often sociably crowded, have undesignated but customary stopping points, and provide a quick means of urban transport. Sometimes too quick: they feature prominently in the accident statistics.

Suburban train services in the Cape Peninsula and Witwatersrand metropolitan areas are extensive, fairly efficient, packed with commuters during the morning (07h00-09h00) and evening (16h00-18h00) rush hours. Criminals were active on some of the lines during 1989 and 1990. The specifics of bus, taxi and train services in the major centres are covered in the relevant Advisories in Part 2.

Tourism and publicity offices

SOUTH AFRICAN TOURISM BOARD Satour maintains regional offices in Pretoria, Bloemfontein, Cape Town, Durban, East London, George, Johannesburg (city and Johannesburg airport), Kimberley, Nelspruit, Pietersburg and Port Elizabeth. Contact addresses and telephone numbers appear in the relevant Advisories in Part 2.

Satour's headquarters are in the Menlyn Park Office Block, corner of Atterbury Road and Menlyn Drive, Menlyn 0081; Private Bag X164, Pretoria 0001; Tel. (012) 47-1131/348-9521.

Satour's representation outside South Africa is expanding; in 1991 its offices abroad included:

Eastern United States: 747 Third Avenue, 20th Floor, New York, NY 10017; Tel. (212) 838-8841.

France: 9 Boulevard de la Madeleine, 75001 Paris; Tel. (09) 4261-8230.

Germany: D-6 Frankfurt/Main 1, Alemannia-Haus, An der Hauptwache 11; postal address: Postfach 101940, 6000 Frankfurt; Tel. (069) 2-0656.

Israel: 14 Hey B'iyar, Kikar Hamedina, Tel Aviv; PO Box 3388, Tel Aviv; Tel. (03) 25-7950.

Italy & Greece: Via M Gonzaga 3, Milan 20123, Italy; Tel. (02) 869-3847/869-3856.

Japan: Akasaka Lions Building, 1-1-2 Moto Akasaka, Minato-ku, Tokyo 107; Tel. (03) 478-7601.

Netherlands, Belgium & Scandinavia: Parnassustoren, Locatellikade 1, 7e etage, 1076 AZ Amsterdam, Netherlands; Tel. (020) 664-6201.

Switzerland & Austria: Seestrasse 42, CH 8802 Kilchberg/Zurich, Switzerland; Tel. (01) 715-1815/16/17.

Taiwan & Hong Kong: Room 1204, 12th Floor, Tower Building, 205 Tun Hau North Road, Taipei 10592, Taiwan, Republic of China; Tel. (02) 717-4238.

United Kingdom: 5-6 Alt Grove, Wimbledon, London, SW19 4DZ; Tel. (081) 944 6646.

Western United States: Suite 1524, 9841 Airport Boulevard, Los Angeles CA 90045; Tel. (213) 641-8444.

Zimbabwe: Mercury House, Gordon Avenue, Harare; PO Box 1343, Harare; Tel. 70-7766/7.

VISITOR'S BUREAUX Major centres and tourist areas have publicity associations or tourist bureaux which provide up-to-date information, free of charge, on local attractions, hotels, restaurants, transport, sport, recreation and so forth.

These offices display the internationally accepted sign for 'Information': a green and white 'i'. Addresses and telephone numbers appear in the relevant Advisories in Part 2.

In centres where there is no bureau, visitors should contact the Town Clerk's office for information and relevant advice.

Game and nature reserves

South Africa has 17 national parks, of which the Kruger is the biggest and best known; scores of provincially controlled game and nature reserves and hundreds of municipal and private reserves.

In addition, there are a number of state forests and wilderness areas, and some fine wildlife and floral reserves in the four formerly 'independent' states within South Africa (Bophuthatswana's Pilanesberg National Park is especially notable).

The Natal and Zululand reserves, administered by the Natal Parks Board, are among the world's most impressive: the region's warm, humid climate and the lush countryside with its wonderful variety of plant life, provide ideal habitats for great numbers of animals and birds. Hluhluwe, for example, is little more than a twentieth the size of the Kruger National Park but contains almost 70% of the total number of the Kruger's species.

The overall emphasis in the Western Cape's many reserves is on the region's magnificent floral heritage.

The major and many of the minor conservation areas are covered in the relevant sections of Part 2, together with the appropriate contact addresses and telephone numbers.

Visitors to the larger parks and reserves stay at enclosed rest-camps, in (usually) thatched rondavels, bungalows, chalets and cottages of varying degrees of sophistication. The bigger and better units will have their own bathrooms (or showers) and kitchens (bedding, linen, cutlery, crockery and fridges are provided); occupants of others have access to communal cooking, eating and washing facilities. Generally the accommodation is reasonably comfortable but without many frills, though there is a growing demand for luxury units, mainly from overseas visitors. Many parks are thus upgrading their facilities.

Some reserves have shops, petrol filling stations, restaurants, swimming pools and other amenities; nearly all offer walking trails; wildlife sanctuaries are traversed by game-viewing roads.

All game parks and nature reserves are easily accessible by road. For visitors who do not have their own transport, there are coach tours, fly-in and fly-drive safaris. Consult a travel agent for details.

GAME LODGES see page 347; and Part 2, page 93.

GAME FARMS There are a great many of these scattered around the Transvaal, Free State and northern KwaZulu-Natal. The game animals are farmed commercially, for their meat and hides. A high percentage of owners provide accommodation and other visitor facilities; some allow hunting on their properties (see below). Among the specialist enterprises are ostrich farms, and numerous crocodile ranches.

HUNTING Conservation programmes have proved very effective in South Africa; game farms (see above) are flourishing, and in consequence there are great numbers of game in the country. In some areas the herds have to be periodically culled in order to maintain the ecological balance.

This opens up opportunities for selective hunting, which is becoming an increasingly prominent element of the tourism industry. Many safari operators offer excellent facilities for game-hunting (and photo-

graphy); a number of them are members of the International Professional Hunters' Association and of the South African Hunters' and Game Preservation Association. The treatment, mounting and shipment of trophies are undertaken by expert taxidermists.

Notable hunting feats achieved in South Africa are recorded in the Rowland Ward Book of Records.

Information on facilities, quotas, fees and so forth is available from Satour, and from the Professional Hunters' Association of South Africa, PO Box 770, Cramerview 2060; Tel. Johannesburg (011) 706-7724.

Outdoor adventure

South Africa's great wilderness areas provide ample opportunities for hiking, camping, mountaineering, rock-climbing, river-riding (see page 134). Some truly splendid nature trails, kayaking (canoeing) trails, horse-riding trails, guided wilderness trails, back-packing trails, snorkelling trails and auto trails have been established.

HIKING One of the fastest-developing forms of outdoor recreation in the country. Since the 1970s the various conservation and tourism authorities have combined to design and build a network of trails called the National Hiking Way, consisting of main, supplementary and connecting routes. The major areas covered are the mountains and coastlines of the south and east, and the Escarpment region of the Eastern Transvaal. The one-thousandth kilometre of the National Hiking Way was completed with the establishment of the Prospectors' Trail in the eastern Transvaal in the mid-1980s.

Individual trails vary from 5 km to more than 100 km, and from the gentle to the strenuous. Facilities *en route* comprise overnight huts with basic cooking and washing facilities.

Information about and maps of individual trails are obtainable for a nominal fee from the National Hiking Way Board, Private Bag X447, Pretoria 0001; Tel. (012) 310-3839.

A number of other wilderness trails traverse mountainous areas, forests, national and provincial parks and reserves. Suggested reading: *The Complete Guide to Walks and Trails in Southern Africa* by Jaynee Levy (Struik), available from major bookstores. Also useful is Satour's *Follow the Footprints*, which contains general information and addresses from which details of the individual trails can be obtained.

OX-WAGON TRAILS A holiday experience unique to South Africa: one hikes across the veld alongside a traditional ox-wagon; sleeps, eats and lives in the pioneering style. Contact Satour for details.

MOUNTAINEERING AND ROCK-CLIMBING There are some grand mountains in southern Africa; the heights of the Drakensberg and the Cape coastal regions are attracting a growing number of climbers. The sport is highly organized within the aegis of the Mountain Club of South Africa, 97 Hatfield Street,

Cape Town 8001; Tel. (021) 45-3412. The club also provides an expert mountain rescue service in co-operation with the police, the air force and the paramedical services.

Related but less exacting is rock-climbing, a mainly informal recreation but in part formalized through the South African Climbers' Club, 71 12th Street, Parkhurst 2153.

General information

AFRICAN TRADITIONAL LIFE South Africa is an industrial country, highly urbanized, and the old ways of Africa are disappearing rapidly. Much of what remains of traditional dance, dress and domestic lifestyles is largely confined to the more remote rural areas, and is therefore not easily accessible to the visitor. Other aspects of the African cultures – notably language and music, custom and belief – are more enduring.

Special shows and displays are staged for the benefit of tourists in the various centres: tribal dancing in some parts of KwaZulu-Natal, on the mines of the Witwatersrand, at Johannesburg's Gold Reef City (see page 43) and at some of the resorts; also exhibitions of beadwork and handicrafts; re-created Zulu, Tsonga and Ndebele villages and so forth. The more prominent venues are covered in Part 2.

CLIMATE A general description of climatic conditions appears in Part 1, page 13. Regional climate profiles are included in the Advisories in Part 2.

CONGRESSES The country plays host to numerous international and local congresses; facilities are generally excellent; nearly all the larger hotels have venues.

Satour issues a biannual South African Congress Calendar, and a South African Congress Venue Directory. Contact Satour's head office (see page 350) or the nearest Satour office.

DIPLOMATIC AND CONSULAR REPRESENTATION Most foreign countries represented in South Africa have established missions in both Pretoria and Cape Town; some are also represented in other centres, notably Durban. Contact telephone numbers are listed in the relevant Advisories (see pages 77 and 305); more comprehensive lists of addresses and telephone numbers appear in the Yellow Pages under Consulates and Embassies.

South African representation abroad is expanding. In 1992 the Republic maintained diplomatic and/or consular missions in Argentina (Buenos Aires), Australia (Canberra, Sydney), Austria (Vienna), Belgium (Brussels), Bolivia (La Paz), Brazil (Brasilia, Rio de Janeiro, Sao Paulo), Canada (Ottawa, Montreal, Toronto), Chile (Santiago), Republic of China (Taipei), Denmark (Copenhagen), Finland (Helsinki), France (Paris, Marseilles), Germany (Bonn, Hamburg, Munich, Frankfurt and Main), Greece (Athens), Guatemala (Guatemala City), Hong Kong, Iceland (Reykjavik), Israel (Tel Aviv), Italy (Rome, Milan), Japan (Tokyo), Luxembourg, Malawi (Lilongwe), The Netherlands (The Hague), Portugal (Lisbon, Madeira), Reunion (La Reunion), Spain (Madrid), Sweden (Stockholm), Switzerland (Berne, Geneva), United Kingdom (London, Glasgow), United States (Washington, New York, Houston, Chicago, Beverley Hills), and Uruguay (Montevideo).

ELECTRICITY Generally, urban power systems are 220/230 volts AC at 50 cycles a second; Pretoria's system generates 250 volts; Port Elizabeth's 220/250 volts. Plugs are 5-amp, two-pin or 15-amp three-pin (round pins).

Not all electric shavers will fit hotel and game park plug points; visitors should seek advice about adaptors from a local electrical supplier.

EMERGENCIES Emergency contact numbers for the police, ambulance and so forth are listed at the front of each telephone directory. The more important ones in the main centres appear in the relevant Advisories in Part 2.

The national number for the police flying squad is 10-111. A national ambulance number, 10-177 recently came into operation.

Among the personal crisis help services are Lifeline (the equivalent of the Samaritans in Britain) and Alcoholics Anonymous. Both are listed in telephone directories.

FOOD AND WINE South African meat, fruit, freshwater and sea fish and shellfish – most notably the crayfish (rock lobster) caught off the Western Cape's coasts – are of the highest quality.

The country's restaurants, many of which are quite superb (local chefs win a surprising number of international competitions) offer the full range of culinary delights, from Continental classics through country fare to the dishes of a score and more exotic peoples.

There's no such thing as 'South African cuisine' in the sense of a single, coherent philosophy of food – the region is ethnically diverse, and eating patterns are drawn from many parts of the world. However, the traditions of some of the colonial and immigrant groups have been especially influential.

Magnificently fiery curries and memorable biryanis can be savoured in KwaZulu-Natal, which has a large Indian population. In the Western Cape, and elsewhere, restaurants serve both Malay cuisine, famed for its fragrant bredies and boboties, and fine 'old Cape' (Dutch/Afrikaner) foods, among which are Karoo lamb, venison (springbok pie is a delicious menu item), sweet potato, pumpkin, as well as a piquant concoction made from waterblommetjies, or 'little water flowers'.

Afrikaner hospitality, especially in the country areas, is legendary; the home-cooked meal you'd eat with the family will certainly be substantial and probably rather stodgy: usual fare comprises splendid portions of good red meat (mutton, lamb and venison invariably feature), sweet potatoes, pumpkin fritters, sweetcorn fritters, mashed vegetables flavoured with cinnamon and sage, milk (or custard) tart, cheesecake, konfyt (various kinds of stickily sweet preserves) and plenty of good, rich coffee to follow.

One of the best-loved of the South African traditions – in fact it's more or less a national institution – is the 'braai' (short for braaivleis), a standard barbecue featuring well-marinated meats (lamb, beef, venison, chicken), potatoes baked in foil, salads, beer and basic conversation. It's usually held in one of the darker, dustier and windier parts of the garden; men and women tend to congregate in their separate groups, the former around the fire.

Traditional African cuisine does not appear on many restaurant menus. The indigenous people have not elevated food to cult status: eating remains very much a practical necessity (and a formidably challenging one in many parts of Africa); the range is limited, the dishes fairly basic.

South African wines are generally excellent, underrated by the world at large and, though prices are rising, still remarkably cheap. Worth obtaining is a handy little volume entitled *The South African Wine Buyer's Guide* by Dave Hughes (published by Struik; available from most of the bigger bookshops).

GAMBLING South Africa has strict gambling laws, but incongruous ones. You may not play games of chance for money, but horse-racing (and betting on horses) is both lawful and enormously popular, and some of the world's most lively and sophisticated casinos flourish in the adjacent 'independent' states, or 'homelands'. Lotteries have been illegal, despite the huge contribution they are able to make to charities. The laws, however, are currently under review.

HANDICAPPED TRAVELLERS Most South African hotels with two stars or more, resorts and the larger game parks and nature reserves have facilities for disabled persons (the Kruger's Skukuza rest-camp offers several specially designed chalets). Accommodation guides, including that produced by Satour for the various touring regions, use the international access symbol to identify the facilities.

Cressida Automatics fitted with hand controls are available from Avis Rent-A-Car in the major centres. SAA and other airlines provide passenger aid units at airports. Wheelchairs and other aids for the disabled can be hired in most of the larger centres.

HEALTH AND FITNESS The major centres are well endowed with fully equipped and expertly staffed health studios, most of which offer aerobics and other fitness classes. For details, consult the hotel reception or the Yellow Pages.

Jogging and cycling are as fashionable in South Africa as they are in any other health-conscious country; clubs are active in most of the larger centres, and they welcome visitors.

HOLIDAYS AND HOLY DAYS Public holidays are currently under review. At the time of writing (1992), there were eleven during the year: New Year's Day

(1 January); Good Friday (29 March); Family Day (1 April); Founders' Day (6 April); Workers' Day (1 May); Ascension Day (9 May); Republic Day (31 May); Kruger Day (10 October); Day of the Vow (16 December); Christmas Day (25 December) and the Day of Goodwill (26 December). In addition, 2 January is accepted as a holiday in the Western Cape; Soweto Day (16 June) is regarded as a commemorative day by large numbers of South Africans. The Jewish, Hindu and Islamic communities observe their traditional holy days.

School holidays The school year is divided into four terms. In the past, the four provinces and the various 'race groups' have all worked to different calendars – a messy and obsolescent set of arrangements that will be rationalized in the future. The peak tourist holiday period runs from mid-December, when the Transvaal schools break up, to the first week in January.

LANGUAGES South Africa's ethnic diversity is reflected in the number of languages and dialects spoken by its peoples.

The two official media are English and Afrikaans. The latter is the mother tongue of the Afrikaners, who comprise some 60% of the country's white population, and of many of the 3-million strong mixed-descent community. A high proportion of other groups – English-speaking whites, black people, and Asians – use Afrikaans as a second or third language.

English is the first language of slightly less than 40% of the whites, and of most of a large and growing number of Asians. It is also the second language of most Afrikaners and mixed-descent people, and of a great many urban blacks.

Other European tongues spoken by minority white groups include Dutch, German, Portuguese, French, Italian and Greek. The main languages of the Asian communities are English, Gujarati, Urdu, Tamil, Hindi and Telegu.

The black peoples of South Africa fall into four major linguistic groupings, which in turn are subdivided into a variety of interrelated languages and dialects, the whole falling within the Bantu family of tongues. The four main groupings are Nguni, Sotho, Venda and Tsonga. Included in the Nguni group are Xhosa (spoken in the Eastern Cape), Zulu (KwaZulu-Natal), South Ndebele and Swazi. With urbanization and greater mobility, however, Zulu is becoming increasingly the preferred medium of communication in the industrial areas of Gauteng.

A bastard language, commonly termed Fanagalo, has evolved within the industrial communities, and especially on the mines, where the variety of tongues spoken often made it difficult for co-workers to communicate. Drawing mainly from Zulu, English and Afrikaans, it has a limited though functional vocabulary and a rudimentary grammatical structure. Its use, though, is now regarded as an affront to dignity and the language is in terminal decline. Finally, there are the Khoisan languages, spoken in remote places by the few remaining peoples of Khoikhoi (Hottentot) and San (Bushman) stock. See also Vocabulary, page 357.

LIQUOR AND LICENSING HOURS Bars usually open at 10h00 and close at 23h00 on weekdays and Saturdays; on Sundays, alcoholic beverages may only be served with meals.

Nightclubs and some city bars remain open until 02h00 and later on weekdays.

Most liquor stores are open from 08h00 to 18h00 or 18h30; a few city outlets stay open until 20h00. Some supermarkets stock beer and wine (but not spirits); they may only sell liquor during licensing hours.

Restaurants may be fully licensed, or licensed to serve only wine and beer, or they may be unlicensed, in which case one takes along one's own beverage. Check before making a reservation.

The liquor and licensing regulations are periodically reviewed; the general trend seems to be towards a more relaxed drinking dispensation.

MEASUREMENT South Africa uses the metric system of weights and measures.

MEDIA Freedom of expression and of the press were restored with the lifting of the state of emergency and its concomitant regulations in 1990.

Newspapers The South African English Language press has an honourable history; generally, newspaper editors have been uncompromising and often courageous in their stand against injustice and the denial of human and political rights.

Major English-language papers include the national weekly *Sunday Times* (with a circulation of well over half a million), the *Sunday Star*, the daily *Star*, *City Press* and the *Sowetan*, all published in Johannesburg, the last two principally for an African readership; the *Pretoria News*; the *Cape Times*, *The Argus* and *Weekend Argus*, published in Cape Town; the eastern Cape's *Herald* and *Post*, published in Port Elizabeth; and the *Sunday Tribune*, the *Daily News* (both published in Durban) and the *Natal Mercury* (Pietermaritzburg).

The leading Afrikaans-language newspapers are the national weekly *Rapport*, with a circulation of close to half a million; and the dailies *Beeld* (Gauteng) and *Die Burger* (Cape Town).

In 1992, most daily newspapers cost 70c to 80c, Sunday newspapers R2 to R2,50.

British newspapers are sold by bookstores in the main centres.

Magazines South African general magazines, especially those with a predominantly female readership, maintain remarkably high editorial and design standards.

The major American magazines are sold in all the bigger bookstores and at other outlets; some stock British, German, French and Italian periodicals.

Radio The South African Broadcasting Corporation (SABC), whose headquarters and main transmitting station are at Auckland Park, Johannesburg, controls the country's radio services, though regional listeners can and do tune in to popular stations operated by the 'independent' republics.

National FM broadcasting services comprise Radio South Africa, English and Afrikaans (both of which tend towards the serious and cultural); Radio Orion (after-midnight music and friendly chat); Radio Allegro (late-night, all-night classical and light-classical music); Radio Lotus (for Indian listeners), and Radio Five, which is lively, youthful and notable for the professionalism of its deejays.

The regional services are Radio Good Hope (Cape Town), Radio Highveld (Johannesburg), Radio Jacaranda (Pretoria), Radio Port Natal (Durban), Radio Oranje (Bloemfontein) and Radio Algoa (Port Elizabeth). Radios Zulu, Xhosa, Sesotho, Lebowa, Setswana, Tsonga, Venda, Swazi and Ndebele beam programmes to predominantly black listeners.

Television The SABC offers two national television services. English- and Afrikaans-language programmes alternate on TV1 (each viewing day is divided equally between the two). Quite a high proportion of the material – until recently mainly American, due to the British Equity ban on the sale of British programmes to South Africa – is dubbed into Afrikaans, some of which can be heard in English on simulcast radio.

The Contemporary Community Values (CCV) service combines African- and English-language entertainment, documentary, educational and news programmes to offer 'something-for-everyone'.

A fifth service, M-Net, is controlled by a consortium of newspaper interests and is available on subscription (in 1991 it had around 580 000 subscribers). M-Net shows entertainment programmes, a lot of sport, some good documentaries and an average of three feature films a day, two of which will usually be repeats. Most of the films are recent or fairly recent releases; many are quite severely edited, to match either M-Net's time-slots or the audience's perceived attention span.

News coverage on the SABC channels is extensive; presentation is sophisticated with, among other things, efficient use being made of line feeds and satellite link-ups. TV1 provides two hours of lunchtime coverage and CCV and hour's late-night international news coverage, both broadcast by America's Cable News Network (CNN).

MEDICAL SERVICES South Africa does not have a 'national health' welfare scheme, and visitors are responsible for their own medical arrangements. They're urged to take out medical insurance prior to departure.

Public hospitals tend to be crowded and the medical and nursing staff are invariably overworked, though the standard of patient care remains remarkably high. Private hospitals generally offer a lot more comfort and individual attention, and are a great deal more expensive.

Private doctors are listed in the telephone directories under 'Medical Practitioners' and, for Afrikaans-speakers, 'Mediese Praktisyns'.

Hospitalization is usually arranged through a medical practitioner, but in an emergency a visitor may telephone or go directly to the casualty department of a General Hospital or, in the smaller centres, to any hospital. Hospitals are listed under 'H' in the telephone directories.

Emergencies Ambulance and other emergency services are listed at the front of the telephone directory. The more important numbers in each city are given in the appropriate Advisories in Part 2.

Pharmacies Most remain open until at least 18h00 on weekdays (13h00 on Saturdays), some until much later; a few provide an all-night and limited Sunday service. The hotel reception, and the hotel porter's office, will have the details. Alternatively, consult the Yellow Pages.

Malaria The disease is largely under control in South Africa, though continentally it is still an extremely serious health problem (in 1986 the World Health Organization estimated that more than 750 000 Africans were dying of malaria each year).

The regions of the Republic where infection is most likely are the northern and Eastern Transvaal and northern KwaZulu-Natal. The risk of contracting the disease, however, is negligible providing you take the standard precautions (see Entering South Africa: health requirements, page 344).

Bilharzia Also known as schistosomiasis, this debilitating, waterborne tropical disease is caused by a parasitical worm that inhabits the rivers and dams of the lower-lying northern and eastern regions.

The transmission cycle is complex: after developing its larval stage in a water snail, the bilharzia fluke may penetrate the skin of a person entering the water, later attacking the bladder, liver and kidneys. The eggs then leave the human body in the waste products, but will only hatch if discharged into fresh water, where the hatchlings will swim around until they find another snail host.

When diagnosed (this can be quite difficult, as the symptoms are often vague), the disease readily responds to drugs.

Precautions: be very circumspect about swimming in rivers and dams – unless there are clear assurances that they are bilharzia-free.

AIDS Although little more than a thousand cases of full-blown Aids had been diagnosed in South Africa by January 1992, the disease is likely to become critical. The incidence of heterosexual Aids, in particular, is increasing exponentially.

The risk of contracting Aids, though, appears to be no greater here than it is in any other country, provided of course that the standard and well-publicized precautions are taken.

Drugs Drug abuse is a growing social problem in South Africa, as it is elsewhere.

Trading in and possession of illegal drugs, including marijuana (also called 'dagga' in South Africa) are criminal offences and carry severe penalties.

Marijuana is the substance most commonly abused. When smoked together with crushed Mandrax (methaqualone), or 'buttons', it is known as a 'white pipe', a combined use that appears to be unique to South Africa. The country has the world's highest incidence of Mandrax abuse.

Heroin and cocaine are latecomers to and remain a very small part of the South African drug scene.

Some appetite suppressants that are prescriptive elsewhere can be bought over the counter in South Africa, as can a host of painkillers and cough medicines containing drugs.

PHOTOGRAPHY Most international film brands and sizes are readily available from photographic shops and department stores; processing is quick (same-day; one-hour at some outlets) and relatively cheap (visitors should enquire whether process charges are included in the price of film).

Note that certain buildings and installations – those relating to defence (military bases, for instance) and internal security (police stations; prisons) – may not be photographed.

Also note that airport security X-ray machines can damage your film. Either pack it in a lead-lined bag or request that it be checked separately.

POSTAL SERVICE Most post offices are open from 08h00 to 16h30 on weekdays and 08h00 to 12h00 on Saturdays. Post offices in city suburbs and the smaller centres close at lunchtime (13h00 to 14h00).

An international priority mail service is available to and from Britain, the United States, Germany, France, Switzerland and a number of other countries.

The South African Post Office also provides facilities for stamp-collectors. Contact: Philatelic Services and Intersapa, Private Bag X505, Pretoria 0001; Tel. (012) 311-3470/1.

RELIGIONS The range of religions practised in South Africa reflects the diverse origins and cultures of its peoples. They include:

Christianity The principal groupings are the Dutch Reformed family of churches (3,5 million members); the Anglican Church (Church of the Province of Southern Africa; 1,3 million members); Roman Catholic (2,5 million), Methodist (2,3 million), and the African Indigenous Churches (see below).

African Indigenous Churches These combine Christianity with some elements of traditional African belief. There are some 2 000 indigenous church groups, most of them in Gauteng (Soweto alone has 500). The largest is the Zion Christian Church, with its own settlement, or headquarters, at Zion City Moria near Pietersburg in the Northern Transvaal. Most of the groups believe in prophet-healers, and some wear brightly coloured uniforms and robes.

Judaism Adherence corresponds with the number of Jewish South Africans – 120 000.

The Islamic faith has some 360 000 adherents, principally within the Indian community of Natal and the mixed-descent community of the Cape (see pages 17 and 279).

Hindus number some 550 000, the vast majority of whom are Indians living in KwaZulu-Natal.

Black traditional beliefs These have four major emphases: belief in a Supreme Being; animism (a conviction that natural objects such as lakes, rivers, trees, stones, and the elements – wind, rain – possess souls); ancestral veneration; and the intercession of spirit mediums, or diviners. The precise affirmation of these beliefs is determined by the history and culture of the many different African groups; the subject is vast, complex and sensitive. It is covered briefly on pages 158 and 211.

SECURITY South Africa is undergoing rapid change; the transition to a fully democratic order has in many ways proved traumatic; there is a great deal of poverty, and the crime rate in some areas has been high. Take the same precautions that you would, say, in Central New York. Specifically:
☆ Busy streets and well-used parks, gardens and other open areas are safe enough, but don't walk alone at night in either city or suburb. Rather call a taxi.
☆ Avoid deserted areas, and the poorer areas, unless you are with a group.
☆ Don't carry large sums of cash around with you.
☆ Don't leave valuables in your hotel room; use a safety deposit box.

SHOPPING The full range of necessities and luxuries is available in South Africa; prices are comparable with and often lower than those in the industrially advanced countries, though some items – electrical appliances and books, for example – are a lot more expensive.

There are modern shopping complexes in and around all the major centres.

Normal shopping and business hours are 08h30 to 017h00 Mondays to Fridays; 08h30 to 13h00 on Saturdays. However, many of the larger supermarkets close later on weekdays and are open on Saturday afternoons, Sundays and public holidays.

Corner cafés – suburban mini-supermarkets – are open from early to late every day of the week throughout the year. They are convenient for milk, confectionery, bread, newspapers, cigarettes and casual purchases· their prices tend to be higher than those of the larger stores.

A General Sales Tax (GST) of 13% has been levied on all sales of goods and services. This is not, usually, reflected in the quoted price.

Sales tax is to be replaced, from the end of 1991, by a Value Added Tax (VAT), a levy on the difference between an item's cost and its pre-tax price. The levy is added on at each stage from factory to shop counter.

Some of the bigger South African retail chains are Woolworths (various departments, including a high-quality supermarket); OK Bazaars (which stocks a wide range of goods at competitive prices); Checkers and Pick 'n Pay (supermarkets); Clicks (general purpose, mainly household goods); Edgars, Truworths, Foschini and Topics (fashion clothing and accessories).

OK's Hyperama, Pick 'n Pay's Hypermarket and Checkers' Warehouse are vast, no-frills, suburban shopping complexes that take bulk-buying, multi-stocking and price-paring to their extremes.

Local products of particular interest to visitors are gold, diamond and semi-precious stone jewellery; copperware; leather (including crocodile skin) and suede goods; items made from karakul wool, ostrich leather and feathers; ceramics, curios and African handicrafts. Among the last two are beadwork, wooden carvings, shields, drums, masks, game animal skins, hand-woven rugs.

Publicity associations have details of what's on offer in the different centres; some of the specifics are covered in the 'City Life' sections of Part 2.

South Africa's 'informal economy' has burgeoned in recent years – the product of widespread unemployment on the one hand and more relaxed trading regulations on the other – and bustling street markets (and craft fairs) now enliven most of the larger centres.

SPORT The country's wonderfully sunny climate favours outdoor activity, and South Africans are enthusiastic sportsmen.

The long years of sporting isolation have, inevitably, affected performance standards; readmittance to the international arena and the removal of race barriers within South Africa will, eventually, allow the country's youth to realize its full potential.

The major spectator sports are soccer, cricket and rugby.

Within the black community, soccer is supreme: there are over 12 000 soccer clubs and nearly a million regular soccer players in South Africa. The country's premier competition is the Castle League, comprising the 22 leading club teams, prominent among which are Kaiser Chiefs, Orlando Pirates, Moroka Swallows, Mamelodi Sundowns, Amazulu, Hellenic (one of the few strong Cape sides), Jomo Cosmos and Wits University. Some of the other professional league teams have splendidly colourful names, among them Dangerous Darkies, Two for Joy, Bluebells, Kroonstad Rabbits and Crystal Brains.

Rugby is especially popular among Afrikaners. The premier provincial rugby competition is the Bankfin Currie Cup (the prefix relates to the current sponsor's name); the top provincial teams are tentatively scheduled to take part in a proposed annual Southern Hemisphere 'Top Ten' tournament. The national team, known for decades as the Springboks, was prominent and sometimes pre-eminent in world rugby until its exclusion in the early 1980s. South Africa was readmitted to the international arena in 1992.

The major provincial cricket competitions are the Castle Cup, the one-day Nissan Shield and the Benson & Hedges day-night series. South Africa made a welcome re-entry into world competition with a short series against India at the end of 1991, followed by participation in the 1992 World Cup.

Golf clubs, of which there are more than 400, welcome visitors; green fees are reasonable, caddies are available and most courses are beautifully maintained. Bowling clubs are equally hospitable.

Watersports attract especially large numbers of participants, not only along the coasts but also on the inland dams and rivers, and the facilities are excellent. Many hotels have their own swimming pools; their managements will help visitors organize angling, sailing and other recreational expeditions. Parts of the Cape and Natal shorelines provide quite magnificent opportunities for surfing.

Jogging and cycling are sociably popular recreations (see Health and fitness, page 353); road-racing is a prominent sport. South Africa has produced some of the world's leading long-distance runners. The premier annual event is the Comrades Marathon, held at the end of May over the 89 km from Pietermaritzburg to Durban (downhill) in odd years and in the reverse direction in even years. Sporting amenities available in the major centres are covered in Part 2.

TELEPHONES The South African telephone system is almost fully automatic; one can dial direct to most centres in South and southern Africa and to most parts of the world. Telephone directories list the dialling codes. Both local and long-distance calls are metered.

Calls from hotels often carry a surcharge; visitors are advised to check the charges that appear on their bills.

Telex and facsimile transmission (fax) facilities are widely available in South Africa.

TIME Throughout the year, South African Standard Time is two hours ahead of Greenwich Mean Time, one hour ahead of Central European Winter Time, and seven hours ahead of the USA's Eastern Standard Winter Time.

VENOMOUS CREATURES The ordinary visitor to South Africa faces little risk from snakes, spiders or scorpions in the main tourist areas; those on safari and on walking trails, though, should obviously be rather more wary, and follow the advice of the group leader.

Snakes There are some 115 species of snake in southern Africa, of which about a quarter are venomous enough to inflict a dangerous bite. The venom may be neurotoxic (affecting the nervous system), haemotoxic (affecting the blood vessels), or cytotoxic (destroying the body's cells). Snakes are shy creatures: they will try to slither out of your way when they sense your presence (and should be allowed to do so), only striking if suddenly disturbed or provoked.

Local back-fanged species include the boomslang and the bird-snake, both highly venomous but, because their fangs are too awkwardly positioned to allow them an efficient grip, rarely cause death or serious injury. Among poisonous front-fanged species are the mambas, cobras, vipers and adders, coral snakes, garter-snakes and sea-snakes.

Anti-snakebite serum is widely available in risk areas; snakebite kits may be bought from pharmacies.

Spiders Around 5 000 species of arachnid (which includes the scorpions) are found in southern Africa. Many will bite if provoked, and some of the bites may be painful. Most dangerous (though rarely fatal to man) is the button spider (Latrodactus).

Scorpions About 175 species are represented in southern Africa, most of them occurring in the hot, dry areas of the subcontinent. All scorpion venom is toxic to the nervous system, but seldom dangerously so.

Bees African bees are notoriously aggressive, and certain types of swarming colony can be dangerous to man and animal. Fortunately, attacks are rare and occur mostly in the remoter areas.

VOCABULARY South Africa is a multilingual country; most South Africans are bilingual (English and Afrikaans) and many speak more than two languages; the thick vowels of the veld can obscure meaning; strange words are used, and visitors may sometimes find conversational English difficult to follow.

There's nothing much one can say about the local accents – newcomers simply have to listen and learn to interpret (the ear becomes attuned surprisingly quickly). A brief glossary of distinctive words, though, may be helpful. These are some of the ones you're more likely to come across:

Amandhla!: Power (to the majority: a rallying cry); *asseblief:* please; *berg:* mountain, hill; *bergie:* Cape Town beggar; *berg wind:* a hot, dry wind from the interior; *biltong:* dried meat, usually in strips; *bioscope:* cinema; *boer:* Afrikaans-speaking farmer, but sometimes used derogatively; *braai:* barbecue; *broek:* pants, sometimes trousers; *dagga:* cannabis, marijuana; *doek:* headscarf worn, mainly, by African women; *dominee:* a Dutch Reformed Church minister; *dorp:* small town; *Egoli:* Johannesburg; *fynbos:* the Cape's distinctive vegetation (heath); *indaba:* a traditional meeting, but the word now denotes any kind of problem; *ja:* yes; *jislaaik!:* exclamation of astonishment; *kaap:* cape; *kaffir:* perjorative word for an African, now forbidden by convention and likely to be forbidden by law; *kloof:* gorge or ravine; *kop:* head, peak, mountain- or hill-top; *koppie:* rocky hillock; *kraal:* small African rural settlement; *krantz:* cliff or crag; *lekker:* nice, delicious, attractive; *man:* used for emphasis in addressing both males and females; *mealie meal:* ground maize; *naartjie:* mandarin orange; *ou:* a person (male); *ouma:* grandmother or old lady; *oupa:* grandfather or old man; *robot:* traffic lights; *samp:* maize meal; *shame!:* sympathetic response to a tale of woe, or towards something cutely endearing; *skollie:* street criminal, usually one of a group; *stoep:* verandah; *tackies:* tennis shoes, sneakers; *tickey-box:* telephone booth or any pay-phone; *totsiens:* goodbye; *velskoens:* tough suede ankle-boots; *toyi-toyi:* ritualistic crowd dance, usually performed at political rallies and protest gatherings; *tsotsi:* street criminal.

NEIGHBOURING COUNTRIES

South Africa shares common borders with Namibia, Botswana, Zimbabwe, Mozambique, Swaziland and Lesotho, the whole forming a wider and increasingly integrated tourist region. Visitors to southern Africa – those with itineraries that go beyond the scope of this book – may find the following introductory pen-profiles useful.

BOTSWANA Formerly the British High Commission Territory (Protectorate) of Bechuanaland and independent since 1966, this vast, land-locked country borders on South Africa (in the south and south-east), Namibia (west and north-west), Zambia (north) and Zimbabwe (north-east and east).

Form of Government Multi-party democracy. The ruling party is the Botswana Democratic Party (initially led by Sir Seretse Khama). Botswana is a member of the Commonwealth, of the Southern African Development Co-ordination Conference (SADCC) and of the SA Customs Union.

Area 581 730 km²; population: 1,4 million (1990 est.), approximately 20% of which is urban; principal towns: Gaborone (capital, est. population 75 000), Francistown, Lobatse; ethnic composition: Tswana 76%; Shona 12%; San (Bushman) 3,5%; Khoikhoi (Hottentot) 2,5%; Ndebele 1,3%; other 4,7%; official language: English; currency: pula, subdivided into 100 thebe.

Economy Mixed, pragmatically managed, regarded by many as a model for other developing African countries. Botswana is fairly heavily subsidized by South Africa and by international agencies; development is dependent on livestock, diamonds, copper, nickel. Tourism is a significant source of foreign exchange. The population remains largely rural and self-employed.

Tourist attractions The magnificent Okavango waterway and swamplands, though these are threatened by invasive cattle-ranching; the immense Kalahari wilderness (it covers 70% of the country); the fascinating Bushman culture; wildlife: there is superb game viewing in the Gemsbok National, Khutse, Chobe, Central Kalahari, Makgadikgadi, Nxai Pan and Moremi parks and the Okavango Delta. The facilities are generally rudimentary; distances enormous; roads are rough; rest-camps isolated, and cautious visitors are advised to put themselves in the hands of a reputable tour or safari operator.

Climate Summer-rainfall region (the rains render some of the roads impassable); summer days can be very hot (up to 38-40 °C); winter days are sunny and warm, the nights can be bitter.

Access from South Africa Scheduled air services to Gaborone, Selebi-Phikwe, Francistown and Maun from Johannesburg international airport; Gaborone is connected with the western Transvaal and northern Cape road networks. The railway line between South Africa and Zimbabwe passes through Botswana, and there are regular passenger services to and from these countries.

Travel documents All visitors require valid passports; Commonwealth and South African nationals do not need a visa, but some other nationals do; check with your travel agent.

Information For visa enquiries contact the Immigration Control Officer, PO Box 942, Gaborone. The Department of Wildlife and National Parks, PO Box 131, Gaborone, Tel. 37-1405, has information on Botswana's national parks and other attractions. Air Botswana's office at Johannesburg airport, Tel. (011) 975-3614, can provide details of flights to and from Gaborone.

LESOTHO This land-locked mountain kingdom forms an enclave within the eastern and central part of South Africa, bordering the Orange Free State (west and north), Natal (north-east and east), Transkei (east and south) and the Cape (south-west). Formerly the British High Commission territory of Basutoland, Lesotho became an independent state in 1966.

Form of Government Constitutional monarchy; in normal times, executive and legislative authority is exercised by a cabinet under the leadership of a prime minister and advised by a National Assembly; authority is currently exercised by a military council led by Major-General Justin Lekhanya, who is also minister of defence and internal security; the council has promised a return to civilian rule.

Area 30 352 km²; population: 1,76 million (1990 est.); growth rate average 2,1-2,4%, population density: 48 per km²; most of the land area lies above the 3 000 m mark; by far the greater proportion of the people live in the fertile corridor along the Caledon River; principal towns: Maseru (capital), Mafeteng, Teyateyaneng; the University of Lesotho is at Roma; ethnic composition: Sotho 99,7% (the Kwena are the largest subgroup); official languages: South Sotho and English; Zulu, Xhosa and Afrikaans are also spoken; currency: loti, subdivided into 100 lisente; the loti is on a par with the SA rand.

Economy Developing mixed economy with agriculture (livestock, maize, wheat) making up a third of the GNP and employing 80% of the workforce. Productivity is low, but economic activity will be stimulated by completion of the giant Lesotho Highlands Water Project. Significant exports: diamonds, wool, mohair. Tourism, remittances of migrant workers and foreign aid funds contribute substantially to foreign earnings.

Tourist attractions Majestic mountain scenery; excellent hotels (and a casino complex) in Maseru; unusually hospitable people; many of whom still wear traditional costume, some of whom use tough little Basuto ponies to get around. The only major wilderness area is the Sehlabathebe national park, within the high Drakensberg mountain range and noted more for its scenic splendours than wildlife.

The roads are generally in poor condition and many

routes can be negotiated only by four-wheel-drive vehicles, though progress on the giant water scheme is prompting road improvement. Beware local laws governing the transportation of liquor.

Climate Summer-rainfall region; the rains render many routes impassable; summer days are cool in the uplands, warm to hot lower down; winter days can be cold and the nights bitter; snow falls on the upper slopes of the Maluti Mountains.

Access from South Africa Scheduled air services from Johannesburg international airport; Maseru is connected with the eastern and north-eastern Orange Free State and the north-eastern Cape road networks, and, tenuously, with Natal via the high and rugged Sani Pass. Most convenient route is from Bloemfontein to Maseru via Ladybrand. The South African rail system links with Maseru.

Travel documents All visitors need valid passports; South Africans and some other nationals require visas (check with your travel agent).

Information Visa applications can be directed to the Lesotho Trade Mission in Johannesburg, Tel. (011) 29-0751; tourist information is obtainable from the Lesotho Tourism Board, 132 Jan Smuts Avenue, Parkwood, Johannesburg, Tel. (011) 788-0742. Lesotho Airways, Tel. (011) 970-1046 has information on flights to and from Maseru. Embassies in Maseru: UK Tel. 2-3961, USA 2-3892, Germany 2-2750.

MOZAMBIQUE The former territory of Portuguese East Africa, elongated in shape, is bordered by South Africa (east and south), Swaziland (south), Zimbabwe (west), Tanzania (north), Malawi (north-east). The entire eastern boundary is defined by the Mozambique Channel of the Indian Ocean.

Mozambique gained its independence in 1975, after a prolonged and bitterly fought civil war between Portugal's 70 000 troops and the Frelimo movement. The new regime adopted Marxist-Leninist policies which, in economic terms, proved a disastrous failure. Moreover, rebel groups known as Renamo or MNR, whose origins lay in the anti-Frelimo covert operations of the Rhodesian security forces in the 1970s, gained strength during the 1980s, provoking a savage conflict that devastated the country.

In 1984, Mozambique and South Africa signed the Nkomati Accord, an agreement that was designed, among other things, to extend friendship, co-operation, economic aid and technical assistance to Mozambique, with special emphasis on the country's communications, power-lines and harbours.

Form of Government One-party republic in which power is vested exclusively in Frelimo; executive: 10-member Political Committee of Frelimo; legislature: 210-member Peoples' Assembly. The country, however, is in transition: in July 1989, Frelimo dropped all references to Marxism and Leninism from the party constitution, and in January 1990, President Joachim Chissano introduced a new (draft) constitution making provision for universal suffrage, a secret ballot and direct election of the president and legislature. The introduction of a promised multi-party political system will hopefully help restore internal peace.

Area 799 380 km²; population: 15 million (1990 est.); growth rate 2,7-3,4%; population density: 17 per km²; principal towns: Maputo (capital; formerly Lourenço Marques), Angoche, Beira, Chimoio, Gogai, Inhambane, Móma, Morrumbala, Quelimane, Tete, Vilanculos, Xai-Xai; ethnic composition (linguistic groupings): Makua-Longwe and Yao (in areas north of the Zambezi River), Tsonga, Karanga, Shona, Nguni (Angoni); Asian and European (Portuguese-speaking) minorities, the latter numbering some 15 000; official language: Portuguese; currency: metical, divided into 100 centavos.

Economy Mozambique is among the world's poorest countries. Technically a developing region, it is plagued by civil war, disintegrating administrative services and lack of skills. The centrally planned economy, based on farming (agricultural management has followed Cuban and Chinese models), international trade and light industries, virtually collapsed during the 1980s.

Mozambique's economic future depends on the restoration of internal peace (a peace initiative was launched in 1990), close South African involvement in the region, development of the railways and harbours, and reactivation of the giant Cahora Bassa hydroelectric installations. The country's to-date unrealized assets include coal (700 million tons of reserves), iron ore (360 million tons), the world's largest tantalite deposits, and significant reserves of natural gas, manganese, uranium, diamonds and asbestos.

Tourist attractions The region has substantial tourism potential. Its game reserves include the splendid (but up to now beleaguered) Gorongoza park; offshore holiday islands are beginning to attract a flow of foreign visitors. Roads are poor and, at the time of writing, highly dangerous. Maputo was once a tropical gem and, if plans materialize, may be so again.

Climate Summer-rainfall region; downpours can be tropically heavy; summers are hot and humid (often uncomfortably so); winters mild.

Access from South Africa Regular scheduled services run between Johannesburg international airport and Maputo. Also on offer are package holidays to the islands off the coast – check with your travel agent. Intending visitors are strongly advised not to attempt a road journey. Daily trains run between Johannesburg and Maputo.

Travel documents All visitors require valid passports and visas. Certificates of inoculation against yellow fever and cholera are usually necessary.

Information The Mozambique Foreign Trade Office, 73 Market St, Johannesburg, Tel. (011) 23-4907 can answer queries about visas, health regulations, etc. South African Airways can provide information about scheduled flights, Tel. Johannesburg (011) 333-6504 or Cape Town (021) 418-1525.

NAMIBIA The republic, formerly German South-West Africa (1884/5-1915), was mandated, as South West Africa, to South Africa by the League of Nations in 1920 and gained its independence in 1990. It is bounded by Angola (north), Zambia (north-east), Bostwana (east), Cape Province (east and south) and the Atlantic Ocean in the west (coastline: 1 489 km). The country's only deep-water port is Walvis Bay, currently a South African enclave; future ownership and use of the port is subject to negotiation.

The early inhabitants were the San (Bushmen), to be followed by the Nama, the Damara, the Ovambo, the Herero and, later, the Basters. Hunters, explorers, traders, missionaries (of the Rhenish Missionary Society) were among the vanguard of white penetration. Walvis Bay and the guano islands were annexed by Britain in 1878; German occupation began in 1884; South African troops under Louis Botha and Jan Smuts conquered the territory in 1915.

Form of government Multi-party democracy.

Area 824 293 km²; population: 1,5 million (1990 est.); annual growth rate: 3,7%; urban population: 25%, increasing at an annual 5,7%; principal towns: Windhoek (capital), Gobabis, Karibib, Keetmanshoop, Lüderitz, Omaruru, Oranjemund, Oshakati, Otjiwarongo, Outjo, Swakopmund, Tsumeb, Walvis Bay; ethnic composition (1986): Ovambo 587 000, Kavango 110 000, Herero 89 000, white 78 000, Nama 57 000, Caprivian 48 000, 'coloured' 48 000, San (Bushman) 34 000, Baster 29 000, Tswana 7 000, other 12 000; official language: English (Afrikaans and German are the dominant spoken languages, however); currency: South African rand. Namibia is unlikely to have its own currency before the end of 1992.

Economy Developing mixed; heavily reliant on uranium mining and the output of the giant alluvial diamond diggings along the southern coast, and to a lesser degree on fisheries – and on agriculture, although the land is arid. International financial aid is vital for development; the tourist industry has great potential. Communications: 2 340 km of railways, 4 318 km of tarred roads; developed air lanes.

Tourist attractions A harsh but varied countryside, much of it desert, most of it both strange and beautiful. Windhoek is a pleasant little city to visit; its citizens are known for their hospitality. The coastal resorts are also welcoming, but the ocean waters tend to be cold. Namibia's pride are its game parks, of which the Etosha is the finest; other major sanctuaries include the Fish River Canyon park, the Kaudom reserve, the Mahango reserve, the Namib-Naukluft park and the Skeleton Coast park. Among the more renowned scenic areas are the Brandberg, the Skeleton Coast and the Fish River Canyon.

Roads are generally in good condition; the main route runs south to north, with subsidiary roads branching off to the small (and mostly isolated) towns.

Climate Dry; what rains there are fall in summer; summer days are hot to very hot, cooler along the coast; winter days sunny and mild, cold at night.

Access from South Africa The main trunk route (the N7) links Cape Town with Windhoek and points beyond; some overland groups start their tours from Johannesburg, travelling through the northern Cape (Kimberley) and Springbok on the western coastal belt before entering Namibia. Windhoek is well connected with the South African air network.

Travel documents Ask a travel agent for details.

Information South African Airways, Tel. Johannesburg (011) 333-6504 or Cape Town (021) 418-1525, has details of scheduled flights to and from Namibia. Namib Air in the Carlton Centre, Johannesburg Tel. (011) 331-6658 or Cape Town (021) 934-0757, can also supply information on flights. The Namibian Trade and Tourism office in St George's Street, Cape Town Tel. (021) 419-3190 has information on all aspects of Namibia.

SWAZILAND This small, land-locked kingdom, formerly a British High Commission territory until it gained its independence in 1968, is bordered by South Africa in the north, west and south, and by Mozambique in the east.

Form of Government Monarchy – supreme power is vested in the king, whose authority is administered by a cabinet presided over by the prime minister; the legislature comprises a Senate and House of Assembly; the monarch is advised by the Liqogo, a personally-appointed council; traditionally, however, the monarch's powers are shared by his mother, or mother-substitute; administrative control resides largely with the aristocracies of the dominant clans, though this authority is, today, balanced by the appointment of commoners to important government posts.

Area 17 364 km²; population: 750 000 (1990 est.); urban population: 8%; principal towns: Mbabane (administrative capital; est. population 40 000), Lobamba (legislative and royal capital), Manzini; ethnic composition: Swazi 84%, Zulu 10%; Tsonga 2,5%; official languages: SiSwati, English; currency: lilangeni (plural: emalangeni); the South African rand is also legal tender; the two units are on a par.

Economy Predominantly a market economy, based largely on subsistence agriculture, retail and wholesale trade, and on some light industry. Exports mainly comprise food and livestock, and crude materials (excluding fuel). The forestry industry is making an increasing contribution to national revenue. Tourism and the remittances of migrant workers are significant sources of income.

Tourist attractions Swaziland is a green and fertile land; much of the scenery is gently pleasant, some of it (in the north and east) spectacularly beautiful. The country has some especially fine hotels and hotel-casino complexes. Among the specific attractions are the Ezulwini ('place of heaven') Valley, the Lebombo range of mountains along the eastern border, the Usutu Forest in the central region, and Piggs Peak and its surrounds in the north. The Mlilwane wildlife sanctuary, the Malolotja reserve and the Hlane National Park are well worth a visit.

Roads are adequate, some barely so, especially during the rainy season (November to March).

Climate Summer-rainfall region; some parts of the north-western uplands receive 2 000 mm and more a year; a temperate climate in the higher areas, subtropical lower down; beware of malaria and bilharzia.

Access from South Africa Swaziland is connected with the South African road network; good roads lead through the Transvaal to ten border posts. There are scheduled air services between various South African centres and Mbabane.

Travel documents All visitors require valid passports; South African and some other nationals do not need visas; some nationals do. Consult your travel agent. Certificates of inoculation against cholera and yellow fever are sometimes necessary for visitors to Swaziland.

Information The Swaziland Tourism Board, 132 Jan Smuts Avenue, Parkwood, Johannesburg, Tel. (011) 788-0742, can answer any queries about the country. Contact the Swazi Trade Mission at 165 Jeppe St, Jeppe, Johannesburg, Tel. (011) 29-9776 for visa applications. Royal Swazi Airways, the national carrier, is at (011) 331-9467/975-8814. The Swaziland Tourist Office in Mbabane is at PO Box 451, Tel. 4-2531. Foreign embassies in Mbabane: UK Tel. 4-2581, USA 4-6441.

ZIMBABWE This republic, formerly the British colony of Southern Rhodesia, is bounded by South Africa (in the south; the Limpopo River forms part of the frontier), Botswana (south-west); Zambia (north and north-west; the Zambezi River is the border), Mozambique (east).

The northern region of Mashonaland was occupied by Cecil Rhodes's British South Africa Company in 1890 (the company later, in 1893, conquered and occupied the south-western region of Matabeleland). The territory became a British colony in 1911; achieved self-governing colonial status in 1924; was a constituent member of Federation of the Rhodesias and Nyasaland from 1953 to 1963. Two years later, Rhodesian Front premier, Ian Smith, unilaterally declared the country's independence (the state, renamed Rhodesia, assumed republican status in 1970). International sanctions, civil war and pressure from South Africa forced the rebel regime to the conference table (at Lancaster House, London) in 1979, and the country achieved legal independence with the electoral victory of Robert Mugabe's Zanu-PF party in 1980.

Form of Government Multi-party democracy. The legislature comprises a Senate and House of Assembly.

Area 390 759 km²; population: 9 million (1990 est.); annual population growth: 3,5%; principal towns: Harare (capital; formerly Salisbury; 1990 est. pop: 1 million), Bulawayo, Chitungwiza (formerly Fort Victoria), Gweru (formerly Gwelo), Mutare (formerly Umtali); ethnic composition: Shona 70%, Ndebele 16%, European 2%; languages: English (official), ChiShona, SiNdebele; currency: Zimbabwean dollar (Z$), divided into 100 cents.

Economy Semi-developed mixed; some state participation. Main trading partners: South Africa (21% of imports, 12% of exports) and United Kingdom (10% of imports, 12% of exports); 30% of the workforce is employed in commercial agriculture (tobacco, maize, cattle-ranching, dairy, coffee, tea, sugar-cane, seed cotton, wheat, sorghum, soya beans, forestry); and a further 30% in subsistence or part-time farming.

Mining accounts for 8% of GNP; the diverse mineral range includes coal, iron ore, limestone, chromite, asbestos, magnesite, bentonite and refractory clays, sulphur, lithium minerals, copper, quartz, nickel, tin, gold, silver, emeralds, corundum, cobalt, tungsten, tantalite, amethyst.

The manufacturing sector is, in the sub-Saharan African context, highly advanced and diversified, partly due to far-reaching import replacement after the 1965 rebellion. Manufactured products include processed agricultural products, crude steel, pig-iron, steel products, cement, electrical and other machinery, textiles and clothing, chemicals, plastics, fertilizers, pesticides, assembled vehicles, pharmaceuticals, ceramic ware. Tourism accounts for a significant proportion of foreign earnings.

Tourist attractions Zimbabwe is a country of great natural beauty; its special drawcards include the Victoria Falls – the 'smoke that thunders' over the Zambezi River; Kariba dam and lake, one of the world's largest man-made stretches of water; Nyanga, the Vumba and the Chimanimani mountains in the lovely Eastern Highlands region; the ruins of Great Zimbabwe. Among the more notable of the country's wilderness sanctuaries – together, they cover more than 12% of the country's area – are the Mana Pools, Victoria Falls and Zambezi national parks in the north, the Matobo National Park near Bulawayo and the famed Hwange National Park in the south-west.

Zimbabwean hotels are of a high standard; the Monomotapa, Meikles and Sheraton in Harare are especially noteworthy. Zimbabwe has a well-developed infrastructure; roads are in excellent condition.

Climate Summer-rainfall region; summers are hot in the lower areas, warm to hot on the Highveld; winter days are sunny and mild, nights chilly.

Access from South Africa The main south-north highway, the N1, leads to the border at Beitbridge and on to Bulawayo (north-west) and Harare (north). Scheduled air and rail services connect these cities with Johannesburg and Pretoria. Direct flights also run between Johannesburg airport and the Victoria Falls.

Travel documents All visitors to Zimbabwe require valid passports; some (including South African passport holders) require visas (check with your travel agent).

Information The Zimbabwe Trade Mission in South Africa, situated in the Sanlam Building, 63 Commissioner St, Johannesburg, Tel. (011) 838-2156, can assist with visas. The Zimbabwe Tourist Development Corporation in the Carlton Centre, Johannesburg, Tel. (011) 331-1541, has information on tourist attractions and other aspects of interest to the visitor. Air Zimbabwe, in the Carlton Centre, Johannesburg, Tel. (011) 331-1541, or at Johannesburg international airport, Tel. (011) 970-1689 or contact South African Airways, Tel (011) 333-6504.

INDEX

PHOTOGRAPHIC CREDITS

Shawn Benjamin Front cover (bottom left), 13, 15, 16, 37, 42, 215, 262, 259 (left), 274 (left), 295, 334; **Ray Bressler** 134; **Gerald Cubitt** Imprint page, 78, 95, 98, 110, 115, 118, 122, 126, 130, 155, 178, 179, 202, 203, 207, 219, 222, 223, 227, 239, 247, 254, 266, 267, 270, 274 (right), 279, 290, 303, 314, 315, 318, 330, 335; **Roger de la Harpe** 6-7, 91, 162, 163, 167, 174, 185, 186 (left), 187, 251, 291, 342-343; **Aubrey Elliott** 158 **John Haigh** Front cover (top left), 278; **Peter Hill** 338; **Peter John** Front cover (middle left); **Walter Knirr** 40; **Jeanie MacKinnon** 83, 131, 242, 259 (right), 306, 326; **Johannesburg Publicity Association** 43, 46; **Jean Morris** 8, 12, 44, 86, 103, 147, 150, 151; **Herman Potgieter** Front cover (bottom right), title page, 33, 45, 47, 48, 50, 51, 54, 71, 74, 126, 166, 210, 250; **Ethel Rosenstrauch** 330, 331; **Percy Sargeant** (the late) 186 (right), 218; **August Sycholdt** Front cover (top right) 36, 66, 67, 70, 154, 159, 174, 198, 230, 234, 235, 238, 282, 286; **Janek Szymanowski** Front cover (middle right), back cover, 57,62, 114, 138, 142, 143, 146, 182, 190, 191, 194, 206, 211, 214, 243, 275, 283, 311; **Mark van Aardt** 38-39, 287, 294, 299, 310, 322, 339

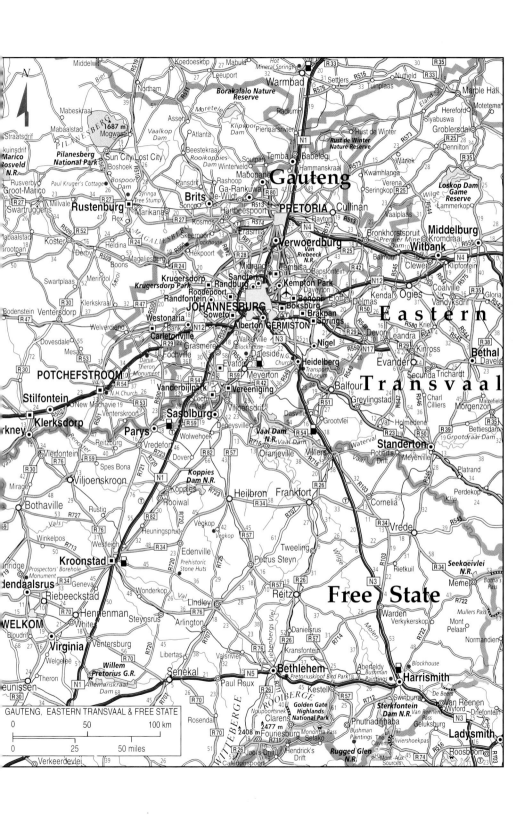

GAUTENG, EASTERN TRANSVAAL & FREE STATE

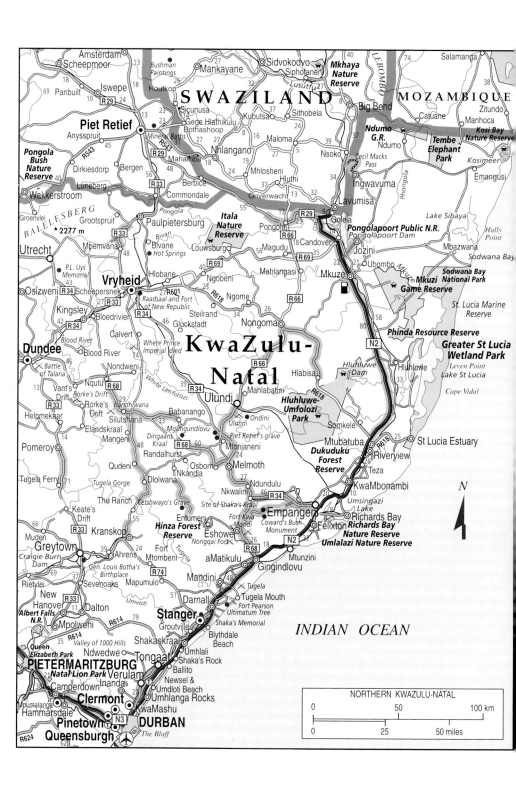

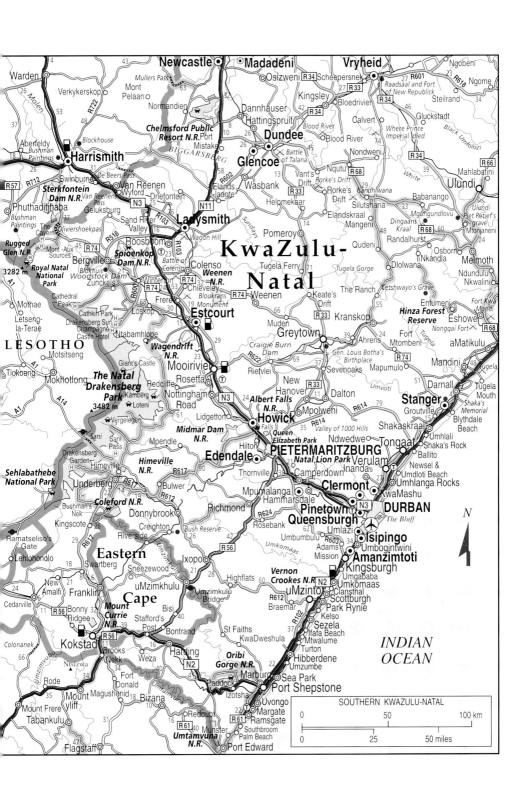

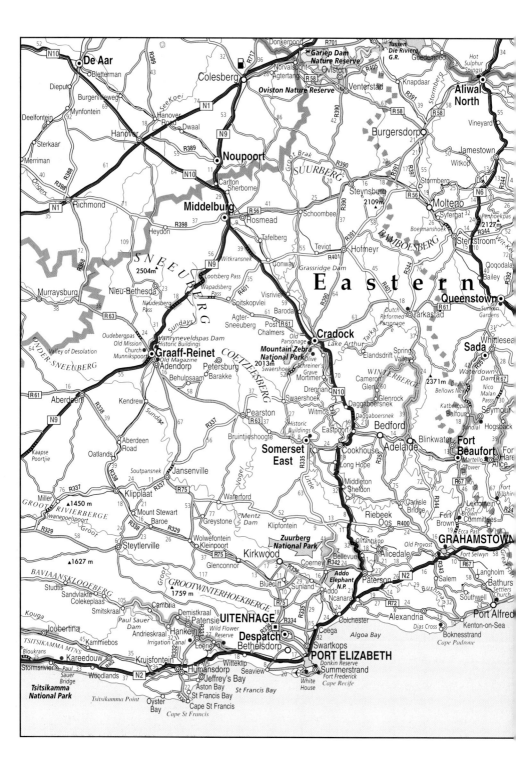

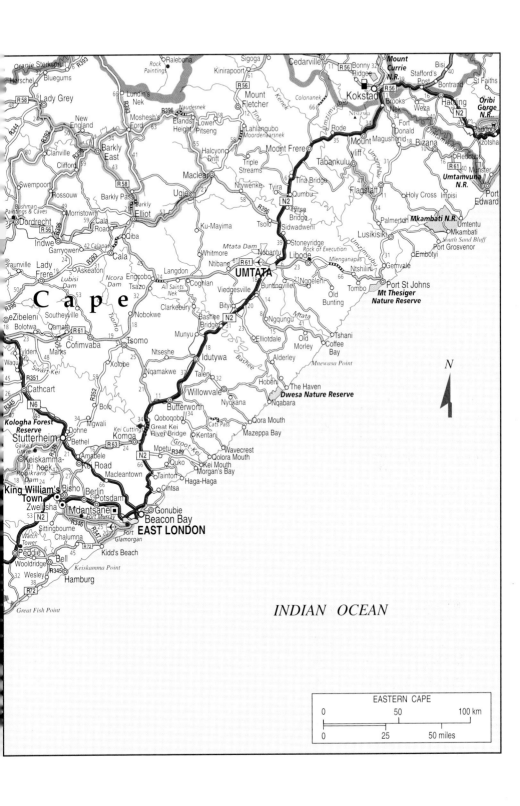

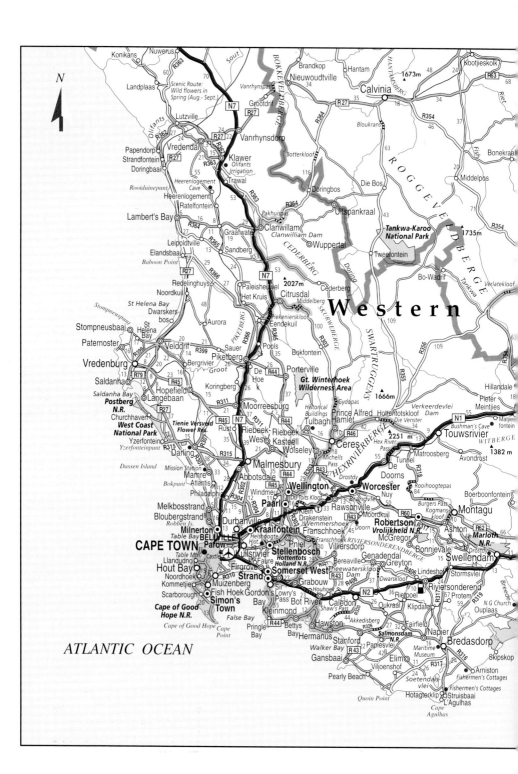